EXAMPLES & EXPLANATIONS

White Collar Crime

EXAMPLES & EXPLANATIONS

White Collar Crime

Julie Rose O'Sullivan
Agnes Williams Sesquicentennial Professor of Law
Georgetown University Law Center

ASPEN PUBLISHING

To contact Customer Service, e-mail customer.service@aspenpublishing.com, call 1-800-950-5259, or mail correspondence to:

Aspen Publishing
Attn: Order Department
1 Wall Street
Burlington, MA 01803

Printed in the United States of America.

1 2 3 4 5 6 7 8 9 0

ISBN 979-8-8920-7069-0

Library of Congress Cataloging-in-Publication Data application is in process.

ABOUT ASPEN PUBLISHING

Aspen Publishing is a leading provider of legal education content and digital learning solutions in the United States and globally. Our innovative products and platforms—designed based on best practices in learning science—engage students and enhance outcomes. From textbooks and audiobooks authored by renowned experts to digital platforms and products like LEAF, Connected eBooks, Connected Quizzing, PracticePerfect, and JD-Next, we empower the next generation of legal professionals with innovative, trusted, and accessible resources.

The Aspen Casebook Series, affectionately known as the "red and black" casebooks among law faculty and students, includes hundreds of highly regarded textbooks across more than 80 disciplines. These range from foundational courses like Torts and Contracts to emerging electives such as Sustainability and the Law of Policing. Our study aids, including the popular *Examples & Explanations* series, help law students master complex topics with clarity and confidence.

Aspen's expertise extends to undergraduate education with our Paralegal, Criminal Justice, and Business Law series, offering the same hallmark quality to a broader audience. JD-Next, our groundbreaking online law school prep course and admissions test, provides a realistic preview of law school, equips students with essential skills for academic success, and evaluates their readiness for legal studies.

Aspen Publishing Is Proud to Be a UWorld Company

Since 2003, UWorld has been a global leader in developing high-quality learning tools for students preparing for high-stakes exams. With a commitment to excellence, UWorld has helped millions of students in undergraduate, graduate, and professional programs in fields such as medicine, nursing, finance, and law achieve their academic and career goals.

Founded by Chandra S. Pemmasani, M.D., during his medical residency, UWorld began focusing on medical education and has since expanded into various academic fields, including law. In 2020, UWorld launched its Legal vertical, starting with its comprehensive Multistate Bar Exam (MBE®) Question Bank, followed by the acquisition of Themis Bar Review, which integrated resources to provide a complete bar exam preparation experience. In 2024, UWorld expanded its offerings by acquiring Aspen Publishing, enhancing its suite of legal education products.

Today, UWorld offers an unparalleled range of study materials that blend active learning methods with expert content, ensuring students and educators can access the most effective resources. From bar preparation to law school success, UWorld is committed to supporting the next generation of legal professionals. Learn more at uworld.com.

To my mentors
Robert B. Fiske, Jr. and John (Jack) P. Cooney, Jr.,
Extraordinary lawyers and even better human beings,
To Graciela (Grace) Rodriguez,
A star of my generation and the best of friends, and
To the future, and my favorite lawyer,
Aedan Rose Collins,
With love, respect, and admiration.

Summary of Contents

Table of Contents

Acknowledgments

I am indebted to many family members, friends, and colleagues for their assistance and encouragement during this project. In particular, I would like to acknowledge Aedan Rose Collins who, as a law student at Georgetown Law Center, suggested I write this book to help students trying master this complex area of law. Special thanks are owed to the friends and expert colleagues who lent me that most precious commodity—their time—to give me their advice, insights, and corrections on the chapters within: Sara Sun Beale, Sam Buell, Randall Eliason, Daniel Richman, and Robert W. Tarun. All errors are, of course, my own. A shout-out is owed to the research assistants who patiently cite-checked these pages, David Lincoln and Tian Zhang. I also appreciate the unflagging help and support of the Georgetown University Law Center librarians and administrative staff, particularly Faculty Manuscript Editor Betsy Kuhn. Finally, and as always, many thanks to Robert F. Muse and Michele A. Roberts, without whose subtle and nimble minds this work would have been much impoverished.

White Collar Crime

CHAPTER 1

Introduction

I. Definition "White-Collar" Crime
II. The Federal Enforcers
III. Prosecutors' Ethical Obligations

I. DEFINITION OF "WHITE-COLLAR" CRIME

There is no generally agreed-upon definition of "white-collar" crime. The term was coined by a sociologist who sought to attack the dominant criminological theories of the day that attributed crime largely to poverty and social disorganization. The sociologist, Edwin H. Sutherland, gathered evidence to show that a large and socially devastating species of violations were committed by persons of seeming respectability and power. Sutherland's focus on the social status of offenders does not fit well with what most practitioners conceive of as white-collar crime. Because of profound changes in the American workplace and the population's access to advanced technology and the Internet, white-collar crime is no longer synonymous with high social standing, extensive education, or financial success; virtually anyone with access to a smartphone or computer can today be a white-collar criminal.

Oftentimes we leave crime definitions to those who are charged with monitoring and combating it. But even the FBI, an otherwise compulsive gatherer of crime data, does not try to define and measure the incidence of "white-collar" crime, nor do other federal agencies. We are left, then, to generalize based on what most practitioners would recognize as white-collar practice. Some describe white-collar offenses as non-violent illegal activities that principally use deceit, deception, concealment, fraud, or misrepresentation to obtain money, property, or some other advantage or to conceal or cover up other wrongdoing. This certainly covers a lot of the landscape, encompassing frauds of every type, as well as false statements, perjury, and obstruction. One can also add that, with the possible exception of professional money launderers and organized cyber-fraudsters, most white-collar offenders are not professional criminals. And although we no longer adopt Sutherland's focus on the perpetrator's position of power or influence, many white-collar cases do involve the defendant's misuse of a position of trust for personal or organizational gain. Public corruption cases fall into this category.

The most obvious harm flowing from white-collar crime is financial: most estimates indicate that the dollar loss attributable to white-collar crime dwarfs the monetary harms caused by all other types of offenses combined. White-collar victims can be private individuals—for example, those bilked by telemarketing, securities, credit card, bank, real estate, or cyber-fraud. Oftentimes, however, the victim is the government. White-collar offenders regularly deceive the government regarding entitlements to government payments, privileges, and public benefits.

Dollars, however, do not begin to measure the total impact of this type of criminal conduct. Many white-collar offenses also threaten the physical well-being of individuals and the public generally. Certainly environmental and Food, Drug and Cosmetic Act cases fall into this category. Another category of potential harms that has lately come to the fore are those endangering U.S. security or other vital national interests. Spying is the most obvious such offense, but Foreign Corrupt Practices Act (FCPA) cases, sanctions evasion, and export control offenses have also become top national security priorities. Notable in this regard are cyberattacks on critical health, election, and financial infrastructure.

Perhaps the greatest harm that white-collar crime poses is to the perceived legitimacy of political, governmental, and financial systems. If members of the public believe that tax evasion is rampant and law enforcement is ineffectual in addressing it, they will feel like suckers for paying their fair share. Should investors decide that the financial markets are rigged or that insider trading is pervasive, they will disdain such markets and turn to other investment opportunities. And if voters believe that politicians are bought and paid for, they will have no incentive to participate in and defend their democracy. In short, a variety of white-collar crimes—including securities fraud and public corruption, antitrust, and tax offenses—undermine public confidence in critical social institutions.

I. Introduction

This volume focuses on *federal* white-collar criminal law and practice for a variety of reasons. Federal criminal law is arguably the single most important white-collar law enforcement system in the country. The largest cases—whether measured by the amount of harm caused, the geographic scope, or the visibility of the wrongdoing—are generally prosecuted in federal courts. The high-profile nature of federal practice is enhanced by the fact that the U.S. Supreme Court decides on the scope of criminal statutes, the meaning of applicable procedural rules, and the constitutionality of federal prosecutorial practices.

Most of the issues raised and examined within are not unique to federal practice and state white-collar practice is extensive. But it is impossible to summarize in one volume the applicable legal rules that control in all the states. That said, those interested in state level practice will find that many of the issues discussed within, and the applicable legal rules, are not in fact very different. Federal statutes, practices, and precedents often serve as models for state actors.

We begin by covering some basics—mens rea, aiding and abetting and attempt liability, double jeopardy constraints on charging, defenses, and the extraterritorial application of U.S. statutes (Chapter 2's General Part). We then delve into issues relating to the reality that corporations are often embroiled in federal white-collar offenses, as perpetrators, instruments controlled by others, or victims. Chapter 3 (Entity Liability) explores the circumstances—including the standards for corporate criminal liability—that often compel corporations to cooperate with the government in seeking a declination or a diversion agreement in lieu of an indictment. It explores the types of diversion agreements available and the Department of Justice's (DOJ's) charging policies. It also discusses some of the issues arising in corporate internal investigations, which are often necessary to inform the corporation's decision regarding what course it ought to adopt in the face of allegations of wrongdoing and, where cooperation is the answer, to effectively meet the DOJ's expectations in this regard.

There are a great variety of white-collar offenses, but space constraints dictate that only the most important or commonly charged can be covered. Chapters 4 to 11 discuss some of the federal code provisions applicable to: Perjury, False Statements, and False Claims; Conspiracy; Mail, Wire, Bank, Health Care, and Securities Fraud; Obstruction of Justice; domestic and transnational Public Corruption; the Racketeer Influenced and Corrupt Organizations Act (RICO); and Money Laundering. It was, of course, possible to fill this volume with substantive offenses, including, for example, tax, environmental, antitrust, and computer crimes. But the effective practice of white-collar crime requires exposure to a great many—for lack of a better term—procedural issues and the remainder of the volume is devoted to those essential subjects.

Because ninety-seven percent of federal criminal cases are resolved by plea, the only process most defendants receive is the grand jury's screening of prosecutorial charging choices. Chapter 12's inquiry into the rules governing the grand jury is also essential because it is the means through which most white-collar crimes are investigated. Chapter 13 concerns discovery issues, which, given plea rates, may seem unnecessary. But these rules often influence other prosecutorial choices, and they illustrate the many advantages the government has in securing information and evidence vis á vis the defense. Virtually the only countervailing advantage the defense has is its ability to deny the government access to critical information through the defendant's assertion of his Fifth Amendment right against compelled self-incrimination. Chapter 15 explores the contours of this important right, as well as the different sorts of immunity that may overcome a potential witness's assertion of her Fifth Amendment right.

Given plea rates, no white-collar book is complete without a discussion of plea bargaining and cooperation agreements, as well as that which defendants often care about most in engaging in such bargaining—sentencing. Chapter 15 covers the U.S. Sentencing Guidelines that apply to both individual and corporate sentencing. The guidelines can, as an initial matter, be difficult to parse but defense counsel in federal cases, in particular, commit professional malpractice if they do not know the guidelines inside and out. Chapter 16 discusses the constitutional constraints on plea bargaining and its mechanics. Finally, in white-collar matters—particularly those involving potential organizational misconduct—it is very common for those under investigation to be subject to parallel civil investigations and lawsuits as well as the scrutiny of federal prosecutors. Chapter 17 discusses some of the challenges defense counsel face in coordinating their client's responses to parallel civil and criminal actions and in minimizing the extent to which actions in one matter prejudice the client in another.

II. THE FEDERAL ENFORCERS

The U.S. Department of Justice (DOJ) is charged with enforcing federal criminal law. Cases come to it from an alphabet soup of agencies some of which have a primarily law enforcement focus and others that have a broader civil and regulatory mandate but also investigate criminal conduct. These include the Federal Bureau of Investigation (FBI), the Drug Enforcement Administration (DEA), the Bureau of Alcohol, Tobacco, Firearms and Explosives (BATFE), the U.S. Marshals Service, the Secret Service, U.S. Immigration and Customs Enforcement (ICE), the U.S. Postal Inspection Service, and the Securities and Exchange Commission (SEC) and many more. Federal prosecutors may also work with state and local law enforcement agencies on individual cases or on task forces. With so many investigators bringing cases to the Department for prosecution, it is impossible for prosecutors to pursue every possible infraction of federal criminal law. Each presidential administration therefore sets the general enforcement priorities for the DOJ's prosecutors.

Within the Justice Department itself (also known as "Main Justice"), a variety of divisions are responsible for criminal matters. The Criminal Division has certain specialized sections, including those that focus on health care fraud and enforcement of the Foreign Corrupt Practices Act, and it exercises general supervision over the enforcement of all federal criminal laws, with the exception of those statutes specifically assigned to Main Justice's specialized Antitrust, Civil Rights, Environment and Natural Resources, and Tax Divisions.

The bulk of federal criminal prosecutions, however, are entrusted to United States Attorneys Offices (USAOs) throughout the country. There are ninety-three United States Attorneys: one for each of the ninety-four federal judicial districts, except for Guam and the Northern Marianas, where a single U.S. Attorney serves both districts. U.S. Attorneys are appointed by the President and confirmed by the Senate. They serve terms of four years or at the President's discretion. In large districts, a USAO may consist of a main office and smaller satellite offices throughout the districts. The USAO will do most of the litigation on behalf of the United States in their district, including appellate work in the circuit courts. Each USAO consists of two major divisions: criminal and civil. The USAOs prosecute cases in their criminal divisions, and both bring and defend civil cases on behalf of the United States in their civil divisions. U.S. Attorneys and some senior DOJ officials are political appointees, but the Assistant U.S. Attorneys (AUSAs) who conduct the day-to-day work of the Department are, by law, hired, promoted, and fired on a non-partisan basis. AUSAs may work as generalists or in specialized sections depending on the USAO's organization.

III. PROSECUTORS' ETHICAL OBLIGATIONS

> The United States Attorney is the representative not of an ordinary party to a controversy, but of a sovereignty whose obligation to govern impartially is as compelling as its obligation to govern at all; and whose interest, therefore, in a criminal prosecution is not that it shall win a case, but that justice shall be done. As such, he is in a peculiar and very definite sense the servant of the law, the twofold aim of which is that guilt shall not escape or innocence suffer. He may prosecute with earnestness and vigor—indeed, he should do so. But, while he may strike hard blows, he is not at liberty to strike foul ones. It is as much his duty to refrain from improper methods calculated to produce

> a wrongful conviction as it is to use every legitimate means to bring about a just one.[1]

This widely-quoted passage reflects the prevailing view that federal prosecutors have a special role in the adversary process. Their obligation to "do justice" is not stated in the text of Rule 3.8, the ABA Model Rule of Professional Conduct provision addressed to the "Special Responsibilities of a Prosecutor." But the commentary to that ethical standard states that

> A prosecutor has the responsibility of a minister of justice and not simply that of an advocate. This responsibility carries with it specific obligations to see that the defendant is accorded procedural justice and that guilt is decided upon the basis of sufficient evidence. Precisely how far the prosecutor is required to go in this direction is a matter of debate and varies in different jurisdictions.

The ABA Standards for Criminal Justice, which, although not legally binding, are often relied upon in discussing the duties of criminal counsel, provide the following standard for the function of the prosecutor:

> The prosecutor is an administrator of justice, a zealous advocate, and an officer of the court. The prosecutor's office should exercise sound discretion and independent judgment in the performance of the prosecution function. . . . The primary duty of the prosecutor is to seek justice within the bounds of the law, not merely to convict.[2]

By contrast, the Standards describe the function of defense counsel as follows:

> The primary duties that defense counsel owe to their clients, to the administration of justice, and as officers of the court, are to serve as their clients' counselor and advocate with courage and devotion; to ensure that constitutional and other legal rights of their clients are protected; and to render effective, high-quality legal representation with integrity.[3]

Federal prosecutors' ethical obligations are further defined in the Citizens Protection Act (CPA), which provides:

> 28 U.S.C. § 530B. Ethical Standards for Attorneys for the Government
>
> (a) An attorney for the Government shall be subject to State laws and rules, and local Federal court rules, governing attorneys in each State where such

1. Berger v. United States, 295 U.S. 78, 88 (1935).
2. ABA Standard for Criminal Justice: The Prosecution Function 3-1.2(b), (c) (4th ed. 2017).
3. ABA Standard for Criminal Justice: The Defense Function 4-1.2(b) (4th ed. 2017).

> attorney engages in that attorney's duties, to the same extent as other attorneys in that State.

This statute is sometimes referred to as the "McDade Amendment"—a reference to its chief sponsor, Congressman Joseph McDade, who was acquitted of federal criminal charges after trial and who complained throughout his case about the excesses of federal prosecutors. The Amendment was adopted to resolve a dispute the Department of Justice was having with state bar organizations and others about federal prosecutors' obligations to comply with state ethical rules. The specific ethics rules involved in the debate were the long-standing bar on lawyers contacting represented parties (the "no-contact" rule)[4] and a rule limiting prosecutors' ability to subpoena lawyers.[5] The McDade Amendment's application to violations of the "no-contact" rule is clear,[6] but its potential effects in other areas in which state ethics rules are more stringent than federal rules or constitutional standards is unclear.

---

4. *See* Model Rule of Prof'l Conduct 4.2 (1983).

5. *See id.* Rule 3.8(e).

6. *See, e.g.*, United States v. Koerber, 966 F. Supp. 2d 1207 (D. Utah 2013) (granting motion to suppress upon a finding that prosecutors and investigators violated Utah's no-contact rule and thus the Citizens Protection Act).

CHAPTER 2

General Part

I. ELEMENTS: ACTUS REUS AND MENS REA

The "elements" of a crime are the skeleton upon which a case is built. Simply put, they are the facts the government must prove beyond a reasonable doubt to secure a conviction. To illustrate the different types of elements, we will look to the crime of perjury (18 U.S.C. § 1621). It requires the government to prove beyond a reasonable doubt the facts that the defendant:

- took an oath
- before a tribunal, officer, or person in any case in which federal law authorizes an oath to be administered
- willfully gave testimony that was
- material
- and false, and
- the defendant knew when he gave the testimony that it was false

The most basic element of a crime is the *actus reus* (guilty act or, in some cases, omission). Due process bars punishing "bad" thoughts alone. To warrant criminal sanction, then, there must be a criminal act—or a failure to act in the face of a duty to do so. For perjury, the actus reus is giving false testimony under oath.

Most violations require that the guilty act be accompanied by the second principal element, a *mens rea* (guilty mind). This culpable mental state, sometimes referred to as "scienter," is identified by statute or judicial implication. As the Supreme Court has frequently asserted, "as a general matter, our criminal law seeks to punish the 'vicious will.' With few exceptions, 'wrongdoing must be conscious to be criminal.'"[1] Thus, criminal law frowns on imposing strict liability, and recklessness and negligence normally do not suffice. In a perjury case, the required mens rea is that the defendant "knowingly" and "willfully" testified falsely.

Some crimes have a "*result*" element—for example, in a murder case, the victim must die for a case to go forward. Another common type of element is the aptly named "*attendant circumstance*" element. This is a fact that must be proved but is neither the actus reus nor the mens rea. A perjury case, for example, requires the government to prove the attendant circumstance that the false testimony was material.

Finally, prosecutors in federal criminal cases are often required to prove a "*jurisdictional*" element (sometimes referred to as the "jurisdictional hook" for the crime). Because the framers chose to leave the police power largely to the states, Congress must find an Article I power to justify its enactment of criminal statutes. Many federal crimes, then, require proof of an element that justifies Congress's exercise of power. For example, Congress employed its Postal Power[2] in enacting the mail fraud statute, and that statute accordingly requires as a jurisdictional element proof of a mailing. Where Congress relied on its Commerce Clause power to enact a criminal statute, the jurisdictional element often takes the form of a requirement that the crime take place "in or affecting interstate commerce." Sometimes, however, the constitutional justification for the crime is established not by a separate element but rather by the nature of the crime. The federal interest in perjury cases, for example, is reflected in the requirement that the offense take place before tribunal or person that is authorized by federal law to administer an oath. Perjury offenses, then, can be viewed as necessary and proper to effectuate the functioning of those federal entities (Congress, the Courts, and Executive Branch departments and agencies) that require that certain actions be taken under oath.

---

1. Ruan v. United States, 597 U.S. 450, 458 (2022) (internal quotation marks omitted). *But see* Counterman v. Colorado, 600 U.S. 66 (2023) (in true-threat cases, the government must prove that the defendant had some subjective understanding of his statements' threatening nature, but the First Amendment requires no more than proof of recklessness).
2. U.S. Const., art. 1, § 8, cl. 7.

This book organizes its discussion of each crime according to the elements of the offense. Because these are the building blocks of the case, prosecutors must be careful to include all the elements of the crime in the indictment.[3] And the Fifth Amendment's due process guarantee and the Sixth Amendment's jury trial right "require criminal convictions to rest upon a jury determination that the defendant is guilty of every element of the crime with which he is charged, beyond a reasonable doubt."[4] In a jury trial, then, each element should be charged and explained to the jury.[5]

In theory, the elements of a crime should be evident from the face of a statute but that is often not the case in federal practice. The federal courts regularly add elements not obvious on the face of the statute and occasionally read elements stated in statutory text right out of it. Reference should be had, then, to the caselaw or to the pattern jury instructions most circuits provide. It is fair to warn readers that the Supreme Court has been less than rigorous in its elements analysis. For example, it has created elements that cannot be easily anchored to the statutory language,[6] has transferred an element identified as part of one statute to a dissimilar statute,[7] and has used the definitional section of one statute to define elements in two other, quite distinct, statutes, with little justification or explanation.[8]

II. MENS REA

Most criminal codes contain a general mens rea provision—like that reflected in Model Penal Code (MPC) § 2.02—that identifies the culpable mental states used in criminal legislation and defines them. Some codes also contain default rules of interpretation of the kind articulated in MPC § 2.02(4), which provides, for example, that "[w]hen the law defining an

3. The Supreme Court granted certiorari in *United States v. Resendiz-Ponce*, 549 U.S. 102 (2007), to determine whether the omission of an element of a criminal offense from a federal indictment can constitute harmless error. Because the Court ultimately concluded that the indictment at issue was not defective, it did not reach the harmless-error question. *Id.* at 109-11. In a subsequent case, however, the Supreme Court cited *Resendiz-Ponce* for the proposition that a "criminal indictment must set forth all elements of the charged crime." *Ruan*, 597 U.S. at 462.

4. United States v. Gaudin, 515 U.S. 506, 510 (1995).

5. *See id.* In *Neder v. United States*, 527 U.S. 1, 4 (1999), the Supreme Court held that the omission of an element in the jury instructions is subject to harmless-error analysis under the constitutional harmless error standard of *Chapman v. California*, 386 U.S. 18, 24 (1967).

6. *See, e.g.*, United States v. Aguilar, 515 U.S. 593 (1995); Staples v. United States, 511 U.S. 600 (1994).

7. *See, e.g.*, Arthur Andersen LLP v. United States, 544 U.S. 696 (2005).

8. *See, e.g.*, McDonnell v. United States, 579 U.S. 550 (2016).

offense prescribes the kind of culpability that is sufficient for the commission of an offense, without distinguishing among the material elements thereof, such provision shall apply to all the material elements of the offense, unless a contrary purpose plainly appears."

Among the most glaring deficiencies of the federal criminal code are its lack of such a general mens rea provision and default interpretive rules, and its failure to define the more than 100 types of culpable mental states scattered throughout the code. Judges have taken up the slack, defining by common law adjudication the requisite mens rea for many federal statutes. This is a critical delegation of power because in many white-collar cases questions of intent predominate. In perjury cases, for example, testifying as to facts that are untrue is not a crime. Providing false testimony is only criminally culpable if the witness *knew* his statements were false; if he was ignorant, mistaken, or spoke negligently or even recklessly in asserting a fact about which he was not certain, he is not guilty of perjury.

A. The Supreme Court's Hierarchy of Mens Rea

The Supreme Court has laid out a hierarchy of mens rea.

1. Acting with **purpose** is the most culpable level of scienter and it is the hardest to prove. "A person acts purposefully when he 'consciously desires' a result."[9] This level of mens rea is not commonly seen in federal statutes.
2. The next most culpable level of mens rea is acting with **knowledge**. "An act is done knowingly if the defendant is aware of the act and does not [act] [fail to act] through ignorance, mistake, or accident."[10] Where what is at stake is "knowledge" of a "result" element—for example, that death will result from the defendant's act in a murder case—one obviously cannot absolutely "know" what the future holds. In those circumstances, a person is said to act "knowingly" if he is aware "that the result is practically certain to follow from his conduct whatever his desire may be as to that result."[11] Congress very frequently uses a "knowingly" mens rea in federal statutes.

9. *Counterman*, 600 U.S. at 79.
10. Ninth Circuit, Manual of Model Criminal Jury Instructions 4.8 (2022 ed.) [hereinafter Ninth Circuit Instructions]; *see also* United States ex rel. Schutte v. Supervalu Inc., 598 U.S. 739, 751 (2023); Seventh Circuit, The William J. Bauer Pattern Criminal Jury Instructions for the Seventh Circuit 4.10 (2023 ed.) [hereinafter Seventh Circuit Instructions].
11. United States v. Bailey, 444 U.S. 394, 404 (1980) (emphasis added and internal quotation marks omitted); *see also* Am. L. Inst., Model Penal Code § 2.02(2)(b) [hereinafter MPC].

3. The third level of culpability is **recklessness**. A defendant acts "recklessly" when he "consciously disregards a substantial and unjustifiable risk that his conduct will harm another."[12] Recklessness shows a lack of concern about risk rather than an awareness of the harm that will ensue, but it is still "morally culpable conduct, involving a 'deliberate decision to endanger another.'"[13] One does not often see a "reckless" mens rea outside of federal regulatory violations.
4. The last level is **negligence**. "A person acts negligently if he *is not* but *should be* aware of a substantial risk" because a reasonable person would be.[14] This is an objective standard that does not require that the defendant be conscious or aware of the wrongful nature of his conduct. It is rarely used in federal criminal law except in criminalized federal regulations.

This hierarchy does not begin to exhaust all the scienter terms used in federal statutes. We will explore within two very popular such terms, "willfully" and "corruptly."

B. Common Mens Rea Issues

Litigants attempting to discern what mens rea applies to a given federal crime face a number of challenges, the most common of which concern:

(1) **Silent Statutes.** Federal statutes not infrequently fail to specify any mens rea requirement. The Supreme Court frowns on strict criminal liability so it generally—but not invariably—presumes that there ought to be a mens rea element, selects one, and reads it into the statute. Normally, where a statute is silent and the Court applies a presumption of mens rea to supply one, it inserts a "knowing" mens rea into the statute.

(2) **Statutory Ambiguity.** Even more commonly, the statute is ambiguous as to which elements an express intent requirement modifies. Statutory ambiguity cases often concern the "knowing" mens rea and essentially pose the question "just what did the defendant have to know?" For example, consider the following statute: "Whoever knowingly sells property stolen from military stores in or affecting interstate commerce" is guilty of a felony. The question is how far down the sentence the "knowing" modifier travels. Does the government have to prove that the defendant knew the property he

12. *Counterman*, 600 U.S. at 79 (internal quotation marks omitted).
13. *Id.*
14. *Id.* at 79 n.5 (emphasis added).

sold was stolen? Does it have to prove that he knew that the items sold were stolen specifically from the U.S. military? Does it have to prove that he knew that his sales were "in or affecting interstate commerce"?

(3) **Definitional Ambiguity.** The same mens rea term can mean different things in different contexts. A couple of terms frequently used in the federal code, "willfully" and "corruptly," do not have one invariable meaning. For example, courts have read "willfully" to reflect three distinct states of mind; which one is appropriate depends on the statutory context in which the term is used.[15]

I. General Interpretive Tools

When courts are called upon to interpret statutes raising mens rea issues, they will bring to bear all the normal tools of statutory construction, beginning by examining the provision's plain language, with reference to dictionary definitions, the rules of grammar, and any common law definition of statutory terms. This textualist analysis also approves reference to statutory context, including the use of the term in other code sections, the statutory structure, and even the titles of code sections.[16] Although a majority of the Court purports to apply a textualist analysis, they often rely on their reading of the legislative intent underlying the statute to avoid the import of the plain meaning of the statute.[17] Of late, the Court has been preoccupied with reading statutes to avoid hypothetical applications of a criminal prohibition that trouble the Justices and with attempting to rewrite overlapping code provisions to avoid redundancy.[18] Actuated by these concerns, for example, the Court famously ruled that a fish is not a "tangible object."[19] The Court will, as appropriate, also lean on such interpretative staples as the rule disfavoring surplusage and that favoring constitutional avoidance. And the Justices will delve into the Latin tool kit and dust off *ejusdem generis*,[20] *noscitur a sociis*,[21] and their ilk.

---

15. *See, e.g.*, Ratzlaf v. United States, 510 U.S. 135, 141 (1994).
16. *See* Yates v. United States, 574 U.S. 528 (2015).
17. *See, e.g.*, *id.*; Fischer v. United States, 603 U.S. 480 (2024).
18. *See, e.g.*, *Fischer*, 603 U.S. 480; Snyder v. United States, 603 U.S. 1 (2024); *McDonnell*, 579 U.S. 550; *Yates*, 574 U.S. 528.
19. *See Yates*, 574 U.S. 528.
20. This canon of construction instructs that "a general or collective term at the end of a list of specific items is typically controlled and defined by reference to the specific classes . . . that precede it." *Fischer*, 603 U.S. at 487 (internal quotation marks omitted).
21. The Court translates this canon to mean that a "word is given more precise content by the neighboring words with which it is associated. That avoid[s] ascribing to one word a meaning so broad that it is inconsistent with the company it keeps." *Id.* (internal quotations marks omitted).

But there are some presumptions and canons of construction that are unique to this context and that federal courts commonly use to create a mens rea requirement where the statute is silent (silent statutes), determine which elements a given term modifies (statutory ambiguity), or which meaning of a given term ought to be used (definitional ambiguity). These are explored below.

C. Presumption of Mens Rea and Exceptions

When addressing mens rea issues specifically, the Court usually starts with "a long-standing presumption, traceable to the common law, that Congress intends to require a defendant to possess a culpable mental state regarding 'each of the statutory elements that criminalize otherwise innocent conduct.'"[22]

First, with respect to silent statutes, the Court often (but not always) applies what it calls a presumption of mens rea when the statute does not specify any scienter, appearing on its face to call for strict liability. In so doing, the Court says it reads into the statute "only that *mens rea* which is necessary to separate wrongful conduct from otherwise innocent conduct."[23] Although Justice Alito has urged the Court to consider reading into statutes a "recklessness" standard rather than the more demanding "knowing" standard, the Court has thus far favored inserting the latter into silent statutes.[24]

Second, with respect to statutory ambiguity problems, the Court uses the presumption to apply a mens rea element that could be read restrictively to modify only one element to apply to other elements in the statute.[25] As the Court explained in *Rehaif v. United States*, 588 U.S. 225 (2019), as "a matter of ordinary English grammar, we normally read the statutory term 'knowingly' as applying to all the subsequently listed elements of the crime."[26] Note, however, that there may be exceptions made when the mens rea term precedes a "long statutory phrase" and the question the Court faces is "how far into the statute the modifier extends."[27]

In applying the presumption in such cases, the Court focuses on what "degree of knowledge [is] sufficient to 'mak[e] a person legally responsible for the consequences of his or her act or omission.'"[28] In particular, the

22. Rehaif v. United States, 588 U.S. 225, 229 (2019).
23. Elonis v. United States, 575 U.S. 723, 736 (2015) (internal quotation marks omitted).
24. *See, e.g.*, *Rehaif*, 588 U.S. at 259 (Alito, J., dissenting); *Elonis*, 575 U.S. at 745-46 (Alito, J., concurring in part and dissenting in part).
25. *See Rehaif*, 588 U.S. at 230.
26. *Id.* at 230 (internal quotation marks omitted); *see Ruan*, 575 U.S. at 458 ("We have . . . held that a word such as 'knowingly' modifies not only the words directly following it, but also those other statutory terms that 'separate wrongful from innocent acts.'").
27. *Rehaif*, 588 U.S. at 230.
28. *Id.* at 229; *see also Ruan*, 597 U.S. at 458.

Court favors applying a presumption of mens rea to elements that separate innocent from wrongful conduct.[29]

For example, in *Rehaif*, the defendant was charged with being an alien in possession of a firearm while being unlawfully present in the United States. A federal statute, 18 U.S.C. § 922(g), provides that "[i]t shall be unlawful" for certain individuals to possess firearms. The provision lists nine categories of individuals subject to the prohibition, including aliens who are "illegally or unlawfully in the United States." A separate provision, § 924(a)(2), adds that anyone who *knowingly* violates the first provision shall be fined or imprisoned for up to ten years. Rehaif had lawfully entered the United States on a student visa. When he failed out of school, his immigration status changed to unlawfully present in the United States. It was at this point that he used two firearms at a shooting range.

The question presented was whether the statute required the government to prove that Rehaif knew not only that he possessed a firearm, but also that he was unlawfully present in the United States. Applying the presumption of mens rea, the Court held that the government had to prove knowledge of both elements. The Court emphasized that, assuming compliance with licensing requirements, "the possession of a gun can be entirely innocent" and therefore it was Rehaif's knowledge of his immigration status that was the crucial element separating innocent from wrongful conduct.[30]

1. Exception 1: Public Welfare Offenses

The Justices "have typically declined to apply the presumption in favor of scienter in cases involving statutory provisions that form part of a 'regulatory' or 'public welfare' program that carry only minor penalties" (public welfare offenses).[31] Public welfare offenses generally concern *malum prohibitum* ("wrong because prohibited") regulatory offenses that involve "dangerous or deleterious devices or products or obnoxious waste materials" of a sort that ought to put the defendant on notice of the regulation.[32]

This is a potentially very broadly applicable exception because of the scope of federal regulations. Congress often enacts legislation that charges executive branch departments or federal agencies with the obligation to issue regulations to implement the statutory policy. At the same time, Congress frequently passes a provision that makes the "knowing violation" of these yet-to-be drafted regulations subject to criminal sanction. Although most people focus on the civil or administrative law content of the regulations that fill the Code of Federal Regulations, it is estimated

---

29. *See Rehaif*, 588 U.S. at 231; *see also Ruan*, 597 U.S. at 458.
30. *Rehaif*, 588 U.S. at 232.
31. *Id.* at 232; *see also Ruan*, 597 U.S. at 459-60.
32. United States v. Int'l Minerals & Chem. Corp., 402 U.S. 558, 565 (1971).

that hundreds of thousands of the regulations are criminally enforceable because of this congressional practice. And many of the statutes that these regulations purport to implement relate to what could generally be called the public welfare, ensuring, for example, that the public is protected from a variety of possible workplace, travel, product, environmental, or other hazards.

If a court is asked to interpret what a "knowing violation" involves, and applies the public welfare doctrine, it will ignore the grammatical import of that phrase, meaning that it will *not* require the government to prove that the defendant knew that he was in violation of the regulation, much less that he knew of the regulations' contents or of their applicability to his activities. All the government must prove is that the defendant knew the general nature of what he was doing.

For example, in *United States v. International Minerals & Chemical Corp*, 402 U.S. 558 (1971), a regulation required that a manufacturer shipping hazardous materials list both the name of the material and its regulatory classification on the shipping documentation. The statute made "knowing violation" of this regulation a misdemeanor. If the Court had applied its normal presumption of mens rea, it would have required that the government prove that the defendant knew the facts that rendered his conduct culpable. Shipping corrosive liquids is not inherently wrongful or illegal. What makes the manufacturer's conduct criminal is its failure to comply with the regulatory labeling requirements; thus, if the court had applied the presumption, it likely would have required the government to prove the defendant's knowledge of its failure to comply with the shipping regulations.

But the public welfare doctrine negates the presumption of mens rea.[33] The *International Minerals* Court applied that doctrine to hold that the government did *not* have to prove that the manufacturer was aware of the applicable regulations or of the fact that it violated the regulation by including the name of the material shipped but omitting the regulatory classification on its shipping documentation. The government did have to prove the basic fact that the company knew that it was shipping a hazardous material. Although the business must "know" something, then, this is in practice a form of strict liability because the government will have little difficulty proving that a company in the business of selling sulfuric acid knows that it is shipping hazardous materials.

The Court has applied the public welfare doctrine to minimize the government's burden of proving scienter in a variety of cases, including those involving possession of an unlicensed hand grenade, sales of controlled substances, shipments of corrosive liquids, and the packaging of misbranded

33. *See Staples*, 511 U.S. at 607 n.3.

or adulterated drugs, and lower courts have applied the doctrine to various environmental statutes.[34]

In separating cases in which the public welfare doctrine is properly invoked from those in which it is not, the Supreme Court has looked to a number of factors that bear on whether the regulation is such that persons subject to it ought to be on notice of its demands. Such factors include the purposes of the legislation, whether the regulations deal with potentially harmful or injurious items, and the highly regulated nature of the materials at issue. In *Staples v. United States*, 511 U.S. 600 (1994), the Supreme Court declined to apply the public welfare doctrine to the regulation of firearms. In so doing, it added two additional factors that would argue against applying the doctrine: the commonplace nature of the activity, in *Staples*, gun ownership, and the potentially harsh penalties available.

In *Staples*, the Court indicated that all these factors go to the ultimate question whether, by virtue of the public welfare doctrine, "the statute potentially would impose criminal sanctions on a class of person whose mental state . . . makes their actions entirely innocent."[35] If so, the Court will decline to use the public welfare doctrine to minimize the government's burden of proving scienter. In some cases in which the Court has declined to apply to the doctrine on this basis, the defendants involved were far from *moral* "innocents." Thus, "innocent" seems to translate into a conclusion that, given the population regulated and the complexity of the regulatory scheme, we cannot fairly expect people to know the content of the regulations.

To the extent one can generalize based on a fairly limited sample, the Court declines to minimize the applicable mens rea through the public welfare doctrine when the regulations at issue govern the behavior of individuals—e.g., the owners of firearms—who can "innocently" (meaning understandably) run afoul of complicated regulatory schemes. In the cases in which the courts generally apply the public welfare doctrine, the defendants are companies or individuals involved in an industry who should know, by virtue of the nature of their business, that they are subject to regulation and have the capacity—and responsibility—to inform themselves of applicable legal standards.

---

34. *See* United States v. Freed, 401 U.S. 601 (1971) (hand grenade); *Int'l Minerals*, 402 U.S. 558 (shipping hazardous materials); United States v. Dotterweich, 320 U.S. 277 (1943) (adulterated and misbranded drugs); United States v. Balint, 258 U.S. 250 (1922) (sales of controlled substances); United States v. Weitzenhoff, 35 F.3d 1275 (9th Cir. 1993) (violation of Clean Water Act required only that they defendant knew he was discharging into navigable waters, not that he was discharging in excess of permitted amounts).

35. *Staples*, 511 U.S. at 614-15.

2. Exception 2: Jurisdictional Elements

According to the Court, "[j]urisdictional elements do not describe the 'evil Congress seeks to prevent,' but instead simply ensure that the Federal Government has the constitutional authority to regulate the defendant's conduct."[36] Because jurisdictional elements do not relate to the culpability of the proscribed conduct, the Court declines to apply the presumption of mens rea to such elements.[37] Thus, for example, the wire fraud statute was passed pursuant to Congress's Commerce Clause powers, and so requires the government to prove that the defendant caused an interstate wiring in furtherance of his scheme to defraud. It is clear, however, that the defendant need not know or intend the jurisdictional wiring or its interstate character; it is sufficient if the requisite wiring was reasonably foreseeable.

D. Ignorance of the Law Is No Excuse

"The general rule that ignorance of the law or a mistake of law is no defense to criminal prosecution is deeply rooted in the American legal system."[38] "This maxim . . . normally applies where a defendant has the requisite mental state in respect to the elements of the crime but claims to be 'unaware of the existence of a statute proscribing his conduct.' "[39] *In short, one generally cannot defend a prosecution by arguing that one did not know that what one did was a crime.*

1. Exception 1: The Statute Makes Knowledge of the Criminal Law Relevant

Ignorance of the law *will* excuse if the law itself permits it to do so. Put another way, the statute itself may impose upon a prosecutor the obligation to prove an accused's knowledge of the law as a specific element of a particular offense. Thus, it is more accurate to say that ignorance of the law is no excuse unless the statute makes knowledge of the law an element of the offense. The mens rea term "willfully" is a prime example of definitional ambiguity in that it has three meanings, one of which illustrates this exception. One definition of "willfully" requires the government to prove that the defendant knew not only what he was doing, and that it was in a general sense bad or "unlawful," but also that the defendant knew that his specific conduct was proscribed by statute.[40]

---

36. *Rehaif*, 588 U.S. 230.
37. *See, e.g., Ruan*, 597 U.S. at 460.
38. Cheek v. United States, 498 U.S. 192, 199 (1991).
39. *Rehaif*, 588 U.S. at 234.
40. *See Ratzlaf*, 510 U.S. at 149 ("To convict Ratzlaf of the crime with which he was charged, violation of 31 U.S.C. §§ 5322(a) and 5324(3), the jury had to find he knew the structuring in which he engaged was unlawful.").

2. Exception 2: The Statute Makes Knowledge of Collateral, Civil Laws Relevant

As the Supreme Court has explained, the maxim "ignorance of the law is no excuse" does not normally apply where a defendant "'has a mistaken impression concerning the legal effect of some *collateral matter* and that mistake results in his misunderstanding the full significance of his conduct,' thereby negating an element of the offense."[41] Many people find this distinction confusing but it is fairly simple: "ignorance of the law is no excuse" does not necessarily apply where the criminal statute makes knowledge of some collateral *civil* regulation, rule, or statute an element of the crime. The bottom line is that "knowing" can be read to require knowledge of a so-called "legal fact," meaning knowledge of some regulation located outside the criminal realm—often in administrative law.

For example, in *Rehaif*, the Supreme Court required the government to prove that the defendant had knowledge of the law: his immigration status as unlawfully present in the United States. This is a legal fact because it requires that the defendant know the content of the immigration provision at issue, but the Court decreed that that legal fact was "collateral," so the "ignorance of the law is no excuse" maxim did not apply.[42] Note that the legal knowledge required—that Rehaif was present in the United States unlawfully—simply required that he be aware of the content of civil law immigration rules; the government did not need to prove that he knew such rules were criminally enforceable.

E. The Rule of Lenity

The rule of lenity, also known as the rule of strict construction, potentially applies to *any* interpretive question raised by a *criminal* statute, not just to mens rea questions.

The rule of lenity is a canon of construction that provides that "when choice has to be made between two readings of what conduct Congress

41. *Rehaif*, 588 U.S. at 234 (emphasis added). The Model Penal Code's way of explaining this distinction is that ignorance or mistake as to a matter of law is a defense if it negatives the mens rea applicable to a given material element of the offense but only if the law as to which the defendant is ignorant or mistaken is not the law defining the offense but rather pertains to some other legal rule. *See, e.g.*, MPC, *supra* note 11, §§ 2.04(1)(a), 2.02(9) & § 2.02 cmt. For example, if a defendant is prosecuted for malicious destruction of property that he honestly but mistakenly believed belonged to him, he may have a defense premised upon his mistake of law. In such circumstances, his mistake concerns not the criminal law under which he is being prosecuted (i.e., is destruction of property a crime) but rather the property law that is made an attendant circumstance by the criminal prohibition (i.e., is this property his or does it actually belong to another).

42. *Rehaif*, 588 U.S. at 235.

has made a crime, it is appropriate, before [the Court chooses] the harsher alternative, to require that Congress should have spoken in language that is clear and definite."[43] In other words, lenity requires that if two readings of an ambiguous statute are equally plausible, courts should endorse the construction that is most favorable to the defense.

This rule is founded first on notice concerns: "'a fair warning should be given to the world in language that the common world will understand, of what the law intends to do if a certain line is passed.'"[44] Second, the legality principal and legitimacy concerns reflected in separation of powers principles justify lenity. The legality principal frowns on judicial law-making because the judiciary does not have the constitutional power or legitimacy to forge criminal norms and judicial interpretation is by definition retroactive; the defendant will only know whether what he did was criminal when the appeals court figures out what the elements of the offense actually are.

The rule of lenity formerly had a real role in statutory interpretation but today it is, in general, an afterthought used to rationalize a result already reached. This is because the "rule applies only when a criminal statute contains a grievous ambiguity or uncertainty, and only if, after seizing everything from which aid can be derived, the Court can make no more than a guess as to what Congress intended."[45] Given the wealth of interpretative aids the Court employs, it is rare that the Justices reach the point of guessing.

F. Remedy for Vagueness or Other Statutory Defects

Where the statutory scheme is such that the line between acceptable business behavior and criminally culpable behavior is not clearly drawn or intuitively obvious, the Court may read a mens rea element into a statute or elevate the existing mens rea. For example, in *United States v. United States Gypsum Co.*, 438 U.S. 422 (1978), in which the Court imposed an intent requirement in prosecutions for price-fixing offenses under the Sherman Act, 15 U.S.C. § 1, the Court explained the necessity of a mens rea requirement as follows:

> ... With certain exceptions for conduct regarded as *per se* illegal because of its unquestionably anticompetitive effects, the behavior proscribed by the [Sherman] Act is often difficult to distinguish from the gray zone of socially acceptable and economically justifiable business conduct.... The imposition of criminal liability on a corporate official, or for that matter on a corporation directly, for engaging in such conduct which only after the fact is determined

43. United States v. Universal C.I.T. Credit Corp., 344 U.S. 218, 221-22 (1952).

44. Marinello v. United States, 584 U.S. 1, 2 (2018).

45. Ocasio v. United States, 578 U.S. 282, 295 n.8 (2016) (internal quotation marks omitted).

> to violate the statute because of anticompetitive effects, without inquiring into the intent with which it was undertaken, holds out the distinct possibility of overdeterrence . . . Further, . . . criminal sanctions would be used, not to punish conscious and calculated wrongdoing at odds with statutory proscriptions, but instead simply to *regulate* business practices regardless of the intent with which they were undertaken.[46]

In extreme cases, where the law governing the offense is very unclear, the defense may have a due process objection to the prosecution on vagueness grounds. Courts will often find that the mens rea element of a statutory scheme saves it from such vagueness attacks. They also use the possible vagueness of the statute in absence of a high level of mens rea to justify reading a heightened intent requirement into the statutory scheme.[47] As the Supreme Court has explained, "'a scienter requirement may mitigate a law's vagueness, especially with respect to the adequacy of notice . . . that [the] conduct is proscribed.'"[48]

G. Specific Mental States: "Knowingly," "Willfully," and "Corruptly"

1. "Knowingly" in General

Where the "*knowing*" mens rea becomes the subject of litigation, it is generally in the context of *silent statutes* or *statutory ambiguity*. When a statute does not provide an express mens rea element, the Supreme Court will use the interpretive methods discussed above to decide whether the statute ought to be construed to impose strict liability or whether some mens rea ought to be read into it. When it chooses to insert a mens rea element into an otherwise silent statute, the Court often requires that the government prove that the defendant "knowingly" engaged in the proscribed conduct.

With respect to statutory ambiguity, many if not most statutes in the federal criminal code require knowledge of *something*—the question is "what does the defendant need to know"? Where a statute is ambiguous in this regard, it is helpful to plot out all the possible elements that the knowing mens rea element may modify and then use the canons of construction outlined above to forecast the arguments of the government and the defense.

For example, consider the National Firearms Act, which provides that "[i]t shall be unlawful for any person. . . to receive or possess a firearm

---

46. *United States Gypsum Co.*, 438 U.S. at 440-42; *see also* Screws v. United States, 325 U.S. 91, 101-02 (1945) (plurality opinion).
47. *See, e.g.*, McFadden v. United States, 576 U.S. 186, 197 (2015); Boyce Motor Lines, Inc. v. United States, 342 U.S. 337, 342 (1952); *Screws*, 325 U.S. at 101-02.
48. Posters 'N' Things, Ltd. v. United States, 511 U.S. 513, 526 (1994).

which is not registered to him in the National Firearms Registration and Transfer Record."[49] Assume that the applicable statutory definition includes machine guns—that is, guns capable of fully automatic firing—as regulated "firearms." Assume further that the defendant has been indicted for unlawful possession of an unregistered machine gun in violation of the Act.

Note that there is no mens rea provision in the statute. The government will argue that Congress intended the statute to be a strict liability offense, likely contending that the public welfare offense justifies such treatment. The defendant will counter with the presumption of mens rea. Assume that the court applies the presumption to insert a "knowing" mens rea into the statute. The question then will be what does the government have to prove the defendant "knew"?

The government will argue for the easiest scienter to prove, requiring only that it demonstrate the simple fact that the defendant knew he had a gun, whatever its nature or capabilities. It will invoke the public welfare doctrine and point to *International Minerals* and like cases in which the Court was satisfied by proof that the defendant knew only that he was dealing with a dangerous or deleterious device.

The defense lawyer will want to increase the government's burden and so will use our interpretive tool kit to push the court to accept a reading further along the spectrum of difficulty. She will argue, then, that the statute requires proof that the defendant knew not only that he had a gun, but also that his gun had all the characteristics that qualified it is a "machine gun" under the statutory definition (i.e., that it was capable of fully automatic firing). She will reason that merely possessing a gun can be entirely innocent; it is the knowledge of the fully automatic firing capacity of the firearm that separates innocent from potentially wrongful conduct. Requiring the government to prove the defendant's knowledge of this specific fact is obviously more difficult.

In support of its position, defense counsel will invoke the presumption of mens rea and the rule of lenity and will argue that this reading is necessary to prevent the statute from convicting "innocents." It will contend that the commonplace nature of gun ownership means that mere possession of a firearm does not raise red flag regarding their regulation. The government will respond, *inter alia*, with the public welfare doctrine, arguing that guns are inherently dangerous and highly regulated devices and, as such, ought to put their owners on notice of their responsibility to learn of and conform to applicable regulations.

Finally, the defense may wish to push the court even further down the difficulty spectrum and argue that the government must prove that the defendant knew the definition of a statutory machinegun or that the

---

49. 26 U.S.C. § 5861(d).

defendant knew that the law required him to register the weapon. These legal facts would be virtually impossible for the government to prove in the usual case. Defense counsel will again rely on the argument that, absent such proof, "innocents" may be rendered liable and cite the rule of lenity. The government will respond by relying on the rule that "ignorance of the law is no excuse." To which the defense will retort that this maxim does not apply when what is at stake is knowledge of collateral legal facts that have nothing to do with the defendant's knowledge of the criminality of his conduct.

This hypothetical is based on *Staples v. United States*, 511 U.S. 600 (1994), in which the parties were fighting over the mens rea appropriately applied to the statute quoted above. The Court applied the presumption of mens rea to create a "knowing" mens rea. When it came to deciding just what the defendant must know, the Court concluded that absent an onerous mens rea requirement, "innocent" gun owners unaware of the fully-automatic firing capacity of their guns would be sanctioned. According, it declined to apply the public welfare doctrine and held that the government had to prove that the defendant knew the specific characteristics of his gun that made it a statutory firearm, that is, that it was capable of fully automatic firing.

a. Proving "Knowledge" Through Conscious Avoidance/Willful Blindness

To ease their burden of showing that the defendant actually, subjectively "knew," federal prosecutors often seek a "willful blindness," "conscious avoidance," or "ostrich" jury instruction. To be perfectly clear, although many refer to this theory as "willful blindness," it is a way to prove *knowledge*; it has nothing to do with the definition or application of a statutory "willfulness" element.

There has been considerable confusion in the courts regarding how to conceptualize this theory of knowledge. Academics often query how one can subjectively "know" something that one is willfully avoiding learning. Probably the most persuasive rationale for the willful blindness theory of "knowledge" is that a defendant who goes out of his way to avoid positive knowledge—particularly one who consciously seeks to create plausible deniability—is as culpable as someone who actually knows.

The Supreme Court set forth its understanding of the requisites of a "willful blindness" jury charge in *Global-Tech Appliances, Inc. v. SEB S.A.*, 563 U.S. 754 (2011). Although the case concerned the mens rea applicable in civil copyright litigation, the Supreme Court relied on what it understood to be the content of the standard in criminal cases. Thus, in *Global-Tech*, the Court decreed that proof of willful blindness has two basic requirements: "(1) The defendant must *subjectively believe* that there is a *high probability* that a fact exists and (2) the defendant must take *deliberate actions* to avoid learning of that fact."[50] The Justices made clear that willful blindness "surpasses recklessness and negligence."[51] Thus a conscious avoidance charge does *not* allow a jury to find that a defendant "knew" something because the jurors think any reasonable person *should* have known (negligence) or that the defendant unreasonably disregarded a substantial and unjustified risk that the fact existed (recklessness). Rather, a "willfully blind defendant is one who takes deliberate actions to avoid confirming a high probability of wrongdoing and *who can almost be said to have actually known the critical facts*."[52]

The defense will generally object—vociferously—to the government's request for a willful blindness jury instruction, contending that there were insufficient "red flags" in evidence to to even suggest that the defendant was willfully blind. The defense's concern is that the instruction, no matter how carefully crafted, actually encourages "the jury to convict based on an *ex post facto* theory (he should have been more careful) or to convict on a negligence theory (the defendant should have known his conduct was illegal)."[53] Unless carefully restricted, the instruction can be perceived to shift the burden to the defendant of proving that—no matter how unreasonable or reckless it may seem—he did not, in fact, "know." Recognizing this, many courts state that willful blindness instructions are appropriately given only in "rare circumstances"[54] but the instruction is in fact widely used and is frequently approved on appeal. If the court determines to give a willful blindness charge, defense counsel will ask the court to underscore that the test is a *subjective* one—not an *objective* test potentially rendering the defendant criminally liable for negligence—and that the jury must find that the defendant *deliberately* took an *affirmative step* to avoid knowledge.

2. "Willfully"

The "willful" mens rea provides a notable example of definitional ambiguity. The caselaw recognizes at least three levels of meaning potentially applicable to this element.

a. Intentional or Non-Accidental

The definition that is easiest for the government to prove provides that a "willful" act is one that "is intentional, or knowing, or voluntary, as distinguished

50. *Global-Tech*, 563 U.S. at 769 (emphasis added).
51. *Id.*
52. *Id.* (emphasis added).
53. United States v. Lighty, 616 F.3d 321, 378 (4th Cir. 2010) (internal quotation marks omitted).
54. *Id.*

from accidental.' "[55] As discussed in Chapter 4 (False Statements), even the Department of Justice does not think this is a sufficiently demanding level of scienter for most types of criminal cases. But, as is discussed in the Chapter 8 (Securities Fraud), the Second and Ninth Circuits have approved a similar instruction in federal securities fraud cases.[56]

b. Awareness of General "Unlawfulness" of Conduct

In *Bryan v. United States*, 524 U.S. 184 (1998), the Court approved a willfulness instruction that required proof that the defendant acted not merely "voluntarily," but also with a "bad purpose," that is, " 'with knowledge that his conduct was unlawful.' "[57] This is the default willfulness instruction.

To be clear, this does not mean that the government has to prove that the defendant knew about the *criminal* law at issue or intended to violate it. This is why the word "unlawful" is used. "Unlawful" means "not lawful" or "illegal." There are many types of laws; indeed, most laws that govern our conduct are civil in nature. Thus, knowing that one is acting unlawfully simply means knowing that one is acting contrary to *some* legal standard, but not what its nature is or how, if at all, it is enforced. For example, in many U.S. jurisdictions, speeding, running a red light, failing to yield, and failing to signal are civil infractions. They can result in fines and points on one's driver's license, but violators cannot be criminally sanctioned in the usual case. Violating these rules, however, does render one's conduct "unlawful" or "illegal."

This distinction may seem a tad precious, in that it draws lines that most non-lawyers would not necessarily intuit. But it is the critical distinction between this default level of "willfulness" and the next level, super mens rea.

c. Super Mens Rea: Awareness That Specific Conduct Is Unlawful

"[I]n some rare instances involving highly technical statutes that present the danger of ensnaring individuals engaged in apparently innocent conduct, . . . 'willfully' has been read to require proof that the defendant actually knew of the specific law prohibiting the conduct."[58] Defendants regularly ask federal courts to read "willfully" to impose this super mens rea requirement,

---

55. United States v. Starnes, 583 F.3d 196, 210 (3d Cir. 2009) (quoting Bryan v. United States, 524 U.S. 184, 191 n.12 (1998)).
56. *See, e.g.*, United States v. Kaiser, 609 F.3d 556, 568 (2d Cir. 2010).
57. *Bryan*, 524 U.S. at 191-92; *see also* Third Circuit Model Criminal Jury Instructions § 5.05 (Feb. 2022) (providing that "willfully" requires the government to prove beyond a reasonable doubt that a defendant "knew that [his or her] conduct was unlawful and intended to do something that the law forbids") [hereinafter Third Circuit Instructions].
58. *Starnes*, 583 F.3d at 211; *see, e.g.*, *Ratzlaf*, 510 U.S. at 149 (anti-structuring statute); *Cheek*, 498 U.S. at 199-202 (criminal tax statute).

which is virtually impossible for the government to meet. And courts regularly decline to do so, noting that the Supreme Court has applied this standard in only two contexts: tax prosecutions and criminal cases brought to enforce the ban on "structuring" cash transactions to avoid currency transaction reporting requirements.[59] The Court justified this super mens rea in these contexts because the regulatory offenses lacked sufficient moral content to put the average citizen on notice, and the regulatory schemes underlying the offences were unusually complex and difficult for the average person to parse. To protect the "innocent," then, the Court imposed this extraordinarily high level of mens rea.

3. "Corruptly"

The word "corruptly" means different things in different contexts and thus is another example of definitional ambiguity. This element is examined at some length in the Chapter 9 (Public Corruption) and Chapter 7 (Obstruction of Justice). The following is a simplified summary.

a. Public Corruption

In public corruption cases, a "corrupt" intent is normally defined as acting knowingly and intentionally, with a bad purpose of accomplishing either an unlawful end or result, or an otherwise lawful end or result by some unlawful method or means.[60] In federal bribery cases under 18 U.S.C. § 201(b)(1)(A), courts generally conflate two elements—the "corrupt" intent requirement and the "*quid pro quo*" element—and end up with an instruction that states: "[a] public official acts 'corruptly' when he or she accepts or receives, or agrees to accept or receive, a thing of value, in return for being influenced with the intent that, in exchange for the thing of value, some act would be influenced."[61]

b. Obstruction of Justice

In the obstruction-of-justice context, there is no one agreed-upon definition of the term "corruptly."[62] Section 1505 of Title 18, which deals with obstruction in the context of congressional investigations and agency proceedings, is the only provision that contains a definition of the term: "[a]s used in section 1505, the term 'corruptly' means acting with an *improper purpose*, personally or by influencing another, including making a false or

59. *See, e.g.*, *Starnes*, 583 F.3d at 211.
60. *See, e.g.*, Third Circuit Instructions, *supra* note 57, 6.18.201B1-3.
61. Ninth Circuit Instructions, *supra* note 10, 10.3.
62. *See* United States v. Fischer, 64 F.4th 329 (D.C. Cir. 2023), *rev'd on other grounds*, 603 U.S. 480 (2024).

misleading statement, or withholding, concealing, altering, or destroying a document or other information."[63]

Probably the most popular instruction in § 1503 and § 1512 cases also equates acting "corruptly" with acting with an "improper" or "wrongful" purpose or motive.[64] Some courts augment this instruction by requiring that, to act corruptly, the defendant must act "knowingly and dishonestly."[65] Still other courts import into their instructions some requirement that the defendant is aware that what he is doing is wrong. Thus, the commentary to the Ninth Circuit's pattern jury instructions notes that "corruptly" means acting with "consciousness of wrongdoing" under § 1512(c).[66] Finally, the Supreme Court has stated that the defendant must act with an intent to obstruct, at least for purposes of § 1503.[67] The following instruction, from the Tenth Circuit, may best capture the gist of these multiple definitions: to act corruptly means to act "with an improper purpose and to engage in conduct knowingly and dishonestly with the specific intent to subvert, impede or obstruct" the relevant proceeding.[68]

4. Specific and General Intent

Two mens rea terms—"specific" and "general" intent—do not appear in the code and are relics of a time when criminal statutes did not contain discrete mens rea elements. Because modern statutes, and courts interpreting them, at least attempt to specify a particular level of "elemental" mens rea, the continuing meaning of the distinction between "general" and "specific" intent is questionable. Indeed, the Supreme Court, recognizing that jury instructions concerning specific intent "have been criticized as too general and potentially misleading," has encouraged courts to "eschew use of difficult legal concepts like 'specific intent' and 'general intent.'"[69] Yet these terms appear with sufficient frequency in federal judicial opinions that they must be addressed.

If one is attempting to place the terms "specific" and "general" intent in the landscape of the Model Penal Code and the Supreme Court's mens rea hierarchy, "[i]n a general sense, 'purpose' corresponds loosely with the common-law concept of specific intent, while 'knowledge' corresponds loosely with the concept of general intent."[70]

---

63. 18 U.S.C. § 1515(b) (emphasis added).
64. *See, e.g.*, *Fischer*, 64 F.4th at 340; United States v. Thompson, 76 F.3d 442, 452 (2d Cir. 1996).
65. *See* United States v. Bedoy, 827 F.3d 495, 510 (5th Cir. 2016); United States v. Gordon, 710 F.3d 1124, 1151 (10th Cir. 2013).
66. Ninth Circuit Instructions, *supra* note 10, 19.5, cmt.
67. *See Aguilar*, 515 U.S. at 599; *see also* Ninth Circuit Instructions, *supra* note 10, 19.3, cmt.
68. *See Gordon*, 710 F.3d at 1151 (internal quotation marks omitted).
69. Liparota v. United States, 471 U.S. 419, 433 n.16 (1985); *see also Bailey*, 444 U.S. at 403-06.
70. *Bailey*, 444 U.S. at 405.

How does this translate into practice? Consider the false statement prohibition, 18 U.S.C. § 1001, which requires the government to prove, *inter alia*, that the defendant make a materially false statement and that he knew the statement to be false at the time he made it. If this were deemed a specific intent crime (the circuits are split on the question), prosecutors would also have to prove that the defendant acted with the *specific intent to deceive*—that it was the *purpose* of his statement to gull his official audience. One can perhaps conceive of scenarios in which a defendant knowingly makes a materially false statement not intending to deceive, perhaps intending to play a prank. But, in general, this additional proof requirement will not be terribly onerous because the jury will be asked to infer a specific intent to deceive from the fact that the defendant knowingly made a materially false statement.

Even if these terms are outdated, the distinction between specific and general intent has some continuing significance. As we shall see *infra*, the rules on when mistakes of fact or law will constitute a defense traditionally are said to differ with the type of intent involved. If the crime is a general intent crime, only reasonable mistakes of fact or law will create an effective defense; by contrast, even unreasonable mistakes of fact or law may be sufficient to defeat a prosecution for a specific intent crime.[71] Federal courts also often indicate that two important defenses—the good faith defense and the reliance on counsel defense—are available only to defeat charges of specific intent crimes.

Examples

1. Manaia Hemi was estranged from his wife. On his Facebook page, he posted very violent threats against his wife and others. For example, he wrote "'[t]here's one way to love you but a thousand ways to kill you. I'm not going to rest until your body is a mess, soaked with blood and dying from all the little cuts.'" He was charged with transmitting in interstate commerce "any communication containing any threat . . . to injure the person of another" under 18 U.S.C. § 875(c). The district court instructed the jury that "[a] statement is a true threat when a defendant intentionally makes a statement in a context or under such circumstances wherein a reasonable person would foresee that the statement would be interpreted by those to whom the maker communicates the statement as a serious expression of an intention to inflict bodily injury or take the life of an individual." On appeal of the defendant's conviction, how would counsel attack the court's scienter instruction?

2. The Department of Agriculture administered the food stamp program. On three occasions Yolotl purchased food stamps from an undercover

71. *See Cheek*, 498 U.S. at 201.

Department of Agriculture agent for substantially less than their face value. At the time, the federal statute governing food stamp fraud, 7 U.S.C. § 2024(b)(1), provided that: "[w]hoever knowingly uses, transfers, acquires, alters, or possesses coupons or authorization cards in any manner not authorized by [the statute] or the regulations" shall be guilty of a federal felony.[72] Yolotl was indicted for acquiring and possessing food stamps in violation of § 2024(b)(1). What would the government and the defense argue is the government's burden of proof with respect to mens rea? What statutory construction aids would they cite to persuade the Court of their positions? How is the Supreme Court likely to come out?

3. Ani Sarkissian is a citizen of Mexico. In 2019, to secure employment, Sarkissian gave her employer a false name, birth date, and Social Security number, along with a counterfeit alien registration card. The Social Security number and the number on the alien registration card were not those of a real person. Sarkissian's employer reported this to U.S. Immigration and Customs Enforcement (ICE). The United States then charged Sarkissian with two predicate crimes, namely, entering the United States without inspection, 8 U.S.C. § 1325(a), and misusing immigration documents, 18 U.S.C. § 1546(a). Finally, and most important for present purposes, it charged her with aggravated identity theft, 18 U.S.C. § 1028A(a)(1).

   The aggravated identity theft statute references a set of predicate crimes, including unlawful activities related to passports, visas, and immigration. It then provides that any person who commits any of those predicate crimes and, in doing so, "knowingly transfers, possesses, or uses, without lawful authority, a means of identification of another person," is subject to a mandatory two-year enhancement to the defendant's underlying sentence. What would the government and the defense argue is the government's burden of proof with respect to mens rea under § 1028A? What statutory construction aids would they cite to persuade the court of their positions? How is the Supreme Court likely to come out?

4A. Rozenn Alana was hired in 1979 by Acme Industries, a defense contractor. Because Alana was to have access to classified material in the course of her employment, she was required to obtain a Department of Defense Security Clearance. To this end, she was asked by Acme to fill out a "Worksheet For Preparation of Personnel Security Questionnaire."

   In response to a question on the worksheet asking whether she had ever been charged with any violation of law, Alana failed to

72. *Liparota*, 471 U.S. at 420 (quoting 7 U.S.C. § 2024(b)(1)).

disclose a prior conviction. An Acme employee typed these representations onto a form entitled "Department of Defense Personnel Security Questionnaire." Alana reviewed the document for errors and signed a certification stating that her answers were "true, complete, and correct to the best of [her] knowledge." After witnessing Alana's signature, Acme's security officer mailed the typed form to the Defense Industrial Security Clearance Office for processing.

Alana's lie regarding her criminal record was revealed and she was charged with violating 18 U.S.C. § 1001. In relevant part, § 1001 requires that the government prove that the defendant "knowingly and willfully" made any materially false, fictitious, or fraudulent statement or representation within the jurisdiction of the executive, legislative, or judicial branches of the U.S. government.

At trial, Alana admitted to having actual knowledge of the falsity of the statement she made to company officials but said she thought she had to make that statement to be consistent with a similar fabrication she had submitted to Acme in her employment application. She testified that she no actual knowledge that her false statement would be transmitted to a federal agency. Is the judge likely to instruct the jury that Alana had to "know" that her statement would be submitted to a federal agency?

4B. What is the likelihood that Rozenn Alana will get a jury instruction on the "willfully" element requiring the government to prove that defendant "must know that it is unlawful to make a false statement"?

5. Shortly after losing his job and accompanying health insurance, Ola Abioye applied for subsidized health insurance coverage provided by the state of Maine to its citizens who fall below specified income levels. To qualify for the subsidy, applicants must fill out a subsidy application. The primary determinants of subsidy eligibility are income and household size.

   In each of three years, Abioye applied for a subsidy. Abioye submitted a subsidy application and signed a verification clause on the application which read in pertinent part: "I understand the questions on this form. All statements and answers I have given are true and complete. . . . I understand it's a crime to knowingly provide false, incomplete, or misleading information on this form and that I could be charged with perjury."

   Each year, Abioye received a subsidy based on his representations on each application that he had no income to report and that he was unemployed, but neither turned out to be true. In 2020, Abioye was charged with three counts of making false statements in receiving health care benefits in violation of 18 U.S.C. § 1035(a)(2). Section 1035(a)(2) provides: "Whoever, in any matter involving a health care benefit program, knowingly and willfully—. . . makes any materially false, fictitious, or fraudulent statements or representations, or makes or uses any materially false writing or document knowing the same to contain any materially false, fictitious, or fraudulent statement or entry, in connection with the delivery of or payment for health care benefits, items, or services," commits a felony.

The trial court instructed the jury that "[a] false statement is made knowingly and willfully if [the defendant] knew it was false or demonstrated a reckless disregard for the truth with a conscious purpose to avoid learning the truth." The court told the jury that "[a] statement is false if it was untrue when made." To decide whether the defendant acted knowingly, the court continued, "you may infer he had knowledge of a fact if you find that he deliberately closed his eyes to a fact that otherwise would have been obvious to him." The jury was reminded that it was "entirely up to [them] to determine whether he deliberately closed his eyes to the fact and, if so, what inference, if any, should be drawn" and to "bear in mind that mere negligence or mistake in failing to learn the fact is not sufficient."

With respect to the willfulness element, the court instructed that the jury had to find that Abioye "made the statement voluntarily and intentionally." The court described "voluntarily and intentionally" to "mean[] that the government must prove beyond a reasonable doubt that Abioye did not make the statement by accident or mistake." As defense counsel, how would you attack these jury instructions on appeal? As the government, what position would you take?

Explanations

1. This case study is drawn from *Elonis v. United States*, 575 U.S. 723 (2015), in which the Court overturned Elonis's conviction, finding this instruction to be incorrect. The case first presents the silent statute problem because the statute does not specify a mental state. The *Elonis* Court cited the general presumption in criminal law that "wrongdoing must be conscious to be criminal."[73] The jury instruction allowed Elonis to be convicted based on how his posts would be understood by a "reasonable person," which is a negligence standard familiar in civil law. The Court held that this was inconsistent with the Court's general requirement that there be some "'*awareness* of . . . wrongdoing."[74] It ruled that there was no dispute that the mental state requirement of § 875(c) would be "satisfied if the defendant transmits a communication for the *purpose* of issuing a threat, or with *knowledge* that the communication

73. *Elonis*, 575 U.S. at 734 (internal quotation marks omitted).
74. *Id.* at 738 (emphasis original).

will be viewed as a threat."[75] Although Justice Alito, concurring in part and dissenting in part, argued for a recklessness standard, the majority declined to decide whether recklessness would suffice, leaving it for the lower court's consideration on remand.

Once the Court decided that some mens rea was required, it faced a statutory ambiguity problem—that is, deciding which elements the mens rea ought to modify. In terms of identifying that which the defendant must "know," the Court applied its usual rule that while a defendant does not have to know his conduct is illegal, he generally must know the facts that make his conduct a crime. It reasoned that the section requires proof that a communication was made and that it contained a threat. It ruled that the "'presumption in favor of a scienter requirement should apply to *each* of the statutory elements that criminalize otherwise innocent conduct.'"[76] The Court reasoned that "communicating *something* is not what makes the conduct 'wrongful.'"[77] Rather, "'the crucial element separating legal innocence from wrongful conduct' is the threatening nature of the communication. The mental state requirement must therefore apply to the fact that the communication contains a threat."[78]

2. This hypothetical is drawn from *Liparota v. United States*, 471 U.S. 419 (1985). This case presents a statutory ambiguity quandary. There is an express mens rea requirement—that the defendant acted "knowingly"—but it is not clear "how far down the sentence" the "knowingly" requirement went—that is, whether the defendant had to know only that he was using, transferring, acquiring or possessing food stamps or whether he also had to know that he was doing so in a manner not authorized by the statute or the regulations.

   The government argued, *inter alia*, that this was a public welfare offense. The Court rejected this argument by noting that "[i]n most previous [public welfare cases], Congress has rendered criminal a type of conduct that a reasonable person should know is subject to stringent public regulation and may seriously threaten the community's health or safety," citing illegal possession of a hand grenade and the shipment of adulterated and misbranded drugs.[79] "'[O]ne would hardly be surprised to learn that" these activities are not "'innocent act[s].'"[80] The Court concluded that "[a] food stamp can hardly be compared to a hand

75. *Id.* at 740 (emphasis added).
76. *Id.* at 737 (emphasis original).
77. *Id.* (emphasis original).
78. *Id.*
79. *Liparota*, 471 U.S. at 433.
80. *Id.*

grenade, . . . nor can the unauthorized acquisition or possession of food stamps be compared to the selling of adulterated drugs."[81]

The *Liparota* Court also rejected the government's argument that requiring proof that the defendant knew that he possessed the food stamps illegally required knowledge of the law, thereby violating the "ignorance of the law is no excuse" maxim. The Court applied the collateral fact exception to that principle because what the defendant had to know was the content of a collateral civil law, not the content of criminal law.

The *Liparota* Court invoked, in resolving the case, the rule of lenity and the background presumption of criminal law requiring mens rea. It held that an individual only violates the statute if the government proves that he knows that he has acquired or possessed food stamps, *and* that he also knows that he has done so in an unauthorized manner. The major force motivating this result (and thus these interpretive aids) was the *Liparota* Court's fear that to construe the statute otherwise would "criminalize a broad range of apparently innocent conduct."[82]

This case presents a good example of the Court's apparent focus in using its "innocence" test. Liparota was hardly a moral innocent. Even if he did not know that what he was doing was proscribed by regulation he had to know that by buying the stamps at less than face value and then presumably using them to secure the full value worth of food, he was both cheating the government and subverting the purposes of the program. Thus, the Court is likely using the word "innocence" to mean "not obviously regulated." At least where regulations are applied to natural persons and not businesses, the public welfare doctrine will not be applied if the regulated parties cannot fairly be presumed to know about the content of a complex regulatory scheme.

3. This case reflects the issues raised in *Flores-Figueroa v. United States*, 556 U.S. 646 (2009), another statutory ambiguity case. The parties agreed that the aggravated identity theft provision applied where the offender knew that he was transferring, possessing, or using *something* without lawful authority. But they disagreed on whether the statute required that "a defendant also know that the *something* he has unlawfully transferred is . . . a real ID belonging to another person rather than, say, a fake ID (i.e., a group of numbers that does not correspond to any real Social Security number)."[83]

---

81. *Id.*
82. *Id.* at 426.
83. *Flores-Figueroa*, 556 U.S. at 648.

Here, even given the presumption of mens rea, the government had a good argument founded on the Court's assertion that it will only supply the mens rea necessary to separate innocent from potentially culpable acts. The government would argue that the defendant's actions were equally culpable given the purposes behind prohibition on identify theft regardless of the happenstance of whether she happened to use the identification of another person or one she simply made up. But the Supreme Court held, relying on "ordinary meaning, in English" and *Liparota*, that the government indeed had to prove knowledge that the identification in fact belonged to "another person."[84] In so doing, the majority noted that "courts ordinarily read a phrase in a criminal statute that introduces the elements of a crime with the word 'knowingly' as applying that word to each element."[85] This provoked Justice Scalia, joined by Justice Thomas, to file a concurrence noting their disagreement with this statement to the extent it was normative as opposed to descriptive. Justice Alito also filed a concurrence, noting that "[i]n interpreting a criminal statute such as the one before us, I think it is fair to begin with a general presumption that the specified *mens rea* applies to all elements of an offense, but it must be recognized that there are instances in which context may well rebut that presumption."[86]

4A. This example is based on *United States v. Yermian*, 468 U.S. 63 (1984). The issue presented was whether the terms "knowingly and willfully" in § 1001 modify the statute's jurisdictional language, requiring the government to prove that false statements were made with actual knowledge of federal agency jurisdiction. The *Yermian* Court noted first that the statutory language requiring that knowingly false statements be made "in any matter within the jurisdiction of any department or agency of the United States" (as the language then stood) is a jurisdictional requirement. It reasoned that "[i]ts primary purpose is to identify the factor that makes the false statement an appropriate subject for federal concern. Jurisdictional language need not contain the same culpability requirement as other elements of the offense. Indeed, we have held that 'the existence of the fact that confers federal jurisdiction need not be one in the mind of the actor at the time he perpetrates the act made criminal by the federal statute.'"[87] Alana's argument that she lacked the requisite "knowing" mens rea would therefore fail.

4B. In *Brogan v. United States*, 522 U.S. 398 (1998), the Supreme Court rejected a defense the lower courts had developed to criminal false statement

84. *Id.* at 657.
85. *Id.* at 652.
86. *Id.* at 660 (Alito, J., concurring in part and concurring in the judgment).
87. *Yermian*, 468 U.S. at 68-69.

liability under § 1001 (explained further in the Chapter 4). Concerned about the enormous scope of potential liability and the possibility that prosecutors would misuse the statute, Justice Ginsberg suggested in her concurrence that it was an open question "whether 'to violate Section 1001, a person must know that it is unlawful to make such a false statement.'"[88] She was in essence inviting defendants to argue that the very rarely applied super mens rea "willfulness" requirement applies in § 1001 cases. Such a requirement would mean that the government must show not only that the defendant knew that her conduct was "bad" and in some general sense "unlawful," but it must also prove that she knew it was unlawful to make a false statement to the government. The Court has only applied this super mens rea in two instances, and both involved the criminalization of highly complex *malum prohibitum* regulatory schemes that had no obvious moral content. The criminal prohibition on knowingly and willfully lying to the government is not that kind of criminal prohibition. To date, defendants have been unsuccessful in pressing this argument.

5. This case study was drawn from *United States v. Russell*, 728 F.3d 23 (1st Cir. 2013). The defense ought to attack the jury instructions used to charge both "knowingly" and "willfully."

   Knowingly: The district court properly understood that the government could prove "knowledge" under a willful blindness theory. But the district court's "willful blindness" charge was clearly deficient—indeed wrong—under *Global-Tech*. The *Global-Tech* Court made it clear that neither negligence nor recklessness will suffice, so the district court's instruction that the knowing element would be satisfied if the defendant either "knew it was false or demonstrated a reckless disregard for the truth" is incorrect.[89] To be safe, courts ought to charge *Global-Tech*'s two-part test, neither of which appeared in the district court's instruction: (1) the defendant must subjectively believe that there is a high probability that a fact exists and (2) the defendant must take deliberate actions to avoid learning of that fact.[90] Many courts charge the jury, as did this court, that they should "'bear in mind that mere negligence or mistake in failing to learn the fact is not sufficient.'"[91] To that caution should be added a reminder that recklessness is also not enough for a conviction.

   Many of the circuits' pattern jury instructions rely on the language used here: "you may infer [the defendant] had knowledge of a fact if you

88. *Brogan*, 522 U.S. 416 (Ginsburg, J., concurring in the judgment).
89. *Russell*, 728 F.3d at 31.
90. *See Global-Tech*, 563 U.S. at 769.
91. *Russell*, 728 F.3d at 31.

find that he *deliberately closed his eyes* to a fact that otherwise would have been obvious to him" and it is "entirely up to [the jury] to determine whether he *deliberately closed his eyes* to the fact and, if so, what inference, if any, should be drawn."[92] The government would argue that that satisfies the *Global-Tech* Court's second requirement of a "deliberate action" to avoid actual knowledge and the defense would argue that it does not. This is an open question that was not raised on appeal.

Willfully: The district court, pursuant to circuit caselaw, applied the least demanding definition of "willfulness": requiring only a finding that the defendant's actions were intentional and not accidental. On appeal, the First Circuit rejected petitioner's argument that § 1035's "willful" element required the government "not only [to] prove that Russell's statements were false and that he knew they were false, but that he also knew that making those false statements was illegal."[93] The U.S. Solicitor General (SG) took the extraordinary step of conceding error in response to Russell's petition for Supreme Court review of the First Circuit's decision. The SG agreed that the general criminal-law interpretation of "willfully" articulated in *Bryan* should govern in the context of § 1001 and § 1035 and explained that:

> The court of appeals correctly noted that in some circumstances, the term means "deliberately and with knowledge." But that interpretation ordinarily applies only in the context of civil statutes. It is different in the criminal law, where this Court has consistently held that a defendant cannot [act willfully] unless he acted with knowledge that his conduct was unlawful.[94]

The Supreme Court granted certiorari, vacated the judgment, and remanded to the First Circuit in light of the SG's confession of error.[95]

III. ROLE IN THE OFFENSE

A. Aiding and Abetting

Unlike conspiracy, aiding and abetting is not a separate and distinct offense from the substantive crime that is its object. It is simply a way to describe the differing roles or contributions various persons performed in committing the substantive offenses. In many civil law systems, the role that the

92. *Id.* (emphasis added).
93. *Id.*
94. Brief of the United States in Opposition, Russell v. United States, 13-7357, 2014 WL 1571932, at *10 (2014) (internal quotation marks omitted).
95. *See* Russell v. United States, 572 U.S. 1056 (2014).

defendant played in committing the crime is important both for conviction and sentencing purposes. Thus, for example, someone who himself commits the criminal act (the principal or perpetrator) would be convicted and sentenced as such. Those who simply induce or solicit the principal to act, or aid or abet him in his criminal scheme, must be convicted for that lesser role and sentenced accordingly.

The federal criminal code, however, makes no distinction between principals and aiders and abettors either for liability or for sentencing purposes. The aiding and abetting statute, 18 U.S.C. § 2, provides that whoever "(a) commits an offense against the United States or aids, abets, counsels, commands, induces or procures its commission, is punishable as a principal."[96] Section 2 also makes liable as principals those who willfully use an intermediary to commit the crime; it states that whoever "(b) willfully causes an act to be done which if directly performed by him or another would be an offense against the United States, is punishable as a principal."

The Supreme Court has explained that § 2 "reflects a centuries-old view of culpability: that a person may be responsible for a crime he has not personally carried out if he helps another to complete its commission."[97] To be clear, an aider and abettor is considered just as culpable as a principal and no distinction whatsoever flows from the distinction under the U.S. Sentencing Guidelines. Thus, the Supreme Court has held, a person may be convicted of aiding and abetting despite the prior acquittal of the principal, because all those participating in the crime are principals and "the fate of other participants is irrelevant" to an aider and abettor's individual responsibility.[98]

To convict a defendant for aiding and abetting a violation, the government must prove that

- a crime was committed[99]
- the defendant took "an affirmative act in furtherance of that offense," and
- in so doing, acted "with the intent of facilitating the offense's commission"[100]

With respect to the requisite act, the defendant is liable for facilitating "any part—even though not every part—of a criminal venture."[101]

96. *See* United States v. Hansen, 599 U.S. 762 (2023) (defining "encourages" and "induces" under 8 U.S.C. § 1324(a)(1)(A)(iv)).
97. Rosemond v. United States, 572 U.S. 65, 70 (2014).
98. Standefer v. United States, 447 U.S. 10, 20 (1980).
99. *See* United States v. Standefer, 610 F.2d 1076, 1087 (3d Cir. 1979), *aff'd on other grounds*, 447 U.S. 10 (1980).
100. *Rosemond*, 572 U.S. at 71.
101. *Id.* at 72.

The defendant need not assist in the accomplishment of each element of the offense. The act "'comprehends all assistance rendered by words, acts, encouragement, support, or presence.'"[102] The act need not itself be criminal. Thus loaning a car to a bank robber with the intent of facilitating the robbery suffices. It also need not be material or integral to the success of the crime. "[A] person's involvement in the crime could be not merely partial but minimal too: The quality [of assistance was] immaterial, so long as the accomplice did *something* to aid the crime."[103]

Because the act requirement is so low, the intent requirement is demanding to prevent "sweep[ing] in innocent bystanders as well as those who gave only tangential assistance."[104] Unless the government can prove that the aider and abettor actually intended to facilitate the crime, ordinary merchants could be liable anytime defendants misused their goods and services in aid of a criminal venture. Thus, for example, the Ninth Circuit's pattern jury instructions provide:

> It is not enough that the defendant merely associated with the person committing the crime, or unknowingly or unintentionally did things that were helpful to that person or was present at the scene of the crime. The evidence must show beyond a reasonable doubt that the defendant acted with the knowledge and intention of helping that person commit [the specified crime].[105]

Although the better practice is to reference § 2 in charging, a defendant does not have to be indicted specifically as an aider and abettor to be convicted as such. Aiding and abetting is implied in every indictment for a substantive offense.[106]

B. Accessory After the Fact

An accessory after the fact "is a person who, knowing that an offense against the United States has been committed by another person, receives, relieves, comforts, or assists that person in order to hinder or prevent that person's arrest, trial, or punishment."[107]

Unlike aiding and abetting, the charge of accessory after the fact is a separate crime, not simply a way of committing the crime committed by the principal offender.[108] Because an accessory after the fact is not an accomplice,

102. Reves v. Ernst & Young, 507 U.S. 170, 178 (1993).
103. *Rosemond*, 572 U.S. at 72 (emphasis original) (internal quotation marks omitted).
104. Twitter Inc. v. Taamneh, 598 U.S. 471, 488 (2023).
105. Ninth Circuit Instructions, *supra* note 10, 4.1.
106. *See* United States v. Frorup, 963 F.2d 41, 42 n.1 (3d Cir. 1992).
107. Third Circuit Instructions, *supra* note 57, 7.08.
108. *See* United States v. Cabrales, 524 U.S. 1, 7-9 (1998).

the defendant has to be charged specifically with being an accessory after the fact under 18 U.S.C. § 3. To be liable as such, the principal offender must have actually committed the crime, and the government must prove that the second crime "facilitated the first or made it profitable by impeding its detection."[109]

Examples

1. Arlo Whitehead, Emery Milton, and Huey Sackville hatched a scheme to cheat at blackjack at Harrah's casino in Lake Tahoe, Nevada. In anticipation, they and Whitehead's wife, Yasuko Himura, practiced playing blackjack at Milton's home. Prior to going to Harrah's, they practiced for three hours. Himura dealt, while the others played and practiced signaling to each other. At one point, Himura chided Milton for his failure to catch the signals Sackville was giving him. On three separate occasions Whitehead, Milton, and Sackville cheated while playing at Harrah's. The government charged the actual cheaters with wire fraud based on a variety of interstate phone calls they placed to arrange the scheme; assume that it can prove these charges. Can Himura be held liable as an aider and abettor?

2. Aysu Ibragimova was a bank teller who embezzled money from her employer. She covered up her wrongdoing by giving another bank employee false information, which that employee—not knowing that the information was false—entered into the books of the bank. Under 18 U.S.C. § 1005, it is a federal crime for an employee of a national bank to intentionally make false entries into the bank's books "with intent to injure or defraud such bank." Can Ibragimova be found guilty under § 2(b) and/or § 3?

Explanations

1. Himura would argue that the government proved only that she dealt cards during the co-conspirator's practice sessions and that this was insufficient to make her an aider and abettor. She would likely lose. "In order to aid and abet another to commit a crime it is necessary that a defendant 'in some sort associate himself with the venture, that he participate in it as in something that he wishes to bring about, that he seek by his action to make it succeed.'"[110] Here, Himura knew of the cheating scheme, helped the co-conspirators perfect their technique, and her coaching is likely sufficient to show that she wished the venture to

109. *Id.* at 8.

110. United States v. Garner, 663 F.2d 834, 839 (1981).

succeed. As indicated above, the amount of assistance can be "minimal" so long as Himura had the requisite intent.

2. Section 2(b) states that a defendant who "willfully causes an act to be done which if directly performed by him or another would be an offense against the United States, is punishable as a principal." Although Ibragimova did not personally make any false entries, she is liable as a principal because she caused such entries to be made by another. The fact that the intermediary she used was innocent does not affect Ibragimova's liability. Indeed, even if a defendant is legally incapable of committing the substantive offense if she acted alone, she may still be liable under § 2(b) if she willfully caused the prohibited action to be committed by intermediaries who have the capacity to commit the crime but lack the criminal intent to be guilty.[111]

   Even though the offense conduct involves concealment of a crime, this could not be charged under § 3 because an accessory after the fact is a person who, knowing that an offense has been committed by *another* person, receives, relieves, comforts, or assists that person in order to hinder or prevent that person's arrest, trial, or punishment.

IV. INCHOATE LIABILITY: ATTEMPTS

There is no one generally applicable attempt statute in the federal criminal code but some specific crimes contain within them authorization for attempt liability.[112] If prosecutors seek to address inchoate criminal conduct where no such authorization exists, they may seek to use other code sections that can be applied to incomplete crimes, such as conspiracy under § 371 (see Chapter 5 (Conspiracy)), "schemes to defraud" under mail and wire fraud (see Chapter 6 (Fraud)), or "endeavors" to commit obstruction (see Chapter 7 (Obstruction of Justice)).

Where "attempts" to commit a crime are proscribed under the relevant statute, the government must prove that:

- the defendant "intended to commit the completed offense"[113] and
- committed "an 'overt act' that constitutes a 'substantial step' toward completing the offense"[114]

111. *See* United States v. Tobon-Builes, 706 F.2d 1092, 1100 (11th Cir. 1983).
112. *See, e.g.*, 18 U.S.C. §§ 1349 (conspiracy and attempt to commit frauds); 1512(b), (c) (obstruction); 1951 (Hobbs Act).
113. *Resendiz-Ponce*, 549 U.S. at 106.
114. *Id.* at 107; *see also Hansen*, 599 U.S. at 775.

A number of courts add that the prosecution must prove that the defendant "acted with the kind of culpability otherwise required for the commission of the crime which he is charged with attempting."[115]

A "substantial step" "demands something more than "'mere preparation'"; it must be "'unequivocal'" and "'significant.'"[116] As the Ninth Circuit instructs:

> A "substantial step" is conduct that strongly corroborated a defendant's intent to commit the crime. To constitute a substantial step, a defendant's act or actions must unequivocally demonstrate that the crime will take place unless interrupted by independent circumstances. Mere preparation is not a substantial step toward committing the crime.[117]

Example

1. In 2021, Baz Tasker entered a port of entry, presented his Mexican birth certificate and told U.S. immigration officials that he wanted to reapply for a resident alien card. Immigration authorities discovered that he had previously been deported, a fact that Tasker readily admitted. There was no evidence that Tasker actually filed any paperwork relating to admission into the United States during this visit.

   The government arrested Tasker for attempting to violate 18 U.S.C. § 1326, which provides that any alien who has been deported and thereafter enters or attempts to enter the United States commits a crime unless, *inter alia*, the alien secures the Attorney General's consent to the alien's reapplication for admission. Tasker had been advised at the time of his deportation that he had to secure such consent to reenter legally.

   The government contends that Tasker's actions constituted an attempt to reenter illegally because he had lost his permanent resident status when he was deported and was told he needed to obtain permission from the Attorney General to reenter. The defendant argues that he was just attempting to use the legal procedure for a new resident alien card so he could reenter lawfully. Should the defendant be liable for attempted re-entry after deportation?

115. United States v. Washington, 106 F.3d 983, 1005 (D.C. Cir. 1977); *see also* United States v. Mandujano, 499 F.2d 370, 376 (5th Cir. 1974).
116. United States v. Taylor, 596 U.S. 845, 851 (2022).
117. Ninth Circuit Jury Instructions, *supra* note 10, 4.4.

Explanation

1. This hypothetical is drawn from *United States v. Morales-Tovar*, 37 F. Supp. 2d 846 (W.D. Tex. 1999). In that case, the district court found that the defendant's and the government's explanations were equally plausible. The court noted that the Fifth Circuit had held that a person who approaches a port of entry and who makes a false claim of citizenship or nonresident alien status "attempts" to enter the United States within the meaning of the statute.[118] But the defendant in this case answered truthfully at every step, providing legitimate identification and other documentation to the immigration inspectors. The court held, then, that the government had failed to demonstrate beyond a reasonable doubt that the defendant was attempting to enter the country, rather than simply seeking to discover what he had to do to re-enter legally. The court also found that the defendant lacked the requisite mens rea. The government must prove that the defendant acted with the degree of culpability required for the commission of § 1326. The court concluded that a showing of specific intent was required to prove attempt-based offenses under § 1326 because, otherwise, "any proactive attempt to follow th[e] legally sanctioned procedure" for seeking permission to to re-enter the United States would "actually be [an] illegal 'attempt' to re-enter."[119] The government failed to show that the defendant specifically intended to re-enter the United States, as opposed to simply attempting to do the paperwork necessary to qualify for re-entry, when he asked to re-apply for a resident alien card.

V. CHARGING AND DOUBLE JEOPARDY

Throughout this volume, the focus is on considering whether as a factual and legal matter certain statutes may be charged and what factors, as a prudential matter, should be considered in making such decisions. But attention must also be paid to *how* certain violations should be charged and, in particular, to the important constraint on prosecutorial charging choices presented by the Double Jeopardy Clause of the Fifth Amendment.

The Fifth Amendment provides that no person shall "be subject for the same offence to be twice put in jeopardy of life or limb."[120] For present purposes we are concerned with two types of double jeopardy problems: "multiple punishment" and "successive prosecution" cases. *Multiple punishment* issues are raised when the government has charged the defendant

118. *See* United States v. Cardenas-Alvarez, 987 F.2d 1129, 1132-33 (5th Cir. 1993).
119. *Morales-Tovar*, 37 F. Supp. 2d at 851.
120. U.S. Const. amend. V.

in one indictment with multiple counts that legally constitute the "same offense." If the defendant were convicted and sentenced on all these counts, then, he would be subjected to multiple punishments for the same offense. *Successive prosecution* problems arise when a defendant is convicted or acquitted of a crime and the government brings another prosecution charging the defendant with the same offense.

Finally, given the increasing geographic scope of many federal crimes, defendants may be charged in different jurisdictions—state and federal or in the United States and in other countries—for the same crime. This raises a "dual sovereignty" issue, discussed within.

A. Multiple Punishment Cases

These cases concern instances in which a variety of charges are included in one indictment, to be tried in one proceeding, and the defendant claims that if he is convicted and sentenced on each charge, he will receive multiple punishments for the same offense in violation of double jeopardy. When a defendant asserts that the charges in a single indictment threaten him with multiple punishment for the same offense, the constitutional test is one of congressional intent—that is, did Congress intend for prosecutors to charge the statutes the way they did. Yes, it is odd that the Fifth Amendment provides no additional protection beyond ensuring that Congress's will is followed. But the Supreme Court has clearly stated that, "[w]ith respect to cumulative sentences imposed in a single trial, the Double Jeopardy Clause does no more than prevent the sentencing court from prescribing greater punishment than the legislature intended."[121] In this context, then, the Double Jeopardy Clause is deemed a restraint upon courts and prosecutors, not on the legislature.[122]

Two different kinds of problems can arise when one is trying to determine whether the indictment poses a risk that the defendant will be twice punished for the "same offense" in a multiple punishment case: the government seeks, in one indictment, (a) to bring multiple counts of the *same criminal statute*; or (b) to charge the same conduct under *different statutes*.

1. Multiple Counts Under the Same Statute

Oftentimes it is not clear whether a given course of conduct warrants a single count of violating a statute or multiple counts. For example, assume that:

121. Missouri v. Hunter, 459 U.S. 359, 366 (1983).
122. *See* Brown v. Ohio, 432 U.S. 161, 165 (1977).

- A defendant employs a single scheme to defraud one victim, but he uses the wires in furtherance of the scheme ten times. Should this be charged as one count of wire fraud or ten?
- A defendant and his co-conspirators make one agreement to commit three different crimes. Should this be charged as one count of conspiracy or three?

These questions raise the issue of what the appropriate "unit of prosecution" is for these statutes. In many cases, the answer is difficult to discern from the face of the statute, forcing one to consult the caselaw. With respect to these statutes, the unit of prosecution for wire fraud is each wiring in furtherance of a scheme to defraud so the defendant can be charged with ten counts even if there is only one scheme and one victim. The unit of prosecution for conspiracy is each agreement; it does not matter how many different crimes are alleged to be the objects of the conspiracy so long as there is only one conspiratorial agreement. Accordingly, the defendant and his co-conspirators would be charged with one conspiracy count that alleges three criminal objects.[123]

"Multiplicity" and "duplicity" are labels used to describe two different sorts of charging errors resulting from a prosecutor's misunderstanding of the appropriate unit of prosecution for a given statute. A multiplicitous indictment is one that charges in separate counts two or more crimes when the unit of prosecution for the statute dictates that only one count is appropriate. In other words, a multiplicitous indictment is one that violates double jeopardy. For example, in the above hypothetical, an indictment that charges three conspiracies—one for each object of a single conspiratorial agreement—would be multiplicitous and jeopardy-barred. An indictment is duplicitous when it joins two or more crimes in a single count. Thus, in the wire fraud case posited, an indictment that charges one wire fraud count encompassing all ten wirings would be duplicitous. Such indictments do not violate double jeopardy, but they may create other problems. Defense counsel ought to lodge objections to multiplicitous or duplicitous indictments before trial; the remedy available depends upon when the problem is identified.

2. Multiple Counts Under Different Statutes Relating to the Same Conduct

The second common issue in multiple punishment cases is presented when the government charges *two different statutes* to address *a single course of conduct* in one indictment. Say, for example, that the government indicts a defendant

123. *See* Braverman v. United States, 317 U.S. 49, 53 (1942).

for perjury (18 U.S.C. § 1623) and making a false statement (18 U.S.C. § 1001) based on the same allegedly false answer during the defendant's grand jury appearance.

It is important to recognize that the Court does not apply a "same-conduct" test in these circumstances.[124] To be crystal clear, the fact that two different statutes are being applied to the same conduct does not matter for double jeopardy purposes. Rather, the question is whether Congress intended that these two statutes could be charged together in these circumstances.

Congress very occasionally expresses its preference. For example, the federal bribery and gratuities statute, in 18 U.S.C. § 201(e), explicitly provides that "[t]he offenses and penalties prescribed in this section are separate and in addition to those prescribed in [the obstruction statutes,] sections 1503, 1504, and 1505 of this title."

In the usual case, Congress has not provided any direction. In such circumstances, courts will examine the usual means of discerning legislative intent—examining the statutes' text and plumbing their legislative history. If the answer remains obscure—as is often the case—courts apply a standard the Court formulated in *Blockburger v. United States*, 284 U.S. 299 (1932). The so-called *Blockburger* test provides that:

> [W]here the same act or transaction constitutes a violation of two distinct statutory provisions, the test to be applied to determine whether there are two offenses or only one, is whether each provision requires proof of a fact which the other does not.[125]

In this multiple punishment context, *Blockburger* is a rule of construction, serving merely "as a means of discerning congressional purpose."[126] It is important to stress that "*Blockburger* calls for a comparison of the *statutorily-prescribed elements* of the offenses, not the *constituent facts either as alleged or proven*."[127]

This sounds much more complicated that it is. To apply the *Blockburger* test, one simply lines up the elements of the two crimes and compares them. If each requires proof of a fact that the other does not, there is no double jeopardy bar. If they have the same elements, they are the same offense. If only one requires proof of a fact that the other does not, they are considered greater and lesser included offenses and sentencing for both would violate double jeopardy.

Return to our hypothetical case in which the prosecutor wishes to charge a defendant under both the perjury and the false statement statutes for a single lie in the course of a grand jury investigation. Absent any other

---

124. *See* United States v. Dixon, 509 U.S. 688, 704 (1993).
125. *Blockburger*, 284 U.S. at 304.
126. Albernaz v. United States, 450 U.S. 333, 340 (1981).
127. United States v. Coachman, 727 F.2d 1293, 1301 (D.C. Cir. 1984) (emphasis added).

indication of congressional intent, we would apply *Blockburger*, and the following indicates that each statute indeed requires proof of a fact that the other does not. Thus, there be no double jeopardy impediment to charging both in one indictment based on the same conduct.

Perjury Elements	**False Statement Elements**
—took an oath —before a competent tribunal, officer or person —willfully gave testimony that was —material —and false, and —the defendant knew when he made the statement that it was false	—knowingly and willfully —made any materially false, fictitious, or fraudulent statement or representation, or —within the jurisdiction of the executive, legislative, or judicial branches of the U.S. government
Elements/facts that must be proven for perjury but not for false statements: —took an oath —before a competent tribunal, officer or person	Elements/facts that must be proven for false statements but not for perjury: —within the jurisdiction of the executive, legislative, or judicial branches of the U.S. government

B. Successive Prosecution Cases

As we have seen, in multiple punishment cases, the Double Jeopardy Clause simply bars courts from imposing greater punishment than the legislature intended. In successive prosecution cases—where the defendant is acquitted or convicted on one charge and the government brings another case against him—different interests are at stake and thus different legal analysis applies. In this context, the Double Jeopardy Clause does not simply serve to ensure that Congress's intention is satisfied. Rather, the Clause prevents the government from "mak[ing] repeated attempts to convict an individual for an alleged offense, thereby subjecting him to embarrassment, expense and ordeal and compelling him to live in a continuing state of anxiety and insecurity."[128] In addition to protecting the defendant's finality interests, the Double Jeopardy Clause also prevents the government from using successive prosecutions to rehearse its presentation, "honing its trial strategies and perfecting its evidence through successive attempts at conviction"[129] because this "enhance[es] the possibility that even though innocent [the defendant] may be found guilty."[130]

128. Green v. United States, 355 U.S. 184, 187 (1957).
129. Tibbs v. Florida, 457 U.S. 31, 41 (1982).
130. *Green*, 355 U.S. at 188.

In multiple punishment cases, the Supreme Court requires courts to apply the *Blockburger* test. But because the focus in such cases is on the defendant's finality interests, not on discerning legislative intent, the *Blockburger* test is usually determinative and whatever congressional purpose appears or can be discerned is irrelevant.

C. Dual Sovereignty

Under the Supreme Court's "dual sovereignty" doctrine, the Double Jeopardy prohibition of the Fifth Amendment does not bar concurrent or successive prosecutions by separate sovereigns. Thus, federal authorities may criminally punish a defendant for crimes and conduct that were previously prosecuted by state authorities (and vice versa), whether or not the first case ended in conviction or acquittal.[131] There may be an exception to this doctrine when "state and federal prosecutions are so intertwined as to undermine the assumption that two supposedly independent criminal actions were prosecuted by separate sovereigns."[132] Although frequently invoked by the defense, this exception is rarely found applicable.[133]

In 2019, in *Gamble v. United States*, 587 U.S. 678 (2019), the Supreme Court reaffirmed its dual sovereignty doctrine in a case involving sequential state and federal prosecutions for the same conduct. The Court emphasized, *inter alia*, that each government could experience a different harm due to the criminal conduct and thus had a legitimate claim to vindication of its own sovereign interests, noting that this "duality of harm explains how 'one act' could constitute 'two offences, for each of which [the offender] is justly punishable.'"[134]

The Court then went on to suggest that this same rationale applies to sequential prosecutions by different sovereign countries. While the Supreme Court did not, given the facts of that case, squarely decide whether the dual sovereignty doctrine applies to sequential foreign and U.S. prosecutions, those courts of appeals that have addressed the issue have determined that it does.[135] Some other nations will apply double jeopardy protections—referred to in international circles as *ne bis in idem* ("not twice in the

---

131. *See, e.g.*, Heath v. Alabama, 474 U.S. 82 (1985); Abbate v. United States, 359 U.S. 187 (1959). The Court has also held that a federal prosecution of a Navajo tribe member was not barred by a previous tribal prosecution. *See* United States v. Wheeler, 435 U.S. 313, 318 (1978); *see also* United States v. Lara, 541 U.S. 193 (2004).
132. United States v. Coonan, 938 F.2d 1553, 1563 (2d Cir. 1991).
133. Defendants may have more success persuading federal prosecutors to leave the prosecution of a matter to state authorities under the Justice Departments' long-standing but non-binding "Petite Policy." *See* U.S. Dep't of Justice, Justice Manual § 9-2.031.
134. *Gamble*, 587 U.S. at 686.
135. *See* United States v. Rashed, 83 F. Supp. 2d 96, 101 (D.D.C. 1999) (collecting cases).

same thing") principles—when successive prosecutions are threatened by different sovereigns relating to the same offense. But in the United States, dual sovereignty principles mean that a foreign prosecution does not foreclose U.S. federal and state prosecutors from pursuing criminal charges against those who have already been convicted or acquitted for the same offense overseas.

Examples

1. Ghufran Samara was interviewed by the Secret Service on two different occasions. On both occasions she made the same false statement, which was material to a pending investigation. Should the prosecutor bring one false statement count under § 1001 or two? Does it matter if the same agents interviewed Samara on both occasions?

2. Shabani Zawadi was arrested and charged with fraud. After his arrest he was released on bond. He twice texted a witness in the case, stating "[t]here is an investigation going on right now. If anyone from the police contacts you, do not answer any questions. You don't know me. It is in all our best interests." After law enforcement discovered these texts, Zawadi was charged with two counts of attempted witness tampering in violation of 18 U.S.C. §§ 1512(b)(2)(A) and 1512(b)(3). Zawadi made a pre-trial motion attacking the two counts of witness tampering as jeopardy-barred. How would a court rule?

Explanations

1. This is a multiple punishment problem that raises the question whether charging multiple counts of the same statute in one indictment is appropriate on the facts. In many instances, the appropriate unit of prosecution may be subject to debate or the application of the relevant rule to the facts may be unclear. The question of how to charge false statement counts under § 1001 is a good example. For instance, where a defendant has made multiple but identical false statements to a variety of governmental actors, should he be charged in separate counts for each iteration of the false statement, or should he be charged in one count for his entire course of conduct?

   After examining the case law, the Eighth Circuit articulated a "unitary harm rule whereby repetition of a false statement which does not 'constitute an additional impairment of . . . governmental functions' should not be charged separately in an indictment."[136] How this applies depends on the facts of the case. It appears that it would matter whether

136. United States v. Graham, 60 F.3d 463, 467 (8th Cir. 1995).

the defendant repeated the same lie to the same agents or to different agents. In *United States v. Salas-Camacho*, 859 F.2d 788 (9th Cir. 1988), the Ninth Circuit held that where a defendant made the same false statement to two different governmental actors, he could be prosecuted for multiple false statement counts. The same court ruled in *United States v. Olsowy*, 836 F.2d 439 (9th Cir. 1988), that a number of separate but identical false statements made by a defendant to a single Secret Service agent could not be the subject of multiple convictions.

2. This is a multiple punishment problem that raises the question whether charging the same conduct under two separate statutes violates double jeopardy. This is a question of legislative intent. In the absence of any specific text or legislative history, courts apply the *Blockburger* test. The question presented, then, is whether § 1512(b)(2)(A) and § 1512(b)(3) each require proof of a fact/element that the other does not. Section 1512(b)(2)(A) makes it a crime to:

   > knowingly use[] intimidation, threaten[], or corruptly persuade[] another person, or attempt[] to do so, or engage[] in misleading conduct toward another person, with intent to . . . (2) cause or induce any person to (A) withhold testimony . . . from an official proceeding.

   Section 1512(b)(3) makes it unlawful to:

   > knowingly use[] intimidation, threaten[], or corruptly persuade[] another person, or attempt[] to do so, or engage[] in misleading conduct toward another person, with intent to . . . hinder, delay, or prevent the communication to a law enforcement officer or judge of the United States of information relating to the commission or possible commission of a Federal offense.

   Recall that we do not care if both counts concern the same activity; instead, we focus only on the elements. This charging choice is not multiplicitous (that is, does not charge in two counts what is one offense) and does not violate the Double Jeopardy Clause because each statutory subdivision requires proof of an element that the other does not.[137] Section 1512(b)(2)(A) requires proof that that the defendant intended to "cause or induce any person to withhold testimony" from an official proceeding but § 1512(b)(3) does not. And while § 1512(b)(3) requires proof that the defendant acted with the intent to "hinder, delay, or prevent the communication . . . of information relating to the commission or possible commission of a Federal offense," § 1512(b)(2)(A) does not. The two counts are therefore not jeopardy barred.

---

137. *See, e.g.*, United States v. Bernhardt, 903 F.3d 818, 824-25 (8th Cir. 2018).

VI. DEFENSES

A defendant has a constitutional right to raise a legally acceptable defense and to present evidence in support of that defense.[138] When a defense is supported by the law and the evidence, the judge should instruct the jury regarding the requisites of the defense.

A. Mistake

In traditional criminal law classes, students are tortured with hypotheticals relating to when, if ever, mistakes of law or fact can excuse criminal liability. For our purposes, however, the basic rule is pretty simple. Ignorance of, or a mistake regarding, law or facts that negates an element of the crime foreclose a conviction. In this sense is it is not truly a "defense"—these assertions, if supported, mean that the government has failed to carry its burden of proof with respect to the element identified.

A few examples may help. A defendant can claim that his mistake regarding the applicable law precludes conviction where knowledge of the law is an element of the crime. This would be the case, for example, where a statute requires that the defendant knew the content of a collateral, civil legal facts—e.g., as in *Rehaif*, that the defendant was not lawfully present in the United States or in *Liparota v. United States*, 471 U.S. 419 (1985), that he possessed food stamps in violation of the applicable regulations.

A defendant can claim that ignorance or mistake of a fact warrants an acquittal when knowledge of that fact is an element of the crime. For example, in *Staples* the Court read the applicable statute to require proof that the defendant knew that his gun was capable of fully automatic firing to be guilty of possession of an unregistered firearm. If the government cannot prove that the defendant possessed such knowledge, he cannot be convicted.

Where the crime at issue is a general intent crime, only reasonable mistakes preclude conviction. But where the defendant is charged with a specific intent offense, even unreasonable mistakes may suffice.

B. Entrapment

The entrapment defense is not founded on any constitutional guarantee. Instead, this defense is considered to be implicit in the federal code. Merely providing someone an opportunity to commit a crime does not constitute

138. *See, e.g.*, Matthews v. United States, 485 U.S. 58, 63 (1988).

entrapment. Even governmental encouragement or inducement to participate in criminal activity is not entrapment if the government can prove beyond a reasonable doubt that the defendant was *predisposed* to commit the criminal act prior to being approached by government agents.[139]

As the Third Circuit's Model Jury Instructions state, "[t]he government is permitted to use undercover agents, deception, and other means of providing opportunities for an unwary criminally-minded person to commit a crime, but the law does not permit the government to induce an unwary innocent into committing a criminal offense."[140] The Instructions go on to state that the defense includes two queries: "First, did the government induce [the defendant] to commit the offense? Second, was [the defendant] predisposed, that is, ready and willing to commit the offense before [he] was first approached by the government?"[141] The government bears the burden of proving beyond a reasonable doubt that the defendant was not entrapped.

Inducements can include "persuasion, fraudulent representations, threats, coercive tactics, harassment, promises of reward or pleas based on need, sympathy, or friendship."[142] "Predisposition" to criminality can be proved by evidence that the defendant readily committed the crime when solicited, or by evidence that the defendant was given the chance to back out of the proposed crime but did not do so.[143] Juries are often instructed to consider a variety factors in deciding whether a defendant was in fact "ready, willing, and able" to commit the crime before the government approach, including "whether the defendant demonstrated reluctance to commit the offense; . . . the defendant's character and reputation; . . . whether government agents initially suggested the criminal activity; . . . whether the defendant engaged in the criminal activity for profit; and . . . the nature of the government's inducement or persuasion."[144]

C. Entrapment by Estoppel

"[E]ntrapment by estoppel" is very different from an "entrapment" defense. This defense applies where the defendant has established by a preponderance of the evidence that:

---

139. *See* Jacobson v. United States, 503 U.S. 540, 549 (1992).
140. Third Circuit Instructions, *supra* note 57, 8.05.
141. *Id.*
142. *Id.*
143. *See* United States v. Rutgerson, 822 F.3d 1223, 1235 (11th Cir. 2016).
144. Ninth Circuit Instructions, *supra* note 10, 5.2; *see also* Third Circuit Instructions, *supra* note 57, 8.05.

> (1) a government official (2) told the defendant that certain conduct was legal, (3) the defendant actually relied on the government official's statements, (4) and the defendant's reliance was in good faith and reasonable in light of the identity of the government official, the point of law represented, and the substance of the official's statement.[145]

In these circumstances, the defendant's ignorance or mistake of law is excusable.[146] Ignorance or mistakes of law might also be forgiven if it is determined that the accused reasonably relied on a statute or judicial precedent later repealed or overturned, or if the legislature failed to make the law adequately known or knowable.

D. Good Faith

Where the government bears the burden of proving a specific intent—to deceive or to defraud, for example—defendants will often defend by asserting that their actions or statements were made in good faith. "A good faith defense is the 'affirmative converse of the government's burden of proving . . . intent to commit a crime.' Acquittal . . . is mandatory because a finding of good faith precludes a finding of fraudulent intent."[147] As such, "good faith" is not truly a "defense" in that it is just a way of saying that the government has not met its burden with respect to scienter. As some instructions explain:

> One who expresses an opinion honestly held by her or belief honestly entertained by her is not chargeable with fraudulent intent even though her opinion is erroneous or her belief is mistaken. And similarly, evidence which establishes only that a person made a mistake in judgment or an error in management or was careless does not establish fraudulent intent. While the term "good faith" has no precise definition, it means among other things a belief or opinion honestly held with an absence of malice or ill will and intention of taking unfair advantage of another.[148]

A good faith belief may defeat a prosecution for a specific intent crime even if it is objectively unreasonable.[149]

---

145. United States v. Stewart, 185 F.3d 112, 124 (3d Cir. 1999) (internal quotation marks omitted).
146. *See, e.g.*, United States v. Penn. Indus. Chem. Corp., 411 U.S. 655 (1973) (holding that party should have been permitted to put on defense that it had been affirmatively misled into believing that its conduct was not criminal by long-standing, official agency interpretation of regulatory requirement).
147. United States v. Cavin, 39 F.3d 1299, 1310 (5th Cir. 1994).
148. *See, e.g.*, United States v. Sayakhom, 186 F.3d 928, 940 (9th Cir. 1999).
149. *See Cheek*, 498 U.S. at 201.

E. Good Faith Reliance on Counsel

The reliance on counsel (and other experts[150]) "defense" also applies to "specific intent" crimes. This is not truly a "defense" in that it, like the good faith "defense," simply means that that the government has failed to prove its burden of showing a wrongful intent. An advice-of-counsel instruction requires the defendant to show that he made a full disclosure of all material facts to his attorney and that he then relied in good faith on the specific course of conduct recommended by the attorney.

Choosing to employ a reliance on counsel defense to a specific intent charge is not without risk because it can often result in a waiver of attorney-client privilege. In *United States v. Bilzerian*, 926 F.2d 1285 (2d Cir. 1991), involving a prosecution for securities fraud, the defendant sought to introduce evidence regarding his allegedly good faith efforts to comply with the securities law in order to negate the element of intent. The Second Circuit held that

> the attorney-client privilege cannot at once be used as a shield and a sword. A defendant may not use the privilege to prejudice his opponent's case or to disclose some selected communications for self-serving purposes. Thus, the privilege may implicitly be waived when defendant asserts a claim that in fairness requires examination of protected communications.[151]

"'The defense of advice of counsel necessarily fails where counsel acts as an accomplice to the crime.' . . . In fact, the advice-of-counsel defense 'presupposes that (1) an attorney-client relationship existed between the defendant and counsel; and (2) the attorney did not act as an accomplice to the defendant's crime.'"[152]

Examples

1. Undercover FBI Agent Marine Davidyan, posing as a member of a drug organization, told D.C. Metropolitan Police Department (MPD) Officer Enara Jasso that she was interested in getting protection from Jasso and other willing police officers for her narcotics activities. Jasso, who was on a list of suspected corrupt officers, expressed her interest and said she knew other potential recruits. Jasso approached MPD Officer Alice Pallesen, who said she had dealt drugs before joining the MPD and was happy to join the group. Finally, Jasso approached MPD Officer Rosemary Chance. Chance

150. *See, e.g.*, United States v. Bishop, 291 F.3d 1100, 1106-07 (9th Cir. 2002).
151. *Bilzerian*, 926 F.2d at 1292.
152. United States v. Kaneshiro, Case No. 1:22-cr-00048-TMB-NC, 2024 WL 1183124, at *4 (D. Hawaii March 19, 2024).

expressed some reservations about joining, stating that she was concerned that this was a new operation in town, and they might invite hostility from existing drug dealers. But after meeting Davidyan, Chance agreed to join the others. Jasso, Pallesen, and Chance were paid to supposedly participate in two drug runs, purporting to pick up drugs at the airport and deliver them to Davidyan's home. Jasso, Pallesen, and Chance were indicted, *inter alia*, for bribery in violation of 18 U.S.C. § 201. Pallesen and Chance presented an entrapment defense, testifying that they were coerced by Jasso into participating. Can this entrapment defense succeed?

2. West Indies Transport, Inc. (WIT) operated several businesses in Florida, including a dry dock, ship repair facility, and barge towing company. To staff these facilities, WIT hired an overseas agent to recruit Filipino workers. The Filipino workers were instructed to apply for D-1 visas intended for non-immigrant foreign maritime crewman, not the H-2 visas required by law. The WIT "crewmen" never put to sea. WIT was charged with aiding and abetting visa fraud in violation of 18 U.S.C. § 2 and § 1546. WIT could prove that ICE extended the Filipino workers' visas based on representations by WIT that the workers would soon be employed as workmen on ocean-going vessels. ICE was not informed that the workers would be living on U.S. soil and working as dock workers in the interim. WIT can also prove that its lawyer told the company that, if it wanted to get visas for the workers, H-2 visas were very difficult to secure but, if one told ICE the "right things," the workers would qualify for the easier to secure D-1 visas. Can WIT prevail by asserting the defenses of entrapment by estoppel and good faith reliance on counsel?

Explanations

1. This problem raises the issue of what is termed "derivative entrapment." Here, the solicitation of Pallesen and Chance was done primarily by Jasso. The caselaw is clear that "'[p]ersuasion, seduction, or cajoling by a private party does not qualify as entrapment.'"[153] Some circuits, however, recognize a derivative entrapment defense under some circumstances when the government agents act through private citizens; others do not.

   Of those jurisdictions that permit the defense, some will only permit the defendant to assert it in cases in which the government acts through a *knowing* agent—such as an undercover agent that the government has recruited for the role. Other circuits hold that a derivative entrapment defense is available even when the government acts through an *unwitting* agent.[154] The basic rationale is that, absent such a defense, the government

153. *Washington*, 106 F.3d at 993.
154. *See id.*

"would be allowed to shield itself from regular entrapment claims by designing sting operations to shift the task of recruiting additional sting targets onto the original targets of the operation."[155] Even in those jurisdictions where an unwitting intermediary suffices, the defense is not be available "'if, in response to pressure put on him by the government, the unknowing intermediary *on his own* induces the defendant to engage in criminal activity.'"[156]

In this case, the government is acting through an unwitting agent of the government, Jasso. Thus in some circuits this defense would fail. If Jasso indeed coerced the others into participating on her own initiative, the defense could not succeed even in those jurisdictions that recognize derivative entrapment by unwitting agents. In any case, entrapment is unlikely to succeed because it appears that Palleson and Chance were "ready, willing, and able" no matter the source of the inducement. Chance showed some hesitation, but her reservations had to do with the likelihood of violence from a rival gang, not qualms about drug dealing. And she seemed to decide to participate without any pressure from the government. She, too, then, would be deemed "ready, willing, and able."

2. Entrapment by estoppel requires that the government official told the defendant that certain criminal conduct was legal, and that the defendant relied in good faith on the government official's statement. This defense, like the good faith reliance on counsel defense, is dependent upon the officials being fully and correctly advised of the underlying facts. WIT did not disclose that the workers would be in the United States and working on the docks before they supposedly would be employed on ships. And there is no evidence that ICE approved this scheme, only that ICE relied on WIT's false representations in issuing the visas.[157]

   With respect to the good faith reliance on counsel defense, it is not clear from the facts whether WIT made full disclosure of the facts to its attorney. But counsel appears to be complicit in the illegal scheme, which would render the defense unavailable. The "advice" given also seems to be a roadmap for committing visa fraud. It is difficult to be believe that a business like WIT relied in good faith on these very hinky instructions.

155. *Id.*
156. *Id.* at 994 (emphasis original).
157. *See* United States v. West Indies Transport, Inc., 127 F.3d 299, 313 (3d Cir. 1997).

VII. EXTRATERRITORIAL APPLICATION OF U.S. STATUTES

Criminal conduct increasingly crosses borders, and enforcement follows. Given this trend, the parties are frequently litigating the issue whether a federal statute applies to foreign conduct. Where, for example, a scam artist, typing on his keyboard in Russia and using a website hosted on a server in another country, defrauds Aunt Milly in Omaha, can federal prosecutors use the wire fraud statute to prosecute him?

A. General Extraterritoriality Analysis

The geographical scope of a criminal statute is a question of congressional intent. Infrequently, Congress provides an express statement regarding its intention. Thus, for example, the money laundering statute, 18 U.S.C. § 1956(f), states that there is extraterritorial jurisdiction over the prohibited conduct when (1) the conduct is committed by a U.S. citizen or, in the case of a non-U.S. citizen, the "conduct occurs in part in the United States" and (2) the transaction involves funds of a value exceeding $10,000. This assertion of extraterritoriality, then, is founded on two very traditional bases recognized in international law: the nationality of the perpetrator and the territory of the sovereign exercising criminal jurisdiction.

Litigation over whether conduct "occurred in part" in the United States has become an important issue in money laundering cases—and its significance extends well beyond that context to a wealth of cases in which the question is whether the crime was "committed" in whole or in part in the United States. As later chapters will reveal, many federal crimes contain a jurisdictional element requiring proof that the instrumentalities of interstate commerce, including interstate wirings, were used. Does the use of U.S. "wires"—by text, email, Internet access or the like—constitute conduct committed on U.S. territory? Generally speaking, the answer is "yes." In money laundering cases and FCPA cases in particular, one very common use of U.S. wires—to send money to, from, or through U.S. correspondent bank accounts—is often asserted to be the requisite conduct occurring on the territory of the United States. Because this issue is frequently raised in money laundering prosecutions, it will be discussed in Chapter 11.

Most federal statutes do not contain any instructions regarding their extraterritorial application. The Supreme Court, however, has provided guidance on the means by which legislative intent is to be discerned. In *Morrison v. National Australia Bank*, 561 U.S. 247 (2010), and its follow-up decisions in *RJR Nabisco, Inc. v. European Community*, 579 U.S. 325 (2016), and *Abitron Austria GmbH v. Hetronic International, Inc.*, 600 U.S. 412 (2023), the Court instructed lower courts to apply a strong presumption against extraterritorial application of geo-ambiguous federal statutes. This presumption can only be rebutted by clear evidence that Congress intended the statute to apply extraterritorially.

The Court sees this as two-step process:

> At step one, we determine whether a provision is extraterritorial, and that determination turns on whether Congress has affirmatively and unmistakably instructed that the provision at issue should apply to foreign conduct. If Congress has provided an unmistakable instruction that the provision is extraterritorial, then claims alleging exclusively foreign conduct may proceed, subject to the limits Congress has (or has not) imposed on the statute's foreign application.
>
> If a provision is not extraterritorial, we move to step two, which resolves whether the suit seeks a (permissible) domestic or (impermissible) foreign application of the provision. To make that determination, courts must start by identifying the "focus" of congressional concern underlying the provision at issue. The focus of a statute is the object of its solicitude, which can include the conduct it seeks to regulate, as well as the parties and interests it seeks to protect or vindicate.[158]

The Supreme Court has yet to apply this analysis in a criminal case. The presumption has been employed to construe the reach of hybrid statutes—that is, statutes that can be applied civilly or criminally, such as the securities fraud statute, § 10(b) of the Securities and Exchange Act of 1934,[159] and the Racketeer Influenced and Corrupt Organizations Act (RICO). But the issue of the extraterritoriality of those statutes came to the Court in civil cases.

In *Morrison*, the plaintiffs were seeking damages for securities fraud, which they alleged occurred in part in the United States, that adversely affected the prices of shares in an Australian bank that the plaintiffs had purchased on a foreign exchange. In determining whether the civil-fraud damages remedy provided in § 10(b) covered such a suit, the *Morrison* Court first applied the presumption against the extraterritorial application of federal statutes and found no clear statement in the statute to rebut the presumption.

Having lost the battle, plaintiffs sought to win the war by arguing that they were not in fact seeking an extraterritorial application of the statute because the fraudulent conduct happened in part in Florida. In assessing whether the case was permissibly domestic or impermissibly extraterritorial, the Court applied its "focus" test. It concluded that the "focus" of § 10(b) was "transactions in securities listed on domestic exchanges, and

158. *Abitron*, 600 U.S. at 417-18. (internal quotation marks omitted).

159. 15 U.S.C. § 78j(b).

domestic transactions in other securities."[160] In other words, unless there is a domestic securities transaction, the case constitutes a forbidden extraterritorial application of the statute.

After *Morrison* was announced, Congress amended the jurisdictional provisions of a number of securities laws in the Dodd–Frank Wall Street Reform and Consumer Protection Act.[161] The amendments left *Morrison*'s holding untouched in private civil securities suits. But with respect to securities fraud cases brought by the SEC and Department of Justice, the Act provides the government jurisdiction to pursue securities violations where the "conduct within the United States . . . constitutes significant steps in furtherance of the violation, even if the securities transaction occurs outside the United States and involves only foreign investors; or . . . conduct occurring outside the United States . . . has a foreseeable substantial effect within the United States."[162]

In 2016, the Court in *RJR Nabisco* ruled on the extraterritorial scope of RICO.[163] RICO complaints generally allege that the defendants conducted an "enterprise" through a "pattern of racketeering activity." Such patterns require proof of two or more violations of qualifying federal or state statutes (aka "predicate acts"). In *RJR Nabisco*, the Court held that RICO has extraterritorial application only where Congress has made the predicate statutes upon which the RICO case is built extraterritorial. *RJR Nabisco* shows that the Court's presumption is not irrebuttable, but its discussion also illustrates how difficult it is to overcome the presumption.

The *Morrison* Court required that, to rebut the presumption against extraterritoriality, the congressional intent for a statute to apply abroad be "'clearly expressed.'"[164] The *RJR Nabisco* Court seemed to take it up a notch, requiring that, to rebut the presumption, Congress must "affirmatively and unmistakably instruct[] that the statute" will apply extraterritorially.[165] It found an obvious textual clue in the fact that some RICO predicates, by their express terms, applied extraterritorially. The Court pointed out that "[a]t least one predicate—the prohibition against 'kill[ing] a national of the United States, while such national is outside the United States'—applies *only* to conduct occurring outside the United States."[166] Congress's incorporation of extraterritorial predicates into RICO, the Court concluded, "gives a clear, affirmative indication that § 1962 applies to foreign racketeering

160. *Morrison*, 561 U.S at 267.
161. Pub. L. No. 111-203, § 929P(b)(2)(A), 124 Stat. 1376, 1865–66 (2010) (codified as amended at 15 U.S.C. § 78aa).
162. *Id.* (quoting 15 U.S.C. § 78aa).
163. 18 U.S.C. §§ 1961–68.
164. *Morrison*, 561 U.S. at 255.
165. *RJR Nabisco*, 579 U.S. 335.
166. *Id.* at 338 (emphasis original) (citing 18 U.S.C. § 2332(a)).

activity."[167] Thus, RICO's unique structure made it "the rare statute that clearly evidences extraterritorial effect despite lacking an express statement of extraterritoriality."[168] Given that the statute applies in part extraterritorially, there was no need to inquire into the statutory "focus." The scope of an extraterritorial statute turns on the limits Congress has (or has not) imposed on the statute's foreign application, and not on the statute's "focus."

B. Potential Applicability of *United States v. Bowman* in Criminal Cases

Prior to the Court's articulation of a muscular presumption against extraterritoriality in *Morrison*, the lower federal courts had been very willing to find that federal criminal statutes applied extraterritorially.

Before *Morrison* and to some extent after it, courts have avoided applying the presumption against extraterritoriality to criminal statutes by relying on a Supreme Court precedent from 1922, *United States v. Bowman*, 260 U.S. 94 (1922). In *Bowman*, the defendants schemed on the high seas and in Rio de Janeiro to defraud a U.S. government-owned corporation. The Court recognized that punishment of crimes against private individuals or their property "must, of course, be committed within the territorial jurisdiction of the government where it may properly exercise it."[169] But, the Court explained, "[t]he same rule of interpretation should not be logically applied to criminal statutes which are, as a class, not logically dependent on their locality for the government's jurisdiction, but are enacted because of the right of the government to defend itself against obstruction, or fraud wherever perpetrated, especially if committed by its own citizens, officers or agents."[170]

As the Supreme Court summarized its *Bowman* holding in *Skiriotes v. Florida*, 313 U.S. 69 (1941), "a *criminal* statute dealing with acts that are *directly injurious to the government, and are capable of perpetration without regard to particular locality* is to be construed as applicable to *citizens of the United States* upon the high seas or in a foreign country, though there be no express declaration to that effect."[171] In the pre-*Morrison* era, the lower courts regularly ignored these limitations, applying *Bowman* to a variety of cases that did not involve fraud or obstruction, did not victimize the U.S. government, and did not involve defendants who were U.S. citizens. Despite the modern Court's emphatic embrace of the presumption, some lower courts continue to resist applying it in criminal cases by taking the position that *Bowman* applies until it is

167. *Id.* at 339.
168. *Id.* at 340.
169. *Bowman*, 260 U.S. at 98.
170. *Id.*
171. *Skiriotes*, 313 U.S. at 73-74 (emphasis added).

expressly overruled.[172] In 2016, for example, the Seventh Circuit refused, despite *Morrison*, to reverse a decision that relied upon *Bowman* to hold a federal criminal statute extraterritorial.[173] Judge Easterbrook explained that "[a] decision such as *Bowman*, holding that criminal and civil laws differ with respect to extraterritorial application, is not affected by yet another decision showing how things work on the civil side."[174]

Example

1. A corporation domiciled in the Bahamas, which maintains its sales offices in Canada, solicits and sells partnerships in a bogus oil investment only to Canadian investors. But in so doing, it communicates by wire with a bank in New York. Can U.S. prosecutors pursue the corporation for wire fraud under 18 U.S.C. § 1343?

Explanation

1. The Supreme Court instructs that courts faced with the issue of the trans-border application of a federal statute begin by applying a strong presumption against extraterritoriality. The first question presented, then, is whether the statute rebuts the presumption by affirmatively and unmistakably evidencing a congressional intent that it apply abroad. There is no express territoriality provision relating to § 1343 so we must turn to the text of the statute.

   The wire fraud statute provides, in relevant part, that

   > Whoever, having devised or intending to devise any scheme or artifice to defraud, or for obtaining money or property by means of false or fraudulent pretenses, representations, or promises, transmits or causes to be transmitted by means of wire, radio, or television communication in interstate or foreign commerce, any . . . signals, pictures, or sounds for the purpose of executing such scheme or artifice [commits a federal felony].

   One might argue that the statute's requirement that the wiring travel in "interstate or *foreign* commerce" rebuts the presumption. But the Supreme Court has "emphatically rejected reliance on such language, holding that 'even statutes. . . that expressly refer to "*foreign* commerce" do not apply abroad.'"[175] Accordingly, the defense would argue that the presumption controls and the wire fraud statute does not apply extraterritorially. The

---

172. *See, e.g.*, United States v. Leija-Sanchez, 602 F.3d 797, 799 (7th Cir. 2010).
173. *See* United States v. Leija-Sanchez, 820 F.3d 899, 900-02 (7th Cir. 2016).
174. *Id.* at 901.
175. *RJR Nabisco*, 579 U.S at 353 (emphasis original).

circuits are currently split on the issue, although the majority hold that § 1343 does not apply overseas.[176] *Bowman* should not apply in this case because the victims of the fraud are private parties, not the U.S. government, and the defendant is not a U.S. national.

If the statute does not apply extraterritorially, we must go on to step two and query whether the facts of the case constitute a domestic or extraterritorial application of the statute. This turns on what the court identifies as the statute's "focus." Wire fraud, according to the Supreme Court, has two elements: (1) a scheme to defraud and (2) an interstate wiring in furtherance of the fraud. Most courts hold that the statutory "focus" is the interstate wiring, but a few have ruled that the focus is the fraud.[177] In the case from which this example is derived, *United States v. Coffman*, 574 Fed. App'x 541 (6th Cir. 2014), the court ruled that the case was not extraterritorial in nature because the defendants used the interstate wires in communicating with a U.S. bank as part of their scheme. Were the statutory "focus" deemed to be the fraud, however, this case would clearly be impermissibly extraterritorial in nature.

---

176. *Compare* United States v. Elbaz, 52 F.4th 593, 602 (4th Cir. 2022), *with* United States v. Georgiou, 777 F.3d 125, 137 (3d Cir. 2015).
177. *Compare* United States v. Napout, 963 F.3d 163, 179 (2d Cir. 2020), *with* United States v. All Assets Held at Bank Julius, 251 F. Supp. 3d 82, 103 (D.D.C. 2017).

CHAPTER 3

Entity Liability

3. Entity Liability

When a crime is committed through an artificial entity, such as a corporation, the government can choose to pursue the individual wrongdoer within the corporation. The fact that the individual acted for the benefit of the corporation and not for personal gain in committing the crime is no defense. The government can also choose to indict the entity itself and the circumstances in which it will do so are the primary focus of this chapter. Finally, in a limited category of cases, some individuals may be held vicariously liable as "responsible corporate officers" even if they did not know about, or participate in, the crimes alleged. The responsible corporate officer doctrine is examined at the conclusion of this chapter.

We need to begin with a reality check. Although the criminal justice system as applied to corporations is formally adversarial, in fact many organizations in the federal government's crosshairs find that it is very difficult to stage a vigorous defense. This flows from a variety of circumstances. As we shall see in this and ensuing chapters, the federal criminal code, as augmented by the hundreds of thousands of criminalized federal regulations, presents prosecutors with a virtually limitless and often malleable selection of possible charges to lodge against corporations. And the extremely broad, judicially-created respondeat standard of corporate criminal liability means that almost any crime that a corporate agent commits in the course of his employment can be imputed to the corporation and result in the organization's criminal conviction.

Even were a corporation to conclude that it has a shot at defending itself against a particular charge or theory of liability, its decision regarding whether to resist a criminal investigation will be hugely affected by the number, range, and seriousness of the consequences that may be visited upon it should it fail in that effort. Although not every conviction is in essence a corporate death sentence, the company will certainly take a pronounced drubbing in a variety of ways, including through: (1) the restitution, fine, and corporate probation provisions of the federal Organizational Sentencing Guidelines; (2) potential debarment from government contracting; (3) possibly ruinous regulatory or licensing repercussions; (4) hits to the company's stock price and market valuation; (5) loss of employees, customers, and financing; and (6) the application of collateral estoppel to foreclose the entity from resisting the civil damages demands of any number of potential public and private plaintiffs.

Corporations will be heavily influenced by their bottom line. They often decide that, whether or not their guilt is contestable, they have no choice but to cooperate fully with the government in hopes of avoiding the wreckage that could result from a criminal conviction. It is very difficult for a public company—especially those in regulated industries or those who do business with the government—to do anything but cooperate in hopes of securing mercy in the form of a declination of criminal charges or a deferred prosecution agreement. A deferred prosecution agreement (DPA) is a popular means of avoiding a criminal conviction; it is simply a negotiated contract between the government and the defense pursuant to which the government agrees not to go forward with the criminal case and the organization promises in return to remedy the harm its conduct caused, pay sanctions, and effect certain internal reforms, including the institution of an effective compliance program to prevent and detect future wrongdoing. As a result, many if not most federal cases against organizations end in a negotiated settlement, many through a DPA. Of the cases actually indicted, over 95% plead out.

This chapter begins with a discussion of the blackletter law of corporate liability. Guilt may not be contested in every case, but the broad standard of liability performs a critical role in forcing corporations to the bargaining table. Discussion then turns to terms normally encompassed in a DPA. The Department of Justice's charging instructions to prosecutors, embodied in the "Principles of Federal Prosecution of Business Organizations," are briefly outlined because they provide the backdrop against which corporations and the government evaluate the corporation's culpability and exposure. Finally, the rationales for, and general operation of, corporate internal investigations are outlined. These investigations are an important part of the dynamic sketched above. They are necessary to provide the entity with the information it needs to anticipate or respond to allegations of wrongdoing and are the means by which the company can give the government the cooperation it demands in return for leniency. Finally, the U.S. Organizational Sentencing Guidelines (Organizational Guidelines) are obviously relevant to the pressures corporations face to cooperate, but they are best explained together with the Guidelines applicable in individual cases (Chapter 15).

I. RESPONDEAT SUPERIOR LIABILITY

Corporations and other legal entities[1] can be held criminally liable in federal court under a respondeat superior ("let the master answer") standard.[2] This is a judge-made doctrine; there is no federal criminal statute that authorizes corporate criminal liability and sets forth a standard for imposing it. In brief, under federal common law, respondeat superior dictates that corporations and other entities can be held criminally liable

1. The same general principles of liability apply to different types of business entities, including partnerships. *See, e.g.*, United States v. A & P Trucking Co., 358 U.S. 121 (1958).

2. *See* New York Central & Hudson River R.R. Co. v. United States, 212 U.S. 481 (1909) (upholding a statute that provided for corporate responsibility under a respondeat superior standard of liability against a due process attack).

- for the criminal actions (or actionable omissions) and culpable state of mind of their agents
- acting within the actual or apparent scope of the agents' employment or authority
- if the agents intend, at least in part, to benefit the corporation
- even though their actions may be contrary to corporate policy or express organizational orders

A. Employees and Agents

Most cases concern the actions of organizational employees, but the criminal conduct of corporate agents can also render the entity liable. It is not necessary for the government to prove that high-ranking persons within the organization approved, acquiesced in, or condoned the criminal activity. The actions of any employee at any level of the corporate hierarchy can bind the corporation as long as she is acting within the scope of her actual or apparent authority and with the appropriate intent. It should be noted, however, the position of the wrongdoing agent may well be important in prosecutor's charging decisions under Justice Department policy and certainly can affect the extent of the sanction imposed under the U.S. Organizational Sentencing Guidelines.

B. Acting Within the Scope of Employment

The first requisite of liability is that the corporate agent act within the scope of her actual or apparent authority. Obviously, one will search in vain for a job description or board of directors' resolution authorizing a corporate agent to engage in criminal wrongdoing. Neither is necessary to hold the corporation vicariously liable. Agents' acts are deemed within the scope of their employment if they are "done on behalf of the corporation and directly related to the performance of the type of duties the employee has general authority to perform."[3] "Apparent authority is the authority which outsiders could reasonably assume that the agent would have, judging from his position with the company, the responsibilities previously entrusted to him, and the circumstances surrounding his past conduct."[4] The defense is rarely able to defeat this element given the capacious definition of agents' scope of authority.

3. United States v. Am. Radiator & Standard Sanitary Corp., 433 F.2d 174, 204-05 (3d Cir. 1970).
4. Id. at 205.

C. With the Intention to Benefit

Both the act and the mens rea of the corporate agent are imputed to the corporation. Commentators complain that a focus only on the actions and the mental state of one employee makes respondeat superior overinclusive because it may render the company liable where the agent is acting out of self-interest and not in the best interests of the corporation. The requirement that an agent be acting with the intent to benefit her principal in committing the crime, then, is designed to ensure that liability is only imposed where the criminal conduct is done to serve corporate interests and is not that of a rogue employee.

In practice, this modest safeguard rarely prevents liability. The caselaw makes clear that the corporation need not actually receive any benefit. And the corporate agent need not be acting solely, or even predominantly, with the intention of benefitting her corporate principal. Courts regularly hold that the conduct of an employee that is actually or potentially detrimental to the corporation may nonetheless be imputed to the corporation if a jury can infer that it was motivated at least in part to benefit the entity.[5]

D. Even If Contrary to Express Corporate Policy/Orders

A corporation can be liable for the actions of its agents within the scope of their employment even though those actions were "contrary to general corporate policy and express instructions to the agent."[6] Although the fact that a crime occurs in violation of policy and despite expensive investments in compliance systems designed to prevent such conduct does not preclude liability under respondeat superior principles, it is a factor in the Justice Department's charging decisions and the size of any criminal fine under the Organizational Sentencing Guidelines.

E. Difficulties Where Responsibility Is Diffused

Under traditional respondeat superior principles, vicarious liability is only appropriate where a primary violator can be identified—that is, when the government identifies an agent who committed the actus reus of the crime with the requisite mental state. If strictly enforced, this rule would preclude liability where no one agent is responsible or where the crime at issue is

5. *See, e.g.*, United States v. Sun-Diamond Growers, 138 F.3d 961, 970 (D.C. Cir. 1998), *aff'd on other grounds*, 526 U.S. 398 (1999).
6. United States v. Hilton Hotels Corp., 467 F.2d 1000, 1007 (9th Cir. 1972).

one of omission rather than commission. But this traditional rule has been relaxed in a variety of ways that ease corporate liability.

Prosecutors do not need to identify a particular person who committed the crime as long as they can show that someone must have done it. Even more significantly, inconsistent verdicts are tolerated. Thus, a corporation can be convicted even if all the individual agents allegedly involved are acquitted. Finally, some circuits have accepted a theory that allows for aggregation of the acts and mens rea of different agents; this is examined below.

I. *Bank of New England:* Collective Knowledge and Flagrant Organizational Indifference

The First Circuit adopted alternative ways of proving that an entity acted knowingly and willfully in *United States v. Bank of New England, N.A.*, 821 F.2d 844 (1st Cir. 1987). The *Bank of New England* standard may be applied in cases involving regulatory offenses but is rarely applied in other contexts.

The Bank of New England was charged with repeatedly failing to file required Currency Transaction Reports (CTRs) when customers engaged in currency transactions exceeding $10,000. The Bank was convicted after trial but all the Bank's employees who knew of the CTR requirement and knowingly and willfully failed to comply with it were acquitted. The First Circuit upheld the Bank's conviction based on an alternative theory through which the requisite mens rea—that the Bank acted "knowingly" and "willfully"—could be demonstrated.

First, the court held that the Bank's "knowledge" was "the sum of the knowledge of all of the employees."[7] Thus, the government could satisfy its burden of proving "knowledge" by either showing that one culpable individual acted within the scope of their employment and with the requisite mens rea under respondeat superior or by showing that various different agents' knowledge cumulatively demonstrated corporate knowledge. Thus, if some of the employees knew of the bank's reporting requirement and others knew that the requisite reports were not being filed, this "collective knowledge" sufficed to demonstrate that the Bank acted "knowingly."[8]

The court further held that there were also two ways the government could prove that the Bank acted "willfully." It could use the normal respondeat superior standard by proving that an agent acting within the scope of her employment acted willfully in failing to file the reports. Or it could show that the bank acted with "flagrant organizational indifference" in avoiding learning about and observing the CTR requirements.[9]

7. *Bank of New England*, 821 F.2d at 855.
8. *Id.* at 855.
9. *Id.*

3. Entity Liability

The First Circuit's ruling in this respect garnered a great deal of attention, but it is a controversial theory. Other federal courts have declined to adopt the First Circuit's "collective knowledge" and "flagrant organizational indifference" theories of proving corporate mens rea.[10]

II. THE IDENTIFICATION PRINCIPLE

There are a variety of other possible corporate liability rules.[11] One that is reflected in the Model Penal Code and has been adopted by some U.S. states and foreign jurisdictions is the identification principle, under which a corporate body will only be liable for criminal conduct committed by one or more high-ranking persons within the company who can be said to be identified with it in that their actions and mental state are deemed those of the company.

This is still a species of vicarious liability but it is narrower in its terms. Model Penal Code § 2.07(1)(c) provides that a corporation can be convicted of a crime when "the commission of the offense was authorized, requested, commanded, performed or recklessly tolerated by the board of directors or by a high managerial agent acting on behalf of the corporation within the scope of his office or employment." The idea is that such high-ranking persons—the corporation's "directing mind"—effectively *are* the company.

Respondeat superior is criticized on many grounds, most particularly because it is overinclusive. It makes no effort to identify truly culpable corporations given its singular focus on the wrongdoing individuals within them. And it provides companies little incentive to invest in costly compliance programs to prevent and detect further wrongdoing. But the identification theory has been criticized as underinclusive. Some question whether a corporation whose policies effectively encouraged lower echelon employees to commit a crime, causing significant harm, should be immune simply because management did not actually know what was going on. Indeed, some charge that this standard incentivizes management to avoid learning of wrongdoing within the entity. Finally, this standard can also be difficult to apply—that is, it may not be obvious in a sprawling company just who is a "high managerial agent" or which officers have a "directing mind."

10. *See, e.g.*, United States v. Science Applications Int'l Corp. 626 F.3d 1257, 1273-76 (D.C. Cir. 2020).

11. *See* U.K. Law Commission, Corporate Criminal Liability: An Options Paper (June 10, 2022).

III. DEFERRED PROSECUTION AGREEMENTS

The genesis of the trend toward the use of diversion agreements can be traced to the demise of Arthur Andersen, LLP. Andersen, a behemoth of an accounting and consulting company, was indicted for obstruction of justice based on the actions of a few employees who destroyed Enron audit records in anticipation of an SEC investigation. A jury found Andersen guilty in June 2002. In part because federal regulations bar felons from the business of auditing public companies, the conviction effectively put Andersen out of business. (Ultimately, the Supreme Court overturned the conviction because of defective jury instructions.[12]) The DOJ was roundly criticized for the harms the criminal prosecution inflicted on the otherwise blameless tens of thousands of Andersen employees who lost their jobs.

After Andersen, the government's use of diversion agreements to resolve criminal cases increased significantly. These agreements provide the government a useful middle path between declining prosecution and obtaining the conviction of a corporation. There are two varieties of these agreements. Non-prosecution agreements (NPAs) are contracts that are reached before any charges are filed and they provide that no charges will be filed if the organization complies with the contract's terms. Deferred prosecution agreements (DPAs) are contracts that contemplate that a criminal complaint will be filed, and that the government will dismiss the complaint if all the organization's contractual undertakings are satisfied. Both NPAs and DPAs—referred to collectively within as diversion agreements—are, quite simply, contracts between the government and the targeted company through which the company agrees to admit wrongdoing and take identified steps to remedy the harm it caused and put in place systems to prevent further wrongs. If the company satisfies the terms of the agreement, criminal charges that have already been filed against it in court will be dismissed (for DPAs) or no formal charges will be filed (for NPAs).

Common provisions in diversion agreements are:

- the company's admission to wrongdoing
- a "non-contradiction" provision under which the organization agrees that neither it nor its agents will make statements "contradicting" anything in the corporation's statement of responsibility
- the organization's agreement to cooperate with the government in ongoing investigations, including those against corporate agents and employees
- the payment of restitution, monetary fines, disgorgement or other penalties

12. *See* Arthur Andersen LLP v. United States, 544 U.S. 696 (2005).

- a corporate undertaking to improve its compliance program, sometimes under the scrutiny of a "monitor" hired and paid for by the company in consultation with the government
- various waivers, including the waiver of indictment, the statute of limitations, and the right to a speedy trial
- a governmental promise that, if the company fully complies with the agreement, it will not proceed with a criminal case against it with respect to the conduct under investigation
- a provision stating that if the company breaches the agreement, it will be subject to prosecution, and that the agreement's statement of facts, which constitutes an admission of guilt, will be admissible
- a provision stating that the agreement does not bind other parties, including other federal agencies.

Many agreements go beyond these basic provisions. Indeed, one of the appealing aspects of diversion agreements is the parties' ability to tailor them to respond to the case and the parties' needs. For example, some diversion agreements contain limitations on business activities and require corporate governance reforms, such as provisions requiring the company to change sales or compensation practices, oust executives or board members, and restrict or modify consulting, contracting, and other arrangements. Corporations may be required to hire outside "monitors," usually law firms, who ensure that the corporation takes the remedial steps identified in the agreement. The particular monitor is selected with the parties' agreement, and the corporation foots the bill for what can be a very expensive undertaking. The durations of NPAs and DPAs vary substantially, from a few months to many years. In recent policy statements, the Department of Justice has indicated that it will deal with companies that breach their agreements more harshly than it has in the past.

Diversion agreements are subject to judicial review only in limited circumstances. NPAs are not subject to any judicial oversight because they are reached before criminal charges are filed and a case commenced. With respect to DPAs, the Speedy Trial Act permits an exclusion from the speedy trial calculation of "[a]ny period of delay during which prosecution is deferred by the attorney for the Government pursuant to a written agreement with the defendant, with the approval of the court, for the purpose of allowing the defendant to demonstrate his good conduct," 28 U.S.C. § 3161(h)(2). All agree that district court judges have the power to adjudicate speedy trial act issues with respect to DPAs, but two district courts were reversed when they attempted to reject a DPA or to supervise its implementation using this authority.[13]

13. *See* United States v. HSBC Bank USA, N.A., 863 F.3d 125, 129, 137 (2d Cir. 2017); United States v. Fokker Servs. B.V., 818 F.3d 733, 738 (D.C. Cir. 2016).

IV. U.S. DEPARTMENT OF JUSTICE CHARGING POLICY

The Department of Justice has long published its "Principles of Federal Prosecution of Business Organizations" (the Principles), which provide non-binding guidance to federal prosecutors who are considering how to resolve an investigation into corporate criminality.[14] Readers are encouraged to read the latest iteration of the policy, which has evolved significantly over time, in its entirety. The following is simply a summary of the most basic provisions.

The Principles instruct prosecutors to weigh the factors normally considered in charging individual cases: "the sufficiency of the evidence; the likelihood of success at trial; the probable deterrent, rehabilitative, and other consequences of conviction; and the adequacy of noncriminal approaches."[15] Because of the nature of corporate crime, however, prosecutors must consider additional factors when conducting an investigation, determining whether to bring charges, and negotiating pleas or other agreements with organizations:

1. the nature and seriousness of the offense, including the risk of harm to the public, and applicable policies and priorities, if any, governing the prosecution of corporations for particular categories of crime
2. the pervasiveness of wrongdoing within the corporation, including the complicity in, or the condoning of, the wrongdoing by individuals in corporate management
3. the corporation's history of misconduct, including prior criminal, civil, and regulatory enforcement actions against it, both domestically and internationally
4. the corporation's willingness to cooperate, including as to potential wrongdoing by its current and former employees, directors, officers, and agents, as well as other individuals and entities that engaged in the misconduct under investigation
5. the adequacy and effectiveness of the corporation's compliance program at the time of the offense, as well as at the time of a charging decision
6. the corporation's timely and voluntary self-disclosure of wrongdoing

---

14. *See* U.S. Dep't of Justice, Justice Manual § 9-28.000 to § 9-28.1740 [hereinafter Justice Manual].
15. *Id.* § 9-28.300.

7. the corporation's remedial actions, including, but not limited to, any efforts to implement an adequate and effective corporate compliance program or to improve an existing one, to replace responsible management, to discipline or terminate wrongdoers, to execute financial compensation measures that punish wrongdoing, or to pay restitution
8. collateral consequences, including whether there is disproportionate harm to shareholders, pension holders, employees, and others not proven personally culpable, as well as impact on the public arising from the prosecution
9. the adequacy of remedies such as civil or regulatory enforcement actions, domestically or internationally, including remedies resulting from the corporation's cooperation with relevant government agencies
10. the adequacy of the prosecution of individuals responsible for the corporation's misconduct, and
11. the interests of any victims, including what steps the corporation has taken to identify potential victims, or other persons or entities who were significantly, even if indirectly, harmed by the criminal conduct, and what steps the corporation has taken to mitigate such harm[16]

One factor that is not normally considered in charging decisions relating to individual offenders is the potential collateral consequences of a criminal disposition to innocent parties. But this has proved to be an important factor in organizational cases in which applicable federal regulations will deprive a felon company, like Arthur Andersen, of its capacity to do business. It has also proved to be a pivotal consideration in cases in which the company does substantial business with the federal government and applicable suspension and debarment regulations would disqualify the company from further contracts. Where, for example, conviction of a pharmaceutical company may debar it from selling its widely prescribed high blood pressure medication to the Medicaid and Medicare programs, the public interest in the continuing availability of the drug may persuade prosecutors that a diversion agreement is the right way to proceed.

The Department of Justice periodically announces new policies and initiatives that may change with the presidential administration. Some notable recent policies include the DOJ Criminal Division's Corporate Enforcement & Voluntary Self-Disclosure Policy, which provides that when a company voluntarily self-discloses misconduct in an FCPA or a Criminal Division matter, fully cooperates, and timely and appropriately remediates in accordance

16. *Id.*

with the Department's standards, there is a presumption that the company will receive a *declination* of prosecution absent aggravating circumstances involving the seriousness of the offense or the nature of the offender.[17] Even if the DOJ concludes, due to the presence of aggravating circumstances, that a criminal resolution is warranted for a company that has voluntarily self-disclosed, fully cooperated, and timely and appropriately remediated, the Criminal Division will recommend a fifty percent reduction of the low end of the entity's fine range under the Organizational Guidelines and will generally not require the appointment of a monitor.

On April 15, 2024, the DOJ's Criminal Division announced a new pilot program designed to incentivize individuals to self-report. "Under this pilot program, individuals with criminal exposure—not including CEOs, CFOs, high-level foreign officials, domestic officials at any level, or individuals who organized or led the criminal scheme—who come forward and report misconduct that was otherwise unknown to the department will be eligible to receive a non-prosecution agreement (NPA) if they meet certain criteria."[18] And on August 1, 2024, the DOJ's Criminal Division launched its new Whistleblower Awards Pilot Program designed to uncover and prosecute corporate crime. "Under this pilot program, a whistleblower who provides the Criminal Division with original and truthful information about corporate misconduct that results in a successful forfeiture may be eligible for an award."[19]

A. Cooperation Credit

As noted in the introduction, most corporations will attempt to cooperate with the government in an effort to avoid criminal indictment. What constitutes "cooperation" has changed over time.

First, perhaps in response to the criticism the Justice Department suffered as a result of the dearth of individual indictments following the 2008 subprime mortgage crisis, the Principles now stress that corporate resolutions cannot substitute for individual accountability. Thus, the Principles state that:

> In order for a corporation to receive any consideration for cooperation under this section, the corporation must identify all individuals involved in or

17. *Id.* § 9-47.120.
18. Criminal Division Pilot Program On Voluntary Self-Disclosures for Individuals, available at https://www.justice.gov/opa/blog/criminal-divisions-voluntary-self-disclosures-pilot-program-individuals
19. Criminal Division Corporate Whistleblower Awards Pilot Program, available at https://www.justice.gov/criminal/criminal-division-corporate-whistleblower-awards-pilot-program

> responsible for the misconduct at issue, regardless of their position, status or seniority, and timely provide to the Department all relevant facts relating to that misconduct. If a corporation seeking cooperation credit declines to learn of such facts or to provide the Department with complete factual information about the individuals involved in or responsible for the misconduct, its cooperation will not be considered a mitigating factor under this section.[20]

Second, the Principles now specify the types of actions that will earn corporations the "[t]he greatest amount of cooperation credit." They include:

1. Timely disclosure of all facts relevant to the wrongdoing at issue, including:
   a. facts gathered during a corporation's internal investigation, if the company chooses to conduct one;
   b. attribution of facts to specific sources, rather than a general narrative of the facts; and
   c. identification of all individuals involved in or responsible for the misconduct at issue, regardless of their position, status, or seniority, including the corporation's officers, employees, customers, competitors or agents and third parties, and all relevant facts relating to the misconduct and the involvement by those individuals;
2. Proactive cooperation, rather than reactive; that is, timely disclosure of all facts that are relevant to the investigation and, where the corporation is aware of opportunities for the Department to obtain relevant evidence not in the corporation's possession and not otherwise known to the Department, timely identification of those opportunities;
3. Timely voluntary preservation, collection, and disclosure of relevant documents and information relating to their provenance, including (a) disclosure of documents located overseas, the locations in which such documents were found, their custodians, and who authored and found the documents, (b) facilitation of third-party production of documents, and (c) where requested, provision of translations of relevant documents in foreign languages;
   a. Where a corporation claims that disclosure of overseas documents is prohibited due to data privacy, blocking statutes, or other reasons related to foreign law, the corporation bears the burden of establishing the prohibition and identifying reasonable alternatives such that the Department receives the necessary facts and evidence to continue its investigations and prosecutions. Moreover, a corporation should work diligently to identify all available legal bases to provide such documents;

20. Justice Manual, *supra* note 14, § 9-28.700.

b. Prosecutors also should consider the extent to which a corporation enforced effective document and data retention policies in order to preserve, collect, and disclose documents, data, and other evidence relevant to the government's investigation (including as to third-party messaging data, regardless of whether the data is kept on corporate or personal devices that are used for work purposes);

4. De-confliction[21] of witness interviews and other investigative steps that a corporation takes as part of its internal investigation, should it conduct one, to prevent the corporation's investigation from conflicting or interfering with the Department's investigation; and
5. Where appropriate and possible, making corporate officers and employees who possess relevant information available for interviews by the Department; this includes, officers, employees, and agents located overseas, as well as former officers and employees, and, where possible, the facilitation of interview[s] of third-party witnesses.[22]

Three aspects of the Principles' cooperation policy have been of vital interest to defense counsel and have evolved over time. The first two areas—concerning corporate payment of individuals' attorneys' fees and joint defenses—became controversial when the Principles provided that prosecutors should inquire "whether the corporation appears to be protecting its culpable employees and agents," explaining that "a corporation's promise of support to culpable employees and agents, either through *the advancing of attorneys fees*, through retaining the employees without sanction for their misconduct, *or through providing information to the employees about the government's investigation pursuant to a joint defense agreement*, may be considered by the prosecutor in weighing the extent and value of a corporation's cooperation."[23] The third area of profound change concerns the Department's stated policy regarding privilege waivers.

1. Payment of Individuals' Attorneys' Fees

In many cases, the organization will pay the attorneys' fees of individual counsel hired by its employees or agents. It often is required to do so by the corporate bylaws or by the individuals' employment contracts. Absent this

21. "Deconfliction" is the practice of having company counsel defer taking certain investigative steps, commonly interviewing company employees, in deference to the government investigators.
22. Justice Manual, *supra* note 14, § 9-28.700.
23. United States v. Stein, 541 F.3d 130, 136 (2d Cir. 2008) (quoting version of the Principles controlling in 2003-06).

funding source, many individuals would have great difficulty paying for their defense efforts.

In *United States v. Stein*, 541 F.3d 130 (2d Cir. 2008), the government was investigating KPMG and some of its employees. The individual employees alleged that the government coerced KPMG into cutting off payment of their attorneys' fees. The district court found that, "but for the [Principles] and the prosecutors' conduct, KPMG would have paid defendants' legal fees and expenses without consideration of cost."[24] The Second Circuit held that KPMG's "adoption and enforcement of a policy under which it conditioned, capped and ultimately ceased advancing legal fees to defendants followed as a direct consequence of the government's overwhelming influence, and that KPMG's conduct therefore amounted to state action."[25] It further ruled "that the government thus unjustifiably interfered with defendants' relationship with counsel and their ability to mount a defense, in violation of the Sixth Amendment, and that the government did not cure the violation."[26]

Subsequently, the DOJ amended the Principles to provide that:

> In evaluating cooperation . . . prosecutors should not take into account whether a corporation is advancing or reimbursing attorneys' fees or providing counsel to employees, officers, or directors under investigation or indictment. Likewise, prosecutors may not request that a corporation refrain from taking such action. This prohibition is not meant to prevent a prosecutor from asking questions about an attorney's representation of a corporation or its employees, officers, or directors, where otherwise appropriate under the law. Neither is it intended to limit the otherwise applicable reach of criminal obstruction of justice statutes such as 18 U.S.C. § 1503.[27]

2. Joint Defenses

A great variety of representation and conflicts issues may arise when acts undertaken in a business context become the focus of a criminal investigation and the business and certain of its officers, directors, employees, or agents are possible subjects or targets. When the government first comes calling, one lawyer or firm may attempt to represent the corporation and the employees allegedly implicated (usually termed "multiple" or "joint" representation). This is ethically permissible in the absence of disabling actual or potential conflicts of interest and with proper disclosure. There are many advantages to such joint representations, including counsel's ability to efficiently and relatively inexpensively investigate the matter and deal with the government; this is particularly true if the corporation and its agents wish

24. *Id.* at 141.
25. *Id.* at 136.
26. *Id.*
27. Justice Manual, *supra* note 14, § 9-28.730.

to present a common, united defense to possible prosecution. It also has an advantage in that under the "no-contact" ethical rule, government attorneys are generally barred from attempting to interview represented witnesses without consulting their lawyers.[28] A joint representation, then, at least in theory means that one firm or lawyer can control the government's access to the company and all its employees, although government lawyers commonly take issue with this application of the rule.

As the investigation progresses, however, and certainly after indictment and at trial, conflicts of interest are virtually inevitable and separate counsel must be hired. At this point, the parties may enter into a joint defense agreement, either informally or in writing. Such agreements are designed to cover the communications among the participants with the joint defense privilege (also known as the common interest rule), which shields from discovery confidential information shared by persons with common or joint interests, typically in litigation or in advance of expected litigation.[29] The doctrine protects both communications between attorneys for joint defense participants and communications between a participant and attorneys for other participants, but it does not protect communications among the clients. Normally the agreement contemplates that the matters discussed will remain privileged unless all participants waive the privilege. And under the terms of typical agreements, those participants who turn state's witness are barred from sharing with the government what they learned from the other participants during the course of the joint defense.

A joint defense potentially gives individual counsel access to invaluable information she would not otherwise have because investigative subjects have no right to discovery or legal process prior to indictment and the grand jury proceedings are shrouded in secrecy. In particular, individual counsel will learn what other witnesses have said and what evidence the government has garnered from other sources, allowing her to better evaluate her client's position and to craft an individual defense. A joint defense certainly allows the group more effectively to track the direction and status of the government's investigative efforts. It may also allow the group to achieve many of the advantages of joint representation while potentially avoiding disqualifying conflicts of interest and other problems. Thus, joint defenses can facilitate the formulation of a common, coherent defense theory and strategy. And they can save clients' money to the extent that joint defense counsel allocate among themselves investigative or trial preparation responsibilities.

---

28. *See* Model Rule of Prof'l Conduct 4.2 (1983).

29. *See generally* Ethical Implications of Joint Defense/Common Interest Agreements, Committee on Professional Responsibility of the Association of the Bar of the City of New York, 51 Rec. Ass'n B. City N.Y. 115 (1996).

Prosecutors usually frown on joint defense agreements. Some believe that they constitute organized obstruction, permitting members to shape their testimony and even coordinate perjury. Others would prefer to keep the progress and substance of their investigation confidential and may prefer a divided rather than a unified defense. Consistent with prosecutors' general distaste for joint defense agreements, the Principles originally allowed prosecutors to consider the existence of a joint defense as evidence of a disinclination to cooperate. But the Principles now state that:

> [T]he mere participation by a corporation in a joint defense agreement does not render the corporation ineligible to receive cooperation credit, and prosecutors may not request that a corporation refrain from entering into such agreements. Of course, the corporation may wish to avoid putting itself in the position of being disabled, by virtue of a particular joint defense or similar agreement, from providing some relevant facts to the government and thereby limiting its ability to seek such cooperation credit. Such might be the case if the corporation gathers facts from employees who have entered into a joint defense agreement with the corporation, and who may later seek to prevent the corporation from disclosing the facts it has acquired. Corporations may wish to address this situation by crafting or participating in joint defense agreements, to the extent they choose to enter them, that provide such flexibility as they deem appropriate.[30]

3. Waivers of Attorney-Client Privilege and the Work Product Doctrine

At one time, prosecutors assessing the corporation's "cooperation and voluntary disclosure" provided that one factor prosecutors could weigh in assessing the adequacy of a corporation's cooperation was the completeness of its disclosure including, if necessary, a waiver of the attorney-client and work product protections. Such waivers could include both the substance of the company's internal investigation and communications between specific officers, directors and employees and counsel.

The defense bar asserted that prosecutors requested such waivers in virtually every corporate investigation (it should be noted that the Justice Department denied this charge). An alliance of business, legal, and civil liberties groups objected to the policy and succeeded in interesting at least some in Congress in "fixing" it through legislation. The Justice Department headed off congressional action by amending its policies.

The Principles' current bottom line is clear: (1) privilege waivers are not (and assertedly have never been) a prerequisite for cooperation credit or for declination of criminal charges; (2) a corporation may freely waive its privileges if it wishes; (3) but that waiver may not be considered when

30. Justice Manual, *supra* note 14, § 9-28.730.

a prosecutor decides whether to give a corporation credit for its cooperation in charging; (4) rather, the critical determinant is whether the entity has provided prosecutors with the facts necessary for them to investigate the matter fairly and responsibly. The policy seemingly permits prosecutors to ask for waivers of "fact" work product and privileged communications, but it provides that corporations "need not produce, and *prosecutors may not request*," such "core" work product and attorney-client privileged materials as attorneys' notes of witness interviews and advice given to the client concerning the legal implications of the putative misconduct at issue "as a condition for the corporation's eligibility to receive cooperation credit."[31]

V. INTERNAL CORPORATE INVESTIGATIONS

There are a wealth of reasons why companies generally conduct internal investigations into non-trivial allegations of corporate misconduct. Such investigations may be required by statute or by industry regulators and associations, such as the New York Stock Exchange, the American Stock Exchange, and the National Association of Securities Dealers. And an investigation of the relevant facts may be necessary for the company to meet whatever reporting requirements constrain it under state or federal law.

Even absent a legal obligation to investigate, the company will want to ensure that whatever wrongdoing has gone on has ceased and investigate whether, absent prompt remedial action such as a restatement of the company's financials, the wrongdoing may morph into other legal problems. The corporation may wish to remediate the wrongdoing in other ways, by proactively compensating victims or cleaning up an environmental spill for example. It will also need to decide whether to cooperate with the government in hopes of securing leniency or even to self-report the violation to the government.

Should the government launch an investigation, the corporation will need to know the facts to formulate an effective defense. If the government's interest becomes public, an investigation may be necessary to reassure various corporate stakeholders—including investors, employees, clients or customers, auditors, regulators and the like. A company's own compliance policy may require an investigation, and its failure to abide by its own policy is sure to paint the corporation as one that is not committed to a culture of compliance. Finally, the Department of Justice's cooperation policy considers whether an investigation

31. *See id.* § 9-28.720(b) (emphasis added). This last injunction is subject to the standard exceptions: where the advice of counsel defense is asserted; where the communications at issue are subject to the crime-fraud exception to privilege rules; and where the conduct at issue constitutes criminal obstruction.

has been launched, and many of the criteria in that policy cannot be met absent such an investigation. The Department of Justice's bottom line is that it wants to know the facts—good, bad, and ugly—about the corporate misconduct and the individuals responsible for it, and those facts can only be uncovered through an internal investigation.

Most internal investigations are triggered by some circumstance that hints at corporate malfeasance, such as questionable stock trading, irregularities discovered during audits, anonymous tips, customer complaints, regulatory inspections, and, of course, the service of civil complaints or criminal grand jury subpoenas. Such circumstances are not always sufficiently serious to require the resources consumed by a full-scale investigation. Some investigations may be conducted by in-house counsel. Where organizational finances permit, large-scale or particularly sensitive investigations are generally conducted by outside counsel from a law firm expert in such inquiries. A variety of circumstances account for this choice, but two stand out.

First, to the extent the investigation is public knowledge and part of the reason for it is to reassure various corporate constituencies and prosecutors, outside counsel's investigative results are likely to be viewed as more credible. The fact that outside counsel is viewed as more independent will also help where the government suspects the involvement of senior management. Second, corporations cannot claim a Fifth Amendment right against compelled self-incrimination and thus it can protect the results of its investigation—at least until it chooses how it will act on the report—only by using lawyers who can shield their work under the attorney-client privilege and work product doctrine. Invocation of the attorney-client privilege and work product doctrine obviously must be based on the provision of legal services. In the United States, unlike many parts of Europe, communications between corporate counsel and employees are covered by the attorney-client privilege and such counsel can claim the protections of the work product doctrine.[32] But in-house counsel are often called upon to give advice in which legal and business considerations are inextricably intertwined, and such materials are not privileged. Courts therefore give more rigorous and skeptical scrutiny to in-house counsels' claims to the protections of the attorney-client privilege and the work product doctrine.

If an outside law firm is engaged, it and corporate representatives—usually the Board or a committee thereof—will first agree on the appropriate scope of the proposed investigation. The lawyers will promptly send out what is known as a litigation hold or preservation letter instructing company employees to preserve potentially relevant evidence, whether it be in documentary form or is electronically-stored information (ESI). The lawyers will then launch their investigative work as quickly as possible. If

32. *See* Upjohn Co. v. United States, 449 U.S. 383 (1981).

the government does not yet know of the misconduct, counsel will want to get a leg up so she can assess the company's exposure and advise it on how to mitigate the risk of discovery and criminal sanction. If the government is already investigating, the time pressures are magnified if the company is to make timely decisions regarding cooperation.

Internal investigations generally focus on two categories of information: physical or digital evidence (including, for example, financial data, memoranda, texts, and emails) and interviews of corporate agents. Because the corporation cannot claim a Fifth Amendment privilege and because mere review by a lawyer of unprivileged documents does not confer upon those documents attorney-client-privileged or work product status, documentary proof generally cannot be shielded from disclosure (although lawyers may claim as protected work product their own choice, categorization, or organization of the key documents).

Witness interviews present a variety of challenges, many of which flow from the fact that counsel's ethical duties are owed to the entity itself, not to any of its constituencies—whether those constituencies are the Board, shareholders, or members of management. Counsel may find themselves in the awkward position of interrogating the general counsel with whom they are coordinating their investigation or the board members who engaged them. When investigating counsel interviews employees or agents of the firm, counsel should give the so-called "*Upjohn* warning,"[33] also referred to as the corporate *Miranda* warning.[34] This warning ensures that the employees do not operate under the misapprehension that counsel represents them and that they control the privilege. Among other things, the warning generally informs the employee that (1) counsel represents the company, not the employee; (2) the interview is protected by the attorney-client privilege, but that the privilege is controlled solely by the company; and (3) the company may choose to waive the privilege and disclose what the employee told counsel to any third party, including the government.

Witness interviews are often critical to understanding the words and numbers contained in the documents or data, putting that evidence in context, and arriving at a reliable narrative of the misconduct and its legal implications. Communications made by corporate employees of any rank to counsel in furtherance of their employer's request for legal advice are protected by the attorney-client privilege.[35] And, to the extent that counsel

---

33. The name is derived from the case, *Upjohn Co. v. United States*, 449 U.S. 383 (1981), in which the Court ruled, *inter alia*, that the communications made between employees and the general counsel of the company during an internal investigation were privileged.

34. *See* Model Rule of Prof'l Conduct 1.13(f) ("In dealing with an organization's directors, officers, employees, members, shareholders or other constituents, a lawyer shall explain the identity of the client when the lawyer knows or reasonably should know that the organization's interests are adverse to those of the constituents with whom the lawyer is dealing.").

35. *See Upjohn*, 449 U.S. at 390-97.

memorializes employee interviews in debriefing memoranda, such memos constitute protected attorney work product.[36]

During the course of the investigation, counsel will likely produce a variety of other analytical or summary work product. One of the first tasks facing counsel will be to get a sense of the cast of characters and the organizational hierarchy. Counsel will prepare a more or less extensive chronology of the relevant events based on documents and witness interviews. Counsel will identify "key" documents and other critical evidence. Certainly, counsel will prepare agendas for meetings, questions for various witnesses, "to do" lists of all sorts, and summary documentation regarding what has been learned and what remains to be uncovered. Legal memos regarding possibly applicable law will be commissioned. Counsel may well hire outside experts, such as forensic accountants, to aid in the interpretation of the data. Finally, counsel will likely write debriefing memos to memorialize, and analyze, all interactions with witnesses and government investigators. Counsel will work hard to ensure that all these materials are protected from disclosure under the attorney-client privilege or the work product doctrine.

At the conclusion of the investigation, or at various stages of it, a report in some form is given to the client. The report will summarize at greater or lesser length what counsel discovered. Note that these reports may make reference to the content of interviews with employees and may contain lawyers' assessments of credibility, but they are very unlikely to contain the lawyers' actual debriefing memos for fear of waiver. The report may include some material reflecting counsel's analytical work product (e.g., organizational charts, identification of "key" documents, a form of chronology). Counsel's report will also generally contain prospective advice, such as recommended steps the corporation might take to remediate any wrongdoing or to prevent future missteps. If, as is often the case, the corporation fears imminent regulatory or prosecutorial scrutiny of the relevant events, the report may suggest a course of action to reduce the corporation's exposure. Where a government investigation has not yet been launched, counsel will have to deal with the agonizing issue of whether the corporation should self-report; where an investigation has been launched, the corporation will need to quickly decide whether and how much to cooperate with relevant authorities.

A. Waiver Issues

Should a prosecutor, or plaintiffs in collateral litigation against the company, seek to subpoena the company for any written reports or records of

36. *See id.*

corporate counsel's investigation, the corporation cannot resist on Fifth Amendment grounds. Investigating counsel's reports to the board of directors—as well as the materials discussed above that were generated during the investigation—are usually covered by the attorney-client privilege or the work product doctrine. The protected nature of such materials is crucial because, absent such protection, the internal investigative report may well provide prosecutors—and civil plaintiffs and regulators conducting parallel litigation against the company—with a roadmap to liability. Counsel will have done the government's work in reviewing masses of data and identifying the important needles in the haystack. They will have gathered the statements of the relevant witnesses, at least some of whom may choose not to speak to government agents. With these materials, the government also would have the expert assessment of experienced criminal counsel regarding the corporation's likely exposure under federal law.

Should the corporate client decide to cooperate with the government, counsel will have to confront a variety of issues relating to possible privilege waivers. In this regard, it is important to recognize that federal law (except in the Eighth Circuit) does not recognize a selective waiver doctrine.[37] Accordingly, *if the holder of the privilege waives it as to the government, it is lost as to all others who may be interested.* This means that privileged materials exposed to the government are potentially discoverable by civil plaintiffs, other government regulators, and any individual corporate employees who are ultimately indicted.[38]

Minimizing the potential for privilege waivers will be a constant issue for investigating counsel. To secure credit for cooperation, the government does not demand privilege waivers, but it does require timely, proactive disclosure of the facts gathered during the investigation. Counsel will therefore need to consider carefully how to turn over the relevant facts without waiving whatever privileges apply to the sources from which those facts are drawn, including reports to the client, witness debriefing memos, summaries of key documents, organizational charts, chronologies, and other analytical work product. If corporate counsel turn over privileged materials, those items will lose their attorney-client privileged status; to the extent they are protected by the work product doctrine, a waiver will be implied where the material is turned over to one deemed an adversary.

The question then becomes the scope of any further waiver. Common law rules developed in this respect, but courts appear to believe that these rules were supplanted in 2008 with the adoption of Fed. R. Evid. 502,

---

37. *Compare* In re Pacific Pictures Corp., 679 F.3d 1121, 1127-28 (9th Cir. 2012), *with* Diversified Indus., Inc. v. Meredith, 572 F.2d 596, 611 (8th Cir. 1978) (*en banc*).
38. *See, e.g.*, In re Columbia/HCA Healthcare Corp. Billing Practices, 293 F.3d 289, 302-04 (6th Cir. 2002). Some courts have indicated that they may recognize limited exceptions to this rule. *See, e.g.*, In re Steinhardt Partners, LLP, 9 F.3d 230, 236 (2d Cir. 1993).

entitled "Attorney–Client Privilege and Work Product; Limitations on Waiver."[39] Rule 502 provides that "when [a] disclosure is made in a federal proceeding or to a federal office or agency and waives the attorney-client privilege or work-product protection, the waiver extends to an undisclosed communication or information in a federal or state proceeding *only* if: (1) the waiver is intentional; (2) the disclosed and undisclosed communications or information concern the same subject matter; *and* (3) they ought in fairness to be considered together" (emphasis added.) As the Advisory Committee Notes state, the Rule "provides that a voluntary disclosure in a federal proceeding or to a federal office or agency. . . generally results in a waiver *only* of the communication or information disclosed."[40] In particular, such disclosure results in a subject matter waiver of undisclosed materials only in those "unusual situations in which fairness requires a further disclosure of related, protected information, in order to prevent a selective and misleading presentation of evidence to the disadvantage of the adversary."[41]

B. Is the Private Investigation "Fairly Attributable" to the Government?

The degree of governmental involvement in the internal investigation must be carefully monitored. No problem should be presented if prosecutors are conducting a parallel investigation and interact with corporate counsel to the degree discussed in the Principles's cooperation policy. But to the extent that the government can be said to have substantially coerced the company or its counsel to do its bidding, or essentially delegated the investigation to private counsel, courts may conclude that the corporate investigation is "fairly attributable" to the government for constitutional purposes. Such a conclusion may have serious consequences for the government's case going forward.

As discussed above, in *Stein*, the conclusion that KPMG's refusal to pay attorneys' fees was "state action" led to a finding that the government had violated the defendants' Sixth Amendment right to counsel. Another example concerns potential Fifth Amendment difficulties. Corporations regularly warn employees that their employment will be terminated if they do not cooperate with the investigation; because the companies are private actors, this does not present Fifth Amendment

39. *See, e.g.*, In re General Motors LLC Ignition Switch Litig., 80 F. Supp. 3d 521, 533-34 (S.D.N.Y. 2015) (although "the parties discuss the common law of waiver in their memoranda of law . . . both sides agree that the waiver analysis is controlled by Rule 502").
40. Fed. R. Evid. 502, cmt. (emphasis added).
41. *Id.*

difficulties. But should a court conclude that the actions of private counsel in obtaining such statements is fairly attributable to the government, these will be deemed compelled statements taken in violation of the Fifth Amendment.[42]

Private conduct is attributed to the government when "'there is a sufficiently close nexus between the state and the challenged action.'"[43] According to the Second Circuit, "'[a] nexus of state action exists between a private entity and the state when the state exercises coercive power, is entwined in the management or control of the private actor, or provides the private actor with *significant encouragement*, either overt or covert, or when the private actor operates as *a willful participant in joint activity* with the State or its agents, is controlled by an agency of the State, has been delegated a public function by the state, or is *entwined with governmental policies.*'"[44]

Courts have only infrequently found that the actions of private counsel are attributable to the government, reserving such a judgment to circumstances in which the government was found to have significantly coerced private counsel or basically deputized them. *Stein* presented a case of coercion. The Second Circuit concluded that KPMG's adoption and enforcement of a policy in which it refused to pay individuals' attorneys' fees "amounted to 'state action' because KPMG 'operate[d] as a willful participant in joint activity' with the government, and because the USAO 'significant[ly] encourage[d] KPMG to withhold legal fees from defendants upon indictment."[45] *United States v. Connolly*, 2019 WL 2120523 (S.D.N.Y. 2019), provides an example of improper delegation of the investigation to private counsel. The court found a sufficiently close nexus based on a finding that "[t]he only conclusion one can draw from [the] evidence is that, rather than conduct its own investigation, the Government outsourced the important developmental stage of its investigation to [the company that was the original target] . . . and then built its own 'investigation' into specific employees . . . on a very firm foundation constructed for it" by the company and its lawyers.[46] In other words, the court concluded, investigating counsel "did everything that the Government could, should, and would have done had the Government been doing its own work."[47]

42. *See* United States v. Connolly, No. 16-Cr-0370 (CM), 2019 WL 2120523, at *14 (S.D.N.Y. May 2, 2019).

43. Blum v. Yaretsky, 457 U.S. 991, 1004 (1982); *see also* Chapter 14 (Fifth Amendment).

44. *Stein*, 541 F.3d at 147 (emphasis original).

45. *Id.*

46. *Connolly*, 2019 WL 2120523, at *12.

47. *Id.*

VI. RESPONSIBLE CORPORATE OFFICER LIABILITY

As noted above, corporate employees and agents are liable for crimes they commit on behalf of an entity. Normally such cases require the government to prove that the agents committed the actus reus of the crime with the requisite mens rea. In a discrete category of cases, however, the Supreme Court has held that an individual corporate officer can be held strictly liable for the criminal actions of subordinates under the "responsible corporate officer" doctrine. That doctrine provides that a corporate executive who has control over activities that lead to a subordinate's violation of a statute may incur liability for failing to fulfill his duty to prevent such misconduct. Where the offense provides for strict liability, the responsible corporate officer can be criminally sanctioned even though he did not personally participate in the wrongdoing and even though he had no personal knowledge of the misconduct perpetrated by his subordinates.

The Court first recognized such liability in *United States v. Dotterweich*, 320 U.S. 277 (1943), in which the president and general manager of a pharmaceutical company was convicted of a misdemeanor violation the Food, Drug, and Cosmetic Act because his company shipped misbranded and adulterated drugs. The Court ruled that Dotterweich could be convicted even if he did not personally participate in or even know about the illegal activity. The Court first noted that the legislation itself "dispenses with the conventional requirement for criminal conduct—awareness of some wrongdoing."[48] The Act was necessary to protect consumers who could not protect themselves and "[i]n the interest of the larger good it put the burden of acting at hazard upon a person otherwise innocent but standing in responsible relation to a public danger."[49] The *Dotterweich* Court concluded that this strict liability offense is committed "by all who . . . have . . . a responsible share in the furtherance of the transaction which the statute outlaws, namely, to put into the stream of interstate commerce adulterated or misbranded drugs."[50]

Later, in *United States v. Park*, 421 U.S. 658 (1975), the Court affirmed the misdemeanor conviction of the president and chief operating office of a national retail food chain under the Food, Drug, and Cosmetics Act for shipping adulterated products. On appeal, the circuit court held that while *Dotterweich* "had construed the statutory provisions under which respondent was tried to dispense with the traditional element of 'awareness of some wrongdoing,' the Court had not construed them as dispensing with the element of 'wrongful action.'"[51] The Supreme Court reversed, essentially

48. *Dotterweich*, 320 U.S. at 281.
49. *Id.*
50. *Id.* at 284.
51. *Park*, 421 U.S. at 666.

holding that Park's "wrongful" conduct was an omission, that is, his "failure to exercise the authority and supervisory responsibility reposed in [him] by the business organization [which] resulted in the violation complained of."[52] It therefore affirmed that "corporate employees who have 'a responsible share in the furtherance of the transaction which the statute outlaws' are subject to the criminal provisions of the Act."[53]

This doctrine remains a threat in certain types of cases, notably those involving prosecutions under the Food, Drug, and Cosmetics Act for shipping misbranded or adulterated drugs, food, and other commodities. It has also been used in environmental prosecutions. Some environmental statutes, like the Clean Water Act,[54] expressly authorize prosecution of responsible corporate officers. When the environmental statute at issue does not impose strict liability—requiring, for example, that the defendant act "knowingly"—courts have held that the responsible corporate officer doctrine does not negate that proof requirement, although proof of such knowledge can be inferred from willful blindness or from circumstantial evidence, such as the "position and responsibility of defendants such as corporate officers."[55]

Examples

1. Jax Hamm was the head of lobbying for an agricultural cooperative, Sun-Diamond Growers of California. Sun-Diamond retained the services of Sandile Ayanda, a partner at the public relations firm of Cleveland Park Associates, to help it with public relations issues. The Secretary of Agriculture, Starr Abbott, was an old college pal of Hamm's with whom Hamm still shared a close friendship. Abbott asked for Hamm's assistance in retiring the campaign debt her brother accrued when unsuccessfully running for Congress. Hamm approached Ayanda and together they hatched a plan to surreptitiously help Abbott's brother. Ayanda asked five of his partners to send $1,000 contributions to the brother's campaign, assuring them that they would be reimbursed. This is illegal under campaign finance law. Ayanda then fraudulently billed Sun-Diamond $5,000 for fictitious expenses incurred while purportedly serving the cooperative. Hamm, who had not shared this scheme with anyone else at Sun-Diamond, approved the expense, Sun-Diamond paid the bill, and Ayanda reimbursed the Cleveland Park Associates partners who made the illegal contributions. The government would like

52. *Id.* at 671.
53. *Id.* at 670.
54. *See* 33 U.S.C. § 1319(c)(3)(A).
55. United States v. MacDonald & Watson Waste Oil Co., 933 F.2d 35, 51, 55 (1st Cir. 1991) (Resource Conservation & Recovery Act (RCRA)).

to charge Sun-Diamond with wire fraud on the theory that it deprived Cleveland Park Associates of the honest services of Ayanda.[56] Assume for present purposes that a case could be made that Hamm's actions constituted honest services wire fraud. As defense counsel for Sun-Diamond, what arguments would you make to resist liability under respondeat superior principles?

2A. Acme Inc. is a large multi-national company that sells computer equipment throughout the Americas. The *Wall Street Journal* (the *Journal*) published an article alleging that Acme's local office in Mexico City had been bribing public officials to obtain government contracts. Acme's board hired the law firm of Muse & Muse to conduct an internal corporate investigation into the report. What are the board and Muse lawyers likely to discuss first?

2B. DOJ prosecutors began issuing grand jury subpoenas for relevant evidence. Acme, in hopes of securing a declination or DPA, assured the Department of Justice that it would cooperate fully with the government investigation. Because prosecutors lack the power to force non-U.S. citizens located abroad to come to the United States for interviews or to give testimony, the prosecutors asked that the company fly Mexican executives from the Mexico City office to the U.S. for interviews with Justice Department personnel and grand jury appearances. The company did so at its own expense. In an effort to meet their de-confliction obligations, Muse lawyers coordinated the timing of interviews they wished to conduct with corporate employees with the prosecutors. Acme refused to pay for individual counsel for the employees and told them that if they did not cooperate fully with the internal investigation and the government, they would be fired. Finally, the company volunteered to waive the attorney-client privilege and work product doctrine protections that might otherwise apply to the conduct of its internal investigation. What are the pros and cons of taking this position with respect to payment of individuals' fees from the defense's point of view? Are the prosecutors in this scenario complying with DOJ policy? Should prosecutors be concerned that this level of corporate cooperation with the government might lead a court to conclude that there is in improper "nexus" between the private and official investigations? How would such a conclusion affect the government?

2C. Assume Muse & Muse talked Acme into paying for private counsel for the individual employees the Justice Department identified as subjects and targets of the investigation. Acme then entered into a joint defense agreement with these individuals, pursuant to which they pooled information and allocated investigative responsibilities. What implications might this have for Acme's ability to gain cooperation credit from the government?

56. See Chapter 6 (Fraud) for discussion of honest services fraud.

2D. As Muse & Muse's investigation progressed, the firm gave Acme's board periodic reports. These reports consisted of oral briefings accompanied by power point presentations that highlighted the facts the firm had discovered and the legal implications of those facts under federal law. The firm also made periodic disclosures of facts to the government. Counsel let prosecutors review but not retain copies of the power point slides. Plaintiffs have launched a shareholder derivative suit against the corporation. They seek disclosure of the power point presentations and any privileged materials or work product that refer or relate to the same subject matter discussed in the slides. Has the company waived applicable privileges and, if so, how broad is that waiver?

Explanations

1. The government would attempt to prove Sun-Diamond's liability by arguing that it is liable under respondeat superior principles for the misconduct of Hamm. The defense would argue that Sun-Diamond is the victim, not the perpetrator. It is inarguably the victim of a $5,000 fraud and is the only party in this story who lost money. Hamm was certainly acting within the scope of his employment, so the defense would depend on an assertion that Hamm was not acting with the requisite intention to benefit his employer: Hamm came up with a scheme to defraud his employer of $5,000 solely to help out a college friend, at Sun-Diamond's expense and not for its benefit. Indeed, the fact that he is a rogue agent rather than a faithful servant is demonstrated by the fact that he was careful not to share his scheme with others at Sun-Diamond and went outside the cooperative to solicit the illegal campaign donations.

   This hypothetical is adapted from *United States v. Sun-Diamond Growers*, 138 F.3d 961 (D.C. Cir. 1998). In that case, the D.C. Circuit affirmed Sun-Diamond's conviction, rejecting these arguments. It did acknowledge that Sun-Diamond's argument had "intuitive appeal" in that it did "look more like a victim than a perpetrator" but the fact that Sun-Diamond employee "hid the illegal campaign contribution scheme from others at the company and used company funds to accomplish it" did not preclude a finding that the employee intended to benefit the cooperative.[57] The court reasoned that part of that employee's job was to cultivate his and Sun-Diamond's relationship with the Agriculture Secretary. "By responding to the Secretary's request to help his brother, [the Sun-Diamond employee] may have been acting out of pure friendship, but the jury was entitled to conclude that he was acting instead, or

57. *Sun-Diamond*, 138 F.3d at 970.

also, with an intent (however befuddled) to further the interests of his employer. The scheme came at some cost to Sun-Diamond but it also promised some benefit."[58]

2A. There will be, at the inception of the relationship, checks for conflicts of interest, execution of a retention and fee agreement, and the dissemination of an appropriate litigation hold. As part of these discussions, the board and outside counsel will agree on the (preliminary) scope of the investigative mandate—for example, whether counsel should confine themselves to looking into this particular allegation or should conduct a broader inquiry. This will turn on the allegations at issue, the corporation's history of similar conduct, and whether other red flags exist. At least where, as here, the DOJ is aware of the allegations through the *Journal* report, sticking one's head in the sand if there are obvious signs that the corruption problem is not confined to Mexico City will not serve the corporation well.

The company and counsel also ought to seriously discuss the possibility of voluntary self-disclosure to the government given the likelihood of an eventual government investigation flowing from the *Journal*'s report. In the past, such disclosures were rarely made or even seriously considered. New DOJ policies, however, promise a declination of charges—not just a DPA—in qualifying cases of voluntary self-disclosure, full cooperation, and effective remediation of the criminal harms caused. But it will be difficult for the company to make a reasonably informed judgment on the risks posed by self-disclosure without at least some preliminary investigative work to ascertain whether there is in fact a problem and how serious and widespread it may be.

2B. The individuals' attorneys' fees for separate counsel may well be expensive. Whether the company can get away with not paying these fees depends on whether such payments are required by the corporate bylaws, employment contracts, or other legal obligations. Even if there is no legal imperative to pay, refusing to pay attorneys' fees is likely to alienate the individual subjects and targets at a point at which investigators most need the information they can provide, and may well drive them out of the defense camp and into cooperation agreements with the government.

The problem asks whether, assuming that the company is seeking cooperation credit toward prosecutors' charging decisions, prosecutors' actions in accepting corporate decisions to withhold payment of individuals' attorneys' fees and to waive applicable privileges violates DOJ policy. The answer is no, assuming the prosecutors did not coerce

---

58. *Id.*

these decisions and did not hint that they were necessary to secure cooperation credit.

This problem also raises the question whether the company's efforts to cooperate are "fairly attributable" to the government. The *Connolly* Court seemed most perturbed by the fact that prosecutors in that case were not "*actually conducting parallel investigations.*"[59] Other courts examining the "nexus" between the private and public investigations for purposes of determining whether the company's actions are fairly attributable to the government focus on the degree of government coercion visited upon the company to take the actions complained of.

This problem presupposes that there is a good faith government investigation ongoing. In such circumstances, de-confliction conversations and efforts to make available company personnel for interviews or grand jury appearances should not be problematic. Nor does there appear to be overt coercion. Given that the company apparently volunteered a privilege waiver and determined on its own to refuse to pay individuals' attorneys' fees, that should not affect the court's "nexus" calculus. If, however, prosecutors essentially strongarmed the company into refusing to pay individuals' attorneys' fees, this would violate DOJ policy and may well be considered state action that violates the individuals' Sixth Amendment rights. If the corporation's conditioning of continued employment on waiver of employees' Fifth Amendment rights is considered to be "fairly attributable" to the government, this would also be constitutionally problematic.

2C. The DOJ policy states that prosecutors should not hold participation in a joint defense against a company when assessing that company's cooperation for charging purposes. That said, the policy also makes the commonsense point that, to the extent that the corporation learns facts from individuals within the joint defense, it may be disabled from turning those facts over to the government as the cooperation policy demands because most joint defense agreements preclude the participants from disclosing anything they learn from others in the course of the joint defense to the government. The DOJ counsels that joint defense agreements be crafted with this in mind. As an alternative to entering into a joint defense, the company can informally undertake to provide such information as it can to the individuals' counsel, consistent with its cooperation obligations to the government, but, absent a joint defense, such communications are potentially discoverable.

59. *Connolly*, 2019 WL 2120523, at *14 (emphasis original).

2D. To the extent that the power point presentations contained attorney-client protected information, allowing prosecutors to read them will constitute a waiver as to the substance of the power points. Any work product in the slides and oral comments will be waived if the government is seen as the corporation's adversary at that point. The plaintiffs in the shareholder derivative suit will get the power points. But they will argue that, by exposing these materials to the government, the company has waived as to the *subject-matter* discussed as well as the particular slides revealed. Rule 502, however, generally limits privilege waivers to the items exposed and only requires further disclosure in unusual situations in which fairness demands it to prevent a selective and misleading presentation of evidence.

CHAPTER 4

Perjury and False Statements and Claims

There are numerous justifications for criminalizing perjury and false statements and claims addressed to the government. When witnesses lie under oath in judicial proceedings they threaten to derail the entire enterprise: securing justice for litigants in civil and criminal trials. Perjury is thought to be troublingly common in federal civil litigation. Because of its sheer volume, as well as prosecutors' suspicions that many perjury allegations are the result of civil lawyers' gamesmanship,[1] perjury in civil litigation is largely left to lawyers and judges to uncover and address during the subject proceedings. But false witness testimony in criminal cases, at least, cannot be shrugged off as easily given that it can result in innocent people suffering the criminal stigma and serving long prison terms.

Lies addressed to executive branch agencies or departments—under oath or otherwise—can result in the extensive waste and diversion of government resources (e.g., the billions of dollars in COVID relief funding lost to fraudsters). Certainly, such lies can frustrate government investigations into vital matters of national interest ranging from criminal activity, to national security, to environmental harms and aviation safety. And lies addressed to Congress can derail that body's ability to gather the information necessary to effective democratic governance and can compromise legislators' ability to exert appropriate oversight over executive implementation of existing programs.

At the same time, Congress and the courts are aware that other important values may be threatened by the overzealous pursuit of "truth" in this context. In perjury cases, for example, courts are reluctant to apply the perjury statutes in a manner that creates a disincentive for witnesses to testify. They have crafted rules intended to ensure that witnesses are not punished for mistaken, unresponsive, or arguably misleading answers, insisting that perjury is reserved for testimony that is intentionally and actually false. In the false statement context, Congress created limitations on the reach of the false statement statute to guard against the possibility that the threat of prosecution would chill constituents' communications with their representatives in Congress or lawyers' zealous advocacy on behalf of their clients in judicial proceedings.

This chapter covers the principal criminal prohibitions that federal prosecutors use to address to perjury, false statements, and false claims: 18 U.S.C. §§ 1621 to 1623, which outlaw perjury and suborning perjury before federal courts, Congress, and in administrative proceedings; 18 U.S.C. § 1001, which proscribes the provision of false statements within the jurisdiction of the executive, legislative, and judicial branches; and 18 U.S.C. § 287, which criminalizes the submission of false claims to any agency or department of the United States. Readers should be aware that there are a wealth of more

1. *Cf., e.g.*, United States v. Lundwall, 1 F. Supp. 2d 249, 254 (S.D.N.Y. 1998).

specific false statements statutes scattered throughout the code; for example, one popular context specific statute is 18 U.S.C. § 1035, which outlaws false statements in connection with a health care benefit program.

I. PERJURY UNDER 18 U.S.C. §§ 1621 AND 1623

When perjury—at bottom, lying under oath in a material way—implicates federal interests, it is most commonly charged under 18 U.S.C. § 1621 and § 1623. Section 1621 has long been prosecutors' primary tool; it applies broadly to material falsehoods made under oath that are used in legislative, administrative, or judicial proceedings. Congress added § 1623 to the Code in 1970 to ease some of the proof problems that make perjury cases hard for the government to win. It is, however, more circumscribed in its coverage: § 1623 applies only to perjury committed before federal courts and grand juries.

The conventional wisdom is that perjury cases are difficult to prove. There is often little in the way of physical evidence to support a perjury charge because many involve lies about what went on in the defendant's head—what he knew or intended. Further, the prosecutor must prove not only that the statement was material, was made in response to a non-ambiguous question, and was actually false (not literally true), but also that the witness knew that the statement was false when it was made—that is, that the witness was not simply mistaken, absentminded, or confused. And jurors can be reluctant to condemn a defendant for something—lying—that many people do daily, bringing to deliberations a "there but for the grace of God go I" sensibility.

The government may therefore seek other means of holding a defendant to account for false testimony. In some circumstances, perjurious testimony can be addressed under the obstruction statutes discussed in Chapter 7. Judges can hold perjurers in criminal contempt upon proof that the witness's lies obstructed the administration of justice.[2] And perjury committed in connection with attempts to conceal another crime can be addressed without initiating a separate prosecution through enhancements applied in the course of the sentencing for the subject crime.[3]

---

2. *See* 18 U.S.C. § 401(1); In re Michael, 326 U.S. 224, 227-28 (1945).

3. As is explored further in Chapter 15 (Sentencing), the U.S. Sentencing Guidelines authorize a sentencing enhancement for the subject crime upon proof that the defendant's perjurious testimony at trial constituted a willful attempt to obstruct justice. *See* U.S. Sentencing Guidelines Manual § 3C1.1 (2023 ed.).

A. Elements

Under § 1621 and § 1623, the government bears the burden of showing that the defendant:

- took an oath
- before a competent tribunal, officer, or person
- the testimony he gave or the writing he certified as true was
- material
- and false, and
- the defendant knew when he made the statement or certified the writing as true that it was false

Both statutes are punishable by a fine, up to five years' imprisonment, or both. Both § 1621 and § 1623 provide for extraterritorial application, stating that their prohibitions are applicable whether the conduct occurred "within or without the United States."[4]

The usual federal definition of materiality applies to both statutes: a misrepresentation is material if it "'has a natural tendency to influence, or was capable of influencing, the decision of' the decisionmaking body to which it was addressed."[5] The differences in the application of, and the proof requirements for, these two statutes are explored below.

1. Competent Tribunal

Section 1621 applies whenever the defendant has taken an oath "before a competent tribunal, officer, or person, in any case in which *a law of the United States* authorizes an oath to be administered" (emphasis added). In *United States v. Hvass*, 355 U.S. 570 (1958), the Court ruled that "[t]he phrase 'a law of the United States,' as used in the perjury statute, is not limited to statutes, but includes as well Rules and Regulations which have been lawfully authorized and have a clear legislative base . . . and also decisional law."[6] Section 1621 therefore applies to any judicial proceedings, congressional investigations, and administrative matters in which the law—broadly defined—authorizes an oath to be administered.

By contrast, § 1623 does not apply in congressional investigations or administrative matters because it is restricted in scope to false declarations "in any proceeding before or ancillary to any court or grand jury of the United States." This includes pre-trial civil depositions and hearings in

4. 18 U.S.C. §§ 1621, 1623(b).
5. Kungys v. United States, 485 U.S. 759, 770 (1988).
6. *Hvass*, 355 U.S. at 504.

criminal cases but excludes an interview in a private attorney's office at which a sworn statement is given.[7]

2. Applicability to Writings

Section 1621 applies where a defendant has made a false certification under oath (or, under 28 U.S.C. § 1746, in an unsworn declaration made under penalty of perjury) as to the truth contained in a writing. A defendant is liable under this section if he, under oath, falsely states (orally or by certification) that "any written testimony, declaration, deposition, or certificate by him subscribed, is true."

A § 1623 case may lie where a witness, in a judicial or grand jury proceeding, under oath (or, under 28 U.S.C. § 1746, in an unsworn declaration made under penalty of perjury), makes any false material declaration or "makes or uses" any other information, including "any book, paper, document, record, recording, or other material," knowing that the declaration is false or the information used contains a false, material declaration.[8]

3. Evidentiary Requirements

Congress enacted § 1623 in "response to perceived evidentiary problems in demonstrating perjury under the existing federal statute, 18 U.S.C. § 1621. As Congress noted, the strict common-law requirements for establishing falsity which had been engrafted onto the federal perjury statute often made prosecution for false statements exceptionally difficult."[9] Congress made a § 1623 case easier for the government to prove in two respects.

First, under § 1621, the government must always prove that a particular sworn statement was actually false. Under § 1623(c)(2), however, the prosecution can meet its burden of proving falsity by "proof that the defendant while under oath made irreconcilably contradictory declarations material to the point in question in any proceeding before or ancillary to any court or grand jury."[10]

Second, the common law "two-witness" rule mandates that "the uncorroborated oath of one witness is not enough to establish the falsity of the testimony of the accused set forth in the indictment as perjury."[11] This rule does not in fact require that two witnesses demonstrate the falsity of the defendant's statements. It is satisfied by the "direct testimony of a second

---

7. *See* Dunn v. United States, 442 U.S. 100, 113 (1979).
8. *See, e.g.*, United States v. Dudley, 581 F.2d 1193 (5th Cir. 1978) (upholding conviction of witness under § 1623(a) who testified regarding falsified document in grand jury).
9. *Dunn*, 442 U.S. at 108.
10. *See* 18 U.S.C. § 1623(c)(2).
11. Hammer v. United States, 271 U.S. 620, 626 (1926); *see also* Weiler v. United States, 323 U.S. 606, 607 (1945).

witness or by other evidence of independent probative value, circumstantial or direct, which is 'of a quality to assure that a guilty verdict is solidly founded.'"[12] The corroborative evidence must support the guilt of the defendant but need not, by itself, be sufficient to support a conviction. Section 1621 retains the two-witness rule, but Congress eliminated that requirement in § 1623 cases.[13]

4. Mens Rea

Both statutes require proof that the defendant made the statement or declaration, or used the information, knowing that it was false. In addition, however, § 1621 requires that the perjury be "willful" while § 1623 does not.[14]

With respect to the "willfulness" requirement, the mens rea materials in Chapter 2 demonstrate that the Supreme Court defines what is meant by "willful" conduct differently according to the type of criminal prohibition at issue or the type of activity regulated. There are three basic meanings of "willful": (1) the lowest connotes only that an act is intentional and voluntary as opposed to accidental; (2) the most common meaning is that the act is done not just voluntarily, but also with a bad purpose, that is, with knowledge that the defendant's conduct is in some general sense "unlawful"; and (3) the most demanding level requires that the defendant actually knew of the specific law he was violating.

It appears that the meaning that is easiest for the government to satisfy—that is, that the conduct is done deliberately and not accidentally—has been applied in the perjury context. For example, The Ninth Circuit's model jury instructions define "willfully" as "deliberately and with knowledge that the testimony was false."[15] The Supreme Court, in *United States v. Dunnigan*, 507 U.S. 87 (1993), instructed that "[a] witness testifying under oath or affirmation violates [§ 1621] if she gives false testimony concerning a material matter with the willful intent to provide false testimony, rather than as a result of confusion, mistake, or faulty memory."[16]

As we shall see, however, the U.S. Solicitor General (SG) conceded error when a similar instruction was applied in a false statement case. The SG asserted that the second meaning of "willfully" was necessary to secure convictions under 18 U.S.C. §§ 1001 and 1035, requiring the government to prove that the defendant acted not merely "voluntarily," but with a "bad purpose," that is, "'with knowledge that his conduct was unlawful.'"[17] It

12. United States v. Weiner, 479 F.2d 923, 926 (2d Cir. 1973).
13. *See* 18 U.S.C. § 1623(e).
14. *See, e.g.*, United States v. Fornaro, 894 F.2d 508, 512 (2d Cir. 1990).
15. Ninth Circuit, Manual of Modern Criminal Jury Instructions 24.15 (2022 ed.).
16. *Dunnigan*, 507 U.S. at 94.
17. Bryan v. United States, 524 U.S. 184, 191-92 (1998).

may be, then, that a direct challenge to the prevailing instruction on the "willfully" element in perjury cases will yield a similar result.

5. Statutory Recantation Defense

Congress created an express recantation defense in § 1623 prosecutions, providing that "[w]here, in the same continuous court or grand jury proceeding in which a declaration is made, the person making the declaration admits such declaration to be false, such admission shall bar prosecution under this section if, at the time the admission is made, the declaration has not substantially affected the proceeding, *or* it has not become manifest that such falsity has been or will be exposed," § 1623(d) (emphasis added). A majority of circuits have read the "or" in the statute to mean "and," requiring the defendant to show both that the declaration did not "substantially affect[] the proceeding" and that the falsehood of the declaration had not become manifest.[18]

Under § 1621, however, the crime is deemed complete the moment the false statement is uttered under oath; accordingly, there is no "recantation" defense in such prosecutions. There may be instances, however, in which juries can be persuaded that a defendant's prompt recantation negates evidence of willfulness.[19]

B. "Defenses": Perjury Traps, Ambiguity, and Literal Truth

Defendants commonly seek to bar prosecution of alleged perjury upon a claim that the government essentially manipulated the circumstances of his testimony to create a "perjury trap" into which the defendant fell. Other defense arguments in perjury cases concern claims that the question to which the defendant allegedly responded was fatally ambiguous and that, in any case, the defendant responded by telling the literal truth. These latter arguments are commonly referred to as "defenses," but they are in fact claims that the government failed in its burden of proving the elements of knowledge and actual falsity.

1. The Perjury Trap

A "perjury trap" is created when the governmental calls the defendant to testify—generally in the grand jury—for the primary purpose of obtaining false testimony that it can later use to prosecute the defendant for perjury.

18. *See, e.g.*, United States v. Sherman, 150 F.3d 306, 313-18 (3d Cir. 1998); *but see* United States v. Smith, 35 F.3d 344, 345-47 (8th Cir. 1994) (reading "or" to mean "or").
19. *See* Beckanstin v. United States, 232 F.2d 1, 4 (5th Cir. 1956).

The defense would claim that the government is seeking to "create" perjury either because it cannot prove whatever crime is under investigation or because it would like to bring a perjury count in addition to the substantive crime under investigation so that the trial jury will infer a consciousness of guilt from the allegedly false denial of wrongdoing. These may be claimed as the prosecutorial motives behind a single invitation to appear before a grand jury or other body requiring sworn testimony. The claim is most often made, however, when the government has repeatedly called a witness back to the grand jury. Defense counsel are not allowed to be present while their clients are testifying in the grand jury and, in most federal circuits, a witness is not entitled to a transcript of his prior grand jury testimony. The defense will argue that no witness can be entirely consistent in how they respond to repeated inquiries over time and that prosecutors are seeking to exploit natural witness mistakes and innocent alterations in the way in which answers were phrased to create the basis for a perjury case.

This is an equitable defense founded on alleged prosecutorial wrongdoing rather than on the defendant's lack of culpability. It is therefore generally grounded in legal theories like abuse of the grand jury or due process. This defense, though frequently aired, is rarely successful.[20] Judges are not particularly sympathetic to such claims when the false testimony is obvious and thus the defense boils down to "I lied under oath, but the government made me do it by asking me to testify repeatedly." Most courts hold that if there is a legitimate basis for the investigation and for the particular questions to which the defendant is alleged to have answered falsely, the defendant is not entitled to relief.

2. Ambiguity

Under both § 1621 and § 1623, a fundamental ambiguity in the question to which the defendant allegedly responded falsely cannot be the basis of a perjury conviction because "a person cannot knowingly give a false reply to a question that defies interpretation despite its context."[21] Where a question is only arguably ambiguous, courts will leave the determination of the defendant's knowledge and understanding to the jury to decide. Reviewing courts will only reverse a perjury conviction on the basis of "fundamental" ambiguity. A question is fundamentally ambiguous when it "is not a phrase with a meaning about which men of ordinary intellect could agree, nor

20. *See, e.g.*, United States v. Williams, 874 F.2d 968, 975 (5th Cir. 1989) (rejecting perjury trap argument even where the prosecutor affirmatively and falsely advised the defendant that he was not the target of the investigation); *but see* Brown v. United States, 245 F.2d 549, 555 (8th Cir. 1957).

21. United States v. Schulte, 741 F.3d 1141, 1150 (10th Cir. 2014).

one which could be used with a mutual understanding by a questioner and answerer unless it were defined at the time it [was] sought and offered as testimony."[22] The challenged question will be evaluated in light of the entire line of questioning and may involve the consideration of extrinsic evidence going to the defendant's likely interpretation of the question.

3. Literal Truth (Actual Falsity)

The government bears the burden of proving that the defendant's testimony was actually false. A defendant may assert a "literal truth" defense, then, when the government is seeking to found its case on a half-truth or a concealment of the truth. The source of this requirement can be found in *Bronston v. United States*, 409 U.S. 352 (1973), in which the defendant was being examined under oath in a bankruptcy hearing. He was asked if he had a Swiss bank account and he responded "no." Because he did not then have such an account, this answer was literally true. He was then asked if he had ever had a Swiss bank account and he answered with a true but non-responsive answer, which was that his company had had such an account. The government argued that his answer was misleading in that although non-responsive it was false by negative implication—that is, by volunteering that his company had had such an account he intended the questioner to conclude that he personally had never had such an account, which was untrue. The Court reversed the defendant's conviction, holding that the defendant's statement must be unmistakably false and that a perjury conviction could not rest on an answer that was literally true but misleading by negative implication.

C. Subornation of Perjury Under 18 U.S.C. § 1622

Section 1622 provides that "[w]hoever procures another to commit any perjury is guilty of subornation of perjury, and shall be fined under this title or imprisoned not more than five years, or both." To convict a defendant of suborning perjury, the government bears the burden of showing

- the testimony of the suborned witness was given willfully, knowing it was false
- the suborner knew that the witness's testimony would be false and knew or intended that the witness would testify with knowledge of its falsity
- the perjury must in fact have been committed

22. United States v. Farmer, 137 F.3d 1265, 1269 (10th Cir. 1998) (internal quotation marks omitted).

This statute is not frequently charged. Prosecutors may prefer to pursue subornation by lodging an obstruction charge for witness tampering under 18 U.S.C. § 1512 because that statute does not require that the subornation be successful—that is, that perjury was in fact committed.

II. FALSE STATEMENT AND CONCEALMENT CASES UNDER 18 U.S.C. § 1001

A. Elements

There are a great many federal criminal statutes that proscribe the provision of false statements in particular contexts, such as in immigration applications, customs declarations, passport or visa documentation, and applications for federal benefits such as Medicare.[23] But most cases involving false statements made to the federal government are pursued under 18 U.S.C. § 1001 because of its simplicity, ease of application, and familiarity.

To secure a conviction under § 1001, the government must prove that the defendant:

- knowingly and willfully
- either
  - falsified, concealed, or covered up by any trick, scheme, or device a material fact
  - made any materially false, fictitious, or fraudulent statement or representation, or
  - made or used any false writing or document knowing the same to contain any materially false, fictitious, or fraudulent statement or entry
- within the jurisdiction of the executive, legislative, or judicial branches of the U.S. government

Violation of this statue is generally punishable by a fine, imprisonment of up to five years, or both.

The statutory prohibition is prefaced by the language "[e]xcept as otherwise provided in this section." This is intended to reference the exceptions Congress carved out with respect to false statements submitted to the judicial and legislative branches in § 1001(b) and (c), respectively. In short,

23. *See, e.g.*, 8 U.S.C. § 1160(b)(7)(A) (applications for immigration status); 18 U.S.C. §§ 541 (entry of goods), 1015 (naturalization, citizenship or alien registry), 1019 (consular officer), 1542 (passport application), 1546 (visas, permits, and other documents); 42 U.S.C. § 1320a-7b (federal health care programs).

§ 1001(b) creates an exception from liability for false statements, representations, writings or documents submitted by a party, or that party's counsel, to a judge or magistrate in a judicial proceeding. Section § 1001(c) provides that the only matters within the jurisdiction of the legislative branch that may be pursued under § 1001 are false statements made with respect to administrative matters and those made in the course of congressional investigations and reviews.

Section 1001 allows prosecutors to proceed under two different theories of liability that have slightly different proof requirements: *false statement (and writing)* cases and *concealment* cases.

In *false statement (and writing)* cases, the statute proscribes materially false statements regardless of whether those statements are oral or written, voluntary or required by law, provided under oath or not. A present statement as to future intent—such as a promise to do that which is not actually intended—can qualify as a false statement of existing fact. In false statement and document cases—as in perjury cases—the government must prove that the statement (or document) is actually "false"—that is, it was literally untrue when made (or used) and the person making (or using) it knew it to be untrue.

At one time, the lower courts created an "exculpatory 'no'" exception that dictated that "a simple denial of guilt does not come within the statute."[24] In *Brogan v. United States*, 522 U.S. 398 (1998), the Supreme Court rejected this exception, holding that any false negative answer—even a simple "no"—in response to a query by the government is a false statement. What is essential in false statement and document cases, like perjury cases, is proof of the actual falsity of the defendant's statement or document.[25]

Concealment cases are appealing to prosecutors in circumstances where the defendant's statement, while highly misleading, was not actually false. Concealment cases require proof that (1) the defendant made an omission of material fact in violation of *a duty to disclose*; and (2) an *affirmative act of concealment*.

A duty to disclose may be imposed by statute, regulation, or the government form at issue, as well as by fiduciary or other relationships of trust and confidence. Thus, for example, where the defendant signs a contract with the government that requires disclosure of certain types of conflicts of interest, she has a duty to disclose the prohibited conflicts.[26] Some courts have emphasized that, to meet the "fair warning" requirement of due process, the duty to disclose must concern "specific requirements for disclosure of

---

24. *See* Brogan v. United States, 522 U.S. 398, 401 (1998).
25. *See, e.g.*, United States v. Safavian, 528 F.3d 957, 967 (D.C. Cir. 2008).
26. *See* United States v. Moore, 446 F.3d 671, 677, 680 (7th Cir. 2006).

specific information," and reject the notion that once one begins speaking when seeking government action, one must "'disclose all relevant facts.'"[27]

To make out a § 1001 concealment case, prosecutors also must demonstrate some "affirmative act" by which a material fact is concealed,[28] as evidenced in the statutory requirement that the defendant conceal by "trick, scheme, or device." The Seventh Circuit's jury instructions explain that a "trick, scheme, or device" includes "any plan or course of action intended to deceive others."[29]

1. Materiality

To be material for purposes of § 1001, a statement must have "'a natural tendency to influence, or [be] capable of influencing, the decision of the decision-making body to which it was addressed.'"[30] There is no requirement that the false writing or document be required by law to be filed. Materiality is a question for jury determination.

This is an objective standard that requires only that the statement is *capable* of influencing the entity to which it was directed; the government is not required to prove that the statement actually influenced the actions of its official audience. Indeed, the government need not prove that the writing was relied upon or even read. It is not necessary that the false statement be at all credible or be believed. And there is no need to prove that the statement caused or was intended to cause any financial or property loss.

2. Mens Rea

a. Knowing

The statute requires that the false statement or act of deceptive concealment be done "knowingly and willfully." At a minimum, it is clear that "[t]o establish a violation of § 1001, the Government must prove beyond a reasonable doubt that the statement was made with knowledge of its falsity."[31]

There is, however, no mens rea requirement with respect to § 1001's jurisdictional element. Until 1996, the statute required that the false statement or concealment occur "within the jurisdiction of any department or agency of the United States"; in 1996 Congress amended the statute to

---

27. *Safavian*, 528 F.3d at 965-65.
28. *See* United States v. London, 550 F.2d 206, 213 (5th Cir. 1977) (cited with approval in United States v. Woodward, 469 U.S. 105, 108 & n.5 (1985) (*per curiam*)).
29. Seventh Circuit, The William J. Bauer Pattern Criminal Jury Instructions of the Seventh Circuit, at 444 (2023 ed.).
30. United States v. Gaudin, 515 U.S. 506, 509 (1995); *see also* United States v. Turner, 551 F.3d 657, 663 (7th Cir. 2008).
31. United States v. Yermian, 468 U.S. 63, 64 (1984).

require that the false statement or concealment occur "within the jurisdiction of the executive, legislative or judicial branches" of the federal government. *United States v. Yermian*, 468 U.S. 63 (1984), was decided under the pre-1996 iteration of the statute. The *Yermian* Court held that the government need not prove that the defendant made the false statement knowing that it was within the jurisdiction of the any "department or agency of the United States"; the same rule applies to the post-1996 iteration of the statute.[32]

The circuits agree that the requisite knowledge can be proved using a willful blindness theory. For example, in *United States v. Puente*, 982 F.2d 156 (5th Cir. 1993), the defendant claimed not to have read the false form at issue in the case and the government was unable to prove that the defendant knew what he was signing. Nonetheless, the Fifth Circuit affirmed Puente's conviction, explaining:

> . . . [Willful blindness] has been held sufficient to satisfy § 1001's scienter requirement so that a defendant who deliberately avoids learning the truth cannot circumvent criminal sanctions. Likewise, a defendant who deliberately avoids reading the form he is signing cannot avoid criminal sanctions for any false statements contained therein. Any other holding would write § 1001 completely out of existence.[33]

b. Willful

As noted above, there are three potential meanings of the "willfully" mens rea. The Department of Justice has taken the position that the least demanding meaning of "willful" is not appropriate for § 1001 cases and that it is the second meaning that controls under § 1001. In *United States v. Russell*, 728 F.3d 23 (1st Cir. 2013), the First Circuit upheld a conviction under 18 U.S.C. § 1035 for "willfully" making false statements in connection with the payment of health care benefits. The court rejected the defense argument that the government had to prove that the defendant was aware of the unlawfulness of his conduct. Instead, the First Circuit, relying heavily on a Ninth Circuit case involving the same issue in a § 1001 case, ruled that proof that the conduct was "deliberate" was sufficient and that the "willfulness" instruction "does not necessarily require knowledge of illegality."[34]

When the defendant sought certiorari, the Department of Justice took the extraordinary step of conceding error, stating that "[t]o find that a defendant 'willfully' made a false statement in violation of Section 1035, a jury must conclude 'that he acted with knowledge that his conduct was unlawful.' The same interpretation should apply to 18 U.S.C. [§] 1001's

32. *See id.* at 74-75.
33. *Puente*, 982 F.2d at 159.
34. *Russell*, 728 F.3d at 32.

materially identical prohibition on 'knowingly and willfully' making a false statement in a matter within the jurisdiction of the federal government."[35] The Supreme Court granted certiorari, vacated, and remanded to the First Circuit for reconsideration in light of the United States' confession of error.[36]

As we saw in Chapter 2, in very rare cases "willfulness" has been read to have a third meaning, requiring the government to prove not only that the defendant knew that the conduct was "unlawful," but also that it violated a specific statute. Although defendants have raised this claim in § 1001 cases, the courts of appeals are unanimous in rejecting it.[37]

c. Specific Intent to Deceive?

In *Yermian*, the Supreme Court stated that § 1001 requires only knowledge and willfulness and that "[n]oticeably lacking from this enactment is any requirement that the prohibited conduct be undertaken with specific intent to deceive the Federal Government."[38] Despite this language, there remains a split in the circuits on the question whether § 1001 requires proof of a specific intent to deceive the false statement's official audience.[39]

In most cases, whether or not this element is required will make little practical difference because the jury will most likely be invited to infer such an intent to deceive from the fact that the defendant made a material misstatement that he knew to be false. Where the existence of a specific intent requirement would make a difference is in the availability of defenses that are said to apply only to specific intent crimes—good faith and reliance on cousel defenses and an unreasonable mistake defense (see Chapter 2's discussion of these defenses).

3. Within the Jurisdiction

Until 1984, some circuits read "within the jurisdiction" to refer only to the power to make final or binding determinations.[40] This significantly limited the scope of the statute. Ultimately, in *United States v. Rodgers*, 466 U.S. 475 (1984), the Supreme Court rejected this definition, choosing instead to read this element broadly.

Rodgers' wife had left him, and Rodgers sought, through deceit, to induce federal investigative agencies find her. He "allegedly lied in telling

35. Russell v. United States, Brief of the United States in Opposition, No. 13-7357, 2014 WL 1571932, at *6 (2014).
36. *See* Russell v. United States, 572 U.S. 1056 (2014).
37. *See, e.g.*, United States v. Starnes, 583 F.3d 196, 210-12 (3d Cir. 2009).
38. *Yermian*, 468 U.S. at 73.
39. *See* United States v. Gonsalves, 435 F.3d 64, 72 (1st Cir. 2006); United States v. Ranum, 96 F.3d 1020, 1029 (7th Cir. 1996) (collecting cases).
40. *See* Friedman v. United States, 374 F.2d 363, 368 (8th Cir. 1967).

the FBI that his wife had been kidnapped and in telling the Secret Service that his wife was involved in a plot to kill the President."[41] The lower courts held that the case failed because the federal agencies involved "'had no power to adjudicate rights, establish binding regulations, compel the action or finally dispose of the problem giving rise to the inquiry.'"[42] For example, lies to an FBI agent would not be considered within its jurisdiction because the FBI generally cannot make final prosecution decisions.

The *Rodgers* Court rejected this "unduly strained" interpretation, noting that:

> Limiting the term "jurisdiction" as used in this statute to "the power to make final or binding determinations" . . . would exclude from the coverage most, if not all, of the authorized activities of many "departments" and "agencies" of the Federal Government, and thereby defeat the purpose of Congress in using the broad inclusive language which it did."[43]

The Court therefore adopted "[t]he most natural nontechnical reading of the statutory language," which was that "jurisdiction" within the meaning of 1001 "covers all matters confided to the authority of an agency or department."[44] Because the FBI is authorized to investigate crimes such as kidnapping and the Secret Service is authorized to protect the President, the false statements at issue in *Rodgers* were within the jurisdiction of the departments and agencies of the United States.

The allegedly false statement may be within the jurisdiction of a federal agency even if it is not submitted directly to the U.S. government. There are a great number of cases, in fact, in which the government has secured convictions founded on false statements made to a state or local government entity relating to matters that involve federal funds or regulations.[45] Even false or fraudulent statements made to private entities can be within the jurisdiction of a federal agency, for example when the federal "agency has given funding to the entity and the fraudulent statements cause the entity to utilize the funds improperly."[46]

Finally, courts have upheld convictions under § 1001 where the false statements were contained in business documents that were not submitted to any federal or state agency but were subject to governmental audit or review. *United States v. Hooper*, 596 F.2d 219 (7th Cir. 1979), for example,

41. *Rodgers*, 466 U.S. at 476.
42. *Id.* at 478.
43. *Id.* at 479, 482.
44. *Id.* at 479.
45. *See, e.g.*, United States v. Pinson, 860 F.3d 152, 170-71 (4th Cir. 2017); United States v. Clark, 787 F.3d 451, 459-60 (7th Cir. 2015).
46. United States v. Ross, 77 F.3d 1525, 1544-45 (7th Cir. 1996). *But see* United States v. Blankenship, 382 F.3d 1110, 1137-41 (11th Cir. 2004).

involved the falsification by university personnel of records required to be maintained pursuant to a federally funded and administered student assistance program. Although the falsified records were never submitted to the federal government, the court found that the statements were made within the jurisdiction of a federal agency because of the agency's audit and inspection authority.[47]

4. Of the Executive, Legislative, or Judicial Branches

Until 1996, § 1001 proscribed false statements made "within the jurisdiction of the any department or agency of the United States." In 1955, the Supreme Court, in *United States v. Bramlett*, 348 U.S. 503 (1955), held that this included false statements made to Congress. The Court rejected the argument that the word "department" was restricted to the executive branch, holding instead that the word "was meant to describe the executive, legislative, and judicial branches of Government."[48]

After *Bramblett*, the courts of appeals were concerned about the potential application of § 1001 in the course of judicial proceedings under the concealment theory. The D.C. Circuit, for example, questioned whether the statute might be interpreted to render conduct criminal that falls well within the bounds of responsible advocacy, querying whether "an attorney 'cover[s] up' when he moves to exclude hearsay testimony he knows to be true, or when he makes a summation on behalf of a client he knows to be guilty?"[49] Accordingly, the unanimous courts of appeals adopted the so-called "judicial function" exception to § 1001. This exception mandated that § 1001 did not apply to the "'judicial' machinery" of the court, but only to false statements made in connection with judicial "administrative" or "housekeeping functions" such as false statements on court forms or misrepresentations regarding counsel's right to practice law.[50] The judicial function exception meant, then, that §1001 did not apply to such matters as falsely denying to a judge that one had forged a document, submission of false letters for consideration by a sentencing judge, and lies at bail hearings.

Finally, in *Hubbard v. United States*, 514 U.S. 695 (1995), the Supreme Court reversed its *Bramblett* decision, holding that "any agency or department of the United States" did not include the judicial branch, which courts interpreted to mean that lies within the jurisdiction of the legislative branch were also outside the scope of § 1001. Congress responded in 1996 by amending the statute to apply to false statements made "in any matter

47. *See Hooper*, 596 F.2d at 222-23; *see also* United States v. Rutgard, 116 F.3d 1270, 1287 (9th Cir. 1997).
48. *Bramblett*, 348 U.S. at 509.
49. Morgan v. United States, 309 F.2d 234, 237 (D.C. Cir. 1962).
50. *Id.*

within the jurisdiction of the executive, legislative, or judicial branch of the Government of the United States," § 1001(a). In so doing, however, Congress qualified the reach of the statute with respect to matters involving the judicial and legislative branches in new subsections § 1001(b) and § 1001(c).

Section 1001(b) qualifies the applicability of § 1001 in judicial proceedings by providing that the statute's prohibition "does not apply to a party to a judicial proceeding, or that party's counsel, for statements, representations, writings or documents submitted by such party or counsel to a judge or magistrate in that proceeding." Note that this exception does not replicate the judicial function exception: It does not distinguish between statements made with respect to "housekeeping" or "administrative" matters and matters going to the "judicial function." Rather, it draws a new line based on the person who is alleged to have made the false statement; parties and their counsel are except from liability for false statements they submit to a judge or magistrate in a judicial proceeding, but non-parties remain liable, even if their false statements go to what was traditionally deemed the "judicial function."

Section 1001(c) created a novel legislative function exception. Under this subsection, the false statement prohibition only applies to "administrative matters, including a claim for payment, a matter related to the procurement of property or services, personnel or employment practices, or support services, or a document required by law, rule, or regulation to be submitted to the Congress or any office or officer within the legislative branch," or "any investigation or review, conducted pursuant to the authority of any committee, subcommittee, commission or office of the Congress, consistent with applicable rules of the House or Senate." Thus § 1001 does not apply to constituent correspondence or other matters that relate to the congressperson's legislative activities.

III. FALSE CLAIMS UNDER 18 U.S.C. § 287

Section 287 is used less frequently than the perjury and false statements provisions. Perhaps that is because the False Claims Act (FCA) can be enforced civilly or criminally, and the government has chosen to focus its energy on the civil cases that have brought in many billions of dollars of damages to the federal fisc. Other statutes—such as the securities fraud, antitrust, and RICO statutes—are hybrids as well but the FCA is unique in providing civil plaintiffs who have not themselves been injured the standing to sue on behalf of the United States to recover damages for false or fraudulent claims upon or against the United States. These plaintiffs, called "relators," recover a bounty for their efforts if they prevail but the government always reaps the largest recovery.[51] These are known as qui tam suits, and they can be initiated by the government or private relators; if the relator's case is a good one, the government can take over the litigation of the case but the relator still receives a portion of any damages. Given our focus on criminal matters, the qui tam provisions will not be further examined within although readers should be aware that representing relators is a booming and potentially very lucrative practice.

To prevail in a criminal false claims prosecution, the government must prove

- the defendant presented a false claim
- against the United States or any department or agency of the United States
- knowing that the claim was false, fictitious, or fraudulent

The penalty proscribed is a fine, not more than five years' imprisonment, or both. Typical false claims cases have involved the filing of false tax returns seeking an unjustified tax refund or the filing of fraudulent claims for Medicare reimbursement for services not rendered.

There is a split in the circuits on whether § 287 requires proof of a specific intent—to defraud when the claim is alleged to be "fraudulent" or to deceive when the claim is alleged to be "false."[52] And the circuits also disagree about whether materiality is an element of a false claims case.[53]

Claims can be made directly to the government or can be made through an intermediary. For example, in a false claims case based on over-charges for Medicaid reimbursement, a court held that the fact that the claims were submitted to insurance companies as contract administrators, not directly to Medicaid, did not undermine the defendant's false claims conviction.[54]

Examples

1. Congress was investigating the distribution of steroids and other performance enhancing drugs (PEDs) by the Bay Area Laboratory Co-operative (BALCO). Thaksin Metharom, a famous baseball player who was the son of another all-star player, was called before a congressional committee to testify. In the committee hearing, and under oath, Metharom denied knowingly using PEDs provided by BALCO and testified that he was

51. *See* 31 U.S.C. §§ 3729 – 3733.
52. *See, e.g.*, United States v. Strong, 114 F.3d 1192, at *2 (7th Cir. 1997) (collecting cases).
53. *See, e.g.*, United States v. Saybolt, 577 F.3d 195, 199-01 (3d Cir. 2009).
54. *See* United States v. Precision Medical Labs, 593 F.2d 434 (2d Cir. 1978).

never offered, supplied with, or administered any human growth hormone, steroids, or any substance that required injection.

One of the exchanges was the following:

> *Congressperson:* Did Greg[, your trainer,] ever give you anything that required a syringe to inject yourself with?
>
> *Metharom:* I've only had one doctor touch me. And that's my only personal doctor. Greg, like I said, we don't get into each others' personal lives. We're friends, but I don't—we don't sit around and talk baseball, because he knows I don't want—don't come to my house talking baseball. If you want to come to my house and talk about fishing, some other stuff, we'll be good friends, you come around talking about baseball, you go on. I don't talk about his business. You know what I mean?
>
> *Congressperson:* Right.
>
> *Metharom:* That's what keeps our friendship. You know, I am sorry, but that—you know, that—I was a celebrity child, not just in baseball by my own instincts. I became a celebrity child with a famous father. I just don't get into other people's business because of my father's situation, you see.[55]

As a prosecutor, how would you charge such a case under § 1621, § 1623 or § 1001? What difficulties would you face in making your case?

2. Mykyta Vasylyk and Victor Wilkins had a two-person law partnership, Vasylyk & Wilkins, through which they practiced trusts and estates law. Vasylyk was the trustee of a trust set up to support a woman who had dementia and was confined to a nursing home. He was suspected of draining that account of millions of dollars. Wilkins was concerned that the unauthorized "loans" he himself had taken from other client trust accounts would be detected if the investigation widened.

   Wilkins was subpoenaed to testify before the grand jury. He asserted his Fifth Amendment right against compelled self-incrimination but the Assistant U.S. Attorney (AUSA) secured an immunity order under 18 U.S.C. § 6002-03 that provided that nothing Wilkins said in the grand jury could be used or derivatively used against him except in a prosecution for perjury, giving a false statement, or otherwise failing to comply with the order. Pursuant to the immunity order, Wilkins appeared in the grand jury, was placed under oath, and had the following exchange with the AUSA:

55. United States v. Bonds, 784 F.3d 582, 583 (9th Cir. 2015) (*en banc*).

AUSA: Are you aware of any thefts from Vasylyk & Wilkins client trust accounts?
Wilkins: What? Sorry I was distracted.
AUSA: OK, I'll repeat my question. Are you aware of any thefts from Vasylyk & Wilkins client trust accounts?
Wilkins: Sorry, can you close those blinds? The sunlight is glaring in my eyes.
AUSA (with evident frustration): OK, the blinds are now closed. Are you aware that your partner, Vasylyk, has been stealing money from his client's trust account?
Wilkins: Yes—I've learned since you started investigating that Vasylyk has been stealing from our clients.

Based on this exchange, can Wilkins be convicted under 18 U.S.C. §§ 1621, 1623, or 1001?

3. Lonnie Haley was convicted of bribery and imprisoned by the State of Connecticut Department of Corrections (CDC), where he was housed as a federal prisoner in the Connecticut Correctional Institution at Somers, Connecticut (Somers). His incarceration at Somers was pursuant to a contract that allowed the federal government to place prisoners within its control into Connecticut correctional institutions. Haley was not scheduled to be released from custody until 2042. While incarcerated, Haley was the law library clerk. He sought to secure additional privileges but to do so he needed his security classification—determined largely on the basis of his remaining sentence—revised. Haley used his access to the library's typewriters and office supplies to send the warden's office two documents supposedly from the U.S. Department of Justice purporting to move his release date up by ten years. Haley's falsification of these documents was obvious, and his ploy was immediately discovered. How would Haley resist an indictment under § 1001? Would he be successful in his arguments?

4. Worknesh Abiodun, a police officer, was called to testify in a grand jury convened to investigate police corruption. In the grand jury, Abiodun was asked about a conversation she had with a drug dealer. Abiodun had been extorting protection payoffs from the drug dealer, but unbeknownst to Abiodun, the dealer had gone to authorities and was cooperating with a police internal affairs investigation when Abiodun spoke to him. Abiodun also did not know her conversation with the dealer was surreptitiously recorded. In the grand jury, Abiodun admitted to having a discussion with the drug dealer but lied about its content. Abiodun later learned from a co-conspirator that her conversation had been taped, and that the prosecutor who questioned her before the grand jury had listened to the tape and knew the true content of the conversation. Abiodun

then requested another opportunity to testify before the grand jury. When she testified the second time, she admitted that her prior testimony had been false, but explained that she had been upset, and had not been certain that she was authorized to divulge confidential police information. Could the government indict Abiodun under § 1621, § 1623, or § 1001 and how might Abiodun defend herself?

5. James Kollie served as a commander of a paramilitary group during the Liberian civil war before fleeing to the United States seeking asylum and permanent residency. His conduct in Liberia, characterized by violence and wanton atrocities, would have precluded immigration relief in the United States. So he repeatedly lied to immigration officials, portraying himself as a persecuted victim. Among other things, in his asylum application (Form I-589 ("Asylum Application")), Kollie answered a question asking whether he had ever belonged to a military or paramilitary group, civil patrol or guerrilla organization by marking "no" on the form. Kollie signed the form under the statement "I certify, under penalty of perjury under the laws of the United States, that this application and the evidence submitted with it are all true and correct." Later, a U.S. immigration official, Gargi Muhammad, interviewed Kollie under oath regarding his application for permanent residency. (Federal law authorizes certain immigration officials, including Muhammad, to administer oaths.) Muhammad read, verbatim, the questions Kollie had answered on his I-589 and asked Kollie if they were true. Kollie orally affirmed that they were. Can Kollie be convicted under § 1621, § 1623, or § 1001?

6. In 2018, Corina Paredes, a Portuguese citizen, entered the United States on a temporary visa. While in the United States, she met Jerald Eldred, an American citizen. At this point, she had overstayed her visa and was about to be deported. She asked Eldred to marry her so that she could remain in the United States. He agreed on two conditions: she would give him $5,000 and no sexual relations would be involved. They were married in New Jersey, after which Paredes gave Eldred the agreed upon amount; they did not consummate the marriage and lived in different cities. The deportation proceedings were reopened after Paredes and Eldred attested to their marriage and produced the marriage certificate. Paredes was then found to qualify for lawful status as the spouse of an American citizen. When the nature of the marriage was revealed, however, the government charged her with violating § 1001 by making false representations as to her marital status. Can it prevail?

7. In 2022, the Naval Criminal Investigative Service (NCIS) opened a criminal investigation into whether Yvette Lamb, then employed as a civil special agent for Army-CID, embezzled Army funds. NCIS advised Lamb of

the allegations, and Army-CID suspended her National Security Clearance and placed her on administrative leave. Lamb resigned from her position after being advised by Army-CID that she was facing termination and that her National Security Clearance had been suspended. Lamb then applied for employment with another federal law enforcement service (FLES) through the USA Jobs website. She submitted through the website an outdated form (verifying federal civilian employment) so she did not have to admit to her resignation. She also submitted an old CV to USA Jobs, which stated that she had an active security clearance. When submitting these materials, the website required that she certify that the information was, to the best of her knowledge, true, complete and made in good faith, and she did so. The grand jury indicted Lamb under § 1001(a)(1) on the theory that she concealed material facts in her application to FLES. How would Lamb defend such a case?

8. Damien Rocha is a colonel in the U.S. army tasked with supervising an official covert intelligence support group which held itself out as a private security firm. In the summer of 2022, the Army scheduled an audit of the firm's accounts. Rocha was required to account for approximately $150,000 that had been advanced to him for operational expenses. In response, he submitted two vouchers. The first claimed that $50,000 was paid to purchase electronic equipment. The government, however, has proof that the electronic equipment was actually paid for by another Army agency. Rocha also submitted a voucher for $1,000 for a plane flight taken for official business. The government claims that Rocha actually paid for the ticket with the miles he had accumulated while traveling on government business. Can Rocha be prosecuted under § 287?

Explanations

1. Prosecutors who have a choice between § 1621 and § 1623 would prefer to proceed under § 1623 because it eliminates the two-witness rule, the government can prove falsity through two irreconcilably contradictory statements, and it does not require proof of willfulness. But because this is a sworn statement before Congress, only § 1621 would apply; § 1623 is restricted to perjury in judicial proceedings.

   The defense is likely to claim that what Metharom said was not actually false. It certainly seems largely non-responsive, but we do not have enough facts to determine whether Metharom was truthful when he stated that "I've only had one doctor touch me. And that's my only personal doctor." Or when he asserted that "Greg, like I said, we don't get into each other's personal lives. . . . I don't talk about his business." The defense will also likely argue that the government cannot successfully prove that Metharom acted "willfully" given his meandering discussion.

But the defense will be most successful in arguing that, even if the answers to these questions were false, they were not material.

In the case from which this problem is adapted, *United States v. Bonds*, 784 F.3d 582 (9th Cir. 2015) (*en banc*), Barry Bonds made this statement under a grant of immunity while testifying in the grand jury, not before Congress as hypothesized here. The jury was faced with an indictment charging Bonds with three counts of perjury in violation of § 1623(a), and one count of obstruction of justice in violation of 18 U.S.C. § 1503. The jury failed to reach a decision on the perjury counts but concluded that the statement quoted above was obstructive. A panel of the Ninth Circuit affirmed but the Ninth Circuit granted *en banc* consideration, ultimately reversing Bonds' conviction amidst a welter of opinions. The *en banc*'s per curiam opinion's reasoning was pithy: "[d]uring a grand jury proceeding, defendant gave a rambling, non-responsive answer to a simple question. Because there is insufficient evidence that [the above quoted statement] was material, defendant's conviction for obstruction of justice in violation of 18 U.S.C. § 1503 is not supported by the record."[56]

Under § 1001, the same defenses would apply—Metharom would argue that his statement was not actually false, that it was not material, and that he did not act willfully. One issue that arises is whether the exception for certain false statements made to Congress under § 1001(c) applies. For matters occurring within the jurisdiction of the legislative branch, the proscription in § 1001(a) applies only to false statements relating to "administrative matters" or those made during "any investigation or review, conducted pursuant to the authority of any committee, subcommittee, commission or office of the Congress, consistent with applicable rules of the House or Senate," § 1001(c). Assuming that this was a valid committee investigation, a false statement that satisfies the other elements of the statute would be prosecutable.

2. The immunity statute expressly provides that nothing Wilkins says in the grand jury can be used or derivatively used against him *except* in a prosecution for perjury or giving a false statement; because of this exception, the immunity grant will provide no impediment to prosecution. Wilkins made a statement under oath in a competent tribunal for purposes of both § 1621 and § 1623. The question is whether he testified falsely. Recall that perjury requires proof of actual falsity, and evasive or squirrely testimony does not suffice. Even if he lied about being distracted or having the sun in his eyes, it is unlikely that the government can prove it or that it will be deemed material. It is only if the government can prove that Wilkins did in fact know of Vasylyk's crimes before the investigation was launched that actual falsity can be shown.

56. *Bonds*, 784 F.3d at 582.

A § 1001 false representations case also requires proof of actual falsity. But the government may be able to rely on a concealment theory under § 1001. Such a case requires that (1) there be some affirmative act of concealment to satisfy the trick, scheme, or device element, and (2) that the defendant had a duty to disclose at the time the statement was made. One could argue that Wilkins affirmatively distracted the questioner through his non-responsive answers; certainly avoiding disclosure of his own crime would be material. But the government would bear the burden of showing that the non-responsive answers were knowing, affirmative acts of concealment. As for a duty to disclose, one could argue that each grand jury witness has a duty to testify truthfully; here, however, that duty is magnified by the immunity order which carries with it such an obligation.

One additional issue is whether the exception Congress built into the statute for certain false statements made during the course of judicial proceedings in § 1001(b) is applicable in this case. Although this concealment might have been exempted under the judge-made "judicial function exception," we know that the Supreme Court rejected that exception in *Hubbard* and that Congress's revision of the statute in response to *Hubbard* did not track the judge-made doctrine. Thus, under the "judicial function exception" courts held that statements made in the course of a judicial proceeding (as here) were exempt from coverage but concealment regarding matters going to the administration of the judicial branch could be prosecuted. The current statute, however, provides an exception only for "a party to a judicial proceeding, or that party's counsel, for statements, representations, writings or documents submitted by such party or counsel to a judge or magistrate in that proceeding," § 1001(b). In this case, the government would not be relying on false statements, representations, or writings; Wilkins is not a "party;" and his statements were made to the grand jury, not a judge or magistrate. Accordingly, a case could proceed assuming the elements were satisfied.

3. Haley would likely be charged for making or using a false writing or document, knowing that it contained a materially false statement under § 1001(a)(3). Haley would resist by asserting that the documents were sent to the warden of the Connecticut institution, not to federal authorities, and that he did not make or use false documents or writings in a matter within the jurisdiction of the executive, legislative, or judicial branches. He would argue that no one believed, let alone relied on, these documents. He might assert that because he had no legal obligation to submit these forms, they could not ground a false statements case. Finally, Haley would contend that he did not violate the statute because he created documents containing false statements that purported to come *from*—and were not, as required by statute, submitted *to*—a federal agency. He would lose on all arguments.

First, in the case from which this case was drawn, the Court held that the concededly false documents were related to "any matter within the jurisdiction" of the executive branch. The fact that the federal agency had a contract with the CDC demonstrated jurisdiction. Under the contract, the federal Bureau of Prisons and Marshal's Service clearly had the power to exercise authority with respect to Haley. Haley's actual parole and release dates were the primary duty of the federal officials. "Merely because the Bureau of Prisons chose to delegate part of this responsibility to a state facility does not remove these matters from its jurisdiction."[57] Second, it is clear that the false statement need not be credible or relied upon to satisfy § 1001. Third, in false statement cases, unlike prosecutions relying on a concealment theory, the government does not have to prove that the defendant was under a legal obligation to speak; qualifying materially false statements can ground a § 1001 case even when volunteered.[58] Finally, "there is no requirement that the false statement be made *to* the federal agency; it need only have been made in 'any matter'" within its jurisdiction.[59]

4. Abiodun's false testimony was made in a competent tribunal under all three statutes. Because her testimony was before the grand jury, § 1001(b)'s exception for a party's testimony before judges or magistrates would not apply. Because it is relying on a false statement (rather than a concealment) theory for purposes of § 1001, the government would have to prove that Abiodun's statement was actually false under all three provisions.

   Under § 1621, the government would meet the burden of showing actual falsity (and the two-witness rule) by introducing Abiodun's initial testimony, her recantation, and the tape of the conversation she had with the drug dealer. Under § 1623, falsity could be proven by the fact that she made two mutually irreconcilable statements. Abiodun will try to claim the recantation defense under § 1623, but most circuits require that she demonstrate that "in the same continuous court or grand jury proceeding in which a declaration is made, the person making the declaration admits such declaration to be false," that "at the time the admission is made, the declaration has not substantially affected the proceeding," *and* that "it has not become manifest that such falsity has been or will be exposed" (§ 1623(d)). Abiodun could not satisfy the latter requirement because it was manifest to Abiodun that the prosecutor knew she had perjured herself.

57. United States v. Davis, 8 F.3d 923, 929 (2d Cir. 1993).
58. *See, e.g.*, *Rodgers*, 466 U.S. 475.
59. *Davis*, 8 F.3d at 929.

There is no recantation defense under § 1621 and § 1001, so Abiodun will also attempt to argue that her recantation undermines any inference that she acted willfully at the time she first testified (proof of willfulness is not required under § 1623). She will contend that she was confused and mistaken, not acting with knowledge that what she was doing was unlawful. If the government is able to strike a deal with the co-conspirator who told Abiodun about the taping, the co-conspirator's testimony is likely to be fatal to this defense.

5. Section 1621(2) authorizes a perjury prosecution where the defendant, "in any declaration, certificate, verification, or statement under penalty of perjury as permitted under section 1746 of title 18, United States Code, willfully subscribes as true any material matter which he does not believe to be true." Kollie could be charged, then, for perjury based on his written statement ("no") in his I-589. Section 1621 applies to sanction perjury in "any case in which a law of the United States authorizes an oath to be administered." The problem stipulates that the oath was authorized by law, so Kollie's false oral statement affirming the truth of the answers in the form, which he made under oath to immigration officer Muhammad, is also subject to prosecution as perjury. The oral statement was actually false, material, and knowingly and willfully made and thus a § 1621(1) case would lie.[60]

   Prosecutors could not use § 1623, however, because it only applies to perjury committed in "any proceeding before or ancillary to any court or grand jury of the United States." An interview in an immigration officials' office, absent some indication of a pending or contemplated grand jury investigation, is unlikely to be considered "ancillary" to a qualifying proceeding.

   Kollie may be prosecuted under § 1001 because, in his initial written application, he made a "false writing or document knowing the same to contain any materially false . . . statement." § 1001(a)(3). He can also be prosecuted for knowingly, willfully, and materially lying to Muhammad in a matter within the jurisdiction of the executive branch under § 1001(a)(2). The fact that he did not lie at length, and merely stated "no" will not save him because the Supreme Court rejected the courts of appeals' "exculpatory no" doctrine in *Brogan*.

   This problem points up the multiplicity and duplicity issues prosecutors may face in charging perjury and false statement cases. For example, does each lie constitute a different perjury count? Should the defendant be charged with two counts or just one based on the lie in the application, reiterated verbatim in the interview? These issues are discussed in Chapter 2.

60. *See* United States v. Jabateh, 974 F.3d 281 (3d Cir. 2020).

6. The statement regarding their marriage was certainly material, and it was made within the jurisdiction of the executive branch (ICE proceedings). The question is whether it was knowingly and willfully made and literally "false." The government may be able to carry its burden if it proves that the marriage is invalid under New Jersey state law and Paredes and Eldred knew that at the time they raised this issue in the deportation proceedings. But if the marriage is formally valid, and thus their representation is true, the motives of the persons involved—to circumvent the immigration laws—are immaterial. The case would also fail for lack of proof that Paredes acted knowingly and willfully; "willfulness" is defined for purposes of § 1001 as acting with knowledge that her conduct was unlawful. Assuming that the marriage was lawful under state law, and Paredes knew that, the government will not be able to carry its burden of proof regarding mens rea.

7. In a § 1001 concealment case, the government must prove that the defendant concealed a material fact within the jurisdiction of the executive, legislative, or judicial branch (1) that she had a duty to disclose; and (2) that she did so using a "trick, scheme, or devise." In exploring whether a concealment violated a duty to disclose, most courts require that the government identify a legal duty to disclose specific information; one cannot simply rely, for example, on vaguely worded ethical standards.[61] With respect to the "trick, scheme, or device" element, courts read this to require an affirmative act of concealment; a passive failure to disclose or silence in the face of unasked questions do not suffice. In this case, Lamb would argue that she had no legal duty to disclose the circumstances surrounding her resignation from Army-CID or the status of her security clearance. She would contend that she engaged in a voluntary communication with the government by deciding to apply for a job and that no legal duty arises out of such voluntary communications. Courts have rejected the proposition that once someone begins speaking to the government, seeking action or in response to questioning, that that person has a duty to disclose all relevant facts. And at least one court could not find any legal authority for a legal duty to supply all relevant information in job applications. But a court would likely find that Lamb had a duty to disclose arising out of her affirmative certification that the materials she had submitted were correct and that this affirmative act of vouching for the contents of her application was a trick, scheme, or device.[62]

61. *See Safavian*, 528 F.3d at 964.

62. *See* United States v. Barrow, Crim. No. 20-cr-127 (CKK), 2021 WL 663188 (D.D.C. Feb. 19, 2021).

8. The defense commonly made in such cases is that materials submitted to reduce liability to the government are not "claims" within the meaning of the statute; only requests for payment of government money or property can be claims. Such arguments are uniformly rejected. Courts assert that liability under § 287 "cannot turn on accounting methods. Regardless of whether a false voucher is submitted for a credit or for reimbursement, the government potentially suffers a monetary loss."[63] It is clear that, with respect to the alleged purchases of electronics equipment, Rocha falsely claimed a reduction in his responsibility for government funds disbursed to him by an amount that he did not actually expend. With regard to the plane ticket, whether this is a false claim depends on the ownership of the ticket—a matter that the court in the case from which this hypothetical was derived did not decide. It concluded that the false statement and claim at issue was "I claim $1,000." If Rocha in fact owned the free ticket, he had a colorable right to reimbursement—that is, reduction of his accountability—for the value of the ticket. Presumably ownership would turn on whether he "owned" the miles he accumulated while traveling for the government. Because the jury was instructed that the ownership did not matter, the conviction could not stand.

63. United States v. Duncan, 816 F.2d 153, 155 (4th Cir. 1987).

CHAPTER 5

Conspiracy

The heart of the crime of conspiracy is an *agreement* between two or more persons to pursue an unlawful purpose—generally, to commit an identified crime such as bribery, fraud, or obstruction. The crime of conspiracy serves two independent values.

First, it is designed to protect society from the perils of criminal partnerships. Conspiracy can be punished as a stand-alone crime whether or not the participants' unlawful ends are achieved because collective criminal action is deemed more dangerous than individual wrongdoing and thus worthy of independent sanction. Coordinated action by a plurality of persons makes it more likely that a criminal plan will be successful due, among other things, to the specialization and economies of scale that group action permits. These same advantages make it possible for groups to engage in more complex, sophisticated, and large-scale victimization than would be possible for an individual acting alone. Research also suggests that individuals are less likely to renounce their criminal plots, and they are more likely to commit additional crimes and take more risks, when they are embedded in a group. In federal law, then, even when the co-conspirators are able to complete the crime that they have conspired to achieve, the conspiracy does not merge into the completed crimes; rather, co-conspirators can be convicted of, and sentenced for, both the conspiracy and the completed crime.[1]

Second, conspiracy serves a preventive function by stopping criminal conduct in its early stages before it has a full opportunity to bloom into actual criminal harms. The co-conspirators do not have to be successful in achieving the criminal aims of their illicit agreement; all that is required for liability is the agreement among a plurality of persons, made with the requisite mens rea, and, depending on the statute, some overt act in furtherance of the conspiracy. Conspiracy is particularly useful in federal criminal prosecutions in which the co-conspirators fail to achieve some or all of their illicit aims because the federal code does not contain a general provision outlawing attempts to commit a crime. Thus, at least in cases in which a criminal agreement can be proved, a conspiracy count serves to address inchoate conduct that in more well-developed code jurisdictions would be charged as an attempt.

There are many specialized federal conspiracy provisions in the federal code. Among the ones discussed in this volume are conspiracies to commit mail, wire, bank, health care, or securities fraud (18 U.S.C. § 1349 (Chapter 6)),[2] witness tampering and obstruction (18 U.S.C. § 1512(k) (Chapter 7)), and money laundering (18 U.S.C. § 1956(h) (Chapter 11));

1. *See* Iannelli v. United States, 420 U.S. 770, 777-78 (1975).

2. Note that § 1349, like some other context-specific conspiracy provisions, reads like a penalty enhancement section rather than as a substantive authorization to pursue criminal conspiracy charges. That is, § 1349 can be construed simply as a statute that makes a conspiracy to commit any of the frauds in Chapter 63 of Title 18 under a general conspiracy statute—presumably 18 U.S.C. § 371—punishable to the same extent as the underlying fraud statute instead of by the up to five years' imprisonment specified in § 371. That said, the

and conspiracies to violate the Hobbs Act (18 U.S.C. § 1951(a) (Chapter 9)) or the Racketeer Influenced and Corrupt Organizations Act (RICO) (18 U.S.C. § 1962(d) (Chapter 10)). The most commonly-charged conspiracy statute, however, is the generally applicable conspiracy prohibition contained in 18 U.S.C. § 371. The elements of a § 371 conspiracy are exceedingly simple: (1) two or more persons agreed to achieve an unlawful objective; (2) the defendant agreed to became a member of the conspiracy knowing of its criminal objective and intending to help accomplish it; and (3) one of the co-conspirators commited an overt act in furtherance of the conspiracy. Courts usually apply the same general conspiracy law principles whether they are addressing § 371 or more specific conspiracy statutes but there are potentially three important differences between § 371 and the more specific conspiracy statutes that litter the code.

First, the statutory maximums are likely quite different. A violation of § 371 is punishable by a fine, not more than five years' imprisonment, or both. Other statutes carry much longer potential sentences; for example, conspiracies to defraud under § 1349 are punishable in the usual case by not more than twenty years' imprisonment for schemes that have as their object mail and wire fraud, twenty-five years for conspiracies to commit securities fraud, and thirty years for conspiracies to commit bank fraud.[3] Second, while § 371 requires that the government prove that one of the co-conspirators took an overt act in furtherance of the conspiracy, many of the specific statutes, such as conspiracies to violate RICO, the Hobbs Act, or the anti-money laundering statute, omit this element.[4]

Finally, as we will see, § 371 gives prosecutors two ways to charge a criminal conspiracy, only one of which other specialized federal conspiracy statutes authorize. The statute provides that "[i]f two or more persons conspire *either* to commit any offense against the United States, *or* to defraud the United States," they have violated federal law. Section 371 cases, then, can be pursued under either the "offense clause" or the "defraud clause." Under the offense clause—as well as other context-specific conspiracy prohibitions—prosecutors charge a conspiracy to commit a specified offense

---

Supreme Court treated a similarly worded conspiracy to commit money laundering section, 18 U.S.C. § 1956(h), as a stand-alone conspiracy statute in *Whitfield v. United States*, 543 U.S. 209 (2005). And courts and prosecutors frequently cite § 1349 as a substantive conspiracy section. Accordingly, this chapter will so treat it and other conspiracy sections that are also, on their faces, phrased as penalty enhancement provisions.

3. *See, e.g.*, 18 U.S.C. §§ 1341 (generally twenty -year maximum), 1343 (same), 1344 (thirty year maximum), 1347 (generally ten year maximum), 1348 (twenty-five year maximum), 1349 (conspiracies to commit §§ 1341, 1343, 1344, 1347, 1348 are subject to the same penalties as those prescribed for the offense, the commission of which was the object of the attempt or conspiracy).

4. *See, e.g.*, *Whitfield*, 543 U.S. 209 (money laundering, 18 U.S.C. § 1956(h)); Salinas v. United States, 522 U.S. 52, 63 (1997) (RICO, 18 U.S.C. § 1962(d)); United States v. Hills, 27 F.4th 1155, 1190 (6th Cir. 2022) (Hobbs Act, 18 U.S.C. § 1951).

against the United States. A grand jury may indict the defendant under a conspiracy provision embedded in a statute that proscribes a particular crime; an example of such a specialized conspiracy provision is § 1956(h), which authorizes punishment of conspiracies to commit money laundering under § 1956. Section 371 is more generous. It allows prosecutors to pursue a conspiracy to commit *any* "offense against the United States," meaning *any* federal criminal prohibition (including those that include embedded conspiracy provisions, like money laundering). These offense clause conspiracy counts would allege, for example, that the defendant conspired to commit an offense against the United States, to wit, to violate the federal bribery statute, 18 U.S.C. § 201.

Section 371 alone permits prosecutors to proceed on another theory: that the defendants conspired to "defraud the United States."[5] Crucially, defraud clause conspiracies do not require that the government prove that the defendants agreed to commit a crime currently outlawed in the U.S. criminal code. As the Supreme Court stated in *Hammerschmidt v. United States*, 265 U.S. 182 (1924), a conspiracy to defraud the United States under § 371 "means primarily to cheat the government out of property or money, but it also means to interfere with or obstruct one of its lawful governmental functions by deceit, craft or trickery, or at least by means that are dishonest."[6] So long as the defendant agreed with others to employ deceit to interfere with a lawful government function or to defraud the government of property, he may be guilty of § 371 conspiracy even if the conduct in which he engaged was not otherwise unlawful under federal law.

Conspiracy charges are deemed the "darling of the modern prosecutor's nursery"[7] because they are relatively simple and easy to prove, can address inchoate as well as completed conduct, and carry with them many very important procedural advantages in terms of joinder, venue, the applicability of the statute of limitations, and the admissibility of evidence. The combination of stringent rules regarding cognizable withdrawals from a conspiracy and the *Pinkerton* doctrine, which makes co-conspirators liable for the substantive crimes committed by their fellows in the course and in furtherance of the conspiracy, mean that defendants often can be held liable for a variety of substantive crimes that were the object of the conspiratorial agreement even if they were not involved in those crimes and their active participation in the conspiracy had ceased at the time they were committed. Accordingly, as the Seventh Circuit has noted, "prosecutors seem to have

5. Such "defraud clause" conspiracies are sometimes known as "*Klein*" conspiracies. *See* United States v. Klein, 247 F.2d 908 (2d Cir. 1957). The appellation "*Klein*" conspiracy is used to describe a subset of conspiracies reflected in the facts of *Klein*: those charging a conspiracy to impede or obstruct the lawful function of the Internal Revenue Service through concealment, for example, of reportable income.

6. *Hammerschmidt*, 265 U.S. at 188.

7. Harrison v. United States, 7 F.2d 259, 263 (2d Cir. 1925) (per J. Learned Hand).

conspiracy on their word processors as Count I; rare is the case omitting such a charge."[8]

I. WHY PROSECUTORS CALL CONSPIRACY "DARLING"

Conspiracy counts give prosecutors many practical advantages in bringing and winning cases. Some of the battles fought over the nature of the conspiratorial agreement and the appropriate scope of a charged conspiracy (discussed within) may only be understood by recognizing the practical stakes of such battles. Accordingly, we begin by exploring this critical background before exploring the elements of conspiracy and related doctrines.

A. Joinder and Severance

Fed. R. Crim. P. 8 governs the joinder of offenses and defendants.[9] Rule 8(a) provides that different crimes may be joined in one indictment if they "are of the same or similar character, or are based on the same act or transaction, or are connected with or constitute parts of a common scheme or plan." Similarly, Rule 8(b) permits different defendants to be charged in one indictment if they are alleged to have "participated in the same act or transaction, or in the same series of acts or transactions, constituting an offense or offenses." Because these rules are heavily transaction-based, where the criminal activities at issue involve disparate crimes by many defendants, the joinder of defendants and crimes in one indictment and trial will be substantially eased by inclusion of a conspiracy charge.

Assume, for example, that the defendant is a member of a criminal gang that engages in a variety of criminal activities—say money laundering, fraud, and theft of government property. Absent a claim that these various activities are tied together in some way, the government would have difficulty proceeding against the defendant with respect to all such activities, or joining him with the rest of the gang, in one indictment or trial. By including a conspiracy count alleging that the gang members agreed to pursue a variety of criminal aims and apportioned the different types of dirty work among the co-conspirators, diverse types of criminal conduct and a variety of otherwise unrelated persons can be pursued together.

Prosecutors will generally strongly prefer to try all potential participants in a criminal enterprise in one go. It would be wastefully time and resource intensive—as well as tedious—to go after each defendant individually

8. United States v. Reynolds, 919 F.2d 435, 439 (7th Cir. 1990).
9. *See also* Fed. R. Crim. P. 14 (relief from prejudicial joinder through severance).

for each crime. Prosecutors also favor joint trials because of their evidentiary advantages. When all the defendants and their varied criminal activities are fair game, prosecutors can present evidence regarding all aspects of the criminal scheme, which is particularly important where the conspiracy involves a variety of criminal activities and actors. In white-collar cases involving wide-ranging criminality or sophisticated financial shenanigans, proof regarding all the activities of all the co-conspirators may be necessary to a full understanding of the role each played as well as the mechanisms they employed.

Defense counsel hate conspiracy charges. With respect to the joinder issue, defense counsel often object to the government's proclivity for joint trials pursuant to which a mass of evidence relating to different crimes is admitted against a number of defendants—all of whom played different roles and have different levels of culpability. They argue that such conspiracy charges create a substantial threat that the jury will not be able to keep straight who is being tried for what and what evidence has been admitted against which defendant. Counsel reasonably fear that such evidentiary spill-over, as well as the defendant's joinder with co-conspirators proved responsible for a variety of wrongdoing in which the defendant did not engage, will inevitably and unfairly prejudice the defendant, particularly when the defendant played a relatively minor role. The defense, then, will often move to sever counts and defendants under Fed. R. Crim. P. 14 as prejudicially joined. They will, however, likely face stiff judicial resistance.

In *Zafiro v. United States*, 506 U.S. 534 (1993), the Supreme Court held that severance is not automatically required when co-defendants have conflicting defenses, asserting that "[t]here is a preference in the federal system for joint trials of defendants who are indicted together."[10] The Court explained that "[j]oint trials 'play a vital role in the criminal justice system'" by promoting "efficiency and 'serv[ing] the interests of justice by avoiding the scandal and inequity of inconsistent verdicts.'"[11] Accordingly, the Court held that "when defendants properly have been joined under Rule 8(b), a district court should grant a severance under Rule 14 only if there is a serious risk that a joint trial would compromise a specific trial right of one of the defendants, or prevent the jury from making a reliable judgment about guilt or innocence."[12]

In theory, the defendant can meet his burden of showing sufficient prejudice flowing from a joint trial by asserting that the fact-finder will be unable to pick its way through the evidence and make an individualized determination as to each co-conspirator.[13] However, "[t]he mere fact that there may be an 'enormous disparity in the evidence admissible against

10. *Zafiro*, 506 U.S. at 537.
11. *Id.*
12. *Id.* at 539.
13. *See id.*; *see also* United States v. Schlei, 122 F.3d 944, 984 (11th Cir. 1997).

[one co-conspirator] compared to the other defendants' is not a sufficient basis" for a severance.[14] Courts often rely on limiting instructions to the jury as a "fix" for prejudicial spill-over. As a practical matter, then, the existence of inconsistent defenses or fears that the jury will not be able to follow limiting instructions regarding what evidence may be considered against which defendant in a sprawling conspiracy trial are generally insufficient to win a severance. "In the context of conspiracy, severance will rarely, if ever, be required."[15]

B. Venue

As the Supreme Court explained in *United States v. Cabrales*, 524 U.S. 1 (1998), "[t]he Constitution twice safeguards the defendant's venue right: Article III, § 2, cl. 3 instructs that 'Trial of all Crimes. . . shall be held in the State where the Crimes shall have been committed'; the Sixth Amendment calls for trial 'by an impartial jury of the State and district wherein the crime shall have been committed.'"[16] Fed. R. Crim. P. 18 echoes these constitutional mandates by providing that the prosecution shall be "in a district where the offense was committed." Venue is not a mere technicality. If the government makes poor venue choices it may burden its witnesses and threaten its ability to secure a sustainable conviction.[17] Defendants have an even greater investment in questions of venue. Should the government choose to indict and try a case far from where the defendant works and resides, the resultant expense, stress, and hardships flowing from maintaining work and familial relationships despite the distance can be devastating for the defendant and his family.[18]

Venue turns on where the crime is deemed to be "committed," which generally turns on the "nature of the crime alleged and the location of the act or acts constituting it."[19] The government bears the burden of proving by a preponderance of the evidence that venue is proper.[20] A conspiracy crime is deemed to be a "continuing offense"[21] that can be tried in any district in which *any* co-conspirator committed *any* overt act—even if there is no evidence that the conspiracy was formed in that district, the defendant has never entered that district, and the people of that district are not those most

14. *Schlei*, 122 F.3d at 984.
15. United States v. Searing, 984 F.2d 960, 965 (8th Cir. 1993); *see also* United States v. DiMarzo, 80 F.3d 656, 659 (1st Cir. 1996).
16. *Cabrales*, 524 U.S. at 6; *see also* United States v. Johnson, 323 U.S. 273, 275 (1944).
17. *See* Smith v. United States, 599 U.S. 236 (2023).
18. *See, e.g.*, United States v. Cores, 356 U.S. 405, 407 (1958).
19. United States v. Anderson, 328 U.S. 699, 703 (1946).
20. *See, e.g.*, United States v. Lanoue, 137 F.3d 656, 661 (1st Cir. 1998).
21. *See e.g.*, 18 U.S.C. § 3237(a).

affected by the conspiratorial wrongdoing.[22] Adding a conspiracy count, then, potentially allows prosecutors a wide choice of venue, meaning that they can choose the location most convenient to them or the district in which jurors are likely to be most sympathetic to the government's case.

C. Statute of Limitations

Where a defendant is charged with conspiracy, the limitations period commences only upon the occurrence of the last overt act committed in furtherance of the conspiracy.[23] Even if the criminal agreement was reached outside the statute of limitations period and the wrongdoing that was the object of the conspiracy would be time-barred if pursued independently, a criminal conspiracy prosecution based on the same agreement and conduct is still viable if one overt act occurred within the statutory period (generally five years[24]).

D. Hearsay Exemption Under Fed. R. Evid. 801(d)(2)(E)

Hearsay evidence is generally not admissible in federal criminal trials. Fed. R. Evid. 801(c) defines hearsay as "a statement, other than one made by the declarant while testifying at the trial or hearing, offered in evidence to prove the truth of the matter asserted." Rule 801(d)(2)(E) goes on to provide, however, that a statement is not hearsay if it is offered against a party and is "a statement by a co-conspirator of a party during the course and in furtherance of the conspiracy." Co-conspirators' statements, if believed, can be very helpful to the government because they often constitute the only direct evidence on such central issues as the defendant's knowledge or intent.

The trial court must determine, under a preponderance of the evidence standard, that a conspiracy existed and that the defendant and the declarant were members of it.[25] The government need not include a conspiracy count in the indictment to take advantage of Rule 801(d)(2)(E). But given that the government will need to prove the existence of a conspiracy to get the co-conspirator's statement into evidence, including a conspiracy charge may ease the admission of this proof and ensure the introduction of other relevant evidence.[26]

---

22. *See, e.g.*, Smith, 599 U.S. at 244 (citing Hyde v. United States, 225 U.S. 347, 365-67 (1912)).
23. *See, e.g.*, Fiswick v. United States, 329 U.S. 211, 216 (1946).
24. *See* 18 U.S.C. § 3282.
25. *See* Bourjaily v. United States, 483 U.S. 171, 175-76 (1987).
26. Fed. R. Evid. 801(d)(2)(E); *see also* U.S. Dep't of Justice, Justice Manual § 9-27.320, cmt. 3 (In considering whether to bring additional charges, "[i]t is proper to consider the

The Supreme Court has held that in making these determinations, courts may consider the proffered hearsay statement itself; they need not look only to independent evidence—that is, evidence other than the statement sought to be admitted.[27] Fed. R. Evid. 801(d)(2) makes clear, however, that while the co-conspirator's statement "must be considered," it "does not by itself establish . . . the existence of a conspiracy or participation in it."

A co-conspirator's statement does not qualify for admission under Fed. R. Evid. 801(d)(2)(E) unless it was made during the course and in furtherance of the conspiracy. Where the record demonstrates that the "central aim of the alleged conspiracy . . . had either never existed or had long since ended in success or failure when and if the alleged co-conspirator made the statement attributed to her," the statement is inadmissible.[28] The Supreme Court has been grudging in its willingness to accept the government's post hoc arguments that efforts to conceal the crime were a part of the ongoing conspiracy.[29] "[A]fter the central criminal purposes of a conspiracy have been attained, a subsidiary conspiracy to conceal may not be implied from circumstantial evidence showing merely that the conspiracy kept a secret and that the conspirators took care to cover up their crime in order to escape detection and punishment."[30] To satisfy the Court, the government must have defined the conspiracy's objectives to require the concealing activity.[31]

II. ELEMENTS OF CONSPIRACY

A. Agreement: Plurality of Persons

An actionable criminal conspiracy requires the agreement of two or more persons to commit a crime (in cases under the specific conspiracy statutes and in § 371 offense clause prosecutions) or to defraud the government (in § 371 defraud clause cases). This agreement is the actus reus of the crime.[32] The defendant needs to know about and agree to the "essential nature" of

---

evidentiary consequences of failing to seek certain charges. For example, in a case in which a substantive offense was committed pursuant to an unlawful agreement, inclusion of a conspiracy count is permissible and may be desirable to ensure the introduction of all relevant evidence at trial.") [hereinafter Justice Manual].

27. *Bourjaily*, 483 U.S. at 178.

28. Krulewitch v. United States, 336 U.S. 440, 442 (1949).

29. *See id.* at 443-44; Lutwak v. United States, 344 U.S. 604, 616-18 (1953).

30. Grunewald v. United States, 353 U.S. 391, 401-02 (1957).

31. *See, e.g.*, Forman v. United States, 361 U.S. 416, 422-23 (1960), *overruled on other grounds by* Burks v. United States, 437 U.S. 1 (1978); *see also* United States v. Upton, 559 F.3d 3 (1st Cir. 2009).

32. *See* United States v. Shabani, 513 U.S. 10, 16 (1994).

the criminal plan but "[a] person may be a conspirator without knowing all the details of the unlawful plan or the names and identities of all the other alleged conspirators."[33] However, "simply being present at the scene of an event or merely associating with certain people and discussing common goals and interests doesn't establish proof of a conspiracy. A person who doesn't know about a conspiracy but happens to act in a way that advances some purpose of one doesn't automatically become a conspirator."[34]

Rarely do co-conspirators reduce their criminal plans to writing, and they have every incentive to hide their plans from anyone who is not complicit. Absent cooperation from one or more co-conspirators or probative co-conspirators' statements admitted pursuant to Fed. R. Crim. P. 801(d)(2)(E), then, agreements are generally proved through circumstantial evidence. Juries will often be asked to infer an agreement on the essential nature of the conspiracy from evidence that the defendants acted with a common purpose, that there was an overlap in the membership and temporal scope of the alleged conspiracy, that the defendants used the same modus operandi, and that the various elements of the plan were interdependent—that is, that the successful operation of the scheme required each conspirator to successfully play their part.

I. Intra-Corporate Conspiracy Doctrine Inapplicable in Criminal Cases

One issue that arises in white-collar cases is what constitutes a plurality of persons in the corporate context. In certain types of civil cases, including some civil RICO suits, antitrust cases, and civil rights actions, federal courts have endorsed the "single entity" or "intra-corporate" conspiracy doctrine.[35] This doctrine rests on the notion that because the conduct of employees acting within the scope of their employment is deemed the act of the corporation under respondeat superior principles, the corporation is not a separate "person" from its employees and agents for conspiracy purposes. Thus, the civil intra-corporate conspiracy doctrine mandates that an actionable conspiracy cannot be proved based solely on the agreement of a corporation and its errant employees because they do not constitute a plurality of persons who independently agree to engage in criminal conduct. Stated differently, the intra-corporate conspiracy doctrine provides that, just

33. Eleventh Circuit Pattern Jury Instructions, Criminal Cases, O13.1 (2022 ed.).

34. *Id.*

35. *See* McAndrew v. Lockheed Martin Corp., 206 F.3d 1031, 1038-39 (11th Cir. 2000). This doctrine sometimes applies in antitrust cases, *see* Copperweld v. Indep. Tube Corp., 467 U.S. 752 (1984), civil rights suits under 42 U.S.C. § 1985, *see* Heffernan v. Hunter, 189 F.3d 405 (3d Cir. 1999), and civil RICO cases, *see* Fogie v. THORN Americas, Inc., 190 F.3d 889 (8th Cir. 1999). Courts, however, refuse to apply these precedents in criminal cases. *See, e.g.*, United States v. St. John, 625 Fed. App'x 661, 665 (5th Cir. 2015); United States v. Hugh Chalmers Chevrolet-Toyota, Inc., 800 F.2d 737, 738 (8th Cir. 1986).

as a natural person cannot conspire with himself, it is not possible for a single legal entity consisting of the corporation and its employees to conspire with itself.

Federal courts reject this doctrine in criminal cases, reasoning that the original purpose behind attribution of employees' conduct to the entity was "to *expand* rather than shrink corporate responsibility"; "'[t]he fiction was never intended to prohibit the imposition of criminal liability by allowing a corporation or its agents to hide behind the identity of the other.'"[36] Courts reason that criminal conspiracies can consist of a corporation and its individual employees or related entities because they together create the group danger at which criminal conspiracy liability is aimed. A few courts have recognized an exception to this rule, however, in cases in which only one human agent is alleged to have entered into the criminal conspiracy with his wholly owned corporation. In *United States v. Stevens*, 909 F.2d 431 (11th Cir. 1990), for example, the Eleventh Circuit concluded that the threat posed to society by conspiracies arises from the meeting of two autonomous minds and that danger is not present when the individual defendant acts for himself and for the wholly owned corporate entity that he controls.[37]

2. The *Sears* Rule Regarding the Plurality Requirement in Sting Cases

An additional issue presented by the plurality requirement arises in cases in which the government conducts "sting" operations. Under the so-called *Sears* Rule, "[t]here can be no conspiracy when the only person with whom the defendant allegedly conspired was a government [agent or informant] who secretly intended to frustrate the conspiracy."[38] Federal courts reason that it "takes two to conspire" and undercovers and informers are not "true" conspirators in that they lack the criminal intent necessary to reach the requisite culpable meeting of the minds.[39] Such cases can only proceed if the undercover or informer agrees with two or more persons who actually intend to make the conspiracy's criminal purpose succeed.

Some states take a different, "unilateral" approach which is also reflected in the Model Penal Code. Under this rule, it is "immaterial to the guilt of a conspirator whose culpability has been established that the person or all of the persons with whom he conspired had not been or cannot be convicted."[40]

---

36. *McAndrew*, 206 F.3d at 1039 (emphasis original).

37. *Stevens*, 909 F.2d at 433-34; *see also* United States v. Peters, 732 F.2d 1004, 1008 n.6 (1st Cir. 1984).

38. Ninth Circuit, Manual of Model Criminal Jury Instructions 11.7 ("*Sears* charge") (2022 ed.) [hereinafter Ninth Circuit Instructions]; *see also* Sears v. United States, 343 F.2d 139, 142 (5th Cir. 1965) (stating rule).

39. United States v. Portela, 167 F.3d 687, 700 n.8 (1st Cir. 1999).

40. *See* Am. L Inst., Model Penal Code § 5.03 & commentary at 399.

3. Wharton's Rule

As noted, a defendant generally can be convicted of both conspiracy to commit a crime and the substantive crime itself. Wharton's Rule constitutes a narrow common law exception. It provides "'[a]n agreement by two persons to commit a particular crime cannot be prosecuted as a conspiracy when the crime is of such a nature as to necessarily require the participation of two persons for its commission.'"[41] "'The basic idea of Wharton's Rule is that where a [substantive] crime requires a plurality of agents for its commission, a charge of conspiracy cannot be used to impose a heavier penalty.'"[42] The Rule acts only as a judicial presumption in the absence of congressional intent to the contrary. Historically, Wharton's Rule was applied to offenses involving two willing participants—such as adultery, incest, bigamy, and dueling—but modern federal courts have been reluctant to extend its application.[43] A number of circuits, for example, have refused to apply Wharton's Rule to bribery prosecutions under 18 U.S.C. §§ 666 and 201.[44]

4. *Gebardi* Rule

It is blackletter law that "[a] person . . . may be liable for conspiracy even though he was incapable of committing the substantive offense."[45] In general, then, conspiracy statutes do not cease to apply simply because the crime is so defined that only certain categories of persons may commit the crime through their own acts. For example, the Hobbs Act makes it unlawful for a public official to knowingly and willfully obtain the property of another under color of official right; the Supreme Court has read this statute to prohibit bribery of public officials. By its terms, the statute authorizes conviction of only the public official—that is, the bribee. But others who cannot themselves violate the statute can be prosecuted for aiding and abetting the public official's violation under 18 U.S.C. § 2 or for conspiring with the public official under the Hobbs Act conspiracy provision or the general conspiracy statute.

In *Gebardi v. United States*, 287 U.S. 112 (1932), the Supreme Court recognized a narrow exception to this general rule. The *Gebardi* exception applies in cases in which it is clear from the structure or history of a legislative scheme that Congress did not intend for persons who could not themselves violate the substantive provisions of a statute to be liable as accomplices or co-conspirators. *Gebardi* itself concerned the Mann Act, which criminalized

41. *Iannelli*, 420 U.S. at 773 n.5 (1975).
42. United States v. McNair, 605 F.3d 1152, 1215 (11th Cir. 2010).
43. *See* United States v. Castro, 887 F.2d 988, 996 (9th Cir. 1989).
44. *See McNair*, 605 F.3d at 1215-16.
45. *Salinas*, 522 U.S. at 64.

transporting in interstate or foreign commerce a woman or girl "for the purpose of prostitution or debauchery, or for any other immoral purpose," with or without the woman's consent.[46] A husband and wife were convicted of conspiring to violate the Mann Act, on the theory that the wife conspired to transport a person—herself—merely by consenting to her husband's transportation of her. The Supreme Court reversed. It reasoned that the statute, by its terms, targets those who do the transporting—whether or not the woman consented—and the statute does not specifically impose any penalty on the women transported. Because Congress contemplated that some women would consent, but the statute discussed no punishment for such women, the Court concluded that Congress intended for the women who crossed state lines voluntarily to be immune from sanction.

Having decided that Congress intended to leave the woman unpunished when she had simply consented in her own illegal transportation, the Court next concluded that she could not be liable for conspiring with the transporter to violate the act. The Court justified this exception to common law conspiracy principles by emphasizing that in the perceived "failure of the Mann Act to condemn the woman's participation in those transportations which are effected with her mere consent," the Court found "evidence of an affirmative legislative policy to leave her acquiescence unpunished."[47] As a consequence, a conspiracy charge could not be used to contravene the immunity that the Mann Act itself conferred.[48]

Gebardi challenges are fairly common but rarely successful. For example, the Supreme Court rejected *Gebardi*'s application to conspiracies to violate the Hobbs Act on an extortion under color of official right theory.[49] Where *Gebardi* has been applied with some success is in the context of the Foreign Corrupt Practices Act (FCPA).

The FCPA outlaws the payment of bribes to foreign officials to obtain or retain business. It specifically identifies various categories of bribers as potential defendants but does not include the *bribees*—the corrupt foreign officials—as potential defendants. In *United States v. Castle*, 925 F.2d 831 (5th Cir. 1991), the Fifth Circuit noted that:

> [T]he very individuals whose participation was required in every case—the foreign officials accepting the bribe—were excluded from prosecution for the substantive offense. Given that Congress included virtually every possible person connected to the payments except foreign officials, it is only logical to

46. *Gebardi*, 287 U.S. at 118 (quoting 18 U.S.C. § 398 (1932)).
47. *Id.* at 123.
48. *Id.* Wharton's Rule was inapplicable in *Gebardi* because Mann Act cases do not always require the willing participation of two persons. A plurality of participants may be present when the woman consents to her transportation, but Mann Act cases can also be made "without the woman's consent as in cases of intimidation or force." *Gebardi*, 287 U.S. at 122.
49. *See* Ocasio v. United States, 578 U.S. 282, 292 (2016).

> conclude that Congress affirmatively chose to exempt this small class of persons from prosecution.[50]

Relying, then, on the "overwhelming evidence of a Congressional intent to exempt foreign officials from prosecution for receiving bribes," the court relied upon *Gebardi* in ruling that the foreign officials alleged to have received bribes could not be prosecuted for conspiring to violate the FCPA.[51]

The *Castle* Rule is widely accepted; another application of *Gebardi* to the FCPA is not. In *United States v. Hoskins*, 902 F.3d 69 (2d Cir. 2018), the Second Circuit applied *Gebardi* to hold that a person who could not himself be convicted under the statute because he does not fit within the statutory definition of covered bribers could not be liable as a co-conspirator with those who could. But the Second Circuit's holding has been rejected by a district court, relying on Seventh Circuit caselaw.[52]

5. Unit of Prosecution

In Chapter 2 (General Part), we discussed the double jeopardy considerations inherent in charging decisions, including the concepts of duplicity and multiplicity. The focus of conspiracy liability is the criminal agreement and thus the agreement is the applicable unit of prosecution. If there are multiple agreements, they should be charged in different counts to avoid duplicity problems. Where one agreement to violate multiple criminal statutes is alleged, that conspiracy should be charged in one count; it would be multiplicitous—and thus violate double jeopardy—to charge separate counts for each of the alleged objects.[53]

B. Scope of the Agreement

The government may be able to prove that a defendant is responsible for a crime, and even that he acted with others. Difficulties may arise, however, where the defendant is alleged to be part of a single, sprawling conspiracy with multiple participants and criminal aims or a conspiracy that morphs over time, evolving, for example, in its personnel or activities. Prosecutors prefer to fold as much criminal conduct as possible under the umbrella of a single conspiracy because this allows them to efficiently try multiple defendants in a single trial and expose the jury to the full array of criminal conduct involved. This practice also, of course, allows the government to exploit

---

50. *Castle*, 925 F.2d at 835.
51. *Id.*
52. United States v. Firtash, 392 F. Supp. 3d 872, 889-92 (N.D. Ill. 2019).
53. *See* Braverman v. United States, 317 U.S. 49, 53 (1942).

the many practical advantages, sketched above, that a broadly defined conspiracy yields.

As noted, the defense will be very concerned when the defendant is lumped into a conspiracy count alleging a wide range of misconduct, some or most of which he had nothing to do with. Defense counsel regularly—and often futilely—object that juries will be unable to keep track of what evidence was admitted against which defendant and that the evidentiary spill-over will unfairly tarnish their client with the acts of others. And, as we shall see, if a defendant is convicted of a conspiracy that alleges an agreement to commit multiple crimes against the United States, and the conspiracy successfully commits those crimes, he may be liable under *Pinkerton v. United States*, 328 U.S. 640 (1946), for all those substantive crimes, thus greatly magnifying his sentencing exposure and the potential collateral consequences of multiple counts of conviction.

Because the consequences of the government's decision regarding the scope of the conspiracy can be so serious, it is *very* common for the defense to attack the indictment as charging one conspiracy when the facts reflect several agreements, not one. As we know, the unit of prosecution is each agreement, and thus charging several agreements in one count is impermissibly duplicitous.[54] Such objections can be lodged before trial, of course, but judges generally decline to rule on such motions before the evidence comes in. After trial, this takes the form of an objection that there has been a material or fatal "variance" between the indictment and the evidence at trial. Such a variance can be the ground of a reversal only if it substantially prejudiced the defendant.

Two Supreme Court cases are often referenced in resolving the question whether a single or multiple conspiracies have been proved. The first, *Kotteakos v. United States*, 328 U.S. 750 (1946), gave us the so-called "wheel" conspiracy. The case involved a scheme through which one broker, Simon Brown, helped a variety of people secure loans based on false and fraudulent information. Brown was the central figure in all the transactions and the thirty-two people he helped to secure loans were alleged to be conspirators with him in a single scheme to violate the National Housing Act. The Supreme Court reversed, holding that the evidence proved multiple different conspiracies, not just one.

The *Kotteakos* Court reasoned that, except for Brown, none of the individuals involved was interested in whether any of the loans went through except his own. None of the individuals, save Brown, by agreement or otherwise, helped others procure loans. The Court likened the scheme to a pattern "of separate spokes meeting in a common center," that is Brown, but "without a rim of the wheel to enclose the spokes" by way of a common overarching

54. *See* charging discussion, covering duplicity and multiplicity objections, in Chapter 2.

agreement.[55] Thus, for a single "wheel" conspiracy to exist, "those people who form the wheel's spokes must have been aware of each other and must do something in furtherance of some single, illegal enterprise. Otherwise, the conspiracy lacks 'the rim of the wheel to enclose the spokes.'"[56] If there is no "interaction between those conspirators who form the spokes of the wheel as to at least one common illegal object, the 'wheel' is incomplete," and multiple conspiracies rather than one have been proved.[57]

The second case, *Blumenthal v. United States*, 332 U.S. 539 (1947), introduced the concept of a "chain" conspiracy. In that case, the indictment charged one conspiracy to sell whiskey at prices above the ceiling set by the Office of Price Administration. The defendant had a scheme, involving a number of middlemen—some of whom did not know his identity—to hide the true price for which he was selling the whiskey. The Supreme Court upheld the conviction of the defendant and all the middlemen on a single conspiracy count on the theory that they had to know that they were indispensable cogs in the machinery through which the illegal scheme was executed. All intended to further the common end of disposing of the whiskey; each middleman aided the common goal by selling his part, but he did so knowing that the total lot to be sold was larger than his portion and thus that he was aiding in the larger plan.

The chain conspiracy theory is very helpful in cases in which persons otherwise unknown to each other are joined in one conspiracy. The key to proving such a conspiracy is establishing the *interdependence* of the participants, meaning that the scheme that is the object of the conspiracy must depend on the successful operation of each link in the chain. "An individual associating himself with a 'chain' conspiracy knows that it has a 'scope' and that for its success it requires an organization wider than may be disclosed by his personal participation. Thus, in a 'chain' conspiracy prosecution, the requisite element—knowledge of the existence of remote links—may be inferred solely from the nature of the enterprise."[58]

To determine whether the evidence demonstrates a single, as opposed to multiple conspiracies, the courts of appeals apply a three-part test. First, they evaluate whether the evidence has demonstrated a common goal among the co-conspirators. This common goal may be stated at a very high level of generality, such as "personal gain."[59] Second, courts look to whether the participants in the various dealings overlap.[60] Finally, courts test whether the evidence shows interdependence among the participants. Some circuits

55. *Kotteakos*, 328 U.S. at 755 (internal quotation marks omitted).
56. United States v. Levine, 546 F.2d 658, 663 (5th Cir. 1977).
57. *Id.*
58. United States v. Elliott, 571 F.2d 880, 901 (5th Cir. 1978) (internal quotation marks omitted).
59. United States v. Shah, 95 F.4th 328, 361 (5th Cir. 2024).
60. *See, e.g.*, *id.*; United States v. Abdelaziz, 68 F.4th 1, 42 (1st Cir. 2023).

describe this as an inquiry into "the nature of the scheme" focusing on whether the evidence shows a common plan wherein the "'activities of one aspect of the scheme are necessary or advantageous to the success of another aspect'" of the scheme or to the overall success of the venture.[61]

C. Knowledge and Intent

The defendant must have knowledge of the conspiratorial agreement and voluntarily join it with the intent to further its aims. At least in theory, this is a demanding level of mens rea. First, the defendant must know the essential nature of the agreement. Where a manager of local division of a large company is paying off public officials to secure government contracts, for example, the manager's supervisor must know that this conduct is occurring to be charged with being in cahoots with him.

Willful blindness may be used to prove knowledge but even that requires proof that (1) the defendant subjectively believed that there was a high probability that a fact existed and (2) the defendant took deliberate actions to avoid learning of that fact.[62] The government may ask the jury to infer that the supervisor knows or is willfully blind to the corruption from the fact that manager is suddenly securing unprecedented numbers of government contracts in a country known for corruption; the inference will be much stronger if the auditors have raised questions about the division's books.

Even then, however, the government must prove the second mens rea element: that the defendant intended to join the conspiracy and to further its aims. In the absence of testimony from a cooperator or admission of helpful co-conspirators' statements, the government will ask the jury to infer such an intent from the circumstances. In our hypothetical case, proof that the supervisor is receiving some professional benefit from the manager's sales "success" and has acted to shield the manager from auditors' inquiries would go a long way toward proving that the defendant joined into a conspiracy with the manager and wanted, for his own reasons, for it to succeed.

If what is alleged is a conspiracy to commit a violation of federal law, either under the specialized federal conspiracy provisions or under the offense clause of § 371, "the fundamental characteristic of a conspiracy is a joint commitment to an 'endeavor which, if completed, would satisfy all of the elements of [the underlying substantive] criminal offense.'"[63] The government, then, must prove "'at least the degree of criminal intent

61. *Shah*, 95 F.4th at 361; *see also* United States v. Allinson, 27 F.4th 913, 922 (3d Cir. 2022).
62. *See* Global-Tech Appliances, Inc. v. SEB S.A., 563 U.S. 754, 769 (2011).
63. *Ocasio*, 578 U.S. at 287 (quoting *Salinas*, 522 U.S. at 65).

necessary for the substantive offense itself.'"[64] But the government has no obligation to demonstrate that each conspirator agreed personally "to commit the crime—or was even capable of committing—the substantive offense . . . It is sufficient that the conspirator agreed that the underlying crime *be committed* by a member of the conspiracy who was capable of committing it."[65]

D. Overt Act

Section 371 requires proof of an overt act done for the purpose of carrying out the conspiracy, that is, an "act to effect the object of the conspiracy." As noted above, many of the specialized, offense-specific conspiracy provisions do not demand such proof.

The overt act is not the actus reus of the crime—the agreement is. As the Supreme Court has explained,

> [i]t is not necessary that an overt act be the substantive crime charged in the indictment as the object of the conspiracy. Nor, indeed, need such an act, taken by itself, even be criminal in character. The function of the overt act in a conspiracy prosecution is simply to manifest 'that the conspiracy is at work,' and is neither a project still resting solely in the minds of the conspirators nor a fully completed operation no longer in existence.[66]

This element is rarely contested because it is so easy to satisfy. Although the overt act requirement is rationalized as necessary to show that an agreement is sufficiently real to warrant criminal liability, proof of an overt act does not require, as does an attempt charge, that the government prove that the co-conspirators made a "substantial step" toward the completion of the crime. All that need be shown is that the overt act was in furtherance of the conspiratorial plan. And that act can be as innocent and otherwise unexceptional as a mailing, wiring, phone call, or meeting.

"The partners in the criminal plan must agree to pursue the same criminal objective and may divide up the work, yet each is responsible for the acts of each other."[67] One overt act committed by any member of the conspiracy, then, is sufficient to support a conviction of all co-conspirators; the government need not prove that each defendant acted to further the criminal agreement.

---

64. Ingram v. United States, 360 U.S. 672, 678 (1959).
65. *Ocasio*, 578 U.S. at 292 (emphasis original).
66. Yates v. United States, 354 U.S. 298, 334 (1957), *overruled on other grounds by Burks*, 437 U.S. 1.
67. *See Salinas*, 522 U.S. at 63-64.

E. *Pinkerton*

In *Pinkerton v. United States*, 328 U.S. 640 (1946), the Supreme Court held that a defendant can be liable for the substantive crimes committed by a co-conspirator as long as the crimes occurred in the course of the conspiracy, were within the scope of the conspiratorial agreement, and could reasonably have been foreseen as "a necessary or natural consequence of the unlawful agreement."[68] *Pinkerton* is founded on agency principles, under which the "conspirators are each other's agents; and a principal is bound by the acts of his agents acting within the scope of the agency."[69]

The implications of the *Pinkerton* rule are not always clear so an example may be helpful. Assume that three co-conspirators agreed to commit a variety of crimes—say mail fraud, money laundering, and bribery—with each co-conspirator designated to perform those actions necessary to bring a discrete crime to fruition. Co-conspirator Rosemary commits the mail fraud, co-conspirator Rita does the money laundering, and co-conspirator Alice is responsible for paying off public officials. All may be charged with one conspiracy count because there was only one agreement even if it has multiple objects. Can each co-conspirator also be charged with and convicted of all three substantive crimes, even though each co-conspirator only committed the single crime allotted to her? The answer is "yes," because under *Pinkerton*, each is responsible for mail fraud, money laundering, and corruption—in addition to conspiring to commit all three offenses—because the crimes were done in the course of and in furtherance of the conspiracy, all were within the scope of the agreement, and all three crimes were certainly foreseeable given the co-conspirators' three-pronged scheme.

Further, co-conspirators are liable under *Pinkerton* regardless of the actual role they played in the conduct of the conspiracy. Thus, low level street dealers and drug kingpins alike are liable for all reasonably foreseeable substantive crimes committed in the course and in furtherance of the conspiracy.[70]

The most common use of *Pinkerton* involves co-conspirators' liability for the substantive crimes that are the object of the conspiracy, as posited above. But *Pinkerton* can also be used to impose liability on all co-conspirators for reasonably foreseeable crimes that are not primary goals of the conspiracy but instead directly facilitate the achievement of such goals. For example, in *United States v. Shabazz*, 887 F.3d 1204 (11th Cir. 2018), the defendant was charged with a conspiracy to defraud the United States by filing false tax returns claiming unearned refunds in the names of persons whose identity the conspirators misappropriated. The Eleventh Circuit upheld the

---

68. *Pinkerton*, 328 U.S. at 648.

69. United States v. Gillespie, 27 F.4th 934, 941 (4th Cir. 2022) (internal quotation marks omitted).

70. *See* United States v. Alvarez, 755 F.2d 830, 849-51 (11th Cir.1985).

co-conspirators' convictions on substantive wire fraud counts, ruling that those crimes were reasonably foreseeable consequences of the conspiracy for *Pinkerton* purposes because "a conspiracy to defraud the government by submitting fraudulent tax returns may naturally involve wire fraud due to the submission of the returns."[71]

F. Impossibility, Termination, and Withdrawal

Prosecutors can secure conspiracy convictions even if the criminal object of the conspiratorial agreement was, or became, impossible for the co-conspirators to achieve.[72] The rationale is that the criminal combination is dangerous whether or not it was capable of achieving its object. Similarly, the Supreme Court has made clear that a conspiracy does not end simply because the government intervenes and, unbeknownst to some of the conspirators, makes the conspiracy's criminal goals incapable of coming to fruition.[73] A conspiracy only "'terminates when the crime or crimes that are its object are committed,'" when the relevant "'agreement . . . is abandoned,'" or, for a particular co-conspirator, that co-conspirator has made an effective withdrawal.[74]

"Since conspiracy is a continuing offense, a defendant who has joined a conspiracy continues to violate the law 'through every moment of [the conspiracy's] existence,' and he becomes responsible for the acts of his co-conspirators in pursuit of their common plot" under *Pinkerton*.[75] A defendant can withdraw from a conspiracy but that does not negate the fact that he is responsible for the criminal actions of the conspiracy prior to his withdrawal. An effective withdrawal has two consequences: it starts the clock running on the time within which the defendant may be prosecuted for statute of limitations purposes; and it ends the defendant's *Pinkerton* responsibility for the substantive crimes of his co-conspirators.

The defendant bears the burden of proving withdrawal,[76] and it is not easy to do so. "Passive nonparticipation in the continuing scheme is not enough to sever the meeting of minds that constitutes the conspiracy."[77] "'[T]o avert a continuing criminality'" there must be "'affirmative action . . . to disavow or defeat the purpose'" of the conspiracy.[78]

---

71. *Shabazz*, 887 F.3d at 1220.
72. *See, e.g.*, United States v. Jimenez Recio, 537 U.S. 270, 275-76 (2003).
73. *See id.* at 274.
74. *Id.* at 276.
75. Smith v. United States, 568 U.S. 106, 111 (2013).
76. *See id.* at 110.
77. *Id.* at 112-13.
78. *Id.* at 113.

The stringent standard for an effective withdrawal from a conspiracy takes on additional importance in light of *Pinkerton*. Assume that a low-level co-conspirator in a Ponzi scheme organized by a plurality of persons contributes to the scheme for six months and then turns his energies to other scams with other actors. As we saw, affirmative acts of withdrawal, not "mere inaction" or the passage of time without active participation in an ongoing conspiracy, are necessary. Unless the defendant can prove effective withdrawal—and simply walking away from a conspiratorial plan is generally insufficient—he will be liable for all the substantive crimes committed by his co-conspirators long after he has ceased to participate and for as long as the conspiracy survives.

III. CONSPIRACY TO COMMIT AN OFFENSE AGAINST THE UNITED STATES UNDER 18 U.S.C. § 371

To secure a § 371 offense clause conspiracy conviction, the government must prove beyond a reasonable doubt that:

- there was an agreement between two or more persons to commit an offense proscribed by federal law
- the defendant became a member of the conspiracy
- knowing that its object was to commit a crime against the United States and intending to help accomplish that object
- one of the members of the conspiracy committed at least one overt act for the purpose of carrying out the conspiracy[79]

An offense clause conspiracy requires an agreement between the defendant and others with a particular kind of object—to commit a crime outlawed under federal law. The "essential nature" of the criminal agreement in offense clause cases must be a joint plan to commit the same offense or offenses. Where there is a question whether the conspirators indeed reached an actionable agreement, courts will examine the gravamen of the federal crime alleged to be the unlawful object.

For example, in *United States v. Stavroulakis*, 952 F.2d 686 (2d Cir. 1992), an undercover agent agreed with Stavroulakis to launder money that was represented to be the proceeds of narcotics sales. Stavroulakis brought a banker, Giziakis, into the conspiracy but Giziakis had scruples about laundering drug money so the undercover and Stavroulakis told him the money was derived from gambling. Upon conviction under § 371 for conspiring

79. *See* United States v. Rigas, 605 F.3d 194, 206 n.9 (3d Cir. 2010) (*en banc*).

to commit money laundering in violation of 18 U.S.C. § 1956, Stavroulakis argued that the conspirators had not agreed upon the essential nature of the plan because they had different understandings regarding the origins of the money to be laundered.

The Second Circuit rejected Stravrolakis's claim after concluding that § 1956 "creates the crime of money laundering, and it takes dead aim at the attempt to launder dirty money. Why and how that money got dirty is defined in other statutes."[80] If the co-conspirators agreed to launder the proceeds of criminal activity, then, they do not need to agree on the nature of the activity that spins off the money to be laundered because § 1956 "was designed to create a new federal crime, rather than to further penalize the underlying criminal conduct."[81] Whatever the co-conspirators' understanding, "[t]he crime is the same: money laundering; the *particular* underlying activity . . . is a necessary, but ancillary, concern."[82]

IV. CONSPIRACY TO DEFRAUD THE UNITED STATES UNDER 18 U.S.C. § 371

To secure a conviction for a defraud clause conspiracy under § 371, the government must prove that:

- there was an agreement between two or more persons to defraud the United States by
  - obstructing the lawful functions of a government entity, department, or agency by deceitful or dishonest means *or*
  - cheating the government out of property or money
- the defendant joined the conspiracy
- knowing that its object was to defraud the United States and intending to help accomplish that object
- one of the members of the conspiracy committed at least one overt act for the purpose of carrying out the conspiracy[83]

The conspiracy can, but need not, have as a goal the deprivation of government property.[84] The fraud covered under the statute also "reaches any conspiracy for the purpose of impairing, obstructing or defeating the

80. *Stavroulakis*, 952 F.2d at 691.
81. *Id.*
82. *Id.* (emphasis original).
83. *See* Ninth Circuit Instructions, *supra* note 38, 11.2; *see also Rigas*, 605 F.3d at 206 n.9.
84. *See* United States v. Johnson, 383 U.S. 169, 172 (1966).

lawful function of any department of the Government."[85] Under the defraud clause, "[n]either the conspiracy's goal nor the means used to achieve it need to be illegal."[86] Rather, "so long as deceitful or dishonest means are employed to obstruct governmental functions, the impairment 'need not involve the violation of a separate statute.'"[87]

Conspiracies to defraud may be proved where the co-conspirators used an innocent party as the conduit for the fraud, but the target of the fraud must be "the United States or an agency thereof" (§ 371). A defraud clause conspiracy cannot stand where the entity defrauded is a private or state entity that simply receives federal funds or is the subject of federal supervision.[88]

The defraud clause lately appears to be experiencing a surge of popularity. Among the recent uses of this theory are: Special Counsel Robert Mueller's allegations that certain Russians conspired to defraud the United States by interfering with the 2016 U.S. Presidential election; the DOJ's indictment of Volkswagen AG for dishonestly interfering with the EPA's implementation of emissions standards under the Clean Air Act; and Special Counsel Jack Sullivan's indictment of President Trump in relation to his alleged efforts to alter the results of the 2020 election.[89]

V. CHARGING CONSPIRACY

A. Co-Conspirators

At least two persons are required to constitute a conspiracy, but the indictment need not name all the members of the conspiracy; "one person can be convicted of conspiring with persons whose names are unknown."[90] In fact, Justice Department policy generally frowns on using the names of unindicted co-conspirators in an indictment because such persons will not have the opportunity to defend the charge and potentially clear their names at trial. The DOJ's Justice Manual therefore provides that "[i]n the absence of some significant justification, federal prosecutors generally should not

85. Tanner v. United States, 483 U.S. 107, 128 (1987) (internal quotation marks omitted); *see also* Dennis v. United States, 384 U.S. 855, 861 (1966).
86. Ninth Circuit Instructions, *supra* note 38, 11.2, cmt. at 218 (internal quotation marks omitted).
87. United States v. Ballistrea, 101 F.3d 827, 832 (2d Cir. 1996).
88. *See Tanner*, 483 U.S. at 129-32.
89. *See* United States v. Internet Research Agency, *et al.*, Case 1:18-cr-00032-DLF (D.D.C. Feb. 16, 2018); United States v. Volkswagen AG, Third Superseding Indictment, Crim. No. 16-20394 (E.D. Mich. Jan. 11, 2017).
90. Rogers v. United States, 340 U.S. 367, 375 (1951).

identify unindicted co-conspirators in conspiracy indictments."[91] Instead, federal prosecutors may refer to co-conspirators who have not been charged, for example, as "Person A" and "Person B," or simply allege that the defendant agreed with another person or persons known or unknown to the grand jury to commit a crime.

B. Charging § 371's Two Clauses

There is a split among the circuits regarding whether the defraud clause and the offense clause of § 371 should be treated as two different means of committing the same offense or as distinct offenses.[92] This question is important for charging, double jeopardy, and jury unanimity purposes.[93]

Where the clauses are thought to constitute simply different means of proving the same "offense," charging one conspiracy with two alternative objects—to defraud the United States and to commit an offense against the United States—is acceptable.[94] In such jurisdictions, then, charging one agreement in two counts—one that has as its object defrauding the United States and the other that has as its object committing a crime against the United States—based on the same facts would be to threaten multiple punishments for the same offense and would thus be jeopardy-barred.[95] And if the two clauses are treated simply as two different means of proving one crime, rather than two separate offenses, the jury need not be unanimous as to which means (defrauding or committing an offense against the United States) was proved so long as they agree that one of them was satisfied.[96]

In those circuits that hold that § 371 creates two discrete crimes—a defraud clause conspiracy and an offense clause conspiracy—charging a single conspiracy to commit both clauses in one count would be impermissible; each should be charged separately. Courts in these circuits have held that charging them as separate counts either in the same indictment or in sequential actions does not violate double jeopardy.[97] And in these jurisdictions the jury would have to be unanimous on whether a conspiracy to

91. Justice Manual, *supra* note 26, § 9-11.130

92. *Compare Rigas*, 605 F.3d at 208 ("Congress enacted § 371 intending to create a single, criminal offense that may be committed in two alternative ways"), *with* United States v. Ervasti, 201 F.3d 1029, 1039 (8th Cir. 2000) ("Though it is not divided formally into subsections, § 371 plainly establishes two offenses").

93. *See, e.g.*, *Rigas*, 605 F.3d at 209-11 (collecting cases).

94. *See id.* at 210.

95. *See* Chapter 2 (discussion of Double Jeopardy rules applicable to charging).

96. *See, e.g.*, Griffin v. United States, 502 U.S. 46, 57-58 (1991); *see also* Schad v. Arizona, 501 U.S. 624, 631 (1991) (plurality opinion) ("We have never suggested that in returning general verdicts in [conspiracy] cases the jurors should be required to agree upon a single means of commission, any more than the indictments were required to specify one alone.").

97. *See Ervasti*, 201 F.3d at 1040; *see also* Chapter 2.

defraud the United States or to commit a crime against the United States (or both) were proved because these would constitute elements of the crimes charged in the separate counts, not simply different means of committing a § 371 conspiracy.

C. Unanimity and Inconsistent Verdicts

The circuits appear to be in agreement that "so long as jurors in a federal criminal trial unanimously agree that the Government has proven each element of a conspiracy, they need not unanimously agree on the particular overt act that was committed in furtherance of the agreed-upon conspiracy."[98] And on appellate review, a court will uphold a general verdict of guilty on a multi-object conspiracy even though there was insufficient evidence to support some of the objects of the conspiracy.[99]

In *United States v. Powell*, 469 U.S. 57 (1984), the Supreme Court held that inconsistent jury verdicts are permissible, arguing that such "inconsistencies" are often likely to be the product of jury lenity rather than an erroneous conviction in light of "the jury's historic function, in criminal trials, as a check against arbitrary or oppressive exercises of power by the Executive Branch."[100] In *Powell*, the defendant was charged with separate counts for possessing cocaine with intent to distribute, conspiring to possess cocaine with the intent to distribute, and using the telephone in committing and in causing and facilitating drug trafficking. The jury acquitted the defendant on the conspiracy and possession counts but convicted on the telephone count.[101] The Court held that, although the verdicts could not be rationally reconciled, this inconsistency was not grounds to vacate the conviction.[102]

Most circuits have read *Powell* to void the "rule of consistency" that previously had required that where all possible co-conspirators are tried together and all but one are acquitted, the remaining conspirator's conviction must be reversed for insufficient evidence. In all save one circuit, then, "the acquittal of all but one co-conspirator during the same trial does not indicate that the jury found no agreement to act."[103] Similarly, when co-conspirators are tried separately, the acquittal of one defendant cannot be used to challenge the conviction of another on inconsistency grounds.[104]

---

98. United States v. Gonzalez, 786 F.3d 714, 718-19 (9th Cir. 2015).
99. *See* Griffin, 502 U.S. at 56-58; United States v. Capozzi, 486 F.3d 711, 717-19 (1st Cir. 2007).
100. *Powell*, 469 U.S. at 65.
101. *Id.* at 59-60.
102. *Id.* at 69.
103. United States v. Crayton, 357 F.3d 560, 565 (6th Cir. 2004); *but see* United States v. Suntar Roofing, Inc., 897 F.2d 469 (10th Cir. 1990).
104. *See* United States v. Senibaldi, 959 F.2d 1131, 1135 (1st Cir. 1992).

Examples

1. Section 8 is a federal housing assistance program that provides vouchers to help low-income individuals pay rent. At the relevant time, the Section 8 program in Washington, D.C., was administered by the Section 8 Division of D.C.'s Department of Public and Assisted Living. Kristian Axelsen headed that division. Gwallter Merricks worked as a Housing Specialist in the Section 8 Division and worked under Axelsen. Under then-existing regulations, Section 8 subsidies could only be provided to D.C. residents who met certain income requirements. There was a substantial waitlist, which was divided into various need categories and listed applicants by the date they applied for the program. The regulations established preferences according to the need categories and, within each category, to applicants who applied earliest. Applicants, unless they were elderly or disabled, were required to apply in person.

   Six years ago, a friend of a friend of Axelsen's, Wen Yu, reached out to him and offered "to make it worth his while" if Axelsen would direct a Section 8 housing voucher to her ex-wife, who lived in Chicago. Yu promised Axelson $1,000, after which Axelsen assisted Yu in filling out the application. Yu, who pleaded guilty to attempted bribery, testified at Axelsen's trial that she mailed Axelsen a check for $1,000 and that Axelsen knew that Yu's ex-wife lived in Chicago. A month after the initial transaction, Yu reached out to Axelsen to secure a Section 8 housing voucher for another Chicago resident. She testified that Axelsen said that he "would do basically what he had done for" the ex-wife. When Yu offered to send him $1,000, Axelsen directed her to send the money to Merricks, "who needed the money" and who would help the friend fill out the application. Yu testified to all the above at Axelsen's and Merrick's trial pursuant to a cooperation deal with the government.

   The government also introduced evidence that, four years ago, Merricks arranged for ineligible D.C. residents—who were either not on the Section 8 waiting list or who were not next in line for subsidies—to receive Section 8 vouchers in return for $500 in cash. Much of this testimony was provided by those who allegedly paid the bribes. These transactions were largely arranged by two "steerers," Hamisi Ibrahim and Bharat Singh, who, in return for a fee, brought those seeking to secure vouchers to the Section 8 office, connected them with Merricks, and gave Merricks the cash. Ibrahim was charged with a bribery conspiracy and did not testify at trial. Singh, who pleaded guilty to attempted bribery, testified that Ibrahim was a friend of Merricks's and that on several occasions he heard Ibrahim tell applicants that Merricks was "splitting the money with Axelsen." According to Singh, Ibrahim made this statement "to convince whoever was getting a Section 8 voucher that it was all good." Another witness—someone who improperly obtained a

Section 8 voucher—testified that she had asked Ibrahim how Merricks could arrange the vouchers and Ibrahim told her that Axelsen "was doing it with her." But the only evidence indicating that Axelsen took any action in support of these applications was two witnesses' statements that Axelsen helped them with their paperwork, for example, by photocopying the documents an applicant brought to support her application. The government introduced evidence that Axelsen had deposited over $6,000 into his children's savings accounts over roughly the same time period.

The U.S. Attorneys Office in Chicago charged Axelsen and Merricks with a single conspiracy, covering both the Chicago and the D.C. schemes, to accept bribes in return for issuing vouchers to ineligible persons. It also brought one count of honest services mail fraud against Axelsen and Merricks based on Yu's mailing of the $1,000 for her ex-wife's Section 8 voucher.[105] Finally, the indictment charged Axelsen and Merricks with two bribery counts based on two $500 payments made to Merricks in the D.C. scheme. Assume that the jury convicted Merricks on the conspiracy, bribery, and mail fraud counts, while Axelsen was acquitted on the bribery and mail fraud counts but convicted of conspiring to accept bribes.

A. Why would the government choose to indict the Chicago and D.C. bribery schemes as one conspiracy?
B. How is Axelsen likely to challenge his conviction on appeal?
C. Can Merricks's conviction for mail fraud be upheld under a *Pinkerton* theory?

2. Forty-three defendants were charged with a single conspiracy to commit mail fraud in violation of 18 U.S.C. § 371. The defendants were alleged to have used the mails in furtherance of a scheme to defraud McDonald's Corporation. During the relevant period, McDonald's conducted a monopoly-style promotional game to attract customers. Customers generally played the game by purchasing food at McDonald's and collecting game stamps that were attached to their meals. Certain game stamps were "winners" worth large amounts of money. An employee of the marketing company that developed and managed the game, Atanase Cristian, was responsible for disseminating the high-value game stamps to McDonald's locations across the country. The indictment alleged that Cristian instead embezzled the winning game stamps and conspired with ten others to act as recruiters who solicited a number of their friends and relatives to submit the stolen winning game stamps by mail to McDonald's and collect the prize money. The prize money was split between Cristian and his

105. See Chapter 6 (Fraud) for a discussion of honest services fraud.

alleged co-conspirators, including the recruiters and the "winners" who had submitted the embezzled stamps.

The government proceeded through trial on the theory that it did not have to prove that Cristian's co-conspirators knew that the stamps were obtained by embezzlement and in fact it did not try to prove such knowledge. Rather, the government alleged that the fraud inhered in the fact that McDonald's prize claim form required winners to certify that they had obtained the stamps through an "authorized, legitimate channel," and the co-conspirators knowingly made false certifications to this effect. Critical to this theory was the allegation that there were only three such authorized legitimate channels recognized under the game rules and the "winners" satisfied none of them: they did not purchase a meal with a winning stamp attached to a McDonald's meal, write McDonald's to obtain a stamp, or cut a game stamp out of a magazine or newspaper. The defense argued that the game rules did not forbid people from giving each other winning stamps. It put on evidence that in fact people were selling stamps on eBay and trading them on McDonald's own website. What challenges should the defense make at the conclusion of the government's case and what objections to the prosecution might a court accept?

3. DOJ Special Counsel Jack Sullivan secured an indictment of President Donald J. Trump charging him, *inter alia*, with a conspiracy to defraud the United States in violation of § 371. Trump ran for re-election to the presidency in 2020 and lost. He wished, however, to remain in power. The superseding indictment filed August 27, 2024 stated that "the Defendant's conspiracy to impair, obstruct, and defeat the federal government function through dishonesty, fraud, and deceit included the following manner and means:
   a. The Defendant and co-conspirators used knowingly false claims of election fraud to get state legislators and election officials to subvert the legitimate election results and change electoral votes for the Defendant's opponent, Joseph R. Biden, Jr., to electoral votes for the Defendant. That is, on the pretext of baseless fraud claims, the Defendant pushed officials in certain states to ignore the popular vote; disenfranchise millions of voters; dismiss legitimate electors; and ultimately, cause the ascertainment of and voting by illegitimate electors in favor of the Defendant.
   b. The Defendant and co-conspirators organized fraudulent slates of electors in seven targeted states (Arizona, Georgia, Michigan, Nevada, New Mexico, Pennsylvania, and Wisconsin), attempting to mimic the procedures that the legitimate electors were supposed to follow under the Constitution and other federal and state laws. . . . The Defendant and co-conspirators then caused these fraudulent electors to transmit

their false certificates to the Vice President, in his capacity as President of the Senate, and other government officials to be counted at the certification proceeding on January 6.

c. The Defendant and co-conspirators attempted to enlist the Vice President, in his ceremonial role as President of the Senate at the January 6 certification proceeding to fraudulently alter the election results. First, using knowingly false claims of election fraud, the Defendant and coconspirators attempted to convince the Vice President to use the Defendant's fraudulent electors, reject legitimate electoral votes, or send legitimate electoral votes to state legislatures for review rather than counting them.[106]

Assuming prosecutors can prove the use of fake electors, and the pressure exerted on the Vice President to accept the fake electors, was the grand jury correct in concluding that the facts make out a colorable claim that Trump engaged in a conspiracy to defraud the U.S. government? Would the government have to prove that this conduct violated another federal statute to prove this § 371 defraud clause conspiracy?

Explanations

1A. The reasons the government would seek to charge the Chicago and D.C. schemes as one conspiracy are many.

Joinder. The Chicago scheme involved different transactions and different bribers than the D.C. scheme. Under the federal joinder rules, it could be difficult to charge these events and persons in one indictment and try them together unless they were joined by a conspiracy count. Because there is one criminal agreement alleged, participants in both schemes can be tried together. Had Yu and Singh not pleaded out, in return for credit for their cooperation, they could have been joined in this conspiracy count even though they never met and were likely unaware of each other's existence.

Bolstering a weak case against Axelsen on the D.C. case. There is very little evidence that Axelsen was a participant in the D.C. scheme but there is direct witness evidence against Axelsen regarding the Chicago bribes. The government, then, needs the jury to hear the Chicago evidence against Axelsen during trial of the D.C. scheme in order to ask the jury to infer that if Axelsen and Merricks did it in Chicago, they were likely doing the same thing in D.C.

106. United States v. Donald J. Trump, Superseding Indictment, Case 23-cr-57-TSC, ¶ 11 (D.D.C. Aug. 27, 2024).

Statute of limitations. The Chicago bribes would be time-barred (one year past the statute of limitations) unless they were joined in a single scheme with the D.C. scheme. If the Chicago and D.C. actions are joined in one conspiracy, the case is timely so long as the last overt act in furtherance of the D.C. scheme was within the five-year statute of limitations, as it was here.

Venue. The case was brought by the Chicago U.S. Attorneys Office and thus will be tried in Chicago. Despite the fact that Axelsen and Merricks have never been to Chicago, they can be forced to defend this criminal case there because venue is proper in any district in which one overt act took place.

Co-conspirators' statements. The best that the government can do in the D.C. case to tie Axelsen to the bribery scheme is to introduce what would otherwise be hearsay testimony—in which Singh and at least one other witness testified regarding what other, non-testifying people said. These statements can come in, however, under Fed. R. Evid. 801(d)(2)(E).

1B. Axelsen's defense would certainly argue (1) that there was a fatal variance in proof in that while only one conspiracy was charged, two separate conspiracies (D.C. and Chicago) were proven; and (2) thus that the court erred in admitting the alleged D.C. co-conspirators' testimony because they were not members of the Chicago conspiracy and their statements were therefore not made during and in furtherance of that conspiracy. The defense would cite what it would characterize as inconsistent verdicts, arguing that Axelsen's conviction for conspiracy cannot be sustained given his acquittal of the substantive bribery counts because if the jury concluded that Axelsen was not bribed in the course of either scheme, it could not have—given the facts of the case—concluded that he *agreed* to be bribed.

In the case from which these facts were derived, *United States v. Gatling*, 96 F.3d 1511 (D.C. Cir. 1996), the court rejected all these objections.

With respect to the variance issue, the court found that the differences in the operation of the schemes (the Chicago interactions were conducted by phone versus in person in D.C.; the amount paid in Chicago was $1,000 versus $500 in D.C.) were "simply differences in their *modus operandi* and not differences in their underlying objective," which could be defined broadly as obtaining money in exchange for section 8 subsidies.[107] In any case, that objective was met in substantially the same way through the operation of the D.C. Section 8 office.

The court also noted the overlap in the main participants, Axelsen and Merricks. Merricks was clearly involved in both schemes and there

107. *See Gatling*, 96 F.3d at 1520.

was strong evidence that Axelsen was involved in the Chicago scheme. The court characterized the evidence of Axelsen's participation in the D.C. scheme as "weak," but it was ultimately persuaded by the deposits of large sums in Axelsen's children's accounts, the testimony of two D.C. residents that he helped them with their paperwork, and the hearsay testimony to the effect that Axelsen was helping Merricks.[108]

Finally, the court acknowledged that the schemes were not interdependent to the degree that would establish a chain conspiracy. "Here, the principal actions required for the success of the Chicago scheme—identifying individuals seeking subsidies, completing the applications, issuing the subsidies and transferring them to Chicago and receiving money—were unrelated to the actions necessary for the success of the D.C. scheme, and vice versa."[109] But there was some interdependence established by the overlap in participation and the "fact that all illegal subsidies were issued by [the Section 8 Office], [and thus] accusations relating to one of the schemes could trigger an investigation that would lead to exposure of both."[110] Finally, because there was one conspiracy, not two, the evidence was properly admitted pursuant to Fed. R. Evid. 801(d)(2)(E).

Courts would reject the claim that these were fatally inconsistent verdicts on the theory that such "inconsistencies" are often likely to be the product of jury lenity rather than an erroneous conviction.

1C. Merricks would claim that his honest services mail fraud conviction should not stand because there is no evidence that he had any involvement in the conduct charged—Axelsen and Yu worked out the exchange of $1,000 for the Yu's ex-wife's voucher and there was no evidence that Merricks had any involvement in the crime. This conviction would stand, however, if the jury convicted based on a *Pinkerton* charge because it could reasonably conclude that this crime was reasonably foreseeable, was consistent with the conspiratorial agreement, and was committed by Merrick's co-conspirator in furtherance of their joint conspiracy.

2. The defense would first argue that the government failed to prove that the alleged co-conspirators "*knowingly* entered into an *agreement* to commit an *unlawful* act."[111] The government was wise not to base its case on an allegation that the conspiratorial aim was defrauding McDonald's by redeeming stolen game stamps. This is because the government failed to prove that the conspirators (aside from Cristian) *knew* that the stamps

108. *Id.* at 1521.
109. *Id.* at 1522.
110. *Id.*
111. United States v. Chandler, 388 F.3d 796, 800 (11th Cir. 2004).

had been obtained wrongly—that is through embezzlement. Thus, a conspiracy count founded on this theory would fail for lack of a *knowing agreement* to an illegal object.

Instead, the government's theory rested ultimately on the winners' knowing agreement to falsely represent themselves to McDonald's as "legitimate" winners. To make its case, the government had to prove that breaching the game rules (if they were in fact breached) constituted a crime—that is, it was fraud. The government contended that even if the defendants had found their winning tickets discarded on the street, their redemption of the tickets by falsely claiming that they obtained them through the legitimate channels set forth in the game rules constituted fraud.

The defendants countered that this underlying fraud theory charged the defendants with a non-crime—that is, violating McDonald's game rules. Thus, there was no agreement to commit an unlawful act. Further, the defense argued that the fact that the rules did not actually forbid transferring the stamps and that McDonald's honored stamps it knew were obtained through on-line trading foreclosed this theory of the case.

In the case from which these facts are derived, *United States v. Chandler*, 388 F.3d 796 (11th Cir. 2004), the Court found the government's case deficient in that, as to the first fraud theory, the government had failed to show a knowing agreement to a scheme to defraud McDonald's by redeeming stolen game stamps because the government did not prove that Cristian's co-conspirators in fact knew that the stamps were embezzled. Second, the court held that the government did not prove an agreement to commit an *unlawful act* because it failed to demonstrate that the defendants violated McDonald's rules or misrepresented themselves as legitimate winners. Evidence that McDonald's knew people were selling stamps on eBay and trading them on McDonald's own website precluded a finding that McDonald's was defrauded by the defendant's certification that they were "legitimate" winners.

Second, the defense would argue that all the defendants were improperly joined in one conspiracy count when multiple agreements were proven; thus, there was a fatal variance between the indictment and the proof that requires reversal. In *Chandler*, the government alleged that even if the co-conspirators did not know that the stamps were wrongfully obtained, they would be liable for fraud by virtue of their false certifications that they had acquired the winning stamps through legitimate channels. The defense argued, however, that the scheme contemplated at least ten different conspiracies consisting of Cristian and each of the ten recruiters and their associated "winners." The court agreed, concluding that "[t]he absence of any evidence of a common goal, overlapping membership among the various spokes of the conspiracy, or interdependence of the spokes reinforces our conclusion that the government failed to prove a single conspiracy."[112]

First, with respect to the common goal criterion, the court believed that, just as in *Kotteakos*, Cristian was the hub of the wheel conspiracy and he worked with ten different recruiters, each of whom constituted a different spoke. And as in *Kotteakos*, there was no proof that these "spokes" had an awareness that there were other spokes, that they interacted in any respect, or that the success of each spoke's scheme depended on the success of the others. Just because they all pursued the same modus operandi did not provide a sufficient basis for inferring a single agreement. Nor did the fact that Cristian and the recruiters had the same goal mean that they had a *common* goal. The single conspiracy theory failed, then, because there was no rim—no common agreement—that bound the spokes together.

Second, there was no evidence of an overlap of membership between the spokes; the only common member was Cristian.

Third, with respect to the interdependence factor, the court ruled that this was not a case where a single scheme could be inferred based on a chain conspiracy theory under *Blumenthal*. Unlike a typical drug distribution conspiracy—in which a mid-level drug retailer knows that there must be an importer or manufacturer of the product above him and street vendors below him even if he does not know their identities—the nature of the alleged scheme is not such that its participants would necessarily know that they are interdependent links in a chain of criminal activity each of which is necessary to make the plan succeed. "The combined efforts of the spokes were not required to [e]nsure the success of the venture. No spoke depended upon, was aided by, or had any interest in the success of the others. Each spoke acted independently and was an end unto itself."[113]

3. The indictment alleges that Trump "did knowingly combine, conspire, confederate, and agree with co-conspirators, known and unknown to the grand jury, to defraud the United States by using dishonesty, fraud, and deceit to impair, obstruct, and defeat the lawful federal government function by which the results of the presidential election are collected, counted, and certified by the federal government."[114] The interference with a legitimate governmental function is alleged to be the effort to derail "a bedrock function of the United States federal government: the nation's process of collecting, counting, and certifying the results of the

112. *Id.* at 811.
113. *Id.*
114. *See* United States v. Donald J. Trump, Superseding Indictment, Case 23-cr-257-TSC, ¶ 7 (D.D.C. Aug. 27, 2024).

presidential election."[115] This certainly seems to be a qualifying "lawful federal governmental function" for purposes of § 371's defraud clause.

We know that prosecutors do not have to show that the government's property interests were affected. But they do need to show that this impairment of governmental functions was achieved through deceit. The deceit charged in the indictment involved false statements regarding the election results: "for more than two months following election day on November 3, 2020, the Defendant spread lies that there had been outcome-determinative fraud in the election and that he had actually won. These claims were false, and the Defendant knew that they were false."[116] Presumably the prosecutors would also rely on the deceit/fraud alleged with respect to attempts to use alternative "fake" slates of electors.

There is no need, under the Supreme Court's caselaw, to prove that the conduct underlying the scheme to defraud the United States violated a specific federal statute or was otherwise illegal. It would be sufficient if the Special Counsel could prove that the conspirators' purpose was to impair, obstruct, or defeat a lawful function of the government through deceitful or dishonest means.

---

115. Id. ¶ 4.
116. Id. ¶ 2.

CHAPTER 6

Fraud

When snail mail was king, so was the mail fraud statute, 18 U.S.C. § 1341. Now that various electronic media (emails, texts, etc.) have displaced the postal service as the prime means of communication, wire fraud, 18 U.S.C. § 1343, has overtaken mail fraud as prosecutors' favorite means of addressing a wide variety of criminal undertakings. Both statutes' applications include a vast array of securities, commodities, real estate, bank, credit card, consumer, and cyber frauds, but also extend to everything from public corruption[1] to smuggling.[2]

The prosecutorial adage is "when in doubt, charge wire fraud" because it is a relatively easy-to-prove crime. Mail and wire fraud, at bottom, have only two elements—a scheme to defraud and a mailing (§ 1341) or wiring in interstate or foreign commerce (§ 1343) in furtherance of the fraud. The principal element—the scheme to defraud—has been construed to be highly elastic, allowing prosecutors to fill perceived gaps in the federal criminal code. Because the federal code lacked any generally applicable statute outlawing state and local corruption, for example, the fraud statutes were pressed into service to prosecute such cases. Mail and wire fraud are also perceived to be the first line of defense when new frauds develop—as they always do—until particularized statutes can be developed. Even then, prosecutors may rely on mail and wire fraud because they are simple, familiar, and may permit the government to avoid the proof requirements of more subject-specific legislation. For example, the wire fraud statute has been used to address a wealth of cybercrime, both before and after Congress enacted the Computer Fraud and Abuse Act.[3]

The wire fraud statute has taken on added importance as technological advances have vastly increased the ability of fraudsters to bilk victims on a global scale. All sorts of modern "flim flams," executed through websites, social media, or using various electronic communications media (texts, emails, faxes), cross national borders. Fraudsters in Russia may bilk retirees in Tulsa and the proceeds of their schemes will often be ping-ponged by wire between offshore banks to avoid seizure and taxes. Although the circuits are split on the question, the better view is that the mail and wire fraud statutes do not apply extraterritorially—that is, they do not apply when the crime takes place overseas.[4] But most of the courts to address

1. *See* McDonnell v. United States, 579 U.S. 550 (2016).
2. *See* Pasquantino v. United States, 544 U.S. 349 (2005).
3. 18 U.S.C. § 1030.
4. *See, e.g.*, United States v. Elbaz, 52 F.4th 593, 602 (4th Cir. 2022) (*en banc*).

the question have held that a mail or wire fraud case is domestic—not extraterritorial—any time the mailing or wiring crosses a United States border.[5] In general, then, as long as there is a mailing or wiring in interstate or foreign commerce that travels across a U.S. border or between two states, a wire fraud case can be made despite the fact that most of the conduct underlying the fraud occurred abroad. And venue in a wire fraud prosecution can be located in any district in which the offense was begun, continued, or completed.[6]

Prosecutors also find these statutes attractive because they may serve as the foundation for more complex charges, such as money laundering[7] (Chapter 11) and Racketeer Influenced and Corrupt Organizations Act (RICO)[8] charges (Chapter 10), which can result in more severe sentences and criminal forfeiture. Mail and wire fraud are in fact the subject of a great deal of civil litigation because they often serve as the predicates for treble damages civil RICO cases. Indeed, the principal reason ordinary commercial, financial, and securities disputes can be bootstrapped into civil RICO cases is Congress's decision to include these infinitely malleable crimes as RICO predicates.[9]

Although mail and wire fraud are the principal focus of this chapter, it is also necessary to briefly discuss two increasingly popular, context-specific fraud statutes: bank fraud (18 U.S.C. § 1344) and health care fraud (18 U.S.C. § 1347). (Securities fraud under 18 U.S.C. § 1348 will be discussed in Chapter 8). These statutes are said to have been inspired by the mail and wire fraud statutes; accordingly, although they are different in structure and elements, courts construing § 1344 and § 1347 often consult mail and wire fraud precedents regarding what constitutes an actionable "scheme to defraud." Both of these statutes can also serve as the basis for a money laundering case, but only bank fraud is a RICO predicate.[10]

I. MAIL AND WIRE FRAUD UNDER 18 U.S.C. §§ 1341, 1343, 1346

According to the Supreme Court, mail and wire fraud have only two elements: (1) a scheme to defraud; and (2) a mailing or a wiring (in interstate

5. *See, e.g.*, *id.* at 602-04; *see also* United States v. Napout, 963 F.3d 163, 180-81 (2d Cir. 2020).
6. *See* 18 U.S.C. § 3237; United States v. Goldberg, 830 F.2d 459, 465 (3d Cir. 1987) (wire transfers of funds from New York to Wilmington passed through the Federal Reserve Bank of Philadelphia so venue proper in the E.D. Pa.).
7. *See* 18 U.S.C. § 1956(c)(7)(A).
8. *See* 18 U.S.C. § 1961(1)(B).
9. *See* Ashland Oil, Inc. v. Arnett, 875 F.2d 1271, 1278-79 (7th Cir. 1989).
10. *See* 18 U.S.C. §§ 1957(c)(7)(A), (F), 1961(1)(B).

or foreign commerce) in furtherance of that scheme. Most of the caselaw concerns the meaning and applicability of the "scheme to defraud" element of mail and wire fraud, and courts have uniformly given this language the same construction whether they are construing § 1341 or § 1343.

A. Scheme to Defraud

To recover for common law fraud, the victim had to prove that: the fraudster made a misrepresentation of material fact; with knowledge that the statement was false; and with the intention that the victim rely on the misrepresentation; the victim justifiably relied on the false statement; and the victim suffered damage as result of that reliance. It is important to note that while the Supreme Court has been very inconsistent in discussing the relevance of the common law of fraud in interpreting the mail and wire fraud statutes,[11] the reality is that "fraud" for purposes of § 1341 and § 1343 bears little relation to its common law cousin. Because the mail and wire fraud statutes proscribe "devis[ing] or *intending to devise* any scheme or artifice to defraud"—thereby addressing inchoate as well as consummated crimes—the government need not prove that the victim relied on the defendant's misrepresentations to his detriment or that any damage ensued.[12] These statutes also reach cases in which fraudulent promises as to future conduct are made, while common law fraud was restricted only to misrepresentations as to past or present circumstances.[13]

The degree to which a statutory "scheme to defraud" has diverged from common law antecedents is most obvious when one considers that, although there is a slight split on the question,[14] most circuits reject a "convergence" requirement—that is, in these jurisdictions, there is no requirement that the person deceived be the victim whose money or property was the object

---

11. *Compare, e.g.*, Bridge v. Phoenix Bond & Indemnity Co., 553 U.S. 639, 652 (2008) ("[M]ail fraud [is a] a statutory offense unknown to the common law. In these circumstances, the presumption that Congress intends to adopt the settled meaning of common-law terms has little pull."), *with* Neder v. United States, 527 U.S. 1, 23 (1999) ("[U]nder the rule that Congress intends to incorporate the well-settled meaning of the common-law terms it uses, we cannot infer from the absence of an express reference to materiality that Congress intended to drop that element from the fraud statutes.").

12. *See Neder*, 527 U.S. at 24-25; *Bridge*, 553 U.S. at 648-49.

13. *See* Durland v. United States, 161 U.S. 306, 313-14 (1896); United States ex rel. O'Donnell v. Countrywide Home Loans, Inc., 822 F.3d 650, 658 (2d Cir. 2016).

14. *Compare, e.g.*, United States v. Greenberg, 835 F.3d 295, 306-07 & n.16 (2d Cir. 2016) (no convergence requirement in the First, Second, Fifth, Seventh, and Eighth Circuits), *with* United States v. Lew, 875 F.2d 219, 221-22 (9th Cir. 1989) (adopting convergence requirement); *see also Bridge*, 553 U.S. at 649 (holding that a plaintiff asserting a RICO claim predicated on a mail fraud scheme in which the misrepresentations were addressed to the government but the plaintiff was deprived of property, need not plead or prove that the plaintiff relied on the defendant's alleged misrepresentation).

of the scheme. To illustrate, suppose that an immigration lawyer lies to the government to secure green cards for clients who otherwise do not qualify for them. The government charges that it is these lies that violate the statute, but under Supreme Court caselaw unissued government benefits, such as green cards, do not constitute "property" for purposes of § 1341 and § 1343. To make out its case, then, the government alleges that it was the lawyer's clients, to whom no lies were directed, that were deprived of their property, that is, the legal fees they paid on the assumption that they were securing legitimate immigration documentation. Most circuits hold that this failure of convergence—the fact that the lies were directed to one party and the property was obtained from another—will not defeat a mail or wire fraud charge. At common law such cases would have been impossible given, among other things, the requirements that the victim rely on the false statements (meaning that the lies were directed to the victim) and that that reliance caused damage to the victim (meaning that the victim also had to be party deprived of his property).

The scheme to defraud element contains within it certain proof requirements:[15]

1. The scheme to defraud must have one of two possible objects: either (a) money or property or (b) the victim's right to the defendant's "honest services"
2. The scheme must involve a cognizable type of fraud (usually a misrepresentation or concealment in the face of a duty to disclose)
3. The fraudulent representation or undisclosed information must be "material" and
4. The defendant must act with a specific intent to defraud

I. Object of the Fraud

There are two permissible objects of a mail or wire fraud case: (a) honest services or (b) money or property. The following discusses the more controversial theory—honest services fraud—first because the government's attempts to expand what may constitute "money or property" fraud have often come in reaction to Supreme Court decisions that made an "honest services" theory unavailable.

15. Some circuit courts now characterize some of the proof requirements inherent in a scheme to defraud—such as the intent to defraud and materiality—as separate "elements" of the offense in their caselaw and pattern jury instructions. Whether or not these are formally recognized as elements does not affect the government's burden: it must prove all the "sub-elements" of the scheme to defraud beyond a reasonable doubt to secure a conviction.

a. Honest Services

Recognizing the protean nature of § 1341 and § 1343, prosecutors sought to use these statutes to address criminal conduct not otherwise covered by the federal criminal code. Most notably, they sought to use mail and wire fraud to address corruption on the state and local level. The federal bribery statute, 18 U.S.C. § 201, is restricted in scope to the corruption of federal officers and employees, and the U.S. Code did not contain a similar, generally applicable provision that could be used to prosecute state and local officials. Turning to § 1341 and § 1343, prosecutors noted that the statutes proscribe, *in the disjunctive*, "devis[ing] or intending to devise any scheme or artifice to defraud, *or* for obtaining money or property by means of false or fraudulent pretenses, representations, or promises." Based on the argument that these alternative bases are independent and must therefore have different meanings, they argued that a "scheme to defraud" must mean something other than a scheme for "obtaining money or property" through fraud. As early as the 1940s, federal prosecutors began charging schemes to defraud that had as their object non-property "intangible" rights such as the public's right to public officials' honest services.

Courts accepted this construction of the statute, and many corrupt public officials were convicted for mail or wire fraud based on the theory that (a) public officials owe a duty of honest service to the public, (b) they breach that duty by accepting bribes or kickbacks, engaging in self-dealing, operating under conflicts of interest, or otherwise violating this duty, and (c) the officials' failure to disclose their breach of duty constituted fraud. Over the course of decades, various other intangible rights were identified including private employers' right to their employees' honest services. Thus, for example, if an employee responsible for buying supplies for a manufacturing company took kickbacks from vendors in return for committing the company to buy the vendors' wares, the employee could be convicted on the theory that (a) the employee owed his employer in the private sector a right to his honest services, (b) accepting kickbacks violated that duty, and (c) the employee's failure to notify his employer of his breach of duty constituted fraud. As may be clear, the honest services theory allowed public and commercial corruption cases to be bootstrapped into fraud cases in which the supposed gravamen of the offense is not the bribe, kickback, or self-dealing but rather the defendant's failure to *disclose* their wrongdoing to those to whom they owed a duty.

It is fair to say that there was a great deal of confusion among the circuits on what gave rise to a duty of honest services, what such a duty entailed, and in what circumstances a criminal conviction could be sustained on such an intangible rights theory. For example, if a public official puts an underqualified relative on the government payroll, is that a sufficient breach of his duty of honest services to warrant a felony conviction for honest services fraud?

Does every breach of a private employer's employment manual—such as using one's work computer for personal purposes—constitute a breach of the employee's duty of honest services worthy of up to twenty years in jail? Finally, after forty-five years of confusion, the Supreme Court threw out these so-called intangible rights theories in *McNally v. United States*, 483 U.S. 350 (1987). The Court chose to read the disjunctive phrases—"devis[ing] or intending to devise any scheme or artifice to defraud, *or* for obtaining money or property by means of false or fraudulent pretenses, representations, or promises"—as a single imperative. Thus, it ruled that a "scheme or artifice to defraud" required that the victims be injured in their property rights. In short, *McNally* held that a scheme to defraud for mail and wire fraud purposes did not include schemes that had as their object ill-defined "intangible" rights and that the statutes proscribed *only* frauds designed to obtain money or property.

Shortly thereafter, Congress overruled *McNally* by enacting 18 U.S.C. § 1346, which defines a "scheme or artifice to defraud" for "the purposes of this chapter" to include a scheme to "deprive another of the intangible right of honest services." "[T]his chapter" refers to Chapter 63 of Title 18 of the U.S. Code, which includes mail, wire, bank, securities, and health care fraud. A scheme to defraud under all of these sections, then, may have as its object the right to honest services, although in practice this theory has been used almost exclusively in mail and wire fraud cases.[16]

Unfortunately, Congress neglected to define "honest services," leaving courts to again confront the types of questions posed above. The courts of appeals each attempted to find a way to confine the scope of "honest services" fraud and, in so doing, generated a mass of hopelessly conflicting caselaw. In private sector cases, questions arose such as whether all employees owe a duty of honest services to their employer or only those employees who have a fiduciary duty to the company or its shareholders, whether the violation of any de minimis duty contained in an employment manual constitutes a breach of honest services, and from what source a duty to disclose arises. In public honest service cases there was similar uncertainty regarding who owes a duty of honest services to the public; in particular, it was unclear whether politically active and influential people who are not actually government employees owe a duty of honest services to the public. Questions also arose as to what constituted a breach and when a duty to disclose arose, specifically whether state laws governing the duties and disclosure obligations of state officials were relevant in defining their duty to disclose for purposes of mail and wire fraud. Many of these questions remain unanswered.

---

16. *But see* United States v. Mahaffy, No. 05-CR-613, 2006 WL 2224518, at *12 (E.D.N.Y. Aug. 2, 2006) (honest services securities fraud case under § 1348).

i. Who Owes a Duty of Honest Services? There remains substantial uncertainty on the basic question of who owes a duty of honest services and from whence such a duty arises.[17] The circuits are split on whether a duty of honest services must arise out of a fiduciary relationship.[18] And it is unclear whether qualifying fiduciary duties may spring only from "positive state or federal law," or whether they can be inferred from "general principles, such as the 'obligations of loyalty and fidelity' that inhere in the 'employment relationship.'"[19] For example, the Ninth Circuit holds that a breach of a fiduciary duty is a necessary element of a honest services case but has also ruled that "a fiduciary duty for the purposes of the Mail Fraud Statute is not limited to a formal 'fiduciary' relationship well-known in the law, but also extends to a trusting relationship in which one party acts for the benefit of another and induces the trusting party to relax the care and vigilance which it would ordinarily exercise."[20]

The Supreme Court has addressed this issue only once since *McNally*, and then unsatisfactorily. The question raised was whether politically powerful individuals who do not hold public office but exert substantial influence over government functions—such as a private person who serves as the chair of a political party—owe a duty of honest services to the public.[21] In *Percoco v. United States*, 598 U.S. 319 (2023), the Supreme Court rejected the argument that "a person nominally outside public employment can *never* have the necessary fiduciary duty to the public."[22] It explained that "individuals not formally employed by a government entity may enter into agreements that make them actual agents of the government" who owe a fiduciary obligation to their principal.[23] And, the Court said, all agree that "individuals who are 'delegated authority to act on behalf' of a public official and to perform government duties have a duty to provide honest services."[24]

The *Percoco* Court ultimately reversed petitioner's conviction, however, ruling that the jury instructions in the case were unconstitutionally vague. The district court had instructed that a private person can be said to have a duty of honest services to the public if two requirements were met: the government proved that he "'dominated and controlled any government business,'" and the people working in government "'actually relied on him because of a special relationship he had with the government.'"[25] The Court

17. *See, e.g.*, United States v. Lusk, Crim. Action No. 2:15-cr-00124, 2017 WL 508589, at *8-11 (S.D.W.Va. Feb. 7, 2017).
18. *See id.* (collecting cases).
19. Skilling v. United States, 561 U.S. 358, 417 (2010) (Scalia, J., concurring in the judgment).
20. United States v. Milovanovic, 678 F.3d 713, 724 (9th Cir. 2012) (*en banc*).
21. *See, e.g.*, United States v. Margiotta, 688 F.2d 108, 113 (2d Cir. 1982), *abrogated by* Percoco v. United States, 598 U.S. 319 (2023).
22. *Percoco*, 598 U.S. at 329 (emphasis original).
23. *Id.* at 329.
24. *Id.* at 330.
25. *Id.* at 330 (quoting jury instructions).

thought this standard was insufficiently clear to provide fair notice, arguing that anyone could be swept up in this definition if they have some degree of ill-defined clout. The statute, so read, would put particularly influential lobbyists and others effectively exercising their First Amendment rights in jeopardy. Unfortunately, the Court declined to suggest an alternative test.

ii. The Scope of Such Duty: Bribery and Kickbacks, Not Self-Dealing. We may not yet know with any certainty who owes a duty of honest services, but the Supreme Court has supplied fairly concrete guidance regarding what conduct constitutes a breach of that duty. In *Skilling v. United States*, 561 U.S. 358 (2010), the Court acknowledged that, without further definition, § 1346 on its face was unconstitutionally vague. It declined to adopt any of the limiting principles identified by the circuits for cabining the scope of the duty of honest services. Instead, it relied on a presumed congressional purpose to outlaw the core conduct prosecuted in pre-*McNally* cases, which the Court identified as bribery and kickbacks. Thus, whether a "right to honest services" fraud count arises in the context of a public corruption prosecution or in a case in which an employee is alleged to have defrauded her private employer, a mail or wire fraud prosecution is only cognizable where the government demonstrates that the defendant breached the victim's right to honest services *through conduct that constitutes bribery or kickbacks*.[26]

Notably, the *Skilling* Court expressly declined to include within the definition of honest services other corrupt activities that had long been prosecuted as honest service fraud, notably cases of corrupt self-dealing and undisclosed conflicts of interest.[27] These cases generally concerned a government or private employee taking actions that furthered "his own undisclosed financial interests while purporting to act in the interests of those to whom he owed a fiduciary duty."[28] Assume, for example, a city mayor secretly creates his own company and, without disclosing his interest, uses the power of his office to funnel city contracts to that company. *Skilling* forecloses the use of honest services to address this type of self-dealing. Similarly, where an employee, unbeknownst to his employer, engages in a side business that compromises his faithful service to his employer, such conflicts of interest do not constitute a breach of his duty of honest services for mail and wire fraud purposes. If the government wishes to pursue these types of cases after *Skilling*, then, it must come up with a way to cast

26. To provide guidance regarding the meaning of kickbacks and bribery, the Court noted that the honest services prohibition draws content from federal statutes proscribing similar crimes, such as kickbacks, 41 U.S.C. § 8701(2), and bribery, 18 U.S.C. §§ 201(b) and 666(a)(2). *See Skilling*, 561 U.S. at 412-13.

27. *See, e.g.*, United States v. Rybicki, 354 F.3d 124, 140-41 (2d Cir. 2003) (*en banc*) (summarizing self-dealing caselaw).

28. *See Skilling*, 561 U.S. at 409.

the conduct as a deprivation of a "money or property" interest cognizable under § 1341 and § 1343.

iii. Kickbacks Defined. A "kickback" scheme "typically involves an employee's steering business of his employer to a third party in exchange for a share of the third party's profits on that business. *See, e.g.*, *Black's Law Dictionary* 948 (9th ed. 2009) (defining "'kickback' as the '*return* of a portion of a monetary sum received, esp. as a result of coercion or a secret agreement')."[29] Kickbacks are covered whether received by private or public employees, and whether or not the payments are directed to persons other than the corrupt employee (for example, to a spouse). In the public context, this would cover various types of patronage schemes that involve a public official awarding a contract to a vendor in return for payments both to the public official himself (through a sham corporation) and others he wants to reward for their political support.

iv. Bribery Defined. With regard to what the *Skilling* Court meant by "bribery," the circuits agree that gratuities cases are not covered; only bribery will suffice. It is also clear that honest services fraud on a bribery theory is not confined—as are 18 U.S.C. § 201 and § 1951—to corruption of public officials.[30] Honest services fraud can address commercial bribery by private employees who owe a duty of honest services to their employer.

Bribery requires that the government prove a *quid pro quo*—that is, a corrupt offer of something of value in *exchange* for *influencing* the public official or private employee in the conduct of his duties. In *McDonnell v. United States*, 579 U.S. 550 (2016), the Supreme Court relied on the federal bribery statute, 18 U.S.C. § 201, to define the requisites of honest services fraud and Hobbs Act prosecutions founded on a bribery theory. It did so upon the *parties' stipulation* that honest service fraud, like the federal bribery statute, requires that the corrupt payment be made or promised in return for influencing an "official act."[31] The Court adopted the bribery statute's definition of that term in 18 U.S.C. § 201(a)(3), which provides that an "official act" has two requirements: (1) a qualifying matter and (2) a decision or action on that matter.[32] This is, of course, a very unusual—to say the least—way to interpret a statute. The fact that the Court accepted the parties' stipulation in this case

29. United States v. DeMizio, 741 F.3d 373, 381 (2d Cir. 2014) (emphasis added).

30. *See* Chapter 9 (Corruption).

31. Courts often rely on Hobbs Act extortion under color of official right (18 U.S.C. § 1951) and federal bribery (§ 201) precedents in defining the scope of bribery for honest services purposes. *See, e.g.*, United States v. Ring, 706 F.3d 460, 466-67 (D.C. Cir. 2013).

32. Section 201(a)(3) provides that the term "official act" means "any decision or action on any question, matter, cause, suit, proceeding or controversy, which may at any time be pending, or which may by law be brought before any public official, in such official's official capacity, or in such official's place of trust or profit."

should not necessarily be read to mandate that the "official act" definition must be satisfied in all honest services bribery cases.

For example, as discussed at greater length in Chapter 9 (Corruption), two types of bribery are covered under the federal bribery statute (§ 201): the offer of anything of value with the intent to influence an "*official act*" (§ 201(b)(1)(A)) *or* the offer of anything of value in return for inducing the public official to "do or omit to do *any act in violation of the lawful duty of such official or person*" (§ 201(b)(1)(C)) (emphases added). In theory, then, prosecutors could rely on the latter theory in an honest services case if they have difficulty proving an "official act." Federal prosecutors seldom rely on § 201(b)(1)(C), however, and thus this theory has not (yet) made its way into the honest services fraud caselaw.

The *McDonnell* Court interpreted the term "official act" narrowly, setting forth a two-part test. With respect to the first element—a qualifying matter—it ruled that the government cannot define the "question, matter, cause, suit, proceeding or controversy" (§ 201(a)(3)) that may be pending or brought before the public official at too great a level of generality. The public official's decision or action must involve a matter that is specific, focused, and concrete.[33] And it must involve a formal exercise of governmental power that is similar in nature to a lawsuit before a "court, a determination before an agency, or a hearing before a committee."[34]The *McDonnell* Court emphasized that simply setting up a meeting, talking to another official, or organizing an event—without more—does not fit the definition.[35] Section 201(a)(3) also requires that the question or matter must be "pending" or "may by law be brought" before "any public official." The Court explained that this means that the question or matter must be within the specific duties of the public official who is performing the official act or before another public official, and it must be "something that is relatively circumscribed—the kind of thing that can be put on an agenda, tracked for progress, and then checked off as complete."[36]

With respect to the second element, the government must prove that the public official agreed to make a decision or take action on the identified matter. Simply hosting a meeting to talk about a question is insufficient, as is expressing general support for a position. But the government can meet its burden if the public official exerts pressure on another official to act or provides advice, knowing or intending that such pressure or advice will form the basis for an official act.

Many critics feared that this narrow definition would make many run-of-the-mill public bribery cases difficult, if not impossible, to prove. But

---

33. *McDonnell*, 579 U.S. at 571.
34. *Id.* at 574
35. *See id.* at 571-74.
36. *Id.* at 570.

post-*McDonnell* circuit court cases indicate that the government, by being thoughtful in identifying what constitutes the "question" or "matter" at issue, can meet their burden.

Thus, for example, in *Unites States v. Van Buren*, 940 F.3d 1192 (11th Cir. 2019), a police officer was convicted of honest services fraud for taking money to conduct an improper license plate search on behalf of the briber, who said he wanted to discover whether a woman he met at a strip club was an undercover police officer. The Eleventh Circuit held that defining the qualifying matter as improperly divulging registration information to a civilian did not meet the *McDonnell* standard because it did not constitute an exercise of governmental power comparable to a lawsuit, hearing, or administrative determination.[37] But the court suggested that the government could have succeeded had it "identified the underlying matter as something like an investigation into illegal activity, such as prostitution, at the strip club," because

> [s]uch an investigation would have been a specific, formal government action, within the ambit of police activity, that is comparable to a lawsuit, hearing, or administrative determination. It could have been put on an agenda, tracked for progress, and marked off as complete. And [the police officer] could have acted *on* the underlying investigation because he could have influenced its findings had he identified an undercover agent in his tag search and revealed her cover [to the briber].[38]

Whether the Supreme Court will impose something akin to an "official act" requirement in honest services cases involving commercial, rather than public, corruption is open to question. It is difficult to see how § 201(a)(3)'s definition of public officials' "official acts" could be easily translated to allegations that a private employee materially breached his duty of honest services to his private employer through undisclosed bribery.

b. Money or Property

The alternative qualifying object of a scheme or artifice to defraud is "money or property." This is a familiar object in that most garden-variety fraud involves a defendant's attempt to obtain, through deceit, "money or property" to which the defendant is not entitled. Traditionally, this meant that the victim lost money as a result of the defendant's fraud. But the government has attempted to use a seemingly endless variety of "property"

---

37. *Van Buren*, 940 F.3d at 1205 (emphasis original), *rev'd on other grounds*, 593 U.S. 374 (2021).

38. *See also* United States v. Burnette, 65 F.4th 591, 604-05 (11th Cir. 2023); United States v. Hills, 27 F.4th 1155, 1177-80 (6th Cir. 2022).

theories to support fraud convictions, citing, for example, a college's interest in its admissions slots,[39] a standardized testing service's right to maintain the integrity of its testing process,[40] a worker's right to compete for a skilled trades designation under a collective bargaining agreement,[41] a bank's right to a fair opportunity to bid to be the repository of state toll revenues,[42] and a seller's right to control the destination of its products after sale.[43] The Supreme Court has, of late, curtailed prosecutorial creativeness in this regard. In so doing, it generally counsels courts to look to "traditional notions of property" in construing these statutes and cautions them to forswear "sweeping expansion[s] of federal criminal jurisdiction in the absence of a clear statement by Congress."[44] The lower courts, then, consult a variety of sources, "including whether the purported property at issue falls within a dictionary definition of that term, whether it has been recognized as property in case law or other legal sources, and whether it exhibits traditional attributes of property."[45]

i. Confidential Business Information. The extent to which the government has used novel "property" theories often aligns with the unavailability of an honest services theory, most notably after *McNally* and before § 1346 overruled it and after *Skilling* significantly narrowed its scope to cases in which the alleged breach of honest services involves bribery or kickbacks. Thus, for example, shortly after the Court rejected intangible non-property right theories in their entirety in *McNally*, the government pressed the Court to recognize that intangible, as well as tangible, property can be the object of mail or wire fraud prosecutions.

In *Carpenter v. United States*, 484 U.S. 19 (1987), the Court accepted this invitation, upholding a conviction founded on a defendant's deceptive misappropriation of "property" in the form of his employer's confidential business information. In *Carpenter*, a *Wall Street Journal* journalist published a popular column that often moved the market in the stocks it discussed. The journalist knew that the *Journal*'s policies forbade employees from trading in advance of publication. He evaded this restriction by tipping his confederates regarding the contents of future columns. The confederates traded to take advantage of the market movements the column precipitated, and they shared their profits with the journalist. The *Journal* was identified as the victim of the scheme to defraud and the fraud alleged was the journalist's failure to tell the *Journal* of his breach of its policies.

---

39. *See* United States v. Abdelaziz, 68 F.4th 1 (1st Cir. 2023) (rejecting theory as overbroad).
40. *See* United States v. Hedaithy, 392 F.3d 580 (3d Cir. 2004) (accepting theory).
41. *See* United States v. Douglas, 398 F.3d 407 (6th Cir. 2005) (accepting theory).
42. *See* United States v. Henry, 29 F.3d 112 (3d Cir. 1994) (rejecting theory).
43. *See* United States v. Bruchhausen, 977 F.2d 464 (9th Cir. 1992) (rejecting theory).
44. Cleveland v. United States, 531 U.S. 12, 24 (2000).
45. *Abdelaziz*, 68 F.4th at 35.

Prior to *McNally*, this could have been charged on the theory that the journalist breached his duty of honest services to the *Journal*. Because *McNally* foreclosed this theory, the government proceeded on a "money or property" theory, which the Court accepted. It found that the *Journal*'s interest in the confidentiality of the contents and timing of the column was a property right, noting that "'[c]onfidential information acquired or compiled by a corporation in the course and conduct of its business is a species of property to which the corporation has the exclusive right and benefit, and which a court of equity will protect through the injunctive process or other appropriate remedy.'"[46]

In the publishing context, this meant that the *Journal* had "property right in keeping confidential and making exclusive use, prior to publication, of the schedule and contents" of the column. The Court cited an earlier case for the proposition that "'news matter, however little susceptible of ownership or dominion in the absolute sense, is stock in trade, to be gathered at the cost of enterprise, organization, skill, labor, and money, and to be distributed and sold to those who will pay money for it, as for any other merchandise.'"[47] The fact that the defendant did not interfere with the *Journal*'s use of the information was irrelevant because the defendant deprived the *Journal* of "its right to exclusive use of the information, for exclusivity is an important aspect of confidential business information and most private property for that matter."[48] Finally, the Court ruled that the intangible nature of this confidential business information—the publication schedule and contents of the column—did "not make it any less 'property' protected by the mail and wire fraud statutes."[49]

Recently, a question has arisen whether theft of confidential *governmental* information constitutes the deprivation of intangible property under a *Carpenter* theory. The Second Circuit has ruled that confidential agency information relating to likely future regulatory action did not constitute property, reasoning that it was not "'stock in trade'" or of commercial value to the government.[50]

ii. Right to Control. Another very commonly used theory of property that developed in the aftermath of *McNally* was drawn from the case itself. After holding that honest services could not be the object of a mail fraud case, the Court noted that there had been no allegation that the victim in that case had actually been cheated of money "[n]or was the jury charged that to convict it must find that the [victim] was deprived of control over how its

---

46. *Carpenter*, 484 U.S. at 26.
47. *Id.*
48. *Id.* at 26-27.
49. *Id.* at 25.
50. *See* United States v. Blaszczak, 56 F.4th 230, 243 (2d Cir. 2022).

money was spent."[51] Taking this hint, the Second Circuit developed a theory recognizing that, because a defining feature of most property is the "right to control" the asset, the "property" protected by the mail and wire fraud statutes includes this interest.

Although this theory was purportedly based on a property interest created by the "right to control" an asset, that is actually a misnomer. The cases were based on the asset holder's right to *the material information* necessary to effectively control the asset—that is, to make discretionary economic decisions regarding the property.

The government regularly employed the "right to control" theory of property, but it did not attempt to defend it before the Supreme Court when it was challenged in *Ciminelli v. United States*, 598 U.S. 306 (2023). And the *Ciminelli* Court made short work of it, ruling that the "so-called 'right to control' "—that is, the "right to valuable economic information needed to make discretionary economic decisions"—is "not an interest that had 'long been recognized as property' when the wire fraud statute was enacted."[52]

The government also attempted to use a right to control theory in cases in which government action was subverted through fraud, but no obvious property interest could be identified and there was no bribe or kickback sufficient to ground an honest services case. The Court rejected this use of the right to control theory in *Kelly v. United States*, 590 U.S. 391 (2020), which involved a plot by various officials to reallocate access lanes to the George Washington Bridge. The officials were counting on the ensuing traffic backups to punish the mayor of the city whose traffic was snarled for a perceived lack of loyalty to the N.J. governor. One of the prosecution's property theories was that the officials deprived the government agency in charge of lane decisions of its right to control the Bridge, effectively "commandeering" the lanes. The Supreme Court rejected the notion that this constituted a property interest, ruling that the plot to reallocate the lanes instead involved "a quintessential exercise of regulatory power."[53]

iii. Government Licenses. One large, contested category of fraud concerned defendants' misleading efforts to secure various types of government licenses, raising the question whether unissued government licenses constituted "property." The Court answered "no" in *Cleveland v. United States*, 531 U.S. 12 (2000). The *Cleveland* defendants wished to obtain state licenses to run a video poker business, but their tax and financial problems undermined their suitability; accordingly, they hid their ownership of the business in their application. The Court reasoned that the mail and wire fraud

51. *McNally*, 483 U.S. at 360.
52. *Ciminelli*, 598 U.S. at 314, 316.
53. *Kelly*, 590 U.S. at 400.

statutes do not reach fraud in obtaining this type of state or municipal license because such a license is not "property" in the government's hands. The State's core concern in issuing such licensees is regulatory. The Court also noted that the State does not benefit financially while the license is in its hands, only *after* it has been issued.

iv. Taxes. In *Pasquantino v. United States*, 544 U.S. 349 (2005), however, the Court held that the right to taxes that should have been paid but were evaded is a cognizable property interest. In that case, the defendants smuggled liquor from the United States into Canada, thereby evading Canadian excise taxes. The Court ruled that the object of the scheme was to deprive Canada of money legally due, and thus the scheme had as its object the deprivation of Canada's "property." This was not treated, then, as an attempt to enforce Canada's regulatory tax policy.

v. Salary. The *Skilling* Court's decision to confine honest service cases to bribery and kickbacks, and to reject cases involving corrupt self-dealing and conflicts of interest, has moved prosecutors to once again push the boundaries of what may constitute property. For example, the government has charged such cases as money or property cases on the theory that the self-dealing public official or employee has cheated the government or the private employer of property in the form of his salary. This theory also found its genesis in *McNally*, in which Justice Stevens argued in dissent that "[w]hen a person is being paid a salary for his loyal services, any breach of that loyalty would appear to carry with it some loss of money to the employer—who is not getting what he paid for."[54]

The Court narrowed the scope of this theory in *Kelly*. In that case, the public officials involved attempted to cover up their misconduct by rationalizing the lane reallocation as an experiment and assigning public employees to work on a made-up study of its effects. The government alleged that the defendants defrauded the government of the salaries paid to the public employees whose services were wasted while they worked on the bogus study. The Court rebuffed the government's theory in that case because "a property fraud conviction cannot stand when the loss to the victim is only an incidental by product of the scheme" to defraud, as it was in *Kelly*.[55]

The *Kelly* Court did acknowledge, however, that a government's right to its employees' time and labor can be the basis of a "money or property" fraud prosecution when it is central to the scheme, such as when a mayor uses deception to get "on-the-clock city workers" to renovate his daughter's

---

54. *McNally*, 483 U.S. at 377 n.10 (Stevens, J., dissenting).
55. *Kelly*, 590 U.S. at 402.

new home,[56] or a city parks commissioner directs his employees to do gardening work for political contributors.[57]

vi. Fraudulent Inducement. In a variety of cases, the circuits have held that "even if misrepresentations result in money or property changing hands, they still may not necessarily constitute fraud."[58] Often these cases concern lies that are used to cause someone to enter into a transaction that they otherwise would not have. For example, in *United States v. Milheiser*, 98 F.4th 935 (9th Cir. 2024), the defendants' sales companies lied in their preliminary sales pitch: they would call a business, falsely state that they were the regular supplier of the business's printer toner, and falsely state that the price of toner was going up but the customer could lock in the current price by ordering that day. The Ninth Circuit reversed their convictions, seemingly on two grounds.

The *Milheiser* court first relied on cases in which courts "rejected the notion that depriving an individual of accurate information" is a property interest protected by the mail and wire fraud statutes.[59] This theory aligns with the rejection of the right-to-control theory of "property" in *Ciminelli*. But the court principally relied on fraudulent inducement cases in which courts reversed convictions not because of the lack of a "property" interest, but rather because the government had failed to prove the intent or materiality elements of "fraud."

These cases, explored further below, hold that, to prove a cognizable fraud, the misrepresentation must go the "'nature of the bargain,' such as a good's price or quantity."[60] Some courts have concluded that there is no "fraud" where there is an *intent to deceive* the victim into engaging in the transaction but no *intent to defraud* by cheating the victim regarding the essentials of the bargain. Alternatively, courts cite a lack of materiality when all that is proven is deceit going to inducement. Because the lies do not go to the essential nature of the bargain—that is, the terms of the deal the victim cared about were presented honestly—they are not *material* for fraud purposes.

In June 2024, the Supreme Court accepted certiorari in *United States v. Kousisis*, 82 F.4th 230 (3d Cir. 2023). The petitioner couched the issue presented as going to the viability of the "fraudulent inducement theory"

---

56. United States v. Pabey, 664 F.3d 1084, 1089 (7th Cir. 2011) (cited with approval in *Kelly*).
57. *See* United States v. Delano, 55 F.3d 720, 723 (2d Cir. 1995) (same).
58. United States v. Milheiser, 98 F.4th 935, 942 (9th Cir. 2024).
59. *Id.* at 942 (citing, for example, United States v. Bruchhausen, 977 F.2d 464 (9th Cir. 1992)).
60. *Id.* at 943 (citing, for example, United States v. Regent Office Supply Co., 421 F.2d 1174 (2d Cir. 1970)).

of money or property fraud.[61] In *Kousisis*, the government alleged that the Stamatios Kousisis and Alpha Painting & Construction Co. defrauded the the Pennsylvania Department of Transportation (PennDOT) by lying to it about Alpha's compliance with a material term in the painting and construction contracts it was awarded. Those contracts required Acme to subcontract with a disadvantaged business enterprise (DBE) for six to seven percent of the projects and specified that a failure to comply with the DBE regulations would constitute a material breach. During the performance of the contracts, the defendants submitted false documentation regarding DBE compliance and that documentation was necessary to get payment from the PennDOT under the contract.

The defendants argued that because PennDOT received the quality of work it wanted at the agreed-upon price, the scheme did not involve an actual or intended money or property loss. The defense relied on *Kelly*'s requirement that the money or property be the object of the scheme. Although lying about the company's compliance with DBE requirements may have gotten it the contract, the object was always to provide the service required, at the quality specified, for the amount agreed upon. All that PennDOT arguably lost was honest dealings and accurate information. The defendant concluded that because the Supreme Court held in *Ciminelli* that the right to economically useful information is not a property interest, this cannot constitute a money or property fraud: the defendants' conduct deprived the government only of a regulatory or policy interest in DBEs, which does not suffice under *Cleveland*.

The Third Circuit rejected these arguments, holding that "the government's money or property was *precisely* the object of" the fraudulent scheme. Put simply, "[the defendants] set out to obtain millions of dollars that they would not have received but for their fraudulent misrepresentation."[62] The court rejected the argument that its theory would essentially turn any intentional breach of contract into a property fraud case, arguing that this argument minimized the nature of the scheme. The defendants did not just scheme to deprive PennDOT of DBE participation. "Rather, they schemed to have Penn DOT pay them millions of dollars that they were clearly not entitled to given their material breach of the contracts."[63]

Although this case apparently will be litigated on the theory that no money or property is at stake where all that is alleged is fraudulent inducement, the case may also turn, as did *Milheiser*, on issues of fraudulent intent or materiality.

---

61. *See* Kousisis v. United States, 144 S. Ct. 2655 (2024).
62. *Kousisis*, 82 F.4th at 240 (emphasis original)
63. *Id.* at 242.

2. Types of Fraud

Fraud can include a variety of chicanery and deceit, ranging from outright untruths, to misleading half-truths,[64] to active concealment of material information, to a passive failure to disclose.[65] The most obvious basis for a fraud prosecution is an outright lie, more politely discussed as a misrepresentation. Such lies can relate to the past or present and can include future promises so long as the defendant, at the time of his undertaking, does not intend to fulfill his promise.

Another type of fraud that is commonly charged but perhaps not as intuitively obvious concerns concealment or omissions where there is a duty to disclose. Not all non-disclosures or omissions of important facts constitute fraud. Where two parties are negotiating at arm's length, for example, they generally have no obligation to show the opposing negotiator all their cards. But where a duty to disclose exists, a failure to share information material to the transaction can constitute fraud. Duties to disclose exist by virtue of statutory or common law legal requirements, with the most frequently cited arising out of a fiduciary or confidential relationship.

Unfortunately, federal courts faced with the question whether a defendant had a duty to disclose in mail and wire fraud cases do not examine the genesis of these duties with any rigor or cite any particular source of law. For example, courts appear to believe, without citing any legal authority, that every employee of a private entity—even those not classified as having fiduciary obligations to the company or its shareholders under corporate law—has a federal law duty to disclose the fact that he or she received a bribe or kickback, and a failure to reveal this information constitutes fraud.

It is very easy to confuse the question whether there is actionable *fraud* by omission (that is, whether the defendant had a duty to disclose), with the separate question, considered above, of whether there is a cognizable *object* of the fraud (that is, whether a defendant has a duty of honest services). But readers are encouraged to separate the two by asking in each case (1) what is the *fraud*—is it a lie or actionable omission and if it is the latter, was there a duty to disclose?; and (2) what is the *object* of the fraud—is it money or property or honest services and if it is the latter, was there a duty of honest services? At least in theory, the questions whether there is a duty to disclose and whether there is a duty of honest services are two distinct issues that may require reference to different sources of law.

As a practical matter, recognizing that these are different questions is important if one wishes to correctly assess whether all elements of a possible fraud prosecution have been met. It may seem logical to treat these questions as the same in cases in which the government charges an honest

64. *See, e.g.*, United States v. Jesenik, Case No. 3:20-cr-228-SI, 2023 WL 3455638 (D. Or. May 15, 2023).

65. *See, e.g.*, United States v. Colton, 231 F.3d 890, 899 (4th Cir. 1991)).

services case grounded on fraud by omission, and courts regularly so conflate them. But the government may base an honest services case on lies, rather than actionable omissions, just as it can found a money or property case on an omission in the face of a duty to disclose.

3. Materiality

In *Neder v. United States*, 527 U.S. 1 (1999), the Supreme Court held that materiality is an element of a "scheme or artifice to defraud" under the mail and wire fraud statutes and must be proven beyond a reasonable doubt to the satisfaction of the jury. This means that, to constitute fraud, the misrepresentation or actionable omission must be one of material fact. Materiality in this context, as well as in the false statements and perjury context, is usually translated into an instruction that the statement or omission is material if "a reasonable man would attach importance to its existence or nonexistence in determining his choice of action in the transaction in question";[66] in other words, a fact is material if it was capable of influencing the decision maker to whom it was addressed.[67] Because this is an objective test, a statement can be material even if the person to whom it was addressed knew or should have known that it was false and did not actually rely upon it.

4. Intent to Defraud

Mail and wire fraud require proof of a specific intent to defraud. What that means depends on whether the case is charged as a money or property case or an honest services case.

a. Money or Property Cases

In money or property cases, most circuits recognize that an intent to *deceive* is not sufficient to meet the specific intent requirement of § 1341 and § 1343; these are not, after all, false statements statutes. Rather, the government must prove an intent to *defraud*, which connotes an intent (in the Second Circuit's language) to "injure,"[68] (in the Fifth and Eleventh Circuits' language), to "harm,"[69] or (in the Ninth Circuit's language) to "cheat."[70] Thus, when the

---

66. *Neder*, 527 U.S. at 22 n.5.

67. *See, e.g.*, Ninth Circuit, Manual of Model Criminal Jury Instructions 15.32, 15.34 (2022 ed.) (false statements or actionable omissions are material if "they had a natural tendency to influence, or were capable of influencing," a person's acts) [hereinafter Ninth Circuit Instructions].

68. United States v. Regent Office Supply Co., 421 F.2d 1174, 1181 (2d Cir. 1970).

69. *See* United States v. Greenlaw, 84 F.4th 325, 350 (5th Cir. 2023); United States v. Takhalov, 827 F.3d 1307, 1313 (11th Cir. 2016), *amended*, 838 F.3d 1168 (11th Cir. 2016).

70. United States v. Miller, 953 F.3d 1095, 1101 (9th Cir. 2020).

government charges that the object of the fraud is money or property, the government must prove that the defendant intended to cheat the victim of money or property by means of a material deception or, put another way, to injure the victim in his property rights through deceit. It is important to remember that although the defendant must harbor this intent to defraud, the government does not have to prove that she was actually successful in harming her victims because § 1341 and § 1343 apply to inchoate schemes to defraud as well as those that have come to fruition.

This intent requirement becomes important in the many cases in which the defendant claims he was only "puffing" ("this book is is the best ever published!") rather than seeking to get something for nothing. It is also important in fraudulent inducement cases.

For example, in *United States v. Regent Office Supply Co.*, 421 F.2d 1174 (2d Cir. 1970), Regent Office Supply, a seller of well-known, nationally advertised brands of stationary products, solicited orders by telephone. To ensure that the company's salespeople could get access to the purchasing agents to whom they wished to sell, they often lied to "get by" the receptionist. Such misrepresentations included, for example, assertions to the effect that the salesperson was able to offer a discount because he was selling the stationary of a friend who had died and whose family was facing financial difficulties. These lies were a preliminary part of their sales pitch, but the salespersons were honest when they discussed the price and quality of the goods on offer.

The Second Circuit held that there was no actionable mail fraud because the government had failed to prove an intent to defraud—translated as an intent to injure or to get something for nothing—because the lies did not go to the nature of the bargain they offered but only to the reason they were able to offer the bargain.[71] The salespeople intended to *deceive* their customers but not to *defraud* them because they did not misrepresent the price or quality of the items offered, or the terms upon which the sale would proceed.

These cases—in which the lies were not sufficiently central or important to the transaction to reveal an intent to injure—arise frequently. Sometimes the defendants, like those in *Regent Office Supply*, couch their defense as one going to the intent element. But in other cases, the defendants argue that the prosecution fails because the misrepresentation or actionable omission failed to satisfy the materiality element. The choice of whether to attack the materiality or the intent to defraud element carries implications in terms of proof.

An intent to defraud is a question of historical fact—it depends upon an analysis of what the defendant subjectively intended. Materiality, by

71. *See Regent Office Supply Co.*, 421 U.S. at 1182.

contrast, is an objective question founded on whether a reasonable person would have found the misrepresentation or omission important in considering a particular course of action. Juries are often invited to infer intent from circumstantial evidence but may have direct evidence if a witness is able testify to the defendant's actual state of mind. With respect to materiality, juries are invited to simply decide what a reasonable person would believe, although witnesses with experience in the type of transaction at issue may be able to testify regarding the importance of the operative facts.

As noted above, although the Supreme Court granted certiorari in *United States v. Kousisis*, 82 F.4th 230, to decide whether the scheme alleged affected the victims' money or property rights, the case could as easily be decided on intent to defraud or materiality grounds. In that case, the defendant lied about compliance with a contractual obligation relating to use of a disadvantaged business enterprise (DBE) for a percentage of the project, but the victims allegedly received the quality of work for which they contracted at the agreed-upon price. If the Court approaches the case by examining these elements, the case would turn on whether DBE compliance was a material term of the contract or whether the defendants' lies regarding DBE compliance for the purposes of being paid under the contract evidence an intent to injure or cheat the victim.

b. Honest Services Cases

In honest services fraud cases the government does not have to prove that the defendants' scheme threatened any financial or property loss. Perhaps because the threatened harm is not tangible or economic in nature, the courts of appeals do not translate the intent to defraud in honest service cases as an intent to injure, harm, or cheat. They hold that the intent to defraud in such cases is satisfied by an intent to deprive another of the intangible right of honest services.[72]

B. Mailing or Wiring in Furtherance

The second element of mail and wire fraud is a mailing or an interstate wiring in furtherance of the fraud. The sole important distinction between the mail and wire fraud statutes relates to the jurisdictional "mailing" and "wiring" elements. This distinction is based on the constitutional foundations of the statutes. Congress originally enacted the mail fraud statute under its Postal Power.[73] Accordingly, the statute covers any mailing through the U.S.

72. *See Rybicki*, 354 F.3d at 145.
73. U.S. const. art I, § 8.

Postal Service, whether it be intra- or interstate. In 1994, however, Congress used its Commerce Clause power[74] to amend the mail fraud statute to cover deliveries by private or commercial interstate carriers. Where the alleged mailing is done through such companies, then, the government will, if challenged, need to prove that *interstate* carriers were used. Congress's enactment of the wire fraud statute was also founded on the Commerce Clause, and thus the government must prove that the charged wiring in fact moved through interstate or foreign commerce in every case.

No mens rea element attaches to this jurisdictional element, however.[75] Thus, for example, the government need not prove that the defendant knew or intended that, in § 1341 cases where private or commercial services are used, the carrier operated in interstate commerce or, in a § 1343 case, the wiring would travel in interstate or foreign commerce.

The mailing or wiring element is generally easy to satisfy. Under the Court's precedents, the mailing or wiring need not contain false or fraudulent communications.[76] Although they are the actus reus of the crime, the mailings or wirings need not be made knowingly or intentionally much less made for the purpose of effectuating the scheme; in short, there is no requirement that the act be done with a criminally culpable state of mind.[77] The statutes permit conviction when the defendant "causes" an interstate wiring or a mailing to be made by another but the Court says that the defendant need not know or intend that the other person make the wiring or mailing; it need only be reasonably foreseeable that the wires or mails will be used.[78] Finally, the Supreme Court requires that the wiring or mailing need only be "incidental" to the scheme, not integral or essential to it.[79]

The Court does require that the mailing or wiring occur before the scheme comes to fruition—that is, before the object of the fraud has been achieved.[80] For example, in *Parr v. United States*, 363 U.S. 370 (1960), several defendants were charged with having fraudulently obtained gasoline through the unauthorized use of a credit card issued to the school district that employed them. The government charged, as the mailing element, the credit card company's use of the mails to bill the school district for the purloined gas. The Court held that these mailings would not suffice because the scheme came to fruition the moment the defendants fueled up their cars and successfully paid for the gas with the credit card; it was immaterial to

74. *Id.* art. I, § 8, cl.3.
75. *See, e.g.*, United States v. Lindemann, 85 F.3d 1232, 1241 (7th Cir. 1996).
76. *See* Schmuck v. United States, 489 U.S. 705, 714-15 (1989).
77. *See id.* 712; *see also* Pereira v. United States, 347 U.S. 1, 8-9 (1954).
78. *See Schmuck*, 489 U.S. at 712.
79. *Id.* at 710-11.
80. *See, e.g.*, United States v. Maze, 414 U.S. 395, 402 (1974); Parr v. United States, 363 U.S. 370, 393 (1960); Kann v. United States, 323 U.S. 88, 95 (1944).

them who bore the ultimate loss—the credit card company or the school district.

In *Schmuck v. United States*, 489 U.S. 705 (1989), however, the Court allowed prosecutors to evade this limitation by recharacterizing the scheme as a continuing one, arguing that future fraudulent transactions might be threatened if the post-transaction wiring or mailing had not gone through. After *Schmuck*, then, prosecutors could successfully use the mailings in *Parr* by charging that the defendants planned to continue misusing their credit cards to purchase gas, and thus the scheme depended in part on the school district receiving and paying the credit card bills through the mails. The Court has also allowed prosecutors to charge mailings or wirings occurring after receipt of the property obtained by fraud if they "'were designed to lull victims into a false sense of security, postpone their ultimate complaint to the authorities, and therefore make the apprehension of the defendants less likely'" than if no jurisdictional acts had taken place.[81]

This element is also important for charging purposes. Mail and wire fraud are punishable by imprisonment of not more than twenty years for each count, which skyrockets to thirty years if the fraud affects a financial institution (and the statute of limitations grows from five to ten years in such cases). Recall our discussion of how double jeopardy issues affect charging choices in Chapter 2. The unit of prosecution for mail and wire fraud prosecutions is each mailing or wiring in furtherance of the fraud. Thus, if a defendant defrauds one victim through one fraudulent scheme but sends and receives one hundred interstate emails in furtherance of the scheme, the defendant can be charged with one hundred counts, each of which carries a potential sentence of twenty years' imprisonment.

Examples

1. Zoi Vlahou, an employee of MegaBank, was responsible for selling the bank's share of a commercial real estate development in Texas. She successfully arranged a sale that exceeded MegaBank's target price by a third. But she also cut himself in on the deal without revealing this to her employer. Thus, she talked the potential buyers into including in their offer letter a term contemplating that Vlahou would buy a minority interest in the property by suggesting that MegaBank wanted her to participate in the deal. She then deliberately misled MegaBank's board of directors and bank officials into believing that the buyer would not close on the deal unless Vlahou was included as a minority partner. Assuming

81. United States v. Lane, 474 U.S. 438, 451-52 (1986); *see also* United States v. Sampson, 371 U.S. 75, 80-81 (1962).

she made an interstate wiring in furtherance of this scheme, can Vlahou be charged with a money or property or honest services wire fraud?

2. Albert Hoxha sought a medical license to practice medicine in Puerto Rico but repeatedly failed the Puerto Rico Board of Medical Examiners' licensing exam. He turned to Zselyke Lengyel, a Board employee who had access to the applicants' files. He paid Lengyel to falsify his scores and, as a result, he received a license to practice medicine through the mails. Can Hoxha be convicted of conspiring to commit honest services fraud? Can he be convicted of mail fraud on the theory that his scheme deprived unsuspecting patients of property in the form of payments they made for his medical services?

3. Afzal Mahmoud, the parent of a high school senior, hired a college admissions consultant to help his child get into competitive colleges. Mahmoud, with the help of the consultant, fraudulently represented his child to be an elite tennis player to gain admission to the University of Southern California (USC). He agreed with the consultant to make payments to university accounts in exchange for the USC tennis coach's help in securing his child's admission as an athletic recruit. In short, the coach was paid off through "donations" to his tennis programs. Can this be charged as money or property fraud?

4. Asier Bengochea, a personal injury lawyer, referred certain of his clients to Maksim Kazlov, a chiropractor, for chiropractic services rendered at inflated prices to be paid out of the clients' insurance settlement proceeds. In return, Kazlov made corresponding payments, equal to five percent of the fees he collected for those services, to Bengochea's relatives at Bengochea's direction. Bengochea did not disclose this arrangement to his clients. Assuming he made an interstate wiring in furtherance of this scheme, can Bengochea be charged with honest services wire fraud? What if, instead of referring clients to Kazlov, Bengochea had set up a chiropractic business under a false name, hired chiropractors, and, without disclosing his interest, referred his clients to this business for treatment at inflated prices?

5. Jingyi Feng is a full-time professor and researcher at Hoya University (HU), a public research university. He is responsible for submitting grant proposals to the U.S. government (USG) through HU and managing USG-funded research. He has received various USG funds to support his research. HU requires its faculty to disclose any conflicts of interest as soon as they become known on a conflict form. Feng applied to one of the People's Republic of China's (PRC's) "talent programs," pursuant to which he was hired as a full-time researcher at a Chinese university and was expected to do research for the benefit of the PRC. At no time did Feng inform HU or the USG of this position or commitment. Feng

then falsely certified on two HU conflicts forms that he did not have any conflicts of interest, certified a lack of conflicts in a USG grant proposal, and falsely told the USG that he was only receiving and expecting to receive USG funding. Assuming that Feng made an interstate wiring in furtherance, can this be charged as either honest services or money or property fraud?

6. Mamun Das, who used to be an employee of the Centers for Medicare and Medicaid Services (CMS), learned of planned changes to Medicaid reimbursement rates from his former colleagues at CMS. Das, in his current capacity as a consultant to various hedge funds, shared this predecisional confidential information with his clients. The clients then sold the stocks of health care companies that would be hurt if these changes were in fact implemented. Assuming that Das made an interstate wiring in furtherance, can this be charged as a money or property wire fraud?

7. Vasil Daskalov was a priest in three different parishes. During his service at these parishes, he entered the churches at night and stole cash that had been collected during Mass. Because he moved from parish to parish, he was successful in hiding his theft until a bookkeeper and pastor in one parish installed a security camera and he was captured on tape stealing the collection money. Daskalov stole, in total, approximately $200,000. He deposited the stolen money in his Wells Fargo bank account, often depositing cash through an ATM in the small hours of the night; such deposits involved the use of the wires. Daskalov had substantial credit card bills because he liked to buy expensive antiques. A couple of days after each deposit of stolen cash, then, Daskalov transferred by wire a similar amount of money from his Wells Fargo account to pay off his credit card debt. Assume that these wires travel in interstate commerce. Can the government successfully charge Daskalov with wire fraud based on his cash deposits and the wirings he made from his bank account to his credit card providers?

8. The Woodcliff Lake School District is funded by taxes assessed for that purpose. By city law, the tax bills are mailed out annually to city residents, and the resulting funds, usually paid by check and returned by mail, are deposited in the District's bank account. Òscar Bernat, a District employee responsible for mailing the tax bills and depositing their proceeds, took some of the resident's checks and deposited them into his personal bank account. Can the government charge mail fraud based on these mailings?

9. Tobias Rask ran a successful nationwide personal injury firm. Unfortunately, he did so without having earned a law degree or passing the bar. He touted his services through his website. Rask contracted hosting services for the website through a company that operated its host

servers in Virginia. Rask's website was replete with fraudulent information regarding his purported credentials and experience. After viewing the website from his home in Tennessee, Stephen Brewer agreed to send $10,000 to Rask in California to retain Rask to represent Brewer's sister. How would one charge this case to satisfy the wiring in interstate or foreign commerce element?

Explanations

1. With respect to the money or property theory, Vlahou could attack the case on three grounds. First, taking a page from *Milheiser* and the defendant's argument in *Kousisis*, Vlahou could argue that the only thing she deprived her employer of was accurate information—that is, the fact that the buyer did not in fact insist on her participation. Because, under *Ciminelli*, the right to economically useful information is not a "property" interest, the case must fail.[82] Second, Vlahou could argue that there was no "fraud" because she did not harbor an intent to defraud—that is an intent to harm, injure, or cheat. Relying on *Regent Office Supply*, she would argue that the government failed to prove the requisite intent to defraud because her lies—in effect, "telling each side of the transaction that the other would walk if she were not given a piece of the deal"—did not evince an intent to injure; "what was crucial was that all the material facts and terms of the actual deal were disclosed."[83] Third, Vlahou could argue that there was no fraud because her misrepresentations were not material to the parties' conclusion of the deal.

   This hypothetical is based on a case in which the Seventh Circuit, chose to reverse on this third ground.[84] It determined that the only way that the defendant misled anyone concerned negotiating positions—that is, he lied to the buyer about the seller wanting him to be part of the transaction and led the seller to believe that the buyer insisted that he have a piece of the deal. But the actual terms of the deal were fully disclosed and subject to negotiation. Accordingly, the defendant did not lie to anyone about material facts.

   This case also raises the question whether Vlahou could be said to have violated her employer's right to her honest services. The Seventh Circuit concluded that although the defendant engaged in self-dealing in violation of his fiduciary duties to his employer, the *Skilling* Court held that such self-dealing cannot be prosecuted as honest services fraud; only proof of bribery or kickbacks will suffice.

---

82. *See, e.g.*, United States v. Yates, 16 F.4th 256 (9th Cir. 2021).
83. United States v. Filer, 56 F.4th 421, 431 (7th Cir. 2022).
84. *See* United States v. Weimert, 819 F.3d 351 (7th Cir. 2016).

2. Lengyel, as a public employee, owed the public a duty of honest services. The *quid pro quo* necessary to bribery is clear: Hoxha paid Lengyel to falsify his test results. Under *Skilling*, this constitutes a breach of his duty of honest services; the breach was not disclosed, making this a fraud case. This hypothetical is drawn from *United States v. Berroa*, 856 F.3d 141 (1st Cir. 2017), in which the First Circuit had little difficulty concluding that honest services fraud, on a bribery theory, had been proved. Note that one could have questioned whether falsifying the test results qualifies as a decision or act on a qualifying matter or question under *McDonnell* but this issue was not addressed by the First Circuit.

   A money or property case is more difficult because *Cleveland* made clear that unissued state and municipal licenses are not property for purposes of the fraud statutes.[85] The government may attempt at an end-run around *Cleveland* by charging that the scheme deprived patients of money or property in the form of fraudulently obtained medical fees. This, however, potentially raises the convergence issue—that is, whether it is permissible to allege that the fraud was addressed to one entity (the Board) while the property was secured from other persons (the patients). Most circuits do not impose a convergence requirement so this theory could work everywhere but the Ninth Circuit.

3. This case is representative of the so-called Varsity Blues prosecutions.[86] In these cases, the government argued that the object of the fraud was property in the form of admissions slots. Courts have held that universities have property rights in their degrees and grading systems.[87] Thus, for example, the Sixth Circuit held that an unissued college degree is a property interest because

   > The number of degrees which a university may award is finite, and the decision to award a degree is in part a business decision. Awarding degrees to inept students, or to students who have not earned them, will decrease the value of degrees in general. More specifically, it will hurt the reputation of the school and thereby impair its ability to attract other students willing to pay tuition, as well as its ability to raise money.[88]

   Similarly courts have accepted the argument that athletic scholarships are "property" because they have economic value: there are a finite number

85. *See Berroa*, 856 F.3d at 149.
86. *See Abdelaziz*, 68 F.4th 1.
87. *See* United States v. Barrington, 648 F.3d 1178, 1191 & n.11 (11th Cir. 2011) (students who hacked into the university's computer and changed students' grades deprived the university of property interest in the form of lost tuition resulting from the unearned hours credited to the students).
88. United States v. Frost, 125 F.3d 346, 367 (6th Cir. 1997) (holding that university had property right in unissued degrees).

of these scholarships and thus giving one student tuition, room, and board means that another will not receive similar benefits.[89]

The Varsity Blue cases raised the question whether offers of admission are different than degrees or scholarships. The government argued that an admissions offer is property because such offers hold economic value of their own—as the case demonstrated, people are willing to pay for them and universities could choose to sell them. The defense argued that an admission offer confers nothing more than the right to agree to the proposed exchange of tuition for education; it is an *invitation* to exchange tuition for an education and a degree, not the transaction itself. An admitted student cannot access the advantages the school offers until she accepts the offer, enrolls, and pays tuition; it is only at this point that a property interest may arise.

The First Circuit rejected both the government's contention that admissions slots always qualify as property for purposes of the mail and wire fraud statutes and the defense's assertion that they can never qualify as property. The court concluded that such bright-line rules fail to account for the variability of admissions slots, both in terms of levels of education (preschool through university), and the types of admissions slots (early admission, rolling admission, and deferred admission) potentially involved. The court ultimately reversed the conviction because of faulty jury instructions but, in so doing, emphasized the "narrowness" of its holding: "We do not hold that admissions slots cannot ever be property. . . . The resolution of [this] question[] will require much more detail, both legal and factual, on the nature of the purported property interest at issue."[90]

4. A lawyer clearly owes a fiduciary duty to his clients, which courts hold translates into both a duty of honest services and a duty to disclose breaches of that duty. This is a classic kickbacks case and thus qualifies as a breach of that duty under *Skilling*. This is a kickback because the lawyer referred business to Kazlov and Kazlov *returned* a portion of the proceeds of that business to Bengochea. Because Bengochea did not tell his clients of the inflated fees or kickback scheme, the arrangement constitutes fraud. The caselaw holds that the fact that Bengochea directed that these monies be paid to other people is irrelevant.

   If, instead, Bengochea created his own chiropractic business and, unbeknownst to his clients, referred them to that business, this is the type of self-dealing *Skilling* said could not be prosecuted as honest services fraud. The difference between this type of self-dealing and a kickback may seem morally inconsequential, but it is legally significant given

89. *See* United States v. Gatto, 986 F.3d 104, 126 (2d Cir. 2021).
90. *Abdelaziz*, 68 F.4th at 34.

the line *Skilling* drew between kickbacks (breach of honest services) and self-dealing (not a breach). A kickback requires a "*return*" of a portion of the business received while self-dealing typically involves receiving the business, and its revenues, directly through undisclosed businesses or transactions.[91]

5. Because *Skilling* holds that the non-disclosure of conflicts of interest is a form of self-dealing that is not covered by honest services fraud in the absence of bribery or kickbacks, this case raises the question whether the government can still bring this case relying on a property theory. The government would allege that the scheme to deprive HU of Feng's salary and the USG of grant money affects cognizable property interests.

   Courts have struggled with this question for many years, but it has taken on added importance because it is a way to avoid *Skilling*'s restriction of honest services cases to bribery and kickbacks and its bar on charging self-dealing or conflicts-of-interests cases as honest services fraud. Prosecutors in need of a property theory have argued that defendants engaged in these types of activities defraud their employers of property in the form of their salaries on the theory Justice Stevens articulated.

   After *Kelly*, we know that the deprivation of salary will not suffice if it is only an incidental by-product of the scheme to defraud; instead, the property at issue must be the object of the fraud. But the *Kelly* Court did recognize that an agent's salary can constitute cognizable property when it is in fact that agent's labor which is sought in the fraudulent scheme.

   In this case, the question is whether lies or actionable omissions regarding one's compliance with an employer's conflict of interest or other disclosure requirements can be charged as a money or property case on the theory that such deceit is aimed at *maintaining* the defendant's salary or benefits—that is, to avoid being fired. Courts disagree. Some courts draw a distinction between a scheme whose object is to obtain a new job or higher salary, which can satisfy the statute, and a scheme to deceive an employer so as to continue drawing an existing salary, which cannot.[92] Some rely on statutory language, arguing that one cannot "obtain" a pre-existing right to a salary.[93] One court, however, has found that a money or property case could proceed on these facts, quoting the Seventh Circuit for the proposition that "'[j]obs are a lot like contracts. Neither is a bag full of money but both are immensely

---

91. *See* United States v. Hausmann, 345 F.3d 952 (7th Cir. 2003).
92. *See, e.g.*, *Yates*, 16 F.4th at 266.
93. *See* United States v. Guertin, 581 F. Supp. 3d 90, 93-94 (D.D.C. 2022), *aff'd*, 67 F.4th 445 (D.C. Cir. 2023).

valuable: a contract is a promise to pay for services rendered, while a job is an exchange of labor for a paycheck.' "[94]

Cleveland may foreclose reliance on the USG grant monies as the "property" involved in the scheme; it is the sort of discretionary decision regarding allocation of government resources that may be characterized as merely an exercise of the regulatory power. There may, however, be an argument that grant funding, as actual money dispensed, looks more like a traditional property interest than a regulatory decision. A distinction similar to the one discussed above may be relevant. If the funding at issue has already been granted, the defendant would argue that his false statements regarding compliance with conflicts of interest policies are not depriving the USG of anything; he is not obtaining property or depriving the USG of property unless the fraud is in connection with future grant applications.

6. This raises the recurring question of the line between governmental property and the government's regulatory function. The government would argue that the Supreme Court has recognized that confidential business information is "property" for purposes of § 1341 and § 1343, citing *Carpenter*, and that the government does not cease to have a property interest in confidential information simply because it is ultimately used for a regulatory purpose. The government cannot be the only employer lacking an economic interest in its work product such that employees may steal and misuse such information with impunity.

   But a divided panel of the Second Circuit has ruled to the contrary, holding that although confidential information may constitute property of a commercial entity, the same is not true of CMS, which is not such an entity. The majority opinion noted that the government's information could not be viewed as its "stock in trade" that had economic value, as in *Carpenter*. It reasoned that "a planned CMS regulation, even if disclosed to outsiders prematurely, remains within the exclusive control of CMS. And if it is prematurely disclosed to others, the disclosure has no direct impact on the government's fisc, although it might well impact CMS's subsequent regulatory choices."[95] Further, "[a]s the Supreme Court recognized in *Cleveland* and emphasized in *Kelly*, the government's right to determine who should get a benefit and who should not. . . do[es] not create a property interest. The information reflecting such a decision and the timing of that disclosure are regulatory in character and do not

94. United States v. Feng Tao, 499 F. Supp. 3d 940, 953 (D. Kan. 2020) (quoting *United States v. Sorich*, 523 F.3d 702, 713 (7th Cir. 2008) ("here the city paid for, and was cheated out of, qualified civil servants")).
95. *Blaszczak*, 56 F.4th at, 244.

constitute money or property of the victim; and they are not a 'thing of value' to CMS that is susceptible to being 'convert[ed].' "[96]

7. This problem presents the question whether the wirings inherent in the deposits of cash and the transfers of funds to pay Daskalov's credit cards were "in furtherance" of the scheme under *Schmuck* and other precedents. Under § 1343, the government must prove that the interstate jurisdictional wirings were made for "the purpose of executing" the scheme or artifice to defraud. The Supreme Court, however, has read the "purpose" mens rea out of the statute. Instead, because this is a jurisdictional element, the Court has decreed that the government does not need to prove that the defendant intended or even knew that the wiring would be made.

   The deposits of the cash and the wirings to pay off Daskalov's credit card debt contained no false statements or representations, but *Schmuck* told us that an actionable wiring or mailing does not itself have to be deceitful. The Supreme Court has also read the "executing" language out of the statute, holding that actionable wirings need not be integral or essential the scheme. The Supreme Court requires only that the wirings be "incidental" to the scheme.

   There remains one potential restriction on this element: under *Schmuck* and earlier precedents, the wirings still have to occur before the scheme comes to fruition. The issues presented are: when did the scheme came to fruition and, if the wirings happened after that point, can the government still prevail by arguing that the wirings were necessary to ensure that the scheme continued or to allay the victims' suspicions?

   The deposit of the money in the Wells Fargo account, at least, can be rationalized as having a sufficient nexus to aid in the execution of the scheme to defraud.[97] In the case from which this hypothetical is drawn, the court concluded that the scheme came to fruition when the priest made off with the donated funds. But it accepted the government's argument that, given that the defendant lived communally with other priests who knew about his modest salary, he had to deposit the cash to avoid suspicion. A reasonable jury could then conclude that the cash deposits, made in the dead of night, were "lulling" wirings in that they were designed to postpone inquiries or keep the ongoing scheme from detection.

   The court also ruled, however, that no reasonable juror could find that the subsequent transfers from the defendant's bank account to pay his credit card bills could have furthered the fraudulent scheme. Once the monies were in his account, the threat of exposure was gone. The

96. *Id.* (internal quotation marks omitted); *cf.* United States v. Rodrigues, 22-CR-00391 (PMH), 2024 WL 113744 (Jan. 10, 2024); United States v. Hird, 913 F.3d 332 (3d Cir. 2019).
97. *See* United States v. Garbacz, 33 F.4th 459 (8th Cir. 2022).

credit card payments were not even incidental to the perpetration of the ongoing scheme because the purchases he made on the credit cards were not part of the fraud. In short, the scheme came to fruition at the point at which the defendant stole the cash, but the cash ATM deposits can be justified as a means of disguising the ongoing scheme; the transfers of money to pay the defendant's credit cards were too just attenuated to satisfy the "in furtherance" requirement.

8. This problem implicates one of the few restrictions the Supreme Court has recognized with respect to what may constitute a valid mailing or wiring. It roughly tracks the scheme alleged in *Parr v. United States*, 363 U.S. 370 (1960). The *Parr* Court held that where the school board was legally required to assess and collect taxes, there was no allegation that the tax bills where "padded" in any unlawful way, and the school board lawfully used the mails for this purpose, such "legally compelled" mailings could not be seen as unlawful "'step[s] in the plot,'" "'part[s] of the execution of the fraud,'" or "'incident to an essential part of the scheme.'"[98] They were, in sum, not made "for the purpose of executing such scheme" within the meaning of the mail fraud statute. The Court concluded by stating:

> we think it cannot be said that mailings made or caused to be made under the imperative command of duty imposed by state law are criminal under the federal mail fraud statute, even though some of those who are so required to do the mailing for the District plan to steal, when or after received, some indefinite part of its moneys.[99]

Many defendants have attempted to use *Parr*'s "required" mailings or wiring exception to avoid liability any time the government relies upon mailings or wirings that are in some sense required by law. Take, for example, a case in which the defendant engages in fraudulent commodities trading and the government relies on the interstate wiring of trade confirmations to customers to meet the wiring in furtherance element. While it is true that these confirmations are required by law, courts agree that not all legally required mailings or wirings are per se exempt. What distinguishes Bernat's case and *Parr* is causation. In Bernat's case and in *Parr*, the tax assessments would have taken place whether or not the defendant had hatched or executed his scheme. But in our hypothesized commodities trading fraud scheme, had the defendants not executed the fraudulent trades, the wirings would have not occurred because there would have been no need for any confirmation.

---

98. *Parr*, 363 U.S. at 391.
99. *Id.*

Where, in short, the government can show that but for the defendant's fraud, these "required" transmissions would not have been made, the wiring in furtherance element is satisfied.[100] Here, no such "but for" causation can be shown. The use of the mails to send out the tax bills and receive the payments would happen whether or not Bernat's scheme was in place. His actions are in the nature of theft or embezzlement rather than fraud.

9. This raises the question of how the government can prove that the wirings traveled in interstate or foreign commerce in a world of digital communications. Most of the digital information one exchanges and accesses is routed through cables and is stored on servers. Consumers do not have a say about which cables or servers are used. The paths that digital information take are largely determined by the technological and business decisions of service providers, not by those availing themselves of email or internet services. Because the routes such messages take are generally not predetermined and predictable, it may be difficult if not impossible for prosecutors to actually trace, for example, the path of an email sent by the defendant to his victims.

   Courts generally say that they will not assume that all email communications or access to websites involve interstate or foreign commerce. Often, they reference the physical location of the sender, recipient, and the providers' servers to determine whether an email or access to a website involved the use of interstate wires. The government will try to prove the email or web access providers' servers are physically located in states other than those in which the victims reside to satisfy the interstate wiring element. In the case upon which this hypothetical is based, the defendant uploaded content to the origin server in Virginia. The Tenth Circuit held that an origin server in Virginia had to transmit the uploaded content over interstate lines to the host server in Tennessee, thus satisfying the interstate wiring element.[101]

II. CONSPIRACY TO COMMIT FRAUD UNDER 18 U.S.C. § 1349

In 2002, Congress enacted § 1349, which provides that "[a]ny person who attempts or conspires to commit any offense under this chapter shall

100. *See* United States v. Ashman, 979 F.2d 469, 483 (7th Cir. 1992).

101. *See* United States v. Kieffer, 681 F.3d 1143, 1154-55 (10th Cir. 2012) (citing Akamai Tech., Inc. v. Cable & Wireless Internet Serv., Inc., 344 F.3d 1186, 1189 (Fed. Cir. 2003), for an explanation of the mechanics of web access).

be subject to the same penalties as those prescribed for the offense, the commission of which was the object of the attempt or conspiracy." This statute, like some other context-specific conspiracy statutes, reads like a penalty enhancement provision rather than as substantive authorization to pursue criminal conspiracy charges. That is, § 1349 could be construed simply as a statute that makes a conspiracy to commit any of the frauds in Chapter 63 of Title 18 under a general conspiracy statute—presumably 18 U.S.C. § 371—punishable to the same extent as the underlying fraud statute instead of by the up to five years' imprisonment specified in § 371. That said, the Supreme Court treated the similarly worded conspiracy to commit money laundering section, 18 U.S.C. § 1956(h), as a stand-alone conspiracy statute.[102] We will therefore join the federal courts and prosecutors who invariably treat § 1349 as a substantive conspiracy section.

Section 1349 makes it a crime to conspire to violate any of the sections contained in Chapter 63 of Title 18 ("Fraud"), including mail, wire, bank, healthcare, and securities fraud. To succeed on a § 1349 count, the government must prove that:

- The defendant agreed with at least one other person
- to commit mail, wire, bank, health care, or securities fraud
- knowing of the unlawful purpose of the agreement, and willfully joining in the agreement with the intent to further the unlawful purpose.[103]

Section 1349 does not require proof of an overt act.[104]

This section gives the government flexibility in charging fraud conspiracies. Thus, for example, if prosecutors plan to charge a defendant with a conspiracy to commit wire fraud, they can use the general conspiracy statute, 18 U.S.C. § 371 (five-year maximum sentence) if they wish to give the defendant a deal, or § 1349 (generally carrying a 20-year maximum) if they are not so inclined.

III. BANK FRAUD UNDER 18 U.S.C. § 1344

The bank fraud statute, § 1344, enacted in 1984, can be violated in two different ways: by executing or attempting to execute a scheme

102. *See* Whitfield v. United States, 543 U.S. 209 (2005).
103. *See* United States v. Greenlaw, 84 F.4th 325, 347 (5th Cir. 2023).
104. *See* United States v. Roy, 783 F.3d 418, 421 (2d Cir. 2015).

- to defraud a financial institution (§ 1344(1)), or
- to obtain money or other property owned by, or under the custody or control of a financial institution, by using false or fraudulent pretenses, representations, or promises (§ 1344(2))

"[F]inancial institution" is broadly defined in 18 U.S.C. § 20; it basically covers federal chartered or insured banks. In *Neder v. United States*, 527 U.S. 1(1999), the Supreme Court ruled that § 1344, like § 1341 and § 1343, contains an implicit materiality requirement, such that the false or fraudulent misrepresentation must be one that has a natural tendency to influence, or is capable of influencing, the decision of the decision-making body to which it was addressed.

Section 1344 was modeled on the mail and wire fraud statutes although its structure is in fact quite different. Courts not infrequently reference precedents decided under § 1341 and § 1343 at least in defining what constitutes a "scheme to defraud" for purposes of § 1344.[105] But bank fraud differs from mail and wire fraud in at least three important respects. First, the statute of limitations is ten years (18 U.S.C. § 3293(1)), not the five years that is normally applicable to non-capital federal felonies like mail and wire fraud (18 U.S.C. § 3282(a)). Second, violations of § 1344 are punishable by a fine, up to thirty years imprisonment, or both, while violations of § 1341 and § 1343 are punishable by "only" up to twenty years' imprisonment, with a maximum sentence of 30 years available only when the fraud can be proved to affect a financial institution.

Third, the unit of prosecution for bank fraud is not as straightforward as it is for § 1341 and § 1341.The bank fraud statute authorizes punishment for each "execution" or attempted "execution" of the scheme to defraud. What constitutes an "execution," however, is not entirely clear. Some courts have accepted charging in which an "execution" is roughly equivalent to acts in furtherance of the scheme,[106] while others have defined an "execution" to include several acts in furtherance of a single scheme.[107]

105. Infrequently, courts have looked to the elements of bank fraud in construing the scope of mail and wire fraud. *See Berroa*, 856 F.3d at 150-54.

106. *See, e.g.*, United States v. Poliak, 823 F.2d 371, 372 (9th Cir. 1987) (holding that each of ten checks deposited in a check-kiting scheme could be charged as a separate "execution" of the scheme).

107. *See, e.g.*, United States v. Lemons, 941 F.2d 309, 318 (5th Cir. 1991) (ruling that each check received by the defendant pursuant to the fraudulent scheme was part of one "execution" of the scheme).

A. Scheme to Defraud a Financial Institution Under § 1344(1)

With respect § 1344(1), the government must prove that the defendant:

- knowingly, and with an intent to defraud
- executed or attempted to execute a scheme to defraud a financial institution (that is, a bank that is federally insured or chartered)
- through a misrepresentation or actionable omission
- of material fact
- and thereby deprive it of something of value

Section 1344(1) requires proof of a specific intent to defraud.[108] As discussed above, in the mail and wire fraud context, courts read this requirement to require proof of an intent to harm, injure, or cheat when the object of the fraud is money or property.

In *Shaw v. United States*, 580 U.S. 63 (2016), the Court upheld a conviction under § 1344(1) of a defendant who stole funds out of a customer account. Shaw argued that his only intent was to steal the customer's money, and he did not deprive, or intend to deprive, the financial institution of its property. It was accepted that the customer's bank suffered no monetary loss because the deposit was federally insured. The Court first took issue with the defendant's premise—that is, that the bank did not have a property interest in its clients' deposits if thefts from customers' account were covered by insurance. It instead ruled that when a customer deposits funds, sometimes the bank becomes the owner of the funds subject to the customer's right to withdraw them; other times the bank simply assumes possession, but even as a bailee, the bank has a "special qualified property" right in the funds.[109] In either case, the bank has a cognizable "property" interest in its customers' deposits.

Second, the Court rejected the defendant's argument based on a subtle distinction between an intent to "deprive the bank of 'something of value'"[110] (that is, money or property) which is required by the statute, and an intent that the "victim bank . . . suffer financial harm,"[111] which is not. Thus, under *Shaw*, this subsection does not require that the government prove that the defendant caused or intended to cause the bank *financial* harm.

---

108. *See, e.g.*, Ninth Circuit Instructions, *supra* note 67, 15.36; Seventh Circuit, The William J. Bauer Jury Instructions of the Seventh Circuit 6.18.1344 (2023 ed.) [hereinafter Seventh Circuit Instructions].
109. *Shaw*, 580 U.S. at 66-67.
110. *Id.* at 72.
111. *Id.* at 68.

Rather, given *Shaw*'s holding that the bank has a property interest in depositors' funds, this element is satisfied "when a defendant engages in deception to deprive a financial institution of its right to use its property, including customer deposit funds that it controls."[112] In short, under *Shaw*, § 1344(1) "demands neither a showing of ultimate financial loss nor a showing of intent to cause financial loss."[113]

B. Scheme to Obtain a Financial Institution's Property by Means of Misrepresentations Under § 1344(2)

With respect to § 1344(2), the government must prove that the defendant:

- knowingly
- executed or attempted to execute a scheme through which the defendant "intend[ed] to obtain any moneys . . . or other property owned by, or under the custody or control of, a financial institution"
- the defendant made a material misrepresentation; and
- the misrepresentation was the "means" by which the defendant intended to obtain bank property.

In relation to the last element—requiring that the property be obtained "by means of" the materially false representation—the Supreme Court, in *Loughrin v. United States*, 573 U.S. 351 (2014), ruled that there must be a more than "oblique, indirect, and incidental" connection between the lies and the obtaining of bank property; "the defendant's false statement [must be] the mechanism naturally inducing the bank (or custodian of bank property) to part with money in its control."[114] But the *Loughrin* Court refused to append additional intent requirements to the statute.

In *Loughrin*, the defendant stole a bank customer's checks and used them to buy merchandise at Target. He planned to return the merchandise for cash. His intent was to defraud Target, not the bank upon which the checks were drawn, the presumption being that the bank would not be out of pocket because its deposits were federally insured. The Supreme Court upheld the conviction, ruling that this subsection and subsection (1) are

112. United States v. Skouteris, 51 F.4th 658, 666 (6th Cir. 2022) (upholding a conviction for a lawyer who fraudulently endorsed clients' settlement checks and deposited them in his own account, stating that a bank, "by accepting a forged check, necessarily distributes its funds to an unauthorized party, preventing the bank from otherwise using those funds while risking liability for the bank itself").

113. *Shaw*, 580 U.S. at 67-68.

114. *Loughrin*, 573 U.S. at 363.

written in the disjunctive and therefore must be read, to the extent possible, to cover different types of criminal activities. It held, then, that subsection (2) does not require that the government prove that the defendant intended to defraud a financial institution.[115]

Examples

1. Many banks will not approve a debit or credit card transaction for marijuana even in states that have legalized the sale of marijuana because the distribution of marijuana is still illegal under federal law. To circumvent this, Niels Snaaijer and Udo Okonkwo—who ran a marijuana dispensary—set up a fictitious business, complete with websites and offshore bank accounts, purporting to sell dog food. In so doing, they lied to the offshore banks and associated credit card processors with whom they set up accounts about the nature of their business. Snaaijer and Okonkwo then used their fictitious business to fool U.S. banks into approving marijuana debit card sales to bank customers by disguising the transactions as sales of dog food. The mechanics of this scheme allowed them to do so indirectly. When a cardholder initiated a purchase, the merchant transmitted information regarding the transaction to the transaction processor. This information included a merchant category code (MCC) describing the product category of the item the customer wished to purchase. The defendants gave their transaction processor a false MCC indicating that the customer was purchasing dog food. The processor passed on the false MCCs to the U.S. banks that issued the debit cards. The banks then approved the transactions and sent the money from their customers' accounts to the defendants' offshore bank accounts. As a result, the U.S. banks processed more than $100 million of transactions that they would have otherwise declined. Can this case be charged as bank fraud under § 1344(1)?

2. Yun Ho was an assistant to a vice president of MegaBank, Samina Misra. Misra maintained a checking account at MegaBank but she lost her ATM card. Misra ordered a new card and selected a PIN number. Unfortunately, she did so while Ho was looking over her shoulder. Misra stored her ATM card in the top drawer of her desk. Ho periodically took the card from her desk and made withdrawals from her account using her PIN number. Can he be prosecuted under § 1344(2)? Assume instead that Ho is responsible for causing funds transfers between MegaBank and affiliated banks. He caused unauthorized wire transfers from MegaBank to his personal offshore bank account. Can he be prosecuted under § 1344(2)?

115. *See id.* at 357-58; *see also Skouteris*, 51 F.4th 667-70; United States v. Bouchard, 828 F.3d 116 (2d Cir. 2016).

Explanations

1. Snaaijer and Okonkwo would first argue that § 1344(1) requires proof of an intent to defraud and thus a bank fraud case would fail because the government cannot prove that the defendants intended to cause harm or injury to the card-issuing banks' money or property. The U.S. banks' customers wanted to buy marijuana and to do so they used their debit cards thereby authorizing the transfer of their own funds on deposit to Snaaijer and Okonkwo. The debit card holders certainly had no objection to these transactions. And, given that the customers had a perfect right to withdraw their funds, the bank had no basis for complaint. The most the banks were deprived of was their "right to control" the assets in their custody. Formerly, courts accepted that the provision of materially false information deprived victims of this "right," and this was treated as a deprivation of a species of property for purposes of the mail and wire fraud statutes. The Supreme Court, however, emphatically rejected this "right to control" property theory in the mail and wire fraud context in *Ciminelli v. United States*, 598 U.S. 306 (2023).

   The government would respond that the object of the scheme was not a right to control or a right to accurate information, but rather the bank's property interest in their customers' deposits. Because the *Shaw* Court recognized that banks have a property interest in such deposits, the defendants' use of deception to deprive the U.S. banks of this property interest manifests an intent to harm or injure the banks in their property interests, whether or not the scheme resulted in financial loss.

   Snaaijer and Okonkwo would then argue that they in fact did not misrepresent anything to the U.S. banks. They will concede that they lied to the offshore banks, but they would rightly contend that these non-U.S. entities, unlike the U.S. banks issuing the debit cards, are foreign entities that are not federally insured or federally chartered and thus are not protected by the bank fraud statute. The defendants would say that they did not lie to the U.S. banks and that the statute requires that the deception be addressed to the same banks that were harmed. If the defendants had instead been charged with mail or wire fraud, this objection would have no force because most circuits accept that § 1341 and § 1343 do not require a "convergence" between the person receiving the misrepresentation and the person who is harmed. Section 1944(1), however, requires that the defendant attempt both to "deceive [a] bank" and to "deprive it of something of value," even if that value does not impose actual financial harm.[116]

116. *Id.* at 72.

The government would respond that even if there is such a convergence requirement, it is met. It was the defendants' intention that their misrepresentations to the offshore banks and transaction processors—the inaccurate MCCs—would be passed on to the cardholders' banks so that the banks would approve the transactions. The inaccurate MCCs were material because the card-issuing banks would not have approved the transactions had they known that marijuana was involved. In the case upon which this hypothetical was based, the district court refused to dismiss the indictment based on the above-described defense arguments.[117]

2. Ho would argue that he did not make any "false or fraudulent pretenses, representations, or promises" within the meaning of § 1344(2) in using Misra's PIN. He did not in fact make a representation of any sort by using the PIN. And the PIN was itself correct—it was not a "lie." In *United States v. Miller*, 70 F.3d 1353 (D.C. Cir. 1995), on similar facts, the D.C. Circuit ruled to the contrary, holding that each time the defendant inserted the stolen card into an ATM, he represented to the bank that "he had the authority to withdraw the funds" from Misra's account.[118] It is clear that the PIN number itself was not "false." But, the court concluded, entry of a PIN number "acts as a sort of electronic signature authorizing an ATM to release available funds."[119] Inputting the PIN without Misra's knowledge or authorization is "tantamount to cashing a check with a forged signature—conduct we have expressly held violates 1344(2)."[120]

   Judge Sentelle objected to the majority's reasoning in *Miller*. He argued that the court's holding that the PIN number constituted a misrepresentation regarding Ho's authority to access the account would criminalize a wide range of conduct far beyond that which Congress would approve. "For example, a person who puts a key in a lock could be said to impliedly represent that he has the authority to open the lock. If he lacks that authority, he becomes liable not only for the consequences of his illegal entry but also for having made a false representation."[121]

   Would the result be different if Ho instead sent unauthorized wire transfers from MegaBank to his own offshore accounts? In such a case, *United States v. Briggs*, 939 F.2d 222 (5th Cir. 1991), the Fifth Circuit held that the defendant had not violated § 1344(2) because the defendant, so far as the record revealed, made no explicit false representations, statements, or promises in carrying out her scheme to send unauthorized wire

117. *See* United States v. Weigand, 482 F. Supp. 3d 224 (S.D.N.Y. 2020).
118. *Miller*, 70 F.3d at 1355.
119. *Id.*
120. *Id.*
121. *Id.* at 1357 (Sentelle, J., concurring in the result).

transfers from her employer's account to her personal accounts.[122] The D.C. Circuit's majority opinion in *Miller* distinguished *Briggs* by explaining that the Fifth Circuit had noted that precisely how the defendant effected the transfers was unclear and had further stated that "'where the defendant falsely represents that she is acting under her employer's authority, we would have little trouble concluding that such conduct is squarely prohibited by the statute.'"[123] The D.C. Circuit, however, failed to respond to the Fifth Circuit's conclusion that "[t]he bare act of instructing a bank to transfer funds is not a factual representation."[124] Accordingly, it "cannot be a *mis*representation, a *false* representation, or *any kind* of misrepresentation."[125]

IV. HEALTH CARE FRAUD UNDER 18 U.S.C. § 1347

Health care fraud encompasses many types of misconduct, usually by health care practitioners and businesspersons in the health care field, aimed at making money by bilking patients, private insurers, or the federal government. Such practices include billing for services that were never rendered, billing for more expensive services or procedures than were actually provided or performed ("upcoding"), performing medically unnecessary services solely for the purpose of generating insurance payments, misrepresenting non-covered treatments as medically necessary, falsifying a patient's diagnosis to justify tests, surgeries, or other procedures that aren't medically necessary, billing a patient more than the required co-pay amount for services, and accepting kickbacks for patient referrals.

Section 1347, enacted in 1996 and amended in 2010, is similar to the bank fraud statute in that it, unlike mail and wire fraud, contains two discrete types of violations. It is violated when a defendant

- knowingly and willfully
- executes, or attempts to execute, a scheme or artifice
  - to defraud any health care benefit program in connection with the delivery of or payment for health care benefits, items, or services, *or*

122. *See Briggs*, 939 F.2d at 226-27.

123. *Miller*, 70 F.3d at 1356 (quoting *Briggs*, 939 F.2d at 227).

124. *Briggs*, 939 F.2d at 226.

125. *Id.*; *see also* Williams v. United States, 458 U.S. 279, 284-85 (1982) (reversing a check kiting conviction under 18 U.S.C. § 1014 because depositing checks knowing that they are not supported by sufficient funds does not constitute a "false statement," reasoning that "a check is not a factual assertion at all, and therefore cannot be characterized as 'true' or 'false.'... Each check [does] not, in terms, make any representation as to the state of [one's] bank balance").

- to obtain, by means of false or fraudulent pretenses, representations, or promises, any of the money or property owned by, or under the custody or control of, any health care benefit program in connection with the delivery of or payment for health care benefits, items, or services.

In § 1347(b), Congress provided that, with respect to violations of this section, "a person need not have actual knowledge of this section or specific intent to commit a violation of this section." In so providing, Congress excluded the possibility that "willfully" would be construed to require the type of "super mens rea" that courts apply in rare circumstances to very complex statutory schemes, as discussed in Chapter 2 (General Part).

In general, the scheme to defraud is interpreted in much the same way as the term is used in mail and wire fraud prosecutions. Some courts recognize that an intent to defraud need not be proved under § 1347(2) in reliance on *Loughrin*.[126]

The term "health care benefit program" is defined to include a jurisdictional nexus to interstate commerce: "any public or private plan or contract, *affecting commerce*, under which any medical benefit, item, or service is provided to any individual, and includes any individual or entity who is providing a medical benefit, item, or service for which payment may be made under the plan or contract" (18 U.S.C. § 24b (emphasis added)). Although the statute was designed primarily to address frauds perpetrated by the medical community, courts have rejected defendants' invitations to read the scope of "health care benefit program" narrowly, concluding, for example, that § 24b does not apply only to health care professionals, nor is it limited to insurance providers or entities funded by an insurer.[127]

A violation of § 1347 is punishable by a fine and not more than ten years' imprisonment, or both. The statutory maximum increases to twenty years if the violation results in serious bodily injury (defined in 18 U.S.C. § 1365), and life imprisonment if the violation results in death. The unit of prosecution for this statute is, like the bank fraud statute, each "execution" or attempted "execution" of the scheme to defraud and courts rely on the bank fraud precedents in resolving claims that indictments are multiplicitous[128] or duplicitous.[129]

126. *See* Seventh Circuit Instructions, *supra* note 108, at 652-53; *but cf.* Ninth Circuit Instructions, *supra* note 67, 15.42 (in generalized instructions for § 1347 including intent to defraud element).

127. *See, e.g.*, United States v. Manamela, 612 Fed. App'x 151, 156 (3d Cir. 2015).

128. *See* United States v. Sosa-Baladron, 800 Fed. App'x 313, 322-24 (6th Cir. 2020); *see also* Chapter 2 (discussion of duplicity and multiplicity).

129. *See* United States v. Kirkham, 129 Fed. App'x 61, 66-69 (5th Cir. 2005).

Examples

1. Loreta Nana and Janice Short participated as passengers in staged auto accidents and fabricated personal injury claims designed to exploit New York's no-fault auto insurance regime. The New York no-fault law requires that every automobile owner maintain an insurance policy that provides those injured in an accident with compensation for economic loss—including the costs of medical treatment, lost wages, and other expenses—without regard to who was at fault in the accident. The law allows those injured in accidents to assign their right to payment for medical expenses to a medical provider.

   Nana and Short were recruited by the fraud's author, Ruslan Saad, to ride in cars that were deliberately crashed into other vehicles. Although no one was hurt in the accidents, Nana and Short sought medical benefits for their non-existent injuries. They were referred to medical clinics in New York City that paid fees to Saad, Nana, and Short for their business. Nana and Short assigned their no-fault insurance benefits to the clinics, which billed the insurance companies directly for their non-existent "treatment" of Nana and Short. To receive the no-fault reimbursements, the clinics generated fictitious treatment records for Nana and Short. Can Nana and Short be prosecuted under § 1347(1)? What defense might they make to such a prosecution?

2. Bryant Nixon worked as a front desk clerk at a methadone clinic operated by Progressive. The clinic provided methadone services in exchange for a fee, usually tendered in cash to Nixon upon the patient's check-in. At the end of the day, Nixon would reconcile the amount of cash gathered with the sign-in sheets and record the amount on the computer. He would then take the cash to the bank to be deposited. Unfortunately, he pocketed large amounts of the cash on the way to the bank. Ultimately, Nixon stole $451,000 in cash from Progressive. Does this constitute health care fraud under 18 U.S.C. § 1347(2)?

Explanations

1. Certainly Nana and Short knowingly and willfully participated in a scheme to defraud insurance companies who paid the clinics' false claims for treatment of fictitious injuries. But, the defense would argue, the statute applies only to frauds perpetrated by health care professionals and the New York no-fault insurance program is not a "health care benefit program."

   In the case from which this hypothetical is derived, *United States v. Lucien*, 347 F.3d 45 (2d Cir. 2003), the Second Circuit relied on the plain language of the statue—including the "[w]*hoever* knowingly and willfully" executes a scheme to defraud a health care benefit program—to hold that the statute applies not only to those medical professionals who bilk benefits programs but also to any others whose conduct otherwise conforms to the elements of the offense.[130]

The Second Circuit also held that payments made pursuant to the requirements of New York's no-fault insurance law involved a "health care benefit program"; it is immaterial that the no-fault law does not operate nationwide and covers only injuries flowing from auto accidents. The Second Circuit reasoned that a "health care benefit program" is defined in § 24(b) as "'*any* public or private *plan or contract* . . . under which *any medical benefit*, item or service is provided to *any* individual.'"[131] Private insurers—bound by the insurance contracts purchased by car owners pursuant to the no-fault law's requirement that they maintain no-fault liability insurance policies—reimbursed the clinics for fraudulently billed expenses supposedly incurred on behalf of Nana and Short. Because Nana and Short received a "*medical benefit*" as a result of the vehicle owners' no-fault *insurance contracts*, a health care benefit program within the meaning of § 24(b) was implicated.

2. Nixon would argue that the theft occurred only after the health care benefit was paid for and delivered and thus was not "in connection with the delivery of payment for health care benefits." The government would respond that a theft from a health care provider that is providing a public or private plan or program is more than a theft from the cash register because the money stolen was intended to pay for a health care benefit program administered by Progressive.

   In the case from which this problem was adapted, the Third Circuit overturned the conviction for lack of fraud. It held that while the government proved theft, it did not prove that the defendant made any type of misrepresentation in connection with the delivery of, or payment for, health care benefits, items, or services. It did not accept the government's theory that by accepting her responsibilities as a front desk clerk, the defendant implicitly promised to deposit the entire amount, rejecting the premise that every employee makes an implicit promise not to steal from their employer. The government's argument that the deposit slip constituted a misrepresentation also did not wash because it correctly reflected the amount of money actually deposited even if it did not reflect the full amount paid to the clinic.[132]

130. *Lucien*, 347 F.3d at 51.
131. *Id.* at 52 (emphasis original).
132. *See* United States v. Jones, 471 F.3d 478 (3d Cir. 2006).

CHAPTER 7

Obstruction of Justice

- B. **Alteration, Destruction, or Falsification, etc. of Records, Documents, and Tangible Objects Under 18 U.S.C. § 1519**
  - 1. **The Differences Between § 1512(c) and § 1519**
    - a. **Attempts**
    - b. **"Other object" vs. "Tangible Object"**
    - c. **Qualifying Conduct**
    - d. **Mens Rea and Intent**
    - e. **"Official Proceeding" vs. "Matter Within the Jurisdiction of Any Department or Agency of the United States"**
- C. **Destruction of Corporate Audit Records Under 18 U.S.C. § 1520**

Chapter 73 of Title 18 provides prosecutors with a selection of overlapping statutes to work with in pursuing obstruction cases. The following focuses on those provisions most frequently used in white-collar cases, omitting, for example, discussion of obstruction by threat of force or physical coercion. Obstruction cases fall roughly into two categories, intransitive and transitive. Intransitive cases are ones in which the *defendant* is personally lying or altering or destroying evidence with a corrupt intent. Transitive cases, by contrast, are cases in which the defendant tampers with *another* witness by tricking or persuading that *other* person to lie or compromise evidence. Transitive obstruction is often called witness tampering for obvious reasons.

An old workhorse, the Omnibus Clause of § 1503, prohibits persons from corruptly endeavoring to "influence, obstruct, or impede" the due administration of justice. Courts have approved the application of the Omnibus Clause to a vast array of conduct, both intransitive and transitive. Section 1503 is limited, however, in one respect: it applies only to cases in which the obstruction is directed at a *pending* judicial proceeding. Another old and broadly applicable provision, the Omnibus Clause of § 1505, also outlaws endeavoring to "influence, obstruct, or impede" but in the context of *pending* agency proceedings and congressional investigations.

In 1982, Congress enacted a new statute, § 1512, which, as originally conceived, was addressed only to transitive obstruction as is demonstrated by its title: "Tampering with a witness, victim, or an informant." Section 1512, then, was designed only to address situations in which the defendant acts on *another person* with the intent to obstruct, recognizing that intransitive obstruction could be dealt with under § 1503 and § 1505. Notably, Congress also provided in § 1512(f) that "an official proceeding *need not be pending* or about to be instituted at the time of" the § 1512 tampering offense (emphasis added).

White-collar witness tampering cases generally involve defendants' use of either corrupt persuasion or misleading conduct directed at another person with the intent to cause or induce that other person to lie, destroy evidence, or otherwise obstruct the conduct of judicial or other proceedings. The only non-coercive tampering covered in the 1982 version of § 1512 was misleading conduct. Thus, prosecutors continued to use § 1503 and § 1505 to fill the gap. Even after Congress added language expanding the scope of § 1512 to include corrupt persuasion in 1988, however, the courts of appeals uniformly concluded that this amendment did not remove prosecutors' ability to address non-coercive witness tampering under § 1503 and § 1505 as well as § 1512.

Prosecutors faced with witness tampering, then, have a great deal of discretion—facts permitting—in choosing among these statutes, and their choice can drastically affect defendants' sentencing exposure: the maximum term of imprisonment for § 1505 is five years, for § 1503 it is ten years, and for § 1512(b) it is twenty years.

In 2002, Congress enacted the Sarbanes-Oxley Act[1] in response to the exposure of Enron's massive fraud and allegations that Enron's outside auditor, Arthur Andersen LLP, had deliberately destroyed potentially incriminating Enron audit records. Enron, a huge energy company, used questionable accounting practices to hide billions of dollars in debt and make it appear as if the company was profitable. Arthur Andersen, then one of the five largest audit and accountancy partnerships in the world, audited Enron's publicly filed financial statements and provided internal audit and consulting services. When questions about Enron's financial condition and accounting practices surfaced, Andersen employees became concerned. The SEC had not yet launched a formal investigation but an in-house lawyer at Andersen deemed such an investigation "highly probable." Because Andersen personnel believed that "the problems are just beginning and we will be in the cross-hairs,"[2] Andersen employees in its Houston office dusted off Andersen's "document retention policy" and engaged in wholesale shredding of an estimated two tons of Enron related documents as well as systematic deletion of email records.[3] Enron declared bankrupty a few months later.

The difficulties the government faced in finding an appropriate obstruction charge to levy against Arthur Andersen revealed critical gaps in the Obstruction Chapter of the federal code. The principal difficulty prosecutors faced was the fact that, while an SEC investigation was threatened and clearly foreseeable, it had not yet commenced at the time of the shredding. Thus,

1. Pub. L. No. 107-204, 116 Stat. 745 (2002).
2. United States v. Arthur Andersen, LLP, 374 F.3d 281, 286 (5th Cir. 2004), *rev'd*, 544 U.S. 696 (2005).
3. *Id.*

they could not proceed under § 1505 because it requires obstruction of a *pending* agency (in Andersen's case, SEC) proceeding. But § 1512, which was then addressed only to witness tampering, was difficult to apply to the the facts, which involved the defendants doing their own shredding rather that persuading *others* to destroy the audit records.

Prosecutors eventually charged Andersen with violating § 1512 under the awkward theory that Andersen tampered with its own employees by corruptly persuading them to destroy documents with the intent to impair their availability in an official proceeding. The jury convicted Andersen after trial, but the Supreme Court reversed, finding the jury instructions deficient.[4] By this point, however, Andersen had collapsed and dissolved, rendering its Supreme Court win the most pyrrhic of victories.

In reaction to the Andersen charging dilemma, Congress, in the Sarbanes-Oxley Act of 2002, added a variety of provisions to the code, most of which, naturally enough, given Arthur Andersen's conduct, concerned intransitive conduct—that is, cases in which the defendants personally destroy, alter, or conceal documents or other objects with the intent to obstruct an official proceeding. The problem is now one of congressional over-kill: at least four "fixes" were made to the statute that introduce substantial redundancy to the Chapter.

First, Congress enacted § 1519, which addresses the destruction, alteration, concealment, or falsification of documents, records or other "tangible objects" in federal investigations and bankruptcies. Second, it added § 1520, which covers the destruction of corporate audit records.

Until recently, the most important provision added in 2002 was § 1512(c), which contains two subsections. The first, § 1512(c)(1), is intransitive in nature and it constitutes a third attempt to "fix" the Andersen problem. Like § 1519, it penalizes those who personally destroy, alter, mutilate, or conceal records, documents, or other objects. It made little sense to locate this intransitive provision in a statute that is designed to deal solely with transitive conduct, but presumably Congress chose to insert this provision into § 1512 because that statute by its terms does not require proof of a pending proceeding and thus would be usable in cases such as Andersen. There is obviously a substantial overlap in the conduct that § 1519 and § 1512(c)(1) cover. As we shall see, in *Yates v. United States*, 574 U.S. 528 (2015), the Supreme Court struggled to find a way to limit that overlap, with questionable success. In so doing, it rather famously arrived at the conclusion that a fish is not a "tangible object."

While § 1512(c)(1) has proved useful, the real star of the show was, until 2024, the second, Omnibus Clause, § 1512(c)(2), which outlaws corruptly "obstructing, influencing, or impeding" an official proceeding

---

4. *See* Arthur Andersen, LLP v. United States, 544 U.S. 696 (2005).

or attempting to do so. Congress obviously borrowed this operative language from § 1503 and § 1505, and the overlap in the applicability of the three Omnibus Clauses was substantial because § 1512(c) covers (like § 1503) judicial proceedings and (like § 1505) congressional and agency proceedings. This subsection constitutes a fourth effort to "solve" one of the difficulties the Andersen prosecutors faced by taking the language of § 1505 and inserting it into a statute that, unlike § 1505, does not require a proceeding to be pending. Because Congress chose to borrow the language of § 1503 and § 1505, it is likely that the intent was to cover, as do those sections, both transitive and intransitive obstruction.[5] Again, the substantial overlap in the coverage of these sections gave prosecutors a great deal of charging discretion and potential leverage in choosing among varying statutory maximum sentences.

Section 1512(c)(2) quickly became a prosecutorial favorite, eclipsing § 1503 and § 1505, because it did not require proof of a pending proceeding, applied to obstruction in judicial, legislative and agency proceedings, and carried a substantial twenty-year maximum sentence. For twenty years, the courts of appeals uniformly read its operative language, like the same language in § 1503 and § 1505, broadly. But, in 2024, the Supreme Court seriously limited the utility of § 1512(c)(2) in *Fischer v. United States*, 603 U.S. 480 (2024), by insisting that § 1512(c)(2)'s broad language be constrained by the scope of § 1512(c)(1). Thus, the terms "influencing, obstructing, or impeding" justice in § 1512(c)(2) are much more limited than the identical language in § 1503 and § 1505. As in *Yates*, the *Fischer* Court was principally concerned with reading § 1512(c)(2) in a way that rationalized the Obstruction Chapter and reduced redundancy in coverage among its sections. Again, its success in this regard is likely to be limited.

This chronology reveals that the obstruction chapter is internally redundant, disorganized, and often arbitrary in terms of coverage and statutory maximum punishments. Although there remains a tremendous amount of overlap among sections, there are also many very small but potentially critical distinctions between them in terms of scope, application, and required elements. These distinctions will certainly tax readers' patience, but they can be case-determinative. The obstruction chapter gives prosecutors great power over defendants' potential sentencing exposure and thus a serious advantage in plea bargaining. But prosecutors are well advised to think very carefully before choosing a charge for the leverage it provides without carefully examining whether the specific, very technical requisites of a particular charge can be sustained on the facts.

---

5. *See* Fischer v. United States, 603 U.S. 480, 491 (2024) (citing a witness tampering case, *United States v. Mintmire*, 507 F.3d 1273, 1290 (11th Cir. 2007), as an example of what is covered by § 1512(c)(2)).

It is important to note that obstructive activities may also be chargeable under different chapters of the Code. For example, § 1503 has been applied to conduct that was also charged as bribery (e.g., payments to a judge for a positive result); perjury (e.g., lying under oath at trial or in the grand jury); contempt (e.g., refusing to testify before a grand jury after immunity has been conferred); and false statements (e.g., lies to federal agents).

I. THE OMNIBUS CLAUSES OF 18 U.S.C. §§ 1503, 1505, AND 1512(c)(2)

The Omnibus Clauses of sections 1503, 1505, and 1512(c)(2) all *appear* to proscribe identical conduct—that is, "corruptly" "influenc[ing], obstruct[ing], or imped[ing]," or endeavoring (§ 1503, § 1505) or attempting (§ 1512(c)(2)) to do so. The differences in application of these statutes will be explored further within but it is worth noting as a preliminary matter some distinctions among them.

First, the authorized maximum term of imprisonment differs widely: five years under § 1505, ten years under § 1503, and twenty years under § 1512.

Second, all three sections address inchoate conduct. Thus, the defendant does not have to be successful in his efforts to obstruct. But § 1503 and § 1505 will be more useful to prosecutors than § 1512(c)(2) in addressing such conduct. Sections 1503 and 1505 reach "*endeavors*" to influence, obstruct, or impede the proceedings while § 1512(c)(2) covers only "*attempts*" to do so. Attempt liability requires proof of a substantial step towards a completed offense but endeavors do not. "[E]fforts to witness tamper that rise to the level of an 'endeavor' yet fall short of an 'attempt' cannot be prosecuted under § 1512."[6]

Third, § 1512 may be more useful when the alleged criminal conduct crosses borders because Congress specified in § 1512(h) that "[t]here is extraterritorial Federal jurisdiction" for offenses under § 1512.

Fourth, § 1503 and § 1512 can serve as RICO predicate acts and thus can be used as the foundation for invoking the powerful RICO remedies but § 1505 cannot.[7] The same is true under the money laundering statute: § 1503 and § 1512 can be the source of the "specified unlawful activity" that is the basis for a money laundering prosecution but § 1505 cannot.[8]

---

6. United States v. Sampson, 898 F.3d 287, 302 (2d Cir. 2018); *see* United States v. Ladum, 141 F.3d 1328, 1337-38 (9th Cir. 1998).

7. *See* 18 U.S.C. § 1961. Sections 1519 and 1520 also cannot serve as RICO predicates. *See id.*

8. See *id.* § 1956(c)(7). Sections 1519 and 1520 do not constitute specified unlawful activity. *See id.*

Fifth, conspiracies to violate all three sections can be charged under 18 U.S.C. § 371, which carries a maximum sentence of five years. But a conspiracy to commit a § 1512(c)(2) offense can also be charged under § 1512(k), which carries a statutory maximum of twenty years.

In very general terms, all three statutes require proof of the following elements: the defendant,

- in a qualifying proceeding or investigation, and
- acting with a corrupt intent
- committed a qualifying obstructive act
- in cases in which there is a nexus between the obstructive act and the proceeding or investigation.[9]

In the following subsections, we will explore the four basic elements common to 18 U.S.C. §§ 1503, 1505, 1512(c)(2) and the differences in how those elements are defined and applied. We will also reference a fourth element—a specific intent to obstruct—that is required by § 1503 and § 1505 but whose application to § 1512(c)(2) is unclear.

A. In a Qualifying Proceeding or Investigation

A notable difference among the three sections is the required object of the obstructive activity:

- § 1503(a) requires that the corrupt influencing, obstructing, or impeding be directed at "the due administration of justice," which is understood to mean a pending federal judicial proceeding
- § 1505 requires that the corrupt influencing, obstructing, or impeding be directed at "the due and proper administration of the law under which any pending proceeding" is being held before U.S. agencies or "the due and proper power of inquiry" in investigations by either House of Congress or committees thereof
- § 1512(c)(2)'s coverage largely replicates that of § 1503 and § 1505; it requires that the corrupt influencing, obstructing, or impeding be in relation to a federal "official proceeding," which is defined as including a proceeding before a judge or court of the United States or a federal grand jury, a proceeding before Congress or an authorized proceeding before a federal government agency

9. The Ninth Circuit, in an attempt to cabin the reach of § 1503, imposed an additional materiality element to this list in a perjury case, although the *en banc* court splintered when attempting to define what materiality means in this context. *See* United States v. Bonds, 784 F.3d 582 (9th Cir. 2015) (*en banc*).

Judicial proceedings within the meaning of § 1503 and § 1512 include not only grand jury investigations and criminal cases, but also civil judicial proceedings.[10]

I. Pending vs. Contemplated Proceeding

One very important difference among these statutes concerns whether the government must prove that the proceedings or investigations identified above are pending or only contemplated.

Although some lower courts question whether the requirement that a proceeding or investigation be pending is consistent with the text of § 1503 and § 1505,[11] the requirement finds its genesis in two Supreme Court opinions. In 1893, the Court ruled in *Pettibone v. United States*, 148 U.S. 197 (1893), that "a person is not sufficiently charged with obstructing or impeding the due administration of justice in a court unless it appears that he knew or had notice that justice was being administered in such court."[12] And the Court, in *United States v. Aguilar*, 515 U.S. 593 (1995), cited *Pettibone* for the proposition that "a person lacking knowledge of a pending proceeding necessarily lack[s] the evil intent to obstruct."[13] Most courts believe, then, that "*Aguilar* reaffirmed the proposition that a defendant may be convicted under section 1503 [and section 1505] only when he *knew* or *had notice* of a *pending* proceeding."[14] As noted in the introduction, this limitation has made some cases—including the Arthur Anderson case—difficult to charge.

By contrast, Congress expressly provided in 18 U.S.C. § 1512(f)(l) that "[f]or purposes of" Section 1512, "official proceeding[s] need not be pending or about to be instituted at the time of the offense." In *Arthur Andersen, LLP v. United States*, 544 U.S. 696 (2005), however, the Court ruled that such proceedings must be contemplated or foreseeable. The Court acknowledged § 1512(f)(l) but reasoned that

> [It is] one thing to say that a proceeding "need not be pending or about to be instituted at the time of the offense," and quite another to say a proceeding need not even be foreseen. A "knowingly. . . corrup[t] persuade[r]" cannot be someone who persuades others to shred documents under a document retention policy when he does not have in contemplation any particular official proceeding in which those documents might be material.[15]

10. *See, e.g.*, United States v. Lundwall, 1 F. Supp. 2d 249, 255 (S.D.N.Y. 1998).
11. *See, e.g.*, United States v. Novak, 217 F.3d 566, 571-72 (8th Cir. 2000).
12. *Pettibone*, 148 U.S. at 206.
13. *Aguilar*, 515 U.S. at 599.
14. United States v. Frankhauser, 80 F.3d 641, 650 (1st Cir. 1996) (emphasis added).
15. *Arthur Andersen*, 544 U.S. at 707-08.

Although the *Arthur Andersen* case involved charges under § 1512(b), courts hold that the government must prove that a proceeding was at least contemplated or foreseeable under § 1512(c) as well.

2. Agency Proceeding: § 1505 vs. § 1512

Section 1505 applies to "proceedings" pending before a department or agency of the United States. In general, the § 1505 cases interpreting the term "proceeding" have concluded that it describes a wide variety of ways in which administrative agencies conduct their business.[16] As the Tenth Circuit summarized, the term "proceeding" under § 1505 is

> [not] limited to something in the nature of a trial. The growth and expansion of agency activities have resulted in a meaning being given to "proceeding" which is much more inclusive and which no longer limits itself to formal activities in a court of law. Rather, the investigation or search for the true facts . . . is not to be ruled as a non-proceeding simply because it is preliminary to indictment and trial.[17]

By contrast, courts have read the term "official proceedings" in the agency context under § 1512(c)(2) to be more limited, which may circumscribe its usefulness in an important context—obstruction committed during investigations by, among others, the FBI and SEC. Courts have read this subsection to require that a particular matter be presented for adjudication and that the decision-making be, at least to some degree, formal and structured. Thus, some courts have refused to find that agencies' informal, routine investigatory activity, even that which relates to decision-making on discrete questions such as a security clearance adjudications or inquiries into violations of agency policy, do not qualify as "official proceedings."

In *United States v. Sutherland*, 921 F.3d 421 (4th Cir. 2019), for example, the Fourth Circuit declared that "FBI investigations . . . are not official proceedings because the statutory language including 'a proceeding before a Federal Government agency which is authorized by law,' § 1515(a)(1)(C), implies some formal convocation of the agency in which parties are directed to appear, instead of any informal investigation conducted by any member of the agency."[18] Much will depend on the specific attributes of any adjudication. Thus, in *United States v. Perez*, 575 F.3d 164 (2d Cir. 2009), the court held that an internal investigation into officers' use of force pursuant to Federal Bureau of Prison rules was "sufficiently formal" to be qualified

16. *See* Rice v. United States, 356 F.2d 709, 712 (8th Cir. 1966).
17. United States v. Browning, 572 F.2d 720, 724 (10th Cir. 1978); *see also* United States v. Leo, 941 F.2d 181, 198-99 (3d Cir. 1991).
18. *Sutherland*, 921 F.3d at 425 (internal quotation marks omitted).

as an "official proceeding" because it "contemplates more than a preliminary investigation; it sets forth a detailed process of review and decision-making," including making required findings.[19]

It may be possible to avoid the circuits' conclusion that FBI investigations are not "official proceedings" for purposes of § 1512(c)(2) through thoughtful pleading. For example, in *United States v. Beach*, 80 F.4th 1245 (11th Cir. 2023), the defendant was convicted under § 1512(a)(2)(A), for threatening to kill a witness who was cooperating with the police against the target of an ongoing investigation. He argued that the investigation was not an "official proceeding." The Eleventh Circuit, however, accepted the government's argument that the FBI investigation was "not the official proceeding in question. The official proceeding would be a trial or grand jury proceeding against" the target being investigated.[20] The court further noted that "[t]hat proceeding need not have already begun," and it was enough that the defendant foresaw such a proceeding.[21]

B. "Corruptly"

In the obstruction-of-justice context, there is no one agreed-upon definition of the term "corruptly." Indeed, in *United States v. Fischer*, 64 F.4th 329 (D.C. Cir. 2023),[22] three different D.C. circuit judges discussed four possible definitions of the term for purposes of § 1512(c)(2) without agreeing on a single variation.

One definition of "corruptly" that is often found in jury instructions for *bribery* defines this mens rea as acting knowingly and intentionally, with a bad purpose of accomplishing either an unlawful end or result, or an otherwise lawful end or result by some unlawful method or means.[23] Justice Scalia, partially concurring in *United States v. Aguilar*, 515 U.S. 593 (1995), would have appended to this definition of "corruptly": "'with a hope or expectation of either financial gain or other benefit to oneself or a benefit of another person.'"[24] Some judges, contending that this is consistent with the common law definition, advocate for this instruction in *obstruction* cases.[25]

By far the most popular instruction in the obstruction-of-justice context equates acting "corruptly" with acting with an "improper" or "wrongful"

19. *Perez*, 575 F.3d at 169.
20. *Beach*, 80 F.4th at 1255.
21. *Id.*
22. This opinion was reversed on other grounds in *Fischer v. United States*, 603 U.S. 480 (2024).
23. *See, e.g.*, Third Circuit Model Criminal Jury Instructions 6.18.201B2-1 (2022 ed.).
24. *Aguilar*, 515 U.S. at 616-17 (Scalia, J., concurring in part).
25. *See, e.g.*, *Fischer*, 64 F.4th at 351-62 (Walker, J., concurring).

purpose or motive.[26] The Supreme Court expressed this more vividly in *Arthur Andersen*, asserting that the meaning of "corruptly" is "clear": "'[c]orrupt' and 'corruptly' are normally associated with wrongful, immoral, depraved, or evil" for purposes of § 1512(b).[27] Some courts augment this instruction by requiring that, to act corruptly, the defendant must act "knowingly and dishonestly."[28] Still other courts import into their instructions some requirement that the defendant be aware that what he is doing is wrong. Thus, the commentary to the Ninth Circuit's pattern jury instructions notes that "corruptly" means acting with "consciousness of wrongdoing" under § 1512(c).[29] Finally, the Supreme Court has stated that the defendant must act with an intent to obstruct, at least for purposes of § 1503.[30] The following instruction, from the Tenth Circuit, may best capture the gist of these multiple definitions: to act corruptly means to act "'with an improper purpose and to engage in conduct knowingly and dishonestly with the specific intent to subvert, impede or obstruct'" the relevant proceeding.[31]

Section 1505 has its own statutory definition of "corruptly," which is attributable to a congressional effort to overturn a D.C. Circuit decision, *United States v. Poindexter*, 951 F.2d 369 (D.C. Cir. 1991). Congress specified that "[a]s used in section 1505, the term 'corruptly' means acting with an *improper purpose*, personally or by influencing another, including making a false or misleading statement, or withholding, concealing, altering, or destroying a document or other information."[32]

C. Commit a Covered Obstructive Act

Courts have routinely interpreted the scope of the primary conduct proscribed in § 1503—corruptly influencing, obstructing, or impeding—very broadly, to "reach[] all corrupt conduct capable of producing an effect that prevents justice from being duly administered, regardless of the means employed."[33] Thus for example, under § 1503 any endeavor to "influence"

26. *See, e.g.*, *id.* at 340-41; United States v. Thompson, 76 F.3d 442, 452 (2d Cir. 1996); *see also* 18 U.S.C. § 1515(b) (for purposes of § 1505, "the term 'corruptly' means acting with an improper purpose.").
27. *Arthur Andersen*, 544 U.S. at 705 (holding that acting "knowingly. . . corruptly" in 18 U.S.C. § 1512(b) requires "consciousness of wrongdoing").
28. *See* United States v. Gordon, 710 F.3d 1124, 1151 (10th Cir. 2013) (§ 1512(c)(2)).
29. Ninth Circuit, Manual of Modern Criminal Jury Instructions 19.5, cmt. (2022 ed.) [hereinafter Ninth Circuit Instructions].
30. *See Aguilar*, 515 U.S. at 599 ("a person lacking knowledge of a pending proceeding necessarily lacked the evil intent to obstruct" under § 1503); *see also* Ninth Circuit Instructions, *supra* note 30, 19.3, cmt. (corruptly "means that the act must be done with the purpose of obstructing justice" for purposes of § 1503).
31. *Gordon*, 710 F.3d at 1151.
32. 18 U.S.C. § 1515(b) (emphasis added).
33. United States v. Silverman, 745 F.2d 1386, 1393 (11th Cir. 1984).

the due administration of justice can qualify no matter how "subtle or circuitous" or "however cleverly or with whatever cloaking of purpose" it is achieved.[34] The terms "obstruct or impede" are similarly capacious and "can refer to anything that blocks, makes difficult or hinders."[35] Certainly § 1503 is construed to cover both transitive and intransitive obstruction.[36] Section 1505 is less frequently invoked but is read to be equally broad in coverage. The D.C. Circuit used a very limited—and questionable—reading of § 1505 to reverse the obstruction conviction of President Reagan's National Security Advisor, Admiral John Poindexter, but it was promptly overruled by Congress.[37]

The types of conduct regularly charged as obstructive acts under § 1503 and § 1505, as appropriate, include the concealment, alteration, fabrication, or destruction of documents or other types of evidence relevant to civil or criminal cases; withholding subpoenaed testimony or documents; perjuring oneself in the grand jury, an administrative or congressional hearing, a deposition, or a trial; lying to investigators; bribing grand jurors into violating grand jury secrecy; paying off judges, investigators, or witnesses; disclosing confidential information to the target of investigations; and suborning perjury or soliciting witnesses to alter, destroy, or fabricate evidence. Even fraud can be obstruction: lawyers who have solicited money from their clients through false promises to "fix" the proceedings or pay off criminal justice officials have been convicted of obstruction.[38]

I. Sections 1503 and 1505 vs. § 1512(c)(2) After *Fischer*

After enactment of § 1512(c), prosecutors preferred to proceed under the Omnibus Clause of § 1512(c)(2) because of its generous maximum penalty and because, unlike § 1503 and § 1505, the government does not have to prove that a proceeding was pending at the time of obstructive activity. The Justice Department read the scope of § 1512(c)(2) very broadly, in line with the generous coverage the Supreme Court and the lower federal courts have given to the identical wording in § 1503's and § 1505's Omnibus Clauses. And, until the Supreme Court's decision in *Fischer v. United States*, 603 U.S. 480 (2024), the circuit courts uniformly accepted the DOJ's broad reading.

---

34. United States v. Roe, 529 F.2d 629, 632 (4th Cir. 1975).

35. Marinello v. United States, 584 U.S. 1, 7 (2018) (internal quotation marks omitted) (describing the scope of 26 U.S.C. § 7212(a), which forbids "corruptly. . . obstruct[ing] or imped[ing], or endeavor[ing] to obstruct or impede, the due administration of [the Internal Revenue Code]," by reference to § 1503).

36. *See, e.g.*, *Sampson*, 898 F.3d at 302-03.

37. *See* United States v. Poindexter, 951 F.2d 369, 279 (D.C. Cir. 1991), *rev'd by statute*, 18 U.S.C. § 1515(b).

38. *See* United States v. Neiswender, 590 F.2d 1269, 1270 (4th Cir. 1979).

For example, the circuits applied § 1512(c)(2) to reach a wide range of obstructive acts, not just those involving tampering with documents or other tangible evidence, including:

> (1) lying in written responses to civil interrogatory questions, (2) soliciting information about a grand jury investigation to evade surveillance, (3) seeking a false alibi witness, (4) tipping off the targets of criminal investigations, (5) asking third parties to create fraudulent physical evidence, (6) giving misleading testimony in a preliminary injunction hearing, (7) attempting to orchestrate a grand jury witness's testimony, (8) making false statements to a grand jury, and (9) burning an apartment to conceal the bodies of two murder victims.[39]

Consistent with the circuits' broad reading of the statute, federal prosecutors used § 1512(c)(2) to charge many defendants who participated in the January 6, 2021 riot at the U.S. Capitol. Juries and judges found these defendants guilty of obstructing an "official proceeding"—that is, Congress's Electoral College voting and certification process—through violence (and thus corruptly). The rioters made a variety of attacks on their convictions but the one that rang the Supreme Court's bell was the argument that the Omnibus Clause in (c)(2) must be limited by the subject matter of (c)(1). Recall that Section 1512(c) proscribes corruptly

> (1) altering, destroying, mutilating, or concealing a record, document, or other object, or attempting to do so, with the intent to impair the object's integrity or availability for use in an official proceeding; *or*
> (2) otherwise *obstructing, influencing, or impeding* any official proceeding.

In June 2024, the Court decided *Fischer*, holding that § 1512(c)(2) is indeed limited by the reach of § 1512(c)(1). It reversed the D.C. Circuit's ruling to the contrary and remanded to that court with instructions to assess the sufficiency of the § 1512(c)(2) charge in the *Fischer* indictment in light of the Court's reading of the statute.

The *Fischer* Court entirely ignored the language of the statute and did not attempt to deal with the fact that the meaning of "corruptly influenc[e], obstruct[], or imped[e]" had—for many decades—been read broadly under the statutes, § 1503 and § 1505, from which Congress borrowed the language of § 1512(c)(2). Rather, it principally relied on the *noscitur a sociis* and *ejusdem generis* canons of construction to support "the common sense intuition that Congress would not ordinarily introduce a general term that renders meaningless the specific text that accompanies it."[40] It concluded

39. *Fischer*, 64 F.4th at 337-38, *rev'd*, 603 U.S. 480.
40. *Fischer*, 603 U.S. at 487.

that "[g]uided by the basic logic that Congress would not go to the trouble of spelling out the list in (c)(1) if a neighboring term swallowed it up, the most sensible inference is that the scope of (c)(2) is defined by reference to (c)(1)."[41] The thrust of the majority's argument was that if it accepted the government's broad reading of (c)(2), it "would largely obviate the need for [the] broad array of other obstruction statutes."[42]

It is not entirely clear what (c)(2) now covers. The Court appears to have two uses in mind. First, "subsection (c)(2) makes it a crime to impair the availability or integrity of records, documents, or objects used in an official proceeding in ways other than those specified in (c)(1)"—that is, *other than* by "altering, destroying, mutilating, or concealing" them.[43] For example, the Court asserted that "it is possible to violate (c)(2) by creating false evidence—other than altering incriminating evidence"—such as by forging a court order.[44] Second, subsection (c)(2) imposes liability for "impairing the availability and integrity of *other* things used in an official proceeding beyond the 'record[s], document[s], or other object[s]' enumerated in (c)(1), such as witness testimony or intangible information," by altering, destroying, mutilating, or concealing them.[45] The Court cited as an example of this latter use a case in which a defendant attempted to orchestrate a witness's grand jury testimony.[46]

To the extent that the Court's aim was to eliminate redundancy in the Obstruction Chapter, its efforts were doomed. Thus, for example, all the conduct that the Court now says is covered by § 1512(c)(2), and indeed the conduct proscribed by (c)(1), can still be prosecuted under a § 1503 and § 1505 where a qualifying proceeding is pending. And, as we shall see, even under the Court's restricted reading, § 1512(c)(2) overlaps in coverage with § 1512(b) and § 1519.

Justice Jackson, who provided the majority its fifth vote, noted in a concurring opinion that Fischer was charged with obstructing a proceeding before Congress, specifically, Congress's certification of the Electoral College vote. "That official proceeding plainly used records, documents, or objects—including, among others, those relating to the electoral votes themselves."[47] Thus, she suggested that on remand the court consider whether Fischer's conduct involved the impairment (or the attempted impairment) of the availability or integrity of such materials in ways other than those specified in (c)(1)—such as, one assumes, by making a violent assault on the Capitol.

---

41. *Id.* at 490.
42. *Id.* at 493.
43. *Id.* at 491 (emphasis added).
44. *Id.* (citing United States v. Reich, 479 F.3d 179, 185-86 (2d Cir. 2007) (Sotomayor, J.)).
45. *Id.* (emphasis original).
46. *Id.* (citing *Mintmire*, 507 F.3d at 1290.
47. *Id.* at 505 (Jackson, J., concurring).

2. Lawful but "Corrupt" Acts

Courts have held that otherwise entirely lawful conduct can be criminally obstructive if it is done with a corrupt intent. For example, if an attorney engages in litigation to "influence" or "impede" a criminal investigation into his client's business affairs, can her otherwise effective advocacy also be the basis for an obstruction conviction? In *United States v. Cueto*, 151 F.3d 620 (7th Cir. 1998), the Seventh Circuit answered "yes," if the lawyer acts with a corrupt intent. In *Cueto*, the lawyer was engaged in various allegedly shady business ventures with his client, and the government alleged that his obstructive activity was motivated by his "personal financial interest in protecting the illegal gambling enterprise" under investigation.[48] The court affirmed the lawyer's conviction, concluding that "[o]therwise lawful conduct, even acts undertaken by an attorney in the course of representing a client, can transgress § 1503 if employed with the corrupt intent to accomplish that which the statute forbids."[49]

This issue occupied center stage in Special Counsel Robert Mueller's investigation into allegations that the Russian government interfered with the 2016 presidential election. Part of that investigation focused on whether President Trump obstructed justice by virtue of a series of actions he took relating to the Russian-interference investigation. Mueller acknowledged that many of the President's actions alleged to potentially be obstructive were otherwise legal and within his presidential powers, including his decision to fire FBI Director James Comey and his requests that Attorney General Jeff Sessions curtail the scope of the Special Counsel's Russia investigation and reverse his decision to recuse himself from it. But Mueller's report asserted that "[a]n improper motive can render an actor's conduct criminal even when the conduct would otherwise be lawful and within the actor's authority."[50] Ultimately the Special Counsel chose not to make a decision on the matter.[51] Attorney General William Barr then declined the case, explaining that the evidence developed during the Special Counsel's investigation was "not sufficient to establish that the President committed an obstruction-of-justice offense,"[52] in part because Barr did not believe that a corrupt intent should make an otherwise lawful but obstructive act criminal.

---

48. *Cueto*, 151 F.3d at 631.
49. *Id.*; *see also* United States v. Cintolo, 818 F.2d 980, 991 (1st Cir. 1987).
50. Special Counsel Robert S. Mueller, III, U.S. Dep't of Justice, Report on the Investigation into Russian Interference in the 2016 Presidential Election, Volume II 9 (March 2019).
51. *See id.* at 2.
52. Attorney General Barr's March 24, 2019 Letter to Congress Summarizing the Mueller Report and Finding That Obstruction Could Not Be Charged at 3 [hereinafter Barr Letter].

3. Obstruction of a Non-Crime

Defendants may be guilty of obstruction where they act to impede investigators' inquiry into a matter that turns out not to be criminal, or at least is not charged as such. For example, Martha Stewart was convicted, *inter alia*, of obstruction of justice under § 1505 in connection with her sale of shares of ImClone Systems Inc. stock, allegedly after a "tip" from ImClone's founder. Although convicted of obstruction in connection with the false explanations she offered to the SEC for her stock sale,[53] she was never indicted for the alleged insider trading that spawned the investigation. (Stewart later settled a concurrent SEC civil enforcement action relating to the alleged insider trading.) Similarly, I. Lewis ("Scooter") Libby, while acting as the Chief of Staff for Vice President Cheney, was alleged to have leaked the identity of a covert CIA agent to the press for political purposes. Federal law criminalizes the intentional, unauthorized disclosure of the identity of such agents in certain circumstances, but Libby was not charged for the leak. Instead, Libby was convicted for, *inter alia*, obstruction under § 1503 based on his lies to federal investigators and the grand jury about the leaks.[54] (President Trump later pardoned Libby.)

Note, however, that where the obstructive act impedes the investigation of something that is not alleged or proved to be a crime, the defense may argue that because the defendant knew that he had not committed a crime, his acts were not done with a corrupt intent. Thus, for example, Attorney General Barr, in declining to bring an obstruction case against President Trump, reasoned in part that "the Special Counsel recognized that 'the evidence does not establish that the President was involved in an underlying crime related to Russian election interference,'" and asserted that, "while not determinative, the absence of such evidence bears upon the President's intent with respect to obstruction."[55]

D. Nexus to a Pending or Contemplated Proceeding or Investigation

The government must prove, as an element of these offenses, a nexus, or causal connection, between the obstructive acts and the judicial proceeding (§ 1503), agency proceeding or congressional investigation (§ 1505), or official proceeding (§ 1512(c)). This nexus requirement is not found in the text of the statutes; the Supreme Court created it in *United States v. Aguilar*, 515

53. *See* United States v. Stewart, 433 F.3d 273, 288 (2d Cir. 2006).
54. *See, e.g.*, United States v. Libby, 429 F. Supp.2d 1, 4 (D.D.C. 2006).
55. Barr Letter, *supra* note 51, at 3.

U.S. 593 (1995), to cabin the scope of § 1503 and ensure that individuals have "fair warning" of what the law proscribes.[56]

In *Aguilar*, a judge lied to agents investigating allegations that he tipped the subject of a federal investigation to the fact that the subject was being wiretapped. Although the judge was advised that there was a pending grand jury, the Court concluded that the evidence was insufficient to show that the judge "knew that his false statement would be provided to the grand jury."[57] This, the Court held, was fatal to the government's case because it had failed to prove that the judge's endeavor to corruptly influence, obstruct, or impede the relevant proceeding had the "natural and probable effect" of interfering with the proceeding or investigation.[58] Stated another way, *Aguilar* demands that the obstructive act "have a relationship in time, causation, or logic with the" proceedings at issue.[59] The defendant need not be successful because an "endeavor" (§ 1503, § 1505) or "attempt" (§ 1512(c)(2)) suffices.

Aguilar makes clear that this is an objective inquiry in cases under § 1503 and § 1505.[60] The *Aguilar* Court, responding to the dissent, posited a case in which the defendant aimed to obstruct but it was unlikely that his false statements would in fact be put before a tribunal. The Court concluded that "[t]he intent to obstruct justice is indeed present, but the man's culpability is a good deal less clear from the statute than we usually require in order to impose criminal liability."[61] In short, the nexus test is an objective inquiry into whether the defendant has acted "in a manner that is *likely* to obstruct justice" and "excludes defendants who have an evil purpose but use means that would only unnaturally and improbably be successful."[62]

By contrast, under § 1512, courts have read this nexus test to contain a subjective component, in part because of the lack of a pending proceeding requirement. Demonstrating the required nexus is not unduly speculative under § 1503 and § 1505 because the government must prove that the judicial or grand jury proceeding (§ 1503) or the agency proceeding or congressional inquiry (§ 1505) was pending at the time of the obstructive conduct and that the defendant knew that the proceeding or inquiry was pending. Recall, however, that § 1512(f)(1) states that "[f]or purposes of" Section 1512, "official proceeding[s] need not be pending or about to be instituted at the time of the offense." So how does one demonstrate a causal nexus to a proceeding that does not yet exist?

The circuits concluded that the nexus requirement did not make sense in this context, but they were overruled by the Supreme Court in *Arthur*

56. *Aguilar*, 515 U.S. at 600 (§ 1503).
57. *Id.* at 601.
58. *Id.* at 599.
59. *Id.*
60. *See, e.g.*, United States v. Smith, 831 F.3d 1207, 1216 (9th Cir. 2016).
61. *Aguilar*, 515 U.S. at 602.
62. *Id.* at 601 (emphasis added and internal quotation marks deleted).

Andersen, LLP v. United States, 544 U.S. 696 (2005). The *Arthur Andersen* Court held that the *Aguilar* nexus test applies to a prosecution under § 1512(b)(2). As noted above, it ruled that a proceeding need not be pending, but it must at least be "contemplated." The Court therefore required the government to prove that the defendant's obstructive conduct had the "natural and probable effect" of interfering with a foreseeable or contemplated proceeding or investigation.[63]

Relying on *Arthur Andersen*, the circuits apply the nexus requirement in § 1512(c)(2) cases.[64] Courts applying the nexus requirement in such cases require that the government prove that the defendant at least foresaw an official proceeding,[65] and "knew that his actions were 'likely' to affect it"[66] or that his conduct was "likely to accomplish his intention" of obstructing the contemplated proceeding.[67]

Where a defendant lies to a court or grand jury or otherwise takes action to directly affect the relevant proceeding, the nexus requirement proves no impediment. Similarly, where the defendant is aware that a grand jury subpoena seeks documents—even if he never read the subpoena and does not know of its exact contents—and then acts to put the documents beyond the grand jury's reach, the nexus element is satisfied.[68] Where the nexus requirement creates difficulties for the government is in cases, like *Aguilar*, where the defendant lies to investigators but there is no proof that he knows that his lies will be repeated by the investigator in a qualifying proceeding. In *Aguilar*, for example, the Court ruled that the nexus requirement was not satisfied because "[w]e do not believe that uttering false statements to an investigating agent—and that seems to be all that was proved here—who might or might not testify before a grand jury is sufficient to make out a violation of the catchall provision of § 1503."[69]

E. Specific Intent

Courts read the passages from *Pettibone* and *Aguilar*, quoted above in the context of the "pending proceeding" requirement of § 1503 and § 1505, to require proof that the defendant specifically intended to obstruct justice.[70]

---

63. *See id.*
64. *See, e.g.*, United States v. Young, 916 F.3d 368, 385 (4th Cir. 2019).
65. *See, e.g.*, United States v. Petruk, 781 F.3d 438, 445 (8th Cir. 2015) (the government must prove that the defendant "contemplated a particular, foreseeable proceeding").
66. United States v. Friske, 640 F.3d 1288, 1292 n.5 (11th Cir. 2011).
67. United States v. White Horse, 35 F.4th 1119, 1122 (9th Cir. 2022).
68. *See* United States v. Quattrone, 441 F.3d 153, 171 (2d Cir. 2006).
69. *Aguilar*, 515 U.S. at 600.
70. *See, e.g.*, United States v. Schwartz, 283 F.3d 76, 105-06 (2d Cir. 2002).

In *Arthur Andersen*, the Court talked about "the requisite intent to obstruct"[71] for purposes of § 1512(b). It is not yet clear whether § 1512(c)(2) carries a specific intent requirement, although there is dicta in circuit cases to that effect.[72]

As discussed Chapter 2 (General Part), recognition of a specific intent requirement affects the defenses available to the defendant. It also is important for purposes of crafting appropriate jury instructions but there is some confusion among the circuits regarding the focus of the specific intent requirement. That is, courts differ on just what the defendant must intend: does the government have to prove that the defendant specifically intended *to obstruct* or is it sufficient that the defendant specifically intended *to engage in the conduct alleged to be obstructive* and should have *reasonably foreseen that the natural and probable consequences of his actions would be to obstruct justice?*[73]

The latter instruction is widely used in charging specific intent,[74] but it should not be. It is likely a misapplication of another instruction that has itself been viewed as concerning: "[i]ntent ordinarily cannot be proved directly, because there is no way of fathoming and scrutinizing the operations of the human mind. . . . You may infer that a person ordinarily intends the natural and probable consequences of acts knowingly done or knowingly omitted."[75] While employing the "natural and probable consequences" language in intent charges may be acceptable when phrased as a general invitation to juries to *infer a specific intent to obstruct*,[76] it is obviously not acceptable to the extent it invites a conviction based on the proposition that specific intent is satisfied by proof that a defendant *knowing performed an act* that he *"should have" reasonably foreseen* would naturally and probably result in the obstruction of justice. This reformulation of the standard instruction in effect substitutes a negligence standard for a specific intent requirement.

71. *Arthur Andersen*, 545 U.S. at 708.
72. *See, e.g.*, *Friske*, 640 F.3d at 1291.
73. *See Aguilar*, 515 U.S. at 611 (Scalia, J., concurring in part). If this language sounds familiar it is because the *Aguilar* Court took the "natural and probable consequences" language—which had long been used in this context as an instruction that eased the government's burden in proving intent—and instead used it to create a new and distinct nexus element.
74. *See, e.g.*, United States v. McBride, 362 F.3d 360, 372 (6th Cir. 2004); United States v. Brenson, 104 F.3d 1267, 1277 (11th Cir. 1997).
75. United States v. Haldeman, 559 F.2d 31, 116 n.235 (D.C. Cir. 1976) (quoting D.C. Jury Instructions No. 3.02) (approving but expressing concerns that the instruction is misleading).
76. *See, e.g.*, United States v. Blair, 661 F.3d 755, 766 (4th Cir. 2011).

7. **Obstruction of Justice**

§ 1503	**§ 1505**	**§ 1512(c)(2)**
influencing, obstructing, or impeding a pending federal judicial proceeding	influencing, obstructing, or impeding a pending proceeding before a U.S. agency or the exercise of the power of inquiry in a pending congressional investigation NB: agency proceeding defined broadly to include, e.g., agency investigations	influencing, obstructing, or impeding a federal "official proceeding," that need not be pending but must be "contemplated," including judicial, congressional, or federal agency proceedings NB: agency proceeding defined narrowly to exclude, e.g., FBI investigations
or endeavoring to do so	or endeavoring to do so	or attempting to do so
covered acts broadly defined to include a variety of transitive and intransitive obstruction; includes all the obstructive acts now covered by § 1512(c) and much more	covered acts broadly defined to include a variety of transitive and intransitive obstruction; includes all the obstructive acts now covered by § 1512(c) and much more	(1) impairing the availability or integrity of records, documents, or objects used in an official proceeding in ways other than by "altering, destroying, mutilating, or concealing" them, such as by creating false evidence (e.g., forging a court order); and (2) impairing the availability or integrity of things other than records, documents, or objects — such as witness testimony or intangible information — by altering, destroying, mutilating, or concealing them (e.g., orchestrating the testimony of grand jury witnesses)
corruptly and with specific intent to obstruct	corruptly and with specific intent to obstruct	corruptly; likely requires specific intent to obstruct
Objective nexus test: the jury must decide whether the defendant's endeavor to corruptly, influence, obstruct, or impede had the "natural and probable effect" of interfering with the pending judicial proceeding	Objective nexus test: the jury must decide whether defendant's endeavor to corruptly, influence, obstruct, or impede had the "natural and probable effect" of interfering with the pending congressional investigation or agency proceeding	Subjective nexus test: the defendant contemplated or foresaw an official proceeding and knew that his actions would likely interfere with it

Examples

1. In August 2024, Special Counsel Jack Smith secured a superseding grand jury indictment charging President Trump, *inter alia*, with conspiring to violate § 1512(c)(2). The indictment charged that Trump obstructed a congressional proceeding in the form of the congressional count and certification of electoral votes on January 6, 2021. This charge was not predicated on the violence visited on the Capitol by the rioters. Rather, the indictment charged that Trump and his co-conspirators organized fraudulent slates of electors in seven targeted states (Arizona, Georgia, Michigan, Nevada, New Mexico, Pennsylvania, and Wisconsin), and "then caused these fraudulent electors to transmit their false certificates to the Vice President, in his capacity as President of the Senate, and other government officials to be counted at the certification proceeding on January 6."[77] It further alleged that Trump and his co-conspirators "attempted to convince the Vice President to use the Defendant's fraudulent electors, reject legitimate electoral votes, or send legitimate electoral votes to state legislatures for review rather than counting them."[78] Please explain why a grand jury could conclude that these facts were sufficient to make out a colorable case against Trump under § 1512(c)(2). How about under § 1503 or § 1505?

2. Acme Corporation was under federal investigation by the SEC and the Department of Justice for securities fraud. Acme engaged Marika Traverso to conduct an internal investigation into the alleged misconduct. Acme hoped to fully cooperate with the government's inquiry to secure regulatory leniency from the SEC and a deferred prosecution agreement or declination from the DOJ. Just in case, Traverso sought to protect her work product and cover all her work with the attorney-client privilege to the extent possible, but she knew that the facts that she discovered were likely to be turned over to the DOJ in return for cooperation credit.

   Acme's Vice President, Montezuma Smythe, was alleged to have been at the center of the fraud. Traverso met with Smythe and gave him the so-called "*Upjohn* Warnings" that white-collar lawyers give their corporate client's employees prior to interviewing them. Traverso's warning went as follows: "I represent Acme, not you. What we say is confidential and protected by the attorney-client privilege, and I urge you to keep this conversation to yourself. But you should know that the privilege is held by Acme and that if it decides to waive the privilege in future—for

---

77. United States v. Donald J. Trump, Case 20-cr-257-TSC, Superseding Indictment ¶ 11(b) (D.D.C. Aug. 27, 2024).
78. *Id.* ¶ 11(b).

example to get cooperation credit from the government—it can do so without your input." Smythe lied to Traverso during this interview. Can Smythe be prosecuted under § 1503, § 1505, or § 1512(c)(2)?

3. Lautaro Kayode was a police commander who presided over an interrogation regime in which suspects were routinely tortured. One of his victims, Mary Chang, sought damages in a civil suit for the physical abuse she suffered while in police custody. While discovery in the civil case was underway, Kayode destroyed investigative notes he kept during the course of his service. Can the government proceed against Kayode under § 1503 or § 1512(c)(2)?

Explanations

1. Because § 1503 requires obstruction of a judicial proceeding, it would not apply. Under § 1505, the government must prove that Trump corruptly influenced, obstructed, or impeded "the due and proper exercise of the power of inquiry under which any inquiry or investigation is being had by either House, or any committee of either House or any joint committee of the Congress." In the congressional context, this section is most often used when a defendant lies, or encourages others to lie, in a congressional hearing or investigation; it is less clear that the counting of electoral votes would qualify as an "inquiry or investigation." That is likely one of the reasons why the Special Counsel chose to rely on § 1512(c)(2).

   The federal courts in D.C. had no difficulty finding that the rioters were intending to obstruct a pending "official proceeding"—that is, Congress's electoral vote count and certification. The question is whether *Fischer* now forecloses the government's obstruction charge against Trump under § 1512(c)(2). Recall the Court's statement that "it is possible to violate (c)(2) by creating false evidence—rather than altering incriminating evidence."[79] In the superseding indictment he secured after the *Fischer* decision came down, the Special Counsel emphasized that the "fake" electoral slate certifications were submitted to, among other government officials, the Vice President in his role as President of the Senate with the intention that they be used in the congressional official proceeding. The grand jury likely concluded, then, that the Special Counsel had established probable cause to believe that the co-conspirators created false evidence in the form of the fake slates of electors' votes with corrupt intention to subvert Congress's electoral count proceeding.

79. *Fischer*, 603 U.S. at 491.

2. The first question is whether a qualifying proceeding or investigation is involved. Under § 1512(c)(2), an SEC investigation is unlikely to satisfy the requirement that the "official proceeding" (in the agency context) be adjudicative and relatively formal. But what constitutes an agency proceeding under § 1505 is construed more broadly; thus, the SEC investigation would satisfy § 1505 if it was pending.[80] Under § 1503, if the DOJ has a sitting grand jury, that would satisfy the pending proceeding requirement. Section 1512(c)(2) would be more helpful if the grand jury is not yet seated but obviously contemplated.

   It is unclear whether Smythe's lies constitute a qualifying obstructive act under *Fischer*'s limiting reading of § 1512(c)(2). The *Fischer* Court said that (c)(2) "ensures that liability is still imposed for impairing the availability or integrity of *other* things used in an official proceeding beyond the "record[s], document[s], or other object[s]" enumerated in (c)(1), such as witness testimony or intangible information."[81] But such "other things" must be "destroy[ed], mutilate[ed], or conceal[ed]." It is not clear whether Smythe could be charged with "conceal[ing]" his own testimony under this subsection. His lies would certainly qualify as obstructive acts under § 1503, however, and, if shared with a pending grand jury, could certainly influence or obstruct the due administration of justice. Smythe is acting corruptly by lying and therefore acting with an improper purpose—to subvert the investigation; he is also acting knowingly and dishonestly and with the intent to benefit himself by hiding his misdeeds.

   The government may struggle if the court were to give an instruction requiring proof that Smythe specifically intended to obstruct justice; the defense may successfully suggest to the jury that it was more likely that he was lying to company counsel to keep his job. Note, however, that at least in the Ninth Circuit, the government may request a jury instruction that states that "[t]he government need not prove that the defendant's sole or even primary intention was to obstruct justice so long as the government proves beyond a reasonable doubt that one of the defendant's intentions was to obstruct justice."[82] The government would fare better were the court to adopt the alternative instruction discussed (and criticized) above; it only requires that the government prove that the Smythe specifically intended to engage in the conduct alleged to be obstructive and should have reasonably foreseen that the natural and probable consequences of his actions would be the obstruction of justice.

   Where the case would likely falter is in proof of the *Aguilar* nexus requirement although, before *Fischer*, prosecutors successfully brought a

80. *See, e.g.*, *Quattrone*, 441 F.3d at 174-75.
81. *Fischer*, 603 U.S. at 491 (emphasis original).
82. Ninth Circuit Instructions, supra note 29, 19.3; *see also* *Smith*, 831 F.3d at 1217-19.

number of cases under § 1512(c)(2) on similar facts. The causal nexus appears both indirect (that is, the false statement was made to company counsel) and contingent (it rests on the likelihood that the company will cooperate with the government and share the false statement with it). In particular, it does not appear that the company has yet agreed to cooperate or share information with the government. Under § 1512(c)(2), the nexus requirement has a subjective component; the jury would be asked to decide whether the *Upjohn* warning was sufficient to show that the defendant knew or should have known of the official proceedings and that his actions were likely to affect it.

In the cases that the DOJ brought on analogous facts, federal prosecutors contended in response to such defense objections that there was an obvious "nexus" between the executives' lies to corporate counsel and the official proceedings (grand jury and the SEC investigations) at issue because the defendants knew or believed that the corporation was cooperating or might cooperate with the government and, in so doing, intended or at least contemplated that counsel would turn over the defendants' false or misleading statements to the grand jury and SEC. The lies would have the "natural and probable" effect on these proceedings because, in this context, private counsel was working as "an arm of the [government]" while conducting their nominally private investigations on behalf of the entity.[83] In one case in which the government also alleged the defendants had lied directly to the SEC, the defendants pleaded guilty to obstruction under § 1512(c)(2) and their pleas were upheld on appeal.[84] Another court upheld the government's theory that lying to corporate counsel where the defendant believed that corporate counsel would be turning over his statements to the government could have the requisite causal nexus to obstruction of an "official proceeding."[85] The defendant went to trial, during which the court dismissed the obstruction count without explanation.

3. Both § 1503 and § 1512(c)(2) apply to judicial proceedings, whether they are civil cases or criminal matters. This hypothetical is a reminder of the degree to which obstruction cases can be brought for misconduct (e.g., lies, document concealment or destruction) occurring during civil discovery.[86] It is designed to illustrate as well that a nexus can exist where the obstructive conduct takes place well before an actual trial. Pre-*Fischer*, a number of circuits upheld convictions under § 1512(c)(2) where

83. United States v. Singleton, Crim. Action No. H-06-080, 2006 WL 1984467, at *6 (S.D. Tex. July 14, 2006).
84. *See* United States v. Kumar, 617 F.3d 612 (2d Cir. 2010).
85. *See Singleton*, 2006 WL 1984467, at *6.
86. *See, e.g.*, United States v. Burge, 711 F.3d 803 (7th Cir. 2013).

the obstructive conduct took place long before any official proceeding, for example in cases in which the defendant tipped off targets of an investigation that a search warrant was about to be executed or where a defendant disclosed an undercover officer's identity to the investigatory subject.[87]

Here, the lawsuit had been filed so a proceeding was pending, and Kayode knew it; § 1503, then, is satisfied. There was certainly an obstructive act that works for purposes of either § 1503 or § 1512(c)(1) (but not (c)(2)): destroying documents. And Kayode acted with a corrupt intent given that he had an improper motive, acted knowingly and dishonesty, and no doubt had a consciousness that what he was doing was wrong Any nexus requirement is satisfied in that the natural and probable result of his document destruction was to obstruct the factfinding and fair adjudication of issues in the civil suit and he was aware of this fact.

II. WITNESS TAMPERING UNDER 18 U.S.C. § 1512(b)

In 1982, Congress removed the express references to intimidating or influencing witnesses in § 1503 and § 1505 and created § 1512. When originally enacted, § 1512 was not intended to safeguard against any type of corrupt conduct that might threaten to derail official proceedings; that was the job of the Omnibus Clauses of § 1503 and § 1505. It was aimed at preventing witness tampering, specifically with protecting witnesses and their safety. Thus, § 1512 originally contained provisions prohibiting tampering with witnesses by killing, intimidation, physical force, threats, misleading conduct, or harassment.[88] With the exception of misleading conduct, all the activities proscribed by the 1982 incarnation of § 1512 involved some element of coercion. This provision did not cover all the non-coercive types of witness tampering that courts had, prior to 1982, recognized as falling within the § 1503's and § 1505's Omnibus Clauses and that were often the subject of white-collar cases.

White-collar witness tampering often involves either misleading potential witnesses or corruptly persuading them to engage in obstruction. Section 1512 covered misleading conduct but not corrupt persuasion. Even after passage of § 1512, then, prosecutors successfully continued to invoke § 1503 to address non-coercive witness tampering such as efforts to urge a witness to give false testimony or withhold or destroy evidence. In 1988, Congress responded to this perceived gap, amending § 1512(b) to add

87. *See, e.g.*, *id.* at 810 (collecting cases).
88. *See* Victim and Witness Protection Act, Pub. L. No. 97-291, 96 Stat. 1249 (1982).

the "corruptly persuades" language. The courts of appeals have uniformly rejected defendants' argument that this constituted an implied repeal of § 1503's and § 1505's coverage of non-coercive witness tampering.[89]

As we have seen, § 1503, § 1505, and § 1512(c)(2) contain a requirement that the government prove that the defendant acted "corruptly," which ensures that juries find that the defendant at least acted with an "improper purpose" in engaging in the conduct alleged to be obstructive. But witness tampering prosecutions under § 1512(b) are different in purpose and effect. Instead of broad prohibition on *any type of activity done with a corrupt intent* that has a nexus to a judicial or official proceeding (§ 1503, § 1505, and, formerly, § 1512(c)(2)), §1512(b) focuses more narrowly on *specific types of presumptively wrongful conduct* through which physical evidence can be compromised or witnesses tampered with.

In short, in witness tampering cases, § 1512(b) *is said to change the focus from corrupt motives to presumptively corrupt methods*. Many of the methods proscribed in § 1512 are inarguably independently wrongful and do not require a corrupt mens rea for jurors to recognize them as such; these would include the use of killing, intimidation, physical force, threats, misleading conduct, or harassment. Where tampering through persuasion is alleged, however, the line between presumptively wrongful conduct and otherwise unobjectionable conduct may be harder to draw. For example, many would argue that defense lawyers regularly attempt to use "persuasion" to "influence" or "impede" investigations or prosecutions on behalf of their clients. That is why, under § 1512(b), only one of the proscribed activities—persuasion—requires proof of a "corrupt" motive. It is also why, as we shall see, Congress added safe harbors designed to protect legitimate defense advocacy.

In sum, where the government wishes to address witness tampering, it has, if appropriate on the facts, a number of charging options:

(1) Section 1512(b), which, in relevant part, provides that persons are liable for

- knowingly
- *corruptly persuad[ing]* another person, or attempt[ing] to do so, *or engag[ing] in misleading conduct* toward another person
- with the intent to

    (1) influence, delay or prevent the testimony of any person in a federal official proceeding

    (2) cause or induce any person to (A) withhold testimony, or withhold a record, document, or other object, from an official proceeding; (B) alter, destroy, mutilate, or conceal an object with intent to impair the object's integrity or availability for

89. *See, e.g.*, *Sampson*, 898 F.3d at 302; *see also Aguilar*, 515 U.S. at 615-16 (Scalia, J. dissenting).

use in an official proceeding; (C) evade legal process summoning that person to appear as a witness, or to produce a record, document, or other object, in an official proceeding; or (D) be absent from an official proceeding to which such person has been summoned by legal process or

(3) hinder, delay, or prevent the communication to a law enforcement officer or judge of the United States of information relating to the commission or possible commission of a federal crime.

- where there is a qualifying nexus between the obstructive conduct a contemplated federal official proceeding

(2) Section 1512(c)(2), which, as construed by the *Fischer* Court, imposes liability for impairing the availability and integrity of things used in an official proceeding other than "record[s], document[s], or other object[s]," "such as witness testimony or intangible information," by altering, destroying, mutilating, or concealing them.[90] The Court cited as an example of this use witness tampering, that is, a case in which a defendant attempted to orchestrate a witness's grand jury testimony.[91]

(3) Sections 1503 and 1505 prohibit corruptly influencing, obstructing, or impeding pending judicial or agency proceedings or congressional inquiries or investigations. The circuits uniformly hold that these sections apply to non-coercive witness tampering, that is, using corrupt persuasion or misleading conduct to take actions such as those identified in § 1512(b)(1)-(3).

Because we have already discussed the elements of §§ 1503, 1505, and 1512(c)(2), this section is confined in its coverage to § 1512(b).

A. Official Proceeding and Nexus

As discussed above, because, for purposes of § 1512, an "official proceeding" need not be pending or about to be instituted at the time of the allegedly obstructive conduct, the statute obviously cannot require actual knowledge of a pending proceeding as do § 1503 and § 1505. Despite this, proof of a nexus to a foreseeable or contemplated proceeding must be shown. And this nexus requirement contains a subjective element requiring proof that the defendant foresaw or contemplated a qualifying proceeding and knew that his actions were likely to affect it.[92]

90. *Fischer*, 603 U.S. at 491.
91. *Id.* (citing *Mintmire*, 507 F.3d at 1290).
92. *See* United States v. Shavers, 693 F.3d 363, 378 (3d Cir. 2012) (nexus requirement applies to § 1512(b)(1) as well as § 1512(b)(2)), *vacated on other grounds*, 570 U.S. 913 (2013).

B. Corrupt Persuasion

"Persuasion" is the only means of witness tampering in § 1512(b) that requires proof of a "corrupt" intent in addition to § 1512(b)'s general "knowing" mens rea. In *Arthur Andersen*, the company was charged with "knowingly corruptly persuading" other persons—that is, its own employees—with the intent to cause those persons to withhold documents from, or alter documents for use in, an official proceeding.[93] The Supreme Court reversed the company's conviction in part because the jury instructions regarding the "knowingly corruptly" mens rea "failed to convey the requisite consciousness of wrongdoing" required for a conviction under § 1512(b).[94] In so holding, the *Arthur Andersen* Court interpreted both "knowingly" and "corruptly." "Knowledge" and "knowingly," the Court said, are "normally associated with awareness, understanding, or consciousness," and "[c]orrupt" and "corruptly" "are normally associated with wrongful, immoral, depraved, or evil."[95] Taken together, "[o]nly persons conscious of wrongdoing can be said to 'knowingly. . . corruptly persuad[e].' "[96]

"Corrupt persuasion" need not be coercive or intimidating; it does not even need to involve an "emotional appeal" or "persistent pleading."[97] It is sufficient to induce, ask, argue, or give reasons, or to coach or remind a witness to attest to facts the defendant and the witness both know are false.

1. Corruptly Persuading to Withhold Testimony

Under § 1512(b), one can be liable for corruptly influencing another with the intent to:

> (2) cause or induce any person to—
>
> (A) *withhold testimony*, or withhold a record, document, or other object, from an official proceeding; or
>
> (3) *hinder, delay, or prevent the communication* to a law enforcement officer or judge of the United States of information relating to the commission or possible commission of a federal crime.

The circuit courts are split on what is required to secure a conviction for corruptly persuading a witness to *withhold* testimony from an official

93. *See Arthur Andersen*, 544 U.S. at 702.
94. *Id.* at 706.
95. *Id.* at 705.
96. *Id.* at 706.
97. United States v. Sparks, 791 F.3d 1188, 1192 (10th Cir. 2015).

proceeding under § 1512(b)(2)(A) or to *hinder reports* to law enforcement under § 1512(b)(3).[98]

In *United States v. Farrell*, 126 F.3d 484 (3d Cir. 1997), the Third Circuit was concerned that, absent greater definition, the "corruptly persuades" language of § 1512(b) is unconstitutionally vague. It reasoned that, given the Supreme Court's insistence that courts should give meaning to all statutory terms, the phrase "corruptly persuades" cannot mean the same thing as the elements of "caus[ing] or induc[ing] any person to . . . withhold testimony" (§ 1512(b)(2)(A)) or persuading "with the intent to hinder communication to law enforcement" (§ 1512(b)(3)) because such an interpretation would render the word "corruptly" meaningless.[99]

Accordingly, the *Farrell* court ruled that "more culpability is required for a statutory violation than that involved in the act of attempting to discourage disclosure in order to hinder an investigation."[100] That "more culpability" is present when a defendant uses obviously unlawful means. Where, for example, a defendant bribes someone to withhold evidence or uses coercive means to do so, the "corruptly" element would be satisfied. But the culpable conduct that violates the "corruptly persuades" clause "does not include [] noncoercive attempt[s] to persuade a co-conspirator who enjoys a Fifth Amendment right not to disclose self-incriminating information about the conspiracy to refrain, in accordance with that right, from volunteering information to investigators."[101] Some courts believe that this rule may only apply where some legitimate privilege exists, although the Third Circuit's statutory construction argument is not limited to such cases.[102]

The Ninth Circuit agrees with the Third Circuit,[103] but the Eleventh and Second Circuits do not.[104] The Eleventh Circuit concluded that the term "corruptly," defined as with an "improper purpose," is not vague and declined to "follow the Third Circuit's lead in imposing a requirement for an additional level of culpability."[105] It argued that "[b]y prohibiting only that persuasion which has an improper purpose, Section 1512(b) does not impermissibly limit protected speech, and provides adequate notice that

---

98. *See, e.g.*, United States v. Bernhardt, 903 F.3d 818, 826 (8th Cir. 2018) (discussing split).
99. *See Farrell*, 126 F.3d at 487.
100. *Id.* at 489.
101. *Id.* at 488.
102. *See id.* at 489 n.3 (noting that "[i]n the absence of a privilege, society has the right to the information of citizens regarding the commission of crime, and it can be argued that discouraging another who possessed no privilege from honoring this civic duty involves some culpability not present when co-conspirators with Fifth Amendment privileges converse"); United States v. Chujoy, 207 F. Supp. 3d 626, 641-42 (W.D. Va. 2016), *aff'd*, 887 F.3d 166, 173-74 & n.3 (4th Cir. 2018).
103. *See* United States v. Doss, 630 F.3d 1181, 1189 (9th Cir. 2010).
104. *See* United States v. Shotts, 145 F.3d 1289, 1300-01 (11th Cir. 1998); United States v. Thompson, 76 F.3d 442, 452-53 (2d Cir. 1996).
105. *Shotts*, 145 F.3d at 1301.

such persuasion is proscribed."[106] The Second Circuit agrees, holding that one can violate § 1512 by suggesting to a co-conspirator that he invoke his Fifth Amendment privilege where the defendant had a self-interested "improper purpose" in making the suggestion—that is, to ensure the witness did not implicate him.[107] In the Eleventh and Second Circuits, then, corruptly persuading a witness to withhold evidence "with an improper purpose"—whether or not the witness has a legal right to do so—would suffice to establish liability.

C. Misleading Conduct

With respect to "misleading conduct," Congress defined this term in 18 U.S.C. § 1515(a)(3) as follows:

(A) knowingly making a false statement
(B) intentionally omitting information from a statement and thereby causing a portion of such statement to be misleading, or intentionally concealing a material fact, and thereby creating a false impression by such statement
(C) with intent to mislead, knowingly submitting or inviting reliance on a writing or recording that is false, forged, altered, or otherwise lacking in authenticity
(D) with intent to mislead, knowingly submitting or inviting reliance on a sample, specimen, map, photograph, boundary mark, or other object that is misleading in a material respect; or
(E) knowingly using a trick, scheme, or device with intent to mislead

Note that, to be liable for witness tampering through "misleading conduct" addressed to a witness, the government need only show that the defendant acted knowingly. There is no requirement that the government also show that he acted "corruptly." Note, too, that while § 1512(b) covers those who "corruptly persuade another person, *or attempt to do so*," it does not expressly provide for attempt liability with respect to "engaging in misleading conduct toward another person."

The distinction between "corruptly persuading" someone and knowingly "misleading" someone is an important one. "*Misleading conduct*" applies to conduct that is *intended to mislead the witness, not to mislead the government*. If a witness *knows* that the defendant is encouraging him or her to tell a false story, this is not a case in which the defendant is "misleading" the witness; rather, it is a case of corrupt persuasion.

106. *Id.*
107. *See, e.g.*, United States v. Gotti, 459 F.3d 296, 342-43 (2d Cir. 2006).

The most obvious case of misleading conduct is where a defendant tells a witness a false story as though it is true, intending that the witness believe the phony tale and, for example, repeat it in the grand jury. There is no "out" under the statute for defendants who falsely deny guilt to family, friends, and associates who may be potential witnesses.

D. Hindering Reports to Law Enforcement Relating to a Federal Offense Under 18 U.S.C. § 1512(b)(3)

Section 1512(b)(3) renders liable those who

- knowingly
- *corruptly persuade* another person, or attempt to do so, *or engage in misleading conduct* toward *another person*
- with the intent to
- hinder, delay, or prevent the communication to a law enforcement officer or judge of the United States of information relating to the commission or possible commission of a federal offense or a violation of conditions of probation supervised release, parole, or release pending judicial proceedings

With respect to violations of § 1512(b)(3) founded on corrupt persuasion, the same circuit split discussed above applies; thus, in the Eleventh and Second Circuits a violation can be proven upon proof that the defendant acted with an "improper motive" in persuading a witness to withhold information from federal officials. But in the Third and Ninth Circuits simply persuading a witness to withhold information with an improper motive will not suffice to satisfy the "corrupt" intent requirement; rather, the government must show that the defendant used improper means, such as bribing the witness, in order to persuade him not to make a report to federal law enforcement.

Of all the acts proscribed in § 1512(b), only § 1512(b)(3) does not require that the allegedly obstructive activity take place in the context of a contemplated "official proceeding." Under § 1512(b)(3), the defendant must have committed the obstructive conduct with the intent to "hinder, delay, or prevent" communication to a federal law enforcement officer or judge of information relating to the commission or *possible* commission of a federal crime. This section does not depend on the existence or immanency of a federal case or investigation but rather on the *possible* existence of a federal crime and the defendant's efforts to derail any inquiry.[108]

---

108. *See, e.g.*, United States v. Carson, 560 F.3d 566, 580-81 (6th Cir. 2009).

The defendant also need not intend specifically to hinder a possible *federal* inquiry. Section 1512(g) provides that "no state of mind need be proved with respect to the circumstance" that the official proceeding is federal in nature or that the law enforcement officer or judge the defendant intends to thwart is a federal officer or judge.

The nexus inquiry articulated in *Aguilar*—that an individual has "knowledge that his actions are likely to affect the judicial proceeding"[109]—does not apply to § 1512(b)(3) because no such proceeding need be proved or even contemplated.[110] But the Supreme Court imposed a nexus requirement of a different kind in *Fowler v. United States*, 563 U.S. 668 (2011), a case charged under § 1512(a)(1)(C), which involved the same conduct—hindering communications to federal law enforcement—but by different means—killing the witness rather using corrupt persuasion or misleading conduct.

In *Fowler*, the Court recognized that when the defendant has in mind a particular law enforcement official to whom he fears the victim may communicate and that official is a federal officer, the application of the statute is clear, whether or not the defendant actually knows that the officer is employed by the federal government. But the more common case may involve a defendant who fears that the witness will report to *some* law enforcement agency in general rather than to any particular person or entity. And in many if not most cases, the defendant has been successful in obstructing the witness's communication to law enforcement, so there is no proof that the communication was made to any federal law enforcement officer.

In such cases, the *Fowler* Court instructed that the government "need not show *beyond a reasonable doubt* (or even that it is *more likely than not*) that the hypothetical communication would have been to a federal officer."[111] Rather, to establish the required federal nexus, the "Government must show *a reasonable likelihood* that, had, e.g., the victim communicated with law enforcement officers, at least one relevant communication would have been made to a federal law enforcement officer."[112] It need only show that the likelihood of the victim communicating with a federal officer was "more than remote, outlandish, or simply hypothetical."[113] In sum, because the statute specifies that the defendant is obstructing a hypothetical communication to a law enforcement officer of the United States, § 1512(b)(3) requires that the government show "a reasonable likelihood that the victim would have communicated with a *federal officer*, not a state or local officer."[114]

---

109. *Aguilar*, 515 U.S. at 599.
110. *See* United States v. Byrne, 435 F.3d 16, 24-25 (1st Cir. 2006).
111. *Fowler*, 563 U.S at 674 (emphasis original).
112. *Id.* at 677 (emphasis original).
113. *Id.* at 678.
114. United States v. Snyder, 865 F.3d 490, 496 (7th Cir. 2017) (emphasis original).

One issue that has arisen with some frequency is whether corrupt persuasion or misleading conduct addressed to state or local police can constitute misleading "another person" within meaning of the statute. Courts agree that the words "another person" are not restricted to civilian witnesses and can include members of state law enforcement, assuming that the other requisites of the statute are met. For example, the First Circuit upheld the conviction under § 1512(b)(3) of two jail guards who fabricated an incident report and made false statements to investigators from the sheriff's department, and the sheriff's report, "containing the false statements, was subsequently obtained by the FBI."[115]

E. Safe Harbors Under 18 U.S.C. §§ 1512(e), 1515(c)

There are two provisions—18 U.S.C. § 1512(e) and § 1515(c)—that are intended to safeguard lawyers from prosecution for allegedly "obstructive" activities related to legitimate advocacy.

The first, § 1512(e) provides an affirmative defense as to which the defendant bears the burden of proof by a preponderance of the evidence. This section only provides protection for those prosecuted under § 1512. Under § 1512(e), a person may lawfully engage in the prohibited means of influencing testimony or withholding documents if his conduct "consisted solely of lawful conduct and . . . the defendant's sole intention was to encourage, induce, or cause the other person to testify truthfully."[116]

The second safe harbor, § 1515(c), provides: "This chapter does not prohibit or punish the providing of lawful, bona fide, legal representation services in connection with or anticipation of an official proceeding." The "chapter" referred to includes §§ 1503, 1505, 1510, 1512, 1519, and 1520. Courts agree that § 1515(c)'s "safe harbor" for legitimate attorney advocacy activities negates the specific intent element of the statute. It is treated as an affirmative defense that the defendant must raise, but because the defense goes to the intent element of the statute, the burden of proof as to its non-applicability is on the government.[117]

Examples

1. Kauan Ngo owns a business that has, with other local firms, engaged in a price-fixing scheme. He heard from another participant in the scheme, Kenojuak Duguay, that the government was investigating and that Duguay had received a grand jury subpoena. Ngo immediately began shredding

115. United States v. Bailey, 405 F.3d 102, 107 n.1 (1st Cir. 2005).
116. *See, e.g.*, United States v. Cruzado-Laureano, 404 F.3d 470, 487 (1st Cir. 2005).
117. *See* United States v. Kloess, 251 F.3d 941, 948-49 (11th Cir. 2001).

documents and deleting incriminating computer files and emails. He asked his business partner, Charity O'Shea, to help him get rid of these materials and she did so. A few days later, two FBI agents stopped by to talk to Ngo but he told them he was too busy to chat. After the FBI agents left, O'Shea asked him what she should do if the FBI tried to talk to her. She later testified in the grand jury that Ngo "said just not to say anything and I wasn't going to be bothered." Can Ngo be charged under § 1503 or § 1512(b) for this conduct?

2. Damien Langlais represented Donagh Sweeney, who had been charged with conspiring to commit money laundering. The government was interested in securing Sweeney's cooperation against his co-conspirators. Langlais believed, incorrectly as it turned out, that Sweeney was better off taking the case to trial and so advised Sweeney to resist the government's overtures and to take the Fifth in the grand jury. Can Langlais be prosecuted under § 1512(b)?

3. Recall Example 2 at the conclusion of Section I, above, regarding lies Acme's vice president, Montezuma Smythe, made to outside counsel to Acme, Marika Traverso, in the course of Traverso's internal investigation. Can Smythe be prosecuted under § 1512(b)?

Explanations

1. There is a pending judicial proceeding—the grand jury—and Ngo knows it. This satisfies both § 1503 and § 1512. At the outset, we should note that Ngo himself had not yet received a grand jury subpoena. Many people, including some lawyers, mistakenly believe that if a person destroys documents or attempts to subvert witness testimony *before* a subpoena or court order issues, that person cannot be prosecuted for obstruction under § 1503. So long as there is proof that a defendant knows of the pending proceeding, however, "the law is clear that neither a subpoena nor a court order directing the production of documents must be issued or served as a prerequisite to a § 1503 prosecution, and that the concealment and destruction of documents likely to be sought by subpoena is actionable under the statute."[118]

   Ngo's Document Destruction: Section 1512(b) applies to witness tampering (transitive obstruction), and because we are presently discussing Ngo's personal document destruction (intransitive obstruction), it does not apply. Rather, this kind of intransitive document destruction could

118. *See, e.g.*, *Lundwall*, 1 F. Supp. 2d at 254.

be addressed under § 1503 or, as we shall see *infra*, § 1512(c)(1) and § 1519. We know that the basic elements of § 1503 would be satisfied. There is a pending official judicial proceeding in the form of a sitting grand jury looking into the matter, and Ngo knew it. Ngo knew that the grand jury was investigating the price-fixing and in fact initiated his obstruction upon hearing that one of his co-conspirators received a subpoena. He acted "corruptly" by any definition: he acted with an improper purpose, dishonestly, and with a consciousness that he knew what he was doing was wrong. He clearly specifically intended to obstruct the grand jury investigation by destroying evidence. The objective and subjective components of the nexus test are satisfied because the natural and probable effect of his document destruction would be to make this information—which he clearly thought would be damaging—unavailable to the grand jury, and Ngo knew that.

O'Shea's Document Destruction: We are now focusing on whether Ngo can be charged with inducing O'Shea to obstruct—that is, with transitive obstruction. This case could be brought under § 1503 because its elements are satisfied (see above discussion) and § 1503 continues to be available to prosecutors to address witness tampering even after the enactment of § 1512.

Under § 1512(b)'s witness tampering provisions, Ngo would be liable for knowingly corruptly persuading O'Shea with the intent to cause or induce her to destroy objects with intent to impair their integrity or availability for use in an official proceeding (§ 1512(b)(2)(B)). It would seem that his conduct would satisfy any definition of "corruptly." Because O'Shea was his business partner, she assumedly knew why they were destroying the records, so this falls under corrupt persuasion, rather than misleading conduct. The fact that she might have been equally complicit in the price-fixing is irrelevant; he asked her to destroy the documents and computer files and she did so.

Ngo's Statement to O'Shea: Again, this presents a potential case of witness tampering. For the above reasons, a case could be charged under § 1503. Ngo could also be charged with "corruptly persuading" O'Shea with the intent to

- cause or induce that person to withhold testimony in a federal official proceeding (§ 1512(b)(2)(A))
- hinder, delay, or prevent the communication to a federal officer of information relating to the possible commission of a federal crime (§ 1512(b)(3)).

As noted above, most of the elements of a § 1512 case are satisfied on the facts. But the case faces two potential problems. First, whether the case succeeds depends on where it is brought because there is a decided circuit split on what is required to show that efforts to persuade another witness to *withhold* evidence are actionable under §§ 1512(b)(2)(A) or 1512(b)(3). This hypothetical was drawn from *United States v. Shotts*, 145 F.3d 1289 (11th Cir. 1998), in which the Eleventh Circuit held that proof of an improper purpose sufficed. Other circuits carve out an exception for defendants who persuade witnesses not to provide testimony, at least where the witnesses have a legal right to avoid cooperating with law enforcement. In the latter circuits, unless a defendant uses corrupt means (such as bribery), he does violate § 1512 if he merely encourages such witnesses to remain silent—even if the defendant intends to hinder a criminal investigation.[119]

The second problem with this case is the thinness of the evidence that Ngo was corruptly persuading O'Shea to withhold testimony or avoid communicating with law enforcement. This hypothetical illustrates that persons seeking to persuade others to obstruct justice often are conscious that their conduct is wrongful and thus use subtle or equivocal language in doing so. Ngo would assert that O'Shea's testimony proves only that O'Shea asked him about talking to the FBI and that he observed that if she did not talk with them, she would not be bothered. This is insufficient to prove that he threatened or intimidated her, offered her any inducement, or persuaded her in any way not to talk to the FBI. The government would respond that the use of the term "bother" referred to the possibility that she would be prosecuted for her role in the price fixing scheme or the evidence destruction. His comment was an attempt to frighten her into not talking to the FBI.

In the actual case from which this hypothetical was derived, a boss gave the advice quoted above to his secretary. The jury was charged that they had to find that the defendant acted "corruptly," meaning that he acted "'knowingly and dishonestly with the specific intent to subvert or undermine the integrity or truth-seeking ability of an investigation by a federal law enforcement officer.'"[120] The court affirmed the defendant's conviction under § 1512(b)(3), concluding that "[w]hile not overwhelming, the jury could reasonably have inferred from this testimony that [the defendant] was attempting with an improper motive to persuade [his secretary] not to talk to the FBI."[121]

2. This case would fail for at least two reasons. First, this is persuasion, but it is not "corrupt" persuasion because it is not done for an improper

119. *See, e.g.*, *Doss*, 630 F.3d at 1189-90.
120. *Shotts*, 145 F.3d at 1301 (quoting jury instructions).
121. *Id.*

purpose. Langlais may have been mistaken—may even have committed malpractice—but he did not act out of self-interest or consciousness that what he was doing was wrong. Second, Langlais could claim the safe harbor of § 1515(c) because his were lawful, bona fide, legal representation services in connection with or anticipation of an official proceeding.

3. We potentially have a choice of "proceedings" to charge. First, an agency (SEC) proceeding is pending. But an "official proceeding" in the agency context under § 1512 is construed to require that some sort of formal agency adjudication be involved; a mere investigation such as this would not suffice.

   Second, we know that the DOJ is involved but we do not yet know if a grand jury has been convened. That does not matter under § 1512: the grand jury need not be pending at the time of the false statement under § 1512(b) as long as it is contemplated, as is likely true here.

   The theory would be that Smythe knowingly engaged in misleading conduct with the intention to "influence" the testimony of company counsel in a federal official proceeding (§ 1512(b)(1)). Smythe "knowingly" engaged in misleading conduct because he "knowingly made a false statement" to company counsel (§ 1515(a)(3)(A)). Proceeding under a "misleading" conduct theory does not require proof of a corrupt intent. Smythe actually communicated his lies, so this is not an unauthorized "attempt." Again, the case would probably turn on whether the government could prove the nexus element—that is, that the defendant's lies had the "natural and probable" effect of interfering with a contemplated grand jury inquiry (objective component) and that he knew that this would be the case (subjective component).

III. PROHIBITIONS OF THE DESTRUCTION, ETC. OF RECORDS AND OBJECTS UNDER 18 U.S.C. §§ 1512(c), 1519, 1520

As discussed above, the Sarbanes-Oxley Act of 2002 was enacted in response to the corporate accounting scandals of the day, the implosion of Enron, and the Arthur Andersen shredding scandal. Prosecutors' attempt to find a charge with which to prosecute Arthur Andersen for destroying Enron-related audit papers revealed a critical gap in the U.S. Code.

In reaction to these pleading difficulties, Congress passed two provisions addressed to the conduct alleged in the Arthur Andersen case: 18 U.S.C. § 1512(c)(1) (Destruction, Alternation or Concealment of Documents of

Objects in Relation to an Official Proceeding) and § 1519 (Destruction, Alteration, or Falsification of Federal Investigation or Bankruptcy Records). Finally, Congress added 18 U.S.C. § 1520, which is specifically addressed to the destruction of corporate audit records.

Where a defendant alters, destroys, mutilates, conceals, falsifies, or makes a false entry into, documents, records, or other objects or otherwise acts to impair their integrity or availability, the government has, depending on the facts, a variety of options:

(1) Section 1512(c)(1) proscribes "corruptly alter[ing], mutilat[ing], or conceal[ing] a record, document, or other object . . . with the intent to impair the object's integrity or availability for use" in congressional, judicial, or agency official proceedings;

(2) In *Fischer*, Supreme Court read the Omnibus Clause of § 1512(c)(2) narrowly in light of (c)(1), so it now outlaws corruptly impairing the availability or integrity of records, documents, or objects in ways other than by altering, destroying, mutilating, or concealing them, or impairing the availability and integrity of things other than records, document, or other objects through alteration, destruction, mutilation, or concealment;

(3) Section 1519 criminalizes "knowingly alter[ing], destroy[ing], or mutilat[ing], conceal[ing], cover[ing] up, falsif[ying], or mak[ing] a false entry in any record, document, or tangible object with the intent to impede, obstruct, or influence the investigation or proper administration of any matter within the jurisdiction of any department or agency of the United States . . . or in relation to or contemplation of any such matter or case";

(4) Sections 1503 and 1505 prohibit corruptly influencing, obstructing, or impeding pending judicial or agency proceedings or congressional inquiries or investigations by the same means.

We have already covered §§ 1503 and 1505. We therefore will focus in this section on §§ 1512(c)(1), 1512(c)(2) as amended by the Supreme Court, 1519, and 1520.

A. Alteration, Destruction, Mutilation or Concealment of Records, Documents, or Objects Under 18 U.S.C. § 1512(c)

To be liable under § 1512(c)(1), the defendant must

- corruptly
- alter, destroy, mutilate, or conceal

- a record, document, or other object, or attempt to do so
- with the intent to impair the object's integrity or availability for use
- in a federal official proceeding

Given that the *Fischer* Court restricted the scope of § 1512(c)(2) by reference to (c)(1), one assumes that to make out a § 1512(c)(2) case after *Fischer*, the defendant must

- corruptly either
  - alter, destroy, mutilate, or conceal something other than a "record, document, or other object" or
  - impair the integrity or availability for use of things other than records, documents, or other objects by altering, destroying, mutilating, or concealing them
- with the intent to impair the evidence's integrity or availability for use
- in a federal official proceeding

The penalty for violating § 1512(c) is a fine, up to twenty years' imprisonment, or both.

As discussed above, § 1512 applies to a range of "official proceedings," including judicial, agency, and congressional proceedings, but the term "proceedings" has been read to require some degree of formality in the adjudication of a particular matter in the agency context. Such official proceedings need not be pending, but they must be foreseeable or contemplated. Both subsections require proof of a corrupt intent; § 1512(c)(1) also requires proof of an intent to impair the integrity or availability of the impaired object in an official proceeding; assumedly § 1512(c)(2) has a similar proof requirement given the Court's *Fischer* analysis.

It is worth noting that an "object" for purposes of 1512(c) has been broadly defined. Indeed, prosecutions under § 1512(c)(1) have regularly involved the destruction of "objects"—including physical evidence like guns and drugs—other than business records.[122] As we shall see, *infra*, the Supreme Court has approved such prosecutions under § 1512(c)(1) while limiting the scope of the term "tangible object" in § 1519 prosecutions to objects that are used to record or preserve information.[123]

122. *See, e.g.*, United States v. Johnson, 655 F.3d 594, 604 (7th Cir. 2011).
123. *See Yates*, 574 U.S. at 532.

B. Alteration, Destruction, or Falsification, etc. of Records, Documents and Tangible Objects Under 18 U.S.C. § 1519

A defendant is liable under 18 U.S.C. §1519 when he

- knowingly
- alters, destroys, mutilates, conceals, covers up, falsifies, or makes a false entry in any record, document, or *tangible object*
- with the intent to impede, obstruct, or influence the investigation or proper administration of any matter within the jurisdiction of *any department or agency of the United States* or any [bankruptcy] case filed under Title 11, or in relation to or contemplation of any such matter or case.

Section 1519 does not contain a materiality requirement.[124] Those found guilty under this section are subject to a fine, imprisonment of not more than twenty years, or both.

Section 1519 "covers conduct intended to impede any federal investigation or proceeding, including one not even on the verge of commencement."[125] Thus, the courts are in accord in holding that the "investigation" or "matter" need not be pending or even contemplated at the time of the obstructive acts.[126] Two courts of appeals have concluded that the government does not have to satisfy the *Aguilar* "nexus" requirement—that is, it need not prove that the defendant's actions had the natural and probable effect of impeding or obstructing the investigation or proper administration of a matter.[127] But the government must prove that that the defendant intended to impede, obstruct, or influence an investigation or matter, whether the defendant acts directly, "in contemplation," or "in relation" to the investigation or matter.[128] The courts of appeals are also in agreement that the government need not prove that the defendant specifically knew that the matter was within the jurisdiction of a federal department or agency.[129]

In *Yates v. United States*, 574 U.S. 528 (2015), the Supreme Court held that fish are not "tangible objects." Yates, a commercial fisherman, caught undersized red grouper in federal waters. To prevent federal officials from confirming that he had improperly harvested the fish, he ordered his crew

124. *See* United States v. Scott, 70 F.4th 846, 855 (5th Cir. 2023).
125. *Yates*, 574 U.S. at 547.
126. *See* United States v. Gray, 642 F.3d 371, 379 (2d Cir. 2011) ("[Section] 1519 does not require the existence or likelihood of a federal investigation.").
127. *See, e.g.*, United States v. Yielding, 657 F.3d 688, 711-13 & n.4 (8th Cir. 2011).
128. *Id.* at 711.
129. *See* United States v. Hassler, 992 F.3d 243, 247 (4th Cir. 2021) (collecting cases)

to throw the suspect catch into the ocean. He was prosecuted under § 1519. The plurality conceded that a fish is indeed an object that is tangible. But it emphasized that § 1519 was passed as part of an Act designed to protect investors and restore public trust in financial markets after the Enron collapse and Arthur Andersen's obstruction. It therefore concluded that "it would cut § 1519 loose from its financial-fraud mooring to hold that it encompasses any and all objects, whatever their size or significance, destroyed with obstructive intent."[130] Relying on various canons of statutory construction, statutory context, and legislative history, the plurality ruled that a "tangible object" within the § 1519's compass is only "*one used to record or preserve information.*"[131] Justice Alito provided the fifth vote, reaching the same conclusion on narrower grounds.

I. The Differences Between § 1512(c) and § 1519

Congress was aware that there was substantial overlap between § 1512(c)(1) and § 1519. Minority Leader Lott introduced § 1512(c)(1) late in the legislative process—after § 1519 was already included in the legislation—explaining that he did so at the President's request.[132] In *Yates*, the dissent posited that the "presence of both § 1519 and § 1512(c)(1) in the final Act may have reflected belt-and-suspenders caution" or simply a wish to satisfy the President.[133] That said, the two provisions are not entirely identical in scope.

a. Attempts

A conviction under § 1519 requires proof that the defendant actually altered, destroyed, mutilated, concealed, covered up, falsified, or made a false entry into a record; an attempt will not do. Section § 1512(c), however, authorizes attempt liability under both its subsections.

b. "Other Object" vs. "Tangible Object"

Under *Yates*, a "'tangible object' for purposes of § 1519 is restricted to objects "used to record or preserve information."[134] By contrast, the *Yates* plurality noted that § 1512(c)(1)'s "reference to 'other object' includes any and every physical object" and thus Yates's conduct could have been pursued

130. *Yates*, 574 U.S. at 532.
131. *Id.* at 549 (emphasis added).
132. *See id.* at 562 (Kagan, J. dissenting).
133. *Id.*
134. *Id.* at 549.

under § 1512(c)(1) if the other elements of that offense could be proved. In short, fish are "objects" but not "tangible objects."[135]

c. Qualifying Conduct

Section 1512(c)(1) covers attempts to "alter, destroy, mutilate, or conceal" a record, document, or other object. Post-*Fischer*, § 1512(c)(2) covers those same acts when they are addressed to evidence other than records, documents, or other objects. Section 1519 can be used to address acts covered by § 1512(c)(1) and more; § 1519 adds liability for those who "cover[] up, falsif[y], or make[] a false entry in any record, document, or tangible object." Under *Fischer*, § 1512(c)(2) also applies to efforts to compromise the integrity or availability for use of any record, document, or tangible object other than by alteration, destruction, mutilation, or concealment. Just what those acts may be will be left to the lower courts to determine going forward but they may include covering up, falsifying, and making a false entry.

Although § 1519 was viewed as Sarbanes-Oxley's "anti-shredding" provision, it is often used to pursue defendants for falsification of documents. In such cases, the government must prove that the defendant knowingly falsified the document—meaning that the "falsification must be done knowingly; an unwitting falsehood will not suffice."[136]

d. Mens Rea and Intent

Both subsections of 1512(c) require proof that the defendant acted corruptly, while § 1519 requires only a knowing mens rea.

Section 1512(c)(1) requires proof that there was a contemplated or foreseeable official federal proceeding and that the obstructive act was done with the intent *to impair an object's integrity or availability for use* in that foreseeable or contemplated official proceeding. We do not yet know whether this intent requirement applies as well to § 1512(c)(2) but given that the *Fischer* Court's analysis, it likely does. By contrast, § 1519 does not require proof that the physical evidence was tampered with to affect a pending or contemplated official proceeding. Rather, the defendant need only compromise the object *with the intent to obstruct the investigation or administration of a qualifying matter*, or in "relation" to, or "contemplation" of, such matter.

135. *Id.* at 542.
136. *Yielding*, 657 F.3d at 711.

e. "Official Proceeding" vs. "Matter Within the Jurisdiction of Any Department or Agency of the United States"

Section 1512(c) applies to "official proceedings," which include judicial, agency, and congressional proceedings while § 1519 applies to obstruction directed at "the investigation or proper administration of any matter *within the jurisdiction of any department or agency of the United States* or any [bankruptcy] case filed under title 11, or in relation to or contemplation of any such matter or case" (emphasis added).

The degree to which the two sections overlap depends on what § 1519's "any matter within the jurisdiction of any department or agency of the United States" means. This language raises two interpretive questions. First, what is meant by "within the jurisdiction"? It seems likely that courts will turn to the Supreme Court's broad interpretation of the same language in 18 U.S.C. § 1001 and hold that that "within the jurisdiction" includes "all matters confided to the authority of an agency or department."[137]

Second, is "department or agency of the United States" restricted only to matters before executive branch departments and federal agencies or does it extend as well to judicial, and perhaps congressional, matters? This question was discussed but not decided in *Yates*. The plurality argued that "the sweeping 'in relation to'" language in § 1519, means that "any matter within the jurisdiction of any department or agency of the United States" includes federal court proceedings.[138] The dissent disagreed with this view.[139] Justice Alito, the deciding vote, concurred on narrower grounds and did not address the issue. Justice Kagan's dissenting opinion has the better of the argument based on existing law.

First, 18 U.S.C. § 1505 applies to congressional investigations and to pending proceedings before "any department or agency of the United States." Under § 1505, the quoted language—mimicked in § 1519—has been read as confined in application to proceedings before executive branch departments (e.g., Department of Justice, IRS, Customs Service) or federal agencies (e.g., SEC).

Second, this language echoes the language of § 1001 before that statute was amended in 1996. Prior to 1996, § 1001 outlawed false statements "within the jurisdiction of any department or agency of the United States." In *Hubbard v. United States*, 514 U.S. 695 (1995), the Supreme Court read the terms "any department or agency of the United States" to *exclude* the judicial branch. The *Hubbard* Court's reasoning also indicated that the Court would read the same language to exclude false statements made to the legislative branch. Congress responded to *Hubbard* in 1996 by amending § 1001 to

---

137. United States v. Rodgers, 466 U.S. 475, 479 (1984).
138. *Yates*, 574 U.S. at 542 n.5.
139. *See id.* at 561 & n.3 (Kagan, J., dissenting).

include false statements made "in any matter within the jurisdiction of the executive, legislative, or judicial branch of the Government of the United States" (§ 1001). Given this recent judicial and legislative interchange, it is reasonable to conclude that Congress intentionally chose language that the Supreme Court had interpreted to *preclude* application of § 1519 to the judicial or legislative branches.

Finally, reading the statute as aimed at obstructive activity that affects the investigation, or proper administration, of any matter within the jurisdiction of executive branch departments or federal agencies is consistent with the context in which the statute was enacted. Section 1519 was written into the statute before § 1512(c)(1) was added. Presumably, then, § 1519 was the provision that Congress thought was responsive to Arthur Andersen's obstructive activity and that activity was intended to impede the investigation of Enron's financials by an executive branch agency—the SEC.

To date, there is little caselaw on this issue. The Eleventh Circuit upheld a conviction based on evidence that the defendant submitted altered records in the course of a judicial proceeding, that is, a grand jury investigation.[140] The court attempted, however, to tie the grand jury as closely as possible to an executive agency investigation in the course of its reasoning by relying on the expansive language of § 1519, which covers "any department or agency of the United States . . . or in relation to or contemplation of any such matter or case." The court reasoned that "[b]ecause the Department of Health and Human Services, which is a 'department or agency of the United States,' conducted the investigation of [the defendant] and the grand jury subpoenaed the missing records '*in relation to or in contemplation of*' this investigation, her failure to produce the records with the photographs intact is obstructive conduct under section 1519."[141]

Reading the scope of § 1519 to be restricted to executive departments and federal agency matters would, to some extent, rationalize these two provisions by reducing the extent to which they overlap. Section 1512(c) would cover judicial and congressional proceedings while § 1519 would apply to certain similar types of obstruction in the context of executive departments and federal agencies.[142] Granted, there would continue to be overlap, as § 1512(c) also applies to agency proceedings. But even so, the two provisions would not be co-terminous in at least one very important

140. United States v. Hoffman-Vaile, 568 F.3d 1335, 1343 (11th Cir. 2009).

141. *Id.* (emphasis added).

142. *See, e.g.*, *Yates*, 574 U.S. at 561 (Kagan, J., dissenting) ("because an 'official proceeding' includes proceedings before a judge or courts of the United States, § 1512(c)(1) prohibits tampering with evidence in federal litigation between private parties. By contrast, § 1519 wouldn't ordinarily operate in that context because a federal court isn't a 'department or agency.'")

respect. Section 1519 covers acts that obstruct "the *investigation* or proper administration of any matter" within the jurisdiction of an executive agency or department but § 1512(c)'s official agency "proceedings" have been read to be limited to formal adjudicatory activities and to exclude investigatory activity. For example, an FBI investigation would be a matter within a federal department's jurisdiction under § 1519, but it is generally not viewed as a sufficiently formal exercise of authority to qualify as an "official proceeding" under § 1512. Because obstructive activity is often addressed to such investigations, this distinction in coverage would be an important one.[143]

The following attempts to compare §§ 1512(c)(1), 1512(c)(2), and 1519 but readers are cautioned that I am speculating about the elements of a (c)(2) case post-*Fischer*.

§ 1512(c)	**§ 1519**
Corruptly	Knowingly
(c)(1) alters, destroys, mutilates, or conceals a record, document, or other object; or (c)(2) alters, destroys, mutilates, or conceals evidence other than a record, document, or other object; or (c)(2) impairs the integrity or availability for use of a record, document, or other object other than by altering, destroying, mutilating, or concealing it	alters, destroys, mutilates, conceals, or covers up, falsifies, or makes a false entry in any record, document, or tangible object
"other object" is not restricted to things used to record or preserve information and includes a variety of tangible items (guns, drugs, fish)	a "tangible object" means one used to record or preserve information (not fish!)
or attempts to do so	no attempt liability
with the intent to impair the object's integrity or availability for use	with the intent to impede, obstruct, or influence the investigation or proper administration of any matter,
in an "official proceeding," which need not be pending but must be contemplated or foreseeable	the relevant matter need not be pending or even contemplated

143. *See, e.g.*, *id.* ("an FBI investigation counts as a matter within a federal department's jurisdiction, but falls outside the statutory definition of 'official proceeding' as construed by courts").

§ 1512(c)	§ 1519
includes judicial, congressional, or federal agency proceedings Agency "proceeding" is read narrowly to exclude investigations	within the jurisdiction of any department or agency of the United States or any bankruptcy case filed under Title 11, or in relation to or contemplation of any such matter or case. Not clear whether department of agency of the United States includes judicial or congressional proceedings or is just confined to matters within the jurisdiction of executive branch departments and federal agencies. Statutory language includes intent to obstruct "investigation" of any matter
Subjective nexus test; the defendant contemplated or foresaw an official proceeding and knew that his actions would likely interfere with it	No proof of nexus required

NB: Sections 1503 and 1505 may also apply to the same circumstances assuming their elements are met.

C. Destruction of Corporate Audit Records Under 18 U.S.C. § 1520

In the Sarbanes-Oxley Act, Congress enacted 18 U.S.C. § 1520, which requires that "[a]ny accountant who conducts an audit of an issuer of securities to which section 10A(a) of the Securities Exchange Act of 1934 (15 U.S.C. [§] 78j-1(a)) applies . . . maintain all audit or review workpapers for a period of 5 years from the end of the fiscal period in which the audit or review was concluded" (§ 1520(a)(1)). Section 1520(a)(2) instructs the SEC to issue such rules and regulations "relating to the retention of relevant records such as workpapers, documents that form the basis of an audit or review" and the like "which are created, sent, or received in connection with an audit or review and contain conclusions, opinions, analyses, or financial data relating to such an audit or review" conducted by a covered accountant. Section 1520 then makes it unlawful for a defendant to "knowingly and willfully violate" subsection (a)(1) or the rules or regulations promulgated by the SEC under (a)(2).[144] Those who violate this provision are subject to a fine, imprisonment of not more than ten years, or both.

144. *See* SEC, Final Rule: Retention of Records Relevant to Audits and Reviews, Release No. 33-8180 etc. (discussing adoption of Rule 2-06 of Regulation S-X effective March 2003), available at https://www.sec.gov/rules/2003/01/retention-records-relevant-audits-and-reviews.

Section 1520 is notably different than the sections discussed above: it does not require proof of a corrupt intent; it does not require that any sort of proceedings be pending or even contemplated; and it imposes no nexus requirement. And it differs from § 1512(c) and § 1519 in that it does not penalize the obstructive act of compromising or destroying physical evidence in identified contexts. Instead, it establishes a positive duty to retain specified records and then penalizes the "knowing and willful" failure to meet that duty.

Examples

1. Sitara Shah learned that she was under investigation by the FBI for attempting to provide material support to a foreign terrorist organization. She read in the newspaper that members of an organization to which she belonged had been indicted by a federal grand jury. As a result, she deleted emails in her inbox that revealed her relationship with the organization. (NB: when one deletes an email, it remains in the "deleted items folder" of one's email account.) Shah also deleted from her hard drive documents that she felt might incriminate her. She then installed a program on her computer called DriveScrubber, which is designed to wipe one's hard drive clean of all deleted information. Normally, when one deletes a file from one's hard drive, that information is not entirely deleted—it remains in the drive's unallocated or "free" space. The deleted file in free space is now available to be overwritten. Instead of waiting for other files to overwrite the "deleted" file, the DriveScrubber program actively overwrites all the data in the free space, thus permanently erasing "deleted" files. Unbeknownst to Shah, however, DriveScrubber did not overwrite the emails in her "deleted items folder." Can the government make a case against Shah under § 1512(c)(1) and § 1519?

Explanations

1. It seems clear that Shah acted with the appropriate mens rea and intent under either section; (1) under § 1512(c)(1) she corruptly attempted to "destroy" or "conceal" a record or object with the intent to impair the object's integrity or availability for use; and (2) under § 1519, she knowingly destroyed or concealed a document or tangible object with the intent to obstruct. A data file would constitute a § 1512(c)(1) "object." Emails and data files also constitute "tangible objects" under § 1519 because they are "used to record or preserve information" under *Yates*.

   For purposes of § 1512(c)(1), it is unlikely that an FBI investigation would qualify as an "official proceeding" given that the caselaw generally demands, in the agency context, that some sort of formal agency adjudication be at least contemplated. The government may argue that a judicial proceeding, in the form of a grand jury, is pending; the government would have to prove that the natural and probable effect of her action was to obstruct the investigation (objective component) and that she knew or could foresee that (subjective component of nexus test under § 1512) based on news reports of indictments in other cases.

By contrast, § 1519 does not require proof of a pending or foreseeable "official proceeding," nor, it appears, does the government have to demonstrate an *Aguilar* nexus. It is unclear whether "any department or agency of the United States" includes judicial proceedings, making reliance on the grand jury troublesome. But § 1519 also covers acts that obstruct "the *investigation* or proper administration of any matter" within the jurisdiction of an executive agency or department. It would therefore apply to an FBI investigation.

Computer Files. Assuming the other requisites of the statutes are met, the government will have little difficulty persuading the judge or jury that the use of the DriveScrubber program actually "destroyed" the files at issue.

Email Messages. The government may be able to show that Shah's deletion of her email messages constituted an *attempt* to destroy them for purposes of § 1512(c)(1), which authorizes attempt liability. But there is no attempt liability under § 1519—the relevant matter has to be actually deleted or concealed. In *United States v. Katakis*, 800 F.3d 1017 (9th Cir. 2015), the § 1519 case upon which this hypothetical is based, the Ninth Circuit held that a single press of an email "delete" button does not "destroy" or "conceal" the email for purposes of § 1519 because all that action does is move an email from one's inbox to one's deleted items folder.[145] Although "concealment" does not require the government to prove that the item will never be found, the Ninth Circuit said that hitting the delete button once was not enough; if she had hit the button twice, thus removing the emails from her "deleted items folder," that might suffice. In short, the Ninth Circuit held that the case failed because deleting the email constituted only an *attempt* to conceal, which is not actionable under § 1519.

145. *Katakis*, 800 F.3d at 1029-30.

CHAPTER 8

Securities Fraud

The Securities and Exchange Commission (SEC) is the primary regulator of U.S. securities markets and is responsible for bringing civil enforcement actions under a variety of federal statutes that govern those markets.[1] (The SEC also has regulatory authority over the anti-bribery and accounting provisions of the Foreign Corrupt Practices Act (FCPA) but that statute is discussed in Chapter 9, which covers transnational corruption.) The Commodity Futures Trading Commission (CFTC) is another important civil regulator with responsibility for futures markets and many derivative contracts covered by another statute, the Commodity Exchange Act.[2]

The U.S. Department of Justice, however, is solely responsible for criminal enforcement of these statutes. Under section 24 of the Securities Act of 1933 ("1933 Act"),[3] section 32 of the Securities Exchange Act of 1934 ("1934 Act")[4] and other federal securities laws,[5] any legal or natural person may be subject to criminal prosecution for "willful" violations of the securities laws, or the rules and regulations promulgated under them.

This chapter will focus on the most commonly charged anti-fraud provisions: § 10(b) of the 1934 Act[6] and Rule 10b-5.[7] Section 10(b) contains the catch-all fraud prohibition that grounds many criminal, and civil, cases. It makes it unlawful "[t]o use or employ, in connection with the purchase and sale of any security . . . any *manipulative* or *deceptive* device or contrivance" prohibited by SEC rules.[8] SEC Rule 10b-5 implements this statutory mandate, making it unlawful to, "in connection with the purchase or sale of any security," (a) "employ any device, scheme, or artifice to defraud," (b) "make any untrue statement of a material fact or . . . omit to state a material fact necessary in order to make the statements made . . . not misleading," or (c) "engage in any act, practice, or course of business which operates or would operate as a fraud or deceit upon any person."[9]

Another statute that deserves attention, 18 U.S.C. § 1348, was enacted in response to the corporate accounting scandals that erupted in 2002. This

1. *See, e.g.*, the Securities Act of 1933, 15 U.S.C. § 77a *et seq.* (regulating issuance of securities), the Securities Exchange Act of 1934, 15 U.S.C. § 78a *et seq.* (regulating the securities market and imposing disclosure requirements), the Trust Indenture Act of 1939, 15 U.S.C. § 77aaa *et seq.* (regulating debt securities), the Investment Company Act of 1940, 15 U.S.C. § 80a-1 *et seq.* (regulating investment companies), and the Investment Advisers Act of 1940, 15 U.S.C. § 80b-1 *et seq.* (regulating investment advisory firms). These statutes have lately been augmented by the Sarbanes-Oxley Act of 2002, the Dodd-Frank Wall Street Reform and Consumer Protection Act of 2010, and the Jumpstart Our Business Startups Act of 2012.
2. 7 U.S.C. § 1 *et seq.*
3. 15 U.S.C. § 77x.
4. *Id.* § 78ff(a).
5. *See, e.g.*, *id.* § 80a-48 (Section 49 of the Investment Company Act of 1940).
6. *Id.* § 78j(b). Enforcement actions are also commonly brought under § 17(a) of the 1933 Act for fraud in connection with the issuance of a security. *See id.* § 77q(a).
7. 17 C.F.R. § 240.10b-5.
8. 15 U.S.C. § 78j(b) (emphasis added).
9. 17 C.F.R. § 240.10b-5.

statute outlaws (1) knowingly engaging or attempting to engage in a fraudulent scheme in connection with commodity options and futures and the securities of certain companies; or (2) by means of deception, fraudulently obtaining money or property in connection with the purchase and sale of such commodities futures or options or securities. Section 1348 is attractive to prosecutors because it eliminates some of the elements required in § 10(b) and Rule 10b-5 cases. Thus, for example, the statute eliminates the requirement that a defendant act "willfully" in violating the securities laws and, at least in cases indicted under § 1348(1), obviates proof that the defendant's fraudulent scheme be in connection with "the purchase or sale" of securities. Section 1348 also allows for potentially longer sentences because its statutory maximum penalty is twenty-five years, in contrast with the twenty years authorized for violations of § 10(b).

Defendants in securities cases are often charged with other crimes of general applicability, such as conspiracy, obstruction, and mail, wire, tax, or bank fraud. In prosecutions involving theories of liability as yet unproven under the securities laws or where there is uncertainty in the application of § 10(b) or § 1348, prosecutors traditionally charged a mail or wire fraud count under 18 U.S.C. § 1341 or § 1343 because such charges do not require proof that a statutorily defined "security" is involved, nor do they require proof of the "in connection with" the "purchase or sale of securities" elements. Whether this practice continues is subject to some question because, as we saw in Chapter 6 (Fraud), the Supreme Court has been reading the scope of the mail and wire statutes narrowly of late.

It is impossible to summarize the extraordinary variety of complex and sophisticated financial schemes underlying securities fraud cases. That said, the FBI and SEC have identified certain recurring types of scams. An old favorite is the Ponzi scheme, named after an early 20th Century con man, Charles Ponzi. In such schemes, organizers gull victims into investing with them by promising high returns with little risk, but the organizers do not in fact invest the funds received. Instead, they use money from new investors to pay earlier investors — to keep them quiet and avoid premature exposure of the scheme — and pocket the rest. Because the scheme has no legitimate investments or returns, it requires the constant investment of new monies to stay afloat. When the organizers cannot recruit new investors, or when large numbers of existing investors attempt to cash out, the scheme will collapse. Bernie Madoff engineered the largest Ponzi scheme in history: it was an estimated $65 billion securities fraud scam.

A pyramid scheme is similar to a Ponzi scheme, but it introduces a twist designed to ease the difficulties the promoters face in constantly securing new victims. Businesses that rely on people to sell to their friends and family and to recruit others to do the same are engaged in what is known as multilevel marketing (MLM). This can be a legitimate business practice but can also be a pyramid scheme. A pyramid scheme is one in which the promoter promises those recruited to sell that they can get rich by making lots of sales but, in reality, they are rewarded only to the extent that they bring in more salespeople. The promoter will require the salespeople to buy excess inventory or pay fees to "earn" the promised rewards. Most salespeople find that no matter how hard they work, they can't sell enough inventory or recruit enough people to make money or even to cover their expenses. In the end, most people lose everything they invested. Some of these pyramid schemes are also Ponzi schemes to the extent that the underlying product or service being sold is fraudulent. Ponzi schemes contemplate that victims' only role will be tendering investment funding, but pyramid schemes generally offer victims the additional opportunity to "make" money by (unwittingly) recruiting more people into the scam.

So-called high yield investment frauds also promise investors a high rate of return with little risk. Such schemes can involve a variety of investment types—such as securities, commodities, and real estate—the common thread being that investors never see the return contemplated. In sum, Ponzi/pyramid schemes and high yield investment frauds target the credulous and induce such persons to "invest" by offering "too good to be true" money-making opportunities.

Then there are the ever-popular advance fee schemes. These induce victims to advance the organizers relatively small sums of money—purportedly to cover such things as processing fees or taxes—in the hope of realizing much larger gains. After the victims send the fees, the organizers make off with the funds and never deliver on the investment. The so-called Nigerian Prince phishing scheme is a notable example.

Another common species of fraud occurs when an officer or director of a corporation misrepresents the business's financial information to its shareholders and the market. Many cases involve corporate efforts to make a company look more valuable or financially stronger than it in fact is. This may require insiders to falsify corporate filings, lie to auditors and outside analysts, or issue false press releases. Such cases may also be founded on "creative" accounting practices that are used to hide losses or lagging revenue numbers. Insiders may be attempting to induce investors to buy shares, thus pushing up the company's share price. In such cases, they are often motivated by fact that the involved executives' personal fortunes are linked to the company's value, for example through compensation schemes that tie executive bonuses to the company's financial performance or stock price. In some cases, insiders will disseminate false or misleading statements to depress a company's share prices, enabling insiders to pick up shares at a low price in anticipation of a later rebound in stock price expected in light of as-yet unannounced earnings or other corporate good news.

A "pump and dump" scheme, by contrast, involves third-party, not insider, misrepresentation. In these types of frauds, a third-party gives out false information about the stock market, a company or an industry.

For example, a fraudster may buy a lot of shares in an unknown company with an attractively low stock price. The buyer will then disseminate false information about the company in an effort to increase demand for the company's shares (the "pump"). Once this demand increases share prices sufficiently, the fraudster will sell his shares (the "dump") for a profit.

Because there are so many varieties of securities fraud, these materials will focus on false statement cases and on the insider trading subset of deceptive device cases.

I. SECTION 10(b) AND RULE 10b-5

Section 10(b) of the Exchange Act, in short, prohibits the use of *manipulative* or *deceptive* conduct in connection with the purchase or sale of securities. *Manipulative* conduct is "virtually a term of art" in securities law and it refers "generally to practices, such as wash sales, matched orders, or rigged prices, that are intended to mislead investors by artificially affecting market activity."[10] Our focus— *deceptive* conduct— includes misrepresentations of material facts (lies) or a failure to disclose material facts necessary to make the statements actually made not misleading (failure to disclose).

More specifically, § 10(b) of the 1934 Act and SEC Rule 10b-5 issued pursuant to § 10(b) prohibit persons from:

- directly or indirectly
- knowingly and willfully
- using
  - any means or instrumentality of interstate commerce or
  - the mails or
  - any facility of any national securities exchange
- to
  - [a] employ any device, scheme, or artifice to defraud
  - [b] make any untrue statement of a material fact or to omit to state a material fact necessary in order to make the statements made, in light of the circumstances under which they were made, not misleading, or
  - [c] engage in any act, practice, or course of business which operates or would operate as a fraud or deceit upon a person
- in connection with the purchase or sale of any security

10. Santa Fe Indus., Inc. v. Green, 430 U.S. 462, 476 (1977).

Courts have often referred to claims founded on Rule 10b-5's subsections (a) and (c)— encompassing the use of schemes to defraud and any act, practice, or course of business operating as a fraud— as "scheme liability," thus distinguishing such claims from "false statement" claims under subsection (b) of Rule 10b-5. Note, however, that each subsection of Rule 10b-5 does not prohibit entirely separate, mutually exclusive categories of conduct.[11] In some circumstances, for example, where someone knowingly disseminates false statements but is not their author, he may not be violating Rule 10b-5(b) but can be found in violation of Rule 10b-5(a) and (c).[12]

Section 32(a) of the 1934 Act criminalizes violations of § 10(b) and Rule 10b-5 as well as the knowing and willful submission of materially false statements to the SEC. It contains the mens rea requirements applicable in criminal prosecutions. Section 32(a) authorizes criminal prosecution of those who:

- "willfully" violate § 10(b) or Rule 10b-5 or
- "willfully and knowingly make[], or cause[] to be made, any statement" in "any application, report, or document required to be filed under this chapter or any rule or regulation thereunder" that is "false or misleading with respect to any material fact"[13]

Section 32(a) provides that those convicted under § 10(b) are punishable by a fine of not more than $5,000,000 for individuals and $25,000,000 for entities, imprisonment of not more than twenty years, or both. But § 32(a) provides a limited immunity from imprisonment, stating that "no person shall be subject to imprisonment under this section for the violation of any rule or regulation if he proves that he had no knowledge of such rule or regulation."[14]

Criminal securities cases require proof of fewer elements than those necessary to a civil damages recovery. In civil cases, plaintiffs must prove, *inter alia*, that they actually purchased or sold securities, that they justifiably relied on the defendant's material misstatement or omission, and that that wrongful conducted caused the plaintiffs' damages.[15] The government need not prove any of these elements in a criminal case. Thus, it is not necessary for prosecutors to show that the victims relied on the defendant's fraudulent statement or omission or that anyone suffered a loss. The government also does not need to prove that the victims actually purchased or sold

11. *See* Lorenzo v. SEC, 587 U.S. 71, 80-81 (2019).
12. *See id.* at 81.
13. 15 U.S.C. § 78ff(a).
14. *Id.*
15. *See* Stoneridge Inv. Partners, LLC v. Scientific-Atlanta, 552 U.S. 148, 157 (2008).

securities.[16] In a concurring opinion in an insider trading prosecution under § 1348, *United States v. Blaszczak*, 56 F.4th 230 (2d Cir. 2022), Second Circuit Judges Walker and Kearse highlighted the anomaly that fewer elements are required to prove a criminal securities fraud case than a civil one. They argued that "traditional notions of fair play are offended by the present incongruence . . . between civil and criminal deterrence" and urged that the courts and Congress address this asymmetry.[17]

Note, too, that the Supreme Court has held that those who merely aid and abet a securities violation cannot be held liable for private civil damages under § 10(b) and rule 10b-5.[18] But prosecutors can bring aiding and abetting charges for violations of the securities laws under 18 U.S.C. § 2 and Congress gave the SEC the power to bring enforcement actions against violators for aiding and abetting a violation of § 10(b) and Rule 10b-5 in § 20(e) of the 1934 Act.[19]

Finally, in *Morrison v. National Australia Bank, Ltd.*, 561 U.S. 247 (2010), the Supreme Court held that § 10(b) and Rule 10b-5 do not apply extraterritorially. Functionally, what that means is that in private civil damages actions the plaintiffs can only pursue causes of action under § 10(b) and Rule 10b-5 when the case is "domestic" in nature. The Court defined such domestic cases as confined to ones involving "transactions in securities listed on domestic exchanges, and domestic transactions in other securities";[20] all other cases constitute improper extraterritorial applications of the statute. However, in the Dodd-Frank Wall Street Reform and Consumer Protection Act ("Dodd-Frank"),[21] Congress provided a different rule for government-initiated securities fraud cases. Thus, where, as is increasingly common, a fraud case crosses borders, the SEC and government prosecutors can bring § 10(b) and Rule 10b-5 cases if they can prove that "conduct within the United States . . . constitute[d] significant steps in furtherance of the violation, even if the securities transaction occur[ed] outside the United States and involve[d] only foreign investors; or . . . conduct [that occurred] outside the United States . . . ha[d] a foreseeable substantial effect within the United States.[22]

16. *See* United States v. O'Hagan, 521 U.S. 642, 664-65 (1997).
17. *Blaszczak*, 56 F.4th at 246.
18. *See* Central Bank of Denver, N.A. v. First Interstate Bank of Denver, N.A., 511 U.S. 164, 177 (1994).
19. 15 U.S.C. § 78t(e).
20. *Morrison*, 561 U.S. at 267.
21. Pub. L. No. 111-203, § 929P(b), 124 Stat. 1376, 1865 (2010) (codified at 15 U.S.C. § 78aa).
22. 15 U.S.C. § 78aa.

A. The "In Connection With" the Purchase or Sale of Securities Requirement

Because § 10(b) proscribes securities fraud, in every criminal case under that section and Rule 10b-5 the government must prove that the fraudulent scheme or untrue statement of material fact was "in connection with the purchase or sale of securities." Note that the government need not prove that the defendant actually participated in a securities transaction so long as he participated in a scheme "in connection with the purchase or sale of any securities."[23] The terms "purchase," "sale," and "security" are defined in the 1934 Act.[24]

The Supreme Court has consistently emphasized that § 10(b) should be construed "'not technically and restrictively, but flexibly to effectuate its remedial purpose.'"[25] It has therefore read the "in connection with" requirement broadly, holding that "it is enough that the fraud alleged 'coincide' with a securities transaction— whether by the plaintiff or by someone else. The requisite showing, in other words, is deception in connection with the purchase or sale of any security, not deception of an identifiable purchaser or seller."[26]

The more straightforward cases concern the dissemination of the false information and allegations that victims relied on such information when engaging in securities transactions. The Second Circuit's decision in *SEC v. Texas Gulf Sulpher Co.*, 401 F.2d 833 (2d Cir. 1968) (*en banc*) is often cited as providing the leading definition of the "in connection with" requirement in this context. In that case, the court found that false and misleading representations are made "in connection" with securities trading "whenever [such] assertions are made . . . in a manner reasonably calculated to influence the investing public."[27] Where the case is founded on public dissemination of false and misleading information, the government must show that the information was material and was disseminated through a medium upon which investors generally rely. The fraudulent information may be contained in prospectuses and other documents used to market securities, press releases, research reports, SEC filings, and financial statements and audit reports. And a sufficient connection between the fraud and the security may be demonstrated by proof that the one of the parties to a securities transaction misled the other about a subject material to the investment decision, that an insider

23. *See id.* § 78j(b).

24. *See id.* §§ 78c(a)(13) (definition of "buy" and "purchase"); 78c(a)(14) (definition of "sell" and "sale"), 78c(a)(10) (definition of "security").

25. SEC v. Zandford, 535 U.S. 813, 819 (2002).

26. Merrill Lynch, Pierce, Fenner & Smith Inc. v. Dabit, 547 U.S. 71, 85 (2006) (internal quotation marks omitted).

27. *Texas Gulf Sulpher Co.*, 401 F.2d at 862.

defendant issued false or misleading statements about his company leading investors to trade on that basis, or that a third-party, such as an accountant or broker, knowingly made false statements intending to influence investment decisions. The "in connection with" requirement, then, can be satisfied whether or not "the makers of a misleading statement also participated in pertinent securities transactions in connection therewith."[28]

It is important to recognize, however, that the "in connection with" requirement is not confined to situations in which one participant in a securities transaction defrauds the counterparty or in which false statements are made to induce victims to engage in securities transactions. For example, in *United States v. O'Hagan*, 521 U.S. 642 (1997), the Court ruled that the defendant committed fraud in connection with a securities transaction when he used confidential information that he misappropriated from his employer to engaging in securities trading. In so doing, the Court rejected O'Hagan's claim that because the fraud operated on the employer who was not in the market for securities, the case was indistinguishable from a case in which a defendant defrauded a bank into giving him the funds that he later used to trade in securities. Then, in *Wharf (Holdings) Ltd. v. United Int'l Holdings, Inc.*, 532 U.S. 588 (2001), the Court held that a broker who sold the victim an option to sell securities while never intending to honor the option and deliver the securities was found to have committed fraud "in connection with" the purchase or sale of securities. Finally, in *United States v. Zandford*, 535 U.S. 813 (2002), the Court held that a broker who sold securities from a client account over which he had discretionary control and pocketed the proceeds conducted a fraud that satisfied the "in connection with" requirement. It rejected Zandford's claim that the securities transaction was lawful and any fraud took place only afterwards when the broker purloined the proceeds of the sales. As the *Zandford* Court summarized the rule emerging from *Wharf* and *O'Hagan*, the "in connection with" requirement simply requires that the fraud and the securities transaction "coincide."[29]

A non-exhaustive list of factors courts look to in determining whether a fraud was "in connection with" the purchase or sale of a security— that is, whether the fraud and trading "coincide"— include "'(1) whether a securities sale was necessary to the completion of the fraudulent scheme; (2) whether the parties' relationship was such that it would necessarily involve trading in securities; (3) whether the defendant intended to induce a securities transaction; and (4) whether material misrepresentations were 'disseminated to the public in a medium upon which a reasonable investor would rely.'"[30] These factors provide only guidance; they are neither mandatory nor exclusive. Given the breadth of the Court's reading of the "in

---

28. *Id.* at 860.
29. *Zandford*, 535 U.S. at 825.
30. SEC v. Pirate Inv. LLC, 580 F.3d 233, 244 (4th Cir. 2009).

connection with" requirement in *O'Hagan*, *Wharf*, and *Zandford*, the defense rarely succeeds in challenging this element.

B. Jurisdictional Element: Use of Instrumentalities of Interstate Commerce or the Mails

Rule 10b-5 dictates that the jurisdictional requirements of prosecutions under § 10(b) and Rule 10b-5 can be met by proof that the defendant engaged in the deceptive conduct proscribed by use of the mails, any facility of any national securities exchange, or any means or instrumentality of interstate commerce. Interstate commerce is defined broadly and includes use of a "telephone or other interstate means of communication" or "any other interstate instrumentality."[31] Traveling in interstate commerce, making telephone calls, engaging in banking transactions, and using the internet, even if "ancillary" to the scheme, will satisfy the jurisdictional element.[32] Just as in the mail and wire fraud context, discussed in Chapter 6, these jurisdictional elements are generally easy to satisfy because the nexus between the fraud and the jurisdictional use of the mails or wires need only be incidental to the fraud.

C. Mens Rea

Section 32(a) contains different mens rea requirements depending upon which clause the government relies upon. If the government bases its criminal case on the first clause of that section— addressing violations of § 10(b) and Rule 10(b)(5)— it need only show willfulness. If, however, the government proceeds under § 32(a)'s second clause, alleging that the defendant made a materially false or misleading statement of material fact in a "filing, application, report, or document required by the securities laws," it must prove that the defendant acted willfully *and* knowingly.[33]

As discussed in Chapter 2 (General Part) the term "willful" has many meanings in federal criminal law. The Supreme Court defines what is meant by "willful" conduct differently according to the type of criminal prohibition at issue or the type of activity regulated. There are three basic meanings of "willful": (1) the lowest connotes only that an act is intentional and voluntary as opposed to accidental; (2) the most common meaning is that the act is done not just voluntarily, but also with knowledge that the defendant's

31. 15 U.S.C. § 78c(a)(17).
32. SEC v. Constantin, 939 F. Supp. 2d 288, 305 (S.D.N.Y. 2013).
33. *See* United States v. Tarallo, 380 F.3d 1174, 1186 (9th Cir. 2004).

conduct is in some general sense "unlawful"; and (3) the most demanding (super mens rea) level requires proof that the defendant actually knew of the specific law he was violating.

The Supreme Court has yet to provide an authoritative reading of the "willful" element in securities law prosecutions, but the Second and Ninth Circuits— which decide the majority of securities law cases— are in accord in holding that the most common meaning— requiring proof that the defendant knew that his conduct was "unlawful"— is inappropriate in the context of securities fraud prosecutions. They hold that that "whatever 'willful' might mean for the purposes of other statutes, for the purposes of Section 32(a), it does not encompass the requirement that the defendant knew he was violating the law."[34]

Instead, the Second and Ninth Circuits require proof that the defendant intentionally undertook an act that he knew to be wrongful.[35] This instruction reflects the easiest (for the government) way to prove that a defendant acted "willfully"— that is, that he acted intentionally rather than accidentally. These circuits do "*not* require that the actor know specifically that the conduct was unlawful,"[36] but they do require that the defendant know he is acting "wrongfully." This may seem like a distinction without a difference, but the words used are important. "Unlawful" is defined as contrary to law. When this term is used in jury instructions, a defendant does not need to know he is violating a criminal law, but he must know that he is acting contrary to some sort of law— be it civil, regulatory or the like. "Wrongful" connotes something more general, that is, a moral or ethical disquiet with the conduct at issue. A defendant should know that his conduct is "bad" even if he does not have to know that it is contrary to law.

Courts also require proof of what is called "scienter," which is defined as a mental state embracing an intent to "'deceive, manipulate or defraud.'"[37] In criminal cases, the Second Circuit has made clear that an "intent to harm is not a component of the scienter element of securities fraud."[38] This is a lower standard that that employed in mail and wire fraud cases, where the requisite specific intent to defraud translates into an intent to injure.[39]

---

34. United States v. Kaiser, 609 F.3d 556, 568 (2d Cir. 2010).

35. *See Tarallo*, 380 F.3d at 1188; *see also* United States v. Newman, 773 F.3d 438, 447 (2d Cir. 2014), *rev'd on other grounds sub nom* Salman v. United States, 580 U.S. 39 (2016) (willfulness is defined "'as a realization on the defendant's part that he was doing a wrongful act under the securities laws'").

36. *Tarallo*, 380 F.3d at 1188.

37. Tellabs, Inc. v. Makor Issues & Rights, Ltd., 551 U.S. 308, 313 (2007); *see also* United States v. Pierre, 22-1274, 2024 WL 676373 (2d Cir. Feb. 20, 2024).

38. *Pierre*, 2024 WL 676373, at *2.

39. *See* Chapter 6 (Fraud) (where the object of the fraud is money or property, an intent to defraud connotes an intent to injure, harm, or cheat).

D. False Statement Cases Under Rule 10b-5(b)

1. Making a False or Misleading Statement

Rule 10b-5(b) prohibits two types of falsity: (1) making[40] "any untrue statement of a material fact"— i.e., false statements or lies; and (2) omitting a material fact necessary "to make the statements made. . . not misleading."[41] In *SEC v. Texas Gulf Sulpher, Co.*, 401 F.2d 833 (2d Cir. 1968), an *en banc* Second Circuit held that Rule 10b-5 is violated whenever assertions are made that "are false or misleading or are so incomplete as to mislead."[42] Courts adjudicating the falsity of representations must inquire "into the meaning of the statement to the reasonable investor and its relationship to truth."[43]

In *Macquarie Infrastructure Corp. v. Moab Partners, L.P.*, 601 U.S. 257 (2024), a civil damages suit, the Supreme Court addressed whether the second prohibition on misleading statements, Rule 10b-5(b), "bars only half-truths or instead extends to pure omissions," defined as occurring "when a speaker says nothing, in circumstances that do not give any particular meaning to that silence."[44] The Supreme Court ruled that "pure" omissions are not actionable under § 10(b) and Rule 10b-5. Thus, an issuer who omits information required by SEC disclosure rules is not automatically liable.[45] An omission may support a fraud claim, however, if the information omitted was necessary to make the issuer's affirmative statements not misleading.[46]

An assertion of opinion can constitute an actionably "false" statement if "the speaker did not hold the belief she professed" or "if the supporting facts she supplied were untrue.[47] The omission of a fact can also make

40. In *Janus Capital Grp., Inc. v. First Derivative Traders*, 564 U.S. 135 (2011), the Court held that, given the text of Rule 10b-5(b), liability as a principal violator under this subsection is limited to persons who "make" a false statement. This was a civil suit and, as noted above, there is no aiding and abetting liability in civil cases and thus who is or is not a principal violator, as opposed to an accessory, is important. One circuit, the Fourth, has held that *Janus Capital* was intended only to restrict the scope of private damages liability and does not apply in criminal cases; the Second Circuit has reserved the issue. *See* Prousalis v. Moore, 751 F.3d 272, 276-79 (4th Cir. 2014); *see also* United States v. Chartier, No. 22-3125(L), 2024 WL 3617023, at *8 n.9 (2d Cir. Aug. 1, 2024). In any case, prosecutors can charge those who aided and abetted a "make[r] of the false statement" under 18 U.S.C. § 2. *See also* Lorenzo v. SEC, 587 U.S. 71, 75 (2019) (those who don't "make" the statement for purposes of Rule 10b-5(b) can be liable under Rule 10b-5(a) and (c)).

41. 17 C.F.R. § 240.10b-5(b).

42. *Texas Gulf Sulphur*, 401 F.2d at 862.

43. *Id.*

44. *Macquarie Infrastructure Corp.*, 601 U.S. at 263.

45. *See id.* at 264.

46. *See id.* at 265.

47. Omnicare, Inc. v. Laborers Dist. Council Constr. Indus. Pension Fund, 575 U.S. 175, 185-86 (2015). *Omnicare* was decided under § 11 of the 1933 Act, but many have lower courts have applied its holding to § 10(b) and Rule 10b-5 cases. *See, e.g.*, City of Dearborn Heights Act 345 Police & Fire Ret. Sys. v. Align Tech., Inc., 856 F.3d 605, 613-14 (9th Cir. 2017).

a statement of opinion, even if literally accurate, "misleading." Thus, "a reasonable investor may, depending on the circumstances, understand an opinion statement to convey facts about how the speaker has formed the opinion— or, otherwise put, about the speaker's basis for holding that view. And if the real facts are otherwise, but not provided, the opinion statement will mislead its audience."[48] In such cases, however, the government would need to "identify particular (and material) facts going to the basis for the issuer's opinion— facts about the inquiry the issuer did or did not conduct or the knowledge it did or did not have— whose omission makes the opinion statement at issue misleading to a reasonable person reading the statement fairly and in context."[49]

2. Materiality

Section 10(b)'s materiality requirement is met when there is "a substantial likelihood" that under all the circumstances the false or misleading statement would have had actual significance in the deliberations of a reasonable investor given the "total mix" of information made available.[50] The materiality element is an objective test that "requires delicate assessments of the inferences a 'reasonable shareholder' would draw from a given set of facts and the significance of those inferences to him."[51] The Supreme Court has repeatedly rejected invitations to adopt a bright-line rule for determining materiality, opting instead for a fact-specific inquiry.[52] When called upon to determine the materiality of contingent information or future events, the Supreme Court, in *Basic Inc. v. Levinson*, 485 U.S. 224 (1988), instructed that, under such circumstances, materiality "'will depend at any given time upon a balancing of both the indicated probability that the event will occur and the anticipated magnitude of the event in light of the totality of the company activity.'"[53]

E. Deceptive Devices: Insider Trading Cases

As noted in the introduction, there are a seemingly endless variety of deceptive devices that contravene the securities law. One high-profile example is the subset of insider trading prosecutions. Here it is important to stress that what is proscribed in the operative portion of § 10(b) are *deceptive* devices

48. *Omnicare, Inc.*, 575 U.S. at 188.
49. *Id.* at 194.
50. Basic, Inc. v. Levinson, 485 U.S. 224, 231 (1988).
51. TSC Indus., Inc. v. Northway, Inc., 426 U.S. 438, 450 (1976).
52. *See, e.g.*, Matrixx v. Initiatives, Inc. v. Siracusano, 563 U.S. 27, 30 (2011).
53. *Basic, Inc.*, 485 U.S. at 238.

or contrivances; it is called securities "fraud" for a reason. So what "fraud" inheres in insider trading?

Obviously, false representations (aka lies) are deceptive and would suffice but they are normally not present in the typical insider trading case. Suppose, for example, a corporate insider decides, based on material non-public information he learned on the job, to buy the corporation's stock from unwitting shareholders. He can do this without dissembling simply by placing an order with a broker or on-line. The fraud in insider trading cases, then, typically relies on another theory of deception: the fact that insider did not *disclose* his trading to the counterparties or his employer *despite a duty to do so.*

As we saw in the context of fraud (Chapter 6) and concealment false statement cases (Chapter 4), it is a commonplace in federal criminal law that if one is engaged in an arm's length transaction, there is no "fraud" in failing to tell the counterparty everything it may wish to know. Fraud only exists when one party fails to disclose in the face of a *duty* to tell the counterparty material facts relevant to the transaction. Fraud in insider trading cases is usually proved by showing that someone traded on material non-public information *in breach of a duty* owed to the persons with whom he transacting or to the persons from who he misappropriated the inside information.

How, then, does a duty to disclose arise? A duty to disclose does not arise simply because the person who is trading is in possession of material non-public information. The federal securities laws do not guarantee that everyone will have equal access to such information. Rather, silence— that is, non-disclosure— is only actionable where the duty to disclose is found in positive law or arises out of a relationship of trust and confidence. It is often said that there are two theories of insider trading— classical theory and misappropriation theory. The only real difference between them lies in the source of the duty that the defendant breaches when trading: in classical theory cases, the defendant is a corporate insider who breaches his duty to the shareholders with whom he is trading while in misappropriation theory cases, the defendant owes a duty to the source of the information that he misappropriates and then trades upon.

In reality, these theories tend to coalesce. Virtually every insider trader liable under the classical theory— that is, an insider who trades on inside information without permission or disclosure in breach of a duty to the shareholders— is also liable under the misappropriation theory because he is essentially stealing the information in breach of his duty to the source of the information— that is, the corporation in which he is an insider. Because courts still distinguish between these two theories, however, these materials will as well.

1. Classical Theory

Under classical insider trading theory, a person has a duty to disclose or refrain from trading on material non-public information when that person is an insider of the company in whose shares he is trading. In such circumstances, the insider has a duty to disclose to prevent him from misusing for personal benefit information shared with him only for corporate purposes and from taking unfair advantage of the shareholders (or shareholders-to-be where he is selling stock) with whom he is trading. Trading on such information qualifies as a "deceptive device" under §10(b) because "a relationship of trust and confidence [exists] between the shareholders of a corporation and those insiders who have obtained confidential information by reason of their position with that corporation."[54]

For many years, the classical theory alone controlled. Thus, for example, in *Chiarella v. United States*, 445 U.S. 222 (1980), the Court reversed the conviction of an employee of a financial printer that had been hired to print corporate takeover bids. The employee bought the shares of the companies targeted for takeover, forecasting correctly that once the bids were announced the share prices would rise. The Court held that although the employee traded on the material non-public information he obtained from these bids in violation of his duty to his employer, he could not be liable under the classical theory because he had no fiduciary duty to, or other relationship of trust and confidence with, the target companies' shareholders within whom he was transacting.

2. Misappropriation Theory

The Court later recognized a second basis for insider trading liability under the "misappropriation theory." Under this theory, a person commits fraud in connection with a securities transaction when, like Chiarella, he misappropriates confidential information for securities trading purposes, in breach of a duty owed to the *source of the information* rather than the shareholders of the companies in whose shares he is trading. "Under this theory, a fiduciary's undisclosed, self-serving use of a principal's information to purchase or sell securities, in breach of a duty of loyalty and confidentiality, defrauds the principal of the exclusive use of that information."[55] In short, rather than premising insider trading liability on a fiduciary relationship between the insider and the shareholders with whom he is trading, the misappropriation

54. Chiarella v. United States, 445 U.S. 222, 228 (1980). Where the insider trading is in connection with a tender offer, the government can rely on another provision, of § 14 the 1934 Act, 15 U.S.C. § 78n(e), and Rule 14e-3(a), 17 C.F.R. § 240.14e-3(a) (prohibiting trading while in possession of material non-public information relating to a tender offer). *See also O'Hagan*, 521 U.S. at 673-77 (Rule 14e-3(a) did not exceed SEC's authority under § 14).
55. *O'Hagan*, 521 U.S. at 652.

theory bases liability for silence on the "fiduciary-turned-trader's deception of those who entrusted him with access to confidential information."[56]

The logic of this extension of insider trading law can be demonstrated by reference to the case in which the Supreme Court accepted this theory of liability, *United States v. O'Hagan*, 521 U.S. 642 (1997). In *O'Hagan*, the defendant was a lawyer at a firm that represented Grand Metropolitan PLC (Grand Met) in connection with its contemplated tender offer for Pillsbury. Plainly the defendant owed a fiduciary duty and a duty to disclose to his firm and its client. But he owed no duty to the Pillsbury shareholders from whom he bought shares. Thus, he would not be liable under the classical theory. But had the firm represented the target, Pillsbury, instead of the entity seeking to acquire Pillsbury, Grand Met, the defendant would have been liable under the classical theory because he would have owed the firm, its client Pillsbury, and the Pillsbury shareholders from whom he was buying shares a duty that he breached through his undisclosed trading. The *O'Hagan* Court reasoned that it made scant sense to reach a different result based on the happenstance that the firm represented the acquiring company rather than the target— in both cases the defendant used information he wrongfully acquired in breach of his duty to his firm and his client. It therefore accepted the misappropriation theory, holding that a cognizable fraud was perpetrated on the *source* of the inside information— the firm and its client— regardless of whether the client was the bidder or target.

The usual misappropriation case concerns the misuse of a business or governmental entity's confidential information by the entity's employee or agent. But misappropriation theory also extends beyond the employment context, for example to a psychiatrist who traded on non-public information he learned from a patient.[57] The SEC issued Rule 10b5-2[58] to clarify under what circumstances certain relationships, such as familial or personal connections, give rise to a duty of trust and confidence enforceable in misappropriation insider trading cases. Rule 10b5–2 identifies three non-exhaustive categories of relationships that give rise to a duty to disclose for misappropriation liability purposes:

> [A] "duty of trust or confidence" exists in the following circumstances, among others:
>
> (1) Whenever a person agrees to maintain information in confidence;
>
> (2) Whenever the person communicating the material nonpublic information and the person to whom it is communicated have a history, pattern, or practice of sharing confidences, such that the recipient of the information knows or reasonably should know that the person communicating the

56. *Id.*
57. *See, e.g.*, United States v. Willis, 737 F. Supp. 269 (S.D.N.Y. 1990).
58. 17 C.F.R. § 240.10b5-2(b).

> material nonpublic information expects that the recipient will maintain its confidentiality; or
>
> (3) Whenever a person receives or obtains material nonpublic information from his or her spouse, parent, child, or sibling; provided, however, that the person receiving or obtaining the information may demonstrate that no duty of trust or confidence existed with respect to the information. . . .[59]

As discussed above, the line between insiders responsible under classical theory and misappropriators under misappropriation theory is not absolute. Where a trader owes a duty to both the shareholders with whom he trades and the source of the confidential information on which he trades, he must make disclosure to both.[60]

3. Temporary Insiders

In a famous footnote in *Dirks v. SEC*, 463 U.S. 646 (1983), the Supreme Court identified an important category of persons potentially subject to insider trading sanction— so-called "quasi-" or "temporary" insiders.[61] The court noted that "[u]nder certain circumstances, such as where corporate information is revealed legitimately to an underwriter, accountant, lawyer, or consultant working for the corporation, these outsiders may become fiduciaries of the shareholders."[62] Such persons assume a duty not because they possess non-public information but instead because "they have entered into a special confidential relationship in the conduct of the business of the enterprise and are given access to information solely for corporate purposes."[63] Where such persons trade on such information, they will be liable assuming that the corporation expected the temporary insider "to keep the disclosed nonpublic information confidential, and that the relationship at least impl[ied] such a duty."[64]

"Temporary insiders are . . . forbidden from trading under both the classical and misappropriation theories without the requisite disclosure."[65] A number of recent cases have raised the issue of when an individual who is formally in an arm's length relationship with the source of the information but is given access to material non-public information pursuant to an express confidentiality agreement can be liable as a temporary insider. In *United States v. Chow*, 993 F.3d 125 (2d Cir. 2021), the defendant objected that the judge was wrong to charge the jury that the non-disclosure agreements

59. *Id.*
60. *See* United States v. Kozinski, 976 F.3d 135, 145 (2d Cir. 2020).
61. *See Dirks*, 463 U.S. at 655 n.14.
62. *Id.*
63. *Id.*
64. *Id.*
65. *Kozinski*, 976 F.3d at 145.

signed in that case, in which "each party agreed not to disclose any confidential or proprietary information of the other," meant that Chow had a duty of non-disclosure as a matter of law.[66] The Second Circuit found this objection "meritless" in reliance Rule 10b5-2's dictate that for purposes of § 10(b), a duty of trust or confidence exists, *inter alia*, "'[w]henever a person agrees to maintain information in confidence.'"[67]

4. Tipper/Tippee Liability

Insider trading cases resting on silence— that is, a failure to disclose that one is trading on non-public information— can only be made upon proof that the defendant breached a duty owed either to the company's shareholders (classical theory) or to the source of the information (misappropriation theory). In *Dirks*, the Supreme Court articulated when an insider or misappropriator can be said to have breached his duty by *tipping* non-public information to persons who trade on it, *rather than by himself trading on it*. It also identified when the *tippees* of the information assume the tipper's duty to disclose or abstain from trading.

a. Breach Through "Personal Benefit"

In *Dirks*, the Court recognized that "[a]ll disclosures of confidential corporate information are not inconsistent with the duty insiders owe to shareholders."[68] The *Dirks* Court explained, for example, that insiders regularly disclose information to market analysists for legitimate purposes. But it may not be clear whether the information disclosed would be considered material non-public information: "Corporate officials may mistakenly think the information already has been disclosed or that it is not material enough to affect the market."[69]

The Court determined that imposing a duty to disclose or abstain from trading only because a person received material non-public information from an insider "could have an inhibiting influence on the role of market analysts, which the SEC itself recognizes is necessary to the preservation of a healthy market."[70] It therefore identified the *purpose* of the "tip" as the determinative question.[71] The test for when a tipper breaches his duty is whether the "insider *personally will benefit*, directly or indirectly, from his disclosure."[72]

66. *Chow*, 993 F.3d at 139
67. *Id.* (quoting 17 C.F.R. § 240.10b5-2(b)(1)); *see also* SEC v. Cuban, 620 F.3d 551 (5th Cir. 2010).
68. *Dirks*, 463 U.S. at 661-62.
69. *Id.* at 662.
70. *Id.* at 658.
71. *See id.* at 662.
72. *Id.* (emphasis added).

The personal benefit test not only was an objective way to separate legitimate disclosures from improper tips, but also was designed to prevent insiders from doing an end run around the insider trading prohibitions by indirectly benefitting from trading that they could not do directly.

With respect to tippee liability, the *Dirks* Court ruled that some tippees assume a duty to the shareholders because the information "has been made available to them *improperly*"[73]— that is, because the tipper breached his fiduciary duty by tipping the information. "Thus, a tippee assumes a fiduciary duty to the shareholders of a corporation not to trade on material nonpublic information only when the insider has breached his fiduciary duty to the shareholders by disclosing the information to the tippee and the tippee knows or should know that there has been a breach."[74] Because the tipper only breaches his duty when he tips for personal benefit, a tippee is only liable when the tipper secured a personal advantage from the tip. "Absent some personal gain [by the tipper], there has been no breach of duty to stockholders. And absent a breach by the insider, there is no derivative breach" when the tippee of the information trades on it.[75]

To determine whether the insider or misappropriator tipped for "personal gain" and thus in breach of his duty, *Dirks* instructs courts to "focus on objective criteria, i.e., whether the insider receives a direct or indirect personal benefit from the disclosure, such as a pecuniary gain or a reputational benefit that will translate into future earnings."[76] A personal benefit "often" can be inferred "from objective facts and circumstances" such as "a relationship between the insider and the recipient that suggests a *quid pro quo* from the latter, or an intention to benefit the particular recipient."[77] A personal benefit that qualifies as a breach of duty can also be inferred "when an insider makes a gift of confidential information to a trading relative or friend"; in such cases, "[t]he tip and trade resemble trading by the insider followed by a gift of the profits to the recipient" of the tip.[78]

Courts have struggled to apply the personal benefit test in cases in which the government relies on a gift theory. In *United States v. Newman*, 773 F.3d 438 (2d Cir. 2014), the Second Circuit attempted to provide some clarity by adopting two limiting principles in such cases. It acknowledged that a factfinder could infer a personal benefit from a gift of confidential information to a trading relative or friend but concluded that such an inference "is impermissible in the absence of proof of [1] a *meaningfully close personal relationship* that generates an exchange that is [2] objective, consequential, and *represents at least*

73. *Id.* at 660 (emphasis added).
74. *Id.*
75. *Id.* at 662.
76. *Id.* at 663.
77. *Id.* at 664.
78. *Id.*

a potential gain of a pecuniary or similarly valuable nature."[79] The Ninth Circuit rejected the second limiting principle, a ruling that the Supreme Court affirmed in *Salman v. United States*, 580 U.S. 39 (2016). In *Salman*, the Supreme Court held that on the facts of that case— a tipper providing inside information to a close trading relative— *Dirks*'s rule was clear: "a tipper breaches a fiduciary duty by making a gift of confidential information to a 'trading relative.'"[80] It rejected the additional proof requirement imposed in *Newman* that the tipper receive something "of a 'pecuniary or similarly valuable nature.'"[81] *Salman* did not, however, address in terms *Newman*'s first requirement of a "meaningfully close personal relationship." It is an open question whether this part of *Newman* remains good law in the Second Circuit and elsewhere.[82]

The Second Circuit has found a personal benefit to be present in cases in which: a tipper hoped to curry favor with his boss;[83] a tippee provided the tipper with requested analyst reports, recommendations of potential partners for the tipper's venture, and introductions to business contacts, and gave him gifts of wine and cigars;[84] and a tippee gave the tipper "an iPhone, live lobsters, a gift card," a jar of honey, and insider information about other stocks.[85]

In cases in which the government is uncertain of its proof regarding "personal benefit" to the tipper, it is likely to charge the case under § 1348 because, as we shall see below, courts have held that the government does not need to prove a personal benefit to prevail on a § 1348 tipping insider trading case.

b. Tippee Knowledge: Tipper Breach or Tipper's Personal Benefit?

Newman, unlike *Salman*, involved another recurring issue: how to determine the liability of tippees where there has been a chain of tipping and thus the defendant tippees are several steps removed from the corporate insiders or misappropriators who were the original source of the information. The government argued in *Newman* that it was sufficient to prove that the defendants traded on material non-public information knowing that the insiders had disclosed that information *in breach of a duty of confidentiality*. The Second Circuit

79. *Newman*, 773 F.3d at 452 (emphasis added).

80. *Salman*, 580 U.S. at 49.

81. *Id.* at 50 (quoting *Newman*, 773 F.3d at 452).

82. In *United States Martoma*, 869 F.3d 58 (2d Cir. 2017), a panel of the Second Circuit ruled that *Newman*'s close personal relationship requirement was no longer good law after *Salman*. *Id.* at 69. After a petition for rehearing *en banc* argued that the panel had no power to effectively overrule *Newman*, however, the panel vacated and amended its opinion, concluding that, given the facts, it did not need to reach the issue. *See* United States v. Martoma, 894 F.3dd 64, 71 (2d Cir. 2018).

83. *See* SEC v. Obus, 693 F.3d 276, 292 (2d Cir. 2012).

84. *See Chow*, 993 F.3d at 142.

85. United States v. Jiau, 734 F.3d 147, 153 (2d Cir. 2013); *see also Martoma*, 894 F.3d at 74.

rejected this theory, holding instead that the government had to prove that the defendant tippees at the end of a chain of tips knew that the original tipper disclosed the inside information *in return for a personal benefit*.[86]

Other courts have reserved the question whether the government must prove only that the tippee knew that the tipper breached a duty when tipping, or whether it must bear the Second Circuit's heavier burden of proving that the tippee knew that the tipper secured a personal benefit.[87]

5. Trading "On the Basis Of"

Insider trading liability requires that the defendant act "on the basis of" material non-public information. The circuits split on what this meant: the Ninth Circuit and others required that the government prove that the defendant actually "used" the information while trading[88] but the Second Circuit and others ruled that it was sufficient if the government proved that the defendant "knowingly possessed" the information.[89]

In 2000, the SEC issued Rule 10b5-1, entitled "Trading 'on the basis of' material nonpublic information in insider trading cases." This rule summarized the "manipulative or deceptive device" employed in insider trading and adopted the "knowing possession" standard.[90] Rule 10b5-1 also provides various affirmative defenses. Thus, for example, a defendant can resist a government case by demonstrating that, before becoming aware of the inside information, the defendant had "[e]ntered into a binding contract to purchase or sell the security," "[i]nstructed another person to purchase or sell the security for the instructing person's account," or "[a]dopted a written plan for trading securities."[91]

It is unclear whether the Ninth Circuit still requires proof that the defendant "used" the information in light of Rule 10b5-1. At least one district court in that circuit applied the "use" standard after Rule 10b5-1 was promulgated[92] and another, noting that this standard may apply in criminal if not civil cases, ultimately concluded that did not need to decide because the facts satisfied both the use and the knowing possession standards.[93]

---

86. *See Newman*, 773 F.3d at 447-48.

87. The Supreme Court noted this issue in *Salman* but concluded that it was not raised on the facts of the case. *See Salman*, 580 U.S. at 45 n.1; *see also* United States v. Salman, 792 F.3d 1087, 1091 n.2 (9th Cir. 2015) (noting but not deciding the issue); *Bray*, 853 F.3d at 28 n.6 (same).

88. *See, e.g.*, United States v. Smith, 155 F.3d 1051, 1067 (9th Cir. 1998).

89. *See, e.g.*, United States v. Rajaratnam, 719 F.3d 139, 158-60 (2d Cir. 2013).

90. 17 C.F.R. § 240.10b5-1.

91. *Id.* § 10b5-1(c)(A).

92. *See* In re Countrywide Fin'l Corp. Secs. Litig., 588 F. Supp. 2d 1132, 1203-04 (N.D. Ca. 2008).

93. *See SEC v. Panuwat*, 21-cv-06322-WHO, 2022 WL 633306, *6 (N.D. Ca. Jan. 14, 2022).

6. Summary of Elements of Insider Trading Liability

Given the above, a defendant can be convicted as a principal in an insider trading case (tipper/tippee liability will be discussed below) if the government can prove:

- The defendant
  - was an insider of the company whose securities were traded
  - was a temporary insider of the company whose securities were traded or
  - was a misappropriator of information from its source, to whom the defendant owed a duty of trust and confidence
- who willfully
- purchased or sold securities
- while in "knowing possession" of (or, perhaps, in the Ninth Circuit, while "using") material, nonpublic information
- without disclosure
- and in so doing used any means or instrumentality of interstate commerce, the mails, or any facility of a national securities exchange

A defendant who "aids, abets, counsels, commands, induces or procures" the commission of an insider trading violation, or "causes an act to be done which if directly performed by him or another" would constitute insider trading, is punishable as an accessory under 18 U.S.C. § 2.

To establish a defendant's principal liability as a tipper, the government would have to prove that

- the tipper was an insider, quasi-insider, or misappropriator
- he willfully tipped material nonpublic information and
- in so doing, acted for personal gain, thus breaching his duties

A tippee will be liable where the government can prove that:

- the tippee obtained material, nonpublic information from the tipper or those to whom the tipper provided such information,
- he knowingly possessed (or, perhaps, in the Ninth Circuit, "used") that information
- when he bought or sold securities
- he knew or "should have known" that the tipper breached his duty[94] (in the Second Circuit, the tippee knew that the tipper "disclosed confidential information in exchange for personal benefit"[95])
- he acted willfully in doing so

94. *Dirks*, 463 U.S. at 660.
95. *Newman*, 773 F.3d at 449.

The government can also rely on aiding and abetting liability under § 2 where a tippee does not himself trade but rather passes the information on to remote tippees.

II. SECURITIES FRAUD UNDER 18 U.S.C. § 1348

Section 1348 renders liable anyone who

- knowingly
- executes, or attempts to execute, a scheme or artifice—
  - (1) to defraud any person in connection with any qualifying commodity future or option or "security"; or
  - (2) to obtain, by means of false or fraudulent pretenses, representations, or promises, any money or property in connection with the purchase or sale of any qualifying commodity future or option or "security"

Congress made violation of § 1348 punishable by a fine, imprisonment for up to twenty-five years, or both. Aiding and abetting cases can be made under 18 U.S.C. § 2 and conspiracies to violate § 1348 can be brought under 18 U.S.C. § 371 or § 1349.

Courts applying § 1348 have identified two general points of reference for litigators contesting its applicability. First, courts have noted that § 1348's text and legislative history reveal that it was modeled on the mail and wire fraud statues and have referenced the caselaw under § 1341 and § 1343 in construing the statute.[96] Second, courts have been inclined to apply § 1348 more broadly than its Title 15 counterpart in reliance on the legislative history of § 1348. Thus, for example, the Second Circuit has noted that § 1348 "was intended to provide prosecutors with a different— and broader— enforcement mechanism to address securities fraud than what had been previously provided in the Title 15 fraud provisions."[97] Finally, courts asked to interpret the meaning of terms that have well-established meanings under the securities laws— for example, the nexus required by the "in connection with" element— reference relevant precedents decided under § 10(b) and Rule 10b-5.[98]

96. *See* United States v. Coscia, 866 F.3d 782, 799 n.71 (7th Cir. 2017).
97. United States v. Blaszczak, 947 F.3d 19, 36-37 (2d Cir. 2019), *vacated and remanded on other grounds*, 141 S. Ct. 1040 (2021).
98. *See, e.g.*, United States v. Hussain, 972 F.3d 1138, 1147-48 (9th Cir. 2020).

A. Securities Fraud under § 1348(1)

Section 1348(1) renders criminally liable a defendant who:

- knowingly
- executes, or attempts to execute, a scheme or artifice to defraud any person
- in connection with
- any commodity for future delivery, or any option on a commodity for future delivery, or any security of an issuer with a class of securities registered under section 12 of the 1934 Act (15 U.S.C. § 78l), or that is required to file reports under section 15(d) of the 1934 Act (15 U.S.C. § 78a(d)).

Section 1348(1) requires proof of a scheme to defraud but not a false statement or material omission.[99] It also requires proof of a fraudulent intent, which, as in mail and wire fraud prosecutions, connotes an intent to injure or cheat. The government must prove that the violation was "knowing," but unlike § 10(b) and Rule 10b-5 cases, § 1348 does not require proof of "willfulness." This subsection requires that the fraud be "in connection with" a security but not in connection with the "purchase or sale" of security as in Title 15 cases.

Also, unlike cases charged under § 10(b) and Rule 10b-5, prosecutors can charge § 1348(1) violations on an honest services theory,[100] the particulars of which are discussed at length in Chapter 6 (Fraud). The honest services theory of fraud had its genesis in mail and wire fraud cases. The object of a cognizable mail or wire fraud must be one of two things: "money or property" or "honest services." We are all familiar with "money or property" fraud: A defendant lies to someone to con her into giving the defendant money or property to which he is not entitled. An "honest services" fraud is not as intuitive, but it is not difficult to understand.

The honest services theory of mail and wire fraud grew out of prosecutors' attempts to find a federal statute with which to attack state and local corruption. Where, you might ask, is the "fraud" in public corruption? Prosecutors charged that (1) public officials owe a duty of honest services to the public; (2) they breach that duty when they receive illegal bribes or kickbacks; and (3) the failure to disclose their breach of duty constituted "fraud." Corruption cases, then, were bootstrapped into fraud cases by the

99. *See Coscia*, 866 F.3d at 796; *see also* United States v. Harra, 985 F.3d 196, 222 n.21 (2d Cir. 2021) (bowing to consensus of sister circuits that § 1348 requires proof of an intent to defraud); United States v. Mahaffy, No. 05-CR-613, 2006 WL 2224518, at *16 (E.D.N.Y. Aug. 2, 2006).

100. *See Mahaffy*, 2006 WL 2224518, at *12.

alleged non-disclosure of a breach of the so-called duty of honest services. Over time, this theory was applied to private employers as well. Thus, private employees owe a duty of honest services to their employers and if they breach that duty and do not disclose the breach, they have defrauded their employer of its right to their honest services.

Congress codified honest services fraud in 18 U.S.C. § 1346, which provides that, "[f]or the purposes of this chapter, the term 'scheme or artifice to defraud' includes a scheme or artifice to deprive another of the intangible right of honest services." "[T]his chapter" means Chapter 63 of Title 18 which contains the mail (§ 1341), wire (§ 1343), bank (§ 1344), health care (§ 1347), and securities (§ 1348) fraud offenses.

Because § 1346 provides that "schemes to defraud" for purposes of § 1348 include schemes to deprive another of the right to honest services, violations of § 1348(1) can be premised on a scheme to deprive the victims of either money or property *or* honest services. Courts will likely turn to mail and wire fraud precedents to determine whether a defendant owes the victim a duty of honest services. This is an area of great uncertainty, but it is safe to say that public officials owe the citizenry a duty of honest services and that most employees owe their employers such a duty. We do know that the Supreme Court, in *Skilling v. United States*, 561 U.S. 358 (2010), severely limited that which will be deemed a violation of a right to honest services. Formerly, such breaches could be alleged based on all kinds of misconduct, including acting under disabling conflicts of interest, or engaging in self-dealing. The *Skilling* Court held that only bribery or kickbacks constitute a breach of honest services.

B. Securities Fraud under § 1348(2)

Section 1348(2) renders criminally liable a defendant who:

- knowingly
- executes, or attempts to execute, a scheme or artifice
- to obtain,
- by means of false or fraudulent pretenses, representations, or promises,
- any money or property
- in connection with
- the purchase or sale of
- any commodity for future delivery, or any option on a commodity for future delivery, or any security of an issuer with a class of securities registered under section 12 of the 1934 Act (15 U.S.C. § 78l), or that is required to file reports under section 15(d) of the 1934 Act (15 U.S.C. § 78a(d)).

In listing the elements of this violation, the Ninth Circuit required proof that "the statements made or the facts omitted as part of the scheme were material."[101] Under § 1348(2), like § 1348(1), the government must prove the defendant's fraudulent intent.[102] Again, this subsection requires only that the defendant act knowingly, not willfully. But it, like Title 15 cases, requires prosecutors to prove that the fraud be "in connection with" the "purchase or sale" of commodity futures or options or securities. Section 1342(2) is limited to cases in which "money or property" is the object of the fraud. It would seem, then, that honest services cases could not proceed under § 1348(2).

C. Scheme or Artifice to Defraud under § 1348(1)

Given that the circuits are looking to mail and wire fraud precedents in construing § 1348, perhaps the most relevant precedent to consult to determine what constitutes a scheme or artifice to defraud under § 1348(1) is *Carpenter v. United States*, 484 U.S. 19 (1987), a pre-*O'Hagan* case. In *Carpenter*, R. Foster Winans was co-author of a Wall Street Journal (*Journal*) investment advice column that did not contain inside information but that, because of its perceived quality and integrity, had an impact on the market prices of the stocks it discussed. Although he was familiar with the *Journal*'s policy that the column's contents were the *Journal*'s confidential information prior to publication, Winans entered into a scheme with others who, in exchange for advance information from Winans as to the timing and contents of the column, bought and sold stocks based on the column's probable impact on the market and shared their profits with Winans.

The government charged the conspirators, *inter alia*, with insider trading and mail and wire fraud. Because Winans did not owe a duty to the shareholders with whom the conspirators were trading, classical insider trading theory was unavailable. The government thus relied on the misappropriation theory, arguing that Winans breached a duty he owed to the source of the information— the *Journal*— and used the information in connection with the purchase or sale of securities. This was the first time the Supreme Court considered the misappropriation theory, but the Justices were deadlocked by a four-four vote. Accordingly, the Court affirmed the insider trading conviction by an evenly divided court and thus without analysis or precedential effect. It was not until 1997 and *O'Hagan* that the Court formally approved the misappropriation theory of insider trading.

---

101. *Hussain*, 972 F.3d at 1146.
102. *See* United States v. Ramsey, Crim. Action No. 19-268, 2022 WL 596378, at *8 (E.D. Pa. Feb. 28, 2022).

The *Carpenter* opinion is important, however, for what the Court said while upholding Winans's convictions for employing a "scheme to defraud" the *Journal* of "money or property" for purposes of mail and wire fraud. Section 1348(1), of course, requires proof of a "scheme to defraud" and § 1348(2) requires that the victim be deprived of "money or property."

Winan first argued that the information he traded on was not "property" for purposes of these statutes. The Supreme Court rejected this argument, holding that "the *Journal*'s confidential business information— the publication schedule and contents of the . . . column"— constituted property protected by the mail and wire fraud statutes.[103] The Court explained that "'[c]onfidential information acquired or compiled by a corporation in the course and conduct of its business is a species of property to which the corporation has the exclusive right and benefit, and which a court of equity will protect through the injunctive process or other appropriate remedy.'"[104] The Court held that the *Journal* had a property right in keeping confidential and making exclusive use, prior to publication, of the schedule and contents of the column, observing "'news matter, however little susceptible of ownership or dominion in the absolute sense, is stock in trade, to be gathered at the cost of enterprise, organization, skill, labor, and money, and to be distributed and sold to those who will pay money for it, as for any other merchandise.'"[105]

The Supreme Court further rejected Winan's argument that the government proved only that he violated workplace rules, not "fraud." It held that the fraud at issue consisted of Winan's deceptive failure to disclose his breach of his duty to the *Journal* to safeguard its confidential information.[106] The Court also noted that the "concept of 'fraud' includes the act of embezzlement, which is the fraudulent appropriation to one's own use of the money or goods entrusted to one's care by another."[107] A "scheme to defraud" for purposes of § 1348(1), then, is likely to reflect Title 15's acceptance of a theory of deception premised on a failure to disclose in the face of an unfaithful employee's duty to do so.

D. Money or Property Under § 1342(2)

Courts are likely to reference mail and wire fraud precedents in determining what constitutes "money or property" for purposes of § 1342(2) because those words are virtually terms of art in such cases. The Second

103. *Carpenter*, 484 U.S. at 25.
104. *Id.* at 26.
105. *Id.*
106. *Id.* at 28.
107. *Id.* (internal quotation marks omitted).

Circuit's reasoning in *United States v. Blaszczak*, 56 F.4th 230 (2d Cir. 2022), is representative.[108]

In *Blaszczak*, the defendant, who used to be an employee of the Centers for Medicare and Medicaid Services (CMS), learned of planned changes to Medicaid reimbursement rates from his former colleagues at CMS. In his capacity as a consultant to various hedge funds, he shared this pre-decisional confidential information with his clients. The clients then shorted the stocks of health care companies that would be hurt if these changes were in fact implemented. Baszczak was charged, *inter alia*, with securities fraud under § 1348 and wire fraud under § 1343.

The question presented was whether the confidential governmental information he shared was "money or property" for purposes of these statutes. The government argued that the Supreme Court has recognized that confidential business information is "property," citing *Carpenter*. Prosecutors argued that the government does not cease to have a property interest in confidential information simply because it is ultimately used for a regulatory purpose, asserting that the government cannot be the only employer lacking an economic interest in its work product such that employees may steal and misuse such information with impunity. But a split panel of the Second Circuit ruled to the contrary, holding that although confidential information may constitute property of a commercial entity, the same is not true of CMS, which is not such an entity. It noted that the government's information could not be viewed as its "'stock in trade'" that had economic value, as in *Carpenter*.[109] Instead, the information reflecting decisions about reimbursement rates and the timing of the disclosure of such decisions was "regulatory in character."[110]

E. "In Connection With" Requirement

The courts are in accord in reading the nexus requirement— that the fraud be in connection with a qualifying commodity future or option or security (§ 1348(1)) or the purchase and sale of a qualifying commodity future or option or security (§ 1348(2))— very broadly.

---

108. The Second Circuit initially concluded, *inter alia*, that the pre-decisional confidential government information was "property." *See* United States v. Blaszczak, 947 F.3d 19 (2d Cir. 2019). The Supreme Court granted certiorari, vacated the judgment, and remanded for reconsideration in light of the Court's decision in *Kelly v. United States*, 590 U.S. 391 (2020). *See* Blaszczak v. United States, 141 S. Ct. 1040 (2021). On remand, the Second Circuit reversed itself on the property question in the case discussed, *United States v. Blaszczak*, 56 F.4th 230 (2d Cir. 2022).

109. 56 F.4th at 243.

110. *Id.* at 244; *cf.* United States v. Rodrigues, 22-cr-00391 (PMH), 2024 WL 113744 (Jan. 10, 2024); United States v. Hird, 913 F.3d 332 (3d Cir. 2019).

Under § 1348(1), the defendants need not have caused or intended to cause *economic* loss to the holder of the securities at issue because the statutory text requires only that the defendant intend to defraud "*any* person in connection with *a security*." *United States v. Mahaffy*, 2006 WL 2224518 (E.D.N.Y. 2006), for example, involved a species of "front running" fraud: the defendant day traders made payments to defendant stockbrokers in return for non-public information relating to pending orders from institutional clients of the brokerage firms for the purchase or sale of large blocks of securities. The day traders used the information to purchase or sell these securities in advance of the brokerage firms' execution of their clients' orders, making a profit when the execution of the brokerage clients' large securities positions moved the market to the traders' advantage. The court rejected the defendants' argument that the case failed because there was no proof that the persons with whom they transacted in buying or selling securities were defrauded. It noted that the statute "defines no such narrow range of prospective victims" and ruled that the requirement that the scheme be "in connection with" a security "is satisfied where, as a result of the scheme, the defendants either benefitted, or attempted to benefit, from trading in securities."[111]

In *United States v. Hussain*, 972 F.3d 1138 (9th Cir. 2020), the Ninth Circuit upheld a conviction under 18 U.S.C. § 1348(2) of a defendant who was the Chief Financial Officer of a company Hewlett Packard (HP) acquired. After the acquisition, it was discovered that the defendant and others had for years fraudulently misrepresented the company's financial status. On the cusp of the acquisition, the defendant had signed a letter warranting that the HP press release announcing the acquisition contained truthful information about the company to be acquired. The government introduced evidence at trial that investors and equity analysts relied on the false statements in the press release. The defendant argued that his verification of the information in HP's press release was too attenuated to constitute a fraudulent scheme "in connection with" HP securities trading. The Ninth Circuit rejected this argument, holding the fraud in the press release met § 1348's "in connection with" requirement. It relied on Supreme Court and Ninth Circuit precedents giving the "in connection with" element of § 10(b) a broad interpretation and noted that Congress could not be unaware of this broad construction in using the same language in § 1348.

The Ninth Circuit relied in particular on caselaw holding that where the fraud alleged involves public dissemination of a document such as a press release, annual report, investment prospectus or other such document on which investors would presumably rely, the "in connection with" requirement is generally met by proof of the means of dissemination and

111. *Mahaffy*, 2006 WL 2224518 at *12.

the materiality of the misrepresentation or omission. Ultimately, the *Hussain* court concluded that because a press release is regularly used to inform the public about an acquisition, it was not a surprise that investors could and would make trading decisions based on its contents.

F. "Securities" and "Commodities"

Under § 1348, the fraud must be in connection with "any commodity for future delivery, or any option on a commodity for future delivery, or any security of an issuer with a class of securities registered under section 12 of the 1934 Act (15 U.S.C. § 78l), or that is required to file reports under section 15(d) of the 1934 Act (15 U.S.C. § 78a(d))."

In practice, the securities covered include the securities of "any company with a class of securities listed on a national securities exchange in the United States, or any company with a class of securities quoted in the over-the-counter market in the United States and required to file periodic reports with SEC."[112] This may include non-U.S. companies, for example foreign firms with American Depository Receipts that are listed on a U.S. exchange.[113]

Section 1348 is not accompanied by a definition of the word "security." One defendant argued that "securities" within the meaning of § 1348 do not include options. Relying primarily on ordinary meaning and the 1934 Act's definition of "security," a district court rejected this argument holding that options for securities fall within § 1348.[114]

When this section was first enacted in 2002, § 1348 did not contain the clauses encompassing commodities futures or options. The statute was amended in 2009 to include these terms,[115] extending the scope of the statute beyond securities fraud regulated by the SEC to frauds covered by the Commodity Exchange Act and enforced by the CFTC.

G. Insider Trading Tipping Cases

Prosecutors will no doubt prefer to use § 1348 when pursuing tipper/tippee cases. As noted above, to prove tipper/tippee liability in an insider trading case under Title 15, the government must prove that the tipper

---

112. U.S. Dep't of Justice & SEC, FCPA: A Resource Guide to the Foreign Corrupt Practices Act 9 (2d ed. 2020). This category of persons is referred to as "issuers" under the FCPA.
113. *Id.* at 10.
114. *Ramsey*, 2022 WL 596378, at *10-*11.
115. *See* Pub. L. 111-21, § 2(e)(1), 123 Stat. 1617, 1618 (2009).

received some "personal benefit" when providing material non-public information. The courts to address this issue thus far have concluded that no such proof requirement exists under 18 U.S.C. § 1348. They reason that the personal benefit test was a court-created doctrine intended to effectuate the statutory purpose of the 1934 Act and that such purposes do not apply in the context of § 1348.[116] They also cite to the congressional intent underlying § 1348 to expand the scope of securities fraud liability.

Examples

1. Lor Ruth was a financial advisor who met Miguelito Aguirre in 2014 while attending Alcoholics Anonymous (AA) meetings. AA is a fellowship of recovering alcoholics who share a desire to stop drinking. AA members are encouraged to reach out to others in the fellowship. As a newcomer, Aguirre sought support from Ruth, who had similar interests and had been sober for decades. For ten years, Ruth informally mentored Aguirre in AA. They attended meetings together and although they went on occasional social outings, sobriety was the primary purpose of their relationship. They both understood that their conversations were private and would not be shared. This comported with the general practice in AA, where "newcomers can turn . . . with the assurance that no newfound friends will violate confidences relating to that person's drinking problem."[117] In early 2024, Aguirre was involved in negotiations to sell the highly profitable company he owned; this information was not public knowledge. During this period, he suffered periodic alcoholic relapses. When Ruth queried him about his binges, Aguirre revealed that he was drinking because of the stress he was under due to his efforts sell his company. Aguirre trusted Ruth to keep this information in confidence. Ruth then purchased a substantial amount of Aguirre's company's stock and, once the sale was announced, sold his shares for a substantial profit. Is Ruth liable for insider trading under § 10(b), Rule 10b-5, or § 1348?

2. Kurt Holmström was the president of a clinical research firm and served as the principal investigator in conducting clinical trials for a new drug developed by a pharmaceutical company, Big Pharma (BP). In this capacity he was responsible for recruiting subjects, monitoring the results of the treatment, and reporting the results of the study. BP paid him a fee of

116. *See Blaszczak*, 947 F.3d at 34-37; United States v. Ramsey, 565 F. Supp. 3d 641, 643-46 (E.D. Pa. 2021).
117. Alcoholics Anonymous, Frequently Asked Questions About AA, 11 (2018), available at https://www.aa.org/frequently-asked-questions-about-aa-formerly-44-questions.

$80,000 for this work. In his contract with BP, Holmström undertook to maintain "in strict confidence" all the information with which he was provided to enable him to perform as principal investigator. Shortly afterwards, he began buying BP stock. When, during the clinical trial period, Holmström received an email informing him that several patients in the trial had suffered serious allergic reactions, Holmström quickly sold his shares. Is Holmström guilt of insider trading under § 10(b), Rule 10b-5, or § 1348? How would he defend such a case?

3. Fikri Demirci was an executive at Acme, Inc. Acme was about to make a significant acquisition that promised to boost its stock price when Demirci went to his high school reunion. He should have known better. While golfing during the reunion weekend, Demirci attempted to make himself look like a mover and shaker by revealing to his foursome that his company was about to make a big acquisition that would move its stock price through the roof. Demirci was bullied and belittled by one of the foursome in high school. He had not seen the classmates in ten years and the tip was intended to show the bully that he had made good. The bully traded on the information and then tipped it to another classmate who was not present, saying that Demirci finally seemed worth knowing. Can the bully and the classmate he tipped be liable as tippees under § 10(b), Rule 10b-5, or § 1348?

4. Era Prifti was the director of the West Virginia Lottery and, as such, was responsible for negotiating and securing contracts on behalf of the Lottery. The Lottery made a confidential decision to expand video lottery gaming in the state. It determined to award a valuable contract to Video Gaming, Inc. (VGI) for these purposes. Before the contract award was announced, Prifti bought 300 shares of VGI stock. Can she be held liable for insider trading under § 10(b), Rule 10b-5, or § 1348? What would Prifti argue in defense?

5. Shu Yun Lin was a corporate executive at Medivation, Inc., a biopharmaceutical company. When she joined Medivation, she signed the company's insider trading policy, which stated in part:

   > During the course of your employment . . . you may receive important information that is not yet publicly disseminated about the Company . . . . Because of your access to this information, you may be in a position to profit financially by buying or selling or in some other way dealing in the Company's securities . . . or the securities of another publicly traded company, including all significant collaborators, customers, partners, suppliers, or competitors of the Company. For anyone to use such information to gain personal benefit . . . is illegal.

In 2023, Lin learned that Pfizer Inc. was contemplating acquiring Medivation. This was treated as highly sensitive, confidential information within the company. Lin immediately purchased out of the money (OTM) call options not of Medivation, but rather of another comparable public company, Incyte Corp. Incyte was a competitor of Mediviation's, and one of the few companies of Mediviation's size that also had commercial-stage oncology drugs A call option is a contract between a buyer and seller that gives the buyer the right to purchase a stock, bond, commodity, or other asset at a specific price, known as the strike price, by a specific date, called the expiration date. The buyer pays the seller a premium for this right and can either exercise the contract or let it expire. If the strike price is lower than the market price of the asset at expiration, the buyer can make a profit by exercising the option and purchasing the asset for less than market value. A call option is OTM if the underlying price is trading below the price at which Lin could exercise her option. Because these options were OTM, Lin was able to pick them up for a song. Following a public announcement that Pfizer had acquired Medivation, Incyte's stock price increased by 8%. Lin exercised her option and earned profits of $100,000. Can Lin be held liable for insider trading under § 10(b), Rule 10b-5, or § 1348? What would she argue in defense?

6. Kim Corwin knew that IMS Health Inc. (IMS) would announce its third-quarter earnings during an analyst conference call scheduled for 6:00 pm EST on October 17, 2023—that is, after the close of the securities markets in New York. IMS hired Thomson Financial to provide investor relations and web-hosting services, which included managing the online release of IMS's earnings reports. Throughout the day on October 17, an anonymous hacker attempted to gain access to the IMS earnings reports by hacking into a secure server at Thompson prior to the report's official release. At 2:15 p.m., the hacker successfully located and downloaded the IMS data from the secure server. Fifteen minutes later, Corwin purchased a large quantity of IMS put options that would expire on October 25, 2023. Put options give the buyer of the option the right, but not the obligation, to sell a specific asset at a predetermined price until a certain date. Put options are generally purchased by those who are betting that the stock price will decline; the option owner hopes to be able to buy shares cheaply after the price goes down and sell them at the higher price contracted for in the option. IMS's disappointing earnings reports were released at 5 pm; the following morning the stock price sank 28%. Within minutes, Corwin sold his put options, realizing a net profit of $300,000 overnight. Can Corwin be held criminally liable under § 10(b), Rule 10b-5, or § 1348?

Explanations

1. Ruth clearly bought securities while in knowing possession of (and using) material, non-public information regarding the prospective sale. He owned no fiduciary duty to the company or the shareholders with whom he transacted. Thus, any insider trading case would have to proceed on a misappropriation theory, which requires proof that he breached a duty of trust and confidence he owed to the source of the material, non-public information. Ruth did not have a fiduciary duty to Aguirre but the Third Circuit held in *United States v. McGee*, 763 F.3d 304 (3d Cir. 2014), that an AA mentorship of the sort hypothesized here constituted a relationship of trust and confidence.

   The SEC, in Rule 10b5-2, identified three non-exhaustive categories of relationships that give rise to a duty to disclose for purposes of misappropriation liability. Even assuming that there is no expectation of confidentiality generally in AA, Rule 10b5-2(b)(2) recognizes a qualifying relationship of trust and confidence where there is a "history, pattern, or practice of sharing confidences" between two parties.[118] In the case posited, Ruth mentored Aguirre for a decade, was entrusted with extremely personal information, and the parties' joint expectation was that information would be kept confidential.

   Ruth would also argue that the inside information about the company exceeded the scope of any confidential relationship born of their membership in AA because the information did not relate to sobriety. This argument was rejected in *McGee* given that the information upon which Ruth traded was shared during a conversation concerning the reasons for Aguirre's failure to remain sober.

   With respect to whether a § 1348 case could be made, that section is not augmented by anything like Rule 10b5-2 and thus who has a duty to disclose a breach of a confidentiality obligation is a matter for common law development. Under mail and wire fraud precedents, "[a] defendant's breach of a fiduciary duty may be a predicate for a violation of the mail fraud statute where the breach entails the violation of a duty to disclose material information. . . . An affirmative duty to disclose need not be explicitly imposed; it may instead be implicit in the relationship between the parties.[119]

   It should also be noted that courts in mail and wire fraud cases have been much less exacting than they are in securities fraud cases when examining who may bear a duty to disclose, the breach of which constitutes fraud. Indeed, they have imposed such a duty on virtually every employee without analysis. Whether courts will be willing to conclude that such a duty arises

118. 17 C.F.R. § 240.10b5-2(b)(2).
119. United States v. Waymer, 55 F.3d 564, 571 (11th Cir. 1995).

out of joint participation in AA and a long-term mentoring relationship is unclear. But one assumes that in securities fraud cases courts will at least reference Rule 10b5-2 (and *McGee*) in interpreting the scope of § 1348.

2. This hypothetical is drawn from *United States v. Kosinski*, 976 F.3d 135 (2d Cir. 2020), in which the principal investigator was convicted under § 10(b). As in that case, Holmström's principal argument would be that he did not owe the BP shareholders with whom he transacted or BP any duty; accordingly, he had no duty to disclose or abstain from trading. There are in fact many cases in which defendants who have entered into confidentiality agreements but are not formally company employees contend that they cannot be convicted of insider trading due to the "arm's length" nature of their business relationship. The Second Circuit has repeatedly rejected this argument.

   In *Kosinski*, the Second Circuit first characterized persons, such as Holmström, who enter into confidentiality agreements as "temporary insiders." The court said that temporary insiders can be liable under both classical and misappropriation theories and, in fact, that Kosinski was responsible under both theories: "he could have been successfully prosecuted under the classical theory (because he failed to disclose to his trading counterparty that he was trading in inside information) and under the misappropriation theory (because he failed to disclose [to the company from which he misappropriated the inside information] that he was trading on inside information that he had been given in confidence)."[120] The court further found that, quite apart from whether the defendant qualified as "temporary insider," his relationship with the drug company was that of a fiduciary, explaining that the "'explicit acceptance of a duty of confidentiality' is itself sufficient to establish the necessary fiduciary duty of trust and confidence."[121]

   For purposes of § 1348, the question again is whether Holmström has a duty to disclose his abuse of confidential information for purposes of § 1348. Although courts are likely to reference whatever caselaw exists in the mail and wire fraud context, one would also assume that they will consider cases like *Kosinski* persuasive precedent.

3. Proceeding under § 10(b) and Rule 10b-5, Demirci was an insider, who tipped material non-public information and the bully, at least, knowingly possessed and used it when he engaged in securities trading. The case, however, raises two issues. The tippee can only be liable if the tipper breached his duty to his company by sharing the information for personal gain, including as a gift, and the tippee knew or "should have

---

120. *Kosinski*, 976 F.3d at 145.

121. *Id.* at 146; *see also Chow*, 993 F.3d at 138.

known" that there has been a breach[122] (which, in the Second Circuit, means the tipper knew that the tippee "disclosed confidential information in exchange for personal benefit"[123]). The first question is whether the tippees knew that the tipper breached his duty by tipping; depending on the sophistication of the tippees— for example, if they were well versed in the financial markets— this may be provable. But in the Second Circuit, the government would have to prove that the tippees knew that the tipper acted for personal benefit, which would be a much heavier burden. The second question is whether the tipper in fact acted for personal benefit or to bestow a gift. Both seem unlikely. Even if the tipper received some vicarious emotional benefit in showing up his high school tormentor, this benefit was not knowingly given by the tippees. And if the sharing of the information is viewed as a "gift," there remains the question whether this theory requires proof of a close personal relationship, which was certainly not present here.

The government could obviate these difficulties by charging the case under § 1348(2). The caselaw thus far holds that the government need not prove that the tipper received a personal benefit to prevail in such insider trading cases.

4. Prifti did not owe any duty to the company or shareholders with whom she transacted and thus could not be charged under classical insider trading theory. After *O'Hagan*, this case would proceed on a misappropriation theory because the Prifti clearly would be found to have a duty to her employer, the state, to safeguard the confidential contract information. She knowingly and willfully bought securities while in knowing possession of and using this information.

   Prifti may argue that application of the misappropriation theory of securities fraud in this case makes no sense because there was no securities-related harm to the victim given that the state was not in market for the securities in which Prifti transacted. She may turn to a case, *United States v. Bryan*, 58 F.3d 933 (4th Cir. 1995), since overruled by *O'Hagan*, in which the Fourth Circuit rejected the misappropriation theory on similar facts. In that case, the court highlighted the fact that the state official was convicted under a misappropriation theory even though the entity deemed defrauded— the state from which he "stole" the information about the impending contract award— was apparently not transacting or planning on transacting in the affected stock. It argued that application of the insider trading prohibition in such circumstances

   > effectively eliminates the requirement that a person in some way connected to a securities transaction be deceived, allowing conviction not only where

122. *Dirks*, 463 U.S. at 660.
123. *Newman*, 773 F.3d at 449.

> the "defrauded" person has no connection with a securities transaction, but where no investor or market participant has been deceived. In allowing the statute's unitary requirement to be satisfied by any fiduciary breach that is followed by a securities transaction (whether or not the breach is of a duty owed to a purchaser or seller of securities, or to another market participant), the misappropriation theory transforms section 10(b) from a rule intended to govern and protect relations among market participants who are owed duties under the securities laws into a federal common law governing and protecting any and all trust relationships.[124]

Prifti may well attempt to borrow Bryan's argument that misappropriation securities fraud cases should fail where there is no securities-related harm threatened to the source of the information. In a classical insider trading case, the defendant is clearly causing harm to the shareholders with whom he is transacting without disclosing material inside information he learned by working, in essence, for them. But in misappropriation cases, there is no securities-related harm to the "victim"— that is, the source of the information— unless the source or someone related to the source is actually trading in the same market as the defendant. Prifti would distinguish *O'Hagan* by noting that there *was* a securities-related harm to the victims in that case. The defendant was a lawyer at a firm that represented Grand Metropolitan PLC (Grand Met) regarding its contemplated tender offer for Pillsbury. The defendant bought Pillsbury stock and made a large profit when Grand Met made its tender offer. In other words, there was a securities-related harm to the firm's client, which sought to purchase the same shares O'Hagan was trading in.

This argument is likely to be couched as one going to the "in connection with" requirement. Although *O'Hagan* is distinguishable on its facts, this defense is inconsistent with the *O'Hagan* Court's reasoning, as summarized above. The Court has endorsed a very broad reading of this element in both *O'Hagan* and *Zandford*. Given the Court's caselaw on the subject, this argument is unlikely to succeed.

This case could not be charged under § 1348(2), at least in the Second Circuit, assuming— as some courts have indicated— that that section should be read in conjunction with the mail and wire fraud statutes. Subsection (2) requires that the defendant execute a scheme to defraud the victim of "money or property." One could argue that the state had a property interest in the confidential information regarding its decision to award a valuable contract to VGI. In *Blaszczak*, however, a panel of the Second Circuit ruled, over a vigorous dissent, that although a private company's confidential business information constitutes "property"

124. *Bryan*, 58 F.3d at 950.

under *Carpenter*, confidential *government* information is not property for purposes of the mail and wire fraud statutes.[125]

With respect to possible charges under § 1348(1), if § 1348 is read in light of §§ 1341, 1343, and § 1346, the only viable object of the scheme to defraud under § 1348(1) would be honest services because, as noted above, a property theory is likely unavailable. But while a public official owes a duty of honest services to the public, the *Skilling* Supreme Court ruled that that duty is only violated by bribery or kickbacks, neither of which is present here.[126]

Note that there have been numerous reports in the press about various members of the U.S. Congress making large profits trading in stocks while in possession, by virtue of their positions, of material non-public information. In 2012, a series of insider trading scandals forced Congress to pass the STOCK Act,[127] which renders it illegal for lawmakers to trade on inside information in certain circumstances. Those members of Congress who choose to participate in equities markets must disclose their transactions. The problem continues, albeit on a lesser scale.[128] As of this writing, a number of proposed reforms have been suggested but not yet adopted.[129]

5. The hypothetical raises the question of whether so-called "shadow" trading— that is, using the material non-public information one learns from one company to trade in the shares of another— violates § 10(b). A call option is a "security" under § 10(b) and Rule 10b-5. Lin is a corporate insider misusing information she learned by virtue of her employment.

   Lin may defend the case first by arguing that the government could not prove materiality because she did not trade in Incyte's securities based on confidential, non-public information about *that security or issuer*. The government would counter by pointing out that § 10(b) prohibits insider trading with respect to "any security" and arguing that information can be material to more than one company. A district court accepted the government's argument in *SEC v. Panuwat*, 2022 WL 633306 (N.D. Ca. 2022), holding that "Rule 10b5-1(a) does not state that the information 'about that security or issuer' must come from the security or issuer itself

125. *See Blaszczak*, 56 F.4th at 243-44.
126. *See* Chapter 6 (Fraud).
127. Pub. Law No. 112-105, 126 Stat. 291 (2012).
128. A 2022 analysis by the *New York Times* found that 97 lawmakers or their families bought and sold stocks that directly intersected with their work on congressional committees. *See Lawmakers still benefiting from share trading in defense stocks*, Federal Times, Apr. 2, 2024, available at https://www.federaltimes.com/federal-oversight/congress/2024/04/01/lawmakers-still-benefitting-from-share-trading-in-defense-stocks/ (last visited June 11, 2024).
129. *See* Congressional Research Service, *Proposals to Limit Financial Activities of Members of Congress: Background and Analysis of Legislative Proposals*, R47818 (Oct. 24, 2023).

in order to be material. It only requires that the information be material and nonpublic."[130] This information was material given that few companies of Mediviation's size had commercial-stage oncology drugs so one could infer that the acquisition of one would make the others more attractive, driving up their stock prices.

Lin would also argue that she did not owe those with whom she transacted a duty and thus classical insider trading liability is inappropriate. She would contend that misappropriation theory is also inapposite because she did not breach any duty to her employer— the source of the information— by trading in its competitor's stock. Lin would likely lose this argument, as the defendant did in *Panuwat*, given that the plain language of the company's insider trading policy covered other public traded companies, including competitors.[131]

Finally, Lin may contend that she did not "knowingly use" the information in trading. There is a split in the circuits on whether the government must show only that the defendant knowingly possessed the information while trading or whether it must show that she actually "used" it in trading. As noted above, the SEC took the position, in Rule 10b5-1, that all the government need prove is that the defendant was "aware of" the material non-public information when trading.[132] In *Panuwat*, the court found that the facts alleged met either standard.

The Ninth Circuit, in endorsing the "use" standard, explained the type of circumstantial evidence that might prove this element: "Suppose, for instance, that an individual who has never before invested comes into possession of material nonpublic information and the very next day invests a substantial sum of money in substantially out-of-the-money call options. We are confident that the government would have little trouble demonstrating 'use' in such a situation."[133] In *Panuwat*, the court was persuaded that the "use" standard could be satisfied because although Medivation had been studying a potential acquisition for a month, it was not until the defendant, who had never traded in Incyte stock previously, received an email saying that the deal was imminent that he bought the Incyte stock. He in fact made the purchase of the options within minutes of reading the email.

6. These "hack and trade" cases are arising with some frequency.[134] A put option is a "security" under § 10(b) and Rule 10b-5. The first question is whether this "device"— computer hacking— is "deceptive." Section

130. *Panuwat*, 2022 WL 633306, *4.
131. *See id.* at *6.
132. 17 C.F.R. § 240.10b5-1(b).
133. *Smith*, 155 F.3d at 1069.
134. *See, e.g.*, United States v. Khalupsky, 5 F.4th 279 (2d Cir. 2021); SEC v. Stone, 22-civ.-3553 (VM), 2023 WL 6387276 (S.D.N.Y. Sept. 29, 2023).

10(b) and Rule 10b-5 are about fraud, which requires proof of deception. Deception is usually proved in one of two ways— through *affirmative misrepresentations (lies)* and *a failure to disclose where there is a duty to do so.* Insider trading cases are normally founded on a failure to disclose but readers should not lose track of the possibility of relying instead on affirmative misstatements.

Corwin had no duty either to the shareholders or the company in whose shares he is trading, or to the source of the information— Thomson. Accordingly, a theory that his failure to disclose his trading in breach of a duty— the theory in most insider trading cases— is not available.

In the case upon which this problem is based, *SEC v. Dorozhko*, 574 F.3d 42 (2d Cir. 2009), then, the SEC did not allege that the defendant remained silent in the face of a duty to disclose or abstain from trading. Rather, it argued that "the defendant affirmatively misrepresented himself in order to gain access to material, nonpublic information, which he then used to trade" and that this misrepresentation constituted a deceptive device or contrivance within the meaning of § 10(b).[135]

The district court held that the alleged hack and trade was a "device or contrivance" within the meaning of the statute. It also held that the device was "in connection with" the purchase or sale of securities because of the close proximity of the hacking to the trading. But the trial court held that something could not be a "deceptive" device absent a breach of a fiduciary duty.

On appeal, the Second Circuit conceded that the Supreme Court's insider trading cases regarding when "silence" constitutes securities fraud establish that non-disclosure in breach of a fiduciary duty to disclose is a deceptive device or contrivance under the securities laws. But the fact that such cases require proof of a fiduciary duty does not mean that such a duty is necessary when the case is founded on *affirmative deception* rather than silence in the face of fiduciary duty to disclose.

The Second Circuit accepted the SEC's argument that a breach of a fiduciary duty was not necessary to prove "deception" where some affirmative misrepresentation is alleged. Turning to the facts of the case, the court discussed the two ways the defendant could have hacked into Thomson's system: (1) providing a false identification and masquerading as another; or (2) exploiting a weakness in the program to cause the program to malfunction in a way that granted the hacker greater privileges. The Second Circuit decided that "misrepresenting one's identity in

135. *Dorozhko*, 574 F.3d at 49.

order to gain access to information that is otherwise off limits, and then stealing that information is plainly 'deceptive' within the ordinary meaning of the word."[136] The court said that it was less clear that exploiting a weakness in the code constitutes deception as opposed to theft. This may be closer to a case in which someone breaks into an investment bank and steals the inside information, which has never been charged as securities fraud.

136. Id. at 51; *see also Khalupsky*, 5 F.4th at 291.

CHAPTER 9

Public Corruption

The term "public corruption" can cover a variety of evils—such as theft, misuse of government assets, and nepotism—as well as bribery. This chapter focuses on the tools prosecutors use in bringing bribery and gratuities cases because it is this form of venality that is the principal focus of most public corruption prosecutions.

Federal prosecutors pursuing public officials for bribery or gratuities violations have a variety of charging options whose applicability depend on the facts of the case. The most obvious candidate is the federal bribery statute, 18 U.S.C. § 201, which applies only to federal officials and employees and those who possess a position of public trust with federal responsibilities (and, since 2023, to foreign officials who corruptly seek a bribe from certain categories of individuals). There is no analogous generally applicable provision in the federal code that can be pressed into service to address domestic bribery or gratuities on the state and local level. To prosecute such cases, prosecutors may rely on the Hobbs Act under 18 U.S.C. § 1951, Federal Program Bribery under 18 U.S.C. § 666, and the Travel Act under 18 U.S.C. § 1952 where the facts permit. Additional potentially applicable statues are explored in other chapters in this volume: honest services mail and wire fraud under 18 U.S.C. §§ 1341, 1343 and 1346 (Chapter 6) and the Racketeer Influenced and Corrupt Organizations Act (RICO) violations under 18 U.S.C. §§ 1961-68 (Chapter 10).[1]

In this chapter we will also explore the Foreign Corrupt Practices Act (FCPA), 15 U.S.C. §§ 78dd1–78dd3, which prosecutors use to address transnational corruption—that is, bribes offered or paid to *foreign* public officials to obtain or retain business. But the FCPA addresses only active bribery—that is, only the persons who offer or make the corrupt payment can be prosecuted. The FCPA cannot be used to pursue passive bribery—that is, the foreign officials who receive the bribes cannot be charged under the FCPA.

To prosecute the corrupt foreign officials, then, federal prosecutors traditionally looked to other statutes, particularly the Travel Act and the anti-money laundering statutes, 18 U.S.C. §§ 1956–1957 (Chapter 11). The Travel Act is useful not only in prosecuting the bribees, but also in pursuing transnational commercial (rather than official) bribery cases, which also are not covered by the FCPA. In 2023, Congress passed the Foreign Extortion Prevention Act which amended the domestic federal bribery statute, 18 U.S.C. § 201, to criminalize foreign officials' demand or acceptance of a bribe in circumstances that would otherwise violate the FCPA. Because this new subsection of § 201(f) contains terms defined in the FCPA, it will be discussed in Part V within, in connection with the discussion of transnational bribery and the FCPA, rather than in Parts I or II, which deal with domestic bribery and gratuity cases under § 201.

I. BRIBERY, 18 U.S.C. § 201(b)

It is important to note at the outset that § 201 covers only the corruption of members of Congress (either before or after such official has qualified), federal officers and employees, and those acting for or on behalf of any department, agency, or branch of the federal government, including the District of Columbia (§ 201(a)(1)). The Court expanded the statue's scope slightly in *Dixson v. United States*, 465 U.S. 482 (1984), by ruling that some state, local, and private actors who assume responsibility for administering

1. Violations of §§ 201, 1951, and 1952 can serve as the predicate acts upon which a RICO case can be built, but § 666 cannot. *See* 18 U.S.C. § 1961.

federal programs may be prosecuted under § 201. The test in such cases is "whether the person occupies a position of public trust with official federal responsibilities."[2]

To secure a conviction for bribery under § 201(b)(1), which targets the *briber*, the government must prove that the defendant:

- corruptly
- directly or indirectly, gave, offered, or promised to any public official
- personally or "to any other person or entity"
- anything of value
- with intent
  - "to influence any official act" (under § 201(b)(1)(A)), *or*
  - "to induce such public official . . . to do or omit to do any act in violation of the lawful duty of such official or person" (under § 201(b)(1)(C)).[3]

Section 201(b)(2) authorizes the conviction of the person *bribed* upon proof of the same circumstances.

Those convicted of bribery are punishable by a fine, imprisonment of up to fifteen years, and disqualification "from holding any office of honor, trust, or profit under the United States" (§ 201(b)). The unit of prosecution under § 201 is each bribe; thus each bribe is a separate offense that will be punished separately.[4]

A. *Quid Pro Quo* and Corrupt Intent

The essence of bribery is the *quid pro quo* (in Latin, "something for something") element—that is, the requirement that the government prove a specific intent to give or receive something of value *in exchange for* being *influenced* in an official act or being *induced* to violate a lawful duty.

Bribery also carries with it a "corrupt" intent requirement, which is often defined as acting knowingly and intentionally, with a bad purpose of accomplishing either an unlawful end or result, or an otherwise lawful end or result by some unlawful method or means.[5] It is this corrupt intent that separates legitimate campaign contributions from illegal bribes.

2. *Dixson*, 465 U.S. at 496.
3. Section 201(b)(2)(B) proscribes payments to public officials to corruptly influence them "to commit or aid in committing, or collude in, or allow, any fraud" on the United States. Such cases are rare and will not be further considered here. *But see* United States v. Wilson, 408 Fed. App'x 798 (5th Cir. 2010); United States v. Lanier, 920 F.2d 887 (11th Cir. 1991).
4. *See* United States v. Anderson, 509 F.2d 312, 333 (D.C. Cir. 1975).
5. *See, e.g.*, United States v. Liebo, 923 F.2d 1308, 1312 (8th Cir. 1991) (FCPA); Third Circuit Model Criminal Jury Instructions 6.18.201B2-1 (Feb. 2022).

Courts often conflate the "corrupt" intent requirement with *quid pro quo* element of the statute.[6] For example, the Ninth Circuit's pattern jury instructions state that "[a] public official acts 'corruptly' when he or she accepts or receives, or agrees to accept or receive, a thing of value, in return for being influenced with the intent that, in exchange for the thing of value, some act would be influenced."[7]

The corrupt intent required may differ slightly depending on whether the government elects to proceed under § 201(b)(1)(A), which requires that the payment be offered in return for an "official act," or § 201(b)(1)(C), which contemplates that the payment be offered in return for an act in "violation of the lawful duty" of the public official. With respect to the former, "corruptly" does not require proof that the agreement contemplated that the bribee violate his duties. Thus, for example, a judge who accepts a litigant's bribe in return for the official act of a ruling in the briber's favor cannot avoid conviction by asserting that his decision was correct on the merits. With respect to § 201(b)(1)(C) cases, however, proof that the corrupt agreement contemplated a violation of the official's duty would be required. In such cases, the government may predicate the alleged violation of duty on federal regulations governing employee conduct so long as the "regulations in question were specific and reasonably related to the alleged misconduct charged."[8]

The corrupt *quid pro quo* agreement generally can be implied or express. Section 201(b)(1) requires only that something of value be offered or promised, not that a bribe actually be paid. The crime is complete for the briber when he makes the offer with the requisite intent; he need not be successful in corrupting the public official. The public official is liable at the point at which he agrees to be influenced in taking an official act in exchange for the bribe; the official act need not be performed for a conviction.

B. The "*Quid*": The Thing of Value

In terms of what may constitute the requisite "*quid*," the "thing of value" offered is read very broadly to include anything of subjective value to the bribee, including money, property, travel, services, a loan, or a promise of future employment.

---

6. *See, e.g.*, United States v. Alfisi, 308 F.3d 144, 149 (2d Cir. 2002) ("The 'corrupt' intent necessary to a bribery conviction is in the nature of a *quid pro quo* requirement").

7. Ninth Circuit, Manual of Modern Criminal Jury Instructions 10.3 (2022 ed.).

8. United States v. Analytics, 687 F. Supp. 87, 90 (S.D.N.Y. 1988); *see also* United States v. Fernandez, Nos.19-15044, 19-15165, 2022 WL 3581793, at *4 (11th Cir. Aug. 22, 2022) ("Although the term 'official duty' is not statutorily defined, its ordinary meaning encompasses a public official's job responsibilities as dictated by governing statutes, rules, and regulations.").

C. The "*Quo*": In Exchange for an "Official Act" Under § 201(b)(2)(A)

The government normally proceeds under § 201(b)(2)(A) in federal bribery prosecutions. In such cases, the "*quo*"—that is, that which is sought to be influenced in exchange for the thing of value—must be an "official act." In *McDonnell v. United States*, 579 U.S. 550 (2016), the Court, upon stipulation by the parties, applied § 201(a)(3)'s definition of an "official act" to Hobbs Act and honest services wire and mail fraud prosecutions. In so doing, the Court read the definition of § 201's "official act" very narrowly, precipitating a host of objections that the Court has made bribery exceedingly difficult to prove.

In *McDonnell*, the Court articulated a two-part test to determine whether a qualifying § 201(a)(3) "official act" has been alleged. First, the government must identify a particular "question, matter, cause, suit, proceeding or controversy" that is specific, focused, and concrete and that involves a formal government action analogous to a lawsuit, hearing, or administrative determination.[9] A "typical meeting, telephone call, or event arranged by a public official" is not such a formal exercise of power.[10] Section 201(a)(3) also requires that the question or matter must be "pending" or "may by law be brought" before "any public official." These terms mean that the question or matter must be within the specific duties of the public official who is performing the official act or another public official and that it must be "relatively circumscribed—the kind of thing that can be put on an agenda, tracked for progress, and then checked off as complete."[11]

Second, the government must prove that the public official agreed to make a decision or take action on the identified question. Simply hosting a meeting to talk about the matter is insufficient, as is expressing general support for a position. But the government can meet its burden if the public official exerts pressure on another official to act or provides advice, knowing or intending that such pressure or advice will form the basis for an official act.

Lower courts applying *McDonnell* appear to believe that, contrary to critics' fears, the two-part test can be met if the government is careful in framing the official "question" or "matter" at issue. Thus, for example, in *United States v. Henderson*, 2 F.4th 593 (6th Cir. 2021), the Sixth Circuit affirmed a bribery conviction (under the Hobbs Act) of a guard who was paid to smuggle contraband into a county jail. The defense had argued that smuggling contraband is not an "official act" under § 201(a)(3), but the government's

9. 579 U.S. at 569.
10. *Id.*
11. *Id.* at 570

theory was that "the question or matter the case raised was whether the inmate should be punished for having contraband and that [the guard] made a decision on that matter when he declined to report the inmate's possession of contraband."[12]

The Sixth Circuit upheld the conviction, ruling that a disciplinary review board proceeding that would have been convened for the possession of contraband "fits within the Supreme Court's explanation of a question or matter as 'similar in nature to a lawsuit before a court, a determination before an agency, or a hearing before a committee.'"[13] The court concluded that "[t]he decision not to act remains a decision, and in this case that decision directly controlled the outcome of the disciplinary board proceeding that would have occurred had the inmate's possession of contraband come to light."[14]

Some bribery schemes involve a direct payment in contemplation of a particular official act in the briber's favor. Many, however, involve a relationship over time, in which the corrupt official may accept a variety of benefits in return for continuing assistance. In response to this reality, courts have long accepted a "stream of benefits" theory (also known as an "as opportunities arise" theory), under which the requisite *quid pro quo* is established by a stream of payments to the public official with the intent to retain the official's services on an "as needed" basis. Under this theory, the government need not prove that a particular benefit was given in exchange for a specific official act, but rather can rest its case on periodic payments made on the understanding that whenever the opportunity presents itself, the public official will perform an official act on the briber's behalf.

The Court has decided two cases that call this theory into question; at the very least, "stream of benefits" instructions must be carefully crafted to pass muster. First, in *United States v. Sun-Diamond Growers*, 526 U.S. 398 (1999), the Court rejected the view that § 201 covers "status" gratuities—that is, a gratuities case cannot stand if all the government can prove is that the payments are made because the public official was worth cultivating or the donor believed that the official might do him possible favors in future. In so doing, the Court implied that a particular official act must be linked to a particular gratuity. Second, defense counsel have argued that after *McDonnell* tightened the "official act" requirement, the stream of benefits theory is no longer viable.

Courts continue to accept this theory, however, as long as the jury instructions make clear that the payments are not simply for unspecified favors in future. Instead, the stream of benefits must be made in contemplation of *specific types of official acts*. Thus, for example, the Second Circuit

12. *Henderson*, 2 F.4th at 598.

13. *Id.*

14. *Id.* at 600.

approved the following jury instruction: the government "does not need to show a direct link between a benefit received and a specifically identified official act. Rather, it is sufficient if [the official] understood he was expected as a result of the payment to exercise *particular kinds* of acts or *influence* on behalf of the payor on an 'as needed' basis or as specific opportunities arose."[15]

D. Alternative "*Quo*": In Exchange for Inducing a "Violation of Official Duty" Under § 201(b)(2)(C)

One way to avoid the rigors of the "official act" definition is to charge that the public official corruptly agreed to accept something of value in exchange not for influencing an official act, as is usually charged under § 201(b)(2)(A), but rather in return "for being induced to do or omit to do any act in violation of the official duty of such official or person" under § 201(b)(2)(C).

With respect to § 201(b)(2)(C), the Second Circuit has explained that "[s]ubsections (A) and (C) undoubtedly overlap in some considerable measure, although resort to (A) seems most appropriate in the case of bribes regarding decisions involving the exercise of judgment or discretion, such as judicial decisions . . ., while use of (C) would be most appropriate in the case of bribes to induce actions that directly violate a specific duty, such as a prison guard's duty to prevent the smuggling of contraband."[16]

In the few cases decided under § 201(b)(2)(C), courts have interpreted the scope of official's lawful duties broadly to include activities traditionally associated with the job. It is a mystery why the government rarely charges bribery cases under this subsection, but *McDonnell*'s narrow reading of the official act requirement may make it more popular.

E. Qualifying Recipients of the Bribe Payments

A bribe need not be promised to or received by the official personally; offers to public officials to give something of value to "any other person or entity" also suffice (§ 201(b)). Bribes can be funneled to spouses, to persons to whom the bribee is indebted, and to charities. Bribe payments may take the form of contributions to campaign committees or political parties, although, as a practical matter, it is much easier to persuade a jury

---

15. United States v. Reichberg, 5 F.4th 233, 247 (2d Cir. 2021) (emphasis added) (honest services bribery case); *see also* United States v. Hills, 27 F.4th 1155, 1179, 1189-90 (6th Cir. 2022) (Hobbs Act bribery case).
16. *Alfisi*, 308 F.3d at 151 n.3.

that an undocumented and surreptitious personal payoff is part of a corrupt arrangement than a duly reported campaign contribution.

II. GRATUITIES, 18 U.S.C. § 201(c)(1)

A gratuity, which is only punishable by a fine, and up to two years' imprisonment, or both, may be objectionable on its own merits, but it can also be thought of as a second-best way of attacking corruption when prosecutors don't have the evidence to prove the more demanding elements of a bribery count. To secure a gratuities conviction under § 201(c)(1)(A), which targets the person making the illegal payment, the government must prove that:

- the defendant knowingly
- directly or indirectly, gave, offered, or promised
- anything of value
- to any public official, former public official, or person selected to be a public official
- "for or because of" any official act performed or to be performed by such public official

To convict the person to whom the gratuity was paid, the government must prove the same circumstances under § 201(c)(1)(B).

A. The Differences Between Bribery and Gratuities Elements

1. Knowing Mens Rea

A gratuity need only be made knowingly. The government does not have to prove a corrupt intent.

2. Nexus: No *Quid Pro Quo* Requirement

The government need not prove the *quid pro quo* that is the essence of bribery. A gratuity need only be offered "for or because of" an official act. But the Supreme Court made this element more difficult to prove in *Sun-Diamond Growers* and *McDonnell*. In *Sun-Diamond*, the Supreme Court construed the "for or because of" an official act requirement to reject the so-called "status" gratuity theory. It made clear that giving public officials something of value simply because they hold a position of power that may ultimately be used for the benefit of the donor does not violate the statute. Rather, the government must link the gratuity to a specific or identifiable official act. And *McDonnell's* rigorous definition of "official act" applies in this context as well.[17]

Given that both bribes and gratuities require the offering of a thing of value and proof that the offer is made in contemplation of a particular type of official act (under § § 201(b)(1)(A)), the distinction between making the payment "for or because of" that act (gratuities) and making it in exchange for influencing the act (bribes) may seem exceedingly subtle if not inexplicable. Perhaps the best way to explain the difference is that, in a bribery case, the briber intends to *corruptly influence* the public official, but no such proof is required in a gratuities case. Thus, if the payment is a no-strings-attached thank you for a past official act or a no-strings-attached anticipatory thank you for some future act that the public official has already decided to take—rather than a corrupt attempt to *influence* the public official to take that official act—it is a gratuity. But rarely are the parties' intentions so clear.

These arrangements often proceed by winks and nods, and the parties to the transactions have every incentive to hide their illegal arrangement. Sometimes, then, prosecutors bring a gratuities count simply because they cannot prove the intent to corruptly influence. For example, assume that the government can prove that something of value was given—say, a Rolex watch—and that the public official took an official action that benefited the giver in some concrete way. If there are no cooperating witnesses or circumstantial circumstances from which a compelling inference can be drawn that the parties saw the payment as a means to *motivate or influence* the official to take particular official act, prosecutors will have to settle for a gratuities count (assuming that they can show a nexus sufficient to establish that the payment was "for or because of" the official act) whatever their personal beliefs regarding the parties' actual purpose.

3. Qualifying Recipients of a Gratuity

The corrupt intent requirement separates legitimate campaign contributions from illegal bribes but the prohibition on gratuities does not require proof of this element. The same result is achieved through the requirement that the gratuity payment be made "to any public official."

Many campaign contributions are made in recognition that the public official has taken, or promises to take, a position on an issue that a donor to the campaign wishes to support. Unlike bribe payments, which can be received by the official personally *or* by "any other person or entity" on

17. Note that prosecutors cannot avoid the strictures of the official act definition in gratuities cases by alleging that the public official was rewarded for "being induced to do or omit to do any act in violation of the official duty of such official or person" because this alternative bribery theory embodied in § 201(b)(2)(C) finds no analog in the gratuities prohibition of § 201(c)(1).

his behalf, gratuities must be received "personally" by the public official (§ 201(c)). Campaign contributions generally will not satisfy this requirement because they are deposited into the accounts of a campaign committee or other entity rather into the official's own personal accounts.

Examples

1. Klavdiya Dimova was employed by the D.C. Department of Consumer and Regulatory Affairs as a contact representative. Her responsibilities included reviewing and processing various license applications, including various licenses needed by hotels. After being informed that Dimova was corrupt, the FBI set up a sting operation. An undercover agent informed Dimova that a hotel needed an elevator license and, possibly, another license for a billiard hall presently doing business within the hotel. Dimova told the agent that she could accept a check for the elevator license fee. She advised, truthfully, that the billiard hall needed its own license. But she then said that the fee—$1,275—had to be paid in cash because the fee was late. Dimova then pocketed the $1,275. Can Dimova be prosecuted under § 201?

2. At the Hunt's Point Terminal Market, brokers, acting as agents of produce growers, sold the produce to wholesalers under contracts that specified the price and quality of the produce to be delivered. If, on delivery, the wholesaler claimed that the produce did not meet the contractual standard, they called on a U.S. Department of Agriculture inspector to verify its condition. The government charged that various wholesalers, including Maquinna Hastiin, paid the USDA inspectors to falsely downgrade their assessments of the quality of the produce, thus allowing the wholesalers to negotiate a lower price. In his defense, Hastiin argued that the inspectors were running an extortion scam, whereby they would only give an honest evaluation of the produce's merit if they were paid. Hastiin argued that he was a victim who was coerced into paying the inspectors to do their jobs correctly, not someone who was seeking to bribe them into giving dishonest valuations. As Hastiin's defense counsel, what statutory element might you use to ground this argument, and are you likely to succeed? Does your answer depend on whether Hastiin is charged under § 201(b)(2)(A) or § 201(b)(2)(C)?

3. Mekaisto Yolotl, a Washington attorney, emailed a professional acquaintance, Ola Abioye, at the Justice Department's Office of Intergovernmental Affairs (OIA) seeking his help in expediting a U.S. Immigration and Customs Enforcement (ICE) review of a visa application for Yolotl's client. Assume that at this time, the OIA supported the DOJ leadership in a number of ways, including coordinating DOJ activities and programs with other agencies like ICE. Abioye agreed to help. He called the secretary of an ICE official and urged her to expedite the application. He then

forwarded Yolotl's email to her, along with a personal note that stated "Thank you for looking into this. I don't know if there is anything that can be done but I said I would look into it. If for any reason nothing can be done, please email me so I can pass that along. Thanks!" The secretary, in turn, passed the email along to five different ICE officials in an effort, she testified, to "make sure action was being taken to answer the request" because it had come from "higher headquarters" at the Department of Justice. Within a single business day, ICE agreed to expedite the application. After hearing news that Abioye's efforts had been successful, Yolotl emailed his client reporting that Abioye had helped and was now looking for tickets to a Washington Wizards basketball game. The client agreed, and Yolotl sent Abioye tickets to a Wizards game on the client's dime. Can Yolotl and Abioye be prosecuted under § 201?

4. The newly elected Ukrainian President, Volodymyr Zelenskyy, urgently sought an invitation to make on official state visit to the White House. Such visits are viewed as the ultimate proof of friendly bilateral relations between the United States and foreign governments and can bolster foreign officials' standing at home and abroad. Such visits can also be helpful in securing specific assistance. According to the House of Representatives' Trump-Ukraine Impeachment Report (Dec. 2019), Zelenskyy also wished to persuade the U.S. President, Donald Trump, to release the military assistance that Congress had authorized for Ukraine, but that Trump had frozen. During a telephone conversation between Zelenskyy and Trump, President Trump demanded that President Zelenskyy publicly announce that Ukraine would be launching criminal investigations into the conduct of former Vice President Joe Biden, the President's principal political rival. Trump believed that such an announcement would benefit him in an upcoming election. The President strongly intimated that the announcement of these investigations was the *quid pro quo* for a White House visit and unfreezing the aid. Could President Trump be indicted for bribery (putting to one side the presidential immunity from prosecution the Supreme Court created in *Trump v. United States*, 603 U.S. 593 (2024))?

Explanations

1. Section 201 normally applies only to federal officials, but the definition includes officials of the District of Columbia. There is no proof that the exchange for the elevator license was corrupt; it appears that Dimova correctly assessed the fee, the FBI paid it by check, and it went into D.C.'s coffers. With respect to the payment of the license fee for the billiard table, the government would argue that the *quid pro quo* element is satisfied because Dimova in fact received a thing of value ($1,275 in cash) in return for performing the official acts of processing and issuing a license.

But Dimova's acceptance of the fees does not meet § 201's corrupt *quid pro quo* requirement. In a similar case, the D.C. Circuit ruled that the *quid pro quo* requirement necessitates an *agreement* between the public official and the briber that the official will perform an official act in return for a *personal benefit*. The evidence showed only that: the payment was made as a fee for the license, not for Dimova personally; the fee was required by the city; she accepted the money ostensibly on behalf of the city; and there is no indication that there was a shared expectation by the parties that the payment would influence Dimova to give the hotel unduly favorable or expedited processing of the license. This evidence supports charging Dimova with embezzlement or stealing from the city, but not bribery. The case might be different had Dimova said to the undercover "you owe $1,275 for the pool table license to the city and $300 to me for making it happen without delay."[18]

2. Hastiin would contend that paying a public official to do his job is not a "corrupt" act within the meaning of the statute. Rather, to act corruptly, Hastiin had to intend to cause the official to misuse his official office. To ground this argument in the statute, he would point out that § 201 requires the government to prove that Hastiin act "corruptly" *and* that there was a *quid pro quo*. Because these are separate elements, they must have distinct meanings. The *quid pro quo* element requires that the payment be made in exchange for influencing an official act and the government could prove that here. "Corruptly," then, must mean something different—something more. In this case, it should require proof that Hastiin corrupted the actual performance of the official act; in other words, that Hastiin intended to cause the inspector to give dishonest evaluations of the produce. If Hastiin in fact was extorted by the inspector into doing his job honestly, no corrupt intent exists.

   In *United States v. Alfisi*, 308 F.3d 149 (2d Cir. 2002), on similar facts, the Second Circuit declined to construe the term "corruptly" to require evidence of an intent to procure a violation of the public official's duty. In so doing, it read "corrupt" intent to require nothing more than proof of a *quid pro quo*, stating that "[t]he 'corrupt' intent necessary to a bribery conviction is in the nature of a *quid pro quo* requirement; that is, there must be 'a specific intent to give . . . something of value in exchange for the official act.'"[19] Thus, under § 201(b)(2)(A)—which is the subsection that the government relies on in almost every case—a case can proceed whether or not the parties intend for the public official to misuse her office or violate her duties.

18. United States v. Dean, 629 F.3d 257, 259 (D.C. Cir. 2011).

19. *Alfisi*, 308 F.3d at 149 (quoting *Sun-Diamond Growers*, 526 U.S. at 404-05); *see also* United States v. Ng Lap Seng, 934 F.3d 110, 144 (2d Cir. 2019) (favorably citing *Alfisi*).

Recall, however, that the statue provides an alternative theory: the government can bring a bribery case on the theory that the thing of value was given with the corrupt intent to induce the public official to "act in violation of [his] official duty" under § 201(b)(2)(C). In such a prosecution, a "corrupt" intent could not be shown where the payments were made to induce the public official to do his job honestly.

Note that, as we shall see, under the FCPA, by contrast, the "corruptly" mens rea is read to require that the offer, payment or promise "be intended to induce the recipient to *misuse* his official position" although the government need not show a breach of a particular duty.[20]

3. The first question presented is whether there was proof of a *quid pro quo* (bribery) or whether the tickets were given "for or because of an official act" (gratuity). A bribery case is unlikely here because there is no obvious proof of an agreement before the fact between Yolotl and Abioye that the tickets would be forthcoming in a corrupt exchange for Yolotl's intervention with the ICE officials; that is, the tickets were not offered in advance to influence Abioye to reach out to ICE decision-makers. These facts are drawn from a case relating to the Abramoff lobbying scandal, *United States v. Ring*, 706 F.3d 460 (D.C. Cir. 2013), in which a conviction was secured on a gratuities theory.

   The defendant in *Ring* also argued that the government had failed to prove an "official act." The D.C. Circuit, in a pre-*McDonnell* decision, noted that attorneys in the DOJ's OIA department litigated on behalf of agency clients and were responsible for reaching across agency boundaries to get things done. In light of the secretary's testimony that, given Yolotl's position, she felt that she could not ignore the request—as well as the swift success of Yolotl's outreach—the court ruled that a rational jury could have concluded that the tickets were given for or because of an "official act."

   Under *McDonnell*, the case will be harder to prove. A decision to grant—and perhaps to expedite—a visa may constitute a "question, matter, cause, suit, proceeding or controversy" that is specific, focused and concrete, and that involves a sufficiently formal government action. The question is whether Abioye made a decision or took action on the identified question. The action sought is not one that he had the power to grant. And simply sending an email expressing general support for the visa grant is insufficient. But *McDonnell* said that the government can meet its burden if the public official exerts pressure on another official to act or provides advice, knowing or

20. *See* U.S. Dept of Justice & SEC, FCPA: A Resource Guide to the Foreign Corrupt Practices Act 13 (2d ed. 2020) [hereinafter *Resource Guide*].

intending that such pressure or advice will form the basis for an official act. Here, the jury would need to decide—in light of what was said during Abioye's call to ICE and in his note—whether he exerted such pressure.

4. The question this problem raises is whether political "logrolling"—exchanging one official act for another—can constitute bribery.

This hypothetical is drawn from the conduct underlying President Trump's first impeachment, for which he was acquitted by the Senate. Proof of a crime is not necessary for an impeachment, and in any case the statutory definition of bribery does not control in impeachment proceedings. Nonetheless, some argued that the President was guilty of bribery. The technical elements of bribery would seem to be satisfied if one accepts the facts in the House Impeachment report: the President demanded something of value (Ukrainian President Zelenskyy's public announcement of two investigations politically beneficial to the President's reelection campaign: one into Joe Biden and a Ukrainian gas company called Burisma, on whose board Biden's son sat, and the other into a discredited conspiracy theory alleging that Ukraine, not Russia, interfered in the 2016 U.S. election) in exchange for taking identified official acts (releasing congressionally approved military aid for Ukraine that Trump had frozen and scheduling a White House meeting with Zelenskyy).

Zelenskyy's public announcement of these investigations would be "someone of value" because Trump apparently believed that the investigations would help him politically. A corrupt intent could be implied from the fact that this *quid pro quo* was offered in return for a personal benefit instead of for consideration related to U.S. interests. With respect to the "official act" requirement, *McDonnell* said that a mere meeting was not a "question" or "matter" within the meaning of § 201(a)(3) but the government would argue that a White House visit is not just any meeting. The decision to invite the head of a foreign nation to make a state visit and to release significant amounts of military aid would seem to qualify as official acts even under *McDonnell*.

But there is a real question whether such logrolling—that is, the trading of official acts—can qualify as bribery. In *United States v. Blagojevich*, 794 F.3d 729 (7th Cir. 2015), the Seventh Circuit said "no." The court was worried about the implications of holding logrolling to be "bribery," seemingly believing that such a rule would criminalize politics as we know it. The court noted in in this regard that neither it nor the government could identify a single case in which logrolling had been the basis of a criminal conviction in the history of the United States. It reasoned that "[i]t would be more than a little surprising to Members of Congress if the judiciary found in the [federal anti-corruption statutes] a rule making everyday politics criminal."[21] Ultimately, the court concluded that bribery's "[c]orruptly" mens rea "refers to the recipient's state of mind and indicates that he understands the payment as a bribe or gratuity. It would not be plausible to describe a political trade of favors as an offer or attempt to bribe the other side."[22] This result would seem intuitively correct, but it is somewhat inconsistent with courts' willingness, discussed above, to treat the "corrupt" element as being satisfied whenever a *quid pro quo* can be proved.

III. EXTORTION UNDER COLOR OF OFFICIAL RIGHT, 18 U.S.C. § 1951 (THE HOBBS ACT)

The Hobbs Act was enacted to combat racketeering in labor-management disputes, but the statute is frequently used to prosecute public corruption cases, particularly those involving state and local officials on the take who cannot be prosecuted under § 201. Section 1951(a) criminalizes "in any way or degree obstruct[ing], delay[ing], or affect[ing] commerce . . . by extortion" or attempting or conspiring to do so.

The problem most people have when first encountering this statute is envisioning how it can be pressed into service, as it regularly is, to sanction bribery given that "extortion" normally connotes the obtaining of something—usually money—through force or threats. Thus, if a public official "extorts" money from someone, normally the coerced payor is treated as a victim. The statute, however, defines "extortion" to mean "the obtaining of property from another, with his consent, induced by wrongful use of actual or threatened force, violence, or fear, *or under color of official right*."[23] The Supreme Court's interpretation of what constitutes "extortion under color of official right" has effectively removed the coercive element and rendered this offense indistinguishable from bribery. Under the Supreme Court's Hobbs Act extortion under color of official right caselaw, then, the public official and the person paying her are treated as equally culpable; the public is the only victim in such cases.

To secure a conviction for Hobbs Act extortion under color of official right (UCofOR), the government must prove that the defendant:

- is a public official who
- knowingly and willfully

21. *Blagojevich*, 794 F.3d at 735.
22. *Id.* at 736.
23. 18 U.S.C. § 1951(b)(2).

- obtained the property of another, with his consent[24]
- under color of official right and
- as a result of the defendant's actions, interstate commerce was obstructed, delayed, or affected.

This statute, unlike § 201 and § 666, authorizes conviction of only the public official, which the caselaw defines as "anyone who actually exercises official powers, regardless of whether those powers were conferred by election, appointment, or some other method."[25] Federal, as well as state and local, public officials are subject to the Hobbs Act. To indict those who are not public officials, including the bribers and others implicated in the scheme, the government must charge them as aiders and abettors of the public official's violation under 18 U.S.C. § 2 or as co-conspirators.[26]

The Hobbs Act is punishable by a fine, up to twenty years' imprisonment, or both. Federal officials who are prosecuted under this statute face five years more jail time than they would under the federal bribery statute, § 201. The statute also outlaws attempts and conspiracies to commit the primary violation, which means that prosecutors have the discretion to charge a conspiracy to commit Hobbs Act extortion under § 371 (carrying a five year statutory maximum) or § 1951 itself (twenty year maximum). A conspiracy count under the Hobbs Act does not require proof of an overt act, while a § 371 conspiracy does.[27]

A. No Pressure or Threat Necessary

Public officials commit extortion "under color of official right" if they take money not due them for the performance of their official duties. Normally one would assume that in an extortion case, the defendant must demand or otherwise solicit the payment, and the payor only surrenders it under threat. But, in *Evans v. United States*, 504 U.S. 255 (1992), the Supreme Court rejected both such requirements and, in so doing, made extortion UCofOR indistinguishable from bribery. In *Evans*, the Court held that the public official need not initiate, solicit, or induce the corrupt transaction; the wrongful acceptance of a bribe

---

24. As used in the Hobbs Act, "with his consent" is "designed to distinguish extortion ('obtaining the property of another, *with his consent*' . . .), from robbery ('obtaining of personal property from the person or in the presence of another, *against his will*'. . .)." Ocasio v. United States, 578 U.S. 282, 297 (2016). Thus, "'consent' simply signifies the taking of property under circumstances falling short of robbery." *Id.*

25. United States v. Freeman, 6 F.3d 586, 593 (9th Cir. 1993).

26. "Acting 'under color of official right" is a requirement of an extortion Hobbs Act offense, substantive or inchoate, [so] [c]onduct by an unsuccessful candidate in an election does not meet that requirement." United States v. Manzo, 636 F.3d 56, 69 (3d Cir. 2011).

27. *See, e.g.*, United States v. Hills, 27 F.4th 1155, 1190 (6th Cir. 2022).

establishes all the inducement that the statute requires. Nor do public officials have to actually threaten to use the power and authority of their office to the payor's detriment. The coercive element inherent in extortion is provided by the public office itself.

B. Conspiracies Can Include Extorter and Extortee

Evidence of just how thoroughly Hobbs Act extortion UCofOR is now indistinguishable from bribery can be found in *United States v. Ocasio*, 578 U.S. 282 (2016). As noted above, the Hobbs Act only applies to the public officials and thus to prosecute the bribers (i.e., in statutory terms, those whose property has been obtained under color of official right), prosecutors generally charge the bribers and the bribee as members of a corrupt conspiracy. In what many would conceive of as the usual extortion case—involving the "wrongful use of actual or threatened force, violence, or fear"[28]—it would be ludicrous to suggest that the extorting party is in an unholy conspiracy with the coerced victim. Indeed, many circuit courts rejected such conspiracy cases, contending that "the Hobbs Act did not permit [the victims] to be convicted of conspiring to extort their own property."[29] But the *Ocasio* Court rejected this reasoning, holding instead that the alleged victims of an extortion UCofOR scheme can be charged as co-conspirators with the public officials who were alleged to have extorted them. In so holding, the Court recognized that "it seems unnatural to prosecute bribery on the basis of a statute prohibiting 'extortion,' but this Court held in *Evans* that Hobbs Act extortion 'under color of official right' includes the 'rough equivalent of what we would now describe as 'taking a bribe.' "[30]

C. *Quid Pro Quo*

Because Hobbs Act extortion UCofOR is treated as bribery, a *quid pro quo* requirement has been read into it. As in § 201(b)(1) cases, a bribe can be paid personally to a public official or to a third party such as a campaign committee. The Supreme Court first addressed the nature of the *quid pro quo* required in *McCormick v. United States*, 500 U.S. 257 (1991), a case in which the alleged bribes took the form of campaign contributions. In that case, the

---

28. 18 U.S.C. § 1951(b)(2).

29. United States v. Gray, 521 F.3d 514, 534 (6th Cir. 2008), *overruled in part*, *Ocasio*, 578 U.S. 282.

30. *Ocasio*, 578 U.S. at 296.

Court acknowledged that campaign contributions can be charged as having been extorted under color of official right, but "only if the payments are made in return for an *explicit promise* or undertaking by the official to perform or not to perform an official act."[31]

Evans, which did not involve campaign contributions, made clear that the bribery scheme need not be successful—that is, proof that the bribee actually misused her power is not necessary where an actionable agreement is proved. But in so doing, the *Evans* Court characterized the *quid pro quo* element in more forgiving (for the government) terms. It stated that the "offense is completed at the time when the public official receives a payment in return for his agreement to perform specific official acts."[32] There remains some confusion among the circuits regarding whether proof of *McCormick*'s "explicit promise" is required or whether the more forgiving *Evans* standard—which would permit agreements to be inferred—controls. The general view is that the more demanding *McCormick* standard applies where the corrupt payment is alleged to take the form of a campaign contribution, and the lesser *Evans* standard can be used in all other contexts.[33]

D. Obtainable Property

Section 1951 UCofOR cases require proof that the defendant "obtain[ed] ... property from another" under color of official right. As a consequence, the Supreme Court holds that only "obtain[able]" property can be extorted.[34] The Court has read "obtainable" property to mean property that can "be exercised, transferred, or sold."[35]

In *Sekhar v. United States*, 570 U.S. 729 (2013), the defendant threatened a public official with exposure of an extramarital affair unless the official recommended to his employer an investment in the defendant's company. The "property" extorted may be tangible or intangible.[36] But, the *Sekhar* Court ruled, given the statutory language, the property must be capable of being "obtained." The *Sekhar* prosecution failed because even if the official's recommendation were deemed "property"—which was unlikely—that property could not "be exercised, transferred or sold."[37]

31. *McCormick*, 500 U.S. at 273 (emphasis added).
32. *Evans*, 504 U.S. at 268.
33. *See, e.g.*, United States v. Ring, 706 F.3d 460, 466 (D.C. Cir. 2013).
34. Scheidler v. NOW, 537 U.S. 393, 402-05 (2003).
35. Sekar v. United States, 570 U.S. 729, 736 (2013).
36. *See, e.g.*, United States v. Cain, 671 F.3d 271, 282-83 (2d Cir. 2012); United States v. Gotti, 459 F.3d 296, 323-24 (2d Cir. 2006).
37. *See Sekhar*, 570 U.S. at 736.

Sekhar was a true extortion case, but this same rule applies even when the extortion theory is UCofOR and the gravamen of the offense is bribery.

E. The *Quo*: Official Act Requirement

In *McDonnell*, the Court, upon stipulation of the parties, applied the "official act" definition of § 201(a)(3) to Hobbs Act UCofOR cases. It is very unusual to import an element from another statute and, simply because the parties agree, impose it in a completely different statutory context. That said, courts seem to believe that the rigorous two-step proof requirements set forth in *McDonnell*—and discussed above—control under § 1951 as well. Courts have accepted that the government may proceed on a stream of benefits theory, described in connection with § 201, but caution should be exercised in crafting these instructions for the reasons articulated above.

F. Jurisdictional Element: Effect on Interstate Commerce

A Hobbs Act extortion UCofOR charge also differs from a § 201 bribery case in that it requires proof of a jurisdictional element: that is, that the extortionate activity "in any way or degree obstruct[s], delay[s], or affect[s] commerce or the movement of any article or commodity in commerce." Section 1951(b)(3) defines commerce broadly to include all commerce "over which the United States has jurisdiction." The Supreme Court holds that this language manifests a congressional purpose to use all its constitutional power,[38] and courts have consistently upheld Hobbs Act convictions where the effect or potential effect on commerce is negligible. For example, the Seventh Circuit upheld the conviction of a state judge who accepted a $1,000–$2,000 bribe from a law firm, ruling that that payment affected interstate commerce by reducing the firm's ability to purchase goods, such as document covers and calculators, in interstate commerce.[39] This jurisdictional element carries no mens rea; thus, the government need not prove that the defendant knew of or intended that interstate commerce be affected.

38. *See Evans*, 504 U.S. at 263 n. 12; *see also* Taylor v. United States, 579 U.S. 301, 305-06 (2016).
39. *See, e.g.*, United States v. Stillo, 57 F.3d 553 (7th Cir. 1995).

Examples

1. Ariadna Tosell purchased a tavern in Chicago and, assisted by Police Officer Arwel Priddy, filled out a liquor license application at the Police Department. She then went to city hall, filed the application, and paid her fee. Officer Priddy was responsible for investigating her application and he inexplicably required her to return with additional information ten to fifteen times. The average liquor license was approved within ten days. After her application had languished for twenty days, Tosell asked Shahid Ahmed, the principal clerk at the liquor license department at the City Collector's Office, about the delay. He said that Priddy wanted $150. Tosell gave Ahmed the money and, one day later, her application was approved. The City Collector's Office could not approve liquor licenses, but it was responsible for processing them, including sending the applications to the various City departments that needed to be consulted (e.g., the police department, the zoning board, etc.). Thus, while Ahmed could not himself approve the license, he could have delayed or at worst "lost" the application. Officer Priddy could recommend that the license not be issued but does not have the power to deny it. Can the government charge Ahmed and Priddy with Hobbs Act extortion UCofOR? Can the government charge a conspiracy to commit bribery among Tosell, Priddy, and Ahmed?

2. The governor of Illinois, Rod Blagojevich, offered to appoint a friend of the newly elected President, Barak Obama, to fill Obama's Senate seat in exchange for Blagojevich's appointment to Obama's cabinet. Can this be prosecuted as Hobbs Act extortion UCofOR?

Explanation

1. First, if the government charges that Ahmed was bribed, it may have difficulties proving (1) a qualifying matter and (2) a decision or action on that matter necessary to the "official act" element.[40] Ahmed's job coordinating the paperwork flow may be a sufficiently focused task but would not seem to involve a formal exercise of governmental power that is similar in nature to a lawsuit before a court, a determination before an agency, or a hearing before a committee.[41] And unless one argues that Ahmed's decision not to "lose" the application constitutes a qualifying action on the matter, there is in fact no identifiable decision involved.

40. *See McDonnell*, 579 U.S. 550.
41. *Id.*

With respect to Priddy, the facts provided do not prove that Priddy was actually involved with the scheme, although one could infer that to be the case given Priddy's seeming foot-dragging during his investigation and the speed with which the license was issued after the $150 payment. The prosecutor may phrase the "question" or "matter" at issue as whether the police department would recommend the application, and Priddy's approval would constitute the requisite "act" under *McDonnell*. The defense would likely argue in response that to constitute a sufficiently formal exercise of power, the "question" must be whether a license should be issued, not whether the Police Department signed off on it. It would argue that there was insufficient evidence that the police department's recommendation was necessary to the issuance of that license; without such a causal connection, Priddy's approval does not meet the official act requirement.

Another question this hypothetical raises is whether the alleged bribe sufficiently "affects commerce." The bribe itself—$150—would not meet the requirement but, in a similar case, the court found a qualifying effect on commerce because, without the license, the briber could not open the tavern for business and thus any purposeful delay in processing the license affected interstate commerce through the unconsummated purchases and sales of liquor sold to and at the tavern.[42]

With respect to whether Tosell, Priddy, and Ahmed can be charged in one conspiracy, we have noted that, unlike 18 U.S.C. § 201 and § 666, which authorize prosecution of both the briber and the bribee, the Hobbs Act imposes liability only on the public officials. To get around this limitation, prosecutors will often charge the briber as a co-conspirator of the public official under either § 1951 or § 371. The Supreme Court approved such conspiracy cases in *Ocasio*. Accordingly, charging Tosell, Priddy, and Ahmed as co-conspirators would be entirely appropriate, assuming the elements of the crime are met.

2. This hypothetical, raises the question whether Blagojevich attempted to use the power of his official office to "obtain[] . . . property" within the meaning of the Hobbs Act. Blagojevich was not, of course, successful but the Hobbs Act authorizes attempt liability. Under the Supreme Court's caselaw, the statute requires that "there must be an 'obtaining': someone—either the extortioner or a third person—must receive the property of which the victim is deprived."[43] In short, the "*quid*" offered in exchange for influencing an official act must take the form of obtainable,

42. *See* United States v. Irali, 503 F.2d 1295, 1301 (7th Cir. 1974).

43. United States v. McFall, 558 F.3d 951, 956 (9th Cir. 2009) (internal quotation marks omitted).

that is transferrable, property. This hypothetical is based on *Blagojevich*, discussed above.

In that case, the Seventh Circuit held that this did not constitute Hobbs Act extortion UCofOR. First, a position in the Cabinet is not "property" from the President's perspective given that "a political office belongs to the people, not to the incumbent (or to someone hankering after the position)."[44] The court reasoned that the President-elect "did not have a property interest in any Cabinet job, so an attempt to get him to appoint a particular person to the Cabinet is not an attempt to secure 'property' from the President (or the citizenry at large)."[45] Further, a Cabinet position is not "obtainable" because it is not "transferrable"; such a job is "not owned by the person with appointing power, and it cannot be deeded over."[46] The court concluded that a Cabinet position "is 'held' or 'occupied' but not 'obtained,' and under *Sekhar* something that cannot be 'obtained' also cannot be the subject of extortion."[47]

IV. FEDERAL PROGRAM BRIBERY, THEFT, AND FRAUD, 18 U.S.C. § 666

A circuit split developed regarding the extent to which state and local officials administering federal programs could be charged under § 201. Before the Supreme Court resolved the split in *Dixson*, Congress enacted 18 U.S.C. § 666, which was designed to make clear that federal law prohibits significant acts of theft, fraud, and bribery involving private or public organizations or state and local governments that receive federal benefits.

The statute contains two principal prohibitions. The first, contained in § 666(a)(1)(A), permits conviction where:

- a public[48] or private organization or a state, local, or Indian tribal government (or an agency thereof) receives, in any one-year period, benefits in excess of $10,000 under a federal program involving a grant, contract, subsidy, loan, guarantee, insurance, or other form of federal assistance other than salary and expense reimbursement, and
- the defendant, as an agent of such organization or government

44. *Blagojevitch*, 794 F.3d at 735.
45. *Id.*
46. *Id.* at 736.
47. *Id.*
48. *See Ng Lap Seng*, 934 F.3d at 122-29 (§ 666 covers public organizations like the U.N.).

- embezzles, steals, obtains by fraud or otherwise without authority knowingly converts or intentionally misapplies
- property valued at $5,000 or more belonging to the recipient entity

Given the focus of this chapter, we shall concentrate on the second prohibition, contained in § 666(a)(1)(B) and § 666(a)(2), which is addressed to program bribery. Liability is appropriate under § 666(a)(1)(B) if:

- an organization or a state, local, or Indian tribal government (or an agency thereof) receives, in any one-year period, benefits in excess of $10,000 under a federal program involving a grant, contract, subsidy, loan, guarantee, insurance, or other form of federal assistance other than salary and expense reimbursement, and
- the defendant, as an agent of such organization or government
- corruptly solicits, accepts, or agrees to accept anything of value from any person
- intending to be influenced or rewarded in connection with any "business, transaction, or series of transactions" of the receiving entity involving anything of value of $5,000 or more

Section 666(a)(2) renders liable the person offering the illegal payment under the same circumstances. A violation of this provision is punishable by a fine, imprisonment of not more than ten years, or both.

A. "Corruptly"

A common instruction under § 666, like § 201, requires that the government prove that the defendant acted "'with the bad purpose of accomplishing either an unlawful end or result, or a lawful end or result by some unlawful method or means.'"[49] It does not require proof that the defendant breached a duty.[50]

B. Organization or Government Receiving "Benefits" Exceeding $10,000

The government must prove, as the first element of every § 666 case, that the victim entity is an organization, government, or agency thereof that receives "benefits" in excess of $10,000 under a federal program

---

49. *Id.* at 142.
50. *Id.* at 142-144 (citing *Alfisi*, 308 F.3d 144).

involving federal "assistance" other than salary or expense reimbursement (§ 666(b)). Because the critical term "benefits" is not defined, this element is litigated with some frequency.

The Supreme Court read the "benefits" requirement broadly in *Fischer v. United States*, 529 U.S. 667 (2000), ruling that health care providers under the Medicare program receive "benefits" within the meaning of the statute. The Court rejected the argument that the Medicare "benefits" go to the elderly and disabled, not the health care organization that simply renders service in return for compensation. The Court reasoned that, given the regulatory structure of the Medicare program and the degree of federal regulation over it, the "payments are made not simply to reimburse for treatment of qualifying patients but to assist the hospital in making available and maintaining a certain level and quality of medical care, all in the interest of both the hospital and the greater community."[51] Medicaid program payments, then, were "benefits" intended to promote the well-being of health care providers in addition to the patients who received care.

Under *Fischer*, the critical question is whether the funds are paid to the entity for significant and substantial non-commercial reasons besides compensation or reimbursement. In making this inquiry, courts examine the "structure, operation, and purpose" of the program, the "conditions under which the organization receives its federal payments," and "whether the recipient's own operations are one of the reasons for maintaining the program."[52] Entities receive a "benefit" under § 666 when they are subject to "substantial Government regulation" that helps them achieve long-term objectives beyond the subject of the immediate transaction. Thus, for example, the Second Circuit ruled that payments to the United Nations that the United States is obligated by treaty to pay as its share of the U.N.'s expenses are a "benefit" because they are intended, *inter alia*, to advance the United States's ongoing foreign policy objectives.[53]

C. No Nexus Between Criminal Conduct and Federal Funds

A second issue that emerged early on was the degree of nexus required between the money pilfered (under § 666(1)(A)) or the "business" that was the object of the bribe (under § 666(1)(B)) and the federal benefits received by the organization or government entity. Thus, for example, a question arose whether the statute prohibits only the theft of federal program funds or whether it bars the misuse of any funds or property of an

51. *Fischer*, 529 U.S. at 679-80.
52. *Id.* at 681.
53. *See* United States v. Bahel, 662 F.3d 610, 629 (2d Cir. 2011).

organization that receives federal benefits. Similarly, the question in the bribery context was whether the corruption charged must compromise some function that is funded by or otherwise involves federal monies or whether the bribery need have no nexus to the federal funding as long as the entity receives $10,000 in benefits.

The Supreme Court has resolved these issues by, again, reading the statute very broadly such that no such nexus need be proved. Thus, in *Salinas v. United States*, 522 U.S 52 (1997), the Court unanimously ruled that federal prosecutors did not need to prove that the bribe charged in some way affected federal funds. And in *Sabri v. United States*, 541 U.S. 600 (2004), the Court held that no nexus between federal funds and the corrupt behavior alleged need be proven. These decisions have been read to mean that if a state, local, or tribal government receives qualifying benefits for any purpose, that receipt subjects all that government entity's agents to liability for any substantial theft, fraud, or bribery affecting the entity's business or transactions—whether or not that particular function receives or involves federal funds.

Every state and virtually every city and county receive funding of $10,000 or more per year from the federal government. Many argue, then, that the Supreme Court's broad reading of the scope of the statute means that § 666, which was originally designed principally to protect the integrity of federal funds, has evolved into a general anti-corruption statute that enables prosecutors to pursue state and local government corruption in much the same way as they address federal corruption under § 201(b).

D. Bribery Only

A circuit split developed over the question whether § 666(a)(1)(B) and (a)(2) covered only bribery or whether gratuities are also subject to prosecution. The statutory language gives mixed signals in this regard. Section 666, like bribery under § 201(b) and unlike gratuities under § 201(c), requires proof of a "corrupt" intent. But it also proscribes promising something of value with the intent to "reward" as well as to "influence" the corrupted agent; bribery, of course, requires an intent to influence while gratuities are "rewards."

In 2024, the Supreme Court resolved the split in *Snyder v. United States*, 603 U.S. 1 (2024), by holding that § 666 covers only bribery and does not make it a federal crime for state and local officials to accept gratuities for their past acts. The Court explained that "[s]tate and local governments often regulate the gifts that state and local officials may accept. Section 666 does not supplement those state and local rules by subjecting 19 million state and local officials to up to 10 years in federal prison for accepting even commonplace gratuities."[54]

E. Agent of the Organization or Government

It is clear that the payment offered or made with the intent to influence or reward must be directed to an "agent" of an organization or government "in connection with any business, transaction, or series of transactions" of the receiving entity. The statute defines an "agent" as a "person authorized to act on behalf of another person or a government and, in the case of an organization or government, [the term] includes a servant or employee, and a partner, director, officer, manager, and representative" (§ 666(d)(1)). Whether such an agency relationship exists is a question of federal law, not contract interpretation, and courts have read the term broadly. Thus, for example, even where a state contractor operates under a contract that provides that he is acting as an independent contractor and not as an agent of the state, he may yet be an "agent" for § 666 purposes if he was authorized to act on behalf of the state.[55]

F. Anything of Value to Influence or Reward a Business or Transaction Valued at $5,000

The statute specifies that that which is influenced or rewarded must be a "business, transaction, or serious of transactions" valued at $5,000 or more not, as in §201, an "official act." Accordingly, § 201(a)(3)'s definition of an "official act," which the Supreme Court chose to read rigorously and to import into the honest services bribery statute (§ 1346) and Hobbs Act extortion under color of official right cases (§ 1951), does not apply to federal program bribery under § 666.[56]

The corrupt payment may be anything of value (the "*quid*") but the "business, transaction, or serious of transactions" sought to be influenced or rewarded (the "*quo*") must be valued at $5,000 or more. Stated another way, the subject matter of the bribe—the "business" or "transaction" sought to be influenced or rewarded—must be valued at $5,000 or more but the bribe itself can be anything of subjective value to the agent. Where the giver

54. *Snyder*, 603 U.S. at 5.
55. *See, e.g.*, United States v. Lupton, 620 F.3d 790, 800-01 (7th Cir. 2010).
56. *See, e.g.*, United States v. Lindberg, 39 F.4th 151, 166 (4th Cir. 2022).

of the corrupt payment receives something of intangible value, however, courts generally will use the bribe amount as a proxy for the value of the "business" or "transaction." Thus, for example, assume that an indicted drug dealer released on bail bribed the probation officer whose duty it was to supervise him to allow the dealer liberties not permitted by the terms of his release. The value of this additional freedom is hard to quantify, so many courts would use the value the parties agreed upon—that is the price of the bribe—in determining whether the "business" or "transaction" was valued at $5,000 or more.[57]

Examples

1. Titas Butkus served as a manager of the Facilities Operation Division of Lockheed Aeronautical Systems (Lockheed). Lockheed is a prime contractor for the U.S. Department of Defense (DOD) and receives millions for selling the DOD airplanes to be used in miliary missions. Butkus's responsibilities included supervising the building, maintenance, and repair projects related to Lockheed's airplane manufacturing facilities. Aybua Kamau, a real estate broker, was a long-time friend of Butkus's and had assisted Lockheed in various real estate matters over the years. Butkus improperly referred work to Kamau and agreed on behalf of Lockheed to pay abnormally high commissions to Kamau. In return, Kamau paid Butkus approximately $15,000. Can a case be made against Butkus and Kamau under § 666?

2. From 2009-2012, the United States government appropriated $150 million in federal funds each year to the Government of the Virgin Islands. During that time, Sukhrab Sultanov served in the Virgin Islands Senate. Sultanov chaired the Senate's Public Safety Committee (PSC). Dimitrij Nikolovski was the president of Acme, a private firm with interests in a variety of businesses in the Virgin Islands. Because of his varied business interests, Nikolovski often wished to promote or defeat proposed legislation on a variety of subjects. As chair of the PSC, Sultanov had the ability to exercise a measure of control over the introduction and progression of bills through the Legislature. Over the course of ten years, Nikolovski regularly gave Sultanov tickets for he and his girlfriend to travel first class to coveted destinations, and paid for their luxury accommodations, lavish meals, and entertainment while on the trips. In return, Sultanov took Nikolovski's "advice" on three pieces of proposed legislation that would have imposed significant regulatory costs on Nikolovski's business

57. *See, e.g.*, United States v. Townsend, 630 F.3d 1003, 1011-12 (11th Cir. 2011).

interests. Nikolovski's committee held hearings after which it issued negative reports on the proposed bills. None of them became law. Can a case be made against Sultanov and Nikolovski under § 666?

Explanations

1. We know that Lockheed earns millions in its contracts with the federal government, but the first issue is whether Lockheed received qualifying "benefits." The statute says that benefits from a federal program can take the form of a "a grant, *contract*, subsidy, loan, guarantee, insurance, or other form of Federal *assistance*" (§ 666(b) (emphasis added)). A federal contract between Lockheed and the DOD for aircraft, on its face, would seem to qualify. And the fact that the government receives some sort of consideration in return for the federal assistance does not mean that § 666 does not apply. For example, § 666 has been applied to a county jail that received federal assistance in exchange for housing federal prisoners[58] and a government-sponsored loan that contemplated that the recipient had to repay the loan amount with interest.[59] But if, as in this case, the contractual relationship between the organization and the government is purely commercial and lacks any semblance of federal "assistance," § 666's threshold showing of a federal benefit is not satisfied.[60]

   If there had been a cognizable "benefit," Butkus, as an agent of the "organization," potentially could be liable for intentional misapplication of Lockheed's funds and for receiving a bribe from Kamau. Kamau in turn could be liable for providing an illegal bribe to Butkus. Butkus is an agent of Lockheed and, under *Salinas* and *Sabri*, the government need not prove that there was any nexus between the federal funds received and the corrupt arrangement. Proof of a corrupt *quid pro quo* is necessary because, under *Snyder*, a § 666 case cannot rest on a mere gratuity. And the exchange must be made with the corrupt intent to reward Butkus in connection with any business, transaction, or series of transactions valued at $5,000 or more. Whether a case could be made, then, depends on whether a *quid pro quo* arrangement can be proven—that is, that the kicked-back funds were offered in a corrupt exchange for Butkus's decision to improperly throw "business" to Kamau at inflated rates. The government would have to prove that the real estate business Butkus threw to Kamau was worth more than $5,000. Given that the kickbacks

58. *See* United States v. Marmolejo, 89 F.3d 1185, 1190-91 (5th Cir. 1996), *aff'd in part sub nom.* Salinas v. United States, 522 U.S. 52 (1997).
59. *See* United States v. Rooney, 986 F.2d 31, 35 (2d Cir. 1993).
60. *See* United States v. Copeland, 143 F.3d 1439, 1441 & n.3 (11th Cir. 1998).

were worth $15,000, it is likely that the business was worth significantly more than that.

2. Courts have had no difficulty finding that funds provided to territorial governments, like those of the Virgin Islands and Puerto Rico, constitute "benefits" within the meaning of the statute. They have similarly rebuffed arguments that the government receiving the money—the state or territory at issue—is a different entity than its Senate or other constituent parts. Thus, the three branches of a state or territorial government constitute one government entity, which is funded by the federal government.[61] State senators, as "representatives" of the "government," also constitute "agents" within the meaning of § 666(d)(1).[62] Consistent with the Supreme Court's proclivity for reading the scope of § 666 broadly, a legislator can be an "individual authorized to act on behalf" of the government; courts generally hold that nothing in the statute requires that the person be authorized to act specifically with respect to the entity's funds. Nor need the government prove, under *Salinas* and *Sabri*, that there was a "nexus" between the bribe and federal benefit funds.[63]

   The government would bear the burden of proving a corrupt *quid pro quo*. The statute requires that the bribe be made in exchange for influencing or rewarding any "business" or transaction" of the covered organization having a value of $5,000 or more. "Business" within the meaning of the statute is not limited to commercial transactions; legislation can constitute "business." Here, the government would have to ask the jury to infer the requisite *quid pro quo* on a "stream of benefits" theory, pursuant to which one need not show that a given payment (e.g., trip) was provided in return for Sultanov's help in killing a specific piece of legislation. Because courts have held that *McDonnell's* rigorous "official act" definition does not apply in this context, concerns about the continuing viability of the stream of benefits theory (discussed above under § 201), are not present. That said, defense counsel should insist on jury instructions like those approved under the § 201, which in this context would require the government to prove that the stream of payments was made for a *specific type of business*—that is, Sultanov's assistance in derailing legislation that would adversely affect Nikolovski's interests—on an "as needed" basis or as specific opportunities arose.

   The "business" that was the reason for the bribe—the value of the legislation to SI—must be more than $5,000. But where the value of the bribe's objective (here, legislation) may be intangible or difficult to

61. *See* United States v. Willis, 844 F.3d 155, 165-67 (3d Cir. 2016).
62. *See id.* at 167.
63. *See* United States v. Gee, 432 F.3d 713, 714 (7th Cir. 2005).

estimate, courts will look to the value of the bribe for guidance; here the court would have to aggregate the value of all the travel received over the course of ten years to see whether it added up to $5,000.[64]

V. TRANSNATIONAL BRIBERY: THE FOREIGN CORRUPT PRACTICES ACT (FCPA), 15 U.S.C. §§ 78dd-1 TO 78dd-3, AND THE FOREIGN EXTORTION PREVENTION ACT, 18 U.S.C. § 201(f)

A. The FCPA

The Foreign Corrupt Practices Act (FCPA), enacted in 1977 and significantly amended over the years, generally prohibits the payment of bribes to foreign officials to assist in obtaining or retaining business. The FCPA can apply to prohibited conduct the world over and extends to a variety of U.S. and non-U.S. companies and their officers, directors, employees, and agents. Persons can be liable under the FCPA for the activities of their agents, including third party agents, consultants, distributors, joint-venture partners, and others.

The FCPA also requires one category of covered persons—issuers—to maintain accurate records and employ a system of internal controls sufficient to, *inter alia*, provide reasonable assurances that transactions and assets are accurately accounted for.[65] Given the focus of this chapter, however, these materials focus only on the anti-bribery provision of the FCPA.

The FCPA is an extraordinarily poorly drafted statute and therefore can be difficult to parse. It is also complex, requiring inquiry into a variety of elements. Readers are encouraged to persevere through the following discussion of the most technical portions—the identification of the potential defendants chargeable under the Act and the actus reus required of each. Once one has a handle on these provisions, the rest is readily understandable to those who have some familiarity with the basics of domestic bribery law.

---

64. *See* United States v. Fernandez, 722 F.3d 1, 13 (1st Cir. 2013).

65. The record-keeping and internal control requirements the FCPA impose on issuers (but not domestic concerns or 78dd-3 persons), *see* 15 U.S.C. § 78m(b)(2), generally fall within the civil enforcement authority of the SEC. They are important to criminal practice, however, for at least two reasons. First, counsel may be able to resolve potential criminal charges by agreeing to a criminal or civil settlement using these provisions—which are seen as less stigmatizing that a "bribery" conviction—as its foundation. Second, the Justice Department can bring criminal charges if it can prove that the defendant *willfully* circumvented or failed to implement a system of internal accounting controls or *willfully* falsified an issuer's books and records.

Until recently, few FCPA cases went to trial; most have settled, often through use of Deferred Prosecution Agreements (discussed in Chapter 4 (Entity Liability)). Because of the relative dearth of caselaw, the following summary often discusses the result in a single circuit because that is the only circuit to have addressed the issue. Recognizing the lack of appellate precedents to guide compliance, the SEC and the Department of Justice have together issued a "Resource Guide" to the FCPA, which is particularly helpful in discerning the federal government's position with respect to the scope of certain elements and in explaining the government's decision-making in particular cases.[66]

To win a conviction under the FCPA's criminal anti-bribery provisions, the government must prove beyond a reasonable doubt the following:

- The defendant falls within one of three categories of persons covered by the FCPA—issuers, domestic concerns, or 78dd-3 persons—or is an agent of same
- The defendant willfully made a payment, or an offer, authorization, or promise to pay, money or anything of value, directly or indirectly (through a third party)
- The defendant made the payment or promise to pay to a covered recipient, meaning:
  - any foreign official
  - any foreign political party or party official
  - any candidate for foreign political office, or
  - any other person while "knowing" that the payment or promise to pay will be passed on to one of the above
- In furtherance of the bribe or offer to bribe, "corruptly" committed the actus reus of the crime. The proscribed act differs depending upon which subsection is invoked (that is, who the defendant is—an issuer, a domestic concern, a 78dd-3 person, or an agent of same) and whether the defendant is a U.S. national
- A qualifying *quid pro quo*, meaning that the thing of value must be offered in exchange for
  - being influenced in the performance of any official act,
  - being induced to do or omit to do any act in violation of the official duty of such foreign official or person,
  - securing any improper advantage, or
  - inducing that person to use his influence with a foreign government to affect or influence any government act or decision
- In order to assist in obtaining or retaining business for, with, or to any person

66. *See Resource Guide, supra* note 20.

A "foreign official" is defined as "any officer or employee of a foreign government or any department, agency, or instrumentality thereof, or of a public international organization, or any person acting in an official capacity for or on behalf of any such government or department, agency, or instrumentality, or for or on behalf of any such public international organization."[67] "Public international organizations" are organizations designated as such by Executive Order.[68] Among the international organizations that currently are designated as "public international organizations" for purposes of the FCPA are the United Nations, the World Bank, the International Monetary Fund, the World Trade Organization, the Organization of American States, and many more.

I. Potential Defendants

The FCPA has one very important limitation in terms of coverage: it can only be used to prosecute those who offer or pay bribes, not the corrupt foreign officials who solicit or receive them. Phrased another way, the FCPA only covers "active bribery"—that is, the bribers—and not "passive bribery"—that is, the bribees. Congress knew that it could reach the foreign officials consistent with international law, at least in some circumstances, but it concluded that the inherent jurisdictional, enforcement, and diplomatic difficulties of applying the FCPA to foreign public officials precluded such coverage.

Over time, the DOJ has used other statutes—most notably the Travel Act (18 U.S.C. § 1952) or the anti-money laundering statutes (18 U.S.C. §§ 1956-1957, discussed in Chapter 11)—to pursue corrupt foreign officials when the elements of those prohibitions could be satisfied.[69] Finally, in December 2023, Congress passed the Foreign Extortion Prevention Act (FEPA) which amends the federal bribery statute, 18 U.S.C. § 201—not the FCPA—to allow prosecutors to indict foreign officials who solicit or accept bribes in circumstances that would otherwise constitute a violation of the FCPA. The Foreign Extortion Prevention Act's § 201(f) will be considered after our FCPA discussion is concluded.

The potential defendants in an FCPA case fall into one of three categories: issuers, domestic concerns, or 78dd-3 persons (and agents of same). Sometimes an individual or entity may fall into more than one category. The safest way to proceed is to ask whether the prospective defendant is an "issuer" first; if it is not an issuer, one queries whether it is a "domestic

67. 15 U.S.C. §§ 78dd-1(f)(1)(A), 78dd-2(h)(2)(A), 78dd-3(f)(2)(A) (emphasis added).
68. *See id.* at §§ 78dd-1(f)(1)(B), 78dd-2(h)(2)(B), 78dd-3(f)(2)(B).
69. *See Resource Guide*, *supra* note 20, at 48-49.

concern"; only if it does not fall into one of the first two categories does one examine whether it qualifies as a 78dd-3 person.

Section 78dd-1 covers "issuers" and their agents. Basically, issuers are any company—whether incorporated under U.S. law or not—that has a class of securities (1) listed on a national securities exchange in the United States, or (2) quoted in the over-the-counter market in the United States and required to file periodic reports with SEC.[70] Natural persons can also be liable under § 78dd-1 because it extends liability to officers, directors, employees, or agents of the issuer acting on its behalf.

Section 78dd-2 covers "domestic concerns" and their agents. Domestic concerns include any company—incorporated in the United States or not—that has its principal place of business in the United States. And, although it is an awkward construction, natural persons can qualify as domestic concerns if they are U.S. nationals or foreign nationals resident in the United States. The bottom line is that domestic concerns are non-issuer U.S.-based persons (individuals and business entities) wherever they are incorporated (businesses).[71] Liability under § 78dd-2 extends as well to any officer, director, employee, or agent of the domestic concern acting on its behalf.

Under § 78dd-3, foreign nationals or businesses (or agents of such nationals or businesses) who are neither "issuers" nor "domestic concerns" but who perform a qualifying act in furtherance of the illicit bribe while in U.S. territory may be liable. Those falling into this category of potential defendants are often referred to as "78dd-3 persons."

Section 78dd-3 was added to the statute in 1998 to implement the Convention on Combating Bribery of Foreign Officials in International Business Transactions adopted by the Organization for Economic Cooperation and Development (OECD), and significantly increased the jeopardy of non-U.S. companies and their agents. Section 78dd-3 reaches individuals who are not U.S. nationals or residents, and companies that are not regulated by the SEC, whose securities are not listed or traded in the United States, and who are neither U.S. companies nor businesses having their principal place of business in the United States if, "*while in the territory of the United States*," they make use of the mails or instrumentalities of interstate commerce or do *any* act in furtherance of the bribe.

Thus, for example, if a French national, living in France and working for a French company that is neither an issuer nor a domestic concern,

70. *See* 15 U.S.C. § 78dd-1(a); Resource Guide, *supra* note 20, at 9-10. This includes foreign companies whose American Depository Receipts are listed on a U.S. exchange. *See Resource Guide, supra* note 20, at 10.

71. *See* 15 U.S.C. § 78dd-2(h)(1); Resource Guide, *supra* note 20, at 10.

travels to New York for a meeting in which bribery of foreign public officials in Indonesia is discussed, he can be liable as a § 78dd-3 person, as can the company for which he works assuming the *respondeat superior* standard of corporate criminal liability is satisfied.

2. Actus Reus or Jurisdictional Act

The conduct that renders a person liable under the statute—that is, the actus reus of an FCPA violation—depends on the defendant's status and whether it is an U.S. person.

a. Issuers and Domestic Concerns

Congress makes a distinction for purposes of defining the requisite actus reus between issuers and domestic concerns that are U.S. persons and those that are not. U.S. persons are nationals of the United States and corporations organized under U.S. law.[72]

Issuers and domestic concerns that *are* U.S. persons are liable if they

- use the instrumentalities of interstate commerce in furtherance of the corrupt payment; *or*
- corruptly do *any act outside the United States* in furtherance of the payment to foreign officials to secure or retain business

It will not be difficult in most cases to find a qualifying use of the instrumentalities of interstate commerce. "[P]lacing a telephone call or sending an e-mail, text message, or fax from, to, or through the United States involves interstate commerce—as does sending a wire transfer from or to a U.S. bank or otherwise using the U.S. banking system, or traveling across state borders or internationally to or from the United States."[73] Even emails sent between persons outside the United States that are routed through or stored on network servers in the United States can constitute qualifying uses of the instrumentalities of interstate commerce.[74]

72. A "U.S. Person" is a natural person who is a "national of the U.S." or any corporation organized under American law. 15 U.S.C. §§ 78dd-1(g)(2), 78dd-2(h)(2). A "national of the U.S.," as defined in 8 U.S.C. § 1101(a)(22), is "(A) a citizen of the United States, or (B) a person who, though not a citizen of the United States, owes permanent allegiance to the United States."

73. *Resource Guide supra* note 20 at 10; *see also* 15 U.S.C. §§ 78c(a)(17), 78dd-2(h)(5), 78dd-3(f)(5).

74. *See* SEC v. Straub, 921 F. Supp. 2d 244, 262-64 (S.D.N.Y. 2013).

The bottom line is that FCPA cases against U.S. persons that are issuers or domestic concerns can be based on a variety of run-of-the-mill corporate conduct that should be fairly easy to identify: they are liable if they or their agents send an email, text, fax or otherwise communicate using the U.S. wires, engage in banking by wire, travel within the United States, or if they take *any* act outside the United States, in furtherance of the bribery scheme.

Issuers and Domestic Concerns who are *not* U.S. persons are liable:

- only if they use the instrumentalities of interstate commerce in furtherance of the corrupt payment

A qualifying jurisdictional act/actus reus in cases involving non-U.S. persons who, as issuers or domestic concerns, have a demonstrable connection to the United States may also be fairly easy to identify. Even if such entities and their agents remain outside the United States, they can still be liable if virtually any banking transfer, email, text, fax, or other use of the wires made in furtherance of the bribery scheme crosses a U.S. border or transits from one state to another.

b. 78dd-3 Persons

What the government must prove with respect to a 78dd-3 person is straightforward because it is inherent in the definition of such persons: they must, *while in the territory of the United States*

- use the mails or any other means or instrumentality of interstate commerce or
- take *any act* in furtherance of the bribe

The Department of Justice has taken the position that this jurisdictional act is satisfied if someone outside the United States "causes" the domestic use of the instrumentalities of interstate commerce or a domestic act in furtherance of the bribe from outside the United States. Although no court has so held, the Second Circuit appeared to reject this position by deciding a case on the assumption that a 78dd-3 person *must actually be on the territory of the United States* when using the instrumentalities of interstate commerce or taking an act in furtherance of the bribe.

In *United States v. Hoskins (Hoskins I)*, 902 F.3d 69 (2d Cir. 2018), the Second Circuit addressed the issue whether a defendant who could not himself be liable under § 78dd-3 could be charged with aiding and abetting or conspiring to commit a violation of § 78dd-3. This question, which the court answered in the negative, assumed that the defendant, a foreign national who never entered the territory of the United States, could not be held liable as a 78dd-3 person even though he repeatedly emailed and called his U.S. co-conspirators from abroad while authorizing the illicit payments. Based on *Hoskins*, then, one could conclude—as most defendants would argue—that a non-U.S. person who is neither an issuer nor a domestic concern can use the instrumentalities of interstate commerce—that is, he can email and call persons in the United States—but he cannot be liable if he was not present on American soil while doing so.

c. Theories to Cover Foreign Nationals Acting Outside the United States

A large percentage of FCPA enforcement actions have been brought against foreign corporations and nationals. But the government has faced challenges in doing so—particularly where the culpable foreign national has never entered the territory of the United States and thus cannot herself be liable under § 78dd-3. The government has addressed this difficulty in two ways.

First, a person may not be a 78dd-3 person if she has never entered the United States, but § 78dd-1 and § 78dd-2 cover not only issuers and domestic concerns but also "agents" acting on their behalf. Agents of issuers and domestic concerns who are not U.S. persons, then, can be liable under § 78dd-1 and § 78dd-2 if they use the instrumentalities of interstate commerce—for example sending an email to the United States—even if they are not themselves on the territory of the United States.

In *Hoskins v. United States* (*Hoskins II*), 44 F.4th 140 (2d Cir. 2022), the Second Circuit set forth three elements that must be proved to demonstrate an agency relationship for purposes of the FCPA: "'(1) a manifestation by the principal that the agent will act for him; (2) acceptance by the agent of the undertaking; and (3) an understanding between the parties that the principal will be in control of the undertaking.'"[75] Factors a court should consider in applying this test include: "'the situation of the parties, their relations to one another, and the business in which they are engaged; the general usages of the business in question and the purported principal's business methods; the nature of the subject matters and the circumstances under which the business is done.'"[76]

The second means prosecutors have used to charge foreign nationals not liable under § 78dd-1, § 78dd-3, or § 78dd-3 is more controversial.

75. *Hoskins II*, 44 F.4th at 149 ("'[a]t common law, agency is the fiduciary relationship that arises when one person (a "principal") manifests assent to another person (an "agent") that the agent shall act on the principal's behalf and subject to the principal's control, and the agent manifests or otherwise consents so to act.'").
76. *Id.* at 150.

Prosecutors have charged persons who would not themselves be liable as issuers, domestic concerns, or 78dd-3 people—or agents of same—as aiders and abettors or as co-conspirators of those who can be liable under these provisions. For example, assume that a French national, living in France and working for a French company that is neither an issuer or a domestic concern and who does not qualify as an agent of an issuer or domestic concern, sends emails and makes telephone calls to employees of a U.S. company in furtherance of a bribery scheme but she never enters the United States. Prosecutors would attempt to charge her as an aider and abettor or co-conspirator of the U.S. company and its employees. This scenario has arisen with sufficient frequency to generate conflicting caselaw.

We know that such an approach works in Hobbs Act extortion UCofOR prosecutions to expand the potential pool of defendants beyond the "public officials" who are targeted by § 1951. But the jury is out on whether this approach will work in FCPA cases. In *Hoskins I*, the Second Circuit, on facts similar to those posited, rejected this practice. It reasoned that, given the care with which Congress delineated those subject to FCPA liability, a person cannot be guilty as an accomplice or co-conspirator of an FCPA crime if he is incapable of committing it as a principal.[77] But a district court in Illinois rejected the *Hoskins* rule as incompatible with Seventh Circuit caselaw.[78]

3. Qualifying Payments

a. "Foreign Officials" and State-Controlled Entities

The ultimate beneficiary of the corrupt payment or offer to pay must be a "foreign official," a foreign political party or official thereof, or any candidate for foreign political office. The term "foreign official" also includes "any officer or employee of a foreign government or any department, *agency*, or *instrumentality* thereof."[79] An issue that has arisen with great frequency is whether commercial entities that are in part government owned or controlled can be deemed an "agency" or "instrumentality" of the government such that their employees qualify as "public officials." Many countries' governments maintain some interest or control over commercial entities perceived to be vital to national interests, such as aerospace or defense manufacturing industries, or transportation and telecommunications utilities.

Under a test articulated by the Eleventh Circuit, commercial entities qualify as "instrumentalities" or "agencies" of a foreign government if

---

77. *See Hoskins I*, 902 F.3d at 95.

78. *See* United States v. Firtash, 392 F. Supp. 3d 872, 891-92 (N.D. Ill. 2019).

79. See 15 U.S.C. §§ 78dd-1(f)(1), 78dd-2(h)(2), 78dd-3(f)(2) (emphasis added).

(1) the entity is "controlled by the government of a foreign country"; and (2) it "performs a function the controlling government treats as its own."[80]

The question whether the entity is "controlled by the government" turns on a number of factors, including:

> the foreign government's formal designation of that entity; whether the government has a majority interest in the entity; the government's ability to hire and fire the entity's principals; the extent to which the entity's profits, if any, go directly into the governmental fisc, and by the same token, the extent to which the government funds the entity if it fails to break even; and the length of time these indicia have existed.[81]

Although there may be exceptions, the SEC and DOJ are unlikely to conclude that a state-controlled entity qualifies as an agency or instrumentality if the government owns less than fifty percent of the company.[82]

To resolve whether the entity performs a function that the government treats as its own, factfinders consider additional factors, including:

> whether the entity has a monopoly over the function it exists to carry out; whether the government subsidizes the costs associated with the entity providing services; whether the entity provides services to the public at large in the foreign country; and whether the public and the government of that foreign country generally perceive the entity to be performing a governmental function.[83]

b. Anything of Value

The "anything of value" offered to the public official can, as in the domestic bribery cases, take many forms. Certainly, cash qualifies, but it is also common for bribes to take the form of expensive gifts like sports cars, furs, or other luxury items. As will be discussed below, the FCPA provides an affirmative defense to liability where the company establishes that the provision of travel, food, and lodging are directly related to the promotion or demonstration of a company's products or services or to the performance of a contract with the foreign government. In many cases, then, companies will attempt to characterize corrupt payments given in the form of, for example, expensive vacations, as necessary to a factory inspection or training visit. But where the official spends little or no time at the company's facilities,

---

80. United States v. Esquenazi, 752 F.3d 912, 925 (11th Cir. 2014).

81. *Id.*; *see also* United States v. Duperval, 777 F.3d 1324, 1333 (11th Cir. 2015).

82. *See Resource Guide*, *supra* note 20, at 21.

83. *Esquinazi*, 752 F.3d at 925; *see also Duperval*, 777 F.3d at 1333.

or visits tourist destinations on the company's dime, such an affirmative defense will fail.[84]

There is no exception for "de minimis" gifts, assuming all other elements are satisfied. But where a small gift is given, especially in a business and cultural context in which such tokens are customarily exchanged, the case will generally be declined for the lack of an obvious corrupt intent. Indicia of appropriate gift-giving are open and transparent exchanges that are properly recorded in the giver's books and are consistent with local law.[85]

c. Payments to Third Parties on the Public Official's Behalf

The FCPA proscribes giving anything of value, "directly or indirectly," to the public official. Thus, companies can violate the FCPA if they make payments or give gifts to third parties, such as a public official's family members. For example, a Hong Kong subsidiary of a foreign bank was convicted under the FCPA for engaging in a systematic practice of hiring and promoting the children of Chinese officials to win business from those officials.[86] Similarly, companies cannot use charitable giving, even to legitimate charitable organizations, as a way of paying off public officials. A company was convicted under the FCPA for donating to a charity headed by a foreign governmental official because, although it was a bona fide charity, the evidence established that the payments were viewed as "dues" the company had to pay to secure the official's help.[87]

d. Payments Funneled Through Third Parties, Including Foreign Subsidiaries

Many companies use local individuals or companies to help them do business in a foreign location. Such advisors or consultants can be invaluable in facilitating transactions and promoting sales. These consultants may provide entirely legitimate services, including language translation, advice regarding the politics and cultural norms prevailing in the country, and help in building important business relationships. But they also create risks. It is very common for bribe payments to be made by or through such intermediaries whether at the organization's express behest, with its tacit approval, or without its knowledge.

The company will be liable if the individual is considered its "agent"; the actions of the company's agents, done within the scope of their employment and to benefit the corporation will be attributed to the company under

84. *See, e.g.*, *Resource Guide*, *supra* note 20, at 15.
85. *See id.* at 14.
86. *See id.* at 16.
87. *Id.*

respondeat superior principles. A company can also be criminally liable for payments offered or made by third parties if others in the company "knew" that the payment would be offered or made for the purpose of obtaining or retaining business.[88]

The FCPA defines a "knowing" state of mind to include willful blindness as well as actual subjective knowledge.[89] "[A] person has the requisite knowledge when he is aware of a high probability of the existence of such circumstance, unless the person actually believes that such circumstance does not exist."[90] Red flags that may be used to prove willful blindness include the payment of excessive commissions to third-party agents, vaguely worded consulting contracts, or evidence that an agent is related to or closely associated with a foreign official or that the consultant was hired at the request of the foreign official. The SEC and DOJ encourage businesses to reduce risks associated with use of third-party agents by adopting an effective compliance program, which ought to include conducting due diligence in hiring local agents.

U.S. companies often attempt to shield themselves from FCPA liability by using a foreign subsidiary to arrange or facilitate the bribe. The company can be liable even where it uses a foreign subsidiary as its intermediary on two theories. First, the parent company itself may have been sufficiently involved—for example, by directing the subsidiary's misconduct—to be directly liable as an issuer or domestic concern. Second, the government may rely on agency principles to make its case. The hallmark of an agency relationships is the principle's control. The "DOJ and SEC evaluate the parent's control—including the parent's knowledge and direction of the subsidiary's actions, both generally and in the context of the specific transaction—when evaluating whether the subsidiary is an agent of the parent."[91] Under *respondeat principles*, the parent will be liable for the actions of its agent subsidiary and its employees, if their actions were within the scope of employment and intended to benefit, at least in part, the parent.

---

88. *See* 15 U.S.C. §§ 78dd-1(a)(3), 78dd-2(a)(3), 78dd-3(a)(3).
89. *See id.* §§ 78dd-1(f)(2), 78dd-2(h)(3), 78dd-3(f)(3).
90. *Resource Guide*, *supra* note 20, at 23. Note that, as discussed *supra* Chapter 2 (General Part), the Supreme Court outlined in *Global-Tech Appliances, Inc. v. SEB S.A.*, 563 U.S. 754 (2011), the two components of a willful blindness charge that apply in the usual federal criminal case: "(1) the defendant must subjectively believe that there is a high probability that a fact exists and (2) the defendant must take deliberate actions to avoid learning of that fact." *Id.* at 769. In the FCPA context, however, the statutory definition would control, and it does not, on its face, require proof of the second element.
91. *Resource Guide*, *supra* note 20, at 28.

4. Willfully and Corruptly

Individual, but not corporate, liability requires proof that the defendant acted willfully.[92] The term "willfully" generally "has been construed by courts to connote an act committed voluntarily and purposefully, and with a bad purpose, i.e., with 'knowledge that [a defendant] was doing a "bad" act under the general rules of law.'"[93] The defendant need not know, however, of the existence of the FCPA or be aware that he is violating the statute.

The word "corruptly" for purposes of the FCPA is defined, in part, much like the word as used in other corruption statutes: "'A person acts corruptly if he acts voluntarily and intentionally, with the improper motive of accomplishing either an unlawful result or a lawful result by some unlawful method or means.'"[94] But FCPA instructions contain an additional requirement—that the defendant intend or desire to wrongfully influence or "'induce the recipient to *misuse* his official position; for example wrongfully to direct business to the payor."[95] Note that this definition differs from that employed in bribery prosecutions under § 201, in which the government need not prove that the defendant intended for the recipient misuse his position, at least where the bribe is offered in exchange for an official act under § 201(b)(1)(A).[96]

Proof of a corrupt intent is sufficient; the FCPA does not require that a corrupt attempt succeed in its purpose. Indeed, the defendant need not even know the identity of the public official at issue. "Thus, an executive who authorizes others to pay 'whoever you need to' in a foreign government to obtain a contract has violated the FCPA—even if no bribe is ultimately offered or paid."[97]

5. *Quid Pro Quo*

As noted above, the required "*quid*"—anything of value—is construed broadly and can be made directly or indirectly for the benefit of the public official or others. With respect to the *quo*, the Second Circuit has held that the "official act" requirement of § 201, defined in § 201(a)(3), interpreted narrowly in *McDonnell*, and applied by the Supreme Court to honest

---

92. *See id.* at 13.
93. *Id.*
94. *Ng Lap Seng*, 934 F.3d at 142.
95. *Resource Guide*, *supra* note 20, at 13 (quoting legislative history, S. Rep. No. 95-114, at 10).
96. *See, e.g.*, *Alfisi*, 308 F.3d 144. The Second Circuit approved an FCPA jury instruction that included the following: "'The term "corruptly" is intended to connote that the offer, payment, and promise was intended to influence an official to misuse his official position.'" *Ng Lap Seng*, 934 F.3d at 142-44. The court further stated, however, that this instruction does not require proof of a "breach of duty." *Id.* at 143.
97. *Resource Guide*, *supra* note 20, at 13.

services and Hobbs Act bribery cases, does *not* apply in the FCPA context.[98] It reasoned that the statute does not prohibit offering anything of value in exchange for an "official act." Rather, it makes it illegal to give a foreign official anything of value

> for purposes of (1) "influencing any act or decision of such foreign official in his official capacity," (2) "inducing such foreign official to do or omit to do any act in violation of the lawful duty of such official," (3) "securing an improper advantage," or (4) "inducing such foreign official to use his influence with a foreign government or instrumentality thereof to affect or influence any act or decision of such government or instrumentality."[99]

And "each of these *quos* [must] serve[] a particular purpose, i.e., to assist the giver in 'obtaining' or 'retaining' or 'directing' business."[100]

6. Business Nexus Requirement: Obtaining or Retaining Business

Many enforcement actions involve bribes to obtain or retain government contracts, but the FCPA also prohibits bribes in connection with gaining a business advantage. For example, the Fifth Circuit, in *United States v. Kay*, 359 F.3d 738 (5th Cir. 2004), held that in some circumstances bribes paid to obtain favorable tax treatment—for example to reduce a company's customs duties and sales taxes on imports—could constitute payments made to "obtain or retain" business within the meaning of the FCPA. The court explained that, in enacting the FCPA, "Congress meant to prohibit a range of payments wider than only those that directly influence the acquisition or retention of government contracts or similar commercial or industrial arrangements."[101] It ruled that:

> The congressional target was bribery paid to engender assistance in improving the business opportunities of the payor or his beneficiary, irrespective of whether that assistance be direct or indirect, and irrespective of whether it be related to administering the law, awarding, extending, or renewing a contract, or executing or preserving an agreement.[102]

The *Kay* Court thus held that payments for favorable tax treatment can violate the FCPA if "[a]voiding or lowering taxes reduces operating costs and thus increases profit margins, thereby freeing up funds that the business is

98. *See Ng Lap Seng*, 934 F.3d at 132.
99. *Id.*
100. *Id.*
101. *Kay*, 359 F.3d at 749.
102. *Id.* at 750.

otherwise legally obligated to expend. And this, in turn, enables it to take any number of actions to the disadvantage of competitors."[103]

Other bribe payments that may satisfy the business purpose test are those made to obtain government action to prevent competitors from entering a market or to avoid a licensing or permit requirement.[104]

7. Exemption and Exceptions

The FCPA exempts from its coverage "facilitating" or "grease" payments to foreign officials "to expedite or to secure the performance of a routine governmental action" involving non-discretionary decisions.[105] Routine governmental action can include such matters as obtaining permits to do business, processing visas and work orders, and arranging for utilities services[106] but does not include "any action taken by a foreign official involved in the decision-making process to encourage a decision to award new business to or continue business with a particular party."[107]

"Grease" or facilitating payments are generally made to expedite ministerial activities undertaken by mid- to low-level foreign functionaries. Even if the payment is made for a routine service, however, it cannot be made to subvert the official's function. "Thus, paying an official a small amount to have the power turned on at a factory might be a facilitating payment; paying an inspector to ignore the fact that the company does not have a valid permit to operate the factory" would not.[108] It is worth noting that such grease payments may not violate the FCPA, but they may be illegal under domestic law and prudent counsel will advise clients to avoid them.

The FCPA also provides for two affirmative defenses. First, a defendant may assert that the payment was lawful "under the written laws and regulations" of the State at issue.[109] The defendant cannot meet her burden merely by showing the activity is not forbidden by written law; the law must affirmatively shield the activity from liability. Given that written laws expressly authorizing bribery are scarce, this exception is rarely used or successful.[110] Second, the FCPA permits a defendant to assert as an affirmative defense that the payment was a reasonable and bona fide expenditure (such as travel and

---

103. *Id.* at 749.
104. *See Resource Guide*, *supra* note 20, at 11.
105. 15 U.S.C. §§ 78dd-1(b), 78dd-2(b), 78dd-3(b).
106. *See id.* §§ 78dd-1(f)(3)(A), 78dd-2(h)(4)(A), 78dd-3(f)(4)(A).
107. *Id.* §§ 78dd-1(f)(3)B), 78dd-2(h)(4)(B), 78dd-3(f)(4)(B).
108. *Resource Guide*, *supra* note 20, at 25.
109. 15 U.S.C. §§ 78dd-1(c)(1), 78dd-2(c)(1), 78dd-3(c)(1).
110. *See* United States v. Kozeny, 582 F. Supp. 2d 535, 537-40 (S.D.N.Y. 2008).

lodging expenses) incurred by or on behalf of a foreign official which was made in connection with the promotion, demonstration, or explanation of the defendant's products or services, or the execution or performance of a contract with a foreign government (or agency).[111] These types of expenditures are common, and the DOJ has provided a great deal of guidance regarding when promotional and contract-related expenses, particularly those for travel and lodging, will be regarded as legitimate.[112]

B. The Foreign Extortion Prevention Act, 18 U.S.C. § 201(f)

In December 2023, Congress passed the Foreign Extortion Prevention Act (FEPA) which amended the federal bribery statute, 18 U.S.C. § 201, to authorize prosecution of corrupt foreign officials where there has been a violation of the FCPA.

Section 201(f) applies to "foreign officials," which are defined to include any official or employee of, or person acting in an official or unofficial capacity for, a foreign government or any department, agency, or instrumentality thereof and any official or employee of, or person acting in an official or unofficial capacity for, a "public international organization" as so designated in an executive order.

To establish a violation of this subsection, the government will have to prove that:

- a foreign official or person selected to be a foreign official
- corruptly
- demanded, sought, received, accepted, or agreed to receive or accept, directly or indirectly,
- anything of value
- personally or for any other person or nongovernmental entity
- by making use of the mails or any means or instrumentality of interstate commerce
- from any issuer, domestic concern, or, while in the territory of the United States, a § 78dd-3 person
- a qualifying *quid pro quo*, meaning that a thing of value must be offered in exchange for
    - being influenced in the performance of any "official act,"

111. *See* 15 U.S.C. §§ 78dd-1(c)(2), 78dd-2(c)(2), 78dd-3(c)(2).
112. *See, e.g.*, *Resource Guide*, *supra* note 20, at 24-25.

- being induced to do or omit to do any act in violation of the official duty of such foreign official or person, or
- conferring any improper advantage
- in connection with obtaining or retaining business for or with, or directing business to, any person

Congress specified that an offense under § 201(f)(1) "shall be subject to extraterritorial Federal jurisdiction" (§ 201(f)(3)).[113] Those found guilty of violating 201(f) can be fined not more than $250,000 or three times the monetary equivalent of the thing of value, imprisoned for not more than fifteen years, or both.

Note that the possible *quo*'s identified in § 201(f) do not precisely track those that are used in FCPA cases.[114] Payments to induce the public official "to use his influence with a foreign government to affect or influence any government act or decision" can be alleged in FCPA cases but is not included in § 201(f).

The definition of a "public official" for purposes of the Act also differs from that used in FCPA cases. Section 201(a)(4) includes "any senior foreign political figure," while the FCPA does not. And the FEPA includes not only persons acting in an official capacity for or on behalf of qualifying governments, instrumentalities of such governments, and international organizations, but also those acting in an unofficial capacity for them. But § 201(a)(4) is narrower in one respect: it does not include foreign political parties or candidates for foreign political office, while the FCPA does.

Examples

1. Serdar Teke was a Turkish national residing in Istanbul. He was hired by Acme, Corp., a company incorporated in Delaware whose shares traded on the New York Stock Exchange (NYSE), as a consultant to help Acme secure a contract worth many millions of dollars from a Turkish airline. The Turkish airline used to be owned by the government but was spun off into a company over which the government still exerts some control. Teke was anxious to establish an ongoing consultancy relationship with

113. Congress included a rule of construction that provides that § 201(f) "shall not be construed as encompassing conduct that would violate [15 U.S.C. §§ 78dd-1, 78dd-2, or 78dd-3] whether pursuant to a theory of direct liability, conspiracy, complicity, or otherwise."

114. The FCPA includes "inducing that person to use his influence with a foreign government to affect or influence any government act or decision" as a possible *quid pro quo* but the FEPA does not.

Acme and knew that Acme was the underdog in the race for the contract. Unbeknownst to Acme, and at the airline President's suggestion, Teke took a portion of his Acme consulting fee and used it to pay the college tuition of the President's daughter. Shortly thereafter, Teke sent an email to Acme saying that he was very hopeful that the company would be successful in obtaining the contract. Could Acme and Teke be liable under the FCPA?

2. A Finnish company, Acme Scandinavia (AS), wished to sell steel in Brazil but Brazilian law imposed prohibitive tariffs on the import of steel. (AS had no securities listed or traded in the United States and its principal place of business was in Finland). AS had a wholly owned subsidiary, ASB, which was incorporated and had its principal place of business in Brazil. A Finnish national who was an employee of ASB, Paavo Laine, agreed to give an influential Brazilian legislator and his family an all-expenses paid trip to Finland to see the company's steel plant in return for his help in reducing the Brazilian tariffs. This trip also included a luxury three-week cruise around various Scandinavian ports to ensure that the legislator understood the company's "cultural milieu." Payment for the trip was wired, at Laine's request, from AS's Finnish bank to the American cruise line's U.S. bank. After the trip, the Brazilian legislator sponsored legislation designed to lower the steel tariffs.

   Pending such legislation, and to test the Brazilian steel market, Laine arranged to pay a Brazilian customs official $2,000 to "forget" to do the paperwork reflecting the import and assessing the required tariff. The customs official insisted on receiving his payment in dollars. At Laine's request, AS wired the official the money from its New York bank account. Could AS and Laine be liable under the FCPA? What if, instead of wiring the money to Laine, AS insisted that Laine go to New York to pick up the $2,000 in cash so there would be no record of the transfer?

3. Acme, which was incorporated and had its principal place of business in Delaware, was a wholly owned subsidiary of an Indonesian company, Acme East (AE). Acme was seeking a contract from the government of Laos to build a dam in that country. It wished to pay off the Laotian public official who was in charge of building the dam. Acme executives were not sure how such payments were best made in Laos. They called Sidik Wibowo, an Indonesian national who was employed by AE and who had a great deal of experience working on projects in Laos. Wibowo gave Acme advice on how to proceed by telephone and email. Ultimately, the bribe was paid, and the public official awarded the contract to Acme. Can Wibowo be prosecuted under the FCPA?

Explanations

1. In this case, the government can likely prove an actionable *quid pro quo* and a business nexus: the offer of a payment was made in exchange for securing an improper advantage and inducing the President to violate his duties by throwing the contract to Acme, both of which result in Acme obtaining business. The payment does not have to go directly to the public official; here, it is enough that the public official directed the payment to his daughter. Teke was acting with a corrupt intent because the parties to the bribe intended that the President misuse his office to give the contract to Acme.

   There are, however, a number of problems with the case. First, there is a real question whether the airline President is a foreign public official. This issue would turn on whether the airline is viewed as an "agency" or "instrumentality" of the Turkish government. Under the Eleventh Circuit's test, this requires proof that (1) the entity is controlled by the government of Turkey; and (2) it performs a function Turkey treats as its own.

   Second, is not at all clear that Acme knew or was willfully blind to the payment made through its intermediary. But if Teke qualifies as Acme's "agent," the company may be liable, under respondeat superior principles, for his actions because his knowledge and intent will be imputed to the company. This agency question will turn on whether the Acme agreed that Teke would act for it, an acceptance by Teke of the undertaking, and an understanding that Acme would control the relationship.

   Acme trades on the NYSE, so it is an issuer, and because it is chartered in the United States, it is a U.S. person. If Teke is an agent of a U.S. issuer, the company will be liable either if he used the instrumentalities of interstate commerce corruptly in furtherance of the corrupt payment or corruptly did any act outside the United States in furtherance of the payment to corrupt officials to secure or retain business. The actus reus requirement would be satisfied by Teke's status update email to Acme or Teke's actions in Turkey.

   With respect to Teke's liability, we will assume he qualifies as an agent of an issuer. He is also a non-U.S. person because of his nationality and residency in Turkey. His actus reus is clear: his email suffices because, given his status, all that need be proven is that he used the instrumentalities of interstate commerce. But if he is not Acme's "agent," he is a 78dd-3 person and cannot be liable because he took no action while on the territory of the United States.

2. Because their shares are not traded on any U.S. exchange and they are foreign corporations with principal places of business abroad, AS and ASB are potentially 78dd-3 companies that are not U.S. persons. Laine, as an employee of ASB, is clearly its "agent" and thus potentially a 78dd-3

person. Given that our focus is on AS, however, the government would have to prove that Laine is acting as an agent of AS in order to have his actions and intention imputed to it. This will turn on whether AS and Laine understood theirs to be an agency relationship in which AS, with Laine's agreement, asserted control over Laine's actions. Given that AS appears to respond with alacrity to Laine's request for the wiring of funds, the parties may well view Laine as AS's agent.

Both the legislator and the customs official are "public officials." The customs official was given $2,000 in return for his help—obviously something of value. The lavish trip planned for the legislator and his family would also qualify as "anything of value" and it is very unlikely—given the inclusion of the legislator's family in the jaunt and the addition of a luxury cruise to the itinerary—to qualify under the affirmative defense for bona fide promotional and contract-related expenses.

Proving a *quid pro quo* and a corrupt intent should not be difficult: these things of value were offered to both officials in return for influencing them to violate their duties. The payment to the customs official would not constitute a grease payment because it is intended not to expedite a non-discretionary and ministerial action but rather to cause the official to fail to do the actions his position requires.

The business nexus requirement is satisfied if the government can show that the legislation is material to making AS's entry into, or its continuation in, the Brazilian steel market feasible. To satisfy the business nexus requirement for the customs official, the government would rely on *Kay* in arguing that avoidance of these tariffs reduced operating costs and made it possible to produce sufficient profit margins to compete with others in the market.

The problem the government will have is in proving the requisite actus reus or jurisdictional act. AS, at Laine's request, clearly used the instrumentalities of interstate commerce (the wiring of money to and from U.S. banks). AS can be liable for the actions of Laine if he was acting as its agent in this matter; it can also potentially be liable for its own actions in wiring the bribe money at Laine's request assuming that it was aware of, or willfully blind to, their corrupt nature. But AS, ASB, and Laine did not use the instrumentalities of interstate commerce *while on the territory of the United States* as required by § 78dd-3. The situation would be different if, as posited, Laine physically travelled to New York to pick up the money because this would be an act in furtherance of the bribe while on the territory of the United States.

3. Acme employees, presumably while in the United States, clearly hatched a scheme to bribe a Laotian public official to obtain a contract with the Laotian government. There seems little doubt that Acme is liable for a FCPA violation in these circumstances. We don't know whether Acme

satisfies the requisites of issuer status, but because it is incorporated and has its principal place of business in the United States, it is at least a domestic concern and a U.S. person. As such, the government need only show that Acme's agents used the instrumentalities of interstate commerce or did any act outside the United States in furtherance of the payment to a public official to secure or retain business. The telephone calls and emails with Wibowo would satisfy the actus reus required.

While the case against Acme would seem to be clear, we have greater difficulty in indicting Wibowo. As a foreign national and non-U.S. resident, he is a potentially a 78dd-3 person. But he could not be convicted under that provision because he has done nothing on the territory of the United States. The government could try to indict him as an agent of the domestic concern, Acme. If he is a non-U.S. person and agent of a domestic concern, his use of the interstate wires in using email and the telephone to communicate with Acme's U.S. team would provide the needed jurisdictional act/actus reus. But it is not clear that the government could prove the elements of "agency": a manifestation by Acme that Wibowo would act for it; acceptance by Wibowo of the undertaking; and an understanding between the parties that Acme will be in control of the undertaking. It seems, rather, as though Wibowo, as an employee of Acme's parent company, lent Acme some advice on corrupt practices in Laos. The government could try to indict Wibowo as an aider and abettor or co-conspirator of Acme, but the Second Circuit, at least, would reject this theory of liability under *Hoskins I*. In *Hoskins I*, the court held that someone who cannot be liable under 78dd-3 cannot be prosecuted for aiding and abetting or conspiring with others to violate that section. The government would meet greater success in proceeding under this theory in the Seventh Circuit.

VI. THE TRAVEL ACT, 18 U.S.C. § 1952

Section 1952 of Title 18 criminalizes interstate or foreign travel or use of the U.S. mail or any facility of interstate or foreign commerce with the intent to promote, manage, establish, carry on or facilitate certain unlawful activities. Enacted in 1961, the Travel Act was intended to help state and local authorities in "dealing with organized criminal activity which, in many instances, had assumed interstate proportions and which in all cases was materially assisted in its operations by the availability of facilities of interstate commerce."[115] The government has relied on § 1952 in corruption cases, both

115. Erlenbaugh v. United States, 409 U.S. 239, 245 (1972).

domestic and transborder, whether or not they have an organized crime nexus because this statute can reach corrupt conduct not chargeable under 18 U.S.C. § 201 or the FCPA.

As relevant here, a defendant is liable under the Travel Act (§ 1952(a)(3)) if he:

- travels in interstate or foreign commerce *or* uses of the mail *or* any facility in interstate or foreign commerce
- with the intent to promote, manage, establish, carry on, or facilitate the promotion, management, establishment, or carrying on, of any "unlawful activity," and
- thereafter knowingly and willfully commits an act, or attempts to perform an act, of promotion, management, establishment, carrying on, or facilitation of the identified "unlawful activity"

The term "unlawful activity" covers a variety of offenses commonly charged in organized crime prosecutions. For white-collar purposes, it is notable that "unlawful activity" includes money laundering under § 1956 and § 1957 and extortion and bribery "in violation of the laws of the State in which committed or of the United States" (§1952(b)). Basically, this statute makes the act of traveling, or using the wires or mails, in furtherance of a bribery, extortion or money laundering scheme punishable by a fine, not more than five years' imprisonment, or both.

The statute requires that the defendant act with the specific intent to commit the bribery, extortion or money laundering but does not require proof of a mens rea in relation to the jurisdictional element of interstate travel, use of the mail, or use of a facility of interstate commerce.[116] Under the Act, the government must prove that the jurisdictional element occurred and "thereafter" the defendant performed or attempted to perform bribery, extortion, or money laundering (§ 1952(a)). Under the Travel Act, the unit of prosecution is each act of interstate travel or use of an interstate facility; each such act or use constitutes a separate offense.[117]

In RICO, Congress decreed that that act be liberally construed. But courts have tended to read the Travel Act less expansively in the belief that "Congress would certainly recognize that an expansive Travel Act would alter sensitive federal-state relationships."[118] Thus, for example, the Supreme Court read the requirement that the defendant travel with intent to "promote, manage, establish, carry on, or facilitate" certain kinds of illegal activity to suggest that the "traveler's purpose must involve more than the desire

116. *See, e.g.*, United States v. Winters, 33 F.3d 720, 722 (6th Cir. 1994).
117. *See* United States v. Jabara, 644 F.2d 574, 577 (6th Cir. 1981).
118. Rewis v. United States, 401 U.S. 808, 812 (1971).

to patronize the illegal activity."[119] It suggested in *Rewis v. United States*, 401 U.S. 808, 812 (1971), that "Congress did not intend that the Travel Act should apply to criminal activity solely because that activity is at times patronized by persons from another State."[120]

The Travel Act is a useful supplemental statute because it addresses individuals and types of corruption that other statutes do not. First, the Travel Act can be used to indict the bri*bees* in transnational bribery cases. As noted above, such persons cannot be liable under the FCPA although the addition of § 201(f) to the Code may obviate this difficulty. Second, § 201, § 1951, and §§ 78dd-1 to 78dd-3 apply only when *public officials* (or their agents) are bribed. They do not address commercial bribery—that is, the bribery of private persons for business. Commercial bribery cases can be pursued, however, under an honest services mail or wire fraud theory (discussed in Chapter 6) or under the Travel Act, assuming the elements of those crimes are satisfied in a particular case. The Travel Act applies because bribery in violation of state law is an "unlawful activity" for purposes of § 1952 and the majority of U.S. states outlaw commercial bribery.[121]

Examples

1. Acme, a California-based company, sells mufflers to Japanese and Korean automobile manufacturers. Acme increased and maintained its sales to these manufacturers by lavishing luxury gifts on their executives and treating them to holidays to Disneyland and Las Vegas, complete with first-class airfare and five-star hotel accommodations. All of these gifts and trips were paid for out of Acme's New York bank accounts. Because the executives are not foreign public officials, Acme cannot be indicted for violating the FCPA. But can the government go forward against the corrupt executives and Acme under the Travel Act?

2. Acme is a U.S. corporation whose shares trade on a U.S. stock exchange. It wired a bribe from its New York bank account to a foreign public official in South Africa who, in return, awarded Acme a government contract to build a dam. Acme is therefore liable under the Foreign Corrupt Practices Act. Is it also indictable under the Travel Act?

119. *Id.* at 811.
120. *Id.* at 812.
121. *See* Perrin v. United States, 444 U.S. 37, 50 (1979) (bribery of private employees prohibited by state criminal statutes violates the Travel Act).

Explanations

1. The Travel Act prohibits the use of "any facility of interstate or foreign commerce" in furtherance of, or with the intent to promote, unlawful activity." "Unlawful activity" includes "bribery . . . in violation of the laws of the State in which committed." The FCPA does not authorize prosecution of the persons—non-governmental commercial actors—receiving the corrupt payment, but the California Code does. The California commercial bribery statute provides that

   > Any employee who solicits, accepts, or agrees to accept money or anything of value from a person other than his or her employer, . . . corruptly and without the knowledge or consent of the employer, in return for using or agreeing to use his or her position for the benefit of that other person, and any person who offers or gives an employee money or anything of value under those circumstances, is guilty of commercial bribery.[122]

   Because the Korean and Japanese executives travelled in interstate and foreign commerce and because Acme used a facility of interstate commerce (banking transfers) to facilitate this commercial bribery scheme, the executives and Acme can be charged under the Travel Act.[123]

2. "Unlawful activity" includes bribery "in violation of the laws . . . of the United States," which, of course, includes the FCPA.[124] Because Acme is an "issuer" and U.S. person that used a facility of interstate commerce (wiring) to facilitate this bribery scheme, an FCPA case can be made and thus a Travel Act charge built upon it is appropriate. Note how extreme such charge nesting can get: because the Travel Act is a RICO predicate act, the government could build a RICO case on this Travel Act predicate, which in turn is based on the FCPA violation.

---

122. Cal. Penal Code § 641.3(a).
123. *See* United States v. Carson, No. SACR 09–00077–JVS, 2011 WL 7416975 (C.D. Cal. Sept. 20, 2011).
124. *See* Chevron Corp. v. Donziger, 974 F. Supp. 2d 362, 595-96 (S.D.N.Y. 2014).

CHAPTER 10

RICO

II. **Procedural Issues, Forfeiture, and Prosecutorial Policies**
   A. **Practical and Evidentiary Considerations**
   B. **Criminal Forfeiture**
   C. **DOJ Approval Requirements and Charging Directions**

In 1970, Congress passed the Racketeer Influenced and Corrupt Organizations (RICO) statute (18 U.S.C. §§ 1961–1968) as part of the Organized Crime Control Act.[1] That Act established new crimes and provided enhanced sanctions and remedies with the goal of eradicating organized crime in the United States. Criminal RICO has become an important prosecutorial tool in pursuing group criminality but has generated a great deal of controversy in part because the statute has regularly been applied to conduct that in no way resembles the traditional organized crime "racketeering" that it was intended to address. Congress's major purpose in defining the activities outlawed in RICO, 18 U.S.C. § 1962, was "to address the infiltration of legitimate business by organized crime."[2] Section 1962 has four subsections, (a)-(d), each of which describes a different violation. The two provisions most pertinent to Congress's principal aim—§ 1962(a) and (b)—are the provisions least frequently invoked. The subsections most frequently charged in white-collar cases are § 1962(c) and (d), and these will be our principal focus.

RICO cases are complex but, at bottom, they are built upon proof that the defendant engaged in a "pattern of racketeering activity" with a specified relationship to a statutory "enterprise." The requisite "pattern of racketeering" requires the commission of, or conspiracy to commit, at least two crimes (often referred to as RICO "predicates").[3] The following materials concentrate on the subsections most used in white-collar cases: § 1962(c), which makes it unlawful for any person employed by or associated with an "enterprise" to conduct the enterprise's affairs through a "pattern of racketeering activity," and § 1962(d), which makes it unlawful for a person to conspire to violate subsections (a), (b), or (c) of § 1962.

RICO is a flexible weapon in part because of the more than 100 serious federal crimes that can serve as RICO predicates, including mail, wire, and bank fraud; obstruction of justice and witness tampering; Hobbs and Travel Act violations; money laundering; and "fraud in the sale of securities" (§ 1961(1)(B), (D)).[4] RICO charges may also be built upon an array of

---

1. Pub. L. No. 91-452, 84 Stat. 941 (1970).
2. United States v. Turkette, 452 U.S. 576, 591 (1981).
3. Civil plaintiffs must allege that two or more crimes were committed as part of a pattern of racketeering and must prove that these predicate acts were committed by a preponderance of the evidence. But the Supreme Court rejected a rule mandating that a private action could proceed only against a defendant who has already been convicted of a predicate act or of a RICO violation. *See* Sedima, S.P.R.L. v. Imrex Co., 473 U.S. 479, 488-93 (1985).
4. With respect to RICO cases founded on securities law violations, note the caveats regarding such cases included in § 1962(a) and § 1964(c).

criminal acts chargeable under state law but included by Congress within the definition of actionable "racketeering activity" (§ 1961(1)(A)). RICO thus "federalizes" traditionally state-law crimes like murder, kidnaping, extortion, robbery, bribery, and dealing in obscene materials. A qualifying "enterprise" is also fairly easy to identify because it can take a seemingly infinite variety of forms, from legal entities such as corporations or government offices to loosely aligned criminal conspiracies. A large percentage of white-collar RICO cases concern either business crime or public corruption by federal, state, and local actors. Using § 1962(c), the theory in these cases is that the defendant conducted an enterprise (e.g., the business or public office) through a pattern of racketeering activity (e.g., wire fraud or bribery).

RICO has proved to be a very attractive tool for prosecutors in major part because of the penalties it affords. RICO violators can be sentenced to a fine, up to twenty years' imprisonment, or both. The statutory maximum increases to a sentence of life imprisonment if the RICO case is based on racketeering activity that carries such a sanction. The defendants may also be convicted of the predicate crimes underlying the RICO count, thus subjecting them to much higher cumulative maximum statutory penalties and the possibility of consecutive sentences.

RICO also authorizes other potent weapons attractive to prosecutors. Under § 1963, defendants convicted under § 1962 "shall forfeit" any interest acquired or maintained in violation of § 1962, any interest in any enterprise operated in violation of § 1962, and any property constituting, or derived from, the proceeds of racketeering activity in violation of § 1962. Under § 1963, prosecutors can secure pre-trial (§ 1963(d)(1)(A)) and even pre-indictment (§ 1963(d)(1)(B)) restraining orders freezing allegedly tainted assets that may be subject to forfeiture. Such orders may be entered even if they freeze funds that the defendant would otherwise use to pay his lawyers or prepare his defense. And upon the government's application, RICO authorizes civil remedies such as divestiture, corporate dissolution, and reorganization (§ 1964(a), (b)).

Finally, RICO cases provide prosecutors many practical boons. RICO indictments give the government significant joinder, venue, and evidentiary advantages. Charging a defendant with "racketeering" carries with it a stigma that stimulates pleas and concerns juries. That stigma, the potentially onerous sentencing consequences of RICO charges, and the many procedural advantages RICO provides combine to give prosecutors a large club with which to force pleas, especially from corporate actors.

Given the above, one might wonder why prosecutors don't attempt to bring RICO charges in virtually all white-collar cases. The answer, as readers shall discover within, is that the RICO statute has many elements and associated legal complexity. Prosecutors, then, must weigh the obvious advantages a RICO charge brings against the possibility that jurors will be hopelessly confused when charged with applying the law to the facts of a case.

RICO is also a hybrid statute—that is, it is capable of civil as well as criminal enforcement. It is viewed as a godsend by civil plaintiffs' lawyers, and for good reason. Section 1964(c) authorizes federal court jurisdiction over civil suits by "[a]ny person injured in his business or property by reason" of a § 1962 violation. As we shall see, many run-of-the-mill fraud or other claims typical in business disputes that would otherwise be tried in state court can easily be bootstrapped into RICO cases. And the incentive to do so is created by 1964(c), which provides that successful RICO plaintiffs "shall recover" treble damages, attorneys' fees, and costs. As a result of the lure of treble damages and fees, civil RICO cases far outnumber criminal ones. Indeed, we will find that much of the caselaw examined or cited within was decided in civil damages actions. One could argue that criminal and civil RICO ought to be construed differently, not least because federal judges regularly attempt to limit the flood of civil RICO suits clogging their dockets by construing the statute narrowly, and their efforts may have the unfortunate result of foreclosing legitimate criminal prosecutions. It is clear, however, that the elements of a RICO case are read the same whether the case is civil or criminal in nature—only the standard of proof differs.[5]

I. PROHIBITED ACTIVITIES: SECTIONS 1962(a), (b), AND (c)

The RICO statute contains three discrete substantive crimes (§ 1962(a), (b), and (c)). The provision outlawing conspiracies to commit these crimes, § 1962(d), is examined *infra*. If one simply reads the statutory language of § 1962(a)-(c), the distinctions between them are not immediately apparent. The best way to discern the differences in the conduct addressed in each subsection is to keep one's eye on *the work that the "racketeering" activity does* in relation to the charged "enterprise" in each subsection.[6]

> (a) It shall be unlawful for any person *who has received any income* derived, directly or indirectly, *from a pattern of racketeering activity to use or invest*, directly or indirectly, *any part of such income*, or the proceeds of such income, *in acquisition of any interest in*, or the establishment or *operation of, any enterprise* which is engaged in, or the activities of which affect, interstate or foreign commerce

5. As is examined *infra*, plaintiffs must also show a domestic injury to recover in extraterritorial civil RICO suits but the government does not bear a similar burden in criminal cases.
6. RICO cases can be built on the collection of an "unlawful debt" arising from illegal gambling or loansharking activities instead of an alleged pattern of racketeering activity. Because white-collar cases relying on this theory are rare, it is not examined within.

The pattern of racketeering in this subsection is spinning off money that is then used to acquire or operate an enterprise. Subsection (a) would apply, for example, if a mobster were to take the proceeds of his drug dealing and buy an apartment complex. Congress was concerned that money that gangsters were earning through their crimes was being invested in legitimate businesses. Racketeers thereby laundered their ill-gotten gains (trading tainted funds for an untainted business asset). And such businesses also were being used as fronts for further criminal activity.

It is important to note for purposes of charging white-collar crimes that this subsection also authorizes liability for those who take the proceeds of their racketeering activity and use those funds to "operate" an enterprise. This subsection, then, can be used to prosecute those who would plow their illicit proceeds back into the conduct of the enterprise's business. For example, consider a utility company that bribes members of the commission that regulates its rates to secure approval of rate increases. One could charge the company with using the income (increased rates) derived from the racketeering activity (bribes) in the continuing operation of the company.

> (b) It shall be unlawful for any person *through a pattern of racketeering activity* to *acquire or maintain*, directly or indirectly, *any interest in or control of any enterprise* which is engaged in, or the activities of which affect, interstate or foreign commerce

The pattern of racketeering here is the means through which the defendant acquires or controls an enterprise. It is not the racketeering earnings that secure the defendant's interest in the enterprise as in (a); rather it is the racketeering activity—for example, predicate crimes such as extortion—that does the job. Subsection (b), then, addresses the more dangerous cases in which business owners are extorted or threatened into ceding ownership or control of their enterprises. For example, subsection (b) would be invoked when a defendant threatens a business owner with violence if he does not sell his business to the defendant. Again, this reflects Congress's principal concern—preventing organized crime from infiltrating legitimate businesses. Where this subsection might be useful in white-collar cases is in the public corruption context. Prosecutors may allege that the defendant bribers used a pattern of bribery to take "control" of an enterprise, that is, the public office they are seeking to corrupt.

Subsections (a) and (b) may be useful in addressing organized crime but they have more limited utility in business crime and public corruption cases. At least in white-collar cases, by far the most useful subsections are § 1962(c) and (d), which are our focus.

> (c) It shall be unlawful for *any person employed by or associated with any enterprise* engaged in, or the activities of which affect, interstate or foreign

> commerce, *to conduct* or participate, directly or indirectly, in the conduct of *such enterprise's affairs through a pattern of racketeering activity*

The racketeering activity in subsection (c) is not an external means of securing an interest in the enterprise, as in (a) or (b), and the enterprise is not the prize to be obtained either through a purchase with tainted funds (§ 1962(a)) or the use of criminal means, such as extortion (§ 1962(b)). Rather, at least in the mob context, the enterprise is the criminal organization itself—the gang, crime family, or tong—that is conducted through a variety of criminal means—racketeering activities such as extortion, bribery, drug trafficking, and the like.

When we leave behind the organized crime context, one can see how easily this subsection can be used to frame white-collar business crime and public corruption cases. Thus, for example, in a case in which a company is scamming its customers, the executives would be charged with conducting the affairs of the business "enterprise" through a pattern of racketeering activity in the form of consumer fraud. In the public corruption context, a corrupt sheriff would be charged with running the sheriff's office "enterprise" through a pattern of bribery.

Under subsection (c), the government must prove:

- the existence of an enterprise
- which affects interstate or foreign commerce
- the defendant "person"
- was "associated with" or "employed by" the enterprise and
- conducted or participated in the conduct of the enterprise's affairs
- through a pattern of racketeering activity

Charging under § 1962(c) can be tricky because of the wealth of elements that must be proved and the extensive caselaw that complicates their application. To summarize the charging challenges—explored at length below—when choosing who to name as the defendant "person," how to characterize the "enterprise," and what predicate acts to charge in a § 1962(c) case, one must consider the following:

- *The distinctiveness requirement*: the defendant "person" cannot be the same individual or entity as the alleged "enterprise"
- *The jurisdictional hook*: the enterprise must affect interstate or foreign commerce
- *The* Reves *requirement*: the defendant "person" must "operate or manage" the enterprise
- *The "pattern of racketeering" requirements*: the pattern must consist of two or more predicate crimes (1) that qualify as such under § 1961, (2) that are separated in time by no more than ten years, (3) that

satisfy the Supreme Court's "relatedness" and "continuity" tests, and (4) one of which occurred within the five-year statute of limitations period.

A. Defendant "Persons"

Under RICO, the defendant "person" "includes any individual or entity capable of holding a legal or beneficial interest in property" (§ 1961(3)). The "persons" that can be charged under RICO, then, include natural persons and a seemingly endless list of entities, including all manner of business organizations and a wide range of other political, commercial, and even religious organizations. The one limitation is that a governmental entity cannot be a defendant "person" under RICO.[7]

B. The "Enterprise"

The term "enterprise" is defined as including "any individual, partnership, corporation, association, or other legal entity, and any union or group of individuals associated in fact although not a legal entity" (§ 1961(4)). This is said to include two categories of associations: (1) organizations such as corporations and partnerships, and other "legal entities"; and (2) so-called "association-in-fact" (AIF) enterprises which include "any union or group of individuals associated in fact although not a legal entity."

1. Legal Entities

In many business crime cases the "enterprise" through which the crimes are committed will be a corporation, partnership, or other legal entity. Note that while government entities cannot be defendant "persons," they can be RICO "enterprises." Thus, in many of the public corruption cases brought under RICO, prosecutors charge that the RICO "enterprise" is the legitimate public entity through which the venal defendants are said to have conducted their corrupt racketeering activities, including police departments, courts, and even governor's offices. For example, a corrupt state governor who accepts bribes in return for directing state business to a particular vendor might be charged as the defendant "person" who is conducting the "enterprise"—the governor's office—through a pattern of racketeering activity in the form of bribery.

7. *See, e.g.*, Gil Ramirez Grp., L.L.C. v. Hous. Indep. Sch. Dist., 786 F.3d 400, 411-12 & n.13 (5th Cir. 2015) (holding school district is not a cognizable defendant "person").

2. Association-In-Fact (AIF) Enterprises

Again, "association-in-fact" (AIF) enterprises include "any union or group of individuals associated in fact although not a legal entity." In *United States v. Turkette*, 452 U.S. 576 (1981), the defendants argued that Congress enacted RICO solely to protect legitimate business enterprises from infiltration by racketeers and thus that RICO does not make criminal participation in "association-in-fact" enterprises that perform only illegal acts and that have not infiltrated a legitimate enterprise. The Court rejected this challenge, holding that the statute applies to both legitimate and illegitimate enterprises. This means that an AIF enterprise need have no connection with a legitimate business; it can consist entirely of a group of conspirators who get together only to commit crimes.

In *Turkette*, the proponents of the suggested limiting construction argued that without it, an "enterprise" would be nothing more than the "pattern of racketeering" in which the defendants engaged, making the "enterprise" element superfluous and the rest of the statutory terms incoherent. In responding to this argument, the Court distinguished an association-in-fact RICO enterprise from the racketeering activity in which it engages in language that is now used to define such AIF enterprises.

The Court explained first that "[t]he enterprise is an entity, for present purposes a group of persons associated together for a common purpose of engaging in a course of conduct."[8] The *Turkette* Court further stated that the enterprise "is proved by evidence of an ongoing organization, formal or informal, and by evidence that the various associates function as a continuing unit."[9] Finally, the Court noted that while proof of the predicate racketeering acts and the enterprise itself "may in particular cases coalesce, proof of one does not necessarily establish the other. The 'enterprise' is not the 'pattern of racketeering activity'; it is an entity separate and apart from the pattern of activity in which it engages."[10]

The AIF's "common purpose" is generally not an obstacle to prosecution because it can be inferred from the participants' coordinated actions in support of identified criminal aims. And it can be expressed very generally; for example, in *United States v. Elliott*, 571 F.2d 880 (5th Cir. 1978), the court was satisfied that "[t]he thread tying all of these [disparate] departments, activities, and individuals together was the desire to make money."[11] The *Turkette* Court's suggestions that an AIF enterprise must have continuity and the associates must function as a continuing

---

8. *Turkette*, 452 U.S. at 583.
9. *Id.*
10. *Id.*
11. *Elliott*, 571 F.2d at 898.

unit also has little teeth in practice. Such continuity exists even if there is a gap in the racketeering activities of the enterprise[12] and the membership of the AIF changes over time.[13] It is also not necessary that every member of the enterprise participated in or even knew about all its activities. It is "sufficient that the defendant kn[e]w the general nature of the enterprise and kn[e]w that the enterprise extend[ed] beyond his individual role."[14]

The *Turkette* Court's statement that the RICO AIF enterprise is an "entity separate and apart from the pattern of activity in which it engages" raised the question whether the existence of an AIF "enterprise" could be inferred solely from the pattern of racketeering through which it operated, or whether some additional showing—such as an "'ascertainable structural hierarchy distinct from the charged predicate acts'"—had to be made.[15] This question provoked a pronounced circuit split, which the Supreme Court resolved in *Boyle v. United States*, 556 U.S. 938 (2009).

The *Boyle* Court held that while an AIF enterprise must have a "structure," it need not be an "ascertainable" structure beyond that inherent in the pattern of racketeering in which it engages.[16] The Court concluded that an AIF enterprise must have only "three structural features: a purpose, relationships among those associated with the enterprise, and longevity sufficient to permit these associates to pursue the enterprise's purpose."[17] And the existence of an AIF enterprise may be inferred from the evidence demonstrating a pattern of racketeering activity.

The facts of *Boyle* demonstrate that the evidentiary bar of proving an AIF enterprise is very low. Boyle and his co-conspirators committed a series of bank thefts over a five-year period. Each theft was planned on an ad hoc basis, with the participants meeting beforehand to plan the crime, gather tools, and assign roles. "The group was loosely and informally organized. It does not appear to have had a leader or hierarchy; nor does it appear that the participants ever formulated any long-term master plan or agreement."[18] Yet the Supreme Court found that an AIF enterprise existed and affirmed Boyle's conviction under § 1962(c).

12. *See, e.g.*, United States v. Olson, 450 F.3d 665, 665-66 (7th Cir. 2006).
13. *Id.* at 665-68.
14. United States v. Rastelli, 870 F.2d 822, 828 (2d Cir. 1989).
15. Boyle v. United States, 556 U.S. 938, 943 (2009).
16. *Id.* at 945-47.
17. *Id.* at 946.
18. *Id.* at 941.

C. Employed by or Associated with the Enterprise (§ 1962(c) Only)

Section 1962(c) alone requires that the defendant "person" be "employed by or associated with" the alleged enterprise. This rarely presents a problem because courts have defined those "employed by or associated with" a legitimate business very broadly. Where the enterprise is a legal entity, the defendant's employment by, or association with it as an employee, agent, or independent contractor can generally be proved through the entity's business records. But "associated" persons can also be "outsiders" who have no formal relationship with the enterprise. And the government does not have to prove that the "associated" persons have a "'stake or interest in the goals of the enterprise.'"[19]

For example, in *Aetna Casualty Surety Co. v. P&B Autobody*, 43 F.3d 1546 (1st Cir. 1994), a number of persons, including Aetna policy holders and the operators of body shops, allegedly submitted false insurance claims to Aetna. The First Circuit held that all these persons were "associated with" Aetna, whether because they had a contractual relationship with it or because each body shop was a place where Aetna employees conducted appraisals and where the insured cars were purportedly repaired.[20] Similarly, where a public official is alleged to have run his official office (enterprise) through a pattern of bribery, courts have no difficulty finding that the outside bribers are, by virtue of their bribes, "associated with" that public office.[21]

Proving that a person is "associated with" an AIF enterprise is even easier. The First Circuit, in *United States v. Marino*, 277 F.3d 11 (1st Cir. 2002), approved a jury instruction that defined "associated with" to mean "'to be joined, often in a loose relationship, as a partner, fellow worker, colleague, friend, companion, or ally. Thus, although a person's role in the enterprise may be very minor, a person will still be associated with the enterprise if he knowingly joins with a group of individuals associated in fact who constitute the enterprise.'"[22]

D. The Distinctiveness Requirement (§ 1962(c) Only)

The so-called "distinctiveness requirement" also applies only to § 1962(c) because of the particular language of that provision. Section 1962(c)

19. United States v. Yonan, 800 F.2d 164, 167 (7th Cir. 1986).

20. *See, e.g.*, *Aetna Casualty Surety Co.*, 43 F.3d at 1559, *abrogated on other grounds*, Salinas v. United States, 522 U.S. 52 (1997).

21. *See, e.g.*, *Yonan*, 800 F.2d at 167-68; United States v. Bright, 630 F.2d 804, 830-31 (5th Cir. 1980).

22. *Marino*, 277 F.3d at 33 (quoting jury instructions).

requires that the defendant "*person*" must be "*employed by or associated with*" the "*enterprise*" whose affairs are conducted through a pattern of racketeering activity.[23] Courts base the so-called "distinctiveness requirement" on the observation that a defendant "person" cannot be "employed by, or associated with," an enterprise consisting only of itself. Consider a case in which the government or civil plaintiffs wish to pursue a partnership for crimes that its partners committed. Courts view it as inconsistent with the terms of the statute to allege that the defendant partnership "person" is employed by or associated with itself—that is an "enterprise" consisting of the partnership. Thus, when charging under § 1962(c), the defendant "person" identified must be distinct from the alleged "enterprise" through which it conducts the racketeering.

This may seem logical and unexceptional, but it has created enormous difficulties for prosecutors and civil plaintiffs in business crime cases. In many such cases, those bringing the case will wish to identify the corporation as the defendant "person" while also alleging that the corporation is the "enterprise" whose affairs were conducted through the pattern of racketeering activity. To illustrate, assume that a company that produces widgets for the Department of Defense regularly defrauds the government by inflating its invoices. Prosecutors may wish to charge the corporation as the defendant "person" in the belief that it was the culpable instrument through which the crimes were committed, especially when the fruits of the fraud ended up in corporate coffers. Civil plaintiffs will wish to charge the corporation as the defendant person because of its deep pockets. Corporations fall within the statutory definitions of both defendant "persons" and a statutory "enterprises."[24] But if the case is charged under § 1962(c), the defendant "person"/the corporation cannot be "employed by or associated with" an "enterprise" that is the corporation even though the corporation was the instrument of the fraud.

The application of the distinctiveness requirement can get very messy and confusing because of the creativity prosecutors and plaintiffs' lawyers use in trying to avoid it. To begin with what is relatively clear, as noted, a corporation cannot be both the defendant "person" and the "enterprise" through which it conducts its racketeering activity.[25] Nor can an individual be both the RICO "person" and a one-man "enterprise."[26] If a sole proprietorship is alleged to be the "enterprise" with which the defendant proprietor was "associated," the distinctiveness question depends on the nature

23. Section 1962(c) provides, in relevant part: "It shall be unlawful for any person employed by or associated with any enterprise engaged in, or the activities of which affect, interstate or foreign commerce, to conduct or participate, directly or indirectly, in the conduct of such enterprise's affairs through a pattern of racketeering activity. . . ."

24. *See* 18 U.S.C. § 1961(3) ("person"), (4) ("enterprise").

25. *See Riverwoods Chappaqua*, 30 F.3d at 344.

26. The definition of "enterprise" expressly includes "any individual" (§ 1961(4)).

of the business. If the sole proprietorship is a "one-man show," the case would fail the distinctiveness requirement, but if the sole proprietorship has employees or other associates, the courts may find that the defendant proprietor is distinct from the business-enterprise that he conducts.[27]

The Supreme Court has held that the distinctiveness requirement is satisfied when a defendant natural person adopts the corporate form to run an enterprise. In *Cedric Kushner Productions, Ltd. v. King*, 533 U.S. 158 (2001), the plaintiff sued Don King, the president and sole shareholder of Don King Productions (DKP), a corporation that promoted boxing matches. The plaintiff—a business competitor—claimed that King conducted the boxing-related affairs of DKP through a pattern of fraud and other RICO predicates. The Court approved the "distinctiveness requirement" the courts of appeals had adopted in light of the language of § 1962(c).[28] But it held that a "corporate owner/employee, a natural person, is distinct from the corporation itself, a legally different entity with different rights and responsibilities due to its different legal status."[29] Thus the suit against the defendant natural "person," Don King, could proceed based on allegations that he ran his one-man corporate "enterprise" through a pattern of racketeering.

A corollary of the *Cedric Kushner* decision is that distinctiveness is satisfied when a group of employees or other individuals associated with a company are alleged to be the defendant "persons" who conducted the affairs of the corporate "enterprise" with which they are associated through a pattern of racketeering activity.[30]

Defendant "Person"	"Enterprise"	Distinct?
Individual	Same individual	No
Corporation	Same corporation	No
Individual (and sole owner/shareholder of one-man corporation)	One man corporation	Yes (*Cedric Kushner*)
Individual employees of company	Company	Yes
Sole proprietor	One-man proprietorship	No
Sole proprietor	Proprietorship with many employees	Yes

The distinctiveness requirement has spawned literally thousands of judicial opinions because prosecutors and plaintiff's lawyers have attempted

27. *See* United States v. Benny, 786 F.2d 1410, 1415-16 (9th Cir. 1986); McCullough v. Suter, 757 F.2d 142, 143-44 (7th Cir. 1985).
28. *See Cedric Kushner*, 533 U.S. at 161-62.
29. *Id.* at 163.
30. *See, e.g.*, Jaguar Cars, Inc. v. Royal Oaks Motor Car Co., 46 F.3d 258, 269 (3d Cir. 1995); Sever v. Alaska Pulp Corp., 978 F.2d 1529, 1534 (9th Cir. 1992).

to use various work-arounds to avoid its limitations. Their primary tool has been the creative use of "association-in-fact" enterprises in charging.[31]

I. Avoiding "Distinctiveness": Association-In-Fact Enterprises

A natural person can be both a defendant "person" and one of a group of natural persons alleged to be the AIF enterprise[32]; indeed, *Turkette* was such a case. As the Eighth Circuit reasoned, an association-in-fact of individuals "is something more than the members of which it is comprised. Although a defendant may not be both a person and an enterprise, a defendant may be both a person and a part of an enterprise."[33]

The same reasoning is not necessarily true when corporations or other legal entities enter the mix. It is clear that AIF enterprises can take some strange, perhaps counterintuitive, forms. They can consist of a group of corporate employees, a company and its employees, a company and its affiliated companies or subsidiaries, a couple of separate corporations, separate corporations and individuals, and a seemingly endless number of permutations of these combinations. A very common way in which prosecutors and plaintiffs' attorneys avoid distinctiveness problems is to charge the corporation as the defendant "person" and as one of a number of legal or natural persons who together constitute an AIF enterprise.[34] But courts do not always view, in the Eighth Circuit's words, such AIF enterprises as "something more than the members of which it is comprised."

Courts generally will not accept pleading in which a corporation is alleged to be both the defendant "person" and a part of an AIF enterprise that consists of nothing more than the corporation and its errant employees. For example, in *Riverwoods Chappaqua Corp. v. Marine Midland Bank, N.A.*, 30 F.3d 339 (2d Cir. 1994), citied by the Supreme Court in *Cedric Kushner*, the

31. In theory, one could charge that a corporation is the RICO "enterprise" and that it is also liable under respondeat superior principles for the actions of the individual "persons" within the corporation who committed the racketeering activity. Courts generally hold, however, that, at least in civil cases, a plaintiff may not use vicarious liability principles to escape the rule that a corporation cannot be both the defendant "person" and the "enterprise" under § 1962(c). *See, e.g.*, Miller v. Yokohama Tire Corp., 358 F.3d 616, 620 (9th Cir. 2004); Brady v. Dairy Fresh Prods. Co., 974 F.2d 1149, 1154 (9th Cir. 1992); Landry v. Airlines Pilots Ass'n, 901 F.2d 404, 425 (5th Cir. 1990).

32. *See* United States v. Fairchild, 189 F.3d 769, 777 (8th Cir. 1999); *see also* St. Paul Mercury Ins. Co. v. Williamson, 224 F.3d 425, 445-47 (5th Cir. 2000).

33. *Fairchild*, 189 F.3d at 777 (internal quotation marks omitted). In *Cedric Kushner*, the Court distinguished this situation from the circumstances of that case by stating that "[i]t is less natural to speak of a corporation 'employed by' or 'associated with' this latter oddly constructed entity" (that is, the corporation and its employees). *Cedric Kushner*, 533 U.S. at 164 (citing *Riverwoods Chappaqua*, 30 F.3d at 344).

34. *See, e.g.*, United States v. Philip Morris USA, Inc., 566 F.3d 1095, 1110-16 (D.C. Cir. 2009) (combinations of individuals and corporations can constitute association-in-fact enterprises).

Second Circuit ruled that the distinctiveness requirement may not be "circumvented" by suing the defendant person corporation and alleging a RICO AIF enterprise that consists merely of the corporate defendant and its own employees or agents carrying on the regular affairs of the defendant.[35] Courts also will not accept pleading in which the corporation is the defendant "person" and an AIF enterprise is alleged that consists only of the persons within the company that conducted the pattern of racketeering activity. The courts reason that if RICO imposed liability on a corporation for the ordinary conduct of an AIF enterprise of its agents and employees, "every claim of corporate fraud would automatically become a violation of RICO."[36]

The results of the distinctiveness question become much more difficult to predict when the AIF enterprise is alleged to be comprised of subsidiaries or affiliated companies, with or without natural persons included in the mix. Indeed, the Sixth Circuit concluded after surveying this caselaw that "[t]he number of different approaches to the distinctiveness analysis roughly mirrors the number of cases that have addressed it."[37]

The Sixth Circuit is alone in holding that a defendant "person" parent corporation is distinct from an AIF consisting of its subsidiaries, relying solely, as did the Court in *Cedric Kushner*, on the separate legal treatment of such entities.[38] Other circuits, including the Second, have rejected a test founded only on legal distinctiveness. Thus, for example, in *U1iT4Less, Inc. v. FedEx Corp.*, 871 F.3d 199 (2d Cir. 2017), the Second Circuit reasoned that "'if a corporate defendant can be liable for participating in an enterprise comprised only of its agents—even if those agents are separately incorporated legal entities—then RICO liability will attach to any act of corporate wrong-doing and the statute's distinctness requirement will be rendered meaningless.'"[39] The Second Circuit believes that where a corporation and its subsidiaries or affiliated companies are "'acting within the scope of a single corporate structure" and are "'guided by a single corporate consciousness'" they are not distinct.[40] In *U1iT4Less*, it therefore held that the alleged defendant persons—a parent corporation and its subsidiary—were insufficiently distinct from the enterprise, alleged to be another subsidiary corporation.

To the extent one can generalize, it appears that the default rule, except in the Sixth Circuit, is that "a parent-subsidiary corporate relationship standing alone" is not sufficient to establish distinctiveness but exceptions

35. *See, e.g.*, *Riverwoods Chappaqua*, 30 F.3d at 344; *see also* Llacua v. Western Range Ass'n, 930 F.3d 1161, 1183-87 (10th Cir. 2019).
36. In re ClassicStar Mare Lease Litig., 727 F.3d 473, 490 (6th Cir. 2013).
37. *Id.* at 491.
38. *See, e.g.*, Fleischhauer v. Feltner, 879 F.2d 1290, 1297 (6th Cir. 1989).
39. *U1iT4LESS*, 871 F.3d at 205-06.
40. *Id.* at 206.

can be made upon a proper showing.[41] Most courts adopt a functionalist approach, focusing on whether the enterprise is "'either formally . . . or practically separable'" from the RICO person,[42] with the object of ensuring that the enterprise "is not simply the same [as the defendant] 'person' referred to by a different name."[43] In these cases, distinctiveness requires that the "defendant conducted the affairs of the [AIF] enterprise rather than simply conducting the defendant[] [corporation's] own affairs."[44]

In performing a functionalist analysis, courts will examine whether those persons and entities included in the AIF are simply doing the corporate defendant "person's" bidding, or whether the AIF has an independent purpose to which these functionally different agents contribute by performing discrete roles or using their separate legal identity to further the racketeering activity.[45]

Some courts delve into the actual functioning and decision-making of the various entities included in the AIF to determine whether the corporation and its affiliated entities are in fact one functional entity.[46] One consideration that is often mentioned is whether the related entities in the AIF add value in ensuring the success of the AIF's common unlawful purpose—for example by allowing the AIF to exploit the separate but related entity to facilitate the racketeering activity.[47] Thus, in *Securitron Mangalock Corp. v. Schnabolk*, 65 F.3d 256 (2d Cir. 1995), the Second Circuit held that, notwithstanding common ownership, two corporations alleged to be the AIF enterprise were distinct from each other "rather than two stacks of stationery."[48] It reasoned that they were "two active corporations that operate[d] independently in different lines of business, receive[d] independent benefits from the illegal acts of the enterprise, and affirmatively *use[d]* their separate corporate status to further the illegal goals of the enterprise."[49]

41. *See, e.g.*, George v. Urban Settlement Servs., 833 F.3d 1242, 1249 (10th Cir. 2016); Fitzgerald v. Chrysler Corp., 116 F.3d 225, 228 (7th Cir. 1997) (concluding that when "a large, reputable manufacturer deals with its dealers and other agents in the ordinary way, so that their role in the manufacturer's illegal acts is entirely incidental, differing not at all from what it would be if these agents were the employees of a totally integrated enterprise, the manufacturer plus its dealers and other agents (or any subset of the members of the corporate family)," do not satisfy distinctiveness requirement).

42. United States v. Mongol Nation, 693 Fed. App'x 637, 638 (9th Cir. 2017).

43. *Cedric Kushner*, 533 U.S. at 161.

44. *George*, 833 F.3d at 1249.

45. *See ClassicStar Mare Lease Litig.*, 727 F.3d at 492; Emery v. Am. Gen. Finance, Inc., 134 F.3d 1321, 1324 (7th Cir. 1998) (no showing that using subsidiaries "somehow made it easier to commit or conceal the fraud").

46. *Riverwoods Chappaqua Corp.*, 30 F.3d at 344-45.

47. *See ClassicStar Mare Litig.*, 727 F.3d at 493.

48. *Securitron Mangalock Corp.*, 65 F.3d at 263; *see also* United States v. Goldin Indus., Inc., 219 F.3d 1271, 1277 (11th Cir. 2000).

49. *U1IT4LESS*, 871 F.3d at 206.

Courts are much more willing to find distinctiveness when a corporation is the defendant person and part of an association-in-fact enterprise that includes the corporation and truly distinct legal entities (that is, not subsidiaries or affiliated companies) and individuals.[50] Thus, for example, the Ninth Circuit ruled that the defendant "person" corporation was distinct from an AIF enterprise consisting of the corporation, the law firms it retained, and expert witnesses retained by the law firms.[51] In so holding, the Ninth Circuit analyzed whether the law firms were truly separate from their corporate client and concluded that "the rules of professional conduct require law firms to be distinct entities and to maintain their professional independence."[52] Where the entities constituting the "association-in-fact" are truly separate entities, courts find no distinctiveness difficulties in cases in which the entities are all charged as defendant persons *and* as members of the association-in-fact enterprise.[53]

Defendant "Person"	Association-in-Fact Enterprise	Distinct?
Individual A	Individual A plus other individuals who together satisfy AIF standard	Yes (*Turkette*)
Corporation	Corporation + employees engaged in wrongdoing	No
Corporation	Employees engaged in wrongdoing	No
Corporation	Corporation + subsidiaries or other affiliated companies (with or without natural persons)	Unclear—fact and jurisdiction dependent
Corporation	Subsidiaries or other affiliated companies (with or without natural persons)	Unclear—fact and jurisdiction dependent
Corporation (and unrelated entities and natural persons)	Corporation + unrelated entities and natural persons	If truly independent, yes

2. Avoiding "Distinctiveness": Section 1962(a)

Another way around the distinctiveness requirement in qualifying cases involves charging under § 1962(a), which makes it unlawful for any person *who has received any income* derived, directly or indirectly, *from a pattern of racketeering* to *use or invest*, directly or indirectly, *any part of such income*, or the proceeds

50. *See, e.g.*, *George*, 833 F.3d at 1250; United States v. Bergrin, 650 F.3d 257, 269 (3d Cir. 2011); Odom v. Microsoft Corp., 486 F.3d 541, 552-553 (9th Cir. 2007).
51. Living Designs, Inc. v. E.I. DuPont de Nemours, 431 F.3d 353, 361-62 (9th Cir. 2005).
52. *Id.* at 362.
53. *See* River City Markets v. Fleming Foods West, 960 F.2d 1458, 1461-62 (9th Cir. 1992).

of such income, in acquisition of any interest in, or the establishment or *operation of, any enterprise* which is engaged in, or the activities of which affect, interstate or foreign commerce. Note that there is some ambiguity in the language of this section because it is unclear whether the defendant person must participate as a principal in the underlying racketeering activity. The plain language suggests, for example, that a financial advisor who assists a drug dealer in investing racketeering proceeds may be liable under this section. The Department of Justice takes the position, as a matter of policy, that "a RICO prosecution under Section 1962(a) will not be approved unless the RICO defendant is actually charged with the underlying pattern of racketeering activity."[54]

What is clear is that this subsection does not contain any language that requires the defendant "person" to be distinct from the alleged "enterprise." It is possible, then, to allege that a corporation is the defendant "person" that has received income directly or indirectly from a pattern of racketeering activity—say, fraud—and has used this income in the "establishment or *operation* of" the corporation/"enterprise."

Resort to § 1962(a) only works, however, where the proceeds of the crime are reinvested in the operation of the defendant corporation. For example, assume that employees of a business conduct the affairs of that business through fraud. If those proceeds are used in the operation of the business, § 1962(a) may be appropriately charged. If, however, the employees are simply using the corporation as an instrument of their fraud and are siphoning off the fraudulent proceeds for their own enrichment, § 1962(a) is unavailable.

3. Corporate Plaintiff/Victims

Thus far we have been dealing with cases in which the corporation is best viewed as either the instrument or perpetrator of the misconduct. But there are cases in which the corporation is truly the victim of employee misconduct. In those cases, the corporate victim of, say, employee embezzlement may wish to sue the employee claiming that the employee-defendant "person" conducted the affairs of the plaintiff-corporate "enterprise" through a pattern of racketeering.

Despite the fact that the language of § 1962(c) does not appear to bar the corporation from being the *plaintiff* and the "enterprise," some courts have—in civil cases—suggested that it would not be possible for the corporation to pursue such a suit.[55] For example, in *Jaguar Cars, Inc. v. Royal Oaks*

54. U.S. Dep't of Justice, Organized Crime & Gang Section, Criminal RICO: 18 U.S.C. §§ 1961-1968; A Manual for Federal Prosecutors 140 (6th ed. May 2016) [hereinafter Manual for Federal Prosecutors].

55. *See, e.g.*, LaSalle Bank Lake View v. Seguban, 54 F.3d 387, 393-94 (7th Cir. 1995).

Motor Car Co., 46 F.3d 258 (3d Cir. 1995), cited by the Supreme Court in *Cedric Kushner*, the Third Circuit explained that:

> [A] victim corporation "drained of its own money" by pilfering officers and employees could not reasonably be viewed as the enterprise *through* which employee persons carried out their racketeering activity. Rather, in such an instance, the proper enterprise would be the association of employees who are victimizing the corporation, while the victim corporation would not be the enterprise, but instead the § 1962(c) claimant.[56]

The Eleventh Circuit, however, has—in a criminal case—rejected this rule, reasoning that "Congress' intention in § 1962(c) to target a specific variety of criminal activity, [includes] the exploitation and appropriation of legitimate businesses by corrupt individuals, not merely the use of an enterprise to swindle third parties."[57]

E. Jurisdictional Hook: The Enterprise Must Affect Interstate Commerce

RICO was passed pursuant to Congress's Commerce Clause power[58] and thus a jurisdictional nexus to interstate commerce must be proved in each case. Under all subsections of § 1962, the government must demonstrate that the enterprise "engaged in" interstate or foreign commerce or "the activities" of the enterprise "affected" such commerce. To be clear, the statute requires that it be the activities or business of the *enterprise*—*not* the pattern of racketeering—that satisfies statute's jurisdictional requirement.[59]

The Supreme Court interpreted this element broadly in *United States v. Robertson*, 514 U.S. 669 (1995), a case in which the defendant was convicted of violating § 1962(a) by investing the proceeds of his drug dealing in an Alaskan gold mine. The Court ruled that it did not have to decide whether the gold mine "affected" interstate commerce because it clearly fell within § 1962(a)'s alternative criterion of "any enterprise . . . engaged in . . . interstate or foreign commerce" by virtue of the fact that the defendant bought equipment and supplies for the mine from out-of-state vendors and on more than one occasion brought out-of-state recruits to work in the mine. A number of circuits have "held, squarely and explicitly, that

---

56. *Jaguar Cars*, 46 F.3d at 267 (emphasis original).
57. United States v. Browne, 505 F.3d 1229, 1273 (11th Cir. 2007) (internal quotation marks omitted); *see also* United States v. Hills, 27 F.4th 1155, 1173-74 (6th Cir. 2022) (discussing split, indicating agreement with *Browne*, but declining to decide the issue as unnecessary to the disposition of the case).
58. U.S. Const. art. I, § 8, cl. 3.
59. *See, e.g.*, United States v. Robertson, 514 U.S. 669 (1995).

a de minimis effect on interstate commerce is all that is required to satisfy RICO's commerce element."[60] Although this is an element that must be pled and proved, then, it rarely presents a contested issue in white-collar cases.

F. Conduct of Enterprise's Affairs (§ 1962(c) Only)

Another element unique to § 1962(c) again derives from its particular statutory language, which requires that a defendant "person" employed by or associated with the enterprise "*conduct or participate*, directly or indirectly, *in the conduct of such enterprise's affairs* through a pattern of racketeering activity" (emphasis added). This language has raised questions regarding when those who are not actually employed by or are otherwise "inside" the enterprise can be liable. For example, where a business goes south allegedly due to wrongdoing, shareholders, creditors, and others may seek to hold outside professionals, such as law and accounting firms—who may be alleged to have facilitated the crime and who are perceived to be perennial deep pockets—liable for a share of the losses. We have discussed above how broadly courts have construed the term "associated with"; rarely, then, can those "outside" the enterprise avoid conviction on this basis.

Those seeking to limit the liability of "outsiders" to the enterprise have had much more success in focusing on the "*conduct or participate in the conduct*" language of § 1962(c). In *Reves v. Ernst & Young*, 507 U.S. 170 (1993), the Supreme Court interpreted this language narrowly, thus shielding tangentially related white-collar professionals from RICO liability. The *Reves* decision, however, spawned a great deal of caselaw regarding its effect on other "outsiders" as well as lower-level employees of the wrongdoing entity.

In *Reves*, Jack White, the general manager of a farmers' Co-op, took large loans from the Co-op to finance his own business venture, White Flame Fuels. When White was arrested for tax fraud, he persuaded the Co-op to purchase White Flame. The Co-op retained as its outside auditor an accounting firm (later merged into Ernst & Young) that was headed by someone who testified on White's behalf in his criminal trial. In auditing the Co-op's books, the accounting firm determined that the value of White Flame depended on when it was acquired. If the Co-op purchased White Flame from White, as was in fact the case, it would be valued at its fair market value—in which case the Co-op would be insolvent. If, however, the Co-op owned the company from its creation, it would be valued at a much higher fixed-asset value—in which case the Co-op was solvent. After consulting with White, the accounting firm chose the latter value. The firm did not disclose to the Co-op's board its conclusion that the Co-op had always owned

60. United States v. Nascimento, 491 F.3d 25, 37 (1st Cir. 2007).

White Flame or that without this choice the Co-op was insolvent. Two years later the Co-op filed for bankruptcy and its trustee sued the accounting firm, among others, under RICO.

The issue presented was whether the defendant outside accounting firm "conducted, or participated in the conduct," of the Co-op's (enterprise's) affairs within the meaning of § 1962(c). The Court read the word "conduct" to "require some degree of direction" and the word "participate" to "require some part in that direction."[61] It said that this language did not limit liability "to those with primary responsibility for the enterprise's affairs" or to persons with a "formal position in the enterprise."[62] It also rejected the D.C. Circuit's requirement that "*significant control*" be proved.[63] But, the Court said, the defendant must take "*some* part in directing the enterprise's affairs" and coined an "operation or management" test as an easy-to-apply formulation of this requirement.[64]

Where the Court's guidance became murky, and thus spawned confusion below, was in its responses to the petitioners' objection that the operation and management test would restrict liability to senior management. The Court answered this by asserting "[a]n enterprise is 'operated' not just by upper management but also by lower rung participants in the enterprise who are under the direction of upper management."[65] It went on to say that "[w]e need not decide in this case how far § 1962(c) extends down the ladder of operation because it is clear that [the outside accounting firm] was not acting under the direction of the Co-op's officers or board."[66]

The United States (participating as an amicus curiae) objected that the Court's test would restrict the degree to which "outsiders" who have no official position in the enterprise can be liable, evidently concerned that an operation or management would limit the government's ability to prosecute public corruption cases. In such cases, those bribing the public officials are inevitably "outsiders" seeking to influence the official's conduct of his office; prosecutors therefore feared that they would have difficulty proving that the bribers "operated" or "managed" the public office alleged to be the "enterprise." The *Reves* Court gave the government a significant one-line gift in response, asserting that "[a]n enterprise also might be 'operated' or 'managed' by others 'associated with' the enterprise who exert control over it as, for example, by bribery."[67]

---

61. *Reves*, 507 U.S. at 179.
62. *Id.*
63. *Id.* at 179 n.4 (emphasis original).
64. *Id.* at 179 (emphasis original).
65. *Id.* at 184.
66. *Id.* at 184 n.9.
67. *Id.* at 184.

1. Lower-Level Employees

The *Reves* Court's statement that "[a]n enterprise is 'operated' not just by upper management but also by lower rung participants in the enterprise who are under the direction of upper management"[68] has caused confusion below because it seems in tension with the *Reves* Court's initial emphasis on direction; it has led some to wonder how lower-level employees can both direct and be directed.

There appears to be great variability in how the *Reves* test is applied to lower-level participants in criminal as well as civil cases. For example, the Second Circuit has stated, in a much quoted passage, that "[s]ince *Reves*, it is plain that the simple taking of directions and performance of tasks that are 'necessary or helpful' to the enterprise, without more, is insufficient to bring a defendant within the scope of § 1962(c)."[69] Other circuits, however, appear to apply less stringent tests. A number of circuits agree that "one may be liable under the operation or management test by 'knowingly implementing decisions, as well as by making them.'"[70] For example, in *United States v. Fowler*, 535 F.3d 408 (6th Cir. 2008), the Sixth Circuit noted that having "some" part in directing the enterprise's affairs can be accomplished "by making decisions on behalf of the enterprise or by knowingly carrying them out."[71] Ultimately this is a highly fact-sensitive inquiry. The Second Circuit has concluded that "the only principle to be drawn from th[e] array of holdings and statements is that the commission of crimes by lower-level employees of a RICO enterprise may be found to indicate participation in the operation or management of the enterprise but does not compel such a finding."[72]

2. Outsiders

Many circuits have characterized *Reves* as "a case about the liability of *outsiders*," because it concerned an independent accounting firm that was deemed not liable because it was "outside the chain of command."[73] In business crime cases, courts consistently hold that "simply performing services for an enterprise, even with knowledge of the enterprise's illicit nature, is not enough to subject an individual to RICO liability under § 1962(c)."[74] Thus,

---

68. *Id.*

69. United States v. Viola, 35 F.3d 37, 40 (2d Cir. 1994), *abrogated on other grounds*, *Salinas*, 522 U.S. 52.

70. United States v. Starrett, 55 F.3d 1525, 1548 (11th Cir. 1995).

71. *Fowler*, 535 F.3d at 418.

72. United States v. Allen, 155 F.3d 35, 42 (2d Cir. 1998). For additional guidance, see Michael L. Thomas, *How Does One Operate or Manage an Enterprise? Insights from* Boyle v. United States, 87 N.Y.U. L. Rev. 284 (2012).

73. United States v. Oreto, 37 F.3d 739, 750 (1st Cir. 1994); *see also Fowler*, 535 F.3d at 418-19.

74. Goren v. New Vision Int'l, 156 F.3d 721, 728 (7th Cir. 1998); *see also* Muskegan Hotels, LLC v. Patel, 986 F.3d 692, 698-99 (7th Cir. 2021) ("A complaint that does no more than

"[f]urnishing a client with ordinary professional assistance, even when the client happens to be a RICO enterprise, will not normally rise to the level of participation sufficient to satisfy the Supreme Court's pronouncements in *Reves*."[75] But lawyers and other professionals are not exempt from liability: "[b]ehavior prohibited by § 1962 will violate RICO regardless of the person to whom it may be attributed, and we will not shrink from finding an attorney liable when he crosses the line between traditional rendition of legal services and active participation in *directing* the enterprise. The polestar is the activity in question, not the defendant's status."[76]

The situation is different in public corruption cases. Prosecutors continue to charge that the government entity corrupted is the "enterprise" through which corrupt public officials conducted a pattern of racketeering activity and often succeed in securing convictions of the bribing "outsiders." Courts generally accept that the "outsider" bribers can (echoing *Reves*) exert some measure of "control" over the conduct of the corrupt official's office "through bribery."[77]

3. Avoiding *Reves*: Redefining the Enterprise

One potential way around the *Reves* "operation or management" test is to redefine the enterprise, once again enlisting the concept of the AIF enterprise to save the day. "Section 1962(c)'s 'conduct' requirement applies without regard to the nature of the enterprise"[78] but the *Reves* test may be easier to satisfy in the AIF enterprise context given *Boyle*. As discussed above, in *Boyle*, the Supreme Court held that an AIF enterprise need only have "three structural features: a purpose, relationships among those associated with the enterprise, and longevity sufficient to permit these associates to pursue the enterprise's purpose."[79] The AIF enterprise has to have a structure, but not an "ascertainable" structure, and the facts of the case itself indicated that a fairly random group of people who periodically and informally convene to commit crimes can constitute an AIF enterprise. Depending upon the size and composition of the AIF, the government may have greater success in applying the *Reves* operation and management test to an AIF that looks like

allege that a law firm performed legal work for an enterprise fails to state a violation of § 1962(c).").

75. Hamdeen v. Lemaire, 112 F.3d 1339, 1348 (8th Cir. 1997).

76. *Id.* at 1349 (emphasis added); *see also* Adam B. Weiss, Note, *From the Bonannos to the Bin Ladens: The* Reves *Operations or Management Test and the Viability of Civil RICO Suits Against Financial Supporters of Terrorism*, 110 Colum. L. Rev. 1123, 1139 (2010).

77. *See, e.g.*, DeFalco v. Bernas, 244 F.3d 286, 311 (2d Cir. 2001). *But see* United States v. Cummings, 395 F.3d 392, 399-400 (7th Cir. 2005) (finding that, through bribery, outsider merely controlled his accomplices within a government enterprise, not the enterprise itself).

78. Walter v. Drayson, 538 F.3d 1244, 1249 (9th Cir. 2008).

79. *Boyle*, 556 U.S. at 946.

little more than a group of persons who together engage in a pattern of racketeering activity.[80]

In short, if the defendant persons have insufficient operation and control over a legal entity such that that entity cannot serve as the RICO enterprise, one may, depending on the facts, simply redefine the enterprise as one over which the defendants do have control. By recharacterizing the enterprise as an AIF, one can perhaps convert an "outsider" into "insider" or a lower-level employee into an essential actor in the scheme for *Reves* purposes.[81] For example, in *Reves*, rather than alleging that the enterprise was the Co-op, the plaintiffs might have had better success had they alleged that the defendant "person" was the accounting firm and that it operated and managed the affairs of an AIF enterprise consisting of the Co-op, the accountants, and Jack White,[82] assuming that they could prove that the AIF was "associated together for a common purpose of engaging in a course of conduct."[83] Presumably the accounting firm could be said to have some ability to "direct" the operation of this association-in-fact enterprise. The case would proceed on the theory that it was this association-in-fact enterprise whose affairs were conducted through a pattern of racketeering activity.

4. Avoiding *Reves*: Using a Conspiracy Charge Under § 1962(d)

Another means of avoiding the strictures of *Reves* is to charge a § 1962(d) conspiracy. The circuits are in accord in holding that the *Reves* operations or control requirement does not apply to a RICO *conspiracy* charge. Thus, a defendant who does not exercise sufficient "operation or management" over the RICO enterprise to be directly liable under § 1962(c) can nevertheless be held liable under § 1962(d) for conspiring with those who do.[84] All that need be proved is that the defendant "knowingly agrees to facilitate a scheme *which includes* the operation or management of a RICO enterprise" by his co-conspirators.[85]

G. Pattern of Racketeering Activity

The meaning of the phrase "pattern of racketeering activity" is the same under § 1962(a), (b), and (c). Section 1961(5) defines the phrase to

---

80. *Id.* at 953-54 (Stevens, J., dissenting); *see also* Thomas, *supra* note 72.
81. *See, e.g.*, *George*, 833 F.3d at 1251-53.
82. The existence of two distinct companies, the Co-op and the accounting firm, would likely meet distinctiveness requirements; they also would likely be found to affect interstate commerce.
83. *Turkette*, 452 U.S. at 583.
84. *See, e.g.*, United States v. Quintanilla, 2 F.3d 1469, 1485 (7th Cir. 1993).
85. United States v. Fernandez, 388 F.3d 1199, 1230 (9th Cir. 2004) (emphasis added).

"require at least two acts of racketeering, one of which occurred after the effective date of this chapter and the last of which occurred within ten years (excluding any period of imprisonment) after the commission of a prior act of racketeering activity." By "acts" the definition means predicate crimes. Those crimes *must* appear in the definition of "racketeering acts" outlined in § 1961 but the two predicate acts need not be similar in nature; indeed, one could be a violation of state law and the other a violation of a federal statute.

The temporal components of this definition are two-fold. First, one act of racketeering must occur after the statute's enactment date in 1970; this requirement was included to avoid *ex post facto* difficulties and has little continuing relevance. The second requires that the two acts of racketeering occur within ten years of each other. This requirement has no relationship to the statute of limitations. Rather, it ensures that the racketeering acts reflect a pattern of wrongdoing rather than isolated crimes committed by the same miscreants.

Over the years, the lower federal courts faced "an extraordinary number of cases" raising the issue of what constitutes a cognizable "pattern of racketeering activity."[86] One reason for this litigation explosion is the scope and nature of the predicate racketeering activities identified by Congress in § 1961. The predicates include "any act or threat involving" a variety of serious state felony offenses, including a variety of offenses not normally within federal criminal jurisdiction.[87] Racketeering activity also includes "any act which is indictable under" a long list of federal statutes.[88]

Perhaps the most important of § 1961's predicates in white-collar cases are the mail and wire fraud statutes (18 U.S.C. §§ 1341 and 1343). These statutes can be applied to an extraordinary variety of activities and are simple to prove. The two principal elements of a wire fraud case are (1) a scheme to defraud; and (2) a mailing or a wiring in interstate or foreign commerce in furtherance of the fraud. Use of the "wires" can include making telephone calls, texts, emails, engaging in banking transactions, and accessing the web. Because each mailing or wiring in furtherance of an alleged fraud constitutes a separate crime, even if each relates to a single scheme to defraud, one rarely has a problem identifying the two predicate crimes required to make out a RICO case; two emails in furtherance of a single continuing scheme to defraud would suffice. Courts have criticized private litigants for turning "garden-variety state law fraud claims into federal RICO actions"[89] by alleging multiple mailings or wirings, thus "bootstrapping ordinary civil fraud cases into RICO suits."[90]

---

86. Ashland Oil, Inc. v. Arnett, 875 F.2d 1271, 1276 (7th Cir. 1989).
87. 18 U.S.C. § 1961(1)(A); *see also id.* § 1961(1)(D).
88. *Id.* § 1961(1)(B); *see also id.* § 1961(1)(C), (E), (F), (G).
89. Jennings v. Auto Meter Products, Inc., 495 F.3d 466, 472 (7th Cir. 2007).
90. *Ashland Oil*, 875 F.2d at 1278; *see also* United States v. Computer Sciences Corp., 689 F.2d 1181, 1189-90 (4th Cir. 1982) (expressing similar concern in criminal case).

In response to the volume of civil RICO cases burdening their dockets, the courts of appeals have attempted to graft onto the statute additional proof requirements. The Supreme Court, bowing to the congressional mandate to read the statute expansively,[91] has generally rebuffed these efforts. For example, in response to the perceived misuse of civil RICO by private plaintiffs, some courts construed RICO to permit private civil actions only against defendants who had been convicted on the predicate criminal charges, and only when a "racketeering injury" could be proved. In *Sedima, S.P.R.L. v. Imrex Co.*, 473 U.S. 479 (1985), the Supreme Court rejected these limitations.[92] Similarly, some lower courts ruled that RICO required proof that either the racketeering enterprise or the predicate acts of racketeering was motivated by an economic purpose. The Court rejected this rule in *NOW v. Scheidler*, 510 U.S. 249 (1994).

The Eighth Circuit came up with another limiting principle, imposing a requirement that a qualifying "pattern of racketeering activity" required proof of multiple illegal schemes. The Supreme Court, in *H.J. Inc. v. Northwestern Bell Telephone Co.*, 492 U.S. 229 (1989) rejected this restriction but imposed its own two-part "pattern" test.

H.J. involved a suit by customers of Northwestern Bell Telephone Co. who alleged that Northwestern Bell bribed members of the public rate-approval body, the Minnesota Public Utilities Commission (MPUC), to secure approval of unreasonable rates for Northwestern Bell's services. A number of bribery counts were alleged to be the predicate acts. The Eighth Circuit dismissed the case, ruling that the case involved a single scheme to defraud and thus did not satisfy that court's "multiple schemes" requirement for a cognizable "pattern of racketeering" activity. The Supreme Court reversed, holding that a single scheme could suffice but that a cognizable pattern of racketeering required proof of "*relatedness*" and "*continuity*."[93]

With respect to the *relatedness* criteria, criminal conduct forms a pattern if "'it embraces criminal acts that have the same or similar purposes, results, participants, victims, or methods of commission, or otherwise are interrelated by distinguishing characteristics and are not isolated events.'"[94] Given the variety of ways in which one can show that two predicate crimes are related, this requirement is not often a problem. The second element, "*continuity*," may be more difficult to satisfy.

91. Section 904(a) of RICO directs that "[t]he provisions of this Title shall be liberally construed to effectuate its remedial purposes." *Turkette*, 452 U.S. at 587. In keeping with this directive, the Supreme Court has consistently read the RICO statute broadly except in *Reves* and, to some extent, H.J.

92. 473 U.S. at 488-93.

93. H.J., 492 U.S. at 239 (emphasis added).

94. *Id.* at 240.

Continuity is "both a closed- and open-ended concept, referring either to a closed period of repeated conduct, or to past conduct that by its nature projects into the future with a threat of repetition."[95] Closed-ended continuity can be demonstrated "by proving a series of related predicates extending over a substantial period of time."[96] Acts extending over a few weeks or months clearly do not meet the closed-ended continuity requirement. Indeed, courts have held that predicate acts spanning less than a year do not satisfy closed-end continuity,[97] but a scheme lasting thirteen months may.[98]

The Court noted that what constitutes open-ended continuity will be heavily fact dependent but cited as an example a "hoodlum" who sold "insurance" to "a neighborhood's storekeepers to cover them against breakage of their windows, telling his victims he would be reappearing each month to collect the 'premium' that would continue their 'coverage.'"[99] Alternatively, the threat of continued criminal activity can be established where discrete predicates "can be attributed to a defendant operating as part of a long-term association that exists for criminal purposes."[100] Allegations of open-ended continuity are helpful because a scheme that covers only a few months can satisfy the continuity requirement in such cases.[101]

H. Mens Rea

It is generally understood that RICO's substantive provisions (§ 1962(a), (b), and (c)) do not contain an independent mens rea requirement.[102] In general, then, the only mens rea that need be proved to obtain a RICO conviction is the mens rea required by the underlying predicate acts.[103]

I. RICO Conspiracy Under § 1962(d)

Section 1962(d) makes it "unlawful for any person to conspire to violate any of the provisions of subsection (a), (b), or (c) of this section." When the

---

95. *Id.* at 241.
96. *Id.* at 242.
97. *See* Cofacredit, S.A. v. Windsor Plumbing Supply Co., 187 F.3d 229, 244 (2d Cir. 1999).
98. *See* Allwaste Inc. v. Hecht, 65 F.3d 1523, 1528 (9th Cir. 1995).
99. H.J., 492 U.S. at 242.
100. *Id.* at 243; *see* United States v. Indelicato, 865 F.2d 1370, 1384-85 (2d Cir. 1989) (*en banc*).
101. *See* United States v. Hively, 437 F.3d 752, 761-62 (8th Cir. 2006).
102. *See, e.g.*, Genty v. Resolution Trust Corp. 937 F.2d 899, 908-09 (3d Cir. 1991); United States v. Biasucci, 786 F.2d 504, 512 (2d Cir. 1986).
103. Cf. United States v. Grote, 961 F.3d 105, 117-22 (2d Cir. 2020) (suggesting that a higher mens rea requirement might be appropriate where the RICO case is founded on the collection of an unlawful debt rather than a pattern of racketeering activity); *see also* United States v. Moseley, 980 F.3d 9, 18-19 (2d Cir. 2020).

government alleges a conspiracy under subsection (d) to violate § 1962(c), it must prove that:

- two or more persons
- knowingly and willfully
- agreed
- to participate, directly or indirectly, in the affairs of an enterprise through a pattern of racketeering activity.

Liability under § 1962(d) is met by knowledge of the corrupt enterprise's activities and an agreement to facilitate those activities.[104] A RICO conspiracy does not require proof of an overt act.[105]

In *Salinas v. United States*, 522 U.S. 52 (1997), a § 1962(d) prosecution, the Supreme Court held that the *Pinkerton* rule applies;[106] this means that co-conspirators must agree on the same criminal plan, and they may divvy up the work, but each is responsible for the reasonably foreseeable acts of the others.[107] The *Salinas* Court read this principle, in the RICO context, to mean that a conspirator under § 1962(d) can be guilty even if he "does not himself commit or agree to commit the two or more predicate acts requisite to the underlying [RICO] offense."[108]

Under *Salinas*, there are two alternative ways to establish a conspiratorial agreement to violate RICO. A defendant must either

- agree personally to commit two predicate acts *or*
- "agree to participate in the conduct of the enterprise with the knowledge and intent that other members of the conspiracy would commit at least two predicate acts in furtherance of the enterprise."[109]

Regardless of the means through which the agreement is proved, the government "'does not have to establish that each conspirator explicitly agreed with every other conspirator to commit the substantive RICO crime described in the indictment, or knew his fellow conspirators, or was aware of all the details of the conspiracy.'"[110] "That each conspirator may have contemplated participating in different and unrelated crimes is irrelevant."[111]

---

104. Smith v. Berg, 247 F.3d 532, 535 (3d Cir. 2001).
105. *See Salinas*, 522 U.S. at 63; *see also* United States v. Churuk, 797 Fed. App'x 680, 688-89 (3d Cir. 2020) (discussing how one determines that an act in furtherance of the conspiracy took place within the limitations period when no overt act need be proved).
106. *See* Chapter 5 (Conspiracy) (discussing Pinkerton v. United States, 328 U.S. 640 (1946)).
107. *See Salinas*, 522 U.S. at 63-64.
108. *Id.* at 65.
109. United States v. Nguyen, 255 F.3d 1335, 1341 (11th Cir. 2001).
110. United States v. Starrett, 55 F.3d 1525, 1544 (11th Cir. 1995).
111. United States v. Pepe, 747 F.3d 632, 959-60 (11th Cir. 1984).

As discussed above, a defendant can be liable for conspiring to violate § 1962(c) even if he does not "participate in the operation or management of the enterprise" sufficiently to be liable under *Reves* for a substantive § 1962(c) violation.

J. Extraterritorial Application

In *RJR Nabisco v. The European Community*, 579 U.S. 325 (2016), the Supreme Court ruled that RICO has limited extraterritorial application: it applies overseas only to the extent that Congress has made the predicate statutes upon which the RICO case is built extraterritorial. Thus, for example, 18 U.S.C. § 1512, which outlaws witness tampering and other obstructive conduct, is listed as a RICO predicate in § 1961. Because § 1512 applies extraterritorially,[112] even obstructive conduct that extends beyond U.S. borders can serve as the basis for RICO liability.

RJR Nabisco was a civil case in which the European Community (EC) sued RJR Nabisco for treble damages for racketeering activity allegedly committed in Europe. The Court went on to hold that even if RICO itself applies to conduct that occurs outside the United States, the section of RICO (§ 1964) that allows private plaintiffs like the EC to file civil suits in U.S. courts does not apply to injuries outside the United States. Instead, to recover in its civil lawsuit against RJR Nabisco, the EC would have to show that it suffered a "domestic injury" within the United States.[113]

II. PROCEDURAL ISSUES, FORFEITURE, AND PROSECUTORIAL POLICIES

A. Practical and Evidentiary Considerations

RICO provides prosecutors with numerous procedural advantages. First, it permits the government to pursue charges that would otherwise be jeopardy- or time-barred. The state law offenses included in § 1961 can serve as RICO predicates regardless of whether the defendant has been criminally prosecuted (and acquitted or convicted) in state court for the same conduct because of the double jeopardy clause's dual sovereignty exception.[114] And

112. *See* 18 U.S.C. § 1512(h).

113. *RJR Nabisco*, 579 U.S. at 354.

114. *See, e.g.*, United States v. Coonan, 938 F.2d 1553, 1562-63 (2d Cir. 1991); *see also* Chapter 2 (discussing Double Jeopardy's dual sovereignty doctrine).

where the federal or state law predicate "racketeering activity" would be time-barred, prosecutors may proceed with a RICO case built upon those crimes if one RICO predicate act happened within the five-year statute of limitations period for the RICO prosecution.[115] This can be further extended by charging a RICO conspiracy because even if all the RICO predicate crimes are time-barred, the case may survive if the conspiracy continues into the limitations period.[116]

RICO also allows the government to avoid rules that would otherwise preclude the joinder of certain offenses or defendants in a single indictment or in a single trial. And during that trial, evidence will be relevant and admissible against the defendants that would be precluded in a non-RICO trial.

Assume, for example, that defendant Alpha was acquitted in state court of murdering four people eight years ago in New York. The government has discovered Alpha's link to an organized crime family and has sufficient evidence to prove that last year he engaged in drug sales in Virginia. The state of New York is jeopardy-barred from retrying Alpha for the murders and the federal government normally has limited jurisdiction over murders. RICO is the answer to these difficulties. The murder charges are not jeopardy-barred in federal court because of the dual sovereignty doctrine[117] and RICO expressly provides that state law murder charges can serve as RICO predicate acts. As long as the drug trafficking offense occurred within five years of indictment, it does not matter how far back the other predicates take place or whether they are time-barred (assuming that the predicate acts are not separated by more than ten years (§ 1961(5)).

Moreover, the federal rules of criminal procedure would normally bar the government from including two such disparate charges in one indictment or trial, but they can be included in a RICO indictment because, as the predicate acts, they constitute elements of the RICO offense.[118] Any venue difficulty that would otherwise arise because the homicides and the drug sales occurred in different districts also disappears because RICO can be tried in any district in which a portion of the crime was committed.[119]

---

115. *See* United States v. Wong, 40 F.3d 1347, 1367 (2d Cir. 1994); *see also* Agency Holding Corp. v. Malley-Duff & Assocs., Inc., 483 U.S. 143, 155-56 (1987) (four-year statute of limitations applies to civil RICO enforcement actions).

116. *See* United States v. Pizzonia, 577 F.3d 455, 463 (2d Cir. 2009).

117. *See, e.g.*, United States v. Burden, 600 F.3d 205, 228-29 (2d Cir. 2010) (acquittal on murder charge did not bar use as a RICO predicate act).

118. *See* Fed. R. Crim. P. 8; *see also* Chapter 5 (Conspiracy) (discussing of joinder rules).

119. *See* Chapter 5 (Conspiracy) (discussing venue rules). Pursuant to 18 U.S.C. § 3237(a), a RICO offense is a "continuing offense," and hence may be brought "in any district in which such offense was begun, continued, or completed." Thus, a RICO prosecution may be brought in any district where some of the enterprise's criminal activity occurred.

At a federal or state trial on charges of drug trafficking alone, evidence of the prior murders would be excluded as irrelevant and highly prejudicial. Attempts to introduce evidence that Alpha is "mobbed up" would certainly be out. In a RICO trial, however, evidence regarding both predicates would be admissible as necessary to prove the elements of the RICO charge—the constituent predicate acts. The RICO charge would allege that the organized crime family is an "enterprise" affecting interstate commerce and that Alpha participated in that enterprise through a pattern of racketeering activity that included the murder and drug dealing. Evidence that Alpha was part of an organized crime family, then, would be relevant and indeed necessary to prove the alleged enterprise, as well as his participation in the racketeering through which the criminal enterprise operated.

Assume now that the government also has proof that defendant Beta has been bribing police officers to turn a blind eye to his car theft ring. In the normal case, neither Beta nor his crimes could appropriately be joined with Alpha's in one indictment and trial.[120] But if the government can prove that Beta is also participating, or conspiring to participate, in the affairs of the same criminal enterprise, he can be indicted and tried with Alpha because they are charged with the same crime—the RICO violation. Although there may be no evidence that Alpha was even aware of Beta's activities, this evidence comes in against Alpha to the extent that bribery is charged as one of the predicate acts of racketeering through which their joint criminal enterprise was conducted.

B. Criminal Forfeiture

Criminal forfeiture is designed to limit the ability of offenders to continue to conduct their racketeering activities and to remove defendants' incentives to engage in future racketeering by threatening their profits. Federal criminal forfeiture is authorized under 18 U.S.C. § 1963 for RICO violations.[121]

Under Fed. R. Crim. P. 32.2(a), if a prosecutor wishes to seek forfeiture, she must include a demand for forfeiture in the indictment against the defendant. A criminal forfeiture must be based on a conviction for the underlying substantive criminal offense and is considered part of the sentence. The government bears the burden of proof beyond a reasonable doubt both as to the defendant's guilt and as to the forfeitability of the subject property. Section 1963(a) dictates that defendants who violate § 1962 "shall" forfeit any interest acquired or maintained in violation of § 1962, any interest in any enterprise operated in violation of § 1962, and

120. *See* Fed. R. Crim. P. 8.

121. For detailed guidance on RICO's forfeiture provision, injunctions, and restraining orders, see Manual for Federal Prosecutors, *supra* note 54, at 220-298.

any property constituting, or derived from, the proceeds of racketeering activity in violation of § 1962.

RICO also permits courts to order forfeiture of "substitute assets" of a defendant when, due to the defendant's action, the property that would have been subject to forfeiture cannot be located, has been transferred to a third party, is beyond the jurisdiction of the court, or has been substantially diminished in value or irrevocably commingled with other property.[122]

To prevent defendants from transferring or hiding assets during the period before forfeiture is ordered, RICO authorizes the government to obtain pre-conviction restraining orders or injunctions preventing defendants from using or dissipating potentially forfeitable property.[123] The government may also seek *pre-indictment* restraining orders or injunctions. Such orders generally issue only after notice and a hearing, at which the government must prove that: (1) there is a substantial likelihood that the government will prevail on the issue of forfeiture and that the failure to issue an order would likely result in the property being made unavailable for forfeiture; and (2) the need to preserve the property outweighs the hardship on any party against whom the order will be entered.[124] The scope of pre-conviction injunctions vary with the underlying criminal offense and the circumstances, but can be quite broad.

The Supreme Court has had no difficulty with the government using these restraining orders to preclude defendants from using potentially forfeitable assets to pay attorneys' fees. In *United States v. Monsanto*, 491 U.S. 600 (1989), the Supreme Court ruled, under a substantially identical criminal forfeiture statute (21 U.S.C. § 853), that "there is no exemption from § 853's forfeiture or pretrial restraining order provisions for assets which a defendant wishes to use to retain an attorney."[125] Further, the Court held, relying upon its contemporaneous decision in *Caplin & Drysdale, Chartered v. United States*, 491 U.S. 617 (1989), that "neither the Fifth nor the Sixth Amendment to the Constitution requires Congress to permit a defendant to use assets adjudged to be forfeitable to pay that defendant's legal fees."[126]

In *Caplin*, the Court held that "whatever discretion § 853(e) provides district court judges to refuse to enter pre-trial restraining orders, it does not extend so far as" to allow a defendant to withhold assets to pay bona fide attorneys' fees.[127] Nor, the Court held, "does the exercise of that discretion

---

122. *See* 18 U.S.C. § 1963(m). Note, however, that the Supreme Court held in *Honeycutt v. United States*, 581 U.S. 443 (2017), that a defendant may not be held jointly and severally liable for property that co-conspirator derived from the crime but that defendant himself did not acquire, at least under the drug forfeiture provision, 18 U.S.C. § 853.
123. *See* 18 U.S.C. § 1963(d)(1).
124. *See id.* § 1963(d)(1)(B).
125. *Monsanto*, 491 U.S. at 614.
126. *Id.*
127. *Caplin*, 491 U.S. at 623.

'immunize' non-restrained assets from *subsequent forfeiture* under § 853(c), *if they are transferred to an attorney to pay legal fees*."[128] *Caplin* thus clarified that the government has the statutory authority to forfeit legal fees already paid upon a conviction of a defendant.

The Court rejected the defendant's contentions that the statute so construed infringed on his Sixth Amendment right to counsel of his choice and his due process rights. Subsequently, however, the Supreme Court held, under a different statute, that the Sixth Amendment prohibits the pre-trial restraint of a defendant's legitimate, untainted assets (i.e., funds not traceable to a criminal offense) needed to retain counsel of choice even if that would result in the defendant having insufficient funds to pay restitution and other financial penalties if convicted.[129] And the defendant may yet claim that RICO's punitive forfeiture violates the Eighth Amendment's prohibition against excessive fines if it is "grossly disproportional to the gravity of a defendant's offense."[130]

C. DOJ Approval Requirements and Charging Directions

Perhaps in recognition of RICO's power and potential for abuse, the Department of Justice requires approval by the Department's Criminal Division prior to the initiation of any RICO criminal information or indictment, or the filing of any civil complaint by the government.[131] It also requires approval from main Justice before attorneys' fee forfeitures may be sought and has issued guidelines for such forfeitures.[132] As a result, the Justice Department has not pursued fee forfeiture actions frequently, though it has done so in extraordinary circumstances.[133]

The Department has also attempted to provide prosecutors some guidance in determining when RICO charges are appropriate; these guidelines are not, however, enforceable against the Department. The policy touches first on federalism issues, noting that RICO "requires particularly careful and reasoned application, because, among other things, RICO incorporates certain state crimes. One purpose of these guidelines is to reemphasize the principle that the primary responsibility for enforcing state laws rests with

128. *Id.* (emphasis added).

129. *See* Luis v. United States, 578 U.S. 5, 23 (2016) (18 U.S.C. § 1345(a)).

130. *See, e.g.*, Alexander v. United States, 509 U.S. 544, 558-59 (1993) (§ 1963 forfeiture); United States v. Bajakajian, 524 U.S. 321, 334 (1998) (§ 982 forfeiture).

131. *See* U.S. Dept of Justice, Justice Manual §§ 9-110.101, 9-110.210 [hereinafter Justice Manual].

132. *Id.* §§ 9-120.100 to 9-120.116.

133. *See, e.g.*, United States v. Moffitt, Zwerling & Kemler, P.C., 83 F.3d 660 (4th Cir. 1996) (pursuing fee forfeiture where fee of $103,800 was paid mainly in $100 bills stacked inside shoeboxes).

the state concerned."[134] DOJ's Justice Manual further notes that "it is the policy of the Criminal Division that RICO be selectively and uniformly used," instructing that "[i]t is the purpose of these guidelines to make it clear that not every proposed RICO charge that meets the technical requirements of a RICO violation will be approved."[135]

The DOJ states that it will not approve "imaginative" prosecutions under RICO that "are far afield from the congressional purpose of the RICO statute"; and "[a] RICO count which merely duplicates the elements of proof of traditional Hobbs Act, Travel Act, mail fraud, wire fraud, gambling or controlled substances cases, will not be approved unless it serves some special RICO purpose."[136] Finally, despite the marked procedural advantages of RICO charges discussed above, the DOJ states that "[o]nly in exceptional circumstances will approval be granted when RICO is sought merely to serve some evidentiary purpose."[137]

Examples

1. Consider the facts of *H.J.* The ratepayers of Northwestern Bell alleged that over a period of years, Northwestern Bell regularly made various cash and in-kind payments to members of the Minnesota Public Utilities Commission (MPUC), which was responsible for determining Northwestern Bell's rates. The allegation was that these gifts (e.g., cash payments, promises regarding future employment, and payments for parties, meals, tickets to sporting events, and airline tickets) influenced the members of the MPUC to approve rates for Northwestern Bell far in excess of a fair and reasonable amount. Assume that the government could prove that these payments constituted bribery under the Minnesota Code. How could the government criminally charge Northwestern Bell under § 1962(a), (b), and (c)?

2. Wongani Afolabi is a partner in the law firm of Hoya Saxa, which has a robust domestic and international practice. Afolabi, feeling that he received an insufficient partnership draw, determined to make up the difference by using firm checks to pay for his personal expenses. Over the course of the last four years, Afolabi wrote firm checks to pay all his credit card bills. Those credit card bills reflected charges for a variety of personal expenses, including meals, dry cleaning, clothes, vacations, etc., totaling approximately $400,000 over four years.

134. Justice Manual, *supra* note 131, § 9-110.200.
135. *Id.*
136. *Id.*
137. *Id.*

On the memo line of the firm checks that Afolabi mailed to pay his bills, Afolabi indicated what professional expenses the checks purported to pay. For example, he would write the client billing number and note something like "deposition expense" or "client travel." These notations were false. Once the checks were cashed, the firm's accounting department would list the purported expense on the clients' draft bills. Afolabi would occasionally write off the charge—that is, omit it from the clients' bills. In those cases, the firm ended up paying for Afolabi's personal expenses. Most of the time, however, Afolabi allowed the bills to go out complete with the false expense statements. Clients paid the bills by check sent through the mails. Assume that the government can prove a multitude of mail fraud counts under 18 U.S.C. § 1341. Can Afolabi be prosecuted under § 1962(a), (b) and (c)? Would this charging be consistent with the DOJ charging instructions?

3. Marina Quiroga was a private investigator employed by the law firm of Hoya Saxa. For the last four years, she assisted the firm's attorneys in preparing for trial in cases in which the attorneys used false witnesses, fabricated evidence, and brought counterfeit claims. Quiroga carried out instructions from the firm partners. In one case Quiroga, at the direction of a firm lawyer, bribed a witness not to testify and instructed two other witnesses to testify falsely. In some instances, she exercised a degree of initiative in carrying out her responsibilities. Thus, in one case, she was instructed to photograph a pothole that supposedly gave rise to a personal injury claim and took it upon herself to enlarge the pothole before photographing it. Erna Wilmer, the firm's bookkeeper, knew about the scheme, but she was not asked to take an active part in the others' nefarious activities other than to record their bribes and other culpable expenditures as legitimate payments on the firm's books. Assume that the firm's many activities will yield many counts of obstruction under § 1503 and § 1512. Can Quiroga and Wilmer be prosecuted under § 1962(c)?

4. Acme, Inc. and Beta, Inc. are both wholesale food distributors. Their Chief Executive Officers got together and agreed to set prices. About six months into the scheme, an investigator at the U.S. Federal Trade Commission called Acme and Beta to inquire about the strange "coincidences" in all their pricing decisions. Acme's CEO conferred with Beta's CEO, and they then directed Acme's Chief Financial Officer to begin wiring bribes to the investigator's offshore bank account. Over the next year and one-half, the CFO wired the investigator a total of $50,000 in ten installments. After a one-year investigation, federal prosecutors believe that they can prove a price-fixing conspiracy in violation of the Sherman Act, 15 U.S.C. § 1, ten counts of bribery in violation of 18 U.S.C. § 201, and ten counts of wire fraud under 18 U.S.C. § 1343. Can they also bring a RICO charge under § 1962(c) against Acme and Beta? How should they charge it?

Explanations

1. Northwestern Bell would be the defendant "person." Bribery under state law is a qualifying predicate act (§ 1961(1)(A)). Note here that, as is explored in Chapter 9 (Corruption), the federal bribery statute, 18 U.S.C. § 201, applies only to federal officials and other persons who occupy a position of public trust with official federal responsibilities. By making state law bribery a RICO predicate, Congress gave prosecutors a weapon with which to attack state and local corruption. The federal bribery statute is also limited to corruption of *public* officials. To the extent state law authorizes prosecutions for commercial as well as official bribery, cases in which a defendant bribes an employee of a private entity to secure its business can be pursued under RICO.

   There is a pattern of racketeering activity because there were more than two instances of alleged bribery and there was relatedness and continuity. The relatedness is proved by the fact the racketeering acts had the same or similar purposes, results, participants, victims, and methods of commission. Closed-end continuity is present because the bribery scheme extended over years. The instances of bribery cannot be separated by more than ten years but given that this was alleged to be a regular practice, that requirement is likely met here. One of the bribes must have occurred within the five-year statute of limitations.

   Under § 1962(a): the government could allege that Northwestern Bell derived income from a pattern of racketeering activity involving the predicate acts of bribery—its increased rates are the proceeds—and used this income to "operate" its business as the "enterprise" (Enterprise = Northwestern Bell). The enterprise, Northwestern Bell, affects interstate commerce. Northwestern Bell would be both the person (defendant) and the enterprise, but the distinctiveness restriction only applies under § 1962(c).

   Under § 1962(b), government could allege that Northwestern Bell acquired an interest in and control of the MPUC through bribery (Enterprise = MPUC). MPUC affects interstate commerce. There is no distinctiveness requirement under § 1962(b), but the defendant person (Northwestern Bell) is distinct from the enterprise (MPUC) in any case.

   Under § 1962(c), the government could not, due to the distinctiveness limitation, allege that Northwestern Bell was the defendant "person" and the "enterprise" through which the company committed its racketeering activity. Instead, prosecutors could allege that the defendant person, Northwestern Bell, participated in the conduct and affairs of MPUC through this pattern of racketeering activity (Enterprise = MPUC). Alternatively, the plaintiffs may charge that the defendant person was Northwestern Bell, and the enterprise was an association-in-fact of Northwestern Bell and MPUC (Enterprise = AIF Northwestern

Bell + MPUC). The government would likely have little difficulty proving the three requirements of an AIF enterprise—a common purpose, relationships among those associated with the enterprise, and longevity sufficient to permit these associates to pursue the enterprise's purpose. Given that these are distinct legal entities, both of which have a vital role in the scheme, this AIF is likely to satisfy the distinctiveness requirement.

The charged enterprise must affect interstate commerce and either Northwestern Bell or an AIF of Northwestern Bell and MPUC would satisfy that requirement. If the enterprise is alleged to be MPUC, the *Reves* test will be satisfied. Recall that the *Reves* Court said that the operation or management requirement can be satisfied by outside bribers (Northwestern Bell) exercising "control" over the conduct of the corrupt officials' office through bribery. Presumably the government will also be able to prove that, if it charges that the enterprise is an AIF of Northwestern Bell and MPUC, Northwestern Bell took part in the operation or management of this unholy alliance.

2. The defendant person would be Afolabi. Mail fraud is a RICO predicate under § 1961.

   Under § 1962(a), one would have to show that Afolabi took the proceeds of his fraud and used it to acquire, establish or operate an enterprise. Here, he did not re-invest the proceeds of his fraud in the firm, so this subsection would be unavailable to the government.

   Under § 1962(b), one would have to show that Afolabi used the fraud to acquire or maintain an interest in or control over the firm. This subsection is also unavailable because it would be difficult to prove that Afolabi controlled the firm through fraud or used mail or wire fraud to take it over.

   Under § 1962(c), the defendant person would be Afolabi and the enterprise would be the firm (Enterprise = Hoya Saxa firm). The government would run into an immediate problem in the Third Circuit which, at least in civil cases, says that because the firm is, at least in part, the victim, § 1962(c) may be unavailable under *Jaguar Cars, Inc. v. Royal Oaks Motor Car Co.*, 46 F.3d 258 (3d Cir. 1995). In the Eleventh Circuit this would not present a problem. Because the firm clients were also victims, however, the suit could proceed on that basis even in the Third Circuit.

   The theory of the case would be that Afolabi was employed by or associated with the firm and he conducted the firm's affairs through fraud. There would be no distinctiveness problem because Afolabi is the defendant person, and the firm is the enterprise. *Reves* would likely not present a problem because in a partnership, partners generally have equal control and voting power and are equally able to bind the partnership. The jurisdictional requirement is met because the firm, which is a robust domestic and international practice, affects interstate commerce. The predicate acts would be multiple counts of mail fraud. There is a qualifying pattern of racketeering because the mail fraud counts were related in that they had similar purposes, results, participants, victims, and methods of commission. And closed-ended continuity was present given that the fraudulent conduct extended for years. Each count cannot be separated by more than ten years but given that this was alleged to be Afolabi's regular way of paying his bills, this requirement is likely satisfied. The alleged conduct occurred within the statute of limitations period.

Regardless of whether this satisfies the requisites of § 1962(c), it may not merit approval under the DOJ policy. There is no "organized" criminal activity here; it is not the kind of case that Congress had in mind in enacting RICO. One partner is defrauding his partners and his clients. This looks like a run-of-the-mill mail fraud case and DOJ frowns on using RICO in such circumstances unless it serves some special RICO purpose. If the prosecutors could persuade Main Justice, which must approve such cases, that there is a special RICO purpose because criminal forfeiture is required to divest Afolabi of his ill-gotten gains, that may warrant approval.

3. In the usual case, the government would name the lawyers, Quiroga, and Wilmer as defendant persons, and the firm as the RICO enterprise through which they engaged in various activities that likely constitute predicate acts of obstruction (Enterprise = Hoya Saxa firm). Obstruction under § 1503 and § 1512 are RICO predicates under § 1961. There is a pattern because the two or more predicate acts occurred within ten years of each other; at least one act of obstruction occurred within the statute of limitations period; the activities alleged are related; and, given the four-year span of the misconduct, the racketeering acts were continuous. The firm is distinct from the individual defendants, it affects interstate commerce, and the partners, at least, will satisfy the *Reves* test. The question this case raises is whether Quiroga and Wilmer, as lower-level participants, can be liable under RICO consistent with *Reves*.

   In the circuits in which lower-level employees can be liable for knowingly implementing decisions made by those managing the enterprise, prosecutors would face no difficulty under *Reves*. One might expect to encounter greater difficulties in the Second Circuit, given that it generally says that the simple performance of tasks under the direction of those operating the enterprise, even if the tasks are "necessary or helpful," is insufficient. In the case upon which this hypothetical is based, *Napoli v. United States*, 45 F.3d 680 (2d Cir. 1995), however, the Second Circuit said it had "no difficulty" in finding that a defendant like Quiroga, who did exercise some discretion in the conduct of her job, could be liable by virtue of the fact that she "provided substantial assistance to the lawyers who conducted the nefarious enterprise" and therefore was "involved in playing a part in the direction of the affairs of the enterprise within the meaning of *Reves*."[138]

Wilmer's role seems less substantial, although she was a professional (bookkeeper) and her role was important to concealment of the scheme. If prosecutors are concerned about whether she satisfies the *Reves* standard, they have other charging options. They could charge her with conspiring to violate § 1962(c) because even though Wilmer does not operate or manage the firm, she can be guilty of conspiracy under § 1962(d) for agreeing with co-conspirators who do operate or manage the enterprise. Alternatively, prosecutors could recast the case to allege that Wilmer and others conducted a pattern of obstructive activity through an AIF enterprise consisting of the firm, the lawyers, Quiroga, and Wilmer.

4. Sherman Act violations under 15 U.S.C. § 1 are not included as predicate acts under § 1961 but federal bribery and wire fraud are. They constitute a pattern of racketeering activity because: there are a total of twenty predicates (ten international wirings and ten bribes); they were committed within ten years of each other; at least one of the predicates occurred within five years of any indictment; the predicate acts are related because they concern the same bribery scheme; and continuity is likely satisfied by the one and one-half year course of the bribery conspiracy.

   The defendant "persons" would be Acme and Beta. The real question is what the government should characterize as the "enterprise," recalling that it must: affect interstate or foreign commerce; satisfy the distinctiveness requirement; and Acme and Beta must operate or manage the enterprise. Both Acme and Beta affect interstate commerce through their business activities. In a case against Acme, Acme cannot be alleged to conduct itself through a pattern of racketeering activity so Acme alone cannot be the enterprise; courts would also reject an AIF enterprise of Acme plus its complicit employees as insufficiently distinct. The same is true of Beta. The enterprise, then, should be an AIF consisting of Acme and Beta (Enterprise = AIF Acme + Beta). Given their price-fixing conspiracy, the government would likely have little difficulty demonstrating the requisites of an AIF enterprise: a common purpose, relationships among those associated with the enterprise, and longevity sufficient to permit these associates to pursue the enterprise's purpose. Alpha and Beta are separate corporate entities that together agreed to bribe a federal official to prevent detection of their joint price-fixing scheme. As such,

138. *Napoli*, 45 F.3d at 683.

charging them together as one AIF is not likely to be seen as an improper circumvention of the distinctiveness requirement. As noted above, where two separate and distinct corporate entities together constitute an AIF enterprise, there is no difficulty in charging them both as defendants *and* as members of the AIF. Alpha and Beta clearly together manage the AIF for their mutual benefit for purposes of *Reves*.

CHAPTER 11

Money Laundering

Money laundering is commonly described as the process by which criminals *conceal* the source, location, or ownership of the money spun off by criminal activity and *cleanse* it of its taint. The object is to hide the questionable provenance of the funds and convert dirty money into legitimate assets that can be used without fear that they will provide an evidentiary trail through which the underlying crimes can be identified and prosecuted. A related process—again focusing on *concealment*—is the use of laundering techniques to avoid applicable currency reporting, record-keeping, or tax laws. Money laundering, then, also helps criminals evade taxes and the possible confiscation of the fruits of their crimes.

This type of laundering is often associated in the popular imagination with drug traffickers or organized crime syndicates. But while white-collar offenders may not be seeking to launder piles of cocaine-crusted $20 bills, they engage in the same process of "cleaning" ill-gotten proceeds, and for the same reasons. The processes they use can be financially sophisticated, lately including the use of cryptocurrency. And the means employed are not confined to shady deals involving offshore banking havens; many major cases have involved the use of the world's biggest banks, wittingly or not, by white-collar criminals who wish to remove the dirt from their loot.

A second activity addressed in U.S. law as money laundering is more accurately described as *criminal financing*. This involves the use of tainted funds to *facilitate or promote* criminal activity, often through the reinvestment of the proceeds of crime to support further wrongdoing. Sometimes, however, the use of "innocent" funds to promote criminal activity is prohibited, for example in cases in which the defendant transfers money overseas to support terrorist activities with otherwise legitimate funds. One can characterize criminal financing as a type of laundering because it, too, involves concealment, albeit of a different nature. Persons attempting to use their money to facilitate or promote criminal activity will seek to obscure the source of the funding in an attempt to maintain their anonymity; that which is concealed, then, is not the crime that produced the money but the person who seeks to promote further crimes.

Although one presumes that money laundering has occurred throughout history, it has only recently been conceived of as a crime separate from the criminal activity that spins off the tainted proceeds. For many years, launderers were charged with conspiring with, or aiding and abetting, those who committed the underlying crimes. In 1970, Congress first attempted to combat money laundering by enacting the Bank Secrecy Act (BSA), which requires financial institutions to file a Currency Transaction Report (CTR) for each cash transaction of $10,000 or more; failure to file such transactions, as well as "structuring" transactions to avoid the requirement,[1] are subject to criminal sanction.[2] The BSA created a formal means by which prosecutors could "follow the money" to uncover traditionally cash-based crimes like illegal gambling or drug trafficking as well as laundering.[3] Although the BSA's requirements, as augmented over time, facilitated the investigation of these activities, the BSA did not outlaw money laundering per se.

In 1986, Congress enacted the Money Laundering Control Act, which for the first time recognized that money laundering is itself a criminal wrong separate and apart from the underlying offense that generated the tainted money. In this Act, Congress gave us two principal prohibitions. The first, 18 U.S.C. § 1956, is the more serious violation and addresses both the concealment and the promotion activities sketched above. The second, 18 U.S.C. § 1957, addresses neither concealment nor criminal financing; rather, it is in the nature of *tainted money-spending* statute. It proscribes knowingly engaging in transactions involving tainted funds. In 1992, Congress enacted 18 U.S.C. § 1960, which sanctions the operation of unlicensed money transmitting businesses, to address laundering done through less traditional, non-bank mechanisms.

Section 1956 contains four distinct ways of proving money laundering:

(1) Subsection 1956(a)(1)—the "transaction" offense"—applies to those who engage in *financial transactions* that they know involve the proceeds of some form of unlawful activity—and that in fact involve the proceeds of "specified unlawful activity"—if they act with the requisite knowledge or intent. In the usual case, they are prosecuted for entering into such transactions with knowledge that the transaction is designed to *conceal* the provenance of the proceeds of "specified unlawful activity" (concealment cases)

1. *See* 31 U.S.C. § 5324.
2. *See id.* § 5322.
3. *See id.* § 5311 *et seq.*

or with the intent to *promote* the carrying on of "specified unlawful activity" (promotion cases).

(2) Subsection 1956(a)(2)—the "transportation" offense—applies to those who *transport or transfer* monetary instruments or funds *across a U.S. border* with the requisite knowledge or intent. Again, most transportation offenses rest on allegations that the transportation was done with knowledge that the transfer represents the proceeds of some form of unlawful activity and is designed to *conceal* the provenance of the proceeds of "specified unlawful activity" (concealment cases) or with the intent to *promote* the carrying on of "specified unlawful activity" (promotion cases). With respect to "transportation" offenses, it is important to understand that such offenses need not involve the physical movement of cash or other property. The use of the word "transportation," then, is intended to underscore that what is required in "transportation" offenses is the movement—by wire as well as by physical means—of monetary instruments or funds over a U.S. border.

(3) Section 1956's third offense is found in sections 1956(a)(2) and 1956(a)(3), which explicitly authorize the use of government sting operations to expose criminal activity.

(4) Section 1956(h) outlaws conspiracies to violate § 1956.

Section 1957 prohibits engaging in transactions involving money that the defendant knows is derived from criminal activity. By outlawing such transactions, Congress hoped to make it difficult for wrongdoers to enjoy the proceeds of their crimes because § 1957 makes *the use* of dirty money illegal. This prohibition is also intended to deter otherwise law-abiding citizens from knowingly engaging in transactions with criminals; an interior decorator who knowingly works with cartel members accepts her fee at her peril.

Sections 1956 and 1957 are prosecutorial favorites for a variety of reasons. From the government's perspective they carry many of the advantages of RICO charges but are simpler to prove and for the jury to understand. They address a broad swath of activities that are commonly seen in many if not most white-collar cases. The laundering must involve certain types of crimes, denominated as "specified unlawful activity" (SUA). But the list of SUAs includes all but one of the crimes that qualify as RICO predicates and many more. Such activities include violations of well used white-collar federal statutes, state statutes, and even a variety of offenses against foreign nations.

As is explored within, the elements of these crimes have also been broadly construed in many cases and thus apply to activities one would not normally conceive of as "money laundering." Thus, for example, one normally expects that, in concealment laundering cases, the crime that spins off the tainted proceeds must be complete before the proceeds can then be cleansed. But courts have been willing to uphold concealment convictions where the underlying crime is not complete or is ongoing. Similarly, one would normally presume that to make a case for promotion laundering, the dirty funds must be used to facilitate future wrongdoing. But many circuits accept that defendants can be held liable for "promoting" already-completed crimes. "Money laundering," under § 1956, then, can include everything from payments to one's co-conspirators while running a clinic that engages in Medicaid fraud to the deposit of bribes in a corrupt official's own bank account. In short, § 1956 can be used to make money launderers of many run-of-the-mill fraudsters or corrupt officials. These creative uses of the statute are largely unconstrained by Main Justice because, unlike RICO prosecutions, most money laundering cases do not require prior DOJ approval.[4]

Money laundering provides prosecutors flexibility in charging cases in which they do not believe that they can secure a conviction on the underlying crime. A defendant need not have been convicted of the underlying criminal offense to be convicted of laundering the proceeds thereof. Instead, the government need only prove that all elements of the underlying offense were committed by someone and that the defendant then laundered the proceeds with the requisite knowledge of their nature. Money laundering charges can be particularly useful when the underlying crimes are time-barred. This is because the statute is concerned only with the conversion of the fruits of earlier crimes into legitimate assets so it is only when the defendants conduct the laundering transactions described by the statute that the statute of limitations begins ticking for purposes of sections 1956 and 1957.

Prosecutors may seek the leverage provided by the harsh penalties and threat of forfeiture that money laundering charges carry. Violations of § 1956(a) are punishable by a fine and up to twenty years' imprisonment or both. (Violations of § 1957 carry a lesser penalty of a fine, up to ten years' imprisonment, or both.) If the launderers are convicted of engaging in the criminal activity that threw off the tainted funds, the statutory maximum penalties stack up and very lengthy sentences are possible. Forfeiture of tainted funds is authorized by 18 U.S.C. § 982, which provides that the

4. *See* Dept of Justice, Justice Manual, § 9-105.300 [hereinafter Justice Manual]. Prosecutors must seek prior authorization from the Criminal or Tax Divisions at DOJ for four types of money laundering prosecutions: where jurisdiction to prosecute is based solely on the extraterritorial provisions; § 1956(a)(1)(A)(ii) cases in which the principal purpose of the financial transaction was to evade taxes; prosecutions of attorneys where the transaction involves attorneys' fees; and prosecution of a financial institution (as defined in 18 U.S.C. § 20 and 31 C.F.R. § 1010.100).

court, in imposing sentence on a person convicted of violations of sections 1956, 1957 or 1960 "shall order that the person forfeit to the United States any property, real or personal, involved in such offense, or any property traceable to such property."[5] The government can also sue those who violate § 1956(a)(1), (a)(2), or (a)(3) and secure a civil penalty of not more than the greater of $10,000 or the funds involved in the transaction (§ 1956(b)). If these threats were not enough, the stigma of the appellation "money launderer" can be used to good effect to induce pleas.

The government has found § 1956 and § 1957 particularly useful in cases where the proceeds of crime cross borders because Congress gave these statutes explicit extraterritorial application in § 1956(f) and § 1957(d). For example, these sections have been pressed into service to hold to account corrupt foreign officials or others who were beyond the reach of the Foreign Corrupt Practices Act. And Congress has given federal prosecutors extraordinary tools to find money secreted abroad for purposes of making these cases. For example, under the Anti-Money Laundering Act of 2020, the government is authorized to subpoena records, even those maintained outside the United States, relating to "any account at [a] foreign bank" that is the subject of a BSA or anti-money-laundering investigation, a civil forfeiture action, or "any investigation of a violation of a criminal law of the United States."[6]

I. MONEY LAUNDERING UNDER 18 U.S.C. § 1956

A. Transaction Laundering Under § 1956(a)(1)

To prove a "transaction" money laundering offense under § 1956(a)(1), the government must demonstrate beyond a reasonable doubt that a defendant:

- conducted or attempted to conduct a financial transaction
- knowing that the property involved in the transaction represented the proceeds of some form of unlawful activity
- the transaction "in fact" involved the proceeds of "specified unlawful activity"; and
- the defendant acted with the requisite knowledge or purpose

5. *See also* 18 U.S.C. § 981 (providing for civil *in rem* forfeiture).
6. 31 U.S.C. § 5318(k)(3).

Section 1956(a)(1) sets forth four alternative means by which the government can demonstrate that the defendant acted with the requisite knowledge or purpose:

- *Promotion*: the defendant conducted the financial transaction "with the intent to promote the carrying on of specified unlawful activity" (§ 1956(a)(1)(A)(i)),
- *Concealment*: the defendant knew that the transaction was "designed in whole or in part" to "conceal or disguise the nature, the location, the source, the ownership, or the control of the proceeds of specified unlawful activity" (§ 1956(a)(1)(B)(i)),
- *Tax fraud*: the defendant conducted the financial transaction with the intent to engage in tax fraud (§ 1956(a)(1)(A)(ii)), or
- *Avoid reporting requirement*: the defendant knew that the transaction was designed to avoid a transaction reporting requirement under state or federal law (§ 1956(a)(1)(B)(ii))

By far the most popular transaction offenses involve promotion or concealment charges. It is important to point out a notable distinction between the mental element required to prove concealment versus promotion. A concealment case requires only proof of the defendant's *knowledge*, that is, that he conducted a financial transaction *knowing* that the property involved in the transaction represented the proceeds of unlawful activity and that he *knew that the transaction was "designed in whole or in part . . . to conceal or disguise"* the nature, location, source, ownership, or control of the proceeds of specified unlawful activity (§ 1956(a)(1)(B)(i)). In concealment cases, the defendant need not *intend* to conceal; he need only know of others' intent to conceal.

By contrast, in a promotion case, proof of intent is required. A defendant can only be liable if he engaged in the transaction, *knowing* that the property involved in the transaction represented the proceeds of some form of unlawful activity and acted "*with the intent to promote the carrying on of specified unlawful activity*" (§ 1956(a)(1)(A)(i)).

1. Actus Reus: A Financial Transaction

The statute defines a "financial transaction"[7] very broadly to include a wide variety of interactions including:

- the movement of funds by wire or other means (§ 1956(c)(4)(A)(i)), transactions in "monetary instruments" like currency, checks, and money orders, investment securities or negotiable instruments

7. *See also* 18 U.S.C. § 1956(c)(3) (defining transaction).

(§ 1956(c)(4)(A)(ii)), or transfers of real property, vehicles, vessels, or aircraft (§ 1956(c)(4)(A)(iii), where such movements, transactions, or transfers in any way or degree affect interstate or foreign commerce, or

- transactions using a "financial institution," including qualifying U.S. and foreign banks, which is engaged in, or the activities of which affect, interstate or foreign commerce in any way or degree (§ 1956(c)(4)(B))

Note that the definition of a "financial institution" for purposes of § 1956(c)(4)(B) includes by reference the BSA's definition of the same term.[8] That term includes informal money transfer systems like hawala (discussed within) and was amended in the Anti-Money Laundering Act of 2020 to address cryptocurrency.[9]

Courts have defined the term "funds" very broadly. For example, one court, in holding that transactions in Bitcoin involve "[f]unds," cited the dictionary definition of the term: "'money, often money for a specific purpose'"; it concluded that "'[m]oney' is an object used to buy things. Put simply, 'funds' can be used to pay for things in the colloquial sense."[10] Bitcoin may not be considered to be a monetary instrument or currency but it represents "funds" because it "can be either used directly to pay for certain things or can act as a medium of exchange and be converted into a currency which can pay for things."[11]

The necessary interstate nexus is met either by showing that the movement of funds "in any manner or degree affected interstate or foreign commerce" or involved a "financial institution" which is defined in such a way as to ensure that such institutions affect interstate or foreign commerce. The relationship that a given transaction or financial institution must have to interstate or foreign commerce is generally characterized in the caselaw as "de minimis." For example, in *United States v. Tarkoff*, 242 F.3d 991 (11th Cir. 2001), a defense lawyer's conviction for money laundering was upheld because of the defendant's and a co-conspirator's travel to Israel to transact business with a bank there, as well as their international phone calls

---

8. A "financial institution" means any financial institution, as defined in 31 U.S.C. § 5312(a)(2), or the regulations promulgated thereunder; and any foreign bank, as defined in 12 U.S.C. § 3101 (§ 1956(c)(6)).

9. *See* 31 U.S.C. § 5312(a)(2). The BSA's definition of a "financial institution" now includes: "a licensed sender of money or any other person who engages as a business in the transmission of currency, funds, *or value that substitutes for currency*, including any person who engages as a business in an informal money transfer system or any network of people who engage as a business in facilitating the transfer of money domestically or internationally outside of the conventional financial institutions system." *Id.* § 5312(a)(2)(R) (emphasis added).

10. United States v. Ulbricht, 31 F. Supp. 3d 540, 570 (S.D.N.Y. 2014) (Silk Road case).

11. *Id.*; *see also* United States v. Iossifov, 45 F.4th 899, 913-14 (6th Cir. 2022).

arranging for funds transfers, and because the transactions involved an Israeli bank that was engaged in and affected foreign commerce.[12]

In short, a qualifying "financial transaction" can take virtually any form that involves the disposition of something of value constituting the proceeds of crime, including the exchange of cash between two individuals, assuming that a de minimis interstate nexus can be proved. "Conducting" a financial transaction is a similarly capacious concept. It includes "initiating, concluding, or participating in initiating, or concluding a transaction" (§ 1956(c)(2)).

2. "Proceeds"

Under § 1956(a)(1), the defendant must believe that the property involved in the transaction is the "proceeds" of "some form of unlawful activity" and the government must prove that the transaction "in fact involves" the "proceeds" of "specified unlawful activity." For twenty years, the statute did not define the critical term "proceeds." A circuit split developed over the meaning of the term and the Supreme Court attempted, without much success, to resolve the split in *United States v. Santos*, 553 U.S. 507 (2007).

Santos operated a lottery that was illegal under state law. He employed a number of "runners" who gathered bets from gamblers and kept a portion of the bets as their commission. They delivered the balance to Santos's "collectors," who in turn delivered the cash to Santos. Santos used the cash to pay the collectors' salaries and to pay off lottery winners. Santos's net profits, then, were what was left after all these obligations were satisfied. Santos was convicted, *inter alia*, of money laundering under § 1956(a)(1)(A)(i) for the various "transactions" in which he paid his employees commissions and salaries and paid off lottery winners.

The case was based on the allegation that Santos was "promoting" not a future, discrete crime, but rather his ongoing lottery scheme. The issue before the Supreme Court was whether the federal money-laundering statute's prohibition of transactions involving criminal "proceeds" applies only to transactions involving criminal *profits* or whether it can apply as well to transactions in criminal *gross receipts*. A plurality of the Supreme Court reversed Santos's conviction, holding that, at least in the circumstances of an illegal gambling business, "proceeds" under § 1956(a)(1) of the money laundering statute meant "profits" and not simply "gross receipts."[13]

This may sound like a simple bookkeeping issue but it in fact has had far-reaching implications for the scope of the statute. As the plurality opinion argued, if "proceeds" simply means "gross receipts," nearly every payment

12. *See Tarkoff*, 242 F.3d at 995; *see also* United States v. Wilkinson, 137 F.3d 214, 220-21 (4th Cir. 1998).
13. *Santos*, 553 U.S. at 514.

made to support an ongoing criminal business—here, for commissions, salaries, and payments to lottery winners—would constitute money laundering, because it could be characterized as a transaction in proceeds designed to "promote" the criminal business. The plurality contended that:

> Few crimes are entirely free of cost, and costs are not always paid in advance. Anyone who pays for the costs of a crime with its proceeds—for example, the felon who uses the stolen money to pay for the rented getaway car—would violate the money-laundering statute. And any wealth-acquiring crime with multiple participants would become money laundering when the initial recipient of the wealth gives his confederates their shares.[14]

To underscore the implications of this decision, the plurality noted that "[t]here are more than 250 predicate offenses for the money-laundering statute and many foreseeably entail such transactions."[15]

The *Santos* dissent argued that "proceeds" meant "gross receipts," not just "profits." Justice Stevens provided the plurality the fifth vote necessary for the judgment, but he opined that "proceeds" could mean different things in different cases. The case, then, did not provide any real guidance to the lower courts.

Another issue that arose regarding the meaning of "proceeds" was whether "indirect" proceeds could serve as the predicate for a money laundering conviction. In these cases, the question was whether money lawfully obtained but unlawfully concealed could constitute "proceeds." For example, one may have perfectly legitimate funds and assets in one's bankruptcy estate. But fraudulent concealment of a bankruptcy estate's assets constitutes a specified unlawful activity. The issue in such a case, then, was whether untainted "property which is required to be included in a bankruptcy debtor's estate but is instead undeclared, and thus [unlawfully] *retained*, is 'proceeds' of a bankruptcy fraud offense under 18 U.S.C. § 152(1)."[16] Many courts rejected the "suggestion that to qualify as 'proceeds' under the federal money laundering statute, funds must have been *directly* produced by or through a specified unlawful activity, and . . . agree[d] that funds *retained* as a result of the unlawful activity can be treated as the 'proceeds' of such crime."[17]

Congress reacted to *Santos* and the "indirect" proceeds issue by amending § 1956 to define "proceeds" as "any property derived from or obtained or *retained, directly or indirectly*, through some form of unlawful activity, *including the gross receipts of such activity*" (§ 1956(c)(9) (emphasis added)). The

14. *Id.* at 516.
15. *Id.* at 516-17.
16. United States v. Yusuf, 536 F.3d 178, 185 (3d Cir. 2008) (emphasis original)
17. *Id.* (emphasis original).

implications of Congress's decision to adopt the broadest reading of "proceeds" in light of the *Santos* plurality's concerns are explored below.

3. Specified Unlawful Activity

The breadth of the money laundering statute is, in theory, constrained by the fact that the laundering activity must conceal the proceeds of, or promote, only certain kinds of crimes, denominated as "specified unlawful activity" (SUA). But, given the breadth of crimes that Congress has identified as SUAs, this element does little to limit the reach of the statute.

In § 1956(c)(7)(A), Congress defined "specified unlawful activity" to includes all the RICO predicates referenced in §1961(1) save one.[18] Recall that Congress included a variety of traditionally state-law crimes like murder, kidnaping, extortion, gambling, arson, robbery, bribery, and dealing in obscene materials or controlled substances (§ 1961(1)(A)) as RICO predicates and thus such crimes also qualify as SUAs. Between the RICO predicates incorporated by reference in 1956(c)(7)(A) and the other federal offenses explicitly listed in the balance of the definition, 1956(c)(7)(B)-(D), "specified unlawful activity" includes a wide variety of white-collar crimes including federal bribery and gratuities (e.g., 18 U.S.C. § 201), federal program theft, fraud, or bribery (§ 666), computer fraud and abuse violations (§ 1030), mail, wire, and bank fraud (§ 1341, § 1343, § 1344), obstruction and witness tampering (§ 1503, § 1512), Hobbs Act extortion (§ 1951), Travel Act violations (§ 1952), certain environmental crimes, fraud in the sale of securities, "any felony violation of the Foreign Corrupt Practices Act" (15 U.S.C. §§ 78dd-1 to 78dd-3), and "[a]ny act or activity constituting an offense involving a Federal health care offense" (§ 1956(c)(7)(F)).

Notably, § 1956(c)(7)(B) includes in the list of specified unlawful activities certain offenses against *foreign* nations. Laundering cases, then, can be founded on transactions in, or the transportation of, the proceeds of crimes committed in another country. SUAs include offenses against a foreign nation involving white-collar criminality, including: public corruption; fraud, or any scheme or attempt to defraud, by or against a foreign bank; and certain smuggling or export control violations. But such offenses against foreign nations only qualify as SUAs if they concern "financial transaction[s] *occurring in whole or in part in the United States*" (§ 1956(c)(7)(B) (emphasis added)).

On the list of offenses against foreign nations that qualify as SUAs are "bribery of a public official, or the misappropriation, theft, or embezzlement of public funds by or for the benefit of a public official"

---

18. Exempted are acts indictable under Title 31, Chapter 53, subchapter 11.

(§ 1956(c)(7)(B)(iv)). As is discussed in Chapter 9 (Corruption), the statute most often applied to transborder corruption of foreign public officials, the Foreign Corrupt Practices Act, does not authorize prosecution of the venal foreign officials themselves, only those who offer such persons bribes. Prosecutors, then, often turn to the money laundering statute to prosecute the foreign officials.[19] Note in this regard that qualifying crimes against foreign states go beyond bribery—which is all that is addressed in the FCPA—to include violations relating to other types of corruption, such as theft and embezzlement from foreign public coffers. It is worth underscoring again, however, that these offenses against foreign nations only qualify as "specified unlawful activity" with respect to "a financial transaction occurring in whole or in part in the United States" (§ 1956(c)(7)(B)).

4. Mens Rea and Actual Proceeds

To prove a transaction violation, the transaction has to "*in fact* involve[]" the proceeds of "specified unlawful activity" (§ 1956(a)(1)). But the statute only requires that the defendant "know" that property involved in the alleged financial transaction represents "the proceeds of *some form of unlawful activity*" (§ 1956(c)(1) (emphasis added)). This means that the government need only prove that "the person knew the property involved in the transaction represented proceeds from some form, though not necessarily which form, of activity that constitutes a felony under State, Federal, or foreign law, regardless of whether or not such activity is [specified unlawful activity]" (§ 1956(c)(1)).

It is worth underscoring the limited nature of this mens rea requirement. The "some form of unlawful activity" standard limits the government's burden of proof regarding the scope of the defendant's knowledge of the nature of the "proceeds." "[S]ome form of unlawful activity" means only that the defendant has to know that the money was the dirty proceeds of some type of felony. He can mistakenly believe that the money is the proceeds of a type of unlawful activity that is not listed as "specified unlawful activity" under money laundering statute. Indeed, he does not even have to know the actual nature of the crime that spun off the money.

The knowledge required by the money laundering statute can be proved through willful blindness or conscious avoidance. Recall that in *Global-Tech Appliances, Inc. v. SEB, S.A.*, 563 U.S. 754 (2011), discussed in Chapter 2 (General Part), the Supreme Court clarified its understanding of the elements of willful blindness to be twofold: "(1) [t]he defendant must subjectively believe that there is a high probability that a fact exists and (2) the defendant must take deliberate actions to avoid learning of that fact."[20] The *Global-Tech* Court

---

19. United States v. Thiam, 934 F.3d 89 (2d Cir. 2019) (affirming money laundering conviction founded on bribery of a public official in the Republic of Guinea).
20. *Global-Tech*, 563 U.S. at 769.

made clear that willful blindness "surpasses recklessness and negligence."[21] Under this formulation, a willfully blind defendant is one "who takes deliberate actions to avoid confirming a high probability of wrongdoing and who can almost be said to have actually known the critical facts."[22]

B. Transportation Laundering Under § 1956(a)(2)

To prove a "transportation" money laundering offense under § 1956(a)(2), the government must prove that the defendant:

- transported, transmitted, or transferred (or attempted to do so)
- monetary instruments or funds
- across the border of the United States
- and, in so doing, acted with the requisite knowledge or purpose

Section 1956(a)(2) sets forth three alternative means by which the government can demonstrate that the defendant acted with the requisite knowledge or purpose:

- *Promotion:* the defendant transported the funds "with the intent to promote the carrying on of specified unlawful activity" (§ 1956(a)(2)(A))
- *Concealment:* the defendant transported funds knowing that the funds involved in the transportation represent the proceeds of some form of unlawful activity and knowing that such transfer is designed in whole or in part to conceal or disguise the nature, location, source, ownership, or control of the proceeds of specified unlawful activity (§ 1956(a)(2)(B)(i))
- *Avoid reporting requirement:* the defendant knew that the transaction was designed to avoid a transaction reporting requirement under State or Federal law (§ 1956(a)(2)(B)(ii)).

The terms "proceeds" and "specified unlawful activity" have the same meaning in this context as they do in transaction cases (discussed above). Again, the overwhelming majority of cases rely on promotion and concealment theories.

---

21. *Id.*
22. *Id.* at 769.

1. Actus Reus: Transporting, Transmitting, or Transferring Monetary Instruments or Funds

While the actus reus of a § 1956(a)(1) case is conducting a "financial transaction" (or attempting to do so), the culpable act at the heart of a § 1956(a)(2) case is the transport, transmission, or transfer (or the attempt to do so) of a "monetary instrument or funds from a place in the United States to or through a place outside the United States or to a place in the United States from or through a place outside the United States." Section 1956(a)(2), as originally enacted, prohibited only the international "transportation" of funds. The statute was amended in 1988 to expressly add the terms "transmit" and "transfer." The amendment was intended to clarify what most courts had already read into the statute—that is, that the section prohibited international wire transfers as well as the physical transportation of monetary instruments or funds.

The statute defines "monetary instruments" to include coin and currency (of any country), traveler's checks, personal checks, bank checks, money orders, and investment securities or negotiable instruments (§ 1956(c)(5)). On the theory that "funds" must mean something different than the items included in the definition of "monetary instruments," all of which "one can *physically* carry," courts have held that "funds" for purposes of subsection (a)(2) generally covers wire transfers.[23]

2. Transborder Transportation

The transborder element requires that the funds or monetary instruments cross a U.S. border—either originating or terminating in the United States. Thus, the Eleventh Circuit held that a defendant could not be convicted under § 1956(a)(2) for transferring funds from one location outside the United States to another country outside the United States because none of the money traversed the U.S. border.[24] Strangely enough, then, what could be viewed as the "international" money laundering prohibition—the transportation offense—is not applicable where the conduct is truly (or entirely) "international" in scope. A "transaction" offense may be cognizable, however, where the laundering transaction occurs entirely overseas assuming that the extraterritoriality provisions of the statue (explored within) authorize the prosecution, and the other elements of the crime are satisfied.[25]

---

23. United States v. Monroe, 943 F.2d 1007, 1015 & n.8 (9th Cir. 1991) (emphasis original).
24. *See* United States v. Kramer, 73 F.3d 1067, 1072-73 (11th Cir. 1996).
25. *See, e.g.*, *Tarkoff*, 242 F.3d at 995-96 (holding that transfers from Curacao to Israel and between accounts in Israel constitute "financial transactions" under 1956(c)(4) and were within the reach of § 1956(a)(1)(B)(i)).

3. "Proceeds" Required for Concealment but Not Promotion

In all transaction cases—whether they are alleged be done for the purpose of concealment or promotion—the transactions must "in fact" involve the proceeds of SUA and the defendant must be aware that the transaction involves the proceeds of some form of unlawful activity. This is not true of all transportation offenses.

Where a *transportation* case is founded on a *concealment theory*, the funds transported across a U.S. border must in fact involve the proceeds of SUA and the defendant must have an awareness that they are the proceeds of some unlawful activity. That is, the government must prove that the defendant transported funds knowing that the funds involved in the transportation represent the proceeds of some form of unlawful activity and knowing that such transfer is designed in whole or in part to conceal or disguise the nature, location, source, ownership, or control of the proceeds of specified unlawful activity (§ 1956(a)(2)(B)(i)). In short, the proof requirements in transportation concealment cases mirror those in transaction cases.

But, in a *transportation* case founded on a *promotion theory*, the government need not prove that the funds transported in fact represent the proceeds of SUA or that the defendant knew that the funds represent the proceeds of some form of unlawful activity. That is, the government need only prove that the defendant transported the funds across a U.S. border "with the intent to promote the carrying on of specified unlawful activity" (§ 1956(a)(2)(A)). In short, a transportation case can be made where the defendant is transporting *clean, untainted* funds over a U.S. border to *promote* an SUA.

Perhaps the easiest way to remember this quirk in the statute is to consider when the United States might wish to proscribe the transfer of *untainted* funds to or from foreign sources with an intent to promote criminal activity. One obvious example concerns terrorism cases. A variety of criminal terrorism violations are included in the list of SUAs, including statutes proscribing material support for terrorism.[26] The United States has an interest in deterring U.S. persons from transferring dirty *or* clean funds overseas to finance terrorism; and it has a compelling interest in preventing overseas sources from sending any kind of funding, whether tainted or not, over a border to finance such activities on U.S. soil.[27] Although not every transportation promotion case will concern terrorism, keeping this example in mind as a paradigmatic case may help readers recall this distinction in transportation promotion laundering cases.

---

26. *See* § 1956(c)(7)(D) (including 18 U.S.C. §§ 2339A, 2339B).
27. *See, e.g.*, United States v. El-Mazain, 664 F.3d 467 (5th Cir. 2011).

C. Government Sting Operations Under § 1956(a)(3) and § 1956(a)(2)

Section 1956(a)(1) transaction cases and § 1956(a)(2)(B) transportation concealment cases require proof that the transaction or transportation in fact involves the proceeds of SUA. Where investigators are conducting a sting operation, such cases fail because the funds are undercover monies supplied by the government rather than dirty money. To fill this gap, § 1956 authorizes sting operations in two provisions—one that is a stand-alone section addressed to transaction laundering, 1956(a)(3), and one that is tucked within the section governing transportation concealment offenses, § 1956(a)(2).

1. Transaction Cases

Section 1956(a)(3) provides the basis for prosecution of transaction cases in which the money "laundered" is government money being used in a sting operation. Section 1956(a)(3) renders liable those who:

- conducted or attempted to conduct a financial transaction
- involving property represented[28] to be the proceeds of specified unlawful activity or property used to conduct or facilitate a specified unlawful activity
- the defendant acted with the requisite knowledge or purpose

Section 1956(a)(3) sets forth three alternative means by which the government can demonstrate that the defendant acted with the requisite knowledge or purpose:

- *Promotion:* the defendant conducted the financial transaction "with the intent to promote the carrying on of specified unlawful activity" (§ 1956(a)(3)(A)),
- *Concealment:* the defendant conducted the financial transaction "with the intent to conceal or disguise the nature, location, source, ownership, or control of property believed to be the proceeds of specified unlawful activity" (§ 1956(a)(3)(B)), or

28. "Represented" means "any representation made by a law enforcement officer or by another person at the direction of, or with the approval of, a Federal official authorized to investigate or prosecute violations of this section." 18 U.S.C. § 1956(3); *see also Castellini*, 392 F.3d at 46-47.

- *Avoid reporting requirement:* the defendant conducted the financial transaction "with the intent" to avoid a transaction reporting requirement under State or Federal law (§ 1956(a)(3)(C))

Note that in the usual transaction concealment case, the defendant need only *know* that the transaction is designed in whole or part to conceal the provenance of the SUA. But in sting cases, § 1956(a)(3)(B) requires that the transaction be conducted with the *intent to conceal*. This is obviously a more demanding mens rea requirement.

2. Transportation Cases

Recall that in *transportation promotion* cases, the government does not have to prove that the money used to "promote" specified unlawful activity was in fact tainted and thus no problems are presented by the government's use of untainted money in sting cases.

Only in *transportation concealment* cases does the statute require proof that the involved funds are the proceeds of SUA. The statute therefore authorizes sting operations in transportation concealment cases in text at end of § 1956(a)(2). It provides that for purposes of such cases, "the defendant's knowledge may be established by proof that a law enforcement officer represented" that the money was the product of SUA, and "the defendant's subsequent statements or actions indicate that the defendant believed such representations to be true."

D. Concealment Cases

In both transaction and transportation concealment offenses, the government must prove that the defendant conducted a transaction or transported funds *knowing* that the funds involved in the transaction/transportation represented the proceeds of some form of unlawful activity and *knowing* that the transaction/transportation is designed in whole or in part to conceal or disguise the nature, location, source, ownership, or control of the proceeds of specified unlawful activity (§ 1956(a)(1)(B)(i), § 1956(a)(2)(B)(i)).[29] The concealment element is generally treated identically in transaction and transportation cases.[30]

In both transaction and transportation concealment cases the funds involved must *in fact* be the proceeds of SUA.

Concealment cases require proof of a design-to-conceal—that is, the animating purpose or design of the transaction or transportation must be to

---

29. *See* United States v. Carr, 25 F.3d 1194, 1204 (3d Cir. 1994).
30. *See id.*

conceal. The Supreme Court discussed this design-to-conceal element in the context of a transportation prosecution in *Cuellar v. United States*, 553 U.S. 550 (2008). Cuellar went to a great deal of trouble to hide $81,000 in a car that he planned to drive from the United States to Mexico. Cuellar's likely purpose in secreting the money was to hide it from border agents, avoid currency reporting requirements, or to otherwise keep it safe from seizure or theft. The Supreme Court reversed his conviction under § 1956(a)(2)(B)(i) because concealment money laundering requires proof that the *purpose* of the transportation—not just its *effect*—is to conceal or disguise one of the listed attributes. In other words, the case failed because the government failed to show that Cuellar *moved the cash over a border in order to conceal it*; simply proving that Cuellar *concealed to the money in order to transport it* was insufficient.[31]

It is important to remember that although the defendant is often the author of the design-to-conceal, he need not be, nor need he share the author's intent to conceal. All that need be proven is that the defendant engages in the transaction or transportation *knowing* that *someone* designed it to conceal.

To prove that the transaction is in fact designed to conceal, the government generally relies both on statements by the defendant or others that indicate such a design and on circumstantial evidence relating to the nature of the transaction or transportation. Juries will be asked to infer an intent to conceal when:

- the transaction was structured in a way to avoid attention
- at the defendant's insistence, unusual secrecy surrounds the transaction
- the illegal funds are funneled through various fictitious business accounts
- illegal profits are deposited in the bank account of a legitimate business (comingling)
- highly irregular transactions lead up to, or are used in connection with, the laundering
- third parties are used to conceal the real owner of funds or property
- the transactions make no business sense and can be explained only by a design to conceal
- money is moved through a large number of accounts, for example by conducting a "shell game" involving multiple intra-conspiracy transfers, or
- there is evidence that the defendants "'intended to and did make it more difficult for the government to trace and demonstrate the [] nature of [the] funds'"[32]

31. *Cuellar*, 553 U.S. at 568.

32. United States v. Singh, 995 F.3d 1069, 1077 (9th Cir. 2021).

The use of anonymous or secretive channels—such as non-traditional payments systems like hawala or the Tor browser—may not alone be sufficient to demonstrate an intent to conceal[33] but juries are entitled to infer that use of such channels is probative of intent.[34] Concealment laundering convictions cannot rest solely on proof that the defendant transferred or spent his money absent *some* inference that the transaction was intended to hide the provenance of the funds. For example, in *United States v. Rockelman*, 49 F.3d 418, 422 (8th Cir. 1995), the Eighth Circuit reversed a money laundering conviction based on insufficient evidence of an intent to conceal because the defendant purchased a cabin with cash, which consisted of illegal proceeds, but he placed the title in the name of his business and made no attempt to conceal either his own identity or the source of the funds.

Courts also hold, however, that "to establish the design element of money laundering, it is not necessary to prove with regard to any single transaction that the defendant removed all traces of his involvement."[35] The question is one of degree and the extent to which one can infer from the transaction that the defendant was seeking to obscure the location and nature of the funds. For example, the Eighth Circuit held in *United States v. Dvorak*, 617 F.3d 1017 (8th Cir. 2010), that a jury could reasonably infer an intent to conceal where a defendant repeatedly deposited fraudulently obtained reimbursement checks into his own checking account and then withdrew the entire amount in cash.[36] But the D.C. Circuit, in *United States v. Adefehinti*, 510 F.3d 319 (D.C. Cir. 2007), reversed a concealment money laundering conviction where the defendant received a check payable to a fictitious third party, falsely endorsed the check in the third party's name, and directed that the proceeds be deposited in the defendant's and his co-conspirator's bank accounts, with a portion being released to the defendant in cash.[37] The D.C. Circuit stressed the facts that the transaction was fairly simple—involving only the cashing and distribution of one check—and that the distribution of the ill-gotten gains was very easy for anyone, including law enforcement, to discover based on the endorsement on the check and the subsequent deposit slips and checks.

33. *See, e.g.*, *Ulbricht*, 31 F. Supp. 3d at 569 ("[A]n allegation that Bitcoins are used as a payment system is insufficient in and of itself to state a claim for money laundering. The fact that Bitcoins allow for anonymous transactions does not *ipso facto* mean that those transactions relate to unlawful activities" but holding that use of Bitcoin exchanges to buy products and services in on-line marketplace constituted "financial transactions").

34. *Singh*, 995 F.3d at 1076-77.

35. United States v. Willey, 57 F.3d 1374, 1386 (5th Cir. 1995).

36. *See Dvorak*, 617 F.3d at 1024.

37. *Adefehinti*, 510 F.3d at 323.

E. Promotion Cases

Transaction and transportation cases can be founded on a defendant's "intent to promote the carrying on of specified unlawful activity." As discussed above, all that needs to be shown in a *concealment* transaction or transportation case is that the defendant *knew* that the transaction/transportation was designed to conceal, but he need not be the author of that design or even share an intent to conceal. Under a *promotion* theory, however, knowledge alone does not suffice. Rather, for purposes of a promotion offense under § 1956(a)(1)(A)(i) or § 1956(a)(2)(A), the government must show that the defendant conducted a financial transaction or transported monetary instruments or funds *with the intent* to promote the carrying on of specified unlawful activity.[38]

1. Transaction vs. Transportation Promotion Offenses

As noted above, there is one important difference between the proof required to make out a transaction promotion case under § 1956(a)(1) as opposed to a transportation promotion case under § 1956(a)(2). Transaction promotion offenses (§ 1956(a)(1)(i)) require proof that the defendant *know* that the property involved in the financial transaction represents the proceeds of some form of unlawful activity *and* conduct a financial transaction that "*in fact involves*" the proceeds of a SUA with an intent to promote a SUA.

Transportation promotion cases (§ 1956(a)(2)(A)) are different in that *there is no requirement that the transportation "in fact involve[]" the proceeds of SUA*. Rather, under § 1956(a)(2)(A), the government need only show that the defendant transported monetary instruments or funds over a U.S. border with the intent to promote SUA. Under § 1956(a)(2)(A), then, a defendant can violate the money laundering statute by sending *clean money* over a U.S. border to promote a SUA.

	§ 1956(a)(1) Transaction	**§ 1956(a)(2) Transportation, including Sting Operations**	**§ 1956(a)(3) Transaction Sting Operations**
Actus Reus	Conduct a "Financial Transaction"	Transport "Monetary Instruments" or "Funds" (or government sting money) across a U.S. border	Conduct a "Financial Transaction" with an undercover

38. *See* United States v. Trejo, 610 F.3d 308, 314 (5th Cir. 2010).

	§ 1956(a)(1) Transaction	§ 1956(a)(2) Transportation, including Sting Operations	§ 1956(a)(3) Transaction Sting Operations
Mens Rea			
Promotion	Knowing that transaction represents the "proceeds" of some form of unlawful activity	No "proceeds" required; can use clean or dirty money; so no knowledge regarding the nature of the funds required	Using money represented to be "proceeds"
	The transaction in fact involves the "proceeds" of SUA		
	Intending to promote SUA	Intending to promote SUA	Intending to promote SUA
Concealment	Knowing that the transaction represents the "proceeds" of some form of unlawful activity	Knowing that transportation represents the "proceeds" of some form of unlawful activity (or believing an undercover's representation to that effect)	Using money represented to be "proceeds"
	The transaction in fact involves the "proceeds" of SUA	The transportation in fact involves the "proceeds" of SUA (or government sting money)	
	Knowing that transaction was designed to conceal	Knowing that the transportation was designed to conceal	Intending to conceal monies believed to be "proceeds"
Avoid Reporting Requirements	Knowing that the transaction represents the "proceeds" of some form of unlawful activity	Knowing that transportation represents the "proceeds" of some form of unlawful activity (or believing undercover's representation to that effect)	Using money represented to be "proceeds"
	The transaction in fact involves the "proceeds" of SUA	The transportation in fact involves the "proceeds" of SUA (or government sting money)	
	Knowing that the transaction was designed to avoid reporting requirements	Knowing that the transaction was designed to avoid reporting requirements	Intending to avoid reporting requirements

	§ 1956(a)(1) Transaction	§ 1956(a)(2) Transportation, including Sting Operations	§ 1956(a)(3) Transaction Sting Operations
Tax Fraud	Knowing that the transaction represents the "proceeds" of some form of unlawful activity The transaction in fact involves the "proceeds" of SUA Intending to commit tax fraud	Not applicable	Not applicable

F. Temporal Issues

When one thinks about "money laundering" and "criminal financing," the usual temporal assumptions are:

Concealment is about *past crimes*	Promotion is about *future crimes*
A past crime threw off tainted "proceeds," which are then laundered in a qualifying "transaction" or "transportation"	Tainted "proceeds" (transaction case)/tainted proceeds or clean funds (transportation case) are used to promote or facilitate a further, future crime

Prosecutors have attempted to use § 1956 in three ways that upset these assumptions and that, when accepted by courts, have vastly expanded the application of this statute in white-collar cases. In particular, prosecutors pushed the concept of "promotion" laundering in a manner that may make a money laundering charge available in many if not most white-collar cases.

1. *Concealment and promotion cases:* the transaction or transportation is *the same transaction* as that throwing off the tainted "proceeds" (so-called "merger cases")
2. *Concealment and promotion cases:* the transaction or transportation is made while the underlying criminal scheme *is ongoing* (another sort of "merger case")
3. *Promotion cases:* the transportation or transaction charged happens after the crime is complete and the allegation is that the transaction *promotes the past crime* (so-called "receipt and deposit cases")

I. Merger Issue #1: Promotion and Concealment in the Same Transaction as That Generating Proceeds

In some cases, the government has alleged that the proceeds were generated *in the same transaction* that is charged as the actionable "promotion" or "concealment." Courts will not accept such charging in transaction or transportation concealment cases, holding that "the laundering of funds cannot occur in the same transaction through which those funds first became tainted by crime."[39] In such cases, courts have also held that use of the money laundering statute is inappropriate where the successful consummation of a crime is the very transaction that is alleged to constitute the laundering of the "proceeds" of that crime.[40]

For example, in *United States v. Christo*, 129 F.3d 578 (11th Cir.1997), the Eleventh Circuit reversed a money laundering conviction where the "withdrawal of funds charged as money laundering was one and the same as the underlying criminal activity of bank fraud and misapplication of bank funds."[41] The court reasoned that "[a] bank fraud offense is not complete until there is an 'execution' of the scheme to defraud. The execution is completed by the movement of money, funds, or other assets from the financial institution."[42] Because the same transaction that moved the funds from the financial institution was alleged to be the laundering transaction, the court concluded that the crimes of bank fraud and misapplication of bank funds were, until the alleged laundering transaction, "incomplete and had generated no proceeds."[43]

The situation is very different in *transportation promotion* cases because, as noted above, § 1956(a)(2) does not require that the monetary instrument or funds sent across a U.S. border to "promote" SUA be the "proceeds" of SUA. In transportation promotion cases alone, then, clean money can be used to promote criminal activity. Because "proceeds" need not be generated in a discrete transaction, courts are willing to accept allegations, for example, that a defendant's single wire transfer—through which he both committed bank fraud *and* moved the stolen funds overseas to promote his crime—was sufficient to sustain a transportation promotion case.[44]

39. United States v. Butler, 211 F.3d 826, 830 (4th Cir. 2000); *see also* United States v. Hall, 945 F.3d 507, 512 (D.C. Cir. 2019) (the offense of money laundering "must be separate and distinct from the underlying offense that generated the money to be laundered").

40. *See, e.g.*, *Butler*, 211 F.3d at 829-30 (collecting cases).

41. *Christo*, 129 F.3d at 580.

42. *Id.*

43. *Id.* at 581.

44. United States v. Piervinanzi, 23 F.3d 670, 680 (2d Cir. 1994); *see also* United States v. Krasinski, 545 F.3d 546, 551 (7th Cir. 2008).

2. Merger Issue #2: Promotion or Concealment in the Context of an Ongoing Scheme

There are actually two types of "merger" questions that arise in the context of ongoing schemes: (a) whether one can launder the "proceeds" of a crime that is not yet complete under either concealment or promotion theories; and (b) whether one can "promote" an ongoing offense by making payments that simply promote its ultimate success.

a. Concealment or Promotion of Proceeds of Incomplete Underlying Crimes

Unfortunately, the statute does not specify when money becomes "proceeds" for money laundering purposes. In many cases, the courts "use the language of time to describe the relationship between the money laundering and the predicate offense—these cases state that the predicate offense must be 'completed' or 'earlier' or 'antecedent.'"[45] It may be best, however, to focus on the transaction at issue rather than temporal circumstances because many circuits have held that qualifying "proceeds" can be derived "from an already completed offense, *or a completed phase of an ongoing offense.*"[46] These cases are heavily fact-dependent, but it is fair to say that in general the underlying crime need not be fully completed—that is, all its elements need not be satisfied—before the laundering can begin.[47] Thus, in temporal terms, a qualifying laundering transaction or transportation can take place before all the elements of the crime generating the offense have been satisfied.

United States v. Mankarious, 151 F.3d 694 (7th Cir. 1998) is representative. In *Mankarious*, the question was when the predicate mail fraud was concluded such that its proceeds could be laundered. In mail fraud cases, the government must prove a scheme to defraud and a mailing in furtherance of the fraud. The Seventh Circuit relied on the mail fraud precedents establishing that a mailing "in furtherance" of a scheme to defraud can occur after the defendant succeeded in defrauding the victim where the government proves that the mailing was designed to ensure that the victim did not realize he have been had or where necessary to ensure that the fraud can continue.[48] Thus, the fraud can throw off the proceeds—the money obtained through fraud—before the crime becomes complete when the mailing element occurs.[49] In this case, then, the court accepted that the

45. United States v. Mankarious, 151 F.3d 694, 703 (7th Cir. 1998).

46. United States v. Szur, 289 F.3d 200, 214 (2d Cir. 2002) (emphasis original).

47. *See* United States v. Castellini, 392 F.3d 35, 48 (1st Cir. 2004) ("'Proceeds' of an illegal activity may be created before the completion of an underlying on-going crime."); *Mankarious*, 151 F.3d at 706.

48. *See* Chapter 6 (Fraud).

49. *See Mankarious*, 151 F.3d at 706; *see also* United States v Bolden, 325 F.3d 471, 487-88 (4th Cir. 2003) (transaction concealment and promotion laundering).

proceeds of the fraud were available and could be laundered before the crime was technically complete.

b. Promotion of Ongoing Underlying Criminal Activity

Recall the Court's concern in in *United States v. Santos*, 553 U.S. 507 (2007). The plurality feared that if "proceeds" meant "gross receipts," virtually every payment of co-conspirators' salaries or other ordinary "business" expenses while conducting an illegal enterprise would violate the money laundering statute. Congress was not impressed. It responded to *Santos* by defining "proceeds" to include "gross receipts," meaning that all such payments—made contemporaneously and during the conduct of the overall scheme—may indeed qualify as transactions that promote the success of the ongoing scheme.

Many lower courts have therefore concluded that the "promotion" element "can be met by transactions that promote the continued prosperity of the underlying offense."[50] This theory of "promotion" helps the government most where the entire scheme is criminal in nature, like a Ponzi scheme. "'When a business as a whole is illegitimate, even individual expenditures that are not intrinsically unlawful can support a promotion money laundering charge.'"[51] Thus, for example, in *United States v Bolden*, 325 F.3d 471 (4th Cir. 2003), promotion and concealment laundering were charged based on transactions that were alleged to allow the defendants to evade Medicaid's regulatory requirements and charge Medicaid inflated costs. The defendants attempted to argue that the payments involved were for legitimate expenses, but the court found that they were part of "a sham business, used solely to deceive Medicaid" and thus were "'integral to the success'" of the scheme.[52]

Where criminal conduct is conducted through a legitimate enterprise, courts may not be willing to find that all business expenses paid in the ordinary course of legal business operations constitute promotion.[53] Thus, for example, if only some doctors within a legitimate health care clinic are scamming Medicare, the payment of the clinic's rent and ordinary salary payments are not likely to be conceived of as promotion laundering. In such circumstances, however, prosecutors may make a promotion case based on payments made to those doctors participating in the fraud to compensate them for their nefarious work or continued participation.

---

50. *Krasinski*, 545 F.3d at 551.
51. United States v. Miles, 360 F.3d 472, 478 (5th Cir. 2004).
52. *Bolden*, 325 F.3d at 489.
53. *See, e.g.*, *Miles*, 360 F.3d at 477.

3. Promotion of a Past Crime

Another prosecutorial theory that threatens to make money laundering virtually indistinguishable from the underlying criminal conduct—and thus chargeable in many if not most white-collar cases—concerns the "promotion" of the completed underlying criminal conduct. The issue, which has arisen in both transaction and transportation offenses, is whether a defendant can be convicted for *promoting* a *completed* crime, or whether he can only be convicted where there is proof that he is seeking to "promote" the commission of *future* "specified unlawful activity." The Second, Third, Fifth, Sixth, and Ninth Circuits hold defendants can be convicted for "promoting" the completed underlying criminal activity, while the Fourth, Eighth, and Eleventh Circuits refuse to accept such pleadings.[54]

A representative transaction case is *United States v. Paramo*, 998 F.2d 1212 (3d Cir. 1999). In *Paramo*, an employee of the IRS sent fictitious tax refund checks through the mails to his co-conspirator, Paramo. Paramo picked up the checks and deposited them in his own bank account. This clearly constituted mail fraud, but is it money laundering? The "transaction" charged here was the deposit of the fraudulently obtained tax refund check. The mail fraud was complete upon the receipt of the check so this deposit is a qualifyingly separate transaction from that which generated any proceeds.

Could one pursue this under a "concealment" theory? No, because Paramo deposited it in his own account and made no other obvious efforts to hide the funds. Do we have evidence that Paramo then used the funds to promote further criminal wrongdoing? No, for all we know it remains in his account today. So how did the government secure a money laundering conviction on these facts? The government's theory was that the transaction—the deposit of the embezzled checks—was necessary to the realization of the profit from the underlying crime. That is, the deposit of the money *promoted the completed mail fraud*.

Paramo, of course, argued that the underlying offense that generated the proceeds—the mail fraud—was complete as of the mailing of the checks and thus that he could not be convicted of money laundering for "promoting" a completed crime. The Third Circuit rejected this argument, holding "because Paramo believed cashing the checks was necessary to realize any

54. *Compare, e.g.*, United States v. Valuck, 286 F.3d 221, 226 (5th Cir. 2002) ("we categorically reject any suggestion . . . that a financial transaction cannot promote a completed illegal activity for purposes of section 1956(a)(1)(A)(i)."); *Piervinanzi*, 23 F.3d at 679; United States v. Paramo, 998 F.2d 1212, 1217-18 (3d Cir. 1993); United States v. Montoya, 945 F.2d 1068, 1076 (9th Cir. 1991), *abrogated on other grounds* in McCormick v. United States, 500 U.S. 257 (1991); with United States v. Jolivet, 224 F.3d 902, 909 (8th Cir. 2000) ("We find no logic in the government's suggestion that Jolivet could promote the carrying on of an already completed crime."); United States v. Heaps, 39 F.3d 479, 484-85 (4th Cir.1994), *abrogated on other grounds by* United States v. Cabrales 524 U.S. 1 (1998).

benefit from the mail fraud, the jury could infer he cashed each check to promote the carrying on of the antecedent fraud."[55]

In the majority of circuits, then, prosecutors can charge a "promotion" money laundering case any time the defendant conducts a financial transaction such as depositing tainted monies in his own bank account or otherwise converting to useable form the proceeds of his crime, even if he is doing so openly and with no intent to conceal. For example, if a corrupt politician deposits his ill-gotten gains in his bank account, in most circuits a money laundering case can be made on the theory that the deposit "promoted" the completed bribery violation because the deposit transaction was necessary for the defendant to realize the benefit of the corrupt scheme.

G. Conspiracy Under § 1956(h)

Section 1956(h) states that anyone who conspires to commit an offense defined in § 1956 or § 1957 "is subject to the same penalties as those prescribed for the offense which was the object of the conspiracy." Congress enacted this specialized conspiracy provision in part to give prosecutors the option of obtaining a greater sanction than that available in run-of-the-mill conspiracies charged under § 371, which carries a statutory maximum penalty of five years' imprisonment.

In *Whitfield v. United States*, 543 U.S. 209 (2005), the Supreme Court held that a conviction for conspiracy to commit money laundering under § 1956(h) does not require proof of an overt act in furtherance of the conspiracy. It also made clear that this conspiracy offense is a stand-alone crime, separate from the substantive money laundering offenses in the same statute.

As discussed in Chapter 5 (Conspiracy) the essence of a conspiracy charge is the defendant's agreement to commit a crime. Just what does that agreement have to encompass in money laundering cases? In *United States v. Stravroulakis*, 952 F.2d 686 (2d Cir. 1992), the issue presented was whether a conspiracy to violate 18 U.S.C. § 1956(a)(3) required that the co-conspirators believe that the money to be laundered is derived from the same specified unlawful activity. In that case, the defendants argued that the defendants did not agree on the essential nature of the conspiratorial plan because one of the conspirators believed the cash stemmed from narcotics transactions while the other believed the money came from illegal gambling.

The Second Circuit held that, "so long as the unlawful source is proven to be one of the illegal activities enumerated in § 1956(c)(7), it is not

---

55. *Paramo*, 998 F.2d at 1217.

essential that the conspirators agree on the same illegal activity."[56] It reasoned that "Section 1956 creates the crime of money laundering, and it takes dead aim at the attempt to launder dirty money. Why and how that money got dirty is defined in other statutes. Section 1956 does not penalize the underlying unlawful activity from which the tainted money is derived."[57] Because the focal point of the statute is the laundering, the court ruled, all the conspirators need agree on is the plan to launder the money, regardless of its alleged source.

H. Extraterritorial Application and Correspondent Banking Transactions

As is discussed at length in Chapter 2 (General Part), the Supreme Court has adopted a very strong presumption against applying federal statutes extraterritorially. Because many federal statutes do not speak in terms to their geographic reach, the presumption will, in many instances, confine the applicability of federal criminal statutes to domestic cases. Sections 1956 and 1957 are unusual in that Congress expressly made them extraterritorial in scope, giving federal prosecutors a useful and malleable statute with which to address overseas criminal conduct.

Section 1956(f) provides that there is exterritorial jurisdiction over conduct prohibited by § 1956 if (1) the conduct is by a U.S. citizen or, in the case of a non-U.S. citizen, "the conduct occurs in part in the United States," and (2) the transaction or series of related transactions involves funds or monetary instruments of a value exceeding $10,000. In short, Congress sought to limit extraterritorial jurisdiction "to situations in which the interests of the United States are involved, either because the defendant is a U.S. citizen or because the transaction occurred in whole or in part in the United States."[58] The $10,000 jurisdictional limit was intended to ensure that extraterritorial jurisdiction "is confined to significant cases."[59]

Although the Department of Justice does not generally require prosecutors to seek DOJ approval before commencing money laundering prosecutions, it does require approval from the DOJ's Money Laundering and Asset Recovery Section prior to commencing an investigation based solely on the extraterritorial jurisdiction provisions of § 1956 and § 1957.[60]

---

56. *Stravroulakis*, 952 F.2d at 691.
57. *Id.*
58. S. Rep. No. 99-433, at 14 (1986).
59. *Id.*
60. *See* Justice Manual, *supra* note 4, § 9-105.300(1).

Extraterritorial prosecutions under § 1956 are readily available if the defendant is a U.S. person. But the DOJ has also used § 1956 against foreign nationals who commit their underlying crimes abroad. Such cases are possible not only because the statute provides an express grant of extraterritoriality, but also because Congress included crimes against foreign states as SUAs that can serve as the foundation of money laundering prosecutions. It is clear that the defendant foreign nationals need not physically be in the United States to satisfy the statute.[61] But if prosecutors wish to proceed against non-U.S. nationals under § 1956, they must identify a qualifying "financial transaction" or a transportation of funds or monetary instruments across a U.S. border that "*occurr[ed] in part in the United States*."

Courts agree that

> [a] transfer from a foreign account to an account in a U.S. financial institution and a transfer from a U.S. account to a foreign financial institution occur in part in the United States under 18 U.S.C. § 1956(f). Further, the legislative history of the statute indicates that Congress intended the provision to apply to situations where 'a person transfers by wire the proceeds of a [crime] from a bank in the United States to a bank in a foreign country.[62]

What troubles many defense lawyers, however, is the the DOJ's position that electronic funds transfers (EFTs) through U.S. *correspondent accounts* "occur in part in the United States."[63] The defense bar complains that this vastly—and unfairly—expands federal prosecutors' international reach. To understand the implications of this position, a brief and highly simplified primer on correspondent banking transactions may be helpful.

In short, correspondent accounts are used to facilitate transborder transactions between banks that do not have a direct relationship. For example, if a Turkish company maintains its accounts at a Turkish bank and wants to make a payment in dollars to a supplier's account at an Indian bank, and the Turkish and Indian bank do not have a direct relationship, the Turkish bank will send the funds through a correspondent bank with which it has a relationship, and that correspondent bank will send it on to the Indian bank if the correspondent bank has a relationship with it. Thus, a typical transaction may proceed as follows:

Turkish Bank transfers funds ➔ Bank of America transfers funds ➔ Indian Bank

61. *See* United States v. Rafoi, 60 F.4th 982, 998 (5th Cir. 2023).

62. United States v. All Assets Held at Bank Julius, 251 F. Supp. 3d 82, 93 (D.D.C. 2017) (quoting S. Rep. 99–443, at 14 (1986)) (collecting cases) (definition of term "transaction" in § 1956(c) indicates that Congress intended § 1956 to cover Electronic Funds Transfers (EFTs)).

63. *See id.* at 93-96 (EFTs through a U.S. correspondent account occur in part in the United States).

If the first correspondent bank, here Bank of American, does not have a relationship with the Indian bank, it will send the money to another correspondent bank with which the Indian bank does have a relationship, assume Wells Fargo, and Wells Fargo will complete the transfer to India.

Turkish Bank transfers funds ➔ Bank of America transfers funds ➔ Wells Fargo transfers funds ➔ Indian Bank

These transactions can take place in many different currencies but because the U.S. dollar is frequently used in international business, dollar payments account for about half of correspondent banking transactions, and the majority of these transactions are done through U.S. correspondent accounts. Given the dominance of the U.S. financial system, prosecutors looking to find a financial transaction or transportation upon which to ground a money laundering case can often find a transfer of funds through a U.S. correspondent account—even if that transfer only spends nanoseconds on "U.S. wires" to make its electronic journey.

Defendants have objected that what looks like two transfers—that is, movement from the Turkish Bank to Bank of America and from Bank of America to the Indian bank—is truly one transfer from Turkey to India. The movement of the money is virtually instantaneous in many cases. They argue that, in general, the payor in Turkey and the payee in India have no idea how the transfer between banks is achieved and do not much care; the journey the money takes is thus not something that the defendants know about, elect, or intend. It is, in effect, collateral to the substance of the transaction and should not serve as the basis for criminal jurisdiction.

To date, however, defense objections have been unsuccessful. The handful of courts to decide the question have found that correspondent banking transactions through U.S. banks are sufficient to satisfy both the statute's requirement of a "financial transaction"[64] and § 1956(f)'s mandate that the transaction or transfer "occur in part in the United States."[65] As one court explained in an analogous context, "international wire transfers do not merely 'ricochet' off of U.S. correspondent banks," but rather, use such banks "as indispensable conduits" and involve "two separate transactions that cross the U.S. border."[66]

64. *See, e.g.*, United States v. Ho, 984 F.3d 191, 204-07 (2d Cir. 2020).

65. *See All Assets Held*, 251 F. Supp. 3d at 93-96 (electronic funds transfers through a correspondent bank account in the United States occur in part in the United States).

66. United States v. Prevezon Holdings, Inc., 251 F. Supp. 3d 684, 693 (S.D.N.Y. 2017).

II. ENGAGING IN A TRANSACTION IN CRIMINALLY DERIVED PROPERTY UNDER 18 U.S.C. § 1957

To secure a conviction under § 1957, the government must prove beyond a reasonable doubt that the defendant:

- knowingly engaged or attempted to engage
- in a monetary transaction
- in criminally derived property with a value of more than $10,000
- knowing that the property was derived from unlawful activity, and
- the property was, in fact, derived from "specified unlawful activity"

The terms "proceeds" and "specified unlawful activity" bear the same meaning as they do under § 1956 (§ 1957(f)(3)).

To understand § 1957's utility, it helps to focus on what it does *not* require in the way of proof. It does *not* require the government to show that the defendant actually laundered the funds or intended to promote or conceal unlawful activity. It does not require that the defendant even know that others are engaging in the transaction to promote or conceal unlawful activity. The most significant difference between § 1957 and § 1956 cases, then, is that § 1957 contains no intent requirement. In such prosecutions, the intent requirements have been replaced with a $10,000 threshold amount for each transaction and a requirement that a financial institution be involved.

The congressional intent under § 1957 was to make it difficult for wrongdoers to enjoy their ill-gotten gains because it is the *use* of criminal proceeds in any qualifying transaction that is illegal. Thus, as the Ninth Circuit has explained:

> [Section 1957] is a powerful tool because it makes any dealing with a bank potentially a trap for the drug dealer or any other defendant who has a hoard of criminal cash derived from the specified crimes. If he makes a "deposit, withdrawal, transfer or exchange" with this cash, he commits the crime; he's forced to commit another felony if he wants to use a bank. This draconian law, so powerful by its elimination of criminal intent, freezes the proceeds of specific crimes out of the banking system.[67]

Congress also intended to deter people, including ordinary citizens with no connection to criminal activity, from engaging in even ordinary

67. United States v. Rutgard, 116 F.3d 1270, 1291 (9th Cir. 1997).

commercial transactions with people they suspect of involvement in criminal activity.

A. Monetary Transaction

The central element of a § 1957 case is a "monetary transaction," which means the deposit, withdrawal, transfer, or exchange in or affecting interstate or foreign commerce of funds or a monetary instrument by, through, or to a financial institution.[68] Like § 1956, this definition includes a jurisdictional element but, unlike § 1956, the definition requires that the transaction involve a "financial institution." In practice, this is not terribly limiting because "financial institutions" include not only banks and credit unions, but also a broad array of other businesses such as car, plane, and boat dealerships, pawn brokers, stockbrokers, travel agents, and persons involved in real estate closings.[69]

The statute states that a "monetary transaction" "does not include any transaction necessary to preserve a person's right to representation as guaranteed by the sixth amendment to the Constitution."[70] Because this provision is limited by what the Supreme Court has said the Sixth Amendment counsel right encompasses, it is generally read as limited to the payment of the defendant's own attorney's fees in a criminal case.[71] Thus, the government cannot charge that a transaction a defendant initiates to pay his lawyer is illegal under § 1957, even if that transfer contains tainted money.

B. Mens Rea and Criminally Derived Property

Section 1957(a) states that a defendant who knowingly engages or attempts to engage in a monetary transaction in "criminally derived property of a value greater than $10,000 and is derived from specified unlawful activity" under the circumstances laid out by statute is guilty of a felony. The term "criminally derived property" means "any property constituting, or derived from, proceeds *obtained from* a criminal offense" (§ 1957(f)(2) (emphasis added)).

---

68. *See* 18 U.S.C. § 1957(f)(1).

69. Under 18 U.S.C. § 1956(c)(6), the term "financial institution" includes (A) any financial institution, as defined in 31 U.S.C. § 5312(a)(2), or the regulations promulgated thereunder; and (B) any foreign bank, as defined in section 1 of the International Banking Act of 1978 (12 U.S.C. § 3101). The businesses identified in the above text can be found in 31 U.S.C. § 5312(a)(2).

70. 18 U.S.C. § 1957(f)(1).

71. *See, e.g.*, United States v. Blair, 661 F.3d 755, 771 (4th Cir. 2011).

The definition of "specified unlawful activity" is the same in § 1956 and § 1957 (§ 1957(f)(3)). The requirement that the property "is derived from specified unlawful activity" means that the statute may not be used for prosecuting persons caught up in a government sting operation, at least where the money supposedly laundered consists entirely of government (and thus presumably untainted) money.

Again, proof of "knowledge" of the illicit nature of the funds may be based upon a defendant's "willful blindness" or "conscious avoidance" of positive knowledge. In § 1957(c), Congress decreed that "[i]n a prosecution for an offense under this section, the government is not required to prove the defendant knew that the offense from which the criminally derived property was derived was specified unlawful activity."

Note that § 1957 specifies that the proceeds must be "obtained" from the criminal conduct, which courts have read to connote "possession of a thing."[72] Courts are rigorous, then, in requiring that "the proceeds of the crime be in the defendant's possession before he can attempt to transfer those proceeds in violation of § 1957."[73]

C. Extraterritorial Application

Section 1957 cases can be brought when the offense (1) takes place in the United States or in the special maritime and territorial jurisdiction[74] of the United States; or (2) takes place outside the United States and such special jurisdiction, but the defendant is a "United States person,"[75] meaning, *inter alia*, a U.S. national,[76] an alien admitted for permanent residence, any person within the United States, and corporations organized under U.S. law.[77]

III. ILLEGAL MONEY TRANSMITTING BUSINESSES UNDER 18 U.S.C. § 1960

Congress augmented § 1956 and § 1957 by prohibiting illegal money transmitting businesses in 18 U.S.C. § 1960. Congress was concerned that drug dealers were increasingly using non-bank financial institutions such

72. *Piervinanzi*, 23 F.3d at 677.
73. *Id.*; *see also* United States v. Gregg, 179 F.3d 1312, 1315 (11th Cir. 1999).
74. *See* 18 U.S.C. § 7 (special maritime and territorial jurisdiction of the United States defined).
75. *See id.* § 3077(2) (defining U.S. person).
76. *See* 8 U.S.C. § 1101(a)(22) ("national" of the United States).
77. *See* 18 U.S.C. § 1957(d).

as money transmitters, check cashers, and foreign exchange dealers to launder and move the proceeds of their drug sales. Section 1960 was drafted to address this perceived hole in the anti-money laundering effort.

Section 1960(a) prohibits conducting, controlling, managing, supervising, directing, or owning all or part of an unlicensed money transmitting business. The critical term, "money transmitting" is defined to include "transferring funds on behalf of the public by any and all means including but not limited to transfers within this country or to locations abroad by wire, check, draft, facsimile, or courier" (§ 1960(b)(2)). Violations of § 1960 are punishable by a fine, imprisonment of not more than five years, or both.

To secure a conviction under this section, the government must prove that the defendant:

- knowingly
- conducted, controlled, managed, supervised, directed or owned all or part of
- a "money transmitting business"[78]
- that affects interstate commerce in any manner or degree and
- is operated as an "unlicensed" money transmitting business, meaning
  - "without an appropriate money transmitting license in State where such operation is punishable as a misdemeanor or a felony under State law, whether or not the defendant knew that the operation was required to be licensed or that the operation was so punishable" (§ 1960(b)(1)(A)),
  - the business fails to comply with applicable federal money transmitting business requirements[79] (§ 1960(b)(1)(B)), or
  - "otherwise involves the transportation or transmission of funds that are known to the defendant to have been derived from a criminal offense or are intended to be used to promote or support unlawful activity" (§ 1960(b)(1)(C)).[80]

Note that unlike sections 1956 and 1957, § 1960 is not tied to a list of "specified unlawful activities" and thus potentially applies to defendants who transmit funds derived from, or in support of, *all* types of federal (and perhaps state or foreign) crimes. And in cases in which the violation is established by the operation of the unlicensed money transmission business in violation of state licensing or federal regulations (under § 1960(b)(1)(A),

78. *See* 31 U.S.C. § 5330(d)(2) (definition of "money transmitting service").
79. *See* 31 U.S.C. § 5330 ("Regulation of money transmitting businesses") and regulations proscribed thereunder.
80. *See* United States v. Bankman-Fried, 680 F.Supp. 3d 289, 311-13 (S.D.N.Y. 2023).

(B)), there is no need to show that the funds being transferred are in any way tainted by crime.

Stated in colloquial terms, "a money transmitting business receives money from a customer and then, for a fee paid by the customer, transmits that money to a recipient in a place that the customer designates,"[81] often outside the United States. Paradigmatic money transmitters are Western Union and PayPal, but § 1960 applies more broadly to include, as detailed below, cryptocurrency transfers and hawala exchanges.

Courts have construed the phrase "on behalf of the public" to mean that the money transmission "occur within a transactional, business dealing or for a member of the broader community rather than within a personal or close relationship."[82] And because an unlicensed money transmitting "business" must be proved, there must be multiple transmissions.[83] Section 1960 only applies to businesses transferring funds that "affect interstate or foreign commerce." In the rare instance where a company only transfers funds within state lines and is not using any form of federal infrastructure, this section would not apply.

A "money transmitting service" includes "not only a transmission of actual currency, but also a transmission of the value of that currency through some other medium of exchange. Nowhere does this definition purport to suggest that a 'money transmitting service' includes only transmissions of actual cash or currency."[84]

The Financial Crimes Enforcement Network ("FinCEN") regulates money transmitters and has issued guidance clarifying when virtual currency exchangers constitute "money transmitters" under its regulations. In short, "[t]he term 'money transmission services' means the acceptance of currency, funds, or other value that substitutes for currency from one person *and* the transmission of currency, funds, or other value that substitutes for currency *to another location or person* by any means."[85] "Transmitting" generally covers accepting virtual currency from one person and sending it on to another, exchanging fiat currency for digital currency or one kind of digital currency for another, and payment processing that involves receiving virtual currency from a vendor's customers and passing fiat currency on to the vendor. Merely accepting currency, funds, or value in exchange for

81. United States v. Velastegui, 199 F.3d 590, 592 (2d Cir. 1999); *see also* United States v. Talebnejad, 460 F.3d 563, 565 (4th Cir. 2006).
82. *Singh*, 995 F.3d at 1077-78.
83. *See Velastegui*, 199 F.3d at 595 n.4; *see also* United States v. Banki, 685 F.3d 99, 114 (2d Cir. 2012).
84. United States v. E-Gold Ltd., 550 F. Supp. 2d 82, 94 (D.D.C. 2008) (quoting 31 U.S.C. § 5330(d)(2)).
85. 31 C.F.R. § 1010.100(ff)(5)(i)(A) (emphasis added).

the provision of goods and services, however, does not qualify as money transmitting.[86]

Thus, an Internet "digital currency" exchange is a "money transmitting business" under § 1960.[87] Courts interpreting the meaning of "money transmitting" (§ 1960(b)(2), "money transmitting business," (31 U.S.C. § 5330(d)(1)), and "money transmitter" (31 C.F.R. § 1010.100(ff)(5)) in other criminal cases have held that:

> [Section] 1960(b)(1)(B) reaches unlicensed operations reaping a commission from exchanging traditional for digital currency . . . ; [an] unlicensed Darknet market that "received cash deposits from . . . customers and then, after exchanging them for Bitcoins, transferred those funds to the customers' accounts" hosted by the market . . . (describing Silk Road)[;] and an online "bank" and "payment processor" that hosted accounts holding virtual currency and processed transactions in virtual currency . . . (describing Liberty Reserve).[88]

The government has relied upon § 1960 to pursue such high-profile targets such as Sam Bankman-Fried and Binance.com, which was one of the the world's large cryptocurrency exchanges and was forced to plead guilty to, *inter alia*, violating § 1960. Binance.com, which had to pay over $4 billion to resolve the case, was alleged to have knowingly facilitated millions of dollars of unlawful cryptocurrency transactions between U.S. persons and those subject to U.S. sanctions.

Section 1960 is particularly useful in dealing with informal money systems such as hawala, a payment system widely used in the Middle East and South Asia for international funds transfers. Although hawala takes many forms, it is generally characterized as a network of hawala brokers or dealers, called hawaladars, who transfer funds from point to point without using formal money transmission channels (banks) and without the physical movement of money. A client may give the funds he wishes to transfer to a hawala broker who will reach out to another broker near the place where the money is to be delivered. The second hawala broker will arrange for delivery of the fund (less fees) in the appropriate currency to the designated recipient. The hawala brokers will then arrange to settle their accounts usually without the actual transfer of funds; they engage in a number of mechanisms to balance their credits and debits, including such practices as invoice manipulation.[89]

---

86. *See id.* § 1010.100(ff)(5)(ii)(F).
87. *See E-Gold*, 550 F. Supp. 2d at 97.
88. *Harmon*, 474 F. Supp. 3d at 102.
89. For example, assume a hawaladar in the United States has arranged for a hawala broker in India to deliver $10,000 to a customer in that country. He now needs to make the Indian

The system is characterized by trust and discretion. The transfers are accomplished with minimal documentation; hawaladars may maintain a log of debts and remittance records only until the debt is paid or the remittance transaction completed. The transfer fees are cheaper than those charged by banks and the transactions are informal and unregulated.

> Hawala is widely used in communities that have limited access to formal banking structures and, for example, is an important vehicle for remittance payments from immigrants to family members in their home countries. But because of its informality, lack of record keeping and government oversight, hawala may be used to transfer illegally derived funds.[90]

The government has used § 1960 to prosecute hawaladars.[91]

A. Section 1960(b)(1)(A)

Section 1960(b)(1)(A) renders liable those who conduct a money transmitting business and operate without an appropriate State money transmitting license. The section expressly states that "such operation" must be punishable as "a misdemeanor or a felony under State law." Prior to the amendment of the statute in 2001, courts held that the defendant must know that the business was an "illegal" money transmitting business—that is, one that was intentionally operated without an appropriate license. Congress amended the statute, however, to clarify that the government does not need to prove that "the defendant knew that the operation was required to be licensed or that the operation was so punishable" (§ 1960(b)(1)(A)). The defendant need only know that he was operating a money transmitting business that was unlicensed.[92] A number of circuits have rejected due process challenges to the statute's lack of a more demanding mens rea.[93]

---

broker whole for this payment in a discrete way and without actually transferring or delivering money through a financial institution. The U.S. hawaladar may do so by under-invoicing, whereby he arranges to send the Indian broker $20,000 worth of goods that that broker wants. The U.S. hawaladar ships the merchandise with an invoice for $10,000. When the Indian broker sends payment of $10,000, having received $20,000 worth of merchandise, their accounts have been settled.

90. *Singh*, 995 F.3d at 1073.

91. *See, e.g.*, *id.*; *Banki*, 685 F.3d 99.

92. *See Talebnejad*, 460 F.3d at 566; *see also* United States v. Elfgeeh, 515 F.3d 100, 132-33 (2d Cir. 2008).

93. *See, e.g.*, *Talebnejad*, 460 F.3d at 568-70; United States v. Dimitrov, 546 F.3d 409, 414-15 (7th Cir. 2008).

B. Section 1960(b)(1)(B)

"Unlawfulness" under § 1960(b)(1)(B) requires proof that the money transmitting business was unlicensed in that it was not registered with the Treasury Department's Financial Crimes Enforcement Network (FinCEN) as required by 31 U.S.C. § 5330. Again, in term of mens rea, the defendant must have known that he or she was operating a money transmitting business and know that the business did not have a license or registration.[94] But this is a general intent crime and does not require proof that the defendant knew of the federal registration requirement.

Examples

1. Josefa Alves was a real estate agent who showed a vacation home to Ellis Bevan. Bevan put an offer on the house, which was listed for $200,000, of $200,000 contingent upon the sellers accepting $100,000 in cash and the closing documents reflecting a purchase price of $100,000. The sellers accepted the deal, and Alves and the selling agent agreed to it on the condition that their commissions were adjusted so that they received the same amount for selling a house supposedly worth $100,000 as they would for a $200,000 house at closing. Bevan secured (apparently legitimately) a mortgage for the remaining $100,000. Bevan, who wished to put the property in his parents' names, explained to Alves that his parents wouldn't accept this gift from him unless they thought he got a real deal on the property. Alves told the sellers' agent after the closing—at which Bevan produced the $100,000 in a brown paper bag stuffed with $20 bills—that she thought Bevan was a drug dealer. Can Alves be convicted of money laundering under § 1956 and § 1957?

2. Daragh Domhnaill owned a property upon which he had taken out two mortgages. After the building on the property burned down, Domhnaill mailed a claim to his insurance company in which he sought recovery for the loss of machinery that was not in fact on the property when the blaze occurred, significantly and fraudulently inflating the insurance pay-out he claimed. Assume that this constitutes mail fraud (18 U.S.C. § 1341) and the fraud was complete the moment Domhnaill mailed in his fraudulent claim. The insurance company issued a check payable to Domhnaill and the two mortgage holders for $260,000.

   Domhnaill talked to the bank manager at his local SunTrust account and the manager told him that, to deposit the check, he needed the two mortgage holders to endorse it. Instead, Domhnaill used the

94. *Talebnejad*, 460 F.3d at 572; *see also* United States v. Keleta, 441 F. Supp. 2d 1, 12 (D.D.C. 2006).

drive-through window and told the teller that the manager had told him orally that Domhnaill's endorsement alone was sufficient. The teller accepted the deposit of the check into Domhnaill's SunTrust bank account without the endorsements of the two mortgage holders. The insurer's bank, Wells Fargo, honored the check and the total amount was transferred out of the insurer's account. Assume that Domhaill thereby committed bank fraud on Wells Fargo (18 U.S.C. § 1344). Note that the Supreme Court has held that banks have a property interest in their depositors' accounts, and thus the fraudulent diversion of customer funds is a qualifying fraud.

Domhnaill then withdrew the entire $260,000 in cash and deposited the funds in a college saving account in his spouse's maiden name at another bank.

Can the government also charge Domhaill with money laundering under 18 U.S.C. § 1956 and § 1957?

3. Il-Seong Gim operated two pain management clinics in the name of Pain Management Inc. in two cities in Texas. He billed state and federal health insurance programs Medicare, Medicaid, and Tricare, for services that were misrepresented to be medically necessary, misrepresented the treatments actually administered to ensure that they were covered, and billed for office visits that did not happen. Gim trained and instructed his employees to perform and fraudulently bill for the same services. Assume that his is therefore guilty of health care fraud under 18 U.S.C. § 1347.

   An FBI agent has put together an analysis showing Gim's receipt and spending of the tainted funds over the course of a five-year period. It established that Gim transferred some of the proceeds of the fraudulent billing scheme from his clinics' operating accounts to his own investment accounts and used tainted funds to purchase property in his name. He also used some of the proceeds of the fraud to pay for business operations, including buying vans used to transport patients to and from his pain management clinics and making irregular payments and loans to the employees participating in the fraud. Can Gim be prosecuted under § 1956 and § 1957?

4. Christina Rolysson worked in the audit department of Beta Bank. After auditing the bank's wire transfer department, she identified weaknesses in its functioning. She decided to exploit that weakness and enlisted a friend, Ile Stefanov, with a bank account in the Cayman Islands to help her. Rolysson made a $2 million wire transfer from a customer account at Beta to Stefanov's account in the Caymans. Assume that Rolysson and Stefanov are guilty of bank fraud under 18 U.S.C. § 1344. Can this transfer also be charged as money laundering under § 1956?

5. Jiang Yu, a citizen of Hong Kong, was the CEO of Beta, Corp., a Chinese oil company. Yu bribed Gérald Monet, the Interior Minister of Narnia, for his help in securing leases for oil wells in Narnia. At Monet's request, the bribe took the form of a supposed charitable contribution to an organization run by Monet's wife. Yu and Monet had a meeting in New York to discuss the payment arrangements. The charity maintains an account at Xanadu Bank in Narnia. Yu caused $500,000 to be wired from Beta's account at HSBC Hong Kong to the charity's account at Xanadu Bank. Because HSBC Hong Kong and Xanadu Bank do not have a relationship, the money was transferred from HSBC Hong Kong to its U.S. correspondent bank, HSBC New York, which then transferred the funds to Xanadu Bank's correspondent bank in the United States, Deutsche Bank New York, before finally arriving in the charity's Xanadu account. Assume that the government believes it can indict Yu for violating the Foreign Corrupt Practices Act (FCPA) but the FCPA does not authorize prosecutions against the corrupt foreign official. Can Monet be prosecuted under § 1956?

6. Neil Durnin operated an underground market on the "Silk Road" website. The Silk Road was designed to operate like eBay: sellers would post goods or services for sale on the website and buyers would purchase the items, which would then be shipped to them. Users left ratings that encouraged others to rely on its vendors. The Silk Road differed from eBay in at least two important respects: (1) this marketplace was only available to those using Tor, a software and network that allows for anonymous, untraceable Internet browsing; and (2) payments could only be made through Bitcoin. The government alleges that the Silk Road was used by narcotics traffickers, hackers, and others to purchase and sell illegal commodities and services.

   To use and hold Bitcoin, purchasers are not required to provide a name, bank account, ID, social security number or name. The payment and receipt of Bitcoin are recorded on Bitcoin's decentralized ledger, also known as the blockchain. When using Bitcoin, the only identifying information for an illicit transaction would be the address of the person receiving the goods, a problem solved by using anonymous P.O. boxes. Silk Road would act as an escrow service between buyer and seller, holding the Bitcoin exchanged, and would profit from commissions taken from every transaction.

   Durnin operated a market in Bitcoin on the Silk Road. He received cash deposits from his customers and then, after exchanging them for Bitcoin, transferred those funds to the customers' Bitcoin wallets on Silk Road, which acted as a third-party agent for a fee. Can the government charge him with operating an unlicensed Money Transmitting Business under 18 U.S.C. § 1960?

Explanations

1. *Section 1956.* The closing on the house qualifies as a financial transaction and it seems clear that the transaction is designed, in whole or in part, to disguise the nature or origins of Bevan's money.[95] This could be inferred from the unusual nature of the transaction. Although Bevans provided an explanation, it is hard to ignore the fact that it allows the buyer to, on paper, spend only $100,000 and get title in others' names to a property worth $200,000—thus disguising the fact that he has converted $100,000 in cash into valuable property. An alternative concealment theory would be that Bevans sought to hide the property by putting it in his parents' names. Trafficking in drugs is a SUA and the $100,000 is stipulated to be drug money, so the transaction in fact involved the proceeds of a SUA. The critical issue here is whether Alves meets the mens rea requirements of a transaction concealment charge.

   Alves does not need to know that Bevan is in fact a drug dealer. She need only know that the money involved in the closing is the proceeds of "some form of unlawful activity." In a case like this, the government is likely to rely on a willful blindness theory to prove that she knew that the transaction was designed to launder. The jury would be asked to infer that she closed her eyes to what otherwise should be obvious given the nature of the transaction and the $100,000 in $20's carried in a brown paper bag to the closing. Alves's statement to the sellers' agent would be the red flag that would secure such a willful blindness jury instruction.

   There is no allegation that Alves was the moving force in designing this transaction or that she in fact intended to conceal the provenance of the money. But the concealment theory does not require that Alves share Bevan's intent—simply that she knew about it. (By contrast, in a transaction promotion case, the government must prove that the defendant actually intended to promote SUA).

   Section 1957. One might at first wonder how the government can prove a "monetary transaction" given that the definition of that term requires the presence of a "financial institution" in the mix. Here, there is no indication that Bevan committed any wrongdoing in securing the mortgage through his bank. But a "financial institution" is defined very broadly to include persons involved in real estate closings and settlements.[96] Thus the closing itself is a transaction in

95. *See, e.g.*, United States v. Campbell, 977 F.2d 854 (4th Cir. 1992).

96. "Monetary transactions" under § 1957 means funds transferred by, through, or to a "financial institution." Section 1957(f)(1) adopts the definition of "financial institution" set forth in § 1956(c)(6), which in turn refers, in part, to 31 U.S.C. § 5312(a)(2). Section 5312(a)(2)(U) defines a "financial institution" to include "persons involved in real estate closings and settlements."

criminally derived property with a value exceeding $10,000. The government would argue that Alves was at the least willfully blind to the illicit nature of the cash Bevans was using to obtain the property, and the $100,000 in fact represents the proceeds of SUA in the form of drug dealing.

2. These facts are designed to illustrate two recurring "timing" problems in § 1956 money laundering cases: (1) discerning when the underlying crime was sufficiently complete to throw off proceeds such that the laundering is a transaction discrete from the underlying crime (the answer to this query depends on the underlying crime alleged); and (2) whether one can "promote" a completed crime (the answer depends on one's circuit). It is also designed to show that the government can avoid potential temporal problems through its charging choices; for example, in this case, by charging that the victim of the bank fraud is Wells Fargo, not Suntrust.

   Section 1956. Deposits and withdrawals of checks and cash constitute financial transactions under the statute. Mail and bank fraud are SUAs. Domhnaill knew that all these transactions involved the proceeds of some kind of unlawful activity—he is the person who crafted the fraudulent insurance claim and knowingly made an end-run around bank rules to deposit the check. And all the transactions would in fact involve the proceeds of specified unlawful activity (mail fraud). Whether the government can show the qualifying knowledge and intent (concealment or promotion) depends on the transaction at issue.

   Deposit of insurance check. If the alleged SUA that generated the tainted proceeds was the mail fraud, the crime would be complete when Domhnaill mailed in the fraudulent claim. The subsequent deposit into the SunTrust account would constitute a distinct transaction involving the proceeds of the fraud. The question would then become whether the government could prove that this transaction was motivated by a desire to conceal the proceeds of the fraud or to promote a crime. Given that Domhnaill deposited the check in his own account at his local bank branch, no intent to conceal likely could be proven. Depending upon the circuit, however, the government may charge that the deposit of the check "promoted" the completed mail fraud because, absent such a deposit, Domhnaill could not have reaped the benefits of his crime. The circuits are split on whether transaction laundering can be charged on the theory the transaction promoted a completed crime.

   If the SUA that generated the tainted proceeds was instead alleged to be to the bank fraud, the crime would not be complete until the insurance check was wrongfully deposited; the deposit, then, would be the point at which the defendant secured the proceeds of the crime. Because the same transaction cannot be charged as the transaction that generates the proceeds and the transaction that launders the proceeds of the crime, this cannot ground a money laundering count.

Withdrawal of cash. If the alleged SUA that generated the tainted proceeds was the mail fraud, the withdrawal is certainly a financial transaction in the proceeds of the mail fraud. Whether such a large cash withdrawal—in light of the subsequent deposit in an account bearing another's name—would evidence an intent to conceal would be a jury question. As discussed above, the D.C. Circuit would likely find that this single transaction would be easy to trace and thus no intent to conceal can be inferred.[97] Perhaps the government could again argue that the withdrawal also "promoted" the completed mail fraud because, absent the withdrawal, Suntrust could have discovered the error and frozen the funds, thus depriving Domhnaill of the benefits of his crime. Because this theory of "promotion" is itself a stretch—rejected by a number of circuits—such a theory seems questionable at best; courts may accept that the laundering transaction—the initial deposit—promoted the mail fraud but subsequent transactions may be viewed as simply too attenuated.

If instead the SUA that generated the tainted proceeds was alleged to be the bank fraud, the defense would likely argue the bank fraud was not complete when the insurance proceeds were deposited into his account; the crime was only complete upon withdrawal because it was only then Suntrust suffered a property loss, i.e., the amount it would have to pay the mortgage holders for allowing Domhnaill to wrongfully deposit the money without their endorsement. Domhnaill would therefore argue that a laundering case cannot proceed based on the withdrawal transaction because the proceeds would be realized in the same transaction as the alleged laundering.

The government would respond that it is not charging that Suntrust was defrauded. Instead, the charge is that Domhnaill knowingly executed a scheme or artifice to defraud the insurer's bank, Wells Fargo, and that that fraud was clearly complete upon deposit. It was at that point that the funds that were supposed to go to the mortgage holders were obtained by Domhnaill. Because banks have a property interest in their depositor's accounts, this would deprive the insurer, and thus Wells Fargo, of that portion of the funds that were supposed to go to the mortgage holders.

The government would likely prevail in its argument that the bank fraud on Wells Fargo was complete when Domhnaill successfully and fraudulently deposited the insurance check. The subsequent withdrawal was a separate transaction and thus could constitute a laundering

97. *See Adefehinti*, 510 F.3d at 323.

transaction. The government would likely fail to prove an intent to conceal for the same reason discussed above. It may, however, be able to argue that because it is the withdrawal (not, as in the mail fraud case, the deposit) that constitutes the laundering transaction, it promoted the underlying bank fraud by allowing Domhnaill to secure and safeguard the proceeds of his bank fraud.

The deposit of cash into the wife's account. The cash was the proceeds of both the mail and bank fraud. A promotion argument based on the above theory is likely unavailable. But concealment could be a viable option. Domhnaill might persuade a jury that simply putting cash into one's kid's college account, which is under one's spouse's name, does not demonstrate an effort to conceal the funds. The fact that the account is in his wife's maiden name makes it a closer case. Ultimately, the government would be best served by attempting to bolster its showing of Domhnaill's intent to conceal.

Section 1957. All of these transactions—the deposit, withdrawal, and re-deposit of these funds—could be charged under § 1957 because Domhnaill knowingly engaged in three monetary transactions in "criminally derived property," meaning "any property constituting, or derived from, proceeds" obtained from an SUA (§ 1957(f)(2)), with a value of more than $10,000. Domhnaill knew that the property was derived from unlawful activity and the funds were in fact the proceeds of specified unlawful activities, to wit, mail and bank fraud.

3. *Section 1956.* Although § 1347 is not a RICO predicate and thus is not an SUA under § 1956(c)(7)(A), and does not appear under the code sections expressly identified by Congress as SUAs in § 1956(c)(7)(D), it is included as an SUA under the general description "any act or activity constituting an offense involving a Federal health care offense" (§ 1956(c)(7)(F)). The FBI's analysis traces the funds used in the transactions at issue and demonstrates that the transactions in fact involve the proceeds of SUA. The potential transactions in these proceeds include the withdrawals from Gim's business account; the deposit of funds into his investment accounts; the purchase of the vans; and the payments and loans extended to his employees. All of these are likely qualifying financial transactions. Because Gim was the author of the scheme, he knew that these amounts were derived from some form of unlawful activity.

   The question is whether the government should proceed on a "concealment" theory, a "promotion" theory, or both. In the case upon which this hypothetical was drawn, *United States v. Valdez*, 726 F.3d 684 (5th Cir. 2013), the Fifth Circuit found the evidence insufficient to prove concealment laundering because all the transactions in property and investments were done openly in the defendant's name; he did not use "false names, third parties, or any particularly complicated financial maneuvers, which are usual hallmarks of an intent to conceal."[98] The court reasoned that it is generally not enough for the government to prove that moving the money around—at least in this limited way—made it more difficult to trace and thus demonstrated an intent to conceal. Rather, the government must prove that the transactions "had the purpose, not merely the effect, of" making it harder for the government to identify the dirty funds.[99]

This problem illustrates another of our temporal problems: whether transactions made during the course of a crime can be said to promote it. Since Congress's amendment to the statute recognizing that "proceeds" can include gross receipts, courts accept that transactions in which the defendant pays business expenses necessary to facilitate an ongoing criminal scheme can constitute promotion laundering. These cases are easiest when the business as a whole is criminal or illegitimate because transactions involving even the most ordinary of business expenses—for example for rent and salaries—can qualify as promotion of the ongoing crime.

With respect to a promotion theory, Gim would argue that the purchase of the vans and the payments to employees were simply legitimate business expenses, relying on cases ruling that such transactions are insufficient to support a promotion money laundering case. As noted, this promotion theory becomes more difficult for the government in cases where there is a facially legitimate business and only some of its activities are criminal. In such cases, courts appear to require some proof that these otherwise seemingly legitimate payments were made specifically to reward subordinates involved in the unlawful scheme or were not in fact legitimate business-related payments. In *Valdez*, for example, the court found that the supposed "payroll" payments were "very irregular," and were made only to those employees who were responsible for essential elements of the fraud (doing the billing, giving the treatments), thus permitting the inference that these payments "to secure loyalty and cooperation in the fraudulent scheme."[100] The court did not address the purchase of the vans but this transaction is unlikely to be viewed as promotion laundering unless the vans were intended to directly facilitate the fraudulent activity rather than the general business of the clinic.

Section 1957. The transfer of the tainted money to Gim's investment account, the purchase of property, and the purchase of the vans[101] would all constitute "monetary transactions" in "criminally derived property"

98. *Valdez*, 726 F.3d at 690.
99. *Id.*
100. *Id.* at 691.
101. See *supra* note 96 for the definitions of monetary transactions and financial institutions. Section 5312(a)(2)(T) defines a "financial institution" to include persons involved in vehicle sales.

with a value of more than $10,000. Gim knew that the property was derived from unlawful activity and the funds were in fact the proceeds of specified unlawful activities, to wit, health care fraud.

4. *Section 1956.* The wire transfer of money would constitute both a qualifying financial transaction under § 1956(a)(1) and a transportation of funds over a U.S. border for purposes of § 1956(a)(2). The transfer of the money to an offshore account in a third party's name in a jurisdiction notorious for its strict bank secrecy laws could be characterized as concealment laundering. The immediate problem, however, is a temporal one: can the transfer of the funds out of the customer account—which is the transaction that constitutes bank fraud—also be characterized as the transfer that launders the proceeds of the bank fraud by putting the money in another name and beyond the reach of U.S. authorities? Can one wire transfer both constitute the crime and the laundering of it? Generally speaking, the answer is "no." The transaction that constitutes the crime must be complete before the laundering transaction can occur.

   All is not lost, however. Recall that transportation promotion cases (§ 1956(a)(2)(A)) are different from transaction promotion cases in that there is no requirement that the transportation "in fact involve[]" the proceeds of SUA; the statute is satisfied where clean money is sent across a U.S. border to promote a SUA. A transportation case could be made out because the money was transferred over a U.S. border; the question is whether such a transfer "promoted" specified unlawful activity. In *United States v. Piervinanazi*, 23 F.3d 670 (2d Cir. 1994), the court affirmed the defendants' conviction on similar facts on the theory that the transaction—the deposit of the purloined funds in the Caymans—promoted the completed crime of bank fraud by making it possible for the defendant to obtain the proceeds of the fraud and to hide it from U.S. authorities. Again, there is a split in the circuits on whether promotion offenses can be founded on promotion of a past crime or whether the government must prove that the transaction or transportation promoted additional, future criminal activity.

   Section 1957. Section 1957 criminalizes knowingly engaging in a monetary transaction in "criminally derived property" that is of a value greater than $10,000 and is derived from SUA. "Criminally derived property" is defined in 1957(f)(2) to mean "any property constituting, or derived from, proceeds *obtained* from a criminal offense" (emphasis added). Courts hold that the word "obtained" entails "possession of a thing" and "'property' implies ownership, or the 'exclusive right to possess, enjoy, and dispose of a thing.'"[102] Thus, the proceeds of the crime

102. *Piervinanzi*, 23 F.3d at 677.

have to be in the defendant's possession before he can attempt to transfer the proceeds in violation of 1957. A § 1957 cases would fail here because the transaction through which the money was "obtained" was the same transaction—the wiring to the offshore account—that is alleged to be the unlawful monetary transaction.

5. There is no evidence that the money used for the bribe was the proceeds of any crime. As a result, the government would have to turn to the one provision that does not require that the transaction/transportation involve the "proceeds" of specified unlawful activity: transportation promotion laundering. Here, the government may charge that funds were transferred over a U.S. border with the intent to promote the SUA of a violation of the Foreign Corrupt Practices Act (15 U.S.C. § 78dd-3).[103] Alternatively, if the court finds this theory questionable because Monet himself could not be charged under the FCPA, the government could charge as the SUA an offense against a foreign nation involving "bribery of a public official" (§ 1956(c)(7)(B)(iv)).

   Section 1956(a)(2) requires, in relevant part, proof that the defendant "transport[ed], transmit[ed], or transfer[ed]" (or attempted to do so) funds "*from* a place in the United States to or through a place outside the United States or *to* a place in the United States from or through a place outside the United States" (emphasis added). Monet will argue that there was no cognizable transfer of funds across the U.S. border because the wiring of the funds does not qualify as a wiring "to" or "from" the United States under § 1956(a)(2), and going "through" the United States by virtue of the correspondent account transfers does not satisfy the statutory terms. He will assert that a movement of funds from one foreign account to another is a single extraterritorial transfer, regardless of the technical movement of funds through U.S. correspondent accounts. The Second Circuit, at least, has rejected this statutory construction argument, concluding "that [a] charged wire transfer, which took advantage of U.S.-based correspondent accounts to conduct a dollar-denominated transaction is [not] barred from coverage under § 1956(a)(2)(A)."[104]

   The specified unlawful activity here concerns extraterritorial conduct—that is the bribery of a foreign public official by a foreign citizen. Courts would likely accept the argument that extraterritorial jurisdiction is appropriate under § 1956(f) because the transaction (exceeding

---

103. *See* Chapter 9 (Corruption) (Yu could be liable under 15 U.S.C. § 78dd-3 because, by virtue of the co-conspirators' meeting in New York, he took action in furtherance of the bribe in U.S. territory). *See* Chapter 9 (Corruption).

104. United States v. Ho, 984 F.3d 191, 204 (2d Cir. 2020).

$10,000) "occur[red] in part in the United States" by virtue of the movement of funds through U.S. correspondent accounts.

6. The first issue is whether Bitcoin qualifies as "funds" for purposes of § 1960. A number of judges have addressed this question, and they have (to date) concluded that Bitcoin does qualify as "funds" for purposes of § 1960. The parties have invited the courts to consult a variety of dictionary definitions and have sometimes referenced federal agencies' (e.g., the IRS's) definitions of related concepts in other contexts. At bottom, the courts have concluded that Bitcoin qualifies as "funds" because it is "'something generally accepted as a medium of exchange, a measure of value, or a means of payment.'"[105] Thus in *United States v. Faiella*, 39 F. Supp. 3d 544 (S.D.N.Y. 2014), Judge Rakoff ruled that Bitcoin "clearly" constitutes "money" or "funds" for purposes of the statute because "Bitcoin can be easily purchased in exchange for ordinary currency, acts as a denominator of value, and is used to conduct financial transactions."[106]

   The second issue is whether running a Bitcoin exchange constitutes running a "transmitting" business. The distinction drawn here is between businesses that merely sell Bitcoin and those that sell money transmitting services to others. The parties often reference the Financial Crimes Enforcement Network's (FinCEN's)[107] guidance in this respect: "[t]he term 'money transmission services' means the acceptance of currency, funds, or other value that substitutes for currency from one person *and* the transmission of currency, funds, or other value that substitutes for currency *to another location or person* by any means."[108] Thus, Durnin would be a money transmitter if he transmits Bitcoin *to another location or person for his customers*.[109] At least one court has rejected an argument that this transmitting business definition requires proof that the transmitting was done for a profit.[110]

   If all Durnin did was sell merchandise in return for payments in Bitcoin,[111] he is not a money transmitter. But, in *Faiella*, the court found that the defendant satisfied the statutory definition because he did more

105. United States v. Murgio, 209 F. Supp. 3d 698, 707 (S.D.N.Y. 2016) (quoting United States v. Faiella, 39 F. Supp. 3d 544, 545 (S.D.N.Y. 2014)); *see also Ulbricht*, 31 F. Supp. 3d at 569-70 (exchanges of Bitcoin in online marketplace constitute "financial transactions" for purposes of § 1956).
106. *Faiella*, 39 F. Supp. 3d at 545.
107. According to its website, "FinCEN is a bureau of the U.S. Department of the Treasury. . . . FinCEN's mission is to safeguard the financial system from illicit use and combat money laundering and promote national security through the collection, analysis, and dissemination of financial intelligence and strategic use of financial authorities."
108. 31 C.F.R. § 1010.100(ff)(5)(i)(A) (emphasis added).
109. *See Murgio*, 209 F. Supp. 3d at 711; *see also Faiella*, 39 F. Supp. 3d at 546 & n.3.
110. *Murgio*, 209 F. Supp. 3d at 711.
111. *See* 31 C.F.R. § 1010.100(ff)(5)(ii)(F).

than that; he received cash deposits from his customers and then, after exchanging those funds for Bitcoin, transferred the funds to the customers' Silk Road accounts. Another court characterized the necessary role as being that of a "middle man." Instead of just buying and selling cryptocurrency, a "money transmitter," as a middle man, typically facilitate transfers between virtual currency wallets or process payments between parties.[112]

112. Murgio, 209 F. Supp. 3d at 714.

CHAPTER 12

Grand Jury Investigations and the Fourth Amendment

Because many, if not most, federal white-collar cases are investigated through the grand jury, this chapter focuses on both the screening and the investigative functions of the grand jury. It addresses the standards that govern prosecutors' use of the grand jury and potential defense challenges to indictments returned by that body. These materials cover the rules that apply to the issuance of grand jury subpoenas ad testificandum (testimonial subpoenas) and duces tecum (subpoenas for non-testimonial evidence such as documents and electronically stored information (ESI)) and discuss some of the tactical challenges that arise in investigations conducted through the grand jury from the perspective of the government and the defense. It explains in some depth the Fourth Amendment issues that arise in this context and summarizes the applicable Fifth Amendment law (which is covered in greater depth in Chapter 14). In so doing, we cover the Fourth Amendment challenges the government faces in securing critical evidence protected by the Stored Communications Act. This chapter concludes by briefly discussing the means by which prosecutors (and the defense) attempt to secure competent evidence from overseas sources.

We should begin with the basics. Petit juries, also known as trial juries, decide both criminal and civil cases. To secure a conviction in a criminal case, a petit jury of twelve persons must unanimously decide that the government met its burden of proving beyond a reasonable doubt that the defendant committed the crime(s) charged.

Grand jurors are called to service in much the same was as petit jurors, but their experience and functions are very different. (Throughout these materials I will describe the particulars of federal grand juries rather than attempt to survey all state jurisdictions.)

- A grand jury hears only criminal cases.
- It consists of 16 to 23 members[1] and boasts a quorum with 16 members present.
- Its "verdict" need not be unanimous. The grand jury can return an indictment by majority vote.
- The grand jury applies a probable cause, not a beyond a reasonable doubt, standard. Prosecutors call witnesses and present other evidence to the grand jury, and the grand jury issues an indictment if it concludes that there is probable cause to believe that a crime was committed and the defendant committed it.
- A grand jury operates in secret. In federal matters, the prosecutor, the grand jurors, the court reporter, and any translator are required to keep confidential "matter[s] occurring before the grand jury."[2] Only

1. Fed. R. Crim. P. 6(a)(1).
2. *Id.* 6(e)(2)(B).

the witness can talk about such matters without fear of criminal or civil sanction.

- The grand jury is an ex parte proceeding; the defense has no right to contest the government's case. Only the grand jurors, the prosecutor, the court reporter, any required translator, and the witness can be present during a grand jury proceeding. Defense counsel cannot be present. Nor can witnesses be accompanied into the grand jury room by their lawyer.
- Grand jurors generally serve for specified periods of time up to 18 months but can serve longer if an extension is granted by a judge. Depending on the nature of the grand jury, they may meet every day or only periodically during their term of service.
- Grand jurors normally consider multiple cases over the course of their term of service.
- Double jeopardy does not attach during grand jury proceedings.[3] The protections afforded by the Double Jeopardy Clause "are implicated only when the accused has actually been placed in jeopardy. This state of jeopardy attaches when a jury is empaneled and sworn, or, in a bench trial, when the judge begins to receive evidence."[4] By contrast, on the very rare occasions that the grand jurors fail to return an indictment (referred to as a "no true bill" or, in earlier times, as an "ignoramus"), there is no double jeopardy or other legal bar to the government returning to the grand jury and re-presenting the case.

The grand jury is a unique device in our federal system. In theory, "it belongs to no branch of the institutional Government, serving as a kind of buffer or referee between the Government and the people."[5] In reality, it is supervised by the courts and directed by prosecutors. The district court selects the grand jurors, impanels them, supervises them, discharges them, conducts any hearings required on grand jury leaks or disqualification of jurors, and the court's processes are required to compel production of subpoenaed testimony or documents. Federal prosecutors participate in the voir dire, give the grand jury instructions on its general operation and standards, instruct the jury on the law, and largely direct and control the grand jury's investigatory function.

The grand jury is said to have two functions, acting as (1) a screening device, and (2) an investigative body.

3. *See* U.S. Const., amend. V.
4. United States v. Martin Linen Supply Co., 430 U.S. 564, 569 (1977).
5. United States v. Williams, 504 U.S. 36, 47 (1992).

I. SCREENING FUNCTION

The Fifth Amendment provides that "no person shall be held to answer for a capital, or otherwise infamous crime, unless on a presentment or indictment of a grand jury."[6] In federal court, then, the accused have a Fifth Amendment right to be indicted by a grand jury for felony offenses. The Fifth Amendment grand jury right is one of the very few criminal procedure guarantees in the Bill of Rights that is not incorporated into the Due Process Clause of the Fourteenth Amendment and thus does not apply to the states.[7] All states provide for grand juries but only about half use them, preferring to screen criminal cases through preliminary hearings.

An indictment, also called a "true bill," is a charging document signed by the government attorney and by the grand jury foreperson if the jury, by majority vote, finds that there is probable cause to believe that a crime was committed and that the charged defendant committed it. A charging document called an "information" can be entered by the prosecutor without consultation with the grand jury in misdemeanor cases. An information is also the charging document used when a defendant waives his right to a grand jury indictment in a felony case.

In exercising its screening function, the task of the grand jury is to "serv[e] the invaluable function in our society of standing between the accuser and the accused, whether the latter be an individual, minority group, or other, to determine whether a charge is founded upon reason or dictated by an intimidating power or by malice and personal ill will."[8] In particular, the grand jury is supposed to serve as a "protective bulwark standing solidly between the ordinary citizen and an overzealous prosecutor."[9] In point of fact, it is believed that federal grand juries return a true bill in over ninety-nine percent of the cases presented to them.

The grand jury's power, although broad, is limited by its screening function, that is, determining whether to indict or decline a case presented to it:

> [T]he grand jury cannot be used solely to obtain additional evidence against a defendant who has already been indicted. Nor can the grand jury be used solely for pre-trial discovery or trial preparation. After indictment, the grand jury may be used if its investigation is related to a superseding indictment of additional defendants or additional crimes by an indicted defendant.[10]

---

6. U.S. Const., amend. V.
7. *See* Hurtado v. California, 110 U.S. 516 (1884).
8. Wood v. Georgia, 370 U.S. 375, 390 (1962).
9. United States v. Dionisio, 410 U.S. 1, 17 (1973).
10. U.S. Dept of Justice, Justice Manual, § 9-11.120 [hereinafter Justice Manual].

A. Rules Relating to Evidence

Because the grand jury is simply a screening device, the Court has rejected rules that would "effectively transform such proceedings into preliminary trials on the merits."[11] In particular, the rules of evidence do not apply in grand jury proceedings. One important consequence is that hearsay is admissible in grand jury proceedings.[12] The government may choose to rely on hearsay testimony, rather than calling the out-of-court declarant, to limit the burden on witnesses, to facilitate an efficient presentation, or to limit the effectiveness of cross-examination should the out-of-court declarant later testify at trial.[13]

The exclusionary rule proscribing the use of evidence seized in violation of the Constitution in the government's case-in-chief does not apply in the grand jury.[14] Thus, evidence seized in violation of the subject's Fourth, Fifth, or Sixth Amendment rights can be used to secure an indictment but not a conviction.

The government has no obligation to seek or provide the grand jury with exculpatory evidence. And, in *United States v. Williams*, 504 U.S. 36 (1992), the Supreme Court held that the federal courts' supervisory powers over the grand jury do not include the power to promulgate a local rule allowing the dismissal of an otherwise competent indictment where the prosecutor has failed to introduce materially exculpatory evidence to the grand jury.[15]

The Supreme Court has explained that "[t]he same rules that, in an adversary hearing on the merits, may increase the likelihood of accurate determinations of guilt or innocence do not necessarily advance the mission

---

11. United States v. R. Enterprises, Inc., 498 U.S. 292, 298 (1991).

12. *See* Costello v. United States, 350 U.S. 359, 359 (1956); *see also* Justice Manual, *supra* note 10, § 9-11.232 ("Each United States Attorney should be assured that hearsay evidence presented to the grand jury will be presented on its merits so that the jurors are not misled into believing that the witness is giving his or her personal account.").

13. As we shall see in Chapter 13 (Discovery), if a trial witness appears in the grand jury, the government will have to turn over to the defense the transcript of that witness's grand jury testimony for impeachment use at trial. If, however, another witness—typically a government agent—instead simply relates to the grand jury what the witness told him, the agent's hearsay testimony is not deemed a statement of the witness that must be produced for impeachment. In those circumstances, the transcript need only be produced if the agent takes the stand at trial.

14. *See* United States v. Calandra, 414 U.S. 338, 351-52 (1974). *But see* Justice Manual, *supra* note 10, § 9-11.231 ("A prosecutor should not present to the grand jury for use against a person whose constitutional rights clearly have been violated evidence which the prosecutor personally knows was obtained as a direct result of the constitutional violation.").

15. *See Williams*, 504 U.S. at 55. *But see* Justice Manual, *supra* note 10, § 9-11.233 ("[W]hen a prosecutor conducting a grand jury inquiry is personally aware of substantial evidence that directly negates the guilt of a subject of the investigation, the prosecutor must present or otherwise disclose such evidence to the grand jury" before seeking an indictment of such person).

of a grand jury, whose task is to conduct an *ex parte* investigation to determine whether or not there is probable cause to prosecute a particular defendant."[16] "Strict observance of trial rules in the context of the grand jury's preliminary investigation 'would result in interminable delay but add nothing to the assurance of a fair trial.'"[17] As a result, "[a]n indictment returned by a legally constituted and unbiased grand jury, like an information drawn by the prosecutor, if valid on its face, is enough to call for trial of the charge on the merits."[18] Courts will not allow an indictment to be challenged "on the ground that there was inadequate or incompetent evidence before the grand jury."[19]

B. Persons Present and Grand Jury Secrecy

Fed. R. Crim. P. 6 governs the conduct of grand jury proceedings. It provides that the only people who may be present while the grand jury is in session are "attorneys for the government, the witness being questioned, interpreters when needed, and a court reporter or an operator of a recording device."[20] This means that counsel may not accompany her client into the grand room, parents cannot accompany testifying children, and marshals cannot be admitted to control a potentially unruly witness.

Fed. R. Crim. P. 6 also contains the grand jury's secrecy mandate. The confidentiality of the proceedings serves a number of distinct interests. First, "by preserving the secrecy of the proceedings, we assure that persons who are accused but exonerated by the grand jury will not be held up to public ridicule."[21] Second, there are a variety of instrumental rationales:

> If preindictment proceedings were made public, many prospective witnesses would be hesitant to come forward voluntarily, knowing that those against whom they testify would be aware of that testimony. Moreover, witnesses who appeared before the grand jury would be less likely to testify fully and frankly, as they would be open to retribution as well as to inducements.[22]

Secrecy also limits the risk that those about to be indicted will flee the jurisdiction or attempt to tamper with evidence or witnesses.

---

16. *R. Enterprises*, 498 U.S. at 298.
17. *Id.*
18. *Costello*, 350 U.S. at 363; *see also* Kaley v. United States, 571 U.S. 320, 328 (2014).
19. *Costello*, 350 U.S. at 363.
20. Fed. R. Crim. P. 6(d)(1).
21. Douglas Oil Co. v. Petrol Stops Northwest, 441 U.S. 211, 219 (1979).
22. *Id.*

Fed. R. Crim. P. 6(e)(2)(B) requires that everyone involved in the grand jury proceedings (government attorneys, jurors, court reporters, and translators) except the witnesses must not "disclose" "a matter occurring before the grand jury" unless one of the exceptions set forth in Rule 6(e) applies. This seemingly simple mandate has given rise to a great deal of fact-specific litigation over what constitutes a "disclosure"[23] and how "a matter occurring before the grand jury" is defined.[24] Examples of "matters occurring before the grand jury" include:

> (1) transcripts of the testimony of witnesses and statements made before the grand jury; (2) internal governmental memoranda that reflect what transpired before the grand jury; (3) witness interviews and auditor's analyses that have been prepared for grand jury use; and (4) information which reveals the identities of witnesses or jurors, the substance of the testimony or evidence, and the deliberations or questions of the grand jury.
>
> In addition, courts have interpreted the secrecy requirement to apply not only to information that has been drawn from transcripts of grand jury proceedings, but also to anything that may tend to reveal what transpired before the grand jury.
>
> As a general proposition, however, physical evidence, such as a document, does not become secret merely because it has been presented to a grand jury, if it was created for purposes other than the grand jury investigation and its disclosure does not reveal matters occurring before the grand jury.[25]

One often used exception provides that a court can order disclosure under Fed. R. Crim. P. 6(e)(3)(E)(i) preliminarily to or in connection with a judicial proceeding. After 9/11, Congress amended Rule 6(e) to add a very broad exception permitting a government attorney, without court order, to "disclose any grand-jury matter involving foreign intelligence, counterintelligence . . ., or foreign intelligence information . . . to any federal law enforcement, intelligence, protective, immigration, national defense, or national security official to assist the official receiving the information in the performance of that official's duties."[26]

Most circuits (except the Fourth) hold that a "proceeding to enforce the secrecy mandate of Rule 6(e)(2) . . . may be initiated by a private plaintiff,"

---

23. *See* United States v. John Doe, Inc. I, 481 U.S. 102 (1987) (a government attorney involved in a grand jury may make continued use of grand jury materials if she is subsequently involved in civil phase of the same or related matter without obtaining court approval because there is no "disclosure" in such circumstances).

24. *See, e.g.*, In re Sealed Case No. 99-3091 (Office of Independent Counsel Contempt Proceeding), 192 F.3d 995 (D.C. Cir. 1999).

25. In re Grand Jury Investigation (90-3-2), 748 F. Supp. 1188, 1207-08 (E.D. Mich. 1990).

26. Fed. R. Crim. P. 6(e)(3)(D); *see also id.* 6(e)(3)(D)(iii) (definition of "foreign intelligence information").

who is usually the target of the investigation aggrieved by the grand jury leak.[27] In certain circumstances—where for example a grand juror discloses grand jury information to the targets of the investigation—the leaking party may be prosecuted for obstruction or other crimes.[28]

II. INVESTIGATIVE FUNCTION

The grand jury is an expensive and awkward investigative body. Where a case can be investigated by agents using other means, the grand jury is generally used only to indict, as in many street crime cases. But the grand jury does provide important investigative advantages, particularly in the secrecy it offers and in the coercive power of grand jury subpoenas. As a consequence of these circumstances and others discussed within, most federal white-collar cases are investigated at least in part by the grand jury.

Cases in which secrecy in the conduct of the investigation is important will often be investigated through a grand jury. The most obvious example is organized crime cases, in which the safety of witnesses is a likely concern. But the secrecy of the proceedings can also be useful in complex, large-scale white-collar cases in which the government would like a cooperating witness to remain undiscovered or otherwise wishes to keep its cards close to its chest.

The coercive power of the grand jury is critical because people generally have no obligation to cooperate with an investigation. They can decline to provide information, whether in the form of oral statements or physical or digital evidence. Federal investigators and prosecutors do not, by virtue of their offices, have the power to compel people to comply with their requests. But they can leverage the coercive power of the grand jury by issuing grand jury subpoenas to compel the production of documents and other physical or electronically-stored evidence (subpoenas duces tecum) and the attendance of the witness who will provide sworn testimony (subpoenas ad testificandum).

Traditionally, the Supreme Court has given grand juries license to "paint with a broad brush."[29] The grand jury "can investigate merely on suspicion that the law is being violated, or even just because it wants assurance that it is not."[30] Thus a grand jury subpoena does not have to be supported, as are warrants, by probable cause because "the very purposes of requesting

27. In re Sealed Case No. 98-3077, 151 F.3d 1059, 1069 (D.C. Cir. 1998). *But see* Finn v. Schiller, 72 F.3d 1182, 1188 (4th Cir. 1996).
28. *See, e.g.*, United States v. Brenson, 104 F.3d 1267 (11th Cir. 1997).
29. *R. Enterprises*, 498 U.S. at 287.
30. United States v. Morton Salt Co., 338 U.S. 632, 642-43 (1950).

the information is to ascertain whether probable cause exists."[31] Grand jury subpoenas can also reach overseas: federal courts are authorized to order the issuance of subpoenas to nationals or residents of the United States who are in a foreign country, requiring their appearance as witnesses or the production of documents or other evidence.[32] These are powerful devices: the failure to obey a grand jury subpoena may be deemed contempt of court[33] and those held in contempt for such failure may be fined or jailed until they comply.[34]

Although denominated as grand jury subpoenas, government attorneys usually draft and issue the subpoenas without necessarily consulting with the grand jury. In white-collar cases, the government attorney normally would negotiate a mutually agreeable date and time for witnesses to appear and testify before the grand jury. Where a subpoena duces tecum is issued, the parties may negotiate to limit the scope of the subpoena, for example by identifying search terms to be used by the defense in scouring databases for responsive materials. The subpoenaed party may often be asked to produce the responsive materials to the investigating agent or the prosecutor rather than to the grand jury itself.

A. Subpoenas Duces Tecum (Documents and Other Objects)

A subpoena duces tecum can be used to secure a wide variety of non-testimonial evidence, including the types of materials necessary to make business crime cases (e.g., bank records, financial information, calendars, tax worksheets, travel documentation, emails, texts, and other communications, and handwritten documents). Prosecutors will use subpoenas duces tecum to secure evidence from those under investigation. But subpoenas may also be used to secure information held by third parties who legally cannot or, for business reasons would prefer not to, comply voluntarily.

The subpoenaed party may make an objection to the scope of the subpoena on Fourth Amendment grounds. The responsive materials may also be withheld if they are subject to a valid claim of privilege, such as the attorney-client privilege, the work product doctrine, or the Fifth Amendment privilege against compelled self-incrimination. In such cases, the subpoenaed

31. *R. Enterprises*, 498 U.S. at 297.

32. *See* 28 U.S.C. § 1783(a); *see also id.* § 1784; Fed. R. Crim. P. 17(e)(2).

33. *See* Fed. R. Crim. P. 17(g); *see also* 28 U.S.C. § 1784.

34. *See* Armstrong v. Guccione, 470 F.3d 89 (2d Cir. 2006) (constitutional and statutory rights not violated by seven-year incarceration for civil contempt for failing to comply with a subpoena).

party is usually expected to document such assertions by providing a privilege log to the government.

1. The Government Perspective

Prosecutors can secure a search warrant for physical or electronically stored evidence, but search warrants are more difficult and time consuming to obtain than subpoenas. Subpoenas can be issued without any showing of cause and without the oversight of the judiciary. With one constitutional[35] and various statutory exceptions,[36] prosecutors can issue a subpoena to hunt down information in an "investigation . . . triggered by tips, rumors, evidence proffered by the prosecutor, or the personal knowledge of the grand jurors."[37] As we shall see, *infra*, a search warrant, by contrast, requires the government to demonstrate to a judicial officer probable cause to believe that the evidence exists in the place indicated. The government must also particularly describe the place to be searched and the items to be seized, which is a more stringent limitation than that applied to test the Fourth Amendment bona fides of a subpoena.

From the government's point of view, serving a subpoena duces tecum for the evidence sought is more efficient and, assuming there are no concerns about witness tampering or document destruction, just as effective. Indeed, in many white-collar cases *someone* will have to cull through thousands of emails or a wealth of other documentation to find the relevant records; a subpoena puts that burden on the party served, rather than, in the case of a warrant, on government agents. And, while the execution of warrants often generates public notice, the fact that a grand jury subpoena has been served is not often publicized by the recipient. One downside of a subpoena, however, is that the defense can lodge a Fifth Amendment objection to the compelled act of producing the required materials but cannot resist a search warrant on Fifth Amendment grounds.[38]

2. The Defense Perspective

The defense also enjoys certain benefits when the government proceeds by subpoena rather than by warrant. Defense counsel cull that which is responsive to the subpoena rather than having government agents make the cut after searching the client's files and databases. This gives the defense the

35. *See* Carpenter v. United States, 585 U.S. 296 (2018), discussed *infra*.
36. *See, e.g.*, The Stored Communications Act (SCA), 18 U.S.C. § 2703, discussed *infra*.
37. *Calandra*, 414 U.S. at 344.
38. *See* Chapter 14 (Fifth Amendment).

ability to object to the scope of the search, and assert applicable privileges *before* the government sees the materials at issue; objections to a search warrant's validity or agents' seizure of privileged materials can only be made after the fact, often in a post-indictment suppression hearing. Indeed, the defendants cannot assert their Fifth Amendment right against compelled self-incrimination to resist execution of the warrant, but they can litigate such claims in response to a subpoena. Finally, the defense often also prefers the secrecy provided by grand jury investigations rather than enduring the public spectacle of agents in raid jackets carrying boxes of materials out of corporate headquarters.

3. The Fourth Amendment

The Fourth Amendment provides as follows:

> [1] The right of the people to be secure in their persons, houses, papers, and effects, against unreasonable searches and seizures, shall not be violated, and [2] no Warrants shall issue, but upon probable cause, supported by Oath or affirmation, and particularly describing the place to be searched, and the persons or things to be seized.

Corporations and other artificial entities can claim rights under the Fourth Amendment.[39] (This in contrast to the Fifth Amendment, which, as we shall see below, such entities cannot claim.)

The reasonableness clause ([1] above) requires that anything that is defined by the Court as a "search" or a "seizure" must be reasonable. The warrant clause ([2] above) lays out the requisites of a valid search or arrest warrant: (a) probable cause, (b) supported by oath or affirmation (c) particularly describing the place to be searched or the persons or things to be seized. It is crucial, however, to understand that the Court reads these two clauses separately. That is, to be constitutionally "reasonable," a qualifying search or seizure does not necessarily require a warrant in every case. For example, the Supreme Court has decreed that arrests in public places and car searches generally do not require a warrant but, absent consent or exigent circumstances, the police need a warrant to cross the threshold of a private home.

The definition of what constitutes a Fourth Amendment "search" is critical because government actions need only be "reasonable" when the defendant proves that the government has conducted a qualifying "search." Unfortunately, what constitutes a "search" within the meaning of the Fourth

39. *See, e.g.*, Hale v. Henkel, 201 U.S. 43 (1906).

Amendment cannot be determined by reference to the dictionary definition of the term.[40]

As we shall see below, in 1886 the Court held that government subpoenas duces tecum constitute Fourth Amendment "searches" and later articulated a standard of reasonableness in that particular context that focused on whether the subpoena was overbroad and oppressive. This line of precedent did not intersect with the analysis the Court employed in all other cases, presumably because the Court believed that there was a significant difference between situations in which the parties themselves searched and produced the materials required by the subpoena and cases in which government agents conducted what was often a much more invasive and disruptive alleged "search."

In the latter category of cases, the question of whether government conduct constitutes a "search" turns on whether the agents invaded the subject's "reasonable expectation of privacy." In the landmark case of *Carpenter v. United States*, 585 U.S. 296 (2018), the Court opened up the possibility that the "reasonable expectation of privacy" standard might also be employed to test what process ought to be applied to subpoenas seeking the disclosure of sensitive information from third parties.

a. General Overbreadth Standard

In a hoary case whose other holdings have been overruled every which way but Sunday, *Boyd v. United States*, 116 U.S. 616 (1886),[41] the Court held a subpoena duces tecum effectuates a Fourth Amendment "search" and thus that the Fourth Amendment applies to court orders in the nature of subpoenas duces tecum in the same manner in which it applies to search warrants. This means that a Fourth Amendment objection is open to those who receive grand jury subpoenas for the production of documents and other tangible things. (Note that, perhaps anomalously, a *testimonial* subpoena is not deemed to be a Fourth Amendment "search or seizure" of the person and thus no Fourth Amendment objection is possible.[42]).

---

40. A Fourth Amendment *seizure* takes place with respect to *property* when the governmental action interferes with the suspect's property or possessory interests in a meaningful way. *See, e.g.*, United States v. Karo, 468 U.S. 705, 712 (1984). With respect to *seizures of persons*, "[a] person is seized by the police and thus entitled to challenge the government's action under the Fourth Amendment when the officer, by means of physical force or show of authority, has in some way restrained [their] liberty," Terry v. Ohio, 392 U.S. 1, 19 n.16 (1968), or, stated differently, when "in view of all of the circumstances surrounding the incident, a reasonable person would have believed that he was not free to leave." United States v. Mendenhall, 446 U.S. 544, 554 (1980); *see also* Torres v. Madrid, 592 U.S. 306 (2021).

41. *See, e.g.*, Fisher v. United States, 425 U.S. 391, 400-01 (1976) (Fifth Amendment analysis does not turn on whether the government is forcing the production of "private" books and papers); Warden v. Hayden, 387 U.S. 294, 301, 310 (1967) (overruling mere evidence rule).

42. *See Dionisio*, 410 U.S. at 9.

One of the ways that *Boyd* has been overruled is in its articulation of what constitutes an "unreasonable" subpoena duces tecum. In *Hale v. Henkel*, 201 U.S. 43 (1906), the Court abandoned the *Boyd* standard and held that the test of a subpoena's Fourth Amendment "reasonableness" turns only on whether it is "far too sweeping in its terms to be regarded as reasonable."[43] In *See v. Seattle*, 387 U.S. 541 (1967), the Court elaborated, holding that, with respect to grand jury or administrative subpoenas, "the Fourth Amendment requires that the subpoena be sufficiently limited in scope, relevant in purpose, and specific in directive so that compliance will not be unreasonably burdensome."[44] In general, if a subpoena has temporal and subject-matter limitations, it will be found reasonable.

The subject of a subpoena can also seek relief under Fed. R. Crim. P. 17(c), which governs the issuance of subpoenas duces tecum in federal criminal proceedings. The Rule provides that "[o]n motion made promptly, the court may quash or modify the subpoena if compliance would be unreasonable or oppressive." In *United States v. R. Enterprises*, 498 U.S. 292 (1991), the Supreme Court declined to adopt the reasonableness standard it applies to trial subpoenas—that is, requiring reasonably specific requests for information that would be both relevant and admissible at trial.[45] The *R. Enterprises* Court instead decreed that when a subpoena is challenged under Rule 17 on relevancy grounds, "the motion to quash must be denied unless the district court determines that there is no reasonable possibility that the category of materials the Government seeks will produce information relevant to the general subject of the grand jury's investigation."[46] It further held that "a grand jury subpoena issued through normal channels is presumed to be reasonable, and the burden of showing unreasonableness must be on the recipient who seeks to avoid compliance."[47]

Returning to our constitutional analysis, the Court has repeatedly held that "Fourth Amendment rights are personal,"[48] and thus has insisted that they "may not be asserted vicariously." It follows that a "person who is aggrieved . . . only through the introduction of damaging evidence secured by a search of a third person's premises or property has not had any of his Fourth Amendment rights infringed."[49] As a practical matter then, if one uses a service provider—say a bank, telephone company, or internet service provider—one has no right, and no standing, to object to a subpoena served on that third-party service provider for one's records.

---

43. *Hale*, 201 U.S. at 77.
44. *See*, 387 U.S. at 544.
45. *R. Enterprises*, 498 U.S. at 297-300.
46. *Id*. at 301.
47. *Id*.
48. Rakas v. Illinois, 439 U.S. 128, 133, 140 (1978).
49. *Id*. at 134.

In sum, a subpoena duces tecum constitutes a Fourth Amendment "search," and as such must be constitutionally "reasonable." Until recently, if a subpoena duces tecum met the *Hale/See* overbreadth standard, that was the end of any Fourth Amendment analysis. And it was clear that a defendant did not have standing to object to a subpoenas duces tecum served on third parties. *In the vast majority of cases, these rules still apply.*

In recent cases specifically involving government attempts to secure cell site location data and access to email, however, courts have been willing to apply what was, until then, a separate line of constitutional analysis: the Supreme Court's "reasonable expectation of privacy" search test. And, in two instances, courts have ruled that where this search test its satisfied the government must secure a court-issued warrant based on probable cause rather than rely on a grand jury subpoena or the other processes authorized by statute.

b. The Reasonable Expectation of Privacy Test and the Third-Party Doctrine

In non-subpoena cases, the concept of a Fourth Amendment search was at one time defined largely by reference to property rights. Thus, for example, were the police to put a wiretap on a telephone line outside a suspect's home, that was not deemed to be a search for constitutional purposes because the official action did not constitute a trespass on the suspect's property. In 1967, however, in response to developments in surveillance technology, the U.S. Supreme Court revolutionized the concept of Fourth Amendment searches by adopting a test that relies principally (though not entirely) on privacy, rather than property, interests.[50]

In *Katz v. United States*, 389 U.S. 347 (1967), the Court found that federal agents had conducted an unconstitutional search when they attached an electronic listening device to the outside of a public telephone booth from which the defendant was conducting his bookie operations. The definition of a Fourth Amendment search that flowed from *Katz* has two components: (1) the government action must invade the defendant's subjective expectation of privacy, and (2) that expectation of privacy must be one that society is willing to accept as reasonable. (This formula also determines whether the defendant has the standing to claim that her rights were violated and thus claim the exclusionary remedy.[51]) A number of conservative Justices have expressed serious doubts about the legitimacy of the *Katz* "reasonable expectation of privacy" standard.[52] Although, at such Justices' urging, the Court has held that property concepts are still relevant to the

50. *See* Katz v. United States, 389 U.S. 347 (1967).
51. *See Rakas*, 439 U.S. at 139-40.
52. *See, e.g., Carpenter*, 585 U.S. at 343 (Thomas, J., dissenting); *id* at 391-94 (Gorsuch, J., dissenting).

question whether a "search" has occurred in a couple of relatively recent opinions,[53] it has not yet chosen to repudiate the *Katz* test.

In applying the *Katz* test, the Supreme Court has long held that one does not have a reasonable expectation of privacy in data held by third parties, including telephone companies and banks. It reasoned that much of this data was actually owned by the service providers who generated it for their own business purposes.[54] More importantly, the Court held that by taking advantage of these services, the customer had knowingly exposed his confidential information to third parties, thus losing any expectation of privacy he could reasonably claim.[55]

This became known as the "third-party doctrine" and it means that those who willingly give their information to third parties do not have the substantive right, or the standing, to object to the third parties' production of the evidence. Then came the digital revolution and the advent of means of communication, searching and providing information, tracking location and habits, and storing information that of necessity involve trusting third party service providers and platforms with information many consumers continue to consider confidential—think, for example, of texts, emails, social media posts to non-public accounts, the terms entered into search engines, and cloud computing storage.

Congress responded by enacting the Stored Communications Act (SCA), 18 U.S.C. §§ 2701-12, which forbids certain third-party service providers from disclosing electronic communications stored with them to the government or others except as authorized by the statute. In 2018, the Supreme Court, in *Carpenter v. United States*, 585 U.S. 296 (2018), did not overrule the third-party doctrine but it indicated that it may not apply in certain categories of cases. Thus, it held that the Fourth Amendment may provide protection greater even than that provided in the SCA for certain highly revealing information held by third parties.

i. Background on the Stored Communications Act

The SCA protects the privacy of electronic communications in storage—that is, wire and electronic communications such as emails and other online messages held by service providers.[56] To the extent that it is more

---

53. *See, e.g.*, Florida v. Jardines, 569 U.S. 1 (2013); United States v. Jones, 565 U.S. 400 (2012).
54. *See* United States v. Miller, 425 U.S. 435, 440-42 (1976) (no reasonable expectation of privacy in bank records).
55. *See id.* at 443; *see also* Smith v. Maryland, 442 U.S. 735, 744 (1979) (no reasonable expectation of privacy in the telephone company's record of the numbers subscriber dialed).
56. The SCA is Title II of three titles in the Electronic Communications Privacy Act of 1986 (ECPA). Title I, often referred to as the Wiretap Act, updated that Federal Wiretap Act of 1968 to deal with the *interception* of computer and other digital or electronic communications in transit rather than in storage. *See* 18 U.S.C. §§ 2511(1)(a), 2516-18. Title III of ECPA requires the government to obtain a court order authoring the use of a pen register (a device that

protective than the Fourth Amendment's protection, the SCA controls; if the SCA's procedures are deemed insufficient to meet Fourth Amendment standards, however, constitutional standards govern.

The SCA controls access to electronic communications held by the *service providers*. It does not apply where the government seizes the subject's laptop or other devices and secures a warrant to search it. It does not apply should a recipient or originator of such communications voluntarily reveal them to the government. It is often difficult, however, to obtain the voluntary production of these records by the recipient or originator of these communications or to obtain the suspect's consent to government access to records of their electronic communications.

The SCA is a very complex statute that can only be sketched here.[57] It regulates the government's ability to compel the production of critical evidence from providers of electronic communications services (ECS)—including cell phone providers, email providers, or social media platforms—and remote computing services (RCS)—such as cloud computing providers—to the public.[58] The distinction between ECSs and RCSs made sense when the bill was drafted in 1986, but it is all but obsolete today; for example, Facebook, like many other social media platforms, is both an ECS and an RCS.[59] The SCA divides the data stored by ECSs and RCSs into content and non-content information and affords greater levels of privacy to the former than the latter. "Content" is defined in § 2510(8) as information "concerning the substance, purport, or meaning" of a communication but does not include the existence of the communication or the identities of the parties to it. Content information, then, generally consists of the actual communications. Non-content information often includes account records relating the user.

Section 2702(a) of the Act generally prohibits ECSs and RCSs from disclosing content information held in electronic storage to any third party, subject to the exceptions provide in § 2702 and to the processes of government compulsion described in § 2703.[60]

---

captures the numbers dialed (and related information) by the subject) and a trap and trace device (a device that captures the numbers and related information from where incoming calls and communications originated). *See id.* §§ 3121–3127.

57. For additional guidance, see Orin S. Kerr, *A User's Guide to the Stored Communications Act, and a Legislator's Guide to Amending It*, 72 G.W. L. Rev. 1208 (2004).

58. ECSs are defined as "any service which provides to users thereof the ability to send or receive wire or electronic communications." 18 U.S.C. § 2510(15). RCSs are those companies who provide to the public "computer storage or processing services by means of an electronic communications system." *Id.* § 2711(2).

59. *See, e.g.*, Crispin v. Christian Audigier, Inc., 717 F. Supp. 2d 965, 977-82 (C.D. Cal. 2010).

60. An ECS provider cannot knowingly divulge the contents of any communication while it holds the communication in electronic storage. 18 U.S.C. § 2702(a)(1). The definition of "electronic storage" is limited to communications either in "temporary, intermediate storage" for transmitting a message or in storage by an ECS as "backup protection." *Id.* § 2510(17). There has been some disagreement about whether emails that have arrived at

Section § 2702(b) allows RCS providers divulge the contents of a communication with the lawful consent of subscriber or the originator or an addressee or intended recipient of such communication.[61] ECS providers may divulge the contents of a communication only to an addressee or intended recipient of such communication or their agent.[62]

Section 2703 specifies the processes by which the government can compel network service providers to disclose electronically stored information. It identifies the three types of process: a warrant, a § 2703(d) court order, and an administrative or grand jury subpoena. A warrant must be issued pursuant to normal procedures by a court of competent jurisdiction; the government must therefore demonstrate probable cause. The government does not need to demonstrate probable cause to secure a § 2703(d) order. The judge can issue such an order upon reasonable suspicion—that is, "specific and articulable facts showing that there are reasonable grounds to believe" that the records requested are "relevant and material to an ongoing criminal investigation," § 2703(d). A grand jury subpoena requires no showing of individualized suspicion or other cause. Section 2705 sets forth the process by which the government can obtain a non-disclosure order delaying notification of the person under investigation that the government has made a request under § 2703.

What form of process is appropriate depends on a number of factors Congress thought related to how private the materials are. For example, the government's ability to compel disclosure of email largely depends on whether it is held by an ECS or a RCS and how long the email has been in electronic storage. Generally, investigators must secure a court-issued warrant for new ECS communications (held for 180 days or less) under § 2703(a). The government can secure private non-content information by asking a court to issue a § 2703(d) order. Finally, the Act permits investigators to use a grand jury subpoena to secure certain types of information that is viewed as less sensitive. Thus, only a grand jury or administrative subpoena is necessary to obtain account information, including the subscriber's name, address, local telephone connection records, length of service and types of services used, telephone number or other subscriber number or identity, and the means of payment for services.[63]

---

their destination and been opened are in "electronic storage." The leading cases hold that an email opened by the user, but still stored by the email provider, is stored for "backup protection" and is thus covered by the Act. *See* Theofel v. Farey-Jones, 359 F.3d 1055, 1075-77 (9th Cir. 2004).

61. 18 U.S.C. § 2702(b)(3).

62. *Id.* § 2702(b)(1); *see also* Facebook v. Pepe, 241 A.3d 248 (D.C. Ct. App. 2020) (consistent with the SCA, provider may not refuse to comply with the defendant's subpoena requiring production of an allegedly threatening Instagram "Story" sent to the consenting defendant by the victim).

63. 18 U.S.C. § 2703(c)(2).

ii. CSLI Data and Email: *Carpenter* and *Warshak*

As noted, under the third-party doctrine, it has long been understood that when one surrendered one's information to a third party, one lost any constitutionally protected expectation of privacy in the materials. Because one only has standing to contest a governmental search or seizure if one can claim such an expectation,[64] in many cases the defendant did not even attempt to contest third party compliance with grand jury subpoenas. Although this is still the rule in the overwhelming majority of cases, the Supreme Court opened up what it deemed a "rare" exception in *Carpenter v. United States*, 585 U.S. 296 (2018).

In *Carpenter*, the government obtained a § 2703(d) court order compelling Carpenter's cell phone provider to produce Carpenter's cell site location information (CSLI) over seven days. With regard to the data at issue, the Court explained that

> Cell phones continuously scan their environment looking for the best signal, which generally comes from the closest cell site. Most modern devices, such as smartphones, tap into the wireless network several times a minute whenever their signal is on, even if the owner is not using one of the phone's features. Each time the phone connects to a cell site, it generates a time-stamped record known as cell-site location information (CSLI).[65]

The *Carpenter* Court applied its "reasonable expectation of privacy test" to determine whether a § 2703(d) court order—issued only upon reasonable suspicion—was constitutionally sufficient to justify the ISP's compelled production of *Carpenter*'s location information over the course of seven days. The Court, ultimately recognizing that "individuals have a reasonable expectation of privacy in the whole of their physical movements,"[66] held that CLSI data for seven days could not be obtained without a warrant. A § 2703(d) court order under the SCA did not meet constitutional muster in this context.

In so holding, the Court had to distinguish two lines of precedent. First, in a series of "beeper" cases, the court held that a person does not have a reasonable expectation of privacy in his location when he travels on public roads because he shares his location with the public—including the police who may surveil him—whenever he leaves his home. The *Carpenter* Court distinguished these cases based on the capabilities of the technology involved:

> Prior to the digital age, law enforcement might have pursued a suspect for a brief stretch, but doing so "for any extended period of time was difficult and costly and

64. *Rakas*, 439 U.S. at 138-39.
65. *Carpenter*, 585 U.S. at 300-01.
66. *Id.* at 310.

> therefore rarely undertaken." For that reason, "society's expectation has been that law enforcement agents and others would not—and indeed, in the main, simply could not—secretly monitor and catalogue every single movement of an individual's car for a very long period."[67]

By contrast, the Court noted, CSLI data reflects a "seismic shift[] in digital technology that made possible the tracking of not only Carpenter's location but also everyone else's, not for a short period but for years and years."[68]

Second, the Court had to distinguish the cases in which it had applied the third-party doctrine. It did so by noting first that cell phone usage is almost ubiquitous among the populace. Most people carry their phones with them wherever they go, and thus when the government "tracks the location of a cell phone it achieves near perfect surveillance."[69] The Court also pointed out that the "time-stamped [CSLI] data provides an intimate window into a person's life, revealing not only his particular movements, but through them his 'familial, political, professional, religious, and sexual associations.'"[70] Further, it cited "the retrospective quality of the data here [which] gives police access to a category of information otherwise unknowable."[71] And finally, the Court emphasized that "a cell phone logs a cell-site record by dint of its operation, without any affirmative act on the part of the user beyond powering up. . . . Apart from disconnecting the phone from the network, there is no way to avoid leaving behind a trail of location data."[72]

Justice Alito, in dissent, noted two ways in which the Court's opinion was "revolutionary."[73] First, noting that "the Court allows a defendant to object to the search of a third party's property,"[74] Alito argued that this violated that Court's long-standing rule that third parties, like the service provider in *Carpenter*, could not assert the constitutional rights of others, and that, because the search was not directed at Carpenter, he had no standing to object.

Second, Alito saw no difference between a § 2703(d) order and a grand jury subpoena. He argued that "the Court ignores the basic distinction between an actual search (dispatching law enforcement officers to enter private premises and root through private papers and effects) and an order merely requiring a party to look through its own records and produce specified documents. The former, which intrudes on personal privacy far more

67. *Id.*
68. *Id.* at 313.
69. *Id.* at 311-12.
70. *Id.* at 311.
71. *Id.* at 312.
72. *Id.* at 315.
73. *Id.* at 362 (Alito, J., dissenting).
74. *Id.*

deeply, requires probable cause; the latter does not."[75] He concluded that "[b]y departing dramatically from these fundamental principles, the Court destabilizes long-established Fourth Amendment doctrine. We will be making repairs—or picking up the pieces—for a long time to come."[76]

In apparent response to Justice Alito's concern that "[h]olding that subpoenas must meet the same [probable cause] standard as conventional searches will seriously damage, if not destroy, their utility,"[77] the Court noted in conclusion that its holding did not imply that:

> all orders compelling the production of documents will require a showing of probable cause. The Government will be able to use subpoenas to acquire records in the overwhelming majority of investigations. We hold only that a warrant is required in the rare case where the suspect has a legitimate privacy interest in records held by a third party."[78]

Predictably, since *Carpenter*, many defendants have argued that they enjoy a reasonable expectation of privacy in a variety of data held by third parties, but courts have been very reluctant to extend *Carpenter*'s reasoning beyond the context of CSLI data. In most cases, then, the *Hale/See* overbreadth standard continues to be the Fourth Amendment test applied to subpoenas. And suspects continue to be barred from contesting subpoenas served on third parties, whether the SCA controls because data is sought from ECSs or RCSs or whether ordinary Fourth Amendment law applies to grand jury subpoenas served on unregulated third parties.[79]

There is one other important (pre-*Carpenter*) case in which a circuit court held that the Fourth Amendment's "reasonable expectation of privacy" standard applied to impose greater process requirements on the government than the SCA mandates: *United States v. Warshak*, 631 F.3d 266 (6th Cir. 2010). In *Warshak*, the government obtained a subpoena under § 2703(d) to compel the defendant's Internet service provider to turn over his emails. Warshak argued that he had a reasonable expectation of privacy in his email and, to the extent that § 2703(d) permitted the ECS to turn over his email only on a showing of reasonable suspicion and with less than a court-issued warrant, it violated his Fourth Amendment rights. The Sixth Circuit agreed with him on both counts.

The Sixth Circuit first noted that the content of snail mail is unquestionably protected by the Fourth Amendment. It concluded that "[g]iven the fundamental similarities between email and traditional forms of

---

75. *Id.* at 361-62.
76. *Id.* at 362.
77. *Id.* at 378 (Alito, J., dissenting).
78. *Id.* at 319.
79. *See, e.g.*, United States v. Soybel, 13 F.4th 584, 590-94 (7th Cir. 2021) (use of pen registers to identify IP addresses visited by the defendant was not a Fourth Amendment search).

communication, it would defy common sense to afford emails less Fourth Amendment protection."[80] Thus, it is "manifest that agents of the government cannot compel a commercial ISP to turn over the contents of email without triggering the Fourth Amendment."[81] In its holding, the court did not distinguish between emails held by ECSs or RCSs, nor did it mention whether the email was in storage more or less than 180 days. The Sixth Circuit simply ruled that a defendant enjoys a reasonable expectation of privacy in his emails vis-à-vis his ISP and thus the government must get a warrant to access such evidence. It concluded that "to the extent that the SCA purports to permit the government to obtain . . . emails warrantlessly, the SCA is unconstitutional."[82] It is important to note, however that other circuits have not rushed to adopt *Warshak*'s reasoning, which the Third Circuit characterized as "closer to a lonely outlier than to a representation of consensus."[83]

4. The Fifth Amendment

The Fifth Amendment states that "[n]o person . . . shall be compelled in any criminal case to be a witness against himself."[84] In summary, the Fifth Amendment's privilege against compelled self-incrimination protects:

(1) natural persons (and sole proprietorships) from being
(2) compelled by the government
(3) to make a testimonial communication, and,
(4) where that testimonial communication takes the form of a compelled act, the information implicitly communicated by that act is not a "foregone conclusion,"
(4) the testimonial communication is a "link in the chain" to incriminating evidence
(5) that can be used against the person in "any criminal case,"
(6) absent a grant of governmental immunity or some other circumstance that bars the government from bringing a criminal case against the person.

Unless all these elements are satisfied, a Fifth Amendment claim of privilege will not be sustained.

Readers are advised to consult Chapter 14, which explains each element of this formula, and particularly its application to subpoenas duces tecum, in some detail.

80. *Warshak*, 631 F.3d at 285-86.
81. *Id.* at 286.
82. *Id.* at 288.
83. Walker v. Coffey, 905 F.3d 138, 148 (3d Cir. 2018).
84. U.S. Const., amend. V.

In summary, corporations and other collective entities have no Fifth Amendment right to claim, and those individuals within the corporation who are tasked with producing corporate records to the grand jury in their representative capacity cannot rely on their personal Fifth Amendment right to resist disclosure.

Individuals and sole proprietorships can assert the Fifth in response to subpoenas duces tecum but the Supreme Court, in *Fisher v. United States*, 425 U.S. 391 (1976), adopted a very literal reading of just what is being "compelled" in such cases. It ruled that the *contents* of the documents sought were not "compelled" because *the government did not force the author to write down her thoughts*. Thus, the *contents of any documentary evidence* are not protected by the Fifth Amendment privilege. This means that the incriminating *contents* of any document or item that the government did not force one to write or create—that is, any document or bit of non-testimonial evidence that pre-dates the subpoena—are not "compelled" and thus are not protected.

But the *Fisher* Court recognized that a subpoena duces tecum does "compel" one to do *something*—that is, it forces one *to turn over, to produce, the subpoenaed documents*. If that *act of producing* the subpoenaed item is both a "*testimonial communication*" and is "*incriminating*," one may have a viable Fifth Amendment claim.

The compelled production of documentary or other physical or virtual evidence constitutes a "testimonial communication" if it implicitly concedes that the item exists, the subpoenaed person possesses it, or that it is responsive or authentic. If any of those facts (existence, possession, responsiveness, or authenticity) would provide a link in the chain of evidence necessary to incriminate the subpoenaed person, the requirement that the production be "incriminating" will be satisfied.

The government has, however, frequently relied on the so-called "foregone conclusion" doctrine to avoid Fifth Amendment claims:

> Under the "foregone conclusion" doctrine, an act of production is not testimonial—even if the act conveys a fact regarding the existence or location, possession, or authenticity of the subpoenaed materials—if the Government can show with "reasonable particularity" that, at the time it sought to compel the act of production, it already knew of the materials, thereby making any testimonial aspect a "foregone conclusion."[85]

Alternatively, under *United States v. Hubbell*, 530 U.S. 27 (2000), if one is responding to a fairly broad subpoena, one can assert that the compelled act of producing the documents is a testimonial communication because

85. In re Grand Jury Subpoena Duces Tecum Dated Mar. 25, 2011, 670 F.3d 1335, 1345-46 (11th Cir. 2012).

the subject will have to use the contents of his mind to sort through his files and identify that which is responsive. And the act of producing such materials will be incriminating because it is a link in the chain to the incriminating contents of the records or to other sources of incriminating evidence.

B. Subpoenas ad Testificandum (Testimony)

With respect to testimonial evidence, investigators may seek to interview potential witnesses, but the witnessses have no obligation to talk. In the grand jury, however, there is no right to silence: the witnesses must either talk or affirmatively assert their Fifth Amendment right or other valid privilege. Thus, through the grand jury, the government will be able to secure information from witnesses who just would prefer not to cooperate—or wish not to be perceived as doing so voluntarily. Other witnesses may be under a legal obligation to keep information confidential in the absence of legal compulsion; a grand jury subpoena unlocks that store of information. Finally, those who are not pure witnesses—that is, persons who may have some criminal culpability—will, if represented by counsel, be advised to take the Fifth. But sometimes they will nevertheless testify and provide investigators with invaluable insights into proposed defenses, give the government the foundation for a perjury prosecution if they lie, and furnish material for impeachment should they later be indicted and take the stand at trial.

In criminal cases, the people investigators and prosecutors will wish to talk to fall into three categories: "*targets*," "*subjects*," and "*witnesses*." These are terms of art that, although imprecise, are important, particularly in giving defense counsel an idea of how culpable the government believes her client to be. The government has no obligation to share this information, however. And the status of a "witness" can change to a "subject" or even a "target" as the investigation progresses.

"*Witnesses*" are persons who have no criminal exposure and who therefore cannot claim a Fifth Amendment right to withhold information from the grand jury. In the Fifth Amendment's language, a grand jury subpoena may be compelling such persons to testify but they are not being asked "to be a witness" against themselves in "any criminal case" because what they say, by definition, is not incriminating to them. "Witnesses" are akin to a bystander at a traffic accident who has no involvement, but who can speak to which driver was at fault.

The Department of Justice defines "subjects" and "targets" as follows:

> A "*subject*" of an investigation is a person whose conduct is within the scope of the grand jury's investigation.
>
> A "*target*" is a person as to whom the prosecutor or the grand jury has substantial evidence linking him or her to the commission of a crime and who, in the judgment of the prosecutor, is a putative defendant. An officer or employee of an organization which is a target is not automatically considered a target even if such officer's or employee's conduct contributed to the commission of the crime by the target organization. The same lack of automatic target status holds true for organizations which employ, or employed, an officer or employee who is a target.[86]

Prosecutors may subpoena subjects and targets to testify before the grand jury, but the subpoenaed persons can assert their Fifth Amendment right to avoid responding to questions. If a witness takes the Fifth before the grand jury, many AUSAs will give the grand jury an instruction that this is the right of every citizen and that the jurors should not draw an adverse inference of guilt from such assertions. But whether the grand jurors follow such instructions is subject to question.

The Department of Justice recognizes that forcing a target to take the Fifth before the grand jury in some cases "may carry the appearance of unfairness."[87] Accordingly, Justice Department policy urges prosecutors to attempt to secure the target's voluntary appearance and, if the target refuses, to only issue a subpoena upon supervisory approval and having considered (1) the importance of the testimony to the investigation; (2) whether alternative sources for the information exist; and (3) whether the answers to the questions sought to be posed will be protected by a valid claim of privilege. The DOJ policy further states that "[i]f a 'target' of the investigation and his or her attorney state in a writing, signed by both, that the 'target' will refuse to testify on Fifth Amendment grounds, the witness ordinarily should be excused from testifying."[88] Prosecutors, however, retain the discretion to call the investigatory target and there is no constitutional bar to their doing so.[89]

1. The Government Perspective

The government's decision regarding what witnesses to call will depend on a variety of factors—most particularly the type of investigation at issue and what is sought to be achieved in the grand jury (i.e., simply securing an indictment or using the grand jury to investigate a case). For example, if a case has been fully investigated by the relevant department or agency, probable cause can be demonstrated by the case agent recounting his investigation

86. Justice Manual, *supra* note 10, § 9-11.151 (emphasis added).
87. *Id.* § 9-11.150.
88. *Id.* § 9-11.154
89. *See* Bank of Nova Scotia v. United States, 487 U.S. 250, 259 (1988).

for the grand jury, and there is no reason to hear from other witnesses, the prosecutor might just call the case agent and ask the grand jury to indict based on his testimony and any physical evidence presented. This is the usual practice in many street crime cases.

Prosecutors may, however, need to call witnesses and subpoena documentary evidence for purposes of the investigation and building of a case—for indictment and trial. For example, prosecutors will rely on testimonial subpoenas to secure the testimony of witnesses who refuse to talk to the government outside the grand jury, to obtain the testimony of those who have been statutorily immunized but will not cooperate and give their statement outside the grand jury, and to obtain evidence that may only be turned over to the government via subpoena. Prosecutors may also call witnesses with an eye to any eventual trial, for example, to lock in the testimony of equivocal or hostile witnesses and to evaluate witness credibility and jury appeal.

What one asks a grand jury witness depends on why one called him and whether he is likely to take the stand at trial. For example, if a prosecutor calls a cooperating witness who is likely to be a trial witness, she generally will wish to ask as little as possible to avoid providing the defense impeachment material.[90] If, however, a prosecutor calls a hostile civilian witness who is expected to testify for the defense, she may wish to conduct an extensive examination to: evaluate the truthfulness of the witness's story as well as her credibility and likely affect at trial; discover the defense's theory of the case so that it can be evaluated and, if rejected, a rebuttal case can be developed; and commit the witness under oath so the government knows what he will say at trial and will be able to cross examine him with any inconsistencies in his story.

2. The Defense Perspective

The generally accepted wisdom is that if a lawyer representing a prospective grand jury witness hears from the government, or concludes based on her own investigation, that the client is a subject or target of the grand jury investigation, the lawyer should advise the client to assert his Fifth Amendment right against compelled self-incrimination if called to testify before a grand jury.

There are many reasons for this default rule. The grand jury is viewed as a creature dominated by the government and, as such, is unlikely to be swayed by even the most persuasive of witnesses. Sending a witness, no matter how well-prepared, into the grand jury without a lawyer (as the rules demand) creates many possibilities for peril. The witness will not be

90. *See supra* note13; *see also* the discussion of "Jencks Act" or "3500" Materials in Chapter 13 (Discovery).

protected by defense objections to misleading, ambiguous, irrelevant, or compound questions from prosecutors. The witness's difficulties may be seriously compounded if she testifies mistakenly—or lies—and the government believes it now has a perjury case. And witnesses often inadvertently waive applicable privileges, like the attorney-client privilege and the work product doctrine. Certainly, if the witness is the subject or target, their testimony will give the government advance notice of the defense's theory, lock it into that theory, and create impeachment material. It is, however, the client's decision whether to claim the Fifth.

Despite the above, "[i]t is not altogether uncommon for subjects or targets of the grand jury's investigation, particularly in white-collar cases, to request or demand the opportunity to tell the grand jury their side of the story."[91] The targets may also "wish to supplement their testimony with the testimony of others."[92] Such persons have no legal right to appear before the grand jury, but the Department of Justice counsels that prosecutors give these requests "favorable consideration," likely because of the many above-described advantages such testimony can provide the prosecution. But the Justice Department instructs prosecutors to keep "in mind that the grand jury was never intended to be and is not properly either an adversary proceeding or the arbiter of guilt or innocence."[93]

3. The Fourth Amendment Right

The Supreme Court has held that the Fourth Amendment simply does not apply to testimonial subpoenas. This is because "a subpoena to appear before a grand jury is not a 'seizure' in the Fourth Amendment sense, even though that summons may be inconvenient or burdensome."[94] As a consequence, a subpoena calling for a witness to appear and give testimony before the grand jury need not be constitutionally "reasonable."

4. The Fifth Amendment Right

A witness called to testify before the grand jury can assert whatever privilege they have, including the attorney-client privilege. The most important of these is the Fifth Amendment privilege against compelled self-incrimination. When applied to testimony, it has a broader scope than many may expect. The privilege "not only extends to answers that would in themselves support a conviction under a federal criminal statute but likewise embraces those which would furnish a link in the chain of evidence needed

91. Justice Manual, *supra* note 10, § 9-11.152.

92. *Id.*

93. *Id.*

94. *See Dionisio*, 410 U.S. at 9.

to prosecute the claimant for a federal crime."[95] Thus, the answer to a prosecutorial query does not have to be an obviously inculpatory admission. An assertion of the privilege could be valid, for example, if an answer to a question posed in the grand jury would lead the government to a witness who could attest to the witness's culpability for a crime.

Because the question may be such that a direct answer may not itself be incriminating but may only be "a link in the chain" to other evidence, whether a witness has a valid claim of the Fifth may not be obvious. The Supreme Court cautions that the Fifth's protection "must be confined to instances where the witness has a reasonable cause to apprehend danger from a direct answer" but, if a court is faced with a contested Fifth Amendment claim, the Court has instructed that, "[t]o sustain the privilege, it need only be evident from the implications of the question, in the setting in which it is asked, that a responsive answer to the question or an explanation of why it cannot be answered might be dangerous because injurious disclosure could result."[96]

5. Advice of Rights

In *United States v. Mandujano*, 425 U.S. 564 (1976), the Supreme Court held that the grand jury is not a venue in which witnesses experience the kind of inherently compelling pressure to speak that concerned the Court in *Miranda v. Arizona*, 384 U.S. 436 (1966). Thus, the familiar *Miranda* warnings need not be given to grand jury witnesses. Indeed, they should not be used because they would be incorrect. Witnesses do not have a right to remain silent: in the grand jury they must speak absent a valid Fifth Amendment or other privilege claim.[97] And grand jury witnesses, prior to indictment, have no Sixth Amendment right to appointed counsel.[98] Finally, once a witness waives his Fifth Amendment right by answering a question, he can be compelled to provide further details; he cannot simply revoke his waiver and remain silent as can those protected by *Miranda*.[99]

In *Mandujano*, the prosecutor warned the witness that he had: a duty to answer questions honestly unless they would require him to incriminate himself; a right to decline to answer questions that would incriminate him; and a right to have a lawyer wait outside the grand jury to consult with the witness. The *Mandujano* Court did not rule on what, if any, warnings might be constitutionally required because it found these warnings were "more than

---

95. Hoffman v. United States, 341 U.S. 479, 486 (1951).
96. *Id.* at 486-87.
97. *Mandujano*, 425 U.S. at 580-81.
98. *Id.* at 581.
99. *See* Chapters 14 (Fifth Amendment) and 17 (Parallel Proceedings).

sufficient" to advise the witness of his "rights and responsibilities."[100] In *United States v.Washington*, 431 U.S. 181 (1977), the Court held that a defendant has no right to be warned in advance of a grand jury appearance that he is a target of the investigation.

It is the policy of the Department of Justice to give subjects and targets an "Advice of Rights" and to warn targets of the investigation that "their conduct is being investigated for possible violation of Federal criminal law."[101] The DOJ's Advice of Rights provides as follows:

- The grand jury is conducting an investigation of possible violations of Federal criminal laws involving: (State here the general subject matter of inquiry, e.g., conducting an illegal gambling business in violation of 18 U.S.C. § 1955).
- You may refuse to answer any question if a truthful answer to the question would tend to incriminate you.
- Anything that you do say may be used against you by the grand jury or in a subsequent legal proceeding.
- If you have retained counsel, the grand jury will permit you a reasonable opportunity to step outside the grand jury room to consult with counsel if you so desire.[102]

C. Prosecutorial Misconduct and Constitutional and Harmless Error

Defendants must lodge any objections to the indictment prior to trial unless the challenge is based on jurisdiction or the indictment's failure to charge a crime.[103] As noted above, very few objections can be made based on evidentiary concerns because in federal court, an "indictment valid on its face is not subject to challenge on the basis of inadequate or incompetent evidence."[104] Defendants often seek dismissal of an indictment based on claims of prosecutorial abuse in the grand jury. These claims commonly rest on alleged violations of Rule 6; for example, the defendant may object that the prosecutor breached grand jury secrecy or called multiple witnesses into the grand jury in one go. One regrettably common prosecutorial error is to instruct witnesses not to share what they said or were asked about in the grand jury with counsel for the target or subjects of the investigation. This

---

100. *Id.* at 580.
101. Justice Manual, *supra* note 10, § 9-11.151.
102. *Id.*
103. *See* Fed. R. Crim. P. 12(b)(3).
104. *See Calandra*, 414 U.S. at 345.

contravenes Fed. R. Crim. P. 6(e)(2)(A) which states that "[n]o obligation of secrecy may be imposed on any person except in accordance with" Rule 6. Or prosecutors can also abuse the grand jury process by, for example, using the grand jury to secure evidence the government wishes to use in a collateral agency civil enforcement action.

Where the defendant seeks a dismissal based on "constitutional" error or error in which "the structural protections of the grand jury have been so compromised as to render the proceedings fundamentally unfair," prejudice may be presumed.[105] Such would be the case, for example, if grand jurors were excluded from service based on their race or gender.[106] Aside from such constitutional errors, however, a defendant seeking dismissal of an indictment on the basis of asserted prosecutorial abuses faces many obstacles, most notably the difficulty of discovering problems in the grand jury process given the grand jury secrecy rules and the absence of a right to pre-indictment discovery.

Another substantial obstacle is reflected in the harmless error standard the Court articulated in *Bank of Nova Scotia v. United States*, 487 U.S. 250 (1988). In that case, the Supreme Court held that where a defendant moves to dismiss an indictment for non-constitutional prosecutorial misconduct in the grand jury, Fed. R. Crim. R. 52's harmless error standard applies. In this context, dismissal of the indictment is appropriate only "'if it is established that the violation substantially influenced the grand jury's decision to indict,' or if there is 'grave doubt' that the decision to indict was free from the substantial influence of such violations."[107]

Despite the fact that prosecutorial abuses are difficult to uncover and must be extreme to qualify for relief, if cognizable misconduct is uncovered, prosecutors may be able to cure the problem by superseding the indictment before another grand jury or re-indicting after an indictment is dismissed. And in *United States v. Mechanik*, 475 U.S. 66 (1986), the Court held that after the defendant was convicted at trial, errors occurring before the grand jury were, by definition, harmless, because the defendant has been convicted by the petit jury hearing competent evidence and applying the more demanding beyond a reasonable doubt standard of proof.

Securing appellate relief will be virtually impossible. "[A]n order denying a motion to dismiss an indictment for an alleged violation of Rule 6(e) does not satisfy [the] 'stringent conditions for qualification as an immediately appealable collateral order,'" and thus cannot be the subject of an

105. *Bank of Nova Scotia*, 487 U.S. at 257.

106. *See, e.g.*, Vasquez v. Hillery, 474 U.S. 254 (1986) (racial discrimination in selection of grand jurors compelled dismissal of the indictment); Ballard v. United States, 329 U.S. 187 (1946) (exclusion of women from the grand jury compelled dismissal).

107. *Bank of Nova Scotia*, 487 U.S. at 256.

interlocutory appeal if the District Court denies the motion prior to trial.[108] And where the defense's motion for dismissal of an indictment due to non-constitutional grand jury abuses is not decided until after trial (whether because belatedly lodged or because the judge took the defense's pre-trial motion under advisement), and the defendant is convicted, *Mechanik* precludes relief.[109]

D. Obtaining Evidence Abroad

The challenges facing the government in investigating transborder criminality, and by the defense in countering such cases, could consume an entire volume, so the following covers only a few important highlights.

Letters rogatory are the traditional means by which evidence can be secured from foreign states. Letters rogatory are

> the medium, in effect, whereby one country, speaking through one of its courts, requests another country acting through its own courts and by methods of court procedure peculiar thereto and entirely within the latter's control, to assist the administration of justice in the former country; such requests being made, and being usually granted, by reason of the comity existing between nations in ordinary peaceful times.[110]

The defense generally must use this mechanism to secure evidence held abroad despite its many shortcomings. Because compliance with letters rogatory is completely discretionary, governments (as well as courts) can refuse to fulfill them or simply not act upon a request without stating a reason. Execution of the request will be accomplished according to local law and requirements, so there is no guarantee that even if responsive evidence is provided, it will be complete or in a form admissible in U.S. proceedings. And finally, once issued, letters rogatory are typically transmitted through governmental channels (from the requesting court to the Justice Department, then from one State Department to another, and back through the Justice Department to the court in the requested country). That journey can take roughly forever.

By contrast, the primary means by which prosecutors secure evidence from abroad are: (1) assistance from foreign enforcement authorities based on formal or informal relationships forged between investigative agencies or prosecutors in the respective jurisdictions; and (2) transfers of evidence

---

108. Midland Asphalt Corp. v. United States, 489 U.S. 794, 799 (1989).

109. *See Mechanik*, 475 U.S. 66.

110. *The Signe*, 37 F. Supp. 819, 820 (E.D. La. 1941).

based upon mutual legal assistance treaties (MLATs) concluded between the United States and scores of foreign states. Neither of these options is open to the defense.

MLATs provide a framework for the exchange of evidence and information relating to a broad range of criminal activity between prosecutorial (rather than judicial) authorities. MLATs are specific to the criminal process and typically include provisions governing multiple valuable forms of assistance from the beginning of an investigation through trial and post-conviction procedures. Prosecutors use these treaties because an MLAT request, unlike letters rogatory, relies on legally binding commitments between states parties to cooperate in sharing evidence. Evidence obtained pursuant to an MLAT is more likely to arrive in the receiving jurisdiction in an admissible form. And because the procedures are centralized and standardized between states parties, requests can be processed far more quickly than are letters rogatory.

If a foreign state is unwilling or unable to provide competent evidence pursuant to a letter rogatory and (for prosecutors) there is no applicable MLAT or other agreement, parties may seek to secure evidence abroad through *domestic* compulsory process. Federal courts are authorized to order the issuance of subpoenas to nationals or residents of the United States who are in a foreign country, requiring their appearance as witnesses or the production of documents or other evidence if the court finds it necessary in the interest of justice.[111] Prosecutors can use this provision to serve grand jury subpoenas on such persons and, after indictment, and the defense can use trial subpoenas issued pursuant to Fed. R. Crim. P. 17 (which are discussed further in Chapter 13 (Discovery)).

But even if the government or the defense wish to subpoena non-U.S. nationals or non-residents overseas, they can still potentially use Rule 17 subpoenas because, as a general matter, courts in the United States may order any person over whom they have personal jurisdiction to disclose or produce evidence within that person's possession, custody, or control, even if the evidence lies outside the territorial jurisdiction of the particular court in question.[112] Thus, if a foreign company has an office in New York, the government and defense can serve subpoenas on that office and require the company to disclose materials it holds abroad.

It is not uncommon, however, for the foreign subpoenaed party to argue that it cannot comply with U.S. subpoenas because it is subject to laws in its home state that preclude the subpoenaed person, under pain of civil or even criminal penalty, from sharing the materials requested. In such circumstances, the foreign person may face a very difficult choice: refuse

111. *See* 28 U.S.C. § 1783(a); Fed. R. Crim. P. 17(e)(2).
112. *See, e.g.*, In re Marc Rich & Co., 707 F.2d 663, 667 (2d Cir. 1983).

to comply with the U.S. court's order and face U.S. contempt sanctions or violate foreign law and risk criminal or civil penalties abroad. U.S. courts faced with this objection engage in a balancing of interests.[113] At least where the subpoenaed materials are sought by prosecutors, U.S. courts, not surprisingly, often given predominant weight to the U.S. sovereign interest in criminal law enforcement.[114]

Most of the cases in which U.S. courts have ordered foreign persons over whom they have jurisdiction to comply with a U.S. subpoena and thereby violate foreign law concern "blocking statutes." Many, like the French blocking statute,[115] impose sanctions on persons who disclose specified materials in response to foreign discovery orders. Although blocking statutes were enacted largely in response to foreign dismay over the scope of U.S. civil discovery, they apply in criminal cases as well. Other foreign laws enforce industry-specific bars, such as statutes that enforce state bank secrecy laws. Data-privacy laws, particularly in Europe, may also act to block compliance with U.S. subpoenas.

This is less of a problem for prosecutors if an MLAT exists with the country involved because MLATs often obligate the requested state to provide U.S. prosecutors with the requested evidence regardless of the limiting provisions of foreign domestic law.

Congress broadened an important means by which white-collar prosecutors can get access to foreign bank records in the Anti-Money Laundering Act of 2020. Formerly, the DOJ could issue subpoenas to any foreign bank maintaining a "correspondent account" in the United States for "records related to such correspondent account[s]."[116] Under the Act, however, the government is now authorized to subpoena records, even those maintained outside the United States, relating to correspondent accounts "or *any account at a foreign bank*" that is the subject of a Bank Secrecy Act or anti-money-laundering investigation, a civil forfeiture action, or "*any* investigation of a violation of a criminal law of the United States."[117]

---

113. *See* Société Nationale Industrielle Aérospatiale v. United States District Court, 482 U.S. 522, 544 n.29 (1987); The Restatement (Fourth) of the Foreign Relations Law of the United States § 426 cmt. (*a*) (2018).

114. *See, e.g.*, In re Grand Jury Proceedings, 691 F.2d 1384, 1391 (11th Cir. 1982) ("Absent direction from the Legislative and Executive branches of our federal government, we are not willing to emasculate the grand jury process whenever a foreign nation attempts to block our criminal justice process.").

115. French Penal Code Law No. 80-538 of July 16, 1980.

116. See Chapter 11 (Money Laundering) for a discussion of correspondent banking.

117. 31 U.S.C. § 5318(k)(3) (emphasis added).

Examples

1. Assume that the government sends Máire O'Brien—a U.S. Representative—a target letter, inviting her to testify before a grand jury investigating allegations that she engaged in public corruption. O'Brien has been elected many times in a competitive House district and believes that she can talk anyone into anything. She wishes to go into the grand jury and tell "her story." You are her attorney, Tamara Zhuk. What do you advise her to do? Can the Assistant U.S. Attorney (AUSA) serve her with a grand jury subpoena if O'Brien declines the invitation to testify?

2. Thom Styles and Ormond Marlow have a two-person law partnership, Styles & Marlow, through which they practice trusts and estates law. Styles is the trustee of a trust set up to support a woman who has dementia and is confined to a nursing home. He is suspected of draining that account of millions of dollars. Marlow is served with a subpoena duces tecum addressed to the firm requiring the production of "any and all documents, data, or other records that refer or relate to client trust accounts." Marlow is also served with a subpoena ad testificandum to appear and testify before the grand jury.

   Marlow is concerned that the unauthorized "loans" he has taken from other client trust accounts will be detected if these documents are produced. (Marlow fully intends to pay these "borrowed" monies back, but he is concerned that the government will conclude that these "loans" constitute theft.) The government is just at the beginning of its investigation and the Assistant U.S. Attorney has advised Marlow that he is considered a witness at this point in time. Can Styles & Marlow and/or Marlow validly seek to resist production of the subpoenaed records based on the Fourth and Fifth Amendments to the U.S. Constitution? Can Marlow assert his Fifth Amendment right to resist testifying?

3. During the course of a grand jury proceeding, an Assistant U.S. Attorney wishes to have two agents read the transcript of a telephone conversation that was intercepted in violation of the Fourth Amendment. Why is this a bad idea?

4. An Assistant U.S. Attorney investigating a criminal tax case was working closely with IRS employees conducting a civil investigation. The AUSA used grand jury subpoenas to gather material for the civil case and disclosed grand jury materials, including the names of targets of the investigation, to the IRS agents. The AUSA subpoenaed seven witnesses for the sole purpose of having them invoke their Fifth Amendment rights in front of the grand jury, thus prejudicing them in the eyes of the jurors. The AUSA told grand jury witnesses that they could not talk to anyone about their testimony. He gave informal immunity to fifteen witnesses. Finally, he had the IRS agents "summarize" evidence falsely and assert

incorrectly that all the summarized evidence had previously been presented to the grand jury. Can the defense secure the dismissal of the ensuing indictment for prosecutorial misconduct?

5. The government was investigating an Internet fraud and had secured IP addresses for the fraudster but was unable to identify a particular person associated with those addresses. They found that the IP addresses corresponded to three coffee shops and could pinpoint the date and approximate time that the fraudulent messages were sent from those coffee shops. Accordingly, they secured an otherwise valid § 2703(d) court order for three "tower dumps." The tower dumps identified the cell phone numbers that accessed the cell phone towers nearest the three coffee shops during the particular timeframe that the fraudsters were working there. When they compared the three lists, the investigators were able to identify one cell phone number that was present at all three locations. After further investigation, they tied the cell phone to Roberta Albanesi and eventually indicted her for fraud. She sought to suppress the evidence yielded by the tower dumps—and the fruit of that evidence—asserting based on *Carpenter* that she had a reasonable expectation of privacy in the data, that a § 2703(d) court order was insufficient to justify such a search, and that without a warrant the collection of the information was unconstitutional. Does *Carpenter* require the suppression of this evidence?

Explanations

1. Zhuk should strongly advise O'Brien to take the Fifth. Federal grand juries' indictment rate is over ninety-nine percent, and the delivery of the target letter indicates that the government has concluded that O'Brien is a "putative defendant." In these circumstances it is exceedingly unlikely that she will talk a grand jury operating under the direction of the AUSA to "no true bill" the case, no matter how strong her powers of persuasion. Remind O'Brien that this is not a level playing field. She would be operating without her lawyer in an unfamiliar, prosecution-dominated legal landscape, not a political contest.

   Zhuk will not be present to object to confusing or misleading questions; to bring out facts necessary to put O'Brien's testimony in context; to limit the examination to avoid questioning on irrelevant, prejudicial, or inculpatory collateral matters; and to steer O'Brien away from responses that may cause a waiver of attorney client or work product privileges.

   The prosecutor will certainly hear "her story"—that is the defense's theory of the case. But the defense will therefore be locked into that theory at an early stage before it has access to many of the facts or a right to discovery. In other words, Zhuk and O'Brien will not know whether the government has facts that will render the defense "story" implausible or impossible to credit. At the very least, this advance notice of the defense will give the government the ability to use the grand jury to build a rebuttal case well in advance of trial.

If O'Brien misspeaks or, God forbid, lies, the prosecutors may add a perjury count to any indictment. Such counts are dangerous because trial juries often conclude that, however confusing the merits may be, lies indicate that the target is conscious that what she did was wrong—essentially helping the government prove the underlying crime's mens rea. And if O'Brien is indicted and wishes to take the stand to tell the petit jury "her story," she can be impeached with any deviations from her grand jury testimony.

Many business executives and political figures will, despite this advice, wish to testify because they fear they will suffer serious employment, professional, or public relations consequences as a result of invoking the Fifth Amendment privilege. For example, some corporate employers who are cooperating with the government will fire any employees who take the Fifth and, because the employers are not government actors, there is no constitutional bar to their doing so. Some clients also insist on testifying to protest their innocence. The decision is O'Brien's. If she decides to testify, Zhuk should (as CYA) write a memo to the files documenting her advice and then prepare O'Brien within an inch of her life for the grand jury appearance.

2. The subpoena is addressed to the firm so Marlow has no standing to object. The firm does have a Fourth Amendment right and likely has a valid claim given the scope of the subpoena. A subpoena duces tecum is a Fourth Amendment "seizure" and thus must be reasonable—which has been read to mean, essentially, not overbroad. The firm practices trusts and estates law so a subpoena that calls for the production of anything related to "client trust accounts" is likely to sweep up a substantial portion of the firm's work; this is not a meaningful subject-matter restriction. Further, there is no temporal limit identified in the subpoena. Given the lack of meaningful subject-matter and temporal limitations, a court would likely conclude that the subpoena is far too sweeping in its terms to be reasonable.

   The firm does not have a Fifth Amendment right and Marlow is not permitted to assert his personal Fifth Amendment right to resist production of firm documents in his representative capacity.

   Marlow can assert his own Fifth Amendment rights with respect to the subpoena ad testificandum. The government's advice that Marlow is a "witness" is not binding—it can and here likely will change. Defense counsel, aware of Marlow's activities, has an obligation to do his own inquiry and knows that if the government sees that Marlow has also been using client accounts as his own piggy bank, he will likely emerge at as a target of the investigation. The fact that the government does not yet know this gives counsel a chance to get ahead of the curve and perhaps, depending on how incriminating the records are and how much evidence the government is likely to find against Marlow, approach the government to strike a cooperation deal.

Counsel will understand that if Marlow takes the Fifth, the government is likely to wonder why—and dig deeper into Marlow's own client accounting. But the potential downsides of a grand jury appearance (documented in Example 1) are too great to do anything other than advise Marlow to take the Fifth with respect to any questions that could furnish a link in the chain of evidence needed to prosecute Marlow for a federal crime. This could mean taking the Fifth with respect to virtually any question relating to the firm's practice and accounting procedures, as well as anything relating to Marlow's own activities. He should also take the Fifth in response to any questions regarding Styles' activities given that the government may have a case that he conspired with, aided and abetted, or was willfully blind to Styles' crimes.

3. The exclusionary rule does not apply in grand jury proceedings so the admission of the evidence seized in violation of the Fourth Amendment is not problematic. Allowing the witnesses to appear before the grand jury in tandem would be a violation of Fed. R. Crim. P. 6(d)(1). But in *Bank of Nova Scotia*, the Supreme Court found that such a breach was not prejudicial because there was "no evidence that the agents' reading in tandem enhanced the credibility of the testimony or otherwise allowed the agents to exercise undue influence."[118] Thus, it is unlikely that this violation would sufficiently prejudice the grand jury's decision to indict to pass the *Bank of Novia Scotia* standard; that is, such a violation likely would not have a substantial influence on the grand jury's decision to indict, and it would not create a grave doubt as to whether it affected the grand jury's decision. That said, as Justice O'Connor explained in her concurrence in *Mechanik*, "[p]rosecutors have been accorded . . . leeway in presenting their cases to the grand jury, but they are bound by a few, clear rules which were carefully drafted and approved by this Court and by Congress to ensure the integrity of the grand jury's functions."[119] Thus, although no remedy may be available, prosecutors have a duty to refrain from such violations in the first instance.

118. *Bank of Novia Scotia*, 487 U.S. at 263.
119. *Mechanik*, 475 U.S. at 74 (O'Connor, J., concurring).

4. These facts were drawn from *Bank of Nova Scotia*. The AUSA violated the secrecy provisions of Fed. R. Crim. P. 6(e) by disclosing the information to the IRS witnesses without securing a court order under Fed. R. Crim. P. 6(e)(3)(E)(i). Calling witnesses to the grand jury to aid in making a civil case is an abuse of the grand jury process. He was also wrong to supplement Rule 6(e)'s secrecy mandate by instructing the witnesses not to talk about what went on in the grand jury.[120] But the *Bank of Nova Scotia* Court held, with respect to these issues, that "it is plain that these alleged breaches could not have affected the charging decision."[121]

   The Court further held that the AUSA did not err in calling witnesses to testify despite their avowed intention to take the Fifth, reasoning that the "Government was not required to take at face value the unsworn assertions made by these witnesses outside the grand jury room."[122] It ruled that the objection based on the "summaries" "boils down to a challenge to the reliability or competence of the evidence presented to the grand jury" and the Supreme Court has "held that such an indictment valid on its face is not subject to such a challenge."[123] Finally, the *Bank of Nova Scotia* Court did not pass on the propriety of the granting informal immunity to so many witnesses, simply concluding that the conduct did not have a substantial effect on the grand jury's decision to indict, and it did not create a grave doubt as to whether it affected the grand jury's decision because the "jurors were made aware that these witnesses had made a deal with the Government."[124]

5. Normally, Albanesi would have no standing to object to a subpoena served on a third party, and the service provider would be unable to assert Albanesi's Fourth Amendment rights. Even if Albanesi had standing, the *Hale/See* overbreadth standard would apply and these are very specific orders that would easily pass that test. Even when the Court uses its "reasonable expectation of privacy" test to determine whether something is a Fourth Amendment "search," the third-party doctrine would typically counsel that because Albanesi made available her CSLI data to her service provider, she has no reasonable expectation of privacy in that data.

   That said, we saw that the *Carpenter* Court identified a "rare" case in which it will apply its reasonable expectation of privacy test to determine whether an individual has a legitimate basis for objecting to the compelled production of particularly sensitive material held by a third

---

120. *See* Fed. R. Crim. P. 6(e)(2)(A).
121. *Bank of Novia Scotia*, 487 U.S. at 259-60.
122. *Id.* at 259.
123. *Id.* at 261.
124. *Id.* at 262.

party. The *Carpenter* Court explicitly took no position on tower dumps. Courts are split on the issue of whether Albanesi has a reasonable expectation of privacy in the data secured such that tower dumps are deemed Fourth Amendment searches requiring a warrant.

Many courts have emphasized that orders authorizing tower dumps capture CSLI "not for one targeted individual for an extended time, chronicling that individual's private life for days, but rather . . . CSLI for a particular *place* at a limited *time*."[125] Thus, "the privacy concerns underpinning the court's holding in *Carpenter* do not come into play here, where the search for data focuses not on 'the whole of [an individual's] physical movements,' but rather on the data that was left behind at a particular time and place by virtue of cell phone tower locations."[126] Courts liken CSLI tower dump to information gathered by "'conventional surveillance techniques' and tools, such as security cameras and fingerprint collections, which capture data for *every* individual who came into contact with the crime scene in the manner revealed by the technology at issue."[127]

Other courts, however, have come out the other way. A district court in Rhode Island opined that the question under *Carpenter* comes down to the "'intimacy, comprehensiveness, expense, retrospectivity, and voluntariness'" of the alleged search.[128] It reasoned that tower dumps do not implicate the whole of a suspect's movements but they do provide "'near perfect surveillance' of a population at a moment in time."[129] Such surveillance could reveal intimate and personal data, for example whom the suspects called, when they called them, and how often, during the date and time identified. The search was not limited to the suspects but rather captured information for all users in the area. The tower dump was "'easy, cheap and efficient' compared to traditional investigative techniques," and "'runs against everyone,'" allowing police to access a great deal of data.[130] And the CSLI data is not voluntarily exposed. Thus, the court concluded, CSLI tower dumps are sufficiently akin to the gathering of CSLI data for a single person over seven days that they, too, should be treated as a practice that invades the suspect's reasonable expectation of privacy and demands a warrant.

---

125. United States v. Walker, No. 2:18-cr-37-FL-I, 2020 WL 4065980, at *8 (E.D. N.C. July 20, 2020) (emphasis original); *see also* State v. Elias, 990 N.W.2d 905 (Neb. 2023).
126. *Walker*, 2020 WL 4065980, at *8.
127. *Id.*
128. United States v. Medina, 712 F. Supp. 3d 226, 242 (D. R.I. 2024), *appeal filed*, No. 24-1282 (1st Cir. Mar. 25, 2024).
129. *Id.*
130. *Id.* at 243.

CHAPTER 13

Discovery and Other Information Gathering Methods

Many white-collar cases are viewed as won or lost at indictment, and thus pre-indictment practice is often the critical phase of white-collar defense work. Yet before indictment, the defense operates at a huge informational disadvantage. It has no entitlement to discovery and no access to compulsory process of a sort enjoyed by the government through the grand jury. At this stage, then, defense counsel must rely on informal or collateral legal mechanisms to secure the information needed to mount an effective defense. These means may include: entering into a "joint defense" with other subjects of the investigation, pursuant to which the joint defense participants may pool information without fear that such sharing will expose the information to discovery by the government or others;[1] schmoozing with the prosecutor in an attempt to figure out what is being investigated and what the government does and does not yet know; lodging Freedom of Information Act (FOIA) requests;[2] using whatever concurrent civil proceedings may be ongoing to obtain discovery pertinent to the criminal case;[3]and depending on the kindness of witnesses to voluntarily share relevant information.

After indictment, the playing field becomes slightly more even, but the government's pre-indictment informational advantage is not erased by existing rules. There are three principal post-indictment disclosure mechanisms: (1) the government's obligations under *Brady v. Maryland*, 373 U.S. 83 (1963), to produce materially exculpatory evidence in the government's possession; (2) Fed. R. Crim. P. 16, which governs (reciprocal) pre-trial discovery obligations; and (3) the *Jencks* Act, 18 U.S.C. § 3500, and Fed. R. Crim. P. 26.2, which govern the (reciprocal) disclosure of witness statements. Motions for bills of particulars under Fed. R. Crim. P. 7(f) are not intended to provide discovery but they can constitute a valuable means of securing

---

1. *See* Chapter 3 (Entity Liability).
2. Defense counsel use the Freedom of Information Act (FOIA), 5 U.S.C. § 552, to obtain materials from relevant governmental agencies, but there are exceptions to FOIA through which prosecutors and agencies may refuse to provide materials relevant to an ongoing criminal investigation. *See id.* § 552(b)(1)(A) (national security exception), § 552(b)(7) (law enforcement investigation exception). Courts may also be reluctant to order, at the behest of a criminal defendant, broader governmental disclosure through FOIA than is available under the criminal discovery rules. U.S. Dist. Court, 717 F.2d 478, 480 (9th Cir. 1983) ("We hold that in criminal cases the Freedom of Information Act does not extend the scope of discovery permitted under Rule 16. The limitations of Rule 16 are controlling.").
3. *See* Chapter 17 (Parallel Proceedings).

more information about the government's theory of the case. Finally, in many white-collar cases, information potentially helpful to the defense may be held by persons or entities who are not involved in the prosecution and who are not subject to the above disclosure rules. Accordingly, these materials touch upon some of the challenges facing defense counsel in obtaining needed evidence from third parties by subpoena under Fed. R. Crim. P. 17.

Four preliminary notes are in order. First, civil practitioners are often shocked by the dearth of discovery available in criminal cases. In federal prosecutions, at least, the defense generally cannot use even the most ordinary of civil pre-trial investigative techniques, such as interrogatories or depositions of potential witnesses.[4] And commonplace trial-related disclosures, such as pre-trial disclosure of witness lists, are not required in federal criminal cases.[5] In the civil context, the discovery rules were overhauled to avoid trial by ambush, reducing the chance that surprise or maneuver, rather than truth, determines the outcome of the case. The same approach has not been adopted in the criminal realm, assertedly for three reasons: pre-trial discovery might result in a perjured defense; an accused, knowing the names of witnesses against him, may interfere with them before the trial; and the constitutional privilege against self-incrimination prevents discovery being a two-way street.

Second, the government has unique access—not available to the defense—to potentially critical evidence: evidence located overseas; and, as outlined in Chapter 12 (Grand Jury), crucial electronic evidence, including the contents of stored texts, emails, voicemail, search requests, and social media accounts. Under the Stored Communications Act (SCA) providers of these services are barred by statute from giving the same evidence to the defense absent the consent of the user or those privy to the conversations.

Third, this information imbalance is not inevitable. This chapter details the minimum disclosures that prosecutors must make consistent with constitutional standards and the federal rules. But federal prosecutors can provide as much disclosure as they wish, consistent with concerns for witness safety and the integrity of evidence. And Department of Justice policy can—and currently does with respect to *Brady* disclosures[6]—require prosecutors to be more generous.

Finally, readers must be aware that there are many levels of rules applicable in the discovery realm and a great deal of variation in those rules among jurisdictions. Circuit courts apply the rules differently, and in many districts U.S. Attorneys Offices, and even individual prosecutors, follow their own

4. Depositions are available only in "extraordinary circumstances" and with the approval of the judge. Fed. R. Crim. P. 15.
5. *See, e.g.*, United States v. Perkins, 994 F.2d 1184, 1190 (6th Cir. 1993).
6. *See* U.S. Dept of Justice, Justice Manual § 9-5.001 [hereinafter Justice Manual].

policies and practices. Ethical standards governing the government's disclosure obligations, in particular, may differ with the jurisdiction.

I. BILLS OF PARTICULARS

Soon after the filing of an indictment or information, the defense often moves for a bill of particulars under Fed. R. Crim. P. 7(f). A bill of particulars "'can be used to ensure that the charges brought against a defendant are stated with enough precision to allow the defendant to understand the charges, to prepare a defense, and perhaps also to be protected against retrial on the same charges.'"[7]

This is not viewed as a discovery device because it is intended to provide the defendant additional specification regarding the nature of the charges in the indictment, not a means of discovering the evidence the government may use to prove those charges. That said, defense counsel will often use such a motion in an effort to learn as much as possible about how the government intends to prove its case. Trial courts have a great deal of discretion in passing on a motion for a bill of particulars and generally are reluctant to accede to defense requests to transform the bill of particulars into a discovery device through which the defense can secure "a preview of [the government's] case or legal theories" or evidentiary detail.[8]

II. *BRADY* MATERIAL

In *Brady v. Maryland*, the Supreme Court held that "suppression by the prosecution of evidence favorable to an accused . . . violates due process where the evidence is material to either guilt or punishment" "irrespective of the good faith or bad faith of the prosecution."[9] To prevail on a *Brady* claim, a defendant must demonstrate that: (1) the evidence at issue was favorable to the accused; (2) the evidence was suppressed by the State, either willfully or inadvertently; (3) the evidence was in the possession of the government, and (4) "prejudice must have ensued," that is, the suppressed evidence must have been "material."[10] "Due process requires that disclosure of exculpatory and impeachment evidence material to guilt or innocence be made in

7. United States v. Mejia, 448 F.3d 436, 445 (D.C. Cir. 2006).
8. United States v. Ragano, 24-cr-00050(HG), 2024 WL 3302673, at *4 (E.D.N.Y. July 3, 2024).
9. *Brady*, 373 U.S. at 87.
10. Strickler v. Greene, 527 U.S. 263, 281-82 (1999).

sufficient time to permit the defendant to make effective use of that information at trial. In most cases, the disclosures required by the Constitution and [DOJ] policy will be made in advance of trial."[11] The burden is on the government "to produce exculpatory materials; the burden is not on the defendant to first point out that such materials exist."[12]

If a *Brady* rule violation is discovered during trial, the court can either declare a mistrial or make such evidentiary rulings as are necessary to cure the violation—for example, by excluding the government evidence that could have been discredited by the information withheld. Because the *Brady* rule inherently involves the defense's ignorance of exculpatory evidence held by the government, however, violations of the *Brady* rule are typically only discovered after the defendant has already been convicted. At this point, the defendant bears the burden of showing that the above four factors have been satisfied. A "*Brady* claim must be established by facts, not speculation," and courts often accept the government's representations with respect to materiality and other elements.[13] If a *Brady* violation is proved, the most common remedies are a reversal of the conviction or a new trial order. Additionally, if prosecutors withheld *Brady* material intentionally or knowingly, they may be subject to professional sanction or, in cases in which the court entered a pre-trial order requiring *Brady* disclosure, a contempt of court citation.

A. Evidence Favorable to the Accused

Information coming within the scope of the *Brady* mandate "includes not only evidence that is exculpatory, *i.e.*, going to the heart of the defendant's guilt or innocence, but also evidence that is useful for impeachment, *i.e.*, having the potential to alter the jury's assessment of the credibility of a significant prosecution witness."[14] *Brady*'s application to materials that will be useful in impeaching the government's witnesses was made clear in *Giglio v. United States*, 405 U.S. 150 (1972), and such materials are often referred to as "*Giglio* material." While Giglio's appeal was pending, his attorney discovered that the government had not disclosed to the defense a promise of immunity made to a key government witness. The Supreme Court ordered a new trial, stating that "[w]hen the 'reliability of a given witness may well be determinative of guilt or innocence,' nondisclosure of evidence affecting

11. Justice Manual, *supra* note 6, § 9-5.001(D) (citing Weatherford v. Bursey, 429 U.S. 545, 559 (1997)).

12. United States v. Harry, 927 F. Supp. 2d 1185, 1213 (D.N.M. 2013).

13. United States v. Nichols, No. 1:21-cr-00117-RCL, 2023 WL 6809937, at *5 (D.D.C. Oct. 16, 2023).

14. United States v. Avellino, 136 F.3d 249, 255 (2d Cir. 1998); *see also* Kyles v. Whitley, 514 U.S. 419, 433 (1995).

credibility falls within" the *Brady* rule.[15] Formal cooperation agreements must be turned over, and a number of circuits have also "found a duty to disclose under *Brady* where there was a tacit agreement promising potential or actual leniency."[16]

The government's duty to comply with *Brady* is a continuing one. And, as *Brady* made clear, prosecutors' obligations exist when the suppressed evidence would be favorable to the defense with respect to either guilt *or* punishment.

B. Suppression of Evidence by the Government

"Suppression" of evidence by the government does not connote intentionality. *Brady* states that the due process disclosure obligation exists "irrespective of the good faith or bad faith of the prosecution." "Suppression" questions instead generally turn on access—that is, whether the evidence is in the possession of the prosecution team and the defense does not otherwise have access to it. It is clear, for example, courts will not find that the government "suppressed" materially exculpatory evidence if the defendant actually had the information prior to trial, either by virtue of a government production or through some independent means.[17]

Some prosecutors seek to meet their *Brady* obligations by electing so-called "open file" discovery. White-collar prosecutions often are exceedingly paper - or data-intensive. In the days when evidence could be found primarily in filing cabinets, prosecutors would sometimes invite defense counsel to peruse cabinets stuffed with documents and call it "open discovery." Now prosecutors may turn over huge masses of electronically stored information (ESI). When swamped with ESI, the defense often argues that too much discovery is as bad as too little and may ask the court to order the government to identify that which is *Brady* within a voluminous data dump. "As a general rule, the government is under no duty to direct a defendant to exculpatory evidence within a larger mass of disclosed evidence."[18] However, some district courts have issued such orders.[19] And some circuits have cautioned that:

> We do not hold that the use of voluminous open file can never violate *Brady*. For instance, evidence that the government 'padded' an open file with pointless or superfluous information to frustrate a defendant's review of the file might

15. *Giglio*, 405 U.S. at 154.
16. Douglas v. Workman, 560 F.3d 1156, 1185 (10th Cir. 2009).
17. *See, e.g.*, Tate v. Wood, 963 F.2d 20, 25-26 (2d Cir. 1992); United States v. Wilson, 901 F.2d 378, 380 (4th Cir. 1990).
18. United States v. Skilling, 554 F.3d 529, 576 (5th Cir. 2009), *aff'd in part and rev'd in part on other grounds*, 561 U.S. 358 (2010).
19. *See, e.g.*, United States v. Saffarinia, 424 F. Supp. 3d 46, 85-91 (D.D.C. 2020).

> raise serious *Brady* issues. Creating a voluminous file that is unduly onerous to access might raise similar concerns. And it should go without saying that the government may not hide *Brady* material of which it is actually aware in a huge open file in the hope that the defendant would never find it.[20]

Initially, the *Brady* rule was only applicable if the defendant made a pre-trial request for information. Then, in *United States v. Bagley*, 473 U.S. 667 (1985), the Supreme Court held that the same standard of materiality applies regardless of whether or not the defense has made a request for *Brady* material. And the Court made clear in *Strickler v. Greene*, 527 U.S. 263 (1999), that "the duty to disclose [*Brady* material] is applicable *even though there has been no request by the accused*."[21] Despite this, many courts require some due diligence from the defense prior to finding that the government is "suppressing" *Brady* materials. As the Seventh Circuit summarized, evidence is suppressed for *Brady* purposes when "(1) the prosecution failed to disclose evidence that it or law enforcement was aware of before it was too late for the defendant to make use of the evidence, and (2) the evidence was not otherwise available to the defendant through the exercise of reasonable diligence."[22]

At least in some jurisdictions, a *Brady* claim will not succeed if the information could have been obtained by the defense from other sources via subpoena.[23] These courts hold that "where counsel is on notice that a witness may have exculpatory information, and has an opportunity to subpoena that witness, there is no obligation for the prosecutor to seek out and provide information to the defendant."[24] The D.C. Circuit appears to reject this rule. In one case, for example, it did not find that the defendant's failure to subpoena a witness precluded his *Brady* claim because the "appropriate way for defense counsel to obtain such information was to make a *Brady* request of the prosecutor, just as he did."[25]

C. Information in the Possession of the Prosecution

Brady applies to any information deemed in the possession of the entire prosecution team, not just information in the prosecuting attorney's files. Indeed, the *Brady* "rule encompasses evidence 'known only to police investigators and not to the prosecutor.' In order to comply with *Brady*, therefore,

---

20. *Skilling*, 554 F.3d at 577; *see also* United States v. Warshak, 631 F.3d 266, 297-98 (6th Cir. 2010).
21. *Strickler*, 527 U.S. at 280 (emphasis added).
22. Boss v. Pierce, 263 F.3d 734, 740 (7th Cir. 2001).
23. *See* United States v. Ellender, 947 F.2d 748, 756-57 (5th Cir. 1991).
24. United States v. Lockhart, 956 F.2d 1418, 1426 (7th Cir. 1992); *see also* United States v. Edwards, 34 F.4th 570, 587 (7th Cir. 2022).
25. In re Sealed Case No. 99-3096 (Brady Obligations), 185 F.3d 887, 897 (D.C. Cir. 1999).

'the individual prosecutor has a duty to learn of any favorable evidence known to the others acting on the government's behalf in th[e] case, including the police.' "[26]

The DOJ instructs that:

> In most cases, "the prosecution team" will include the agents and law enforcement officers within the relevant district working on the case. In multi-district investigations, investigations that include both Assistant United States Attorneys and prosecutors from a Department litigating component or other United States Attorney's Office (USAO), and parallel criminal and civil proceedings, this definition will necessarily be adjusted to fit the circumstances. In addition, in complex cases that involve parallel proceedings with regulatory agencies (SEC, FDIC, EPA, etc.), or other non-criminal investigative or intelligence agencies, the prosecutor should consider whether the relationship with the other agency is close enough to make it part of the prosecution team for discovery purposes.[27]

An important question in white-collar cases is whether agencies charged with civil enforcement of a particular statutory regime, or other government agents who engage in parallel civil investigations of the same misconduct for which the defendant was indicted, are deemed to be part of the prosecution team for *Brady* purposes. Some circuits have yet to provide express guidance on when knowledge of *Brady* material can be imputed from one government agency to another.[28] Other circuits differ on how rigorously they evaluate the "question of how much knowledge possessed by various arms of the State should be imputed to the prosecution."[29]

One fairly typical, if not particularly illuminating, test queries whether the agency is conducting a "joint investigation" with the Department of Justice.[30] Among the factors one would look to in resolving this question are whether the other agency: participated in witness interviews; reviewed documents gathered by, or shared documents with, the prosecution; was involved in presenting the case to the grand jury; played a role in the development of a prosecutorial strategy; or accompanied prosecutors to court proceedings.[31] The Department's Justice Manual also details a range of factors to be considered in determining whether to review information held by another agency.[32] It cautions, however, that prosecutors ought to be sure "they understand the law in their circuit and their office's practice regarding

26. *Strickler*, 527 U.S. at 280-81.
27. Justice Manual, *supra* note 6, § 9-5.002.
28. *See* United States v. Ingarfield, No. 20-cr-146 (RA), 2023 WL 3123002, at *3 (S.D.N.Y. April 27, 2023).
29. *See* United States v. Combs, 267 F.3d 1167, 1174 (10th Cir. 2001) (discussing various circuits' conflicting standards).
30. *Ingarfield*, 2023 WL 3123002, at *3; *see also* United States v. Hwa, 18-cr-538 (MKB), 2021 WL 11723583, at *55 (E.D.N.Y. Sept. 3, 2021).
31. *See Ingarfield*, 2023 WL 3123002, at *3.
32. *See* Justice Manual, *supra* note 6, § 9-5.002.

discovery" and encourages them to "err on the side of inclusiveness when identifying the members of the prosecution team for discovery purposes" in order "to avoid future litigation over *Brady* and *Giglio* issues and avoid surprises at trial."[33]

If the prosecution team—however defined—does not have the information the defense seeks, courts generally hold that the prosecutor is under no obligation to seek it out. As the Eighth Circuit has explained, "[t]he government has no 'affirmative duty . . . to take action to discover information which it does not possess.' . . . In addition, the 'prosecutor has no duty to undertake a fishing expedition in other jurisdictions in an effort to find impeaching evidence.'"[34]

Given this rule, the question whether prosecutors are deemed in "possession" of information obviously takes on greater import. As we shall see, absent a finding that the prosecution team "possesses" the information requested and a concomitant governmental obligation to disclose under *Brady*,Fed. R. Crim. P. 16, or the *Jencks* Act, defense counsel may not be able to secure the needed information through other means because of the limitations of the only legal tool left to the defense, Fed. R. Crim. P. 17 trial subpoenas (considered *infra*).

D. Prejudice or Materiality

The question whether the government improperly withheld *Brady* material often turns on the very fact-specific question of "prejudice," more often termed "materiality."[35] In *United States v. Bagley*, the Court held that "evidence is material only if there is a reasonable probability that, had the evidence been disclosed to the defense, the result of the proceeding would have been different. A 'reasonable probability' is a probability sufficient to undermine confidence in the outcome."[36] This test requires that the materiality of the suppressed evidence be considered collectively, not item by item.[37]

In *Kyles v.Whitley*, 514 U.S. 419 (1995), the Court clarified that:

> Although the constitutional duty is triggered by the potential impact of favorable but undisclosed evidence, a showing of materiality does not require demonstration by a preponderance that disclosure of the suppressed evidence would have resulted ultimately in the defendant's acquittal. . . . *Bagley*'s touchstone of materiality is a "reasonable probability" of a different result, and the adjective is important.[38]

---

33. *Id.*
34. United States v. Jones, 34 F.3d 596, 599 (8th Cir. 1994).
35. *See, e.g.*, Turner v. United States, 582 U.S. 313, 324-25 (2017).
36. *Bagley*, 473 U.S. at 682.
37. *Kyles*, 514 U.S. at 436.
38. *Id.* at 434.

The *Kyles* Court also stressed that materiality is not a sufficiency of evidence test: "A defendant need not demonstrate that after discounting the inculpatory evidence in light of the undisclosed evidence, there would not have been enough left to convict."[39] "One does not show a *Brady* violation by demonstrating that some of the inculpatory evidence should have been excluded, but by showing that the favorable evidence could reasonably be taken to put the whole case in such a different light as to undermine confidence in the verdict."[40]

The Court's test sounds like a harmless error standard, and it is in fact the means by which *Brady* claims are tested on appeal. "Once a reviewing court applying *Bagley* has found constitutional error there is no need for further harmless-error review."[41] But the test is also the standard by which prosecutors must make their *forward-looking* decisions whether or not to turn over potentially exculpatory information. And they are required to make these judgments before trial or at least in time for the defense to have the opportunity to effectively use the information at trial.

This is a difficult and highly artificial inquiry in a number of respects. Prosecutors must attempt to forecast how their case will go in and guess at the likely cumulative effect of withholding various individual items of exculpatory evidence. This difficulty is exacerbated by the fact that, before trial, prosecutors may not know what the defense's theory is, and the defense has no obligation to share it with the government. Finally, this exercise requires significant psychological discipline, as well as imagination, if it is to be done fairly. It must be acknowledged that prosecutors, by virtue of their training, experience, and investment in their cases, often do not see or deeply discount the exculpatory nature of the evidence at issue.

As difficult as it may be for prosecutors to apply the *Brady* standard in certain cases, prosecutors' *Brady* obligations are both fundamental to just results and non-negotiable. As the results of the efforts of the Innocence Project and others attest, there is ample evidence that individuals whom prosecutors, juries, and judges believed to be guilty beyond a reasonable doubt have in fact been wrongfully accused, convicted, and jailed. Prosecutors should approach their *Brady* obligations with this troubling fact front and center. Many *Brady* violations flow from misjudgment or negligence rather than game-playing but nothing excuses the demands of due process. The best advice to prosecutors, then, is that absent serious concerns about witness safety or the continuing integrity of evidence, if it does not "hurt" to turn it over, turn it over; if it does "hurt" to turn it over, turn it over because it is likely to be *Brady*. Or as the Supreme Court puts it, "the prudent prosecutor will resolve doubtful questions in favor of disclosure."[42]

---

39. *Id.* at 434-35.
40. *Id.* at 435.
41. *Id.*
42. United States v. Agurs, 427 U.S. 97, 108 (1976).

Most commentators, and many judges, believe that we are facing an epidemic of *Brady* violations.[43] There has been a disheartening stream of high-profile cases that imploded because of prosecutorial *Brady* violations, including the prosecution of Senator Ted Stevens and the "Fat Leonard" Navy corruption cases. Judges are taking these violations very seriously. Judge Sullivan in the District of D.C. commissioned an investigation by private counsel into the non-disclosure of *Brady* materials and published the findings. Judge Nathan, after vacating a conviction after a jury verdict due to *Brady* violations, issued a scathing opinion detailing the prosecution's errors and ordered all Assistant U.S. Attorneys (AUSAs) in the Southern District of New York to read her opinion and certify that they had done so.[44]

E. Waivers and Pre-Plea *Brady*

Given that guilty plea rates in federal criminal cases hover around ninety-seven percent, the question whether the government must make pre-plea disclosure of materially exculpatory information is an important one. To avoid the issue, federal prosecutors regularly require defendants, as a condition of the plea deal, to agree to what are known as "*Brady*" waivers, discussed further in Chapter 16 (Plea Bargaining).

Such a waiver was at issue in *United States v. Ruiz*, 536 U.S. 622 (2002). The *Ruiz* Court recognized that "[o]f course, the more information the defendant has, the more aware he is of the likely consequences of a plea, waiver, or decision, and the wiser that decision will likely be."[45] But it held that "the Constitution does not require the prosecutor to share all useful information with the defendant" and, in particular, does not require pre-plea disclosure of *Giglio* materials.[46]

At issue in *Ruiz* was whether the government had to provide the defendant with any witness impeachment materials it had in its possession in order to ensure that the defendant's subsequent plea was voluntary. The Court said "no," reasoning that the law ordinarily considers a waiver knowing, intelligent, and voluntary if "the defendant fully understands the nature of the right and how it would likely apply *in general* in the circumstances—even though the defendant may not know the *specific detailed* consequences of invoking it."[47]

---

43. *See, e.g.*, United States v. Olsen, 737 F.3d 625, 626 (9th Cir. 2013) (Kozinski, J., dissenting from denial of rehearing *en banc*) ("There is an epidemic of *Brady* violations abroad in the land. Only judges can put a stop to it.").
44. *See* United States v. Nejad, 487 F. Supp. 3d 206 (S.D.N.Y. 2020).
45. *Ruiz*, 536 U.S. at 629.
46. *Id.*
47. *Id.* (emphasis original).

The *Ruiz* Court conducted a balancing of interests analysis, in which it discounted the value of impeachment material to the defense. It is not clear whether the Court would strike a different balance if what was at stake is substantive evidence of innocence. The Court dismissed the defendant's concern that, in the absence of impeachment information, innocents will plead guilty by noting that "the proposed plea agreement at issue here specifies [that] the Government will provide 'any information establishing the factual innocence of the defendant' regardless."[48]

F. Ethical Rules and the McDade Amendment

In Chapter 1 (Introduction), we generally discussed prosecutors' ethical obligations and 28 U.S.C. § 530B (the "McDade Amendment"), which subjects attorneys for the federal government to "State [ethics] laws and rules, and local Federal court [ethics] rules, governing attorneys in each State where such attorney engages in that attorney's duties." The constitutionally required *Brady* disclosure standard is less generous to the defense than that applied in reigning ethical standards, which generally do not include a "materiality" requirement. Thus, Model Rule of Professional Conduct 3.8(d) requires prosecutors to "make timely disclosure to the defense of all evidence or information known to the prosecutor *that tends to negate guilt* of the accused or *mitigates the offense*, and, in connection with sentencing, [to] disclose to the defense and to the tribunal all unprivileged *mitigating information* known to the prosecutor" (emphasis added).

In short, *Brady* provides the constitutional floor below which prosecutors cannot go, but in the many jurisdictions that have adopted Rule 3.8, prosecutors must follow its more demanding standard lest they violate § 530B and face possible ethics charges.[49]

III. PRE-TRIAL DISCOVERY: FED. R. CRIM. P. 16

"There is no general constitutional right to discovery in a criminal case, and *Brady* did not create one."[50] Because "'the Due Process Clause has little to say regarding the amount of discovery the parties must be afforded,'"[51]

48. *Id.* at 631.
49. *See* In re Kline, 113 A.3d 202 (D.C. Ct. App. 2015); ABA Standing Comm. on Ethics & Prof'l Responsibility, Formal Op. 09-454 (July 8, 2009) (Rule 3.8(d) requires disclosure of exculpatory information whether or not it is material).
50. *Weatherford*, 429 U.S. at 559.
51. *Id.*

the parties' discovery obligations are controlled by federal rule—Fed. R. Crim. P. 16.

Although *Brady*'s disclosure obligations are not dependent on a defense request, the defense must make a request for discovery under Rule 16 to trigger the government's disclosure obligations. Compliance with this request by the government, and a reciprocal government request for Rule 16 discovery, creates a defense obligation to make more limited discovery to the government under Rule 16(b).

Fed. R. Crim. P. 12(b)(3) requires motions for Rule 16 discovery to be made before trial; the court may control the timing of discovery motions under Rule 12(c). Under Rule 16(c), both parties are under a continuing obligation to disclose any additional evidence or material as they discover it. Disputes about discovery often take the form of a motion for a protective order under Rule 16(d)(1) or a motion to compel or for sanctions under Rule 16(d)(2). If the government fails to meet its Rule 16 discovery obligations, a convicted defendant can only secure relief by showing that his failure to obtain the requested materials affected his substantial rights, thereby overcoming Fed. R. Crim. P. 52(a)'s harmless error standard. An error affects the defendant's substantial rights if it "affected the outcome of the district court proceedings."[52]

When one looks at the substance of Rule 16, the items required to be disclosed might seem somewhat random. But the various types of materials covered by this rule share certain characteristics. In general, Rule 16 dictates that a defendant should not be surprised by the evidence against him where the evidence is particularly powerful; belongs to the defendant; requires pre-trial investigation or pre-trial motion practice to deal with the use or admissibility of the evidence; and/or is not susceptible to manipulation or intimidation by the defendant.

A. The Government's Discovery Obligations

1. Defendant's Statements

Rule 16(a)(1)'s disclosure obligation is confined to statements made by the defendant. It does *not* extend to providing other witnesses's statements; these are covered by the *Jencks* Act and Fed. R. Crim. P. 26.2.

Disclosure to the defense of the defendant's own admissions, particularly those in the nature of a confession, is appropriate because they can be very powerful evidence. Turning these statements over in pre-trial discovery will also expedite the litigation of motions to suppress the statements on constitutional or other grounds. Finally, these statements are largely

52. United States v. Olano, 507 U.S. 725, 734 (1993).

immune from any efforts the defendant may make to impair the integrity of this evidence.

Rule 16(a)(1)(A) & (B) requires the government to disclose the following to the defense:

1. The substance of any relevant *oral statement* made by the defendant if:
   - the defendant has made a Rule 16 request
   - the statement was made before or after arrest
   - in response to interrogation by a person
   - the defendant knew was a government agent
   - if the government intends to use the statement at trial

Rule 16(a)(1)(A) does not impose on the government the burden of writing down and turning over everything the defendant said in an interview. But fairness requires that those oral statements that the government believes are important enough for use at trial be reduced to writing and turned over to the defense. The rule specifies that the defendant must know that he is talking to a government agent, presumably putting the defendant on notice that what he said could be used against him. The drafters also apparently did not want to impose on the government an obligation to produce every statement the defendant made to any witness. Statements made to undercovers and confidential informants obviously do not qualify.

2. the portion of *any written record* containing the *substance* of any relevant *oral statement* made by the defendant if:
   - the defendant has made a Rule 16 request
   - the statement was made before or after arrest
   - in response to interrogation by a person
   - the defendant knew was a government agent

Rule 16(a)(1)(B)(ii) is a variation on Rule 16(a)(1)(A). Here, the defendant's oral statements made to a known government agent have already been reduced to writing, thus potentially enhancing the reliability of the government's narrative. These statements must be produced even if the government does not intend to use the statement at trial, in its case in chief or in rebuttal.

3. any relevant written or recorded statement *by the defendant* if:
   - the defendant has made a Rule 16 request
   - the statement is within the government's possession, custody, or control; and
   - the attorney for the government knows—or through due diligence could know—that the statement exists

Rule 16(a)(1)(B)(i) is usually read to mean something reduced to writing by the defendant or signed or otherwise approved by him. It would apply, for example, if the defendant was interviewed and signed or adopted the transcript or summary of the interview. This section is not usually read to include an agent's written report of an oral statement that is not signed or otherwise adopted by the witness/defendant.

Because this is a statement the defendant authored or adopted, it is especially powerful evidence. Thus, it must be produced even if the statement was not made contemporaneously with an arrest, was not made in response to interrogation by a known government agent, and even though the government does not intend to use it at trial. Because this rule would cover any statement by the defendant, whether or not made to law enforcement personnel, it would apply, for example, to a defendant's deposition transcript in civil litigation, or a defendant's signed employment application or application for government benefits, so long as such statements are relevant, in the government's possession, and the AUSA knows, or should know, that the statements exist.

4. the defendant's recorded testimony before a grand jury relating to the charged offense.

Rule 16(a)(1)(B)(iii) is truly a subcategory of Rule 16(a)(1)(B)(i) but this subsection makes explicit the government's authority to disclose matters occurring before the grand jury that would otherwise be subject to grand jury secrecy rules. Not all the government's grand jury presentation must be disclosed—only the defendant's testimony.

If the defendant is an organization, the government must disclose to the defendant any oral or written statement (as described above) if the government contends that the person making the statement:

> (i) was legally able to bind the defendant regarding the subject of the statement because of that person's position as the defendant's director, officer, employee, or agent; or
> (ii) was personally involved in the alleged conduct constituting the offense and was legally able to bind the defendant regarding that conduct because of that person's position as the defendant's director, officer, employee, or agent.[53]

2. The Defendant's Prior Record

Rule 16(a)(1)(D) provides that, "[u]pon a defendant's request, the government must furnish the defendant with a copy of the defendant's prior

53. Fed. R. Crim. P. 16(a)(1)(C).

criminal record that is within the government's possession, custody, or control if the attorney for the government knows—or through due diligence could know—that the record exists."[54] The defense needs this information to make informed choices and critical decisions. The length of the defendant's rap sheet will affect his sentencing exposure under the U.S. Sentencing Guidelines; this information, then, will be important in informing the defendant's decision-making on governmental plea offers. Defense counsel will also need to know whether the defendant has a record before advising the defendant whether he should take the stand, given that a defendant's rap sheet generally can only be used at trial to cross-examine him if he testifies. Because the defendant's criminal record is in the government's control, it is unlikely to be subject to compromise by the defendant. And the defense may wish to make a pre-trial motion to exclude the use of the defendant's record on cross-examination.

3. Documents and Objects

Under Rule 16(a)(1)(E), the government must permit the defendant to inspect and to copy or photograph books, papers, documents, data, photographs, tangible objects, buildings or places, or copies or portions of any of these items, if

- the defendant has made a request
- the item is within the government's possession, custody, or control and
  - (i) the item is material to preparing the defense
  - (ii) the government intends to use the item in its case-in-chief at trial, or
  - (iii) the item was obtained from or belongs to the defendant

a. Items "Material to Preparing the Defense" Under Rule 16(a)(1)(E)(i)

This category of information is more limited in scope than its language may suggest. First, in *United States v. Armstrong*, 517 U.S. 456 (1996), the Court held that the defendant was not entitled to discovery regarding his constitutional claim that he was selected for prosecution because of his race. The court read the term "defense" to mean only those items that "refute the Government's arguments that the defendant committed the crime charged."[55] Stated another way, Rule 16(a)(1)(E)(i) only requires disclosure of materials that rebut the government's arguments that the defendant committed the offenses in the indictment. A selective prosecution claim, in

54. *Id.* 16(a)(1)(D).
55. *Armstrong*, 517 U.S. at 462.

the *Armstrong* Court's view, did not meet this criterion. Courts have also held that Rule 16(a)(1)(E)(i) does not authorize discovery relating to allegedly abusive or illegal investigative practices by the government.[56]

A second limitation on the scope of Rule 16(a)(1)(E)(i) concerns the meaning of "material." Many courts have adopted the following formulation as the standard: "For the defendant to show materiality under this rule, '[t]here must be some indication that the pretrial disclosure of the disputed evidence would have enabled the defendant significantly to alter the quantum of proof in his favor.' "[57] Most courts read this, consistent with *Brady*, to mean "exculpatory." Thus, the Second Circuit has ruled that:

> Evidence that the government does not intend to use in its case in chief is material if it could be used to counter the government's case or to bolster a defense; information not meeting either of those criteria is not to be deemed material within the meaning of the Rule merely because the government may be able to use it to rebut a defense position.[58]

This would not include, for example, inculpatory information or material that the defense would like to have in advance of trial to determine if the government can counter an anticipated defense argument.[59]

The D.C. Circuit, however, relying on the standard quoted above, ruled that:

> This language does not mean that inculpatory evidence may never be material. To the contrary, a defendant in possession of such evidence may "alter the quantum of proof in his favor" in several ways: by preparing a strategy to confront the damaging evidence at trial; by conducting an investigation to attempt to discredit that evidence; or by not presenting a defense that is undercut by such evidence.[60]

The D.C. Circuit concluded that the "rule as written does not compel the conclusion that inculpatory evidence is immune from disclosure. Inculpatory evidence, after all, is just as likely to assist in 'the preparation of the defendant's defense' as exculpatory evidence."[61] Thus, in the D.C. Circuit, evidence is "material" under Rule 16 "'as long as there is a strong indication that it will play an important role in uncovering admissible evidence, aiding

56. *See* United States v. Sanders, 106 F.4th 455, 473-74 (6th Cir. 2024) (*en banc*).
57. United States v. Caro, 597 F.3d 608, 621 (4th Cir. 2010).
58. *See* United States v. Stevens, 985 F.2d 1175, 1180 (2d Cir. 1993); *see also Sanders*, 106 F.4th at 475.
59. *See Stevens*, 985 F.2d at 1180.
60. United States v. Marshall, 132 F.3d 63, 68 (D.C. Cir. 1998).
61. *Id.* at 67.

witness preparation, corroborating testimony, or assisting impeachment or rebuttal.' "[62]

b. Items the Government "Intends to Use in its Case-in-Chief" Under Rule 16(a)(1)(E)(ii)

This is a critical category of discovery. Rule 16(a)(1)(E)(ii) requires the government to make pre-trial disclosure of items it "intends to use in its case-in-chief"—meaning its prospective trial exhibits. In document-intensive white-collar cases, disclosure of the government's trial exhibits can give the defense an extremely helpful preview of the government's case.[63]

c. Items Obtained from or That Belong to the Defendant Under Rule 16(a)(1)(E)(iii)

Providing defense access to items that were obtained from or belong to the defendant can include evidence seized from the defendant during an arrest or pursuant to a search warrant. In many such cases, the defense will already know about the seized materials. The information disclosed pursuant to Rule 16(a)(1)(E)(iii) may be helpful to the defense, however, when the government alleges that certain inculpatory items—such as pornography or records of fraudulent activity—belonged to the defendant despite the fact that they were seized from anonymized on-line accounts or devices that the defendant denies owning.

4. Reports of Examinations and Tests

If the government conducts physical or mental examinations or scientific tests or experiments, the defense will likely wish to hire its own experts to replicate the examinations or tests. Such examinations or tests can take time, and thus these matters are more efficiently dealt with before trial.

62. *Id.* at 68.

63. Another type of trial-related disclosure is imposed on the government by the Rules of Evidence rather than Rule 16. Under Fed. R. Evid. 404(b)(3), upon the request of the defendant, prosecutors are required to "provide reasonable notice" of any evidence of the defendant's prior crime or wrongs "that the prosecutor intends to offer at trial, so that the defendant has a fair opportunity to meet it." The prosecutor must explain, in writing and generally before trial, the purpose for which this evidence is tendered. This requirement applies to the prosecution "regardless of how it intends to use the extrinsic act evidence at trial, i.e., during its case-in-chief, for impeachment, or for possible rebuttal." Fed. R. Evid. 404(b), 1991 amend. adv. comm. notes.

Accordingly, under Rule 16(a)(1)(F), the government has an obligation to allow the defendant to inspect and to copy or photograph the results or reports relating to any such examinations, tests, or experiments if

- the defendant makes a request
- the item is within the government's possession, custody, or control
- the attorney for the government knows—or through due diligence could know—that the item exists and
- the item is either
  - material to preparing the defense or
  - will be used by the government in its case-in-chief at trial

5. Expert Witnesses

Under Rule 16(a)(1)(G), upon the defense's request the government must give to the defendant a written summary of any expert opinions (and related materials) that the government intends to use during its case-in-chief at trial or plans to introduce in its rebuttal case.

6. Government Information Not Subject to Disclosure

Except as otherwise expressly permitted in Rule 16, Rule 16(a)(2) states that the rule generally does "not authorize the discovery or inspection of reports, memoranda, or other internal government documents made by an attorney for the government or other government agent in connection with investigation or prosecuting the case." In other words, the government's work product is not subject to disclosure. Rule 16 also does not authorize or compel the disclosure of grand jury or *Jencks* Act material relating to statements made by prospective government witnesses.[64]

B. The Defense's Reciprocal Discovery Obligations

The defense has no obligation—consistent with the defendant's Fifth Amendment right—to provide the government with the defendant's prior statements. Nor does it have to turn over the defendant's rap sheet. It does have a contingent obligation to turn over three types of materials.[65]

64. *See* Fed. R. Crim. P. 16(a)(2), (3).

65. The defense is also obligated to provide the government pre-trial notice of its intention to rely on certain types of defenses under Fed. R. Crim. P. 12.1 (alibi defense); Fed. R. Crim. P. 12.2 (insanity defense or expert testimony on defendant's mental condition); Fed. R. Crim.

1. Documents and Objects

Under Rule 16(b)(1)(A), if the defendant requests disclosure of the documents and objects described in Rule 16(a)(1)(E), the government complies, and the government makes a reciprocal request, the defendant must permit the government to copy or photograph books, papers, documents, data, photographs, tangible objects, buildings or places, or copies or portions of any of these items, if

- the item is within defense's possession, custody, or control and
- the defendant intends to use the item in his case-in-chief at trial

2. Reports of Examinations and Tests

The defendant must permit the government to inspect and to copy or photograph the results or reports of any physical or mental examination and of any scientific test or experiment if:

- the defendant made a request for such material under Rule 16(a)(1)(F)
- the government complied with the request
- the government makes a reciprocal request
- the item is within the defendant's possession, custody, or control
- the defendant intends either
  - to use the item in the defendant's case-in-chief at trial or
  - to call the witness who prepared the report and the report relates to the witness' testimony

2. Expert Witnesses

Under Rule 16(b)(1)(C), the defense must give the government a written summary of any expert opinions (and related materials) that the defendant intends to use as evidence at trial if

- the defendant made a similar request of the government under Rule 16(a)(1)(G), the government complied, and it made a reciprocal request, or
- the defendant has given notice under Rule 12.2(b) of an intent to present expert testimony on the defendant's mental condition and the government requested the summary

---

P. 12.3 (claim of actual or believe exercise of public authority on behalf of law enforcement or federal intelligence agency).

3. Defense Information Not Subject to Disclosure

Under Rule 16(b)(2), except for scientific or medical reports, the rule "does not authorize the discovery or inspection of . . . reports, memoranda, or other documents made by the defendant, or the defendant's attorney or agent, during the case's investigation or defense." It also does not authorize disclosure of a statement made to the defendant or the defendant's lawyer by a government or defense witness, or a prospective government or defense witness.

IV. *JENCKS* ACT OR 3500 MATERIALS: WITNESS STATEMENTS

In *Jencks v. United States*, 353 U.S. 657 (1957), the Supreme Court held that federal criminal defendants are entitled under certain circumstances to receive, for impeachment purposes, relevant statements of government witnesses. Congress codified this decision, with certain alterations, in the *Jencks* Act, 18 U.S.C. § 3500. The *Jencks* Act, as translated into Fed. R. Crim. P. 26.2, is the means by which witness statements—other than those of the defendant—may be obtained from the prosecution by the defense; such statements are not subject to disclosure in discovery under Rule 16(a)(2). Qualifying witness statements are often called "*Jencks*" or "3500" material. Like Fed. R. Crim. P. 16, the disclosure obligations of the *Jencks* Act and Fed. R. Crim. P. 26.2 are triggered only by a timely defense request.

Recall that the defense in a criminal case does not have access to the tools that civil litigants regularly employ to ferret out the substance of their opponent's case. Critically, they cannot depose the government witnesses or serve them with interrogatories to find out what they are likely to say at trial. Unless the government's witnesses are willing to be interviewed by the defense—and they have no obligation to do so—the only notice the defense has of what the government's witnesses are likely to say will be found in whatever *Jencks* Act statements they have made. And, as was recognized in *Jencks*, these statements can be a critical source of impeachment material. If a government witness testifies inconsistently with her grand jury testimony or comes up with new facts not provided in her deposition in a parallel civil case, the defense can use that to attack the witness's credibility.

As important as this category of information is, the *Jencks* Act is, in essence, an anti-discovery statute. It is designed to make clear that the government cannot be forced to produce this critical category of materials prior to the conclusion of witnesses's direct examination at trial. Thus, § 3500 provides that, in any federal prosecution, "no statement or report in the possession of the United States which was made by a Government witness or prospective Government witness (other than the defendant)" and which relates to the subject matter as to which the witness testified "shall be the subject of subpoena, discovery or inspection until said witness has testified on direct examination in the trial of the case."

To qualify for *Jencks* Act disclosure, the material must

- be in the possession of the government
- the defense must make a timely request
- the material must relate to the subject-matter of the testimony, and
- the material must constitute a "statement" within the meaning of the Act

Fed. R. Crim. P. 26.2 adopts the same requirements and definition of "statement" found in the *Jencks* Act but extends its coverage by providing for reciprocal disclosures by the defense of witness statements, and by requiring the provision of witness statements not only at trial, but also at various types of hearings.

The *Jencks* Act does not in so many words say that it is the exclusive means by which defendants can secure witness statements from the government for purposes of impeachment. But the Court, in passing on the issue, found that "some things too clearly evince a legislative enactment to call for a redundancy of utterance."[66] When querying what is covered by the Act, one may wish to consult Congress's purposes in enacting it. Congress not only "strongly feared that disclosure of memoranda containing the investigative agent's interpretations and impressions might reveal the inner workings of the investigative process and thereby injure the national interest," but also felt that it would be "grossly unfair to allow the defense to use statements to impeach a witness which could not fairly be said to be the witness' own rather than the product of the investigator's selections, interpretations, and interpolations."[67]

This concern about fairness to witnesses informs courts' decisions on the much-litigated issue of what constitutes a witness "statement." Section 3500(e) defines a statement as:

(1) A "written statement made by [the trial] witness and signed or otherwise adopted or approved by him."[68] Into this category would fall things like a statement given to the police that the witness signed or adopted, writings by others approved by the witness, and, where an agent is the witness, any search or arrest warrant affidavits she swore out.

---

66. Palermo v. United States, 360 U.S. 343, 350 (1959).
67. *Id.*
68. 18 U.S.C. § 3500(e)(1); *see also* Fed. R. Crim. P. 26.2(f)(1).

(2) A "stenographic, mechanical, electrical, or other recording, or a transcription thereof, which is a *substantially verbatim* recital of an oral statement made by said witness and *recorded contemporaneously with* the making of such oral statement."[69] Examples of materials that fall into this category are a cooperator's prior testimony in a related trial or in the grand jury, the taped confession of a cooperating co-defendant, a transcript of the witness's deposition testimony in a parallel civil case, and a cooperating witness's plea colloquy.

(3) "A statement, however taken or recorded, or a transcription thereof, if any, made by said witness to a grand jury."[70] This provision requires the government to provide a transcript of the grand jury testimony of any of its trial witnesses. As was noted in the Chapter 12 (Grand Jury), prosecutors may decide to use hearsay recitals of a witness' prospective testimony rather than calling the witness herself to the grand jury to avoid producing potential impeachment material in its *Jencks* Act production.

The second definition of "statements" is the most difficult to apply because there is substantial ambiguity regarding what constitutes a "virtually verbatim" and "contemporaneous" statement. The government routinely resists producing FBI reports of witness statements (recorded on FBI form 302 and thus often referred to as "302s"), arguing that 302s do not satisfy either requirement. One thing is clear, however: the government has no general obligation to take witnesses statements down in a way that fits within the statutory definition of a "statement."[71]

One notable issue arising under the *Jencks* Act concerns the timing of disclosure. In many white-collar cases, the "*Jencks*" or "3500" material may be voluminous. If it is in fact turned over to the defense at the conclusion of a witness's direct examination, there may be insufficient time for the defense to read, digest, and effectively use it in cross-examining the witness.[72] Courts may grant defense counsel a recess to study the material,[73] but recesses disrupt the flow of the trial proceedings and burden all involved. Some district courts have attempted to order the government to make early disclosure of *Jencks* material, but the circuit courts have made clear that such orders are "plainly inconsistent with the language of the Act."[74] District courts, however, can and do strongly "encourage" early disclosure[75] and have many ways to make prosecutors' lives difficult if they do not heed the court's "suggestion."

---

69. 18 U.S.C. § 3500(e)(2) (emphasis added); *see also* Fed. R. Crim. P. 26.2(f)(2).
70. 18 U.S.C. § 3500(e)(3); *see also* Fed. R. Crim. P. 26.2(f)(3).
71. *See* United States v. Brimage, 115 F.3d 73, 76-77 (1st Cir. 1997).
72. *See, e.g.*, United States v. Holmes, 722 F.2d 37, 40-41 (4th Cir. 1983).
73. *See* Fed. R. Crim. P. 26.2(d).
74. United States v. Lewis, 35 F.3d 148, 150 (4th Cir. 1994).
75. *See, e.g.*, *id.* at 151.

Prosecutors have the discretion to make early disclosure and sometimes do so. Some prosecutors, for example, will make pre-trial disclosure of *Jencks*; others have a policy of producing all the *Jencks* material once jeopardy has attached in the trial (in a jury trial, once the jury is sworn). There appears to be very little consistency in federal practice in this regard.

One recurring issue relating to the timing of *Jencks* disclosure arises when information constitutes both *Brady/Giglio* material (in that it is, for example, materially impeaching) and *Jencks* material. Most courts hold that "'[w]hen *Brady* material sought by a defendant is covered by the *Jencks* Act, . . . the terms of that Act govern the timing of the government's disclosure.'"[76]

V. FED. R. CRIM. P. 17 SUBPOENAS

As outlined above, materials important to the formulation of an effective defense may be held by government actors who are only indirectly involved in the prosecution of the criminal case. Further, it is often the case that important documents are held by non-governmental third parties. These third-party materials may not only provide fodder for the defense theory and possible impeachment material, but they may also yield critical information about the government's theory of the case when they are obtained from regulatory enforcement authorities whose investigations parallel prosecutorial efforts. Discovery of documents under Rule 16(a)(1)(E) does not reach documents held by non-parties except insofar as the prosecution might have gathered material from them for use in its investigation or they are deemed part of a joint investigation.

The primary means by which the defense may seek to obtain materials from persons not subject to *Brady*, Rule 16, or *Jencks* Act requirements is Fed. R. Crim. P. 17, which governs the issuance of trial subpoenas in criminal cases. Under Fed. R. Crim. P. 17(c) the defense can subpoena witnesses "to produce any books, papers, documents, data, or other objects the subpoena designates." In *Bowman Dairy Co. v. United States*, 341 U.S. 214 (1951), the defendant attempted to subpoena the prosecution for documents not then subject to discovery under Rule 16. The Supreme Court rebuffed this attempt, explaining that a Rule 17 subpoena duces tecum is "not intended to provide an additional means of discovery"; rather, the rule was intended simply "to expedite the trial by providing a time and place *before* trial for the inspection of subpoenaed materials" in Rule 17(c)(1).[77]

In *United States v. Nixon*, 418 U.S. 683 (1974), the Court imposed a rigorous standard for the pre-trial issuance of Rule 17 subpoenas. *Nixon* was a

76. United States v. Davis, 306 F.3d 398, 421 (6th Cir. 2002).
77. *Bowman Dairy Co.*, 341 U.S. at 220 (emphasis added).

criminal case against former government officials and presidential campaign officials for, *inter alia*, conspiracy to defraud United States and to obstruct justice. The special prosecutor caused a third-party subpoena duces tecum to be issued directing President Nixon to produce tape recordings and documents relating to conversations he had with his aides and advisors. The *Nixon* Court held that, to require production of these materials prior to trial,

> the moving party must show: (1) that the documents are evidentiary and relevant; (2) that they are not otherwise procurable reasonably in advance of trial by exercise of due diligence; (3) that the party cannot properly prepare for trial without such production and inspection in advance of trial and that the failure to obtain such inspection may tend unreasonably to delay the trial; and (4) that the application is made in good faith and is not intended as a general "fishing expedition."[78]

In short, courts have applied *Nixon* to require the defense to show "(1) relevancy; (2) admissibility; (3) specificity."[79] Those served with Rule 17 subpoenas can put the defense to its burden of proving these elements by proceeding under Rule 17(c)(2), which provides that "[o]n motion promptly made, the court may quash or modify the subpoena if compliance would be unreasonable or oppressive."

Application of the demanding *Nixon* standard makes it difficult for the defense to compel disclosure of materials potentially important to the defense that are held by third-parties. For example, courts regularly hold that Rule 17 subpoenas may only be used to secure materials that themselves would be admissible as evidence. Notably, "[c]ourts have consistently interpreted the admissibility standard of Rule 17(c) to preclude production of materials whose evidentiary use is limited to impeachment."[80] "In this respect, Rule 17(c) can be contrasted with the civil rules which permit the issuance of subpoenas to seek production of documents or other materials which, although not themselves admissible, could lead to admissible evidence."[81]

It should be noted that at least one district court has held that the *Nixon* standard applies only when a subpoena is served on a party and a less demanding standard should apply when the subpoena is issued to third parties.[82] Although other courts have not rushed to embrace this ruling, the opinion is both well-reasoned and consistent with Supreme Court precedent. As Judge Scheindlin noted, the advisory committee note accompanying Rule 17 when it was enacted states that "'[t]his rule is substantially the

78. *Nixon*, 418 U.S. at 699-700.
79. *Id.* at 700.
80. United States v. Cherry, 876 F. Supp. 547, 553 (S.D.N.Y. 1995) (collecting cases).
81. *Id.* at 553.
82. *See* United States v. Tucker, 249 F.R.D. 58 (S.D.N.Y. 2008).

same as rule 45(b) of the Federal Rules of Civil Procedure,' which permits parties in a civil action to obtain discovery from non-parties by way of a subpoena. This . . . may indicate that the rule drafters initially thought Rule 17(c) would govern discovery from non-parties, while Rule 16 would govern discovery from the Government."[83]

The court further reasoned that *Bowman Dairy* involved the defendants' attempt to subpoena the *prosecution* for documents not then subject to discovery under Rule 16. The Court's statement that Rule 17 is not a discovery device should be read in light of the Court's evident belief that the defense was trying to do an end run around the limitations of Rule 16. In *Nixon*, the Special Prosecutor issued a trial subpoena to a third party—President Nixon—for evidence. The *government* argued "that the evidentiary requirement of *Bowman Dairy Co.* . . . does not apply in its full vigor when the subpoena duces tecum is issued to third parties rather than to government prosecutors."[84] The *Nixon* Court responded that it did not need to decide whether a lower standard applies to third-party subpoenas because the relevance and evidentiary nature of the tapes were sufficient to meet the higher standard.

As another district court concluded after discussing Judge Scheindlin's reasoning with approval:

> [I]t remains ironic that a defendant in a breach of contract case can call on the power of the courts to compel third-parties to produce any documents "reasonably calculated to lead to the discovery of admissible evidence," Fed. R. Civ. P. 26(b)(1), while a defendant on trial for his life or liberty does not even have the right to obtain documents "material to his defense" from those same third-parties. Applying [a lesser] standard to subpoenas *duces tecum* issued to third parties under Federal Rule of Criminal Procedure 17(c) would resolve that puzzle at great benefit to the rights of defendants to compulsory process and at little cost to the enforcement of the criminal law, since Rule 17 permits the government to issue subpoenas as well.[85]

A. Obtaining Evidence from Overseas

The defense is at an informational disadvantage in its access to two potentially important sources of information: evidence located abroad, and evidence covered by the Stored Communications Act (SCA), 18 U.S.C. § 2702(a).

As is discussed at some length in Chapter 12 (Grand Jury), when pertinent information is located abroad, the government primarily relies on

83. *Id.* at 62.
84. *Nixon*, 418 U.S. at 699 n.12.
85. *United States v. Rajaratnam*, 753 F. Supp. 2d 317, 320 n.1 (S.D.N.Y. 2011).

(1) its contacts with foreign investigative agencies and prosecutors to secure information without using formal legal process, and (2) U.S. Mutual Legal Assistance Treaties (MLATs) to secure in a timely way admissible evidence from countries with whom the United States has such treaties. The defense has access to neither of these important sources of information and evidence. It is generally barred from using MLATs and must proceed through the time-consuming letters rogatory process, in which the provision of the requested information rests in the discretion of the requested country. In some circumstances, however, the defense can make use of domestic process, in the form of Rule 17 subpoenas, to compel U.S. nationals or residents overseas to appear or produce documents and to secure evidence located overseas by serving U.S. branches of foreign companies over which U.S. courts have jurisdiction.

B. Access to Electronic Communications Under the Stored Communications Act (SCA)

The SCA prohibits the providers of electronic communication services (ECSs)—including cell phone and email providers and social media platforms—and remote computing services (RCSs)—including cloud computing providers—from disclosing the contents of certain stored electronic communications to any third party, except in very limited circumstances.[86] ECSs and RCSs are the guardians of a great deal of potentially critical evidence, including email and attached documents, voicemail messages, texts, and social media posts.

As discussed in Chapter 12 (Grand Jury), § 2703 of the Act specifies the three types of process through which the government can compel ECSs and RCSs to disclose electronically stored information: a warrant, a § 2703(d) court order, and an administrative or grand jury subpoena. Critically, however, the SCA does not provide the defense in a criminal case with similar access.[87]

If the material is in the government's hands, it will have to produce it if it falls within the prosecution's *Brady*, Rule 16, or *Jencks* Act obligations. If it is not in the government's possession, the defense must proceed more indirectly to obtain the materials protected by the SCA. It can secure

86. ECSs are defined as "any service which provides to users thereof the ability to send or receive wire or electronic communications." 18 U.S.C. § 2510(15). RCSs are those companies who provide to the public "computer storage or processing services by means of an electronic communications system." *Id.* § 2711(2). "Content" is defined in § 2510(8) as information "concerning the substance, purport, or meaning" of a communication but does not include the existence of the communication or the identities of the parties to it.

87. *See, e.g.*, Facebook, Inc. v. Wint, 199 A.3d 625 (D.C. 2019) (providers may not disclose communications covered by the SCA to comply with criminal defendants' subpoenas).

certain information under the exceptions provided in § 2702(b)(3). Under that section, RCS providers may divulge the contents of a communication with the lawful consent of subscriber or the originator or an addressee or intended recipient of such communication.[88] ECS providers may divulge the contents of a communication to an addressee or intended recipient of such communication or their agent.[89]

If such consents are unavailable, the defense may have to get creative. In civil cases, litigants have attempted to subpoena the (non-consenting) sender, recipient, addressee or RCS subscriber on the theory that the information is in such person's "possession, custody, or control" within the meaning of Rule of Civ. P. 45.[90] The theory is that the court can order such persons to consent given their "control" over the protected materials. In at least one case, this argument succeeded.[91] Rule 17, unlike the applicable civil rule, does not specify that subpoenas can require the production of materials within the "possession, custody, or control" of the subpoenaed party so whether this theory will work is subject to question.

It should be noted, however, that courts are unlikely to accept the argument that because the government can secure SCA-protected materials through warrant, court order, or subpoena, those materials are in the government's "control" such that it has an obligation to produce them under Rule 16 or other disclosure rules.[92]

Examples

1. Hùng Mai was one of a number of individuals running an illegal Ponzi scheme. He entered into a cooperation agreement with the government. Before trial, and while he was in jail on another charge, he asked a friend to set up a Facebook account for him under an alias. Against prison rules, he used a smuggled cell phone to post status updates. Defense counsel for an alleged co-conspirator, Seong-Ho Han, told prosecutors about the account and said that a witness had told counsel about one post that

88. 18 U.S.C. § 2702(b)(3). Note that some courts have held that such consent can be implied. Thus, for example, the California Supreme Court held that § 2702(b)(3)'s lawful consent exception applies to allow providers to disclose communications like Facebook posts or MySpace comments configured by the user to be public. *See* Facebook, Inc. v. Superior Court, 417 P.3d 725, 743-44 (Cal. 2018).

89. 18 U.S.C. § 2702(b)(1); *see also* Facebook v. Pepe, 241 A.3d 248 (D.C. Ct. App. 2020) (consistent with the SCA, provider may not refuse to comply with the defendant's subpoena requiring production of an allegedly threatening Instagram "Story" sent to the consenting defendant by the victim).

90. *See* Fed. R. Civ. P. 45(a)(1)(A)(iii).

91. *See* Flagg v. City of Detroit, 252 F.R.D. 346 (E.D. Mich. 2008).

92. *Cf. Mejia*, 448 F.3d at 444 (rejecting argument that, because the government has the power to secure materials through an MLAT, it should be tasked with doing so to comply with its discovery obligations under Fed. R. Crim. P. 16).

said "I'm not gonna hurt my friends but I'm gonna make Han pay." The government plans to have Mai testify against Han at trial. Han's counsel demands that the government get from its cooperator, and disclose to the defense, the contents of Mai's Facebook account. Does the government have an obligation under *Brady* to do so? Might the government at least have to turn over the posts as *Jenks* material? How else can the defendant get access to these posts?

2. The government failed to turn over to the defense the result of polygraph examination it had administered to a prosecution witness that showed deception as to certain questions. Assume that, in this state, polygraph examinations are inadmissible in evidence and cannot be used even for impeachment purposes. Did the government violate *Brady* by suppressing the polygraph results?

3. Nikon Naumov was the Chief Operating Officer of Acme, Inc., a financial services company, but was fired when an internal investigation by an outside law firm revealed that he had made materially false statements to potential investors.

   Naumov felt betrayed by his friend, the Chief Executive Officer of Acme, Neasa Fannon, for whom he had covered up some shady practices at Acme. In anger, Naumov called a friend at the FBI and reported that Acme was defrauding its investors. Naumov provided the FBI with handwritten notes, purportedly authored by Fannon, that directed Naumov to cover up the fraud. Acme is now cooperating with the government in an effort to secure a deferred prosecution agreement.

   An Assistant U.S. Attorney reviewed the materials and agreed to a cooperation agreement in which Naumov would plead guilty to a misdemeanor in return for his cooperation. FBI agents then spent nine days debriefing him, during which they took twenty-five pages of notes and at the end of which they wrote a six-page memorandum of the witness interview on FBI form 302. The AUSA reached out to the enforcement division of the SEC, notified SEC personnel of the investigation, and shared the 302 with them. The SEC personnel said that they would launch their own investigation and asked the AUSA to keep them informed. The SEC ultimately declined to bring an enforcement action against Acme.

   The FBI arranged for Naumov to meet with Fannon and talk with her about the fraud while Naumov wore a wire that permitted agents to record what was said. After the taped conversation, during which the Fannon denied the alleged fraud, Naumov sent a text message to a former work colleague, Maud Elwyn, saying that he had gotten Fannon back for firing him.

   The government and the defense each submitted the handwritten notes Naumov turned over to the FBI to their own expert document examiners for handwriting and other analyses. The government's examiner's report was inconclusive; she could not opine with any certainty about the author of the notes or anything else. The defense made a request for the government's report but the government said it had no obligation to turn it over. The defense expert could not provide a definitive answer on the handwriting question, but she detected Fannon's fingerprints on the notes.

After further investigation, the government secured an indictment of Fannon for securities fraud. Naumov was not called as a witness in the grand jury, but an FBI agent testified as to what Naumov had told the Bureau.

The government, pursuant to Fannon's discovery request, informed counsel that Fannon has no rap sheet but defense counsel knew that she had a marital battery conviction in another state. Before trial, Naumov sent the AUSA a letter complaining that government had not followed through on its promise to protect him from the media fall-out and to help him in his proposed civil action against Acme for wrongful termination. Naumov followed up this letter by texting the same complaints to the FBI case agent. The government plans to call Naumov as a witness at trial.

You are counsel for Fannon. Please explain what items the government must disclose pursuant to *Brady*, Rule 16, and the *Jencks* Act; in what circumstances the defense must turn over items to the government under Rule 16 and the *Jencks* Act; and what other items the defense will seek and how it will obtain them.

Explanations

1. Under *Brady/Giglio*, the government must turn over to the defense materially exculpatory impeachment material in the possession of the prosecution "team." It does not, however, have an obligation to go out and secure such materials if they are not in the team's possession. This problem raises the question of whether cooperating witnesses are part of the government team for *Brady* purposes, such that the government must secure and turn over the posts, assuming that in the total mix of information, they are materially impeaching. If Mai is not part of the team, the government has no such obligation.

   In *United States v. Meregildo*, 920 F. Supp. 2d 434 (S.D.N.Y. 2013), the district court held that the government had no obligation to turn over the Facebook posts of a cooperating witness because that witness was not a member of the prosecution team. The court reasoned that:

   > When the Government uses an informant as a government agent and directs him to gather information, a court may hold the Government responsible for his actions. But in most cases witnesses and agents perform separate functions. Agents investigate. Witnesses relate information they observe.

> Prosecutors do not direct witnesses to investigate, and witnesses do not advise prosecutors on trial strategy. As such, cooperating witnesses are rarely members of the prosecution team.[93]

It concluded that "[t]he fact that a cooperating witness[] signs a plea agreement and testifies at trial does not transform him from a criminal into a member of the prosecution team."[94]

Rule 16 does not apply because this is a witness statement and, per Rule 16(a)(2), the Jencks Act is the means by which such statements can be obtained.

The post would likely qualify as a *Jencks* Act "statement" because it was a "written statement made by" Mai if he is called at trial. But *Jencks* only requires disclosure if the witness statement is in the government's possession.

If the government is not required to turn over the posted information under *Brady/Giglio* or *Jencks*, the SCA bars ECSs and RCSs from disclosing the contents of non-public Facebook accounts to the defense in these circumstances, and a Rule 17 subpoena does not overcome that protection. As a practical matter, the defense will be best served by using informal means—that is, asking Mai's lawyer or others who can themselves access the Facebook account to provide copies of postings. (NB: A lawyer would run into ethical problems if she sought access by sending a friend request under an assumed name.)

2. These facts were drawn from *Wood v. Bartholomew*, 516 U.S. 1 (1995). The Ninth Circuit granted a writ of habeas corpus holding that, even though under state law the polygraph examinations were inadmissible, the information could have been material under *Brady* because it could have affected defense counsel's pre-trial investigation and strategic decision-making. The Supreme Court reversed, reasoning that because the results of a polygraph test were not admissible, they were not "evidence" at all and their disclosure "could have had no direct effect on the outcome of the trial, because respondent could have made no mention of them either during argument or while questioning witnesses."[95] Nor, according to the Court, was it evident how it could have affected counsel's preparation or trial strategy.

   The circuits are split on how stringently to read *Wood*. For example, one circuit has read *Wood* to hold that inadmissible statements are immaterial under *Brady* "as a matter of law."[96] Others have found that inadmissible evidence can be material if it "could have led to the discovery

93. *Meregildo*, 920 F. Supp. 2d at 444.
94. *Id.* at 445.
95. *Wood*, 516 U.S. at 6.
96. Hoke v. Netherland, 92 F.3d 1350, 1356 n.3 (4th Cir. 1996); *see also* United States v. Morales, 746 F.3d 310, 314-15 (7th Cir. 2014) (collecting cases).

of admissible evidence."[97]Current DOJ policy suggests that prosecutors produce more than the Supreme Court's *Brady* caselaw would require:

> Recognizing that it is sometimes difficult to assess the materiality of evidence before trial, prosecutors generally must take a broad view of materiality and err on the side of disclosing exculpatory and impeaching evidence. While ordinarily, evidence that would not be admissible at trial need not be disclosed, this policy encourages prosecutors to err on the side of disclosure if admissibility is a close question.[98]

3. This problem raises a variety of issues under *Brady*, Rule 16, *Jencks*, and Rule 17.

Internal Investigative Report

The defense will want the report documenting that Naumov was complicit in investor fraud for impeachment purposes. If the government has possession of the report, relevant portions of it should be turned over as likely *Brady/Giglio*. (Note that whether the government has suppressed *Brady* information depends on an assessment of whether all the exculpatory items, in total, are likely "material"; thus, for present purposes we can only isolate items as "likely" *Brady* or *Giglio* material.)

If the government does not have physical possession of the report, the defense is likely to argue that, by virtue of Acme's cooperation with the government, the parallel Justice Department and private investigations should be considered to be a "joint" endeavor and thus Acme must be considered part of the prosecution team for *Brady* purposes. One court has found that the "joint investigation" analysis does not apply to private parties, just to other governmental agencies.[99]

The defense is also likely to argue that, given Acme's stated policy of cooperation, the government has the right to obtain materials in Acme's possession and thus these materials should be considered within the government's "control" for Rule 16 purposes. It would contend that the report is "material to preparing the defense" under Rule 16(a)(1)(i). Although this argument has worked before, the weight of authority seems to require that the government have actual possession of materials for it to have Rule 16 obligations to disclose them.[100]

If the government does not possess the report and thus does not have to disclose it under *Brady/Giglio* or Rule 16, the defense can seek to obtain

---

97. Johnson v. Folino, 705 F.3d 117, 130 (3d Cir. 2013).

98. Justice Manual, *supra* note 6, § 9-5.001.

99. *See Hwa*, 2021 WL 11723583, at *55 (Goldman Sachs Group is not part of the prosecution team for *Brady* purposes simply because it entered into a DPA with the government).

100. *See id.* at 51-60 (holding that "Rule 16 does not require the Government to produce materials possessed by a third party simply because it may have a legal right to obtain such materials pursuant to a cooperation agreement").

it through Rule 17 subpoena. (Assume for the moment that no attorney client privilege or work product issues are presented.) Acme can resist the production to the extent that Fannon only wishes to use the information to impeach Naumov, on the ground that the subpoena does not seek admissible evidence. If, however, Fannon plans to blame the fraud entirely on Naumov, this evidence may be relevant to her substantive defense.

Handwritten Notes

The problem presupposes that the defense has custody of the notes, enabling it to provide them to its expert. But if it did not, and assuming a defense request, the handwritten notes should be produced under Rule 16. They could fall under a number of potential categories: Under Rule 16(a)(1)(B)(i) these may constitute "relevant written or recorded statement by the defendant"; under Rule 16(a)(1)(E) these may be subject to disclosure if the government plans to use them as exhibits at trial; and under the same rule, they may also be deemed to be obtained from or belonging to the defendant.

Cooperation Agreement, Naumov Letter to the Government, and Naumov Text

A cooperation agreement is classic *Brady/Giglio* material, and, given the apparent importance of Naumov's evidence, it will be material to impeach his testimony. In his letter to the government, Naumov alleges that the prosecutors made additional promises to him—to protect him from the press and to help him in his civil suit—that are not usually part of a cooperation agreement. This letter should be turned over on the same theory.

Rule 16(a)(2) provides that the Rule does not "authorize the discovery or inspection of statements made by prospective government witnesses except as provided in" the *Jencks* Act. In short, Rule 16 does not apply because *Jencks* does.

The letter is *Jencks* material under § 3500(e)(1): A "written statement made by [the trial] witness and signed or otherwise adopted or approved by him." For the same reasons, Naumov's text message to the case agent must be disclosed.[101] If the material is deemed both *Brady/Giglio* and *Jencks*, it is likely that the *Jencks* Act will control the timing of the disclosure—that is, it will be produced only after the witness has testified on direct.

---

101. *See* United States v. Suarez, Crim. No. 09-932 (JLL), 2010 WL 4226524, at *4 (D.N.J. Oct. 21, 2010) ("[R]egardless of the content of the text messages, the Court can at least be certain here that the agents and cooperating witness each adopted and approved each message sent when they affirmatively chose to transmit it. Thus, the Court deems the text messages 'statements' under the *Jencks* Act").

FBI Rough Notes and 302

It is unlikely that these notes contain materially exculpatory information for *Brady* purposes. They are not subject to production under Rule 16 because, again, that rule does not apply where the *Jencks* Act does.

The agents' rough notes of the interview certainly are in the possession of the prosecution team and are relevant to the subject-matter of Naumov's testimony, so assuming a defense request, this will be *Jencks* Act material if the notes are deemed a "statement" within the meaning of the Act. Section 3500(e)(2) provides that a *Jencks* Act statement includes a "stenographic, mechanical, electrical, or other recording, or a transcription thereof, which is a *substantially verbatim* recital of an oral statement made by said witness and *recorded contemporaneously with* the making of such oral statement." The government will fight to withhold the FBI agents' rough notes because, it will argue, twenty-five pages of notes cannot possibly constitute a "substantially verbatim recital" of what was said over a nine-day debriefing. The government will also fight to withhold the resulting six-page 302 report because it both is not substantially verbatim and was not recorded contemporaneously with the interview.

Recording of Wired Conversation

The contents of the recording are materially exculpatory and thus *Brady* material. Rule 16(a)(1)(A), governing the disclosure of the substance of the defendant's oral statements, does not apply because the defendant did not know she was speaking to a government agent and the government is unlikely to introduce this in its case-in-chief given that Fannon's statements were exculpatory. But, assuming that Fannon made a Rule 16 request, it is covered by Rule 16(a)(1)(B)(i) because it is relevant written or *recorded* statement by the defendant in the government's possession. It is not Jencks Act material because the government cannot call Fannon as a witness at trial.

Test Results

Assuming that the defense made a request for the handwriting test results, the government is under no obligation to disclose its report under Rule 16(a)(1)(F) because the results were indeterminant and thus unlikely to be either material to preparing the defense (exculpatory) or to be used by the government in its case-in-chief at trial (inculpatory). The government will not have an obligation to disclose expert testimony under Rule 16(a)(1)(G), even with a defense request, because the indeterminate response means that the government will not call a handwriting expert during its case-in-chief at trial or during rebuttal.

With respect to the fingerprint evidence, the defendant only has a reciprocal obligation to turn over reports of its tests if the defendant made a request for the government's test results under Rule 16(a)(1)(F), the government complied with the request, the government made a reciprocal request, and the defendant intends either to use the report in the defendant's case-in-chief at trial or to call the witness who prepared the report and the report relates to the witness' testimony. Because the discovery of the defendant's handwriting on the documents is inculpatory, the defense will not be using the report at trial or calling an expert. The defense, then, does not have a disclosure obligation under Rule 16(b)(1)(B) or Rule 16(b)(1)(C).

GJ Transcript

The testimony is unlikely to contain materially exculpatory information and thus is probably not *Brady* material. Again, Rule 16 does not apply to witness statements.

The agent's testimony is not *Jencks* material under § 3500(e)(3) because only the grand jury testimony of *the witness* in the grand jury is a covered "statement." Because Naumov was not called as a grand jury witness, there is nothing to produce. Were the agent called to testify at trial, the grand jury transcript of his testimony would have to be disclosed.

Rap Sheet

Even if the defense made a Rule 16 request for the defendant's rap sheet and the government complied, the defense has no reciprocal obligation under Rule 16(b) to provide the government with the defendant's criminal history.

Subpoena to SEC

The defense will likely wish to secure the SEC's investigative file in the hopes that the SEC's declination will provide the basis for a defense. Given the limited interaction between the SEC and the AUSA, the DOJ and SEC were not conducting a "joint investigation." It is unlikely, then, that the SEC will be deemed part of the prosecution team for *Brady* purposes or that the files will be deemed within the prosecution's possession, custody, or control under Rule 16. And the defense is unlikely to be successful in securing the SEC's information through a Rule 17 subpoena without being able to demonstrate that the specific SEC materials will be relevant and admissible. A hunch that there may be items useful to the defense in the SEC file given its decision not to go forward with an enforcement action is clearly insufficient to meet the defense's burden.

Naumov Text to Elwyn's Phone

If the government has a copy of the text, it should turn it over as likely *Brady/Giglio* material and also as a *Jencks* Act statement. If the government does not have a copy, it theoretically could use the processes of the SCA to get the text message, but it is unlikely to wish to do so given that the content of the text hurts its case. And the government has no obligation to seek out or secure exculpatory evidence for the defense.

If the government does not have possession of the text, Fannon will wish to subpoena Elwyn under Rule 17 for the text message to support her argument that Naumov is seeking revenge, not justice. If Elwyn contests the subpoena, it is unlikely that a court will enforce the subpoena because the text is only useable for impeachment of Naumov. If Elwyn no longer has access to the the text, the SCA will prevent Elwyn's service provider from complying with a defense Rule 17 subpoena for the text's contents absent Elwyn's consent.

CHAPTER 14

The Fifth Amendment and Immunity

The Fifth Amendment provides that no person "shall be compelled in any criminal case to be a witness against himself."[1] As we shall see, the protections of the Self-Incrimination Clause are both narrower and broader than many would assume given the plain language of the Fifth Amendment. In summary, the Fifth Amendment's privilege against compelled self-incrimination protects:

(1) natural persons (and sole proprietorships) from being
(2) compelled by the government
(3) to make a testimonial communication, and,
(4) where that testimonial communication takes the form of a compelled act, the information implicitly communicated by that act is not a "foregone conclusion,"
(4) the testimonial communication is a "link in the chain" to incriminating evidence
(5) that can be used against the rights holder in "any criminal case,"
(6) absent a grant of governmental immunity or some other circumstance that bars the government from bringing a criminal case against the rights holder.

Unless all these elements are satisfied, a Fifth Amendment claim of privilege will not be sustained.

These elements are examined individually in sections I to V below. Many find confusing their application to the compelled production of non-testimonial evidence, such as documents and other physical or digital evidence. Accordingly, a summary laying out how all these elements apply in that context is provided in section VI.

Miranda v. Arizona famously gave suspects subjected to police custodial interrogation a "right to silence" but, for the reasons laid out in section

1. U.S. Const., amend. V.

VIII, *Miranda* often does not apply in business crime cases. There is no absolute right to silence outside of *Miranda*-land. The government can overcome a witness's valid claim of the Fifth Amendment privilege—that is, force her to speak under pain of a contempt sanction—by granting the witness statutory immunity. The process by which immunity is negotiated, and the different types of immunity, are explored in section VII.

I. NATURAL PERSONS AND SOLE PROPRIETORSHIPS

Only natural persons and sole proprietorships[2] may claim the Fifth Amendment privilege against compelled self-incrimination. In what has come to be known as the "collective entity doctrine," the Supreme Court has held that "artificial entities," including corporations and partnerships, "are not protected by the Fifth Amendment."[3]

Further, a corporate officer cannot resist producing subpoenaed corporate records by asserting his personal Fifth Amendment right—no matter how incriminating the records are to him—because "the custodian of corporate or entity records holds those documents in a representative rather than a personal capacity" and thus has no privilege to assert.[4] The D.C. Circuit has also applied this rule to government employees, holding that "[j]ust as corporate records belong to the corporation and are held for the entity by the custodian only in an agency capacity, so government records do not belong to the custodian, . . . but to the government agency. Their production thus falls outside the Fifth Amendment privilege, which is a personal one."[5]

This rule applies whether the subpoena is addressed to the corporation or to the individual in his capacity as a custodian of corporate records.[6] But because the individual is acting as a corporate representative, the government cannot make evidentiary use of the fact that the individual delivered the documents to the grand jury against him.[7]

2. *See* United States v. Doe, 465 U.S. 605 (1984) (*Doe I*).
3. Braswell v. United States, 487 U.S. 99, 102 (1988).
4. *Id.* at 109-10.
5. In re Sealed Case (Government Records), 950 F.2d 736, 740 (D.C. Cir. 1991).
6. *See Braswell*, 487 U.S. at 108-09.
7. *Id.* at 117-18.

II. COMPELLED BY THE GOVERNMENT

A. What Constitutes Compulsion

In general, a witness is "compelled" when physically or legally forced to comply with a government request. In white-collar cases, the most common form of compulsion is a grand jury or trial subpoena for testimony (subpoena ad testificandum) or for the production of documents or other tangible objects (subpoena duces tecum). Compulsion can also take the form of a deposition subpoena, civil investigative demand (CID), administrative summons, or other legal process. The recipient of such process must comply with it or risk being held in contempt or suffering other sanctions.

In addition to direct compulsion, the Supreme Court has occasionally, albeit rarely, prohibited practices that it deems coercive because they make the exercise of the privilege simply too "costly." Thus, if an individual faces sanctions with particularly serious economic consequences, such as the loss of government employment or state contracts, if he takes the Fifth, his statements will be deemed compelled and will be excluded.[8] Similarly, the Court has barred judges and prosecutors from inviting jurors to draw an adverse inference from the defendant's failure to testify in a criminal trial, stating that such comments are "a penalty imposed by courts for exercising a constitutional privilege" and improperly "cut[] down on the privilege by making its assertion costly."[9] But not all "costly" assertions of the Fifth warrant relief. For example, as is discussed at greater length in Chapter 17 (Parallel Proceedings), the decision-maker in a *civil* case may draw an adverse inference against a party for taking the Fifth so long as that inference is not determinative, meaning that it alone is not the basis for judgment.[10]

Finally, the Court, in *Miranda v. Arizona*, determined that "custodial interrogations" by police are inherently coercive and require additional protections to safeguard suspects' ability to decide whether to assert their Fifth Amendment right. These protections are discussed *infra*, section VIII.

---

8. *See* Lefkowitz v. Turley, 414 U.S. 70 (1973); Uniformed Sanitation Men Ass'n v. Comm'r of Sanitation, 392 U.S. 280 (1968); Garrity v. New Jersey, 385 U.S. 493 (1967); Spevack v. Klein, 385 U.S. 511 (1967).

9. *See* Griffin v. California, 380 U.S. 609, 614 (1965).

10. *See* Baxter v. Palmigiano, 425 U.S. 308, 318-19 (1976); LaSalle Bank Lake View v. Seguban, 54 F.3d 387, 390-92 (7th Cir. 1995).

B. Compulsion by a State Actor

The compulsion to speak or provide evidence must be the result of state action. As noted above, if the government presents one with the choice of providing evidence or losing one's government job, that constitutes sufficient state compulsion to justify a Fifth Amendment remedy.[11] But if a corporate employer gives employees a similar choice—as corporations often do if they are cooperating with the government—the employees generally will have no Fifth Amendment recourse. Courts have also declined to expand the category of "state actors" to include professional self-regulatory organizations that may be investigating the defendant and may impose their own sanctions.[12]

There is a limited exception to this rule where the actions of a private employer or organization are "fairly attributable to the government."[13] Private conduct is attributed to the government only when "there is a sufficiently close nexus between the state and the challenged action"—a showing that has been difficult to make in the normal case.[14]

Investigations increasingly cross borders, raising the question of which country's action is necessary to ground a Fifth Amendment claim. The Supreme Court holds that a witness generally cannot assert a Fifth Amendment claim of self-incrimination in U.S. courts based on his real and substantial fear of criminal prosecution in another country.[15] But the Second Circuit has ruled that the Fifth Amendment prohibition on the use of compelled testimony in U.S. courts applies even when it was a foreign sovereign that compelled the testimony so used.[16]

C. The Rights Holder Must Be Compelled

As Justice Holmes asserted, "[a] party is privileged from producing the evidence but not from its production."[17] The protection afforded by the Self-Incrimination Clause of the Fifth Amendment, then, is a "personal privilege"; it "adheres basically to the person, not to information that may

11. *See Garrity*, 385 U.S. 493.
12. *See, e.g.*, D.L. Cromwell Investments, Inc. v. NASD Regulation, Inc., 279 F.3d 155, 161-62 (2d Cir. 2002).
13. Desiderio v. Nat'l Ass'n of Secs. Dealers, Inc., 191 F.3d 198, 206 (2d Cir. 1999).
14. *See* Chapter 17 (Parallel Proceedings). Although it is difficult to prevail on such claims, it can happen. *See* United States v. Connolly, No. 16 Cr. 0370 (CM), 2019 WL 2120523, at *10-14 (S.D.N.Y. May 2, 2019); United States v. Stein, 440 F. Supp. 2d 315 (S.D.N.Y. 2006), *aff'd*, 541 F.3d 130 (2d Cir. 2008).
15. *See* United States v. Balsys, 524 U.S. 666 (1998).
16. *See* United States v. Allen, 864 F.3d 63 (2d Cir. 2017).
17. Johnson v. United States, 228 U.S. 457, 458 (1913).

incriminate him."[18] Where the defendant is not personally "compelled" to provide the incriminating information, he has no claim.

It is therefore clear that one person cannot assert the Fifth Amendment privilege of another. This is both because constitutional rights are personal and because a subpoena duces tecum addressed to a third party does not "compel" the rights holder to do anything; it is the third party who must produce the documents. For example, when the government subpoenas an entity that may hold the suspect's data—for example, her bank—the suspect generally does not have the right to object. The bank may object to the subpoena on other grounds but cannot assert the suspect's Fifth Amendment right to resist production.

There may be limited exceptions to this rule.[19] One important caveat concerns subpoenas served on lawyers for their clients' documents. Where a lawyer is subpoenaed for materials her client turned over to her for the purpose of securing legal advice, the materials will not be protected under the Fifth Amendment because an attorney cannot assert the privilege of her client.[20] But the Supreme Court has held—as a matter of attorney-client privilege law—that if the client turns over documents or other evidence to the attorney for purposes of securing legal advice, those materials will be privileged in the attorney's hands to the same extent they would have been privileged under the Fifth Amendment in the client's hands.[21]

D. Material Seized by Warrant Is Not Compelled

Because it is the rights holder who must be "compelled," an individual whose property is searched or seized by investigators pursuant to a search warrant may not claim that the Fifth Amendment requires the suppression of any items seized. In *Andresen v. Maryland*, 427 U.S. 463 (1976), the Court held although the Fifth Amendment can protect an individual from complying with a *subpoena* for the production of his personal records in his possession, "a seizure of the same materials by law enforcement officers [pursuant to a *warrant*] differs in a crucial respect[:] the individual against whom the search is directed is not required to aid in the discovery, production, or authentication of incriminating evidence."[22] In short, a target cannot resist a search warrant based on his Fifth Amendment right because he is not being

18. Couch v. United States, 409 U.S. 322, 328 (1973).
19. *See* Fisher v. United States, 425 U.S. 391, 398 (1976) (noting suggestion that exceptions may exist where "constructive possession is so clear or relinquishment of possession so temporary and insignificant as to leave the personal compulsion upon the taxpayer substantially intact").
20. *Id.* at 402.
21. *Id.* at 402-05.
22. *Andresen*, 427 U.S. at 473-74.

"compelled" to do anything by the warrant. The investigating agents executing the warrant will do the searching and seizing.

E. If the Government Didn't Make You Write It, What You Wrote Is Not Compelled

Many find the application of the "compulsion" element to documents and other tangible objects counterintuitive. To illustrate, let us assume that the government subpoenas one's diary, which is chock full of confessions regarding one's life of crime. One might assume that the diary's author could resist the subpoena simply on a showing that she is being required to turn over something that is clearly incriminating. Not so. In *Fisher v. United States*, 425 U.S. 391 (1976), the Court adopted a very crabbed reading of just what is being compelled by a subpoena duces tecum or summons. It ruled that the *contents* of the documents sought were not "compelled" because *the government did not force the author to write down her thoughts*. (Really? Yes.) Thus, the *contents of the diary* are not protected by the Fifth Amendment privilege.

What does this mean? It means that the incriminating *contents* of any document or item that the government did not force one to write or create—that is, any document or bit of non-testimonial evidence that predates the subpoena—are not "compelled" and thus are not protected.

Does this mean that one has *no* Fifth Amendment claim when the government subpoenas existing documents or other types of physical or digital evidence that the government did not force one to write or create? No. The *Fisher* Court recognized that a subpoena duces tecum does compel one to do *something*—that is, it forces one *to turn over, to produce, the documents*. If that compelled *act of producing* the subpoenaed item is both a "*testimonial communication*" and is "*incriminating*," one may have a viable Fifth Amendment claim unless the information conveyed is already known to the government and thus is a "*foregone conclusion*." These elements are explored below.

III. TO PROVIDE A TESTIMONIAL COMMUNICATION

The Supreme Court's caselaw clearly provides that only "testimonial communications" are covered, although at least two Justices have questioned this limitation.[23] The Court believes that the heart of the Fifth Amendment privilege lies in its protection against the state "obtaining evidence against an accused through the 'cruel, simple expedient of compelling it from his

23. *See* United States v. Hubbell, 530 U.S. 27, 49 (2000) (Thomas, J., concurring).

own mouth.'"[24] The most obvious example of a "testimonial communication" is a witness's oral testimony. "The vast majority of verbal statements thus will be testimonial and, to that extent at least, will fall within the privilege."[25] This element is clearly satisfied, then, whenever a witness seeks to resist a testimonial subpoena (subpoena ad testificandum).

There are also circumstances, however, in which a compelled *act* can be considered a "testimonial communication." The fundamental problem with forcing someone to speak is compelling him to "*disclose the contents of his own mind.*"[26] A variety of compelled acts do not require such mental exertion; they simply require exposure of an immutable physical characteristic—such as one's fingerprints, one's voice, or one's handwriting. But the Court has recognized that sometimes a compelled act can require witness to use his mind to assist the prosecution in convicting him of a crime.

To illustrate the distinction, Justice Stevens was fond of a using a metaphor that courts have relied on since: the government can force a witness "to surrender a key to a strongbox"[27] because it is a compelled act with no real communicative content; a witness cannot be compelled "to reveal the combination to his wall safe—by word or deed" because the latter would require the defendant to use the contents of his mind to comply.[28]

The test the Court has articulated for when a compelled "act" constitutes a "testimonial communication" is whether it implies assertions of fact. That is, to be testimonial, an accused's act "must itself, explicitly or implicitly, relate a factual assertion or disclose information."[29] This issue often arises in three contexts: when someone seeks to resist an order requiring them to (A) take an act such as giving a handwriting exemplar, donning a piece of clothing, or submitting to a blood draw; (B) produce documents or other tangible objects pursuant to a subpoena duces tecum; and (C) provide access to a device, such a phone or computer, or decrypt data on such devices, by entering a password or providing a biometric identifier.

A. Compelled Acts That Are Used as Evidence

The Supreme Court has held that the Fifth Amendment generally does not apply to orders directing the suspect to take actions like providing a voice exemplar because such acts do not disclose the contents of the witness's

---

24. Schmerber v. California, 384 U.S. 757, 763 (1966).
25. Doe v. United States, 487 U.S. 201, 213-14 (1988) (*Doe II*).
26. Curcio v. United States, 354 U.S. 118, 128 (1957) (emphasis added).
27. *Hubbell*, 530 U.S. at 43.
28. *Doe II*, 487 U.S. at 219 (Stevens, J., dissenting).
29. *Id.*

mind or "'any knowledge he may have.'"[30] The suspect is "required to use his voice as an identifying physical characteristic, not to speak his guilt."[31] Or, as the Court later explained,

> When an accused is required to submit a handwriting exemplar he admits his ability to write and impliedly asserts that the exemplar is his writing. But in common experience, the first would be a near truism and the latter self-evident. . . . [A]though the exemplar may be incriminating to the accused and although he is compelled to furnish it, his Fifth Amendment privilege is not violated because nothing he has said or done is deemed to be *sufficiently* testimonial for purposes of the privilege.[32]

As a result, in addition to being forced to provide voice[33] and handwriting[34] exemplars, a suspect may be compelled to furnish a blood sample,[35] to stand in a lineup,[36] and to wear particular clothing.[37] The Supreme Court also holds that the privilege "'offers no protection against compulsion to submit to fingerprinting, photography, or measurements, . . . to appear in court, to stand, to assume a stance, to walk, or to make a particular gesture."[38]

B. Compelled Acts of Producing Documents and Other Tangible Evidence

Other acts, such as the act of producing documents pursuant to a subpoena duces tecum, *can* implicitly communicate facts or information sufficient to constitute "testimonial communications." Recall that in *Fisher*, the Court held that if the government did not force one to write or create evidence, the contents are not "compelled"; thus, the contents of most documents are not protected. The *Fisher* Court did acknowledge, however, that a subpoena duces tecum does "compel" something—that is, the act of producing the covered materials. For present purposes, then, the question is whether this compelled act of production constitutes a "testimonial communication."

The *Fisher* Court ruled that the compelled production of an accountant's work papers pursuant to an IRS summons "tacitly concedes the *existence* of the papers demanded and their *possession* or *control* by the taxpayer. It also

30. *Id.* at 211.
31. United States v. Wade, 388 U.S. 218, 222-23 (1967).
32. *Fisher*, 425 U.S. at 411 (emphasis added).
33. *See* United States v. Dionisio, 410 U.S. 1, 7 (1973).
34. *See* Gilbert v. California, 388 U.S. 263, 266-67 (1967).
35. *See* Schmerber v. California, 384 U.S. 757, 765 (1966).
36. *See* United States v. Wade, 388 U.S. 218, 221 (1967).
37. *See* Holt v. United States, 218 U.S. 245, 252-53 (1910).
38. *Schmerber*, 384 U.S. at 764.

would indicate the taxpayer's belief that the papers are those described in the subpoena," that is, that they are *responsive* to the subpoena.[39] Finally, the compelled production of documents and other tangible objects can implicitly communicate that the materials are *authentic*.[40]

In *United States v. Hubbell*, 530 U.S. 27 (2000), the Supreme Court added another basis for arguing that the compelled act of producing documents or other tangible objects pursuant to a subpoena duces tecum is a "testimonial communication." In that case, Hubbell had produced volumes of documents pursuant to a very broad subpoena under a grant of "act of production" immunity under 18 U.S.C. § 6002. The question presented was whether evidence that the government obtained by reading the materials Hubbell produced and then following the leads they provided to other sources of incriminating evidence constituted a prohibited "derivative use" of the materials produced.[41] The Court answered that question in the affirmative, and its reasoning in doing made Fifth Amendment claims much easier to sustain in this context.

Justice Stevens, writing for the Court in *Hubbell*, held that the compelled act of production in that case was a "testimonial communication" because it was a very broad subpoena and "[i]t was unquestionably necessary for respondent to make extensive use of 'the contents of his own mind' in identifying the hundreds of documents responsive to the requests in the subpoena."[42] Where the government serves, as it usually does, a broadly worded subpoena, then, the witness can argue that his response is a testimonial communication—without regard to concessions regarding the existence, possession, responsiveness, or authenticity of the material subpoenaed—because he had to use the contents of his mind to identify the responsive materials.

C. Compelled Provision of Access Codes and Decryption Keys

In cases in which the government seeks to force a suspect to open or decrypt devices upon which data is stored (e.g., smartphones, laptops), the question presented is often whether such compelled acts constitute "testimonial

39. *Fisher*, 425 U.S. at 410 (emphasis added).
40. *See id.* at 412-13.
41. *Hubbell* concerned what constitutes derivative use in a case where the defendant produced the documents pursuant to the grant of "act of production" immunity under 18 U.S.C. § 6002. But because the Supreme Court holds that the scope of use and derivative use immunity is co-extensive with the scope of the Fifth, *see* Kastigar v. United States, 406 U.S. 441 (1972), *Hubbell* provides guidance on what a defendant can assert is covered by the Fifth Amendment in the first instance.
42. *Hubbell*, 530 U.S. at 43.

communications." This has been the subject of a great deal of litigation, which, unfortunately, has provided few definitive answers. It is fair to say, however, that much will depend on whether the device or the data is protected by an alphanumeric password or by a biometric identifier (such as a fingerprint, facial recognition, or the like). An additional distinction may be drawn depending on *how* the police seek to compel access or decryption—for example, whether they seek to compel the suspect to orally provide the password or to force the suspect to enter the password outside their presence and turn over the opened device.

Most courts—including two circuit courts and six State Supreme Courts—hold that a defendant cannot be forced to provide police with an alphanumeric passcode to access a device or decrypt data because this would constitute a compelled testimonial communication.[43] How they have arrived at this conclusion, however, varies. Where the police try to force suspects to verbally provide them with the code, this has been characterized as "[o]rdinary testimony," not an "act," and thus clearly covered.[44] In cases in which the courts do not specify how the police wish to compel access, and they assume what is required is an act, courts generally rule for the suspect on the ground that such compelled acts force the subject to disclose information from his mind[45] because "[c]ommunicating or entering a passcode requires facts contained within the holder's mind—the numbers, letters, or symbols composing the passcode."[46]

Some courts rely primarily on Justice Steven's metaphor to find that this constitutes a "testimonial communication" because forcing the suspect to provide a memorized alphanumeric password is akin to compelling a suspect to share the combination to a safe rather than the key to a lockbox.[47] Other courts instead rely on *Fisher* and *Hubbell*, finding that the act of producing the access code is testimonial because it tacitly communicates information: the subject possesses the access code, it is authentic, he has access to the data on the laptop, and perhaps, by inference, that the laptop and the

---

43. *See, e.g.*, United States v. Apple MacPro Comp., 851 F.3d 238, 247-48 (3d Cir. 2017); In re Grand Jury Subpoena Duces Tecum Dated Mar. 25, 2011, 670 F.3d 1335, 1346 (11th Cir. 2012); People v. Sneed, 230 N.E.3d 97, 113 (Ill. 2023); State v. Andrews, 234 A.3d 1254, 1273 (N.J. 2020); Comm. v. Jones, 117 N.E.3d 702, 709 (SJC 2019); State v. Valdez, 552 P.3d 159, 167 (Utah 2023); Seo v. State, 148 N.E.3d 952, 955 (Ind. 2020); Comm. v. Davis, 220 A.3d 534, 548 (Pa 2019);

44. *Valdez*, 552 P.3d at 168; *see also* United States v. Shvartsman, 23-cr-307 (LJL), 2024 WL 1193703, at *23 (S.D.N.Y. Mar. 20, 2024); *Davis*, 220 A.3d at 548.

45. *See Davis*, 220 A.3d at 548. *But see Sneed*, 230 N.E.3d at 114 (compelling suspect to enter a passcode does not reveal the contents of his mind because "'a cell phone passcode is a string of letters or numbers that an individual habitually enters into his electronic device throughout the day'" and it "'may be used so habitually that its retrieval is a function of muscle memory rather than an exercise of conscious thought.'").

46. *Andrews*, 234 A.3d at 1273.

47. *See id.*; *Davis*, 220 A.3d at 548.

data within it are his or that he has custody and control over them.[48] The Eleventh Circuit relied on both analyses, concluding that forcing a suspect to provide a decryption key is akin to providing the combination to a safe and that "decryption and production would be tantamount to testimony . . . of [the subject's] knowledge of the existence and location of potentially incriminating files; of his possession, control, and access to the encrypted portions of the drives; and of his capacity to decrypt the files."[49]

A few courts, however, have reached a different result, at least where the means the police employ does not require the suspect to share the password with the government.[50] The Fourth Circuit, for example, has ruled that where the defendant was forced to enter her access passcode into a phone outside the sight of the officer, the act was not a testimonial communication. "Unlike a circumstance, for example, in which she gave the passcode to the agent for the agent to enter, here she simply used the unexpressed contents of her mind to type in the passcode herself."[51] Because the contents of her mind were never communicated to the government, the compelled act of unlocking her phone was like turning over the key to a strongbox.[52]

Fewer jurisdictions have definitively resolved the question whether the Fifth Amendment allows suspects to resist compulsory biometric authentication, and there is less judicial consensus on the subject.[53] A few courts have held that these are testimonial acts. They note that unlocking a device with a biometric identifier is the functional equivalent of compelling the person to turn over an alphanumeric code, which most courts have held to be privileged.[54] They contend that there should not be a constitutional difference in treatment of these two means of access. They also argue that, under the *Fisher/Hubbell* act of production cases, a "successful finger or thumb scan confirms ownership or control of the device, and . . . the authentication of its contents cannot be reasonably refuted."[55] Finally, such courts rely on policy, pointing to the disturbing amount of a data held on cell phones and computers and thus the extent of the invasion that this forced act would entail. One court, in distinguishing the Supreme Court's ruling that the Fifth Amendment provides no protection against compelling a suspect to submit to fingerprinting, argued that "the Court could not have anticipated the

---

48. *See, e.g.*, *Sneed*, 230 N.E.3d at 115; *Seo*, 148 N.E.3d at 955-58.

49. In re Grand Jury Subpoena Duces Tecum Dated Mar. 25, 2011, 670 F.3d at 1346.

50. *See Valdez*, 552 P.3d at 167-71 (discussing different circumstances).

51. United States v. Oloyede, 933 F.3d 302, 309 (4th Cir. 2019).

52. *Id.*

53. *See, e.g.*, In re Search Warrant No. 5165, 470 F. Supp. 3d 715, 725-26 (E.D. Ky 2020) (collecting cases); In re Search Warrant Application for Cellular Tel. in U.S. v. Barrera, 415 F. Supp. 3d 832, 838 (N.D. Ill. 2019) (same).

54. *See, e.g.*, United States v. Wright, 431 F. Supp. 3d 1175, 1187 (D. Nev. 2020); In re Residence in Oakland, CA, 354 F. Supp. 3d 1010, 1015-16 (N.D. Ca. 2019).

55. *In re Residence in Oakland, CA*, 354 F. Supp. 3d at 1016.

creation of the iPhone nor could it have anticipated that its holding would be applied in such a far-reaching manner."[56]

A probable majority of courts, however, refuse to recognize such acts as testimonial, ruling, for example, that the compelled act of putting one's finger on an iPhone touchpad is not protected.[57] Courts adopting this view see no problem with treating alphanumeric codes and biometric identifiers differently given the distinction the Court has drawn between forced non-testimonial acts like the provision of handwriting or voice exemplars and acts that have some potential testimonial significance, such as an act of production pursuant to a subpoena duces tecum.

The Ninth Circuit is the only federal circuit court to resolve this issue to date and its reasoning is representative. In *United States v. Payne*, 99 F.4th 495 (9th Cir. 2024), the Ninth Circuit likened using a thumbprint to unlock a phone to turning over a key to a safe, arguing that it involves no "mental process" or "cognitive exertion" on the subject's part.[58] It also relied on the Court's compelled act cases, reasoning that "the use of Payne's thumb to unlock his phone appears no different than a blood draw or fingerprinting at booking."[59]

The defendant attempted to rely on the *Fisher/Hubbell* act of production precedents, asserting that forcing him to provide access was a testimonial act because it simultaneously confirmed ownership and authentication of the phone's contents. The Ninth Circuit rejected this argument by concluding that the defendant "was never compelled to acknowledge the existence of any incriminating information. He merely had to provide *access* to a *source of potential information*," in much the same way that the compelled act of submitting to a blood draw only allows the government access to the suspect's blood.[60] In both cases, "[t]he officers [a]re left to identify any incriminating evidence through their own investigation."[61] The court reasoned that this is "decidedly unlike *Hubbell*, where the subpoena respondent was implicitly conceding the 'existence, authenticity, and custody' of specific documents that prosecutors could use in building its case against the respondent."[62]

The Ninth Circuit cautioned, however, that "Fifth Amendment questions like this one are highly fact dependent and the line between what is testimonial and what is not is particularly fine."[63] It suggested that its

---

56. In re Application for a Search Warrant, 236 F. Supp. 3d 1066, 1073 (N.D. Ill. 2017).
57. *See, e.g.*, United States v. Payne, 99 F.4th 495 (9th Cir. 2024); In re Search Warrant Application for Cellular Tel., 415 F. Supp. 3d at 842; State v. Diamond, 905 N.W.2d 870, 875 (Minn. 2018).
58. *Payne*, 99 F.4th at 511.
59. *Id.* at 509.
60. *Id.* at 511 (emphasis added).
61. *Id.*
62. *Id.* at 511-12.
63. *Id.* at 513.

result may have been different had the officer required the subject to "independently select the finger that he placed on the phone."[64]

D. The Foregone Conclusion Doctrine

1. The Doctrine as Applied to Subpoenas Duces Tecum

The *Fisher* Court held the compelled production of materials pursuant to a subpoena duces tecum could constitute a "testimonial communication" where that act implicitly communicated that the materials existed, that the witness possessed them, or that they were responsive or authentic. But it went on to articulate a limit that has taken on great practical significance.

In *Fisher*, the Court held that the witness in that case could not resist the forced production of his accountant's workpapers because, *inter alia*,

> [i]t [was] doubtful that implicitly admitting the existence and possession of the papers [rose] to the level of testimony within the protection of the Fifth Amendment. The papers belong to the accountant, were prepared by him, and are the kind usually prepared by an accountant working on the tax returns of his client. Surely the Government is in no way relying on the "truth-telling" of the taxpayer to prove the existence of or his access to the documents. The existence and location of the papers are a *foregone conclusion* and the taxpayer adds little or nothing to the sum total of the Government's information by conceding that he in fact has these papers.[65]

The government has frequently relied on the so-called "foregone conclusion" doctrine to avoid Fifth Amendment claims:

> Under the "foregone conclusion" doctrine, an act of production is not testimonial—even if the act conveys a fact regarding the existence or location, possession, or authenticity of the subpoenaed materials—if the Government can show with "reasonable particularity" that, at the time it sought to compel the act of production, it already knew of the materials, thereby making any testimonial aspect a "foregone conclusion."[66]

It is important to note that the foregone conclusion doctrine does not apply in cases involving actual testimony as opposed to compelled acts. The government cannot argue that a *witness's testimony* is "insufficiently testimonial" and thus a foregone conclusion because it already has a good idea of what that witness will say.

---

64. *Id.*; *see also* In re Search Warrant Application for [redacted text], 279 F. Supp. 3d 800, 803-04 (N.D. Ill. 2017).
65. *Fisher*, 425 U.S. at 411 (emphasis added).
66. In re Grand Jury Subpoena Duces Tecum Dated Mar. 25, 2011, 670 F.3d at 1345-46.

The circuits generally apply a "reasonable particularity" standard to test whether that doctrine applies. Under this standard,

> The government [i]s not required to have actual knowledge of the existence and location of each and every responsive document; the government [i]s required, however, to establish the existence of the documents sought and [the subpoenaed party's] possession of them with "reasonable particularity" before the existence and possession of the documents could be considered a foregone conclusion and production therefore would not be testimonial.[67]

It is unclear how, if at all, the foregone conclusion doctrine applies to the new theory of testimonial communications introduced by *Hubbell*. *Hubbell* suggests that those who receive broadly worded subpoenas duces tecum subpoena can argue that their act of production is necessarily testimonial because they have to use the contents of their minds to determine what was responsive to the subpoena. Presumably when the subpoena is very particular—only calling, for example, for the production of a particular laptop—the government would argue that the defendant does not have to use the contents of his mind to produce the laptop; its production, then, would be insufficiently testimonial, and thus a foregone conclusion.

2. The Doctrine as Applied to Forced Access or Decryption

It is also not clear whether and how the "foregone conclusion" doctrine applies when the government seeks to force a suspect to provide access to a device or decrypt its contents.[68] This is a very important question, at least in the many cases involving alphanumeric access and decryption codes, because of the number of courts that have found compelled production of these codes to be protected "testimonial communications."

A number of State Supreme Courts have refused to apply the doctrine, arguing that it is a very limited exception applicable only to subpoenas for business records, and that applying it to cell phones, which are capable of storing massive amounts of information, would "allow the exception to swallow the constitutional privilege."[69] By contrast, other courts have concluded that "there is nothing in the history of the foregone conclusion doctrine to suggest that it does not apply to acts of producing passcodes to cell phones."[70]

---

67. In re Grand Jury Subpoena, Dated April 18, 2003, 383 F.3d 905, 910 (9th Cir. 2004).

68. *See Sneed*, 230 N.E.3d at 115-18 (discussing split); *see also Apple Mac Pro Comput.*, 851 F.3d at 247-48 & n.7.

69. *Davis*, 220 A.3d at 549; *see also Seo*, 148 N.E.3d at 959 (extending the foregone conclusion doctrine to this case "fails to account for the ubiquity and capacity of smartphones," may "prove unworkable," and "runs counter to U.S. Supreme Court precedent.").

70. *Sneed*, 230 N.E.3d at 118; *see also Andrews*, 234 A.3d at 1273.

The applicability of this doctrine also depends on how the government is seeking to compel access or decryption. For example, where the government is forcing the suspect to verbally disclose his password, some courts have concluded that the act of production precedents, and the foregone conclusion doctrine, simply do not apply.[71] It applies only where the government seeks to "compel *physical acts* that *implicitly* convey information," not where the suspect is actually forced to speak.[72] But where the government simply seeks to compel the suspect to act—for example, to turn over an unlocked cell phone—the foregone conclusion might apply.

Even where the foregone conclusion applies, courts disagree about that which the government must "know" to satisfy its requirements.[73] Some courts hold that the production of the passcode is tantamount to producing the device's contents. They believe that a suspect surrendering an unlocked smartphone implicitly communicates, at a minimum, three things: "(1) the suspect knows the password; (2) the files on the device exist; and (3) the suspect possessed those files."[74] To prevail, then, the government must show that it knew with reasonable particularity that the encrypted files existed, they were located on the device, and the suspect had the password and thus could decrypt such files.[75]

Other courts have concluded that what is being communicated by the forced access or decryption is not "I know these files exist on this device"; it only is "I know the password/decryption key."[76] Such courts require only a showing that at the time the government sought to compel access to or decryption of a device, it knew with reasonable particularity that "(1) the passcode existed, (2) the passcode was within defendant's possession or control, and (3) the passcode was authentic."[77]

IV. THAT IS INCRIMINATING

Just how incriminating must the evidence be to sustain a Fifth Amendment claim? In this respect, the caselaw provides broader protection than the plain text may indicate. The Fifth Amendment privilege "not only extends

71. *See, e.g.*, United States v. Gray, 21-cr-713 (PAE), 2024 WL 1526368, at *3 (S.D.N.Y. April 9, 2024); *Valdez*, 552 F.3d at 171-73.

72. *Gray*, 2024 WL 1526368, at *3.

73. *Compare* In re Grand Jury Subpoena Duces Tecum Dated Mar. 25, 2011, 670 F.3d at 1346, *with* United States v. Smith, 706 F. Supp. 3d 404, 408-09 (S.D.N.Y. 2023).

74. *Seo*, 148 N.E.3d at 957.

75. See In re Grand Jury Subpoena Duces Tecum Dated Mar. 25, 2011, 670 F.3d at 1346, 1349.

76. *See, e.g.*, *Smith*, 706 F. Supp. 3d at 408-09; *Andrews*, 234 A.3d at 1273-74; *Jones*, 117 N.E.3d at 717.

77. *Sneed*, 230 N.E.3d at 118; *see also Andrews*, 234 A.3d at 1273 ("the foregone conclusion test applies to the production of the passcodes themselves, rather than to the phones' contents").

to answers that would in themselves support a conviction under a federal criminal statute but likewise embraces those which would *furnish a link in the chain of evidence* needed to prosecute the claimant for a federal crime."[78] Thus, the answer to a query does not have to be the obviously inculpatory admission that "I shot the sheriff." An assertion of the privilege would be valid, for example, if an answer to a question posed in the grand jury would lead the government to a witness who could attest that I indeed shot the sheriff.

Because the question may be such that a direct answer may not itself be incriminating but may be "a link in the chain" to other evidence, whether a witness has a valid claim of the Fifth may not be obvious. Courts adjudicating contested assertions of the Fifth cannot ask the witness for an explanation of why the answer might lead to incriminating information because the witness's explanation would constitute a waiver of his Fifth Amendment right. The Supreme Court cautions that the Fifth's protection "must be confined to instances where the witness has reasonable cause to apprehend danger from a direct answer" but "[t]o sustain, the privilege, it need only be evident from the implications of the question, in the setting in which it is asked, that a responsive answer to the question or an explanation of why it cannot be answered might be dangerous because injurious disclosure could result."[79]

As discussed above, *Fisher* held that the contents of the pre-existing records in that case were not compelled and thus not protected. It went on to hold, however, that the act of producing documents or other tangible objects is compelled by a subpoena and that such acts of production could constitute a qualifying testimonial communication when the acts implicitly communicated information regarding the existence, possession, responsiveness, and authenticity of the subpoenaed materials and that information was not a foregone conclusion.

Under *Fisher*, one could not test whether the "incriminating" element was satisfied by reference to the records' contents because those contents were not compelled. Thus, a Fifth Amendment claim could only be sustained where the fact implicitly communicated by the act of production—the existence, possession, responsiveness, or authenticity of the documents—was incriminating.

One can conceive of some fairly unrealistic circumstances where this might be the case. For example, if a subpoena required one to produce "any and all marijuana plants in your possession, custody or control," one would have a valid Fifth Amendment claim because that which is compelled and implicitly communicated—that one has possession of a pot plant—is incriminating under federal law. Or assume that the subpoena calls for "any and all documents that refer or relate to your money laundering activity." If

78. Hoffman v. United States, 341 U.S. 479, 486 (1951) (emphasis added).
79. *Id.* at 486-87.

one produces the documents, one is implicitly saying that these are responsive and thus relevant to one's money laundering activities, a concession that would be incriminating.

In general, however, it is rarely the case that the subject of a subpoena can show that the fact that his business records existed, he possessed them, they were responsive and authentic was incriminating without reference to their contents. As the Court noted in *Fisher*, even assuming that the taxpayer's act of producing his accountant's workpapers had "some minimal testimonial significance, surely it is not illegal to seek accounting help in connection with one's tax returns or for the accountant to prepare workpapers and deliver them to the taxpayer."[80] The Court ruled that it was "quite unprepared to hold that either the fact of existence of the papers or of their possession by the taxpayer poses any realistic threat of incrimination to the taxpayer."[81] This would be true in many white-collar cases. The fact that one has bank or telephone records generally is not incriminating given that what is in those records was, under *Fisher*, deemed irrelevant to the Fifth Amendment inquiry.

After *Fisher*, then, conventional wisdom held that it was nearly impossible to successfully assert a Fifth Amendment claim in response to a grand jury subpoena duces tecum. For reasons discussed in Chapter 12 (Grand Jury), white-collar prosecutors rely heavily on grand jury subpoenas, rather than search warrants, to secure evidence—at least where there is no concern about evidence tampering. The advantages of proceeding by grand jury subpoena are many: subpoenas can be issued without approval by a judicial officer and with little investment of prosecutors' or investigators' time and effort; probable cause need not be demonstrated; and the Fourth Amendment limitations on the scope of subpoenas are more forgiving than the Fourth Amendment warrant clause's "particularity" requirement applicable to search warrants. Under *Fisher*, as a practical matter the Fifth Amendment provided no more protection for documents called for by subpoena than those seized pursuant to search warrant. Accordingly, documents were routinely produced to grand juries by the individual subjects or targets of investigations.

All this changed, however, when the Supreme Court decided *Hubbell*. In that case, for the first time, counsel argued that the "link in the chain" doctrine applied to subpoenas duces tecum as well as to testimony. And the Court accepted this argument. It held that because the defendant's act of production was both testimonial and a link in the chain of evidence to other sources of evidence, the defendant had a valid claim. Hubbell used the contents of his mind to compile the responsive documents and that constituted a testimonial communication that was a *link in the chain* leading

80. *Fisher*, 425 U.S. at 412.
81. *Id.*

to the incriminating *contents* of the records and in turn to other sources of admissible evidence.[82]

This alteration in the application of the "incriminating" element of our formula in *Hubbell* made it far easier to demonstrate that the testimonial communications implicit in the act of production are "incriminating" because the link in the chain analysis makes the incriminating contents relevant. Those contents may themselves be incriminating, or they may lead the government to find the self-same incriminating documents from other sources. In either case, a valid claim of the Fifth is now possible. The application of the "link in the chain" standard in this context resulted in a complete about-face in the presumed availability of the Fifth Amendment to shield documents in the face of a subpoena duces tecum. After *Hubbell*, any time the government serves a fairly broad subpoena duces tecum on a natural person or sole proprietorship, a Fifth Amendment claim is possible. Prosecutors are leaning heavily on the foregone conclusion doctrine to defeat such claims. Where they cannot sustain their burden under this doctrine, however, they must—where they can demonstrate probable cause—seek a search warrant to obtain the evidence.

V. AND CAN BE USED AGAINST THE WITNESS IN A "CRIMINAL CASE"

The compelled statement must be capable of use against the witness in "any criminal case." The Court's interpretation of this element also provides more protection than the language of the Fifth Amendment may suggest. The government compulsion does not have to be exercised during *one's own "criminal case."* When the Fifth Amendment says "in any criminal case," it refers to the *potential eventual use* of the compelled testimonial or physical evidence, not the type of proceeding in which the evidence was first compelled. Thus, the Court has held that the Fifth Amendment "not only protects the individual against being involuntarily called as a witness against himself in a criminal prosecution but also privileges him not to answer official questions put to him in any other proceeding, civil or criminal, formal or informal, where the answers might incriminate him in future criminal proceedings."[83] A witness may therefore assert his Fifth Amendment right in many venues, including when subpoenaed by Congress, when noticed for a civil

82. *See, e.g.*, United States v. Ponds, 454 F.3d 313, 321 (D.C. Cir. 2006) (*Hubbell* indicates that "the Supreme Court understands the contents of the documents to be off-limits because they are a derivative use of the compelled testimony regarding the existence, location, and possession of the documents.").
83. *Lefkowitz*, 414 U.S. at 77.

deposition, or when subpoenaed to testify before a grand jury, so long as the statement may eventually be used in a "criminal case."

It is important to again emphasize, however, that the right against compelled self-incrimination is not a right to silence. That is, if there is no possibility that the compelled statements or evidence can be used against the defendant in a criminal case, the person seeking to resist testifying or producing evidence cannot claim the Fifth Amendment privilege. For example, if the statute of limitations has run on criminal charges or the defendant has been pardoned, she cannot resist governmental efforts to compel from her information relevant to those charges. And, to be clear, the Fifth Amendment does not protect against the forced production of embarrassing or personally damaging information, or even information that could result in significant consequences in civil proceedings, if that information cannot be used against the witness in "any criminal case." Finally, the government can ensure that the witness is not compelled to be a witness against himself by immunizing the witness—with or without the witness's consent—under applicable statutes, in federal court, 18 U.S.C. §§ 6002 to 6003.

The above concerns the circumstances in which one can *assert* the right; there is a further question regarding in what procedural circumstances the compelled statement is inadmissible—that is, what constitutes a "criminal case." Some circuits hold that certain pre-trial proceedings—such as suppression and probable cause hearings—qualify as part of the "criminal case" and thus that use of the compelled statements in these venues is forbidden. Other circuits, however, hold that the Fifth Amendment is a "trial right" and that pre-trial proceedings do not qualify as a "criminal case" for such purposes.[84]

VI. SUMMARY WITH RESPECT TO COMPELLED ACTS AND SUBPOENAS DUCES TECUM

In many white-collar cases, the government will seek through a grand jury subpoena duces tecum, a CID, or other process to compel the production of a variety of materials—financial data, tax information, emails, texts, calendars, travel documentation and the like (referred to within, whether maintained in physical or digital form, as documents). The Supreme Court treats forced compliance with such government demands—that is, the production of the subpoenaed materials—as as a compelled act. The question is when this compelled act is deemed a testimonial communication that is incriminating within the meaning of the Fifth Amendment.

84. *See, e.g.*, Vogt v. City of Hays, 844 F.3d 1235, 1240-41 (10th Cir. 2017) (collecting cases).

The reason that that the Fifth Amendment law in this context is difficult to parse is because the *Fisher* Court articulated an analysis that is, for many, counterintuitive, and the Court then effectively overruled *Fisher* in *Hubbell*, by seemingly following its dictates but adding two critical elements.

Fisher provides that:

1. If the government does not compel one to write or generate the *contents* of the subpoenaed documents, the content of those documents is *not* "*compelled*" and thus one cannot assert the Fifth Amendment even if those contents are incriminating. (Thus, for example, the government did not force me to confess my sins in my diary, so those contents are not "compelled" and thus not privileged.)
2. The only thing that is "*compelled*" by a subpoena duces tecum is the *act of producing the documents*. (Where my diary is subpoenaed, I am required under pain of contempt to produce it to the government.)
3. The *act of producing* the documents can be a "*testimonial communication*" within the meaning of the Fifth Amendment if that act implicitly communicates to the government that the documents subpoenaed *exist*, that the subpoenaed party *possesses* them, that they are *responsive* to the subpoena, and that they are *authentic*. (By turning over my diary, I am implicitly conceding that it exists, I possess it, it is responsive to the subpoena, and it is authentic.)
4. Where the government already knows these facts with reasonable particularity, the production of the materials is insufficiently testimonial, and the *foregone conclusion doctrine* defeats a claim of privilege. (If my roommate told the government that I keep the diary and she can authenticate it, I have no privilege because of the foregone conclusion doctrine.)
5. It is those compelled testimonial communications that must be "*incriminating*." If the facts of existence, possession, responsiveness, and authenticity are not incriminating, the Fifth Amendment does not apply. (Even without my roommate's betrayal, there is nothing incriminating in conceding the existence, possession, responsiveness, or authenticity of a diary without reference to the contents so I have no valid Fifth Amendment claim).

Because it is rare that conceding that financial data, bank records, travel documentation, or the like exist, are possessed, are responsive and authentic is incriminating, it was the rare case that Fifth Amendment claims succeeded in business crime cases before *Hubbell* was decided. Even if the witness could make such a showing, the government could still prevail by showing that it knew of the materials with reasonable particularity before the subpoena was served, thus rendering any testimonial communication inherent in the act of production a foregone conclusion.

Hubbell added the following two elements to the *Fisher* analysis—which significantly strengthened witnesses's Fifth Amendment claims:

1. One does not need to rely only on the implied "testimonial communications" identified in *Fisher* (existence, possession, responsiveness and authenticity) to support a Fifth Amendment claim. After *Hubbell*, one forced to respond to a fairly broad subpoena can argue that compelled act of production is a "testimonial communication" because it is necessary for the subpoenaed party "to make extensive use of 'the contents of his own mind' in identifying" the documents responsive to the requests in the subpoena.[85]
2. Even more importantly, *Hubbell* introduced to this context the "link in the chain" analysis previously used only to test the "incriminating" nature of testimonial evidence. The *Hubbell* Court held that the government improperly used the materials produced under a grant of immunity because it found other sources of evidence by reading the materials produced. Thus, the incriminating contents are now once again relevant despite *Fisher*'s ruling that they are not themselves compelled. If the compelled act of production provides a link in the chain to the contents, which in turn lead prosecutors to other sources of this incriminating evidence, the subpoenaed party has a valid Fifth Amendment claim.

What this has meant is that those seeking to resist subpoenas duces tecum now often have a valid claim of the Fifth.

Examples

1. Taher Khoroushi was an accountant at Acme Corporation. Acme discovered that someone had been embezzling from the corporation through unauthorized transfers to an offshore account. The general counsel of the company was charged with investigating the thefts. His suspicions centered on Khoroushi, who had recently purchased an expensive home that seemed disproportionate to his income. Company counsel reported the theft to the police and informed them of his suspicions. When Khoroushi found out, he cleaned out his desk and quit. He then received a grand jury duces tecum requiring him to produce "any and all documents, data, or other materials" (1) that Khoroushi removed from the Acme Corporation or (2) referring or relating to his home purchase and any bank accounts he held over the past year. Can Khoroushi successfully resist producing these materials based on his Fifth Amendment right?

85. *Hubbell*, 530 U.S. at 43.

2. Gwallter Merricks was suspected of tax evasion and the government sought to obtain evidence from offshore banks where it believed he had accounts. It sought a court order requiring him to sign a form that stated:

   > I, Gwallter Merricks, do hereby direct any bank or trust company at which I may have a bank account of any kind to deliver copies of all documents in its possession or control that relate to said account to the grand jury sitting in the Southern District of New York. This directive has been executed pursuant to a certain order of the court in connection with a grand jury investigation. This shall be construed as consent with respect thereto.

   Can Merricks decline to sign the form based on his Fifth Amendment right?

3. The grand jury was investigating a massive Ponzi scheme. Subpoenas had issued for some twenty witnesses, but only eleven had been served; as the prosecutor put it, he was "having trouble finding some big shots." The prosecutor requested a bench warrant for one such witness, William Weisberg.

   In response to subpoena, John Hoffman—who has a lengthy rap sheet—appeared in the grand jury. The pertinent interrogation, in which he refused to answer certain questions based on his Fifth Amendment rights, follows:

   > "Q. Do you know Mr. William Weisberg?
   > "A. I do.
   > "Q. When did you last see him?
   > "A. I refuse to answer.
   > "Q. Have you seen him this week?
   > "A. I refuse to answer.
   > "Q. Do you know that a subpoena has been issued for Mr. Weisberg?
   > "A. I heard about it in Court.
   > "Q. Have you talked with him on the telephone this week?
   > "A. I refuse to answer.
   > "Q. Do you know where Mr. William Weisberg is now?
   > "A. I refuse to answer."

   Will a judge sustain Hoffman's privilege claims?

4. Federal authorities believed that the Devont'e Walker was engaging in cyberfraud, using a website to solicit contributions to a fake charity. Based on a reliable tip from Walker's former girlfriend, agents arrested Walker. They also executed a search warrant for his residence and during the search they seized a laptop.

4A. Investigators secured an order compelling Walker to unlock the computer using his alphanumeric code. What analysis would courts use in deciding that Walker cannot be compelled to provide them access to his computer?

4B. Assume that instead of an alphanumeric passcode, Walker opens his computer by using his thumbprint. What analysis would courts use in holding that the government can force him to put his thumbprint on the pad and thus open the computer?

4C. Computer forensic examiners discovered that most of the contents of the laptop were encrypted with software that is impossible to circumvent. The relevant computer files could not be accessed and viewed unless the authorized user first entered the correct password to unlock the encryption. What analysis would courts use in deciding that the government cannot force Walker to decrypt his data over his Fifth Amendment claim?

4D. On the day of his arrest, Walker was interviewed by law enforcement officials after having been advised of his *Miranda* rights and waiving them. In response to questioning, Walker said that he was able to decrypt the computer, but he refused to divulge any further information. How, if at all, does this change your Fifth Amendment analysis?

Explanations

1. With respect to the materials Khoroushi removed from his office, we know that current employees who turn over corporate documents pursuant to subpoena in their representative capacity cannot claim a Fifth Amendment right even if the documents incriminate them personally. This problem raises the question whether a corporate employee who is fired or leaves his job after a grand jury investigation has commenced and takes with him corporate records that might incriminate him can resist production of those records based on his personal Fifth Amendment right. The circuits are split on the question. The Second Circuit has held that an ex-employee may assert his personal privilege in such circumstances because "once the agency relationship terminates, the former employee is no longer an agent of the corporation and is not a custodian of the corporate records."[86] But the Eleventh Circuit has held that it is "the immutable character of the records as corporate which requires their production and which dictates that they are held in a representative capacity."[87]

   Khoroushi can attempt to assert the privilege with respect to any personal information he took from the office, and to his mortgage and

86. In re Three Grand Jury Subpoenas Duces Tecum Dated Jan. 29, 1999, 191 F.3d 173, 181 (2d Cir. 1999).
87. In re Grand Jury Subpoena Dated Nov. 12, 1991, 957 F.2d 807, 812 (11th Cir. 1992).

banking information, because they are not corporate records, and he would not be producing them in his representative capacity. Whether he will be successful in claiming the privilege will turn on whether his act of producing these materials was both a testimonial communication and incriminating. He would argue that because his act of production would implicitly communicate that the materials exist, he possesses them, and they are responsive and authentic, it is a testimonial communication. Alternatively, he can argue under *Hubbell* that the subpoena was sufficiently broad that he had to use the contents of his mind to produce the requested materials. In either case, Khoroushi would argue that these testimonial communications would be incriminating because they would provide a link in the chain leading to inculpatory evidence—that is, the contents of the documents and any other inculpatory evidence the government could find by examining the documents. But if the government can show with reasonable particularity that it already knew that he possessed these records, the foregone conclusion doctrine forecloses his claim.

2. The contents of the foreign bank records are not privileged because they are not "compelled" by the government. The foreign banks also cannot invoke the Fifth Amendment because artificial entities have no Fifth Amendment right, and they cannot assert Merricks' rights because such rights are personal. And Merricks cannot use his Fifth Amendment right to prevent the banks from producing the bank records because he is not being "compelled" to do anything.

   The issue this hypothetical raises concerns Merricks' sole remaining claim: that he has a Fifth Amendment right to refuse to comply with the court order forcing him to execute the form. That which the government is compelling him to do is an act—that is, signing the form. The problem comes down to whether, by signing the form, Merrick is making a "testimonial communication"—that is, whether executing the form "communicates any factual assertions, implicit or explicit, or conveys any information to the Government."[88]

   In *Doe v. United States*, 487 U.S. 201 (1988) (*Doe II*), the Supreme Court held that forcing the defendant to sign such a form does not violate his Fifth Amendment rights because his signature does not constitute a "testimonial communication" given the contents of the form. The Court explained that the consent directive itself is not "testimonial" because it was "carefully drafted not to make reference to a specific account, but only to speak in the hypothetical. Thus, the form does not acknowledge that an account in a foreign institution is in existence or that it is

88. *Doe II*, 487 U.S. at 215.

controlled" by the defendant.[89] The form does "direct" the bank to disclose account records that "may exist" but "directing the recipient of a communication to do something is not an assertion of fact or, at least in this context, a disclosure of information."[90] The form does not state that Merricks "consents" to the release of records, merely that the directive "shall be construed as consent." And it specifically says that it is signed pursuant to court order, so it "sheds no light on his actual intent or state of mind."[91] In these circumstances, the Court reasoned that compelling the act of providing a signature was no more "testimonial" than compelling a handwriting exemplar.

3. Here, Hoffman, a natural person, is clearly being compelled to make a testimonial communication: he has been subpoenaed to testify before the grand jury. This hypothetical turns on whether another element of our Fifth Amendment formula is satisfied: that is, whether the compelled testimony is "incriminating." The facts are drawn from *Hoffman v. United States*, 341 U.S. 479 (1951), in which the Court articulated its "link in the chain" standard for what is an incriminating answer. The Court also instructed judges that they cannot force a defendant to explain why his answer might be incriminating, for fear of a forced waiver. It noted, then, that "it need only be evident from the implications of the question, in the setting in which it is asked, that a responsive answer to the question or an explanation of why it cannot be answered might be dangerous because injurious disclosure could result."[92]

   The *Hoffman* Court upheld the claim of privilege, providing a good example of the kind of guesswork judges must engage in to apply this standard. The Court asserted that the judge in the case should have recognized that "one person with a police record summoned to testify before a grand jury investigating the rackets might be hiding or helping to hide another person of questionable repute sought as a witness."[93] The Court then hypothesized that the questions, if answered affirmatively,

   > would establish contacts between petitioner and Weisberg during the crucial period when the latter was eluding the grand jury; and in the context of these inquiries the last question might well have called for disclosure that Weisberg was hiding away on petitioner's premises or with his assistance. Petitioner could reasonably have sensed the peril of prosecution for federal offenses ranging from obstruction to conspiracy.[94]

89. *Id.*
90. *Id.* at 217.
91. *Id.* at 216.
92. *Hoffman*, 341 U.S. at 486-87.
93. *Id.* at 488.
94. *Id.*

4A. In holding that forcing a suspect to unlock a device using an alphanumeric access code is a "testimonial communication," most courts reason that forcing someone to remember and disclose or use a memorized alphanumeric code forces a suspect to use the contents of his mind and is therefore protected. Some courts rely on the *Fisher/Hubbell* line cases. They reason that this compelled act is a "testimonial communication" because, by allowing access to the device or decrypting the data, the subpoenaed party implicitly acknowledges that she has the code or decryption key, she has access to the device, and perhaps one could infer that she owns or controls the computer and its contents. Other courts rely heavily on Justice Stephens' metaphor, concluding that the forced sharing of a memorized alphanumeric password is more like forcing a suspect to reveal the combination to a safe (which, because it requires the defendant to use the contents of his mind, would be testimonial communication) than compelling him to turn over a key to the strongbox (not a testimonial communication). To succeed on this claim, the rights holder would have to demonstrate that conceding these facts is incriminating in that they would be a link in the chain of evidence needed to convict. Where there is incriminating material on the laptop, the incrimination element would be satisfied.

4B. Courts holding that the suspect has no Fifth Amendment right in this context would argue that compelling someone to provide biometric identifiers—such as one's fingerprint or face—communicates only "this is my fingerprint" or "this is my face," which does not require use of the suspect's mind. This information is, in any case, self-evident and thus insufficiently testimonial. In this regard the compelled provision of biometric data is indistinguishable from other types of compelled acts that the Court has said are unprotected—such as providing fingerprints or voice or handwriting exemplars. Those courts that rely heavily on Justice Steven's metaphor would argue that compelling one to show one's thumbprint or expose one's fact is more akin to forcing the subject to turn over the key to a lockbox than compelling the subject to turn over the combination of the safe.

4C. The question presented is whether requiring the provision of a decryption code should be treated as different than forced access to the device. To the extent that the decryption key is a memorized alphanumeric code, the analysis would likely be the same as that sketched out above.

Additional arguments are possible, however. The ACLU and the Electronic Frontier Foundation have contended that Justice Steven's metaphor is inapposite because decryption is neither a key nor a combination. They contend that "encrypting electronic data does not simply lock it up; it scrambles the data into an unreadable format. Likewise, decrypting the data does not simply unlock it; rather decryption transforms the scrambled data into readable" data.[95] Decrypting data is "an act of translation and transformation."[96] Because compelling someone to decrypt electronic data, then, "amounts to a command to explain the data,"[97] these amici argue, decryption clearly requires using the contents of one's mind and is a testimonial communication.

4D. The answer would depend on whether: (1) the court is one that accepts the applicability of the foregone conclusion doctrine in this context; and (2) if it does, what the court concludes is the substance of the implied testimonial communication for purposes of applying the doctrine. Assuming the court is willing to apply the foregone conclusion doctrine, some courts believe that all that is communicated by decryption is "I have the decryption key"; in such jurisdictions the foregone conclusion doctrine would apply here because, by virtue of Walker's statements, the government knows that Walker has the key and can decrypt the device. But if the court believes that the foregone conclusion doctrine only applies when the government can show, with reasonable particularity, that files exist on the hard drive, the suspect possessed them, and they are authentic, the interrogation was likely insufficient to give the government this information.

VI. IMMUNITY

In the white-collar context, Fifth Amendment issues are frequently exposed at the grand jury stage. The government will often seek the testimony of persons who may be involved to a greater or lesser degree in the criminal wrongdoing under investigation. If a witness has a valid Fifth Amendment claim, and the government believes that it needs his testimony, it may confer immunity to secure that witness's testimony. There are at least three types of immunity, listed below from the least protective to the most protective from the defense's point of view.

(1) Use immunity protects the witness only from the government's use of the witness's actual evidence. Thus, the government could not advert to the witness's testimony in any way, nor use the documents or other evidence the defendant produced pursuant to the immunity grant. But the government can use that compelled testimony or those subpoenaed documents to

95. Brief of Amici Curiae ACLU et al., Mass. v. Gelfgatt, SJC-11358, at 1 (Oct. 28, 2013).
96. Id. at 4.
97. Id. at 1.

pursue *other* admissible evidence and testimony. For example, assume that the defendant testifies pursuant to subpoena under a grant of use immunity to two facts about which the government previously had no idea: that he has a bank account at Sun Trust and that his sister was a witness to his crime. The government cannot use his statements to this effect against him at trial, but it can introduce any evidence it secures from Sun Trust or from his sister. Use immunity is insufficient to supplant a defendant's right against self-incrimination in U.S. courts but it satisfies a similar guarantee in U.K. courts.[98]

(2) Use and derivative use immunity ensures that neither the compelled testimony *nor evidence derived from it* will be used in a prosecution against the immunized witness. Not only is the government barred from using the witness's own compelled statements, but it is also barred from using those statements as leads to other admissible evidence. In the example posited above, then, any evidence the government secured from Sun Trust and the sister's evidence could not be used against the witness because they would constitute "derivative use" of the witness's compelled testimony. This is the type of immunity provided by federal statute, 18 U.S.C. § 6002.

(3) Transactional immunity means that an individual cannot be prosecuted for a transaction or matter about which his testimony relates. It shields an individual from prosecution for any matters disclosed under the grant of immunity *even if the government can secure sufficient evidence to convict from different, independent sources*. In our example, the government would be barred from prosecuting the defendant even if it could prove the case beyond a reasonable doubt without reference to what the witness said or derivative evidence such as the bank account records and any information the sister may provide. Many states provide this type of immunity, but the federal immunity statute is more limited in its protection.

A. Formal Immunity Under 18 U.S.C. § 6002

The federal immunity statute, 18 U.S.C. § 6002, provides for use and derivative use immunity:

> the witness may not refuse to comply with the [immunity] order on the basis of his privilege against self-incrimination; but no testimony or other information compelled under the order (or any information directly or indirectly derived from such testimony or other information) may be used against the witness in any criminal case, except a prosecution for perjury, giving a false statement, or otherwise failing to comply with the order.[99]

98. *See Allen*, 864 F.3d at 76.
99. 18 U.S.C. § 6002.

The Supreme Court, in *Kastigar v. United States*, 406 U.S. 441 (1972), upheld the constitutionality of this statute, ruling that use and derivative use immunity is "coextensive with the scope of the privilege."[100] Statutory immunity orders can be used to overcome Fifth Amendment claims with respect to compelled testimony (testimonial immunity) and the compelled production of documents and other tangible objects ("act of production" immunity).

Individuals may, of course, agree to a grant of immunity but they need not. The government can force individuals to speak if it undertakes, pursuant to a formal court order obtained under 18 U.S.C. § 6003, not to use and derivatively use his statements or any documents he produces under compulsion. In criminal cases, a court order is required, but the decision to seek an immunity order is viewed as within the discretion of the executive branch[101] and the statute therefore provides that district courts "shall issue . . . such order" upon the government's request.[102] Congress (under § 6002(3))[103] and federal agencies (under § 6002(2)),[104] can also compel a witness to speak by giving them use and derivative use immunity. As we shall see, where Congress or agencies grant immunity to pursue their own investigations, it can seriously complicate prosecutors' job in bringing a subsequent criminal case because they are bound by the use and derivative use bar.

Under § 6002, a witness can be compelled to provide testimony "in a proceeding before or ancillary to" a court or grand jury of the United States. Such "ancillary" proceedings include a pre-trial deposition but not an interview in a prosecutor's office.[105] Importantly, a statutory immunity grant does not compel the witness to cooperate with the government, for example, by allowing herself to be prepared for trial testimony.

Cooperation can be negotiated, of course. The Department of Justice vastly prefers that its culpable witnesses take a guilty plea in return for a cooperation agreement because prosecutors will wish to hold such persons responsible for their own wrongdoing. And witnesses who have conceded their guilt for the same crime about which they are testifying are less likely to be viewed in askance by the jury than those to whom the government has given immunity; certainly, they will be less vulnerable on cross-examination

---

100. *Kastigar*, 406 U.S. at 453.

101. The government generally has no obligation to immunize witnesses that the defense identifies as potentially useful but that threaten to take the Fifth if called to testify. *See* United States v. Turkish, 623 F.2d 769, 774-76 (2d Cir. 1980). In "extraordinary circumstances," however, courts may require prosecutors to confer use immunity at the defense's request. United States v. Praetorius, 622 F.2d 1054, 1064 (2d Cir. 1979); *see also* United States v. Ebbers, 458 F.3d 110, 119 (2d Cir. 2006).

102. 18 U.S.C. § 6003(a).

103. *See also id.* § 6005.

104. *See also id.* § 6004.

105. *See, e.g.*, Dunn v. United States, 442 U.S. 100, 111 (1979).

to suggestions that they are lying like rugs to save their own skins. But the need for the witness's testimony and other factors may persuade prosecutors to consider providing the witness immunity.

Depending on the relative bargaining position of the parties, the prosecutor may agree to give an individual formal, statutory immunity under § 6002 in exchange for cooperation or she can agree, pursuant to a contract between the government and defense, to give the defendant informal (also known as "letter" or "pocket") immunity whose contours are negotiated but can include a grant of transactional immunity.

I. *Kastigar* Procedures to Enforce Use and Derivative Use Immunity Orders

As a practical matter, it is fairly easy to identify and prevent "use" of the witness's immunized testimony. For example, judges will readily refuse to permit the government to use at trial testimony the witness gave under a grant of immunity before the grand jury. Where enforcement of an immunity order becomes more difficult is in policing the government's "derivative use." Recall the above hypothetical in which an immunized witness testifies about where he banks and tells the government about a witness, his sister, who can provide inculpatory testimony. Assume that the government is prosecuting the witness and attempts to put into evidence the witness's bank statements, which it secured from his bank, and call the witness's sister to testify against him. Prosecutors may assert that they secured the relevant bank statements and talked to the sister *before* they heard from the immunized witness—that is, that this evidence does not reflect derivative use of the witness's testimony. How would the defense prove to the contrary given that only the government truly knows when and how it secured its evidence?

The answer is that the defense does not have to. In response to defense concerns that § 6002 immunity would be meaningless without an effective means of policing prosecutors' compliance with it, the *Kastigar* Court constructed important procedural safeguards. Once a defendant has testified under a grant of immunity, the government has

> "the burden of showing that [its] evidence is not tainted by establishing that [it] had an independent, legitimate source for the disputed evidence." This burden of proof . . . is not limited to a negation of taint; rather, it imposes on the prosecution the affirmative duty to prove that the evidence it proposes to use is derived from a legitimate source wholly independent of the compelled testimony.[106]

---

106. *Kastigar*, 406 U.S. at 460.

A trial court will normally hold a hearing (a "*Kastigar* hearing") for the purpose of allowing the government to affirmatively demonstrate, by a preponderance of the evidence, that it obtained all of the evidence it proposes to use from sources independent of the compelled testimony. A prosecutor's or agent's representation that he did not make any use of the immunized testimony, standing alone, is insufficient to meet the government's burden.[107] A *Kastigar* hearing can be held at any point but is usually conducted pre-trial.

If the government fails to meet its burden, there can be drastic consequences. The indictment can be dismissed if the grand jury evidence was tainted. If forbidden use or derivative use is only discovered later, during or after trial, a defendant may be entitled to a new trial. Dismissal of the indictment or vacation of the conviction is not necessary, however, where the proscribed use is found to be harmless beyond a reasonable doubt.

2. Derivative Evidence: Indirect Evidentiary Use and Non-Evidentiary Use

One type of "indirect evidentiary" use that has generated some controversy is the use of immunized testimony by other witnesses "to refresh their memories, or otherwise to focus their thoughts, organize their testimony, or alter their prior or contemporaneous statements."[108] Sometimes prosecutors or others may ask witnesses to refresh their recollections by reviewing statements made by the immunized party.[109] But the most famous instance in which prospective trial witnesses were "tainted" by exposure to immunized testimony arose out of the Iran-Contra scandal. Pursuant to a § 6002 order, Congress immunized Oliver North, a Marine Lt. Colonel and National Security Council staff member under President Reagan, and forced him to testify in a congressional hearing that was televised. Despite prosecutors' best efforts to ensure that neither they nor their witnesses were exposed to North's televised appearance, some of the trial witnesses watched the hearing and heard North's testimony.

In *United States v. North*, 910 F.2d 843, 860 (D.C. Cir) (*North I*), the D.C. Circuit noted first that "[i]f the government uses immunized testimony to refresh the recollection of a witness (or to sharpen his memory or focus his thought) when the witness testifies before a grand jury considering the indictment of a citizen for acts as to which the citizen was forced to testify, then the government has clearly *used* the immunized testimony."[110] It then required prosecutors to meet a demanding two-part showing to meet their

107. *See, e.g.*, *Allen*, 864 F.3d at 69.

108. *See* United States v. North, 910 F.2d 843, 860 (D.C. Cir) (*North I*), *modified*, *North II*, 920 F.2d 940 (D.C. Cir. 1990).

109. *See, e.g.*, *Allen*, 864 F.3d 75-79.

110. *North I*, 910 F.2d at 861.

Kastigar burden in these circumstances: (1) the prosecutor must prove that there is an independent source for all matters on which the witness testifies; and (2) the prosecutor must prove that any witness exposed to the compelled statement has not shaped or altered her testimony in any way, either directly or indirectly, as result of that exposure.[111] North's conviction was overturned because the government could not meet the second requirement. As a practical matter, it may be impossible for the government to affirmatively prove that any witnesses exposed to compelled testimony were not consciously or unconsciously affected by it.

The Second Circuit employs the same test[112] but the Ninth Circuit declined to impose the second part of the *North* test, holding that:

> [I]t is the law of our circuit that the prosecutor's *Kastigar* burden is met if the substance of the exposed witness's testimony is based on a legitimate source that is independent of the immunized testimony. Ensuring that the content of a witness's testimony is based on personal knowledge provides the required Fifth Amendment protections and meets the *Kastigar* requirement that the defendant's compelled statements shall not be used against him in subsequent criminal proceedings.[113]

"Non-evidentiary use" is a broader category of potential "derivative use" that focuses on the affect that exposure to the immunized testimony may have on the decision-making of the prosecutors and investigators who have been exposed to it. When those prosecutors and investigators are deciding whether to prosecute the immunized witness, or formulating their trial strategy against him, they may consciously or unconsciously use the witness's immunized testimony for "assistance in focusing the investigation, deciding to initiate prosecution, refusing to plea bargain, interpreting evidence, planning cross-examination, and otherwise generally planning trial strategy."[114] Non-evidentiary use also may include use of immunized testimony to: "help explicate evidence heretofore unintelligible"; to "expose as significant facts once thought irrelevant (or vice versa)"; to "indicate which witnesses to call, and in what order"; and to assist "in developing opening and closing arguments."[115] "*Kastigar* does not define, except perhaps by implication, what non-evidentiary use of compelled testimony might be nor does it expressly discuss the permissible scope of such use."[116]

111. *See Allen*, 864 F.3d 92-93.
112. *See id.*
113. United States v. Koon, 34 F.3d 1416, 1432-33 (9th Cir. 1994), *aff'd and rev'd in part on other grounds*, 34 F.3d 1416 (9th Cir. 1994) (*en banc*).
114. United States v. McDaniel, 482 F.2d 305, 311 (8th Cir. 1973).
115. *North I*, 910 F.2d at 857-58.
116. *Id.* at 858.

The issue of whether and in what circumstances non-evidentiary use is proscribed has divided courts.[117] Most of the caselaw concerns what the prosecutor or investigator must show to demonstrate that their exposure to the immunized testimony did not taint their decisions.[118] At bottom, the issue is whether the government must merely show an independent basis for all its evidence, or whether it must go further and demonstrate that government agents' thought processes were unaffected. The debate is important because, again, in most cases it would be impossible for the government to affirmatively prove that those prosecutors or investigators exposed to the testimony were not affected by it. Requiring such proof would effectively bar such government employees from involvement in any subsequent indictment or prosecution of the immunized witness.

3. Federalism Issues

In *Murphy v. Waterfront Comm'n*, 378 U.S. 52 (1964), the Supreme Court held that if a state compels a witness to speak by giving him immunity—whether transactional or use and derivative use—the Fifth Amendment precludes federal officials from using or derivatively using the state-compelled testimony in a federal criminal prosecution. And the reverse is true. If federal prosecutors give a defendant statutory immunity under § 6002, state prosecutors may not use or derivatively use the evidence federal prosecutors secured in a state prosecution.

B. Cooperation: Negotiations and Proffers

Cooperation deals can be initiated in a variety of ways. The prosecutor may reach out to a witness who is sufficiently involved in the crime to provide needed testimony but who is perceived to be the least culpable of the participants. Alternatively, if defense counsel is satisfied that his client has criminal exposure and that the government can easily make a case against him, counsel and his client may reach out to the prosecutor to attempt to secure some kind of deal.

The defense's object is to secure the greatest possible protection from criminal sanction or punishment. Immunity, then, will be the most desirable result (we will discuss, *infra*, the advantages of formal versus informal immunity from the defendant's perspective). But immunity is seen as the last resort for the government. The government grants immunity to serious offenders reluctantly because prosecutors do not like to allow obviously culpable individuals to avoid punishment; the public and jurors may be

117. *See id.* at 857-60 (collecting authorities).
118. *See, e.g.*, United States v. Crowson, 828 F.2d 1427, 1429-30 (9th Cir. 1987).

indignant if a guilty witness avoids conviction and punishment; and witnesses given immunity (as opposed to being forced to plead guilty to some charge as part of a cooperation deal) will be easier for defense counsel to impeach and may harm, rather than enhance, the government's case. The government, then, will prefer that the cooperating witness take a plea to a negotiated charge.

Prosecutors generally will not offer a deal—much less grant immunity—to someone they have not interviewed. They will require a so-called witness "proffer" to evaluate the witness's culpability, usefulness to the case, and credibility before negotiating any type of cooperation agreement. If the possibility of an immunity deal is on the table, the government needs a proffer to evaluate the factors prosecutors must consider in assessing whether granting statutory immunity or entering into a non-prosecution agreement (a grant of informal transactional immunity) is in the interests of justice, among them (1) the importance of the investigation or prosecution to effective enforcement of the criminal laws; (2) the value of the person's testimony or information to the investigation or prosecution; (3) the person's relative culpability in connection with offense; and (4) the interests of any victims.[119]

If the government insists on a proffer, the witness is protected by Fed. R. Crim. P. 11(f) and Fed. R. Evid. 410, which state that the content of the defendant's statements made during such proffer sessions are inadmissible for most purposes against the defendant. But federal prosecutors will wish to alter these protections to give potential cooperators what the government views as the appropriate incentives—that is, to agree to be interviewed *and* to be truthful during the proffer. Prosecutors, then, will generally insist that proffers be conducted pursuant to a so-called "Queen for a Day" agreement,[120] in which the witness waives the protection of Fed. R. Crim. P. 11(f) and Fed. R. Evid. 410.[121]

Proffers do not guarantee that the parties will reach a deal; the witness, then, must be given some incentive to talk. Understanding that culpable witnesses are unlikely to spill their guilty guts to prosecutors without some protection, "Queen for a Day" agreements often provide that prosecutors cannot use what is said in the proffer in their case-in-chief or at

---

119. *See* U.S. Department of Justice, Justice Manual §§ 9-23.210 (immunity), 9-27.620 (non-prosecution agreement).

120. It appears that this appellation is derived from a popular radio and then TV show, "Queen for a Day," that ran from 1945 to 1960. Basically, contestants—all women—were invited to share with the audience recent financial, family, or emotional hardships. Audience applause determined who was the "winner"—that is, the contestant with the most heart-wrenching story. That woman was robed, crowned, and then awarded prizes that were designed to ease the difficulties she had shared. *See* https://en.wikipedia.org/wiki/Queen_for_a_Day.

121. In United States v. Mezzanatto, 513 U.S. 196 (1995), the Supreme Court held that a defendant may waive the Rule 410 and Rule 11(f) bar on the admissibility of statements made during plea discussions for purposes of impeachment or rebuttal.

sentencing—with certain exceptions designed to keep witnesses honest. Guilty suspects often have a natural inclination to minimize their guilt, shift culpability onto others, or outright lie to avoid prosecution. To deter suspects from blowing smoke throughout the proffer, Queen for a Day agreements generally provide that the government can use the suspect's statements (1) to prosecute him for false statements or obstruction if he lies during the proffer, (2) to provide leads to other evidence, and (3) to cross-examine the suspect if he should testify.

Some proffer agreements contain a further clause that gives defense lawyers pause. This provision allows the government to use the statements the witness makes during the proffer to rebut any evidence or arguments offered by or on behalf of the witness at any stage of his criminal prosecution (including bail, all phases of trial, and sentencing) in any prosecution brought against him. Assuming the parties do not reach any kind of deal after the proffer and the case goes to trial, this provision may significantly hamstring defense counsel during openings, closings, and witness examinations if counsel's arguments or questions arguably contradict statements made during the defendant's proffer.

C. Informal ("Letter" or "Pocket") Immunity

As noted, formal immunity does not impose a condition of cooperation; it requires only that a witness to be truthful when subpoenaed to testify. To obtain the witness's cooperation, the government may agree to enter into a contractual immunity deal with the witness ("informal," "letter," or "pocket" immunity agreements). The scope of informal immunity can take any form the parties negotiate—that is, it can provide, use, use and derivative use, or transactional immunity.

In terms of enforcing such agreements, the Court held in *Santobello v. New York*, 404 U.S. 257 (1971), that a defendant must be given "what is reasonably due" under the plea agreement; a concurring opinion suggested that due process requires the prosecution to meet its obligations under a plea agreement.[122] If the defendant breaches the agreement, the sanction for breach is that which is specified in the immunity agreement. Such agreements usually provide that if a cooperator breaches an informal immunity agreement, the government can prosecute the cooperator for any crimes known to the government—including those covered by the agreement—and all the information the cooperator provided can be used against him.[123] Informal immunity agreements will usually contain a variety of waivers, for example, of applicable statutes of limitations and double jeopardy.

---

122. *See Santobello*, 404 U.S. at 262; *see also id.* at 265 (Douglas, J., concurring).
123. *See, e.g.*, Ricketts v. Adamson, 483 U.S. 1 (1987).

Informal immunity may be conferred where the defense has a great deal of bargaining power and insists the witness receive protections not provided by formal immunity. But it is also often used when a witness is technically a "subject" of the investigation, in that she potentially has some exposure, but the prosecutor is confident that she is not sufficiently important to warrant actual prosecution. To secure her grand jury testimony over a claim of the Fifth in an expeditious way, the government may provide her with a non-prosecution agreement contingent on truthful testimony.

D. Advantages and Disadvantages of Formal vs. Informal Immunity

1. The Defense

The principal advantage of informal immunity to the defendant is the potential it offers for protection greater than that available under § 6002. Independent Counsel Ken Starr, for example, gave Monica Lewinsky both transactional and use and derivative use immunity in return for her cooperation in his investigation of President Clinton. The flexibility of such agreements is another advantage. The immunity contract can, for example, prohibit the government from sharing information with foreign prosecutors. And witnesses can negotiate for clemency for others. Starr agreed not to prosecute Lewinsky's parents as part of her immunity deal. Another advantage is the penalty for a failure to comply with one's obligations. If an immunized witness refuses to testify, he can be held in contempt and jailed. Under an informal immunity agreement, the government's only recourse is to pursue whatever sanction the agreement provides as a remedy.

Potential downsides largely flow from the fact that *Kastigar*'s protections are only applicable where the defendant is *compelled* to give testimony *over* a claim of privilege. Where the prosecution and defendant enter into agreement in which the defendant trades his Fifth Amendment privilege and cooperation for some type of immunity, he has waived his Fifth Amendment rights. Whatever he decides to say under a cooperation agreement is not "compelled" within the meaning of the Fifth Amendment. As a consequence, (1) if the agreement simply contains use immunity, no court will require that the government also provide derivative use immunity; and (2) if the defendant contends that the government breached an informal use and derivative use immunity agreement, the defendant is not entitled to a *Kastigar* hearing, and the government does not bear the burden of making an affirmative showing that its evidence was untainted, unless the parties agree to this in the agreement.

Because defendant has waived his Fifth Amendment rights and there is no "compulsion" to speak, the protections afforded by *Murphy v. Waterfront*

Commission also do not apply. Informal immunity contracts only bind the government in the district in which it is granted. Thus, unless the immunity contract so specifies, any other jurisdiction not party to the agreement is free to use or derivatively use the witness's testimony if the immunizing authority chooses to share it.

Finally, a defendant subject to a statutory immunity order cannot be held in breach or otherwise sanctioned for a failure to "cooperate" if he satisfies his obligation to give truthful testimony when subpoenaed to do so. An informal immunity agreement, by contrast, is usually contingent upon the witness's full and complete cooperation or his truthful testimony for the government. Thus, if a defendant fails to give the prosecutor his full "cooperation" or disagrees regarding what "cooperation" means, he may be held in breach of the agreement and prosecuted to the full extent of his culpability with his own statements and the evidence he proffered.

2. The Government

Prosecutors may prefer to give a witness informal immunity because in the immunity agreement the government can require certain types of cooperation that statutory immunity does not, including that the witness: make him/herself available whenever necessary for debriefing or witness preparation, turn over documentary or other physical evidence, or endeavor to secure the cooperation of others (e.g., family members, business associates). As noted, *Kastigar's* protections, and the limitations of *Murphy v. Waterfront Commission*, do not apply unless the parties include them in the agreement. It also must be acknowledged that some federal prosecutors will prefer informal immunity because it entails much less paperwork, avoids burdensome Department of Justice approval requirements, and can be done quickly.

Formal immunity, however, does offer prosecutors at least one advantage: Where formal, statutory immunity is ordered, the immunity order may be enforced by civil or criminal contempt sanctions (including jailing). Such sanctions are not available to coerce compliance with informal immunity contracts.

VIII. *MIRANDA* AND CUSTODIAL INTERROGATIONS

Miranda v. Arizona, 384 U.S. 436 (1966), requires that police warn suspects of their *Miranda* rights before interrogating them[124] and holds that any ensuing statements are admissible only if the government can show that the suspect

124. The basic *Miranda* warning provides as follows: "You have the right to remain silent. Anything you say can and will be used against you in a court of law. You have the right to an

made a knowing, intelligent, and voluntary waiver of his Fifth Amendment rights. The *Miranda* Court created a Fifth Amendment right to appointed counsel that is found nowhere in the text of that amendment, and a right to silence that does not apply outside the *Miranda* context. The suspect can revoke his waiver at any time and assert these rights. If a suspect invokes his rights, questioning must cease and resumption of the interrogation can happen, if at all, only after certain requisites are satisfied.[125]

Critically, however, *Miranda*'s protections are only available where the suspect is subjected to a "*custodial interrogation*." The legal test for *Miranda* "custody" is whether the suspect was "taken into custody or otherwise deprived of his freedom of action in any significant way."[126] What the *Miranda* Court was concerned about was "incommunicado" interrogation by the police in the "unfamiliar," police-dominated, and "menacing" environs of a stationhouse.[127] In such circumstances, the *Miranda* Court concluded that, unless the *Miranda* guarantees were employed "to dispel the compulsion inherent in custodial surroundings, no statement obtained from the defendant can truly be the product of his free choice."[128]

In many white-collar cases, subjects and targets are simply not subjected to this kind of intimidating interrogation at a police station. Interviews are often conducted at the suspect's home, place of business, or in a conference room, none of which bear any relationship to the type of oppressive, police-dominated environment envisioned in *Miranda*.

"Custodial interrogations" are also rare in many business crime cases because, finances permitting, the defense is paid for by the company, and counsel are often hired when the first subpoenas fly. Agents may wish to interview the suspect, but counsel will have advised their clients—and the government—that such informal chats are at an end. As Justice Jackson famously advised, "[a]ny lawyer who has ever been called into a case after his client has 'told all' and turned any evidence he has over to the Government, knows how helpless he is to protect his client against the facts thus disclosed."[129] Accordingly, "[a]ny lawyer worth his salt will tell the suspect in no uncertain terms to make no statement to the police under any circumstances."[130] As a result, any questioning by government agents or

---

attorney. If you cannot afford an attorney, one will be provided for you. You have the right to stop answering questions at any time."

125. *See* Edwards v. Arizona, 451 U.S. 477 (1981) (consequences of invocation of the right to counsel); Michigan v. Moseley, 423 U.S. 96 (1975) (consequences of invocation of the right to silence).

126. *Miranda*, 384 U.S. at 444.

127. *Id.* at 457.

128. *Id.* at 458.

129. Watts v. Indiana, 338 U.S. 49, 59 (1949) (Jackson, J., concurring in part).

130. *Id.*

prosecutors in such cases will be done, if at all, only on a negotiated basis and with counsel present.

Miranda protections may apply, however, in white-collar cases in which defendants are not as well-heeled and thus cannot afford counsel or the defendant is arrested and interrogated before defense counsel is hired.

The only arguably "coercive" environment a typical suspect in a business crime case may be subjected to is an appearance before the grand jury, but the Supreme Court has held that a grand jury is not a "custodial interrogation" for *Miranda* purposes.[131] *Miranda* warnings would, in any case, be highly misleading in the grand jury context because the witness has no right to remain silent—only a right to speak or assert the Fifth—and no right to an appointed lawyer under the Sixth Amendment because adversary proceedings have not commenced against him.[132] And, as we shall see below, a suspect who begins talking in the grand jury may not be allowed to simply revoke his waiver and refuse to answer any further questions.

IX. WAIVER

The stringent waiver standards set forth by the Supreme Court in *Miranda* apply only when a defendant is subjected to a "custodial interrogation" by government agents. In that discrete context, the government must demonstrate that the suspect was given *Miranda* warnings, and he knowingly, intelligently, and voluntarily waived his rights within the meaning of *Johnson v. Zerbst*, 304 U.S. 458 (1938). In all other contexts, including when a client is being deposed or is testifying in the grand jury or at trial, the *Zerbst* standard is not applied to test whether a defendant's statements comport with the Fifth Amendment. In short, a waiver of Fifth Amendment rights outside of *Miranda*-land need only be voluntary; it need not be knowing and intelligent.[133]

With respect to the question of what is "voluntary," the fact that the witness has been compelled to testify in the grand jury or at trial does not make his testimony involuntary; the presupposition is that in both venues the witness can freely claim his Fifth Amendment right. The Supreme Court has explained that "'[t]he [Fifth] Amendment speaks of compulsion. It does not preclude a witness from testifying voluntarily in matters which may incriminate him. If, therefore, he desires the protection of the privilege, he must claim it or he will not be considered to have been "compelled" within

131. United States v. Mandujano, 425 U.S. 564, 579-80 (1976).
132. *See* Chapter 12 (Grand Jury).
133. *See* Garner v. United States, 424 U.S. 648, 654 n.9 (1976) (footnote omitted) (emphasis added).

the meaning of the Amendment.'"[134] Generally speaking, then, a witness who answers a question, even if the witness is not aware of the danger of incrimination or possibility of waiver, will be deemed to have acted voluntarily and to have waived the privilege. Witnesses under examination outside of a custodial interrogation generally must use the privilege or lose it.

Rogers v. United States, 340 U.S. 367 (1951), demonstrates that the witness's waiver may extend beyond the question asked and answered. In *Rogers*, a witness testified before a federal grand jury that as Treasurer of the Communist Party of Denver she had turned membership records over to another person. The witness then refused to name the person to whom she had given the records, claiming her Fifth Amendment privilege. The Supreme Court rejected her claim of privilege, compelling her to reveal the name of the person in possession of the records. The Court held that "[d]isclosure of a fact waives the privilege as to details."[135] It found that, on these facts, the witness's privilege was not implicated because answering the question would not incriminate her further.[136]

Under *Rogers*, courts hold that "'where criminating facts have been voluntarily revealed, the privilege cannot be invoked to avoid disclosure of the details'" unless an answer would put the witness in further legal peril.[137] "As to each question to which a claim of privilege is directed, the court must determine whether the answer to that particular question would subject the witness to a 'real danger' of further crimination."[138]

Although *Rogers* concerned the scope of a waiver in the context of sequential questions in a single grand jury appearance, courts often apply the *Rogers* analysis in determining whether a witness's statement in one proceeding constitutes a waiver for purposes of later proceedings. In making this determination, however, a clear majority of courts apply an irrebuttable presumption of further incrimination where the witness is asked to reiterate his earlier statement in a "separate proceeding."[139] Although not relying upon the above rule, the Supreme Court has also made clear that the privilege against self-incrimination survives a guilty plea, holding that a defendant who had pleaded guilty can assert her Fifth Amendment right not to testify at sentencing and that a sentencing judge may not draw an adverse inference from her assertion of her right.[140]

---

134. Minnesota v. Murphy, 465 U.S. 420, 427 (1984) (quoting United States v. Monia, 317 U.S. 424, 427 (1943)).
135. *Rogers*, 340 U.S. at 373.
136. *See id.* at 374-75.
137. *Id.* at 373.
138. *Id.* at 374.
139. United States v. Johnson, 488 F.2d 1206, 1210 (1st Cir. 1973); *see also* United States v. James, 609 F.2d 36, 45 (2d Cir. 1979). *But see Ellis v. United States*, 416 F.2d 791 (D.C. Cir. 1969) (not applying such a presumption).
140. Mitchell v. United States, 526 U.S. 314 (1999).

X. THE REQUIRED RECORDS EXCEPTION

The Supreme Court created the so-called required records doctrine in *Shapiro v. United States*, 335 U.S. 1 (1948). In that case, the recipient of an administrative subpoena for his business records sought to resist production based on the Fifth Amendment. The records in question were required to be maintained under the Emergency Price Control Act (EPCA). The Court determined that the EPCA constituted a valid exercise of regulatory power and that the record-keeping provisions were central to its objectives. It held that the Fifth Amendment did not apply in these circumstances, observing that the required records had "public aspects," and as such, they could be considered quasi-public records. In subsequent cases, the Court clarified the three requirements necessary to application of the public records exception: "'(1) the purposes of the government inquiry must be *essentially regulatory*; (2) information is to be obtained by requiring the preservation of records of a kind which the regulated party has *customarily kept*; and (3) the records themselves must have assumed *public aspects* which render them at least analogous to a public document.'"[141]

The rule applies as well to claims founded on the incriminating nature of the "act of production." In response to such a claim, for example, the Seventh Circuit explained that:

> [t]he voluntary choice to engage in an activity that imposes record-keeping requirements under a valid civil regulatory scheme carries consequences, perhaps the most significant of which, is the possibility that those records might have to be turned over upon demand, notwithstanding the Fifth Amendment privilege. That is true whether the privilege arises by virtue of the contents of the documents or the act of producing them.[142]

One example of the utility of this exception to the government is the Second Circuit's ruling in *In re Grand Jury Subpoena Dated Feb. 2, 2012*, 741 F.3d 339 (2d Cir. 2013). A grand jury subpoenaed Doe for his foreign bank account records. Doe refused to comply based on his Fifth Amendment right and was held in contempt. The Second Circuit upheld the contempt sanction based on its application of the required records exception to the recordkeeping requirements of the Bank Secrecy Act. That Act requires beneficiaries of foreign bank accounts to retain records containing basic information about their accounts.[143] Congress enacted a statement of purpose for

141. In re Special Feb. 2011-1 Grand Jury Subpoena, 691 F.3d 903, 906 (7th Cir. 2012) (emphasis original); *see also* Grosso v. United States, 390 U.S. 62, 67-69 (1968).
142. In re Special Feb. 2011-1 Grand Jury Subpoena, 691 F.3d at 909.
143. *See* 31 C.F.R. § 1010.420.

the Act that explained that this required information is designed to facilitate "criminal, tax, or regulatory investigations or proceedings, or [] the conduct of intelligence or counterintelligence activities."[144] The Second Circuit pointed out that there is nothing inherently suspect or illegal about holding foreign bank accounts. In response to arguments that the statute itself mentions that the recordkeeping is necessary for criminal enforcement of its requirements, the Second Circuit, relying in part on the consensus of sister circuits, held that the fact that "a statute relates both to criminal law and to civil regulatory matters does not strip the statue of its status as essentially regulatory."[145]

Examples

1. Recall our first example, above, in which Taher Khoroushi was an accountant at Acme Corporation. Acme discovered that someone had been embezzling from the corporation through unauthorized transfers to an offshore account. The general counsel of the company was charged with investigating the theft. His suspicions centered on Khoroushi, who had recently purchased an expensive home that seemed disproportionate to his income. Company counsel reported the theft to the police and informed them of his suspicions. When Khoroushi found out, he cleaned out his desk and quit. He then received a grand jury duces tecum requiring him to produce "any and all documents, data, or other materials" (1) that Khoroushi removed from the Acme Corporation or (2) referring or relating to his home purchase and any bank accounts he held over the past year. If the government responded to Khoroushi's Fifth Amendment objection by securing a § 6002 order immunizing Khoroushi's act of production in response to the subpoena, how, if at all, could the government use the materials he produced?

2. Halimah Wibawa is a federal prosecutor who is investigating a securities fraud case. She believes that she can prove that the comptroller of Acme, Inc., Endel Ilves, with other executives, disseminated false information regarding Acme's financial health through press releases and SEC filings. Ilves's counsel, Roman Plank, concludes that Wibawa has an airtight securities fraud case against Ilves and, with Ilves' approval, reaches out to Wibawa to offer Ilves's cooperation against Acme's President and the chairman of its board. Wibawa wisely insists on a proffer. She presents Plank with a Queen for a Day Proffer Agreement that provides that

144. 31 U.S.C § 5311.

145. In re Grand Jury Subpoena Dated Feb. 2, 2012, 741 F.3d at 349 (internal quotation marks omitted); *see also* United States v. Chabot, 793 F.3d 338 (3d Cir. 2015).

(1) In any prosecutions brought against Ilves by this Office, except as provided below, the Government will not offer in evidence on its case-in-chief, or in connection with any sentencing proceeding for the purpose of determining an appropriate sentence, any statements made by Client at the meeting, except in a prosecution for false statements, obstruction of justice or perjury with respect to any acts committed or statements made during or after the meeting or testimony given after the meeting.

(2) Notwithstanding item (1) above, in any prosecution brought against Client, the Government may use statements made by Client at the meeting and all evidence obtained directly or indirectly therefrom for the purpose of cross-examination should Client testify.

2A. Ilves asks Plank—with some exasperation—why he should explain to the prosecutor just how guilty he is when he has no guarantee that the government will give him any kind of deal. How should Plank explain to Ilves what the Queen for a Day means and why it is in his best interests to agree to it?

2B. The parties executed the Queen for a Day agreement and, in the proffer, Ilves told Wibawa that Acme's President ordered him to falsify the press release and the SEC filings. The government and Ilves then entered into a deal pursuant to which he received an order of immunity under § 6002 in return for his cooperation. The cooperation agreement provided that Ilves must tell the truth, and stipulated that if Ilves breached the agreement, the government's obligations under the agreement ceased. The government could then pursue Ilves for any and all crimes about which it had knowledge, including perjury and securities fraud. Ilves testified in the grand jury regarding the conduct of the fraud, and Acme President's role in it; his description in the latter regard was consistent with his proffer. At trial, Ilves took the stand and admitted his own culpability, but he testified that Acme's President was ignorant of the fraud. Wibawa thinks that Ilves lied in his trial testimony. She wishes to prosecute him for perjury and for the underlying securities fraud. How is she constrained by the proffer, cooperation agreement, and the immunity grant? What constraints, if any, will *Kastigar* impose on Wibawa going forward?

2C. Assume that Wibawa and Ilves entered into the cooperation agreement described above but instead of providing that Ilves would receive a formal immunity order under § 6002, the agreement granted Ilves informal contractual use and derivative use immunity in return for his cooperation. Can Wibawa share Ilves' grand jury[146] and trial testimony with state prosecutors who wish to use the evidence against Ilves in a state-law securities fraud prosecution? If Wibawa later decides to prosecute Ilves and Ilves believes that she derivatively used his testimony to secure evidence she proposes to use at trial, what recourse does he have?

Explanations

1. *Hubbell* held that the materials produced pursuant to act of production immunity under § 6002 cannot themselves be used in evidence. Furthermore, to the extent that they constitute a link in the chain to other sources of incriminating evidence, this would constitute derivative use and would be barred. Thus, any personal items Khoroushi took with him from Acme could not be used against him, nor could the government use leads it learned from reading the documents. The same is true of Khoroushi's own banking information and documentation regarding his house purchase. The government could not use those materials in evidence, nor could it use any documents it later secured from the bank or closing agent if it knew to ask for those documents only after reading the materials Khoroushi produced pursuant to the immunity grant.

2A. Ilves's question is a logical one and it illustrates how challenging defense counsel's role is in this context. Defense counsel must: forecast correctly and in a timely way that the government is likely to make a case against the witness and that it is best for the witness to attempt to sell a deal rather than fighting further; argue for the best possible terms in the proffer session while oftentimes not knowing precisely what the defendant's true bargaining position is because of the lack of discovery about what the government has or knows; preparing the client to reveal all honestly and completely to the prosecutor—all the while maintaining the attorney-client relationship and, in particular the witness's trust and confidence in counsel's loyalty and zealousness.

Counsel must persuade the client that the bottom line is threefold: the government has an airtight case against him; his only hope for avoiding prosecution and jail time is cooperation; and no such deal is possible without a proffer. This proffer does protect him insofar as he is honest, and honesty is essential. A dishonest proffer will be far

146. Assume that she secured an appropriate order under Fed. R. Crim. P 6. *See* Chapter 12 (Grand Jury).

worse for Ilves than no proffer at all because he will lose any chance of cooperation *and* it will open him up to prosecution for false statements or obstruction. Finally, if Ilves lies, a deal fails to materialize, and Ilves wishes to take the stand in his own defense at trial, Ilves can be cross-examined with any proffer statements inconsistent with his testimony.

2B. Wibawa believes that Ilves lied at trial, not in his proffer or grand jury appearance. If she charges him with perjury, Wibawa will likely wish to use at trial what was said in the proffer session as well as Ilves' grand jury testimony to demonstrate that his trial testimony was irreconcilable with his earlier statements.

Perjury Prosecution:

The Queen for Day Agreement expressly provides that, in the event Ilves lies during the proffer, the government can use whatever he said in a prosecution for perjury or false statements committed during the proffer or in "testimony given after the meeting." The proffer agreement, then, presents no obstacle.

Nor does the cooperation agreement. If the government can prove that he lied at trial, this is a breach of that agreement and voids the government's obligations under it. The remedy for breach is that the government can go after Ilves for perjury and securities fraud and use everything he said in the course of his cooperation for that purpose.

With respect to the immunity grant, § 6002 says that the government cannot use or derivatively use any evidence the defendant provides under compulsion of the order "except a prosecution for perjury, giving a false statement, or otherwise failing to comply with the order." Wibawa, then, can indict Ilves for perjury assuming she can prove that this trial testimony is false, and she can use his grand jury and trial testimony to prove her case.

Securities Fraud:

Assuming Wibawa also wishes to charge Ilves for his participation in the securities fraud, the Queen for a Day agreement bars her from using statements he made during the proffer regarding the securities fraud in such a prosecution except on cross-examination should he take the stand. The cooperation agreement presents no bar because, again, Ilves' lies under oath constitute a breach of the agreement and, in such circumstances, the government can go after Ilves for securities fraud.

The government secured a formal order of immunity under § 6002, and that will present Wibawa with difficulties in a securities fraud prosecution. Wibawa cannot use or derivatively use what Ilves said in the grand jury or at trial regarding his role in the securities case. She will bear the affirmative burden, in a *Kastigar* hearing, of demonstrating under a preponderance standard that all the evidence that she will use against him at his securities fraud trial was obtained independently of his compelled grand jury and trial testimony.

This problem also raises the issue of potential "nonevidentiary use" of the immunized testimony. Wibawa was exposed to Ilves' immunized testimony. In some circuits this may "taint" her participation in any prosecution of Ilves for securities fraud unless she can affirmatively prove that her thought processes in deciding to indict Ilves or in structuring her case have not been affected by his testimony.

2C. The defendant agrees, in an informal immunity agreement, to waive his Fifth Amendment right and cooperate in return for the contractual—not statutory—immunity grant. He is therefore not being "compelled" to do anything, and *Kastigar* and *Murphy* do not protect him. Unless the government agrees in the immunity deal that such protections will apply, they do not. Wibawa, then, can share his testimony with anyone she wishes if the agreement contains no restrictions. And *Murphy* would not bar the state prosecutors' use of his grand jury and trial testimony against him. Even if Ilves believes that Wibawa improperly derivatively used evidence he provided during his cooperation, he is not entitled to a *Kastigar* hearing at which the government would have to affirmatively demonstrate that its evidence was untainted. The government does, however, have a duty to fulfill its promises[147] and a court may decide that, as a remedial measure, it will follow *Kastigar's* rules in determining whether the government breached is contractual obligations.

147. *See Santobello*, 404 U.S. at 262.

CHAPTER 15

U.S. Sentencing Guidelines

3. Identification and Application of the Minimum and Maximum Multipliers

In the Sentencing Reform Act of 1984 (SRA), Congress precipitated a profound change in the federal criminal system by establishing the U.S. Sentencing Commission and tasking it with formulating guidelines designed to control judicial discretion in sentencing.[1] The Commission, pursuant to this congressional delegation, promulgated the U.S. Sentencing Guidelines (Guidelines or USSG), which took effect for the sentencing of individuals in 1987 and for corporations and other organizational defendants in 1991.

"The efficacy of any sentencing system cannot be assessed absent agreement on the purposes and objectives of the penal system. And the responsibility for making these fundamental choices and implementing them lies with the legislature."[2] Congress, then, first required that the Commission establish sentencing policies and practices designed to assure that the purposes of sentencing—as set forth in 18 U.S.C. § 3553(a)—were met. Section 3553(a) mandates that courts impose a criminal sentence "sufficient, but not greater than necessary," to comply with the need for the sentence imposed "to reflect the seriousness of the offense, to promote respect for the law, and to provide just punishment of the offense" (retribution or "just deserts"); "to afford adequate deterrence to criminal conduct" (deterrence); "to protect the public from further crimes of the defendant" (incapacitation); and to provide the defendant with needed educational or vocational training, medical care, or other correctional treatment in the most effective manner" (rehabilitation). Congress qualified the last clause—concerning rehabilitative concerns—by decreeing that in determining whether to impose a term of imprisonment and, if so, its length, courts should recognize that "imprisonment is not an appropriate means of promoting correction and rehabilitation."[3]

A second directive flowed from one of the principal impetuses behind this sentencing revolution: studies that showed troubling disparities among sentences imposed on similarly situated defendants, with particularly harsh sentences being visited upon Black defendants. The Commission was charged with promoting reasonable uniformity and proportionality in sentencing by "narrowing the wide disparity in sentences imposed for similar criminal

---

1. The U.S. Sentencing Commission (Commission) is a permanent independent agency in the judicial branch. The Commission's seven voting members are appointed by the President and confirmed by the Senate and serve staggered six-year terms. Three of the members must be federal judges and no more than four may belong to the same political party. The Commission continues to refine the Guidelines, conducts training, and collects, analyzes, and distributes a broad array of information and data on federal sentencing practices.
2. Harmelin v. Michigan, 501 U.S. 957, 998 (1991) (Kennedy, J., concurring in part and concurring in the judgment).
3. 18 U.S.C. § 3582(a); *see also* 28 U.S.C. § 994(k); Tapia v. United States, 564 U.S. 319 (2011).

offenses committed by similar offenders"[4] while imposing "appropriately different sentences for criminal conduct of differing severity."[5]

A third congressional mandate flowed from another concern that spurred congressional reform efforts—a perceived lack of honesty and transparency in sentencing. Congress wished to move from a system in which sentences were essentially indeterminant to one in which the offender received a certain sentence and served that full sentence.

In pre-Guidelines practice, the sentence a defendant actually served was the result of the virtually unconstrained discretion of three actors: the prosecutor who chose the charges and thus the applicable statutory maximum punishment; the judge who chose the sentence within the often generous limit set by the statutory maximum (e.g., zero to twenty years); and the U.S. Parole Commission, which had the power, after sentencing, to decide when offenders were actually released from prison, often well before the expiration of their formal sentences. In the Sentencing Reform Act, Congress not only charged the Commission with constraining judges' discretion, but it also eliminated parole in the federal system, thus ensuring that a prisoner would be released only upon the completion of his sentence less any credit earned by good behavior while in custody.

To understand the Commission's choices in writing the Guidelines, one must understand one final challenge it faced in following Congress's mandate to ensure uniformity and proportionality in sentencing: taking account of the potential disuniformity that could result from prosecutorial charging choices. The Act obviously contemplated constraining or eliminating the outsized discretion exercised by two of the three actors who previously determined the length of an offender's actual sentence: judges and the Parole Commission. The only actor whose discretion the Act did not constrain was the Department of Justice. Congress and the Commission did not, and probably constitutionally could not, directly limit the charging practices of prosecutors. The Commission did, however, design the Guidelines in such a way as to blunt the extent to which prosecutors' choices could affect defendants' sentences. Some of the Guideline provisions novices find most puzzling and difficult—the "relevant conduct" and "grouping" rules—can only be understood with this background in mind.

The fruit of the Commission's work was a complex set of rules that, in the normal case, provided the sentencing judge with a narrow range (e.g., six to twelve months) within which he or she was *required* to sentence the defendant. Judges could, in extraordinary cases, "depart" from the Guidelines range, but the U.S. Sentencing Commission had rules and policies to guide departures, and appellate courts were diligent in their de

4. U.S. Sentencing Guidelines, ch. 1, pt. A, former intro. comm. (2023 ed.) [hereinafter USSG].
5. *Id.*

novo review of district courts' discretionary departure judgments. In short, although denominated as "Guidelines," these rules were in fact mandatory.

The Guidelines survived a number of constitutional challenges—both to the institutional arrangement by which they were promulgated[6] and to the operation of the Guidelines themselves. Finally, however, in January 2005, the U.S. Supreme Court held that the *mandatory* sentencing Guidelines violated the Sixth Amendment in *United States v. Booker*, 543 U.S. 220 (2005).[7] The remedy the Court adopted was not to invalidate the Guidelines, but rather to strike only those statutory provisions that rendered them mandatory.

After *Booker*, then, the very general guidelines provided in 18 U.S.C. § 3553(a) control federal criminal sentencing. Section 3553(a) provides that the U.S. Sentencing Guidelines still operate, but they are advisory only. Further, the *Booker* Court decreed that district court's sentencing determinations were subject only to "reasonableness" review on appeal. In 2007, the Supreme Court decided *Gall v. United States*, 552 U.S. 38 (2007), and *Kimbrough v. United States*, 552 U.S. 85 (2007), in which it underscored that "reasonableness" means "abuse of discretion," and that it contemplates substantial appellate deference to district courts' exercises of sentencing discretion.[8] Courts of appeals rarely reverse a sentence as "unreasonable."

Post-*Booker*, § 3553(a) may be the theoretical touchstone for sentencing, but the Guidelines in fact continue to be a critical factor in parties' decision-making at all stages of federal criminal cases—from bail, to plea bargaining, to sentencing after trial or plea, to appellate review of trial courts' sentencing decisions.

Pre-trial detention decisions turn on two factors: risk of flight and dangerousness to the community.[9] It is common, then, to perform at least a rudimentary Guidelines analysis to evaluate, for example, whether a wealthy sixty-year-old defendant (with a passport and an offshore bank account) who is facing 121–151 months in jail is likely to flee.

When it comes to plea negotiations, defendants understandably are very concerned with their sentencing exposure. Federal statutes give little guidance on sentencing to structure the parties' negotiations. They simply provide a maximum term of imprisonment, which is usually very generous, authorizing, for example, a term of imprisonment from zero to twenty years. The Guidelines, then, provide the reference point against which the parties negotiate for a sentencing result that both parties can live with. Indeed, the federal rules expressly provide for bargaining in the facts and factors that

---

6. *See* Mistretta v. United States, 488 U.S. 361 (1989).

7. The Court applied the same analysis to organizational defendants in *Southern Union Co. v. United States*, 567 U.S. 343 (2012).

8. *See also* Holguin-Hernandez v. United States, 589 U.S. 169, 174 (2020); Spears v. United States, 555 U.S. 261 (2009) (*per curiam*).

9. *See* 18 U.S.C. § 3142(e)(1).

drive Guidelines sentences,[10] and Guidelines stipulations are a common part of federal plea agreements. Judges are also advised to consult the Guidelines in deciding whether the parties' proffered plea deal will comport with the uniformity and proportionality goals of the SRA.[11] Given that approximately ninety-seven percent of federal criminal cases plead out, the Guidelines' role in plea bargaining is more significant that their role in sentencing after trial.

Should a case proceed to trial and a conviction ensue, the Supreme Court has repeatedly instructed that district courts "should begin all sentencing proceedings by correctly calculating the applicable Guidelines range. As a matter of administration and to secure nationwide consistency, the Guidelines should be the starting point and the initial benchmark."[12] And it appears that, for the most part, judges are following the "advisory" Guidelines range—or are deviating from it at the request of the government—in about seventy-five percent of cases.[13] Because there is a great variation around the country in the extent to which judges follow the Guidelines, however, this average conformance figure is somewhat misleading.[14] Notably, conformance also depends on the type of prosecution at issue; research demonstrates that many defendants in major white-collar cases receive shorter sentences than the Guidelines range would suggest.[15]

Finally, the Guidelines can determine appellate outcomes. Some circuit courts apply a "presumption of reasonableness" when reviewing district court's within-Guidelines sentences, a practice the Supreme Court ruled was consistent with the Sixth Amendment in *United States v. Rita*, 551 U.S. 338 (2007).[16]

In short, despite *Booker*, those who practice federal criminal law must know how to use—and some would say abuse—the Sentencing Guidelines.

I. RELEVANT STATUTES

As discussed above, now that the Guidelines are advisory only, 18 U.S.C. § 3553(a) controls federal sentencing.[17] But § 3553(a) requires sentencing

10. *See* Fed. R. Crim. P. 11(c); *see also* Chapter 16 (Plea Bargaining).
11. *See* USSG, *supra* note 4, § 6B1.2.
12. *Gall*, 552 U.S. at 49; *see also Kimbrough*, 552 U.S. at 108-109; *Rita*, 551 U.S. at 352
13. *See* U.S. Sentencing Comm'n, 2023 Sourcebook of Federal Sentencing Statistics, Table 29 [hereinafter 2023 Sourcebook].
14. *See id.* Table 30.
15. *See* U.S. Sentencing Comm'n, The Influence of the Guidelines on Federal Sentencing: Federal Sentencing Outcomes, 2005-2017, 7, 27-32 (2020).
16. This presumption is only appropriate on appellate review, as the Supreme Court subsequently emphasized in *Nelson v. United States*, 555 U.S. 350, 352 (2009).
17. Congress has also identified by statute the factors to be considered in determining whether to impose a fine, its amount, and methods for payment in 18 U.S.C. § 3572. Section 3572 instructs a sentencing court to consider, *inter alia*, the income, earning capacity, and

judges to consider the Sentencing Guidelines and the Supreme Court requires the judges to start with a Guidelines analysis.

When one is doing a Guidelines analysis, other statutes become relevant—notably the statute(s) of convictions and other sentencing provisions discussed below. First, it is critical to understand *that the maximum or minimum sentence prescribed by the offense of conviction always trumps the Guidelines sentencing range*. The Commission could not alter the determinative effect of the count of conviction at the end of the Guidelines process because this effect is mandated by statute. Thus, the floor below which the sentence may not go, regardless of the applicable sentencing range determined under the Guidelines, is set by any statutory mandatory minimum for the offense of conviction.[18] Similarly, the ceiling that the sentence may not exceed, again regardless of the Guidelines' calculus, is set by the statutory maximum sentence prescribed for the offense of conviction by Congress. For example, if a Guidelines calculation yields a range of about ten years, but the prosecutor only chooses to charge one count of conspiracy under 18 U.S.C. § 371, which carries a statutory maximum of five years, the sentencing court *cannot* sentence the defendant to any more than five years.

To compute the statutory maximum, one simply adds up the statutory maximums for all the counts in the indictment. If the indictment contains one count of conspiracy under § 371, the statutory maximum is five years but if it contains two such counts, the maximum is ten years.

Additional sentencing statutes to which one should refer in performing a sentencing analysis are:

18 U.S.C. § 3559 (Sentencing classification of offenses). This provision is important for purposes of assessing whether a defendant is statutorily eligible for probation (under 18 U.S.C. § 3561 (discussed below)) and determining the potential term of post-incarceration supervised release (under 18 U.S.C. § 3583 (discussed below)).

18 U.S.C. § 3561(a) (Sentence of probation). This section provides that a sentence of probation is authorized *except* in certain circumstances. The object of defense counsel in many white-collar cases (and other cases as well, of course) is to attempt to secure a sentence of probation, as opposed to a sentence involving incarceration. Defendants are eligible, under the Guidelines, to a sentence of straight probation if they are in Zone A of the Guidelines sentencing grid found in Chapter Five (generally, if they have a range of zero to six months).[19] However, given that the statutes always

---

financial resources of the defendant; the burden that a fine will impose on the defendant; the pecuniary loss suffered by virtue of the offense and the need to deprive the defendant of its ill-gotten gains; whether the defendant can pass on the fine to other persons; whether restitution has been ordered; the size of the organization and any measures taken by the organization to prevent a recurrence of the offense. For some inexplicable reason this code section is rarely referenced in corporate sentencing.

18. *See* USSG, *supra* note 4, § 5G1.1.

19. *See id.* § 5C1.1(b).

trump the Guidelines, a defendant cannot receive probation, regardless of his Guidelines range, if the statute says he is not entitled to it because of the "class" of his felony conviction.

18 U.S.C. § 3571 (Sentence of fine). Generally, for an individual convicted of a felony, the maximum fine is the *greatest* of (1) the amount specified in the offense of conviction if the statute specifies one, (2) $250,000, or (3) under subsection (d), twice the gross gain or loss. (The same is true for organizations, but the default figure is $500,000.)

18 U.S.C. § 3663(a)(1)(A) (Order of restitution). If a defendant is convicted of an offense under Title 18, restitution is authorized by this section.

18 U.S.C. § 3583 (Inclusion of a term of supervised release after imprisonment). This statute provides guidance on the term of supervised release to which a defendant may be subject after his term of imprisonment is over.

18 U.S.C. § 3013(a)(2) (Special assessment on convicted persons). The court must impose a special assessment of $100 for each felony offense if the defendant is an individual ($400 for organizational defendants).

II. OUTLINE OF INDIVIDUALS' GUIDELINES ANALYSIS

Before considering how Guidelines sentencing works, it is helpful to understand the procedural context. The rules that apply at sentencing are significantly laxer than those that apply in criminal—or civil—trials. The Federal Rules of Evidence do not apply at sentencing, and thus facts that significantly increase the defendant's sentence may be based on hearsay.[20] Sentencing judges need only apply a preponderance of the evidence standard to enhance a defendant's sentence on the basis of facts that are not elements of the offense (extra-element facts) and thus were not proved beyond a reasonable doubt at trial.[21] Such facts may include the defendant's

20. *See, e.g.*, United States v. Umaña, 750 F.3d 320, 346-48 (4th Cir. 2014) (Sixth Amendment's Confrontation Clause inapplicable at sentencing so hearsay admissible to persuade sentencers to impose the death penalty).

21. Because a jury's acquittal only demonstrates that the jury found that the defendant was not guilty beyond a reasonable doubt, the acquittal does not necessarily mean that the government did not prove its case by a preponderance of the evidence. The Supreme Court held in *United States v. Watts*, 519 U.S. 148, 156 (1997) (*per curiam*) that a sentencing court may consider conduct for which the defendant was acquitted at trial as relevant conduct under the Guidelines so long as the conduct was proved by a preponderance of the evidence to the satisfaction of the sentencing judge. On April 17, 2024, the U.S. Sentencing Commission voted unanimously to largely prohibit conduct for which a person was acquitted in federal court from being used in calculating a sentence range under the federal Guidelines. This amendment becomes effective November 1, 2024, unless Congress takes action to the contrary. The amendment revises USSG, *supra* note 4, § 1B1.3 by adding a new subsection (c), which provides that "[r]elevant conduct does not include conduct for which the defendant

motive, the vulnerable nature of his victims, or the amount of loss or harm caused. Indeed, the facts a judge can consider in formulating an appropriate sentence include uncharged criminal conduct that the Guidelines make relevant. A defendant has no constitutional right to confront the witnesses against him or to cross-examine the sources of the facts upon which his sentence rests.

A. Chapter Five: The Sentencing Table

Readers are strongly advised to reference the actual Guidelines Manual, available on the Commission's website,[22] throughout this discussion. Readers are also cautioned that the Guidelines appear at first glance to present practitioners with a math exercise—one simply totes up the points that go into an offense level and criminal history category and that suffices. As one digs deeper, however, one sees that there are a great number of interpretive questions that can arise: Who is a "vulnerable victim"? What constitutes the use of "sophisticated means" in the commission of a crime? Defense counsel will litigate these questions vigorously because each point potentially means additional months of imprisonment. When seeking definitional guidance, one should initially consult the application notes that follow each Guideline section. But there is conflicting case law on many Guidelines interpretive questions and thus practitioners must also consult the applicable law in their circuit. (Practice tip: the Commission intentionally made its numbering system unique to ease users' burden in conducting legal research.)

To begin, one should turn to the Sentencing Table set forth in Guidelines Chapter Five, Part A. This chart demonstrates that a defendant's Guidelines sentencing range is a function of two factors—the defendant's "offense level" and his "criminal history category." The sentencing range lies at the intersection of the offense level (vertical axis) and the criminal history category (horizontal axis) applicable to a given defendant. For example, if a defendant has an offense level of 15 and a criminal history category of I, the Guidelines advise that a term of imprisonment of between eighteen and twenty-four months (not years!) is appropriate.

The bulk of the Guidelines Manual consists of instructions on how to determine what offense level and criminal history category govern in a given case. USSG § 1B.1 provides instruction on how one should proceed. Generally, one works sequentially through the chapters in the Guidelines Manual. Chapter One contains definitions and application instructions.

---

was criminally charged and acquitted in federal court unless such conduct also establishes, in whole or in part, the instant offense of conviction." *See also* (new) Application Note 10 to § 1B1.3.

22. *See* https://www.ussc.gov/guidelines/2023-guidelines-manual-annotated

Chapters Two and Three are largely concerned with computing the defendant's offense level. Chapter Four provides guidance in discerning the defendant's criminal history category.

The criminal history category is supposed to reflect the *defendant's disposition to criminality or dangerousness*.

The offense level, by contrast, is designed to measure *the seriousness of the crime of conviction*. The offense level is largely determined by reference to three factors: (1) the "base offense level" which is prescribed by the Chapter Two guideline applicable to the offense of conviction; (2) the "specific offense characteristics" which are again included in the applicable Chapter Two guideline; and (3) any "adjustments" from Chapter Three that are appropriately assessed given the circumstances of the offense.

B. Chapter Two: Base Offense Level and Specific Offender Characteristics

The effect of the offense(s) for which the defendant was convicted is confined in effect to the *beginning* and the *end* of the Guidelines calculation. At the *beginning* of a Guidelines calculation, one must first determine which Chapter Two Guideline applies. The offense(s) of conviction presumptively determines which Chapter Two Guideline(s) will control, and thus in most cases which "base offense level" and which "specific offense characteristics" apply.[23] As noted above, the charged offense also determines the statutory maximum or minimum that, at the *end* of the sentencing analysis, may trump whatever Guidelines range is applicable.

To begin computing a defendant's offense level, then, one identifies the offense of conviction and looks it up in the index provided in Guidelines' Appendix A. The index specifies the offense Guideline section(s) in Chapter Two applicable to the statute(s) of conviction. If more than one Guideline section is referenced for a particular statute, one uses the Guideline most appropriate for the offense conduct charged in the count of which the defendant was convicted. Thus, for example, if the defendant is charged with obstruction under § 1503, § 1505, or § 1512(b) or (c), one is directed to USSG § 2J1.2. If one turns to Chapter Two, Part J, one will see that this part concerns "Offenses Involving the Administration of Justice" and that § 2J1.2 covers obstruction of justice. If one flips through Chapter Two, one will see that the offenses are generally organized by subject-matter. Thus, for example, white-collar practitioners will spend a great deal of time in

23. In some circumstances, a cross-reference will refer the parties to another Guideline. *See* USSG, *supra* note 4, § 1B1.5.

Chapter Two, Part B, which covers "Basic Economic Offenses" and Part C, which applies to public corruption violations.

Turning to the applicable Chapter Two Guideline, one first ascertains the "base offense level," which is a number reflecting the seriousness of the offense of conviction. Some offenses have one base offense level, and others have a choice depending on the facts of the case. Although it may seem like this base offense level is simply an arbitrary number plucked from thin air, the Commission says that it relied on pre-Guidelines sentencing data to arrive at a number that it thought reflected judges' historical judgment regarding the relative culpability reflected in the commission of a given crime.

One then turns to identifying the applicable "specific offense characteristics." Specific offense characteristics allow the sentencing judge to adjust the defendant's base offense level in light of the circumstances of the crime. These are facts that—although not elements of the crime—the Commission or Congress identified as aggravating or mitigating the seriousness of the crime. For example, in most economic crime cases, the Guidelines require one to reference a loss table that graduates the number of points one adds as a specific offense characteristic on the theory that the amount of harm caused should be a significant driver of sentences. Similarly, in drug cases, the specific offense characteristics largely center on the type and quantity of the drugs involved.

Recall that one of the challenges that the Commission faced in constructing the Guidelines was attempting to dampen the effect that prosecutorial charging choices could have on sentencing results. Its classification of applicable Chapter Two Guidelines reflects this concern. Thus, the Commission attempted to group together like offenses into discrete Chapter Two Guidelines so the same Guidelines analysis would apply regardless of what related offenses a prosecutor chose to charge.

For example, we have seen that regardless of whether a prosecutor charges obstruction under § 1503, § 1505, or § 1512(b) or (c), the judge will use the same Guidelines to identify the defendant's offense level and specific offender characteristics. In economic crime cases, one guideline (§ 2B1.1) determines the base offense level for a very large variety of offenses, including the myriad offenses relating to fraud or deceit as well as theft, embezzlement, receipt of stolen property, and property destruction. As a result, in 2023, seventy percent of all federal criminal sentences were largely determined by the few Guidelines sections relating to drug (over 30.1 percent), immigration (28.4 percent), firearms (13.6 percent) and economic crime (7.9 percent) offenses.[24]

---

24. *See* 2023 Sourcebook, *supra* note 13, Table 20.

A prosecutor's decision to charge one code section rather than another, then, may have little sentencing consequence beyond dictating the (usually generous) statutory maximum applicable. But the Commission's categorization system does not completely eliminate prosecutors' ability to manipulate which Chapter Two Guideline applies through its charging theory. Thus, if the prosecutor charges a "money or property" wire or mail fraud,[25] Appendix A counsels that we turn to § 2B1.1 (economic crimes), which instructs judges to use a base offense level of 6 or 7, depending on the offense charged. But if she instead charges the case under an "honest services" fraud theory, one would rely on § 2C1.1 (public corruption), which starts with a base offense level of 12 or 14, again depending on the precise crime at issue.

C. Chapter Three: Adjustments

Once the Chapter Two offense level is determined by adding the applicable Chapter Two Guideline's specific offense characteristics to the base offense level, one must turn to Chapter Three to determine whether any "adjustments" are appropriately assessed in a given case. These adjustments further customize treatment of the offense at issue, requiring courts to distinguish between offenders based upon facts that were not necessarily proved beyond a reasonable doubt at trial, including: the nature of the victim and the defendant's motivation in selecting that victim or committing the crime; the defendant's aggravating or mitigating role in the offense; or the defendant's abuse of a position of trust or a special skill in the course of the offense. The Chapter Three adjustments potentially allow for the enhancement of a defendant's offense level based on uncharged criminal conduct that is connected to the conviction offense. For example, even if a defendant is not charged with obstruction of justice or perjury, a judge who finds by a preponderance of the evidence that the defendant "willfully obstructed or impeded . . . the administration of justice with respect to the investigation, prosecution, or sentencing" of the offense of conviction, may increase the defendant's offense level by two levels.[26]

---

25. *See* Chapter 6 (Fraud) (discussing "money or property" versus "honest services" theories of fraud).

26. USSG, *supra* note 4, § 3C1.1; *see also* United States v. Dunnigan, 507 U.S. 87, 96-98 (1993) (rejecting the claim that allowing sentencing adjustment for perjury chilled the exercise of the defendant's Sixth Amendment right to testify on her own behalf).

D. Relevant Conduct

Now for the difficult part. Chapters Two and Three tell a court what factors—such as the amount of loss caused or a defendant's obstructive conduct—should be considered in computing a sentence. Section 1B1.3's "relevant conduct" rules tell the court what conduct committed by the defendant or his accomplices—and during what time period—may be considered in applying these factors. The relevant conduct rules have two fairly straightforward dimensions: the temporal dimension and the accomplice attribution dimension. A more difficult to master "third dimension" is considered separately.

1. Temporal Dimension

The conduct that may be considered by a judge in applying Chapters Two and Three includes actions "that occurred during the commission of the offense of conviction, in preparation for that offense, or in the course of attempting to avoid detection or responsibility for that offense."[27]

2. Accomplice Attribution Dimension

The second, or accomplice attribution, dimension of relevant conduct provides that a defendant is responsible not only for "all acts and omissions committed, aided, abetted, counseled, commanded, induced, procured, or willfully caused by the defendant,"[28] but also all acts and omissions of others that were "within the scope of the jointly undertaken criminal activity," "in furtherance of that criminal activity," and "reasonably foreseeable in connection with that criminal activity."[29] This means, for example, that when the sentencing judge is determining what "loss" figure to use for purposes of 2B1.1(b)(1)'s loss chart, she will use all the loss caused by the defendant *and* his coconspirators (whether or not conspiracy is charged or proved) if she is satisfied by a preponderance of the evidence that their conduct was in furtherance of a joint criminal plan and was reasonably foreseeable in connection with the criminal activity the defendant agreed to undertake.

This provision has the potential to vastly increase a defendant's Chapter Two offense level. For example, assume that the defendant is part of a large gang that sells drugs. He makes sales of $20,000, but the group in aggregate sells $1 million. The total amount of drugs would be used in computing his

27. USSG, *supra* note 4, § 1B1.3(a)(1).
28. *Id.* § 1B1.3(a)(1)(A).
29. *Id.* § 1B1.3(a)(1)(B); *see also id.* § 1B1.3, App. N. 3.

Chapter Two specific offense characteristic relating to the amount and type of drugs involved in his offense if his co-conspirators' sales were "within the scope of the jointly undertaken criminal activity" and reasonably foreseeable in light of the activity the defendant agreed to undertake.

This accomplice attribution dimension of relevant conduct also applies to Chapter Three adjustments. Thus, if one of our defendant's compatriots threatens a defecting gang member who is cooperating with the police, and that threat is within the scope of the conspiracy and reasonably foreseeable, the defendant can be assessed an obstruction of justice adjustment under Chapter Three even if he had nothing to do with the witness intimidation.

E. The Third Dimension: Relevant Conduct and Grouping

Readers are cautioned that the Guidelines sections discussed below, sections 1B1.3(a)(2), 3D1.2(d), and 3D1.3(b), are both facially incomprehensible and absolutely essential for white-collar practitioners to understand. Defense counsel, in particular, risk malpractice if they do not master the mechanics of these sections.

Let's start with the problem the Commission was trying to solve and work backwards to the arcane text of sections 1B1.3(a)(2), 3D1.2(d), and 3D1.3(b). Let us assume that a defendant defrauded ten victims of $1 million each through wire fraud. Further assume that the government could bring one count of wire fraud relating to an interstate email sent to one of the victims or it could bring ten counts based on emails between the perpetrator and all his victims. Should the sentence the offender receives depend on whether the prosecutor chooses to charge one count or ten? The Commission sought to dampen the effect of prosecutorial charging choices in cases in which the perceived harm from the crime is reflected primarily in an aggregated quantity—in economic crime cases, the loss from the offense and in drug cases, the total amount of the particular drug involved. Thus, it decreed that when such "aggregable" offenses are at issue, the sentencing range should be the same regardless of whether the prosecutor chose to charge one count or ten, with the sentencing range turning ultimately on the total quantity of economic loss or drugs at issue.

Sections 1B1.3(a)(2), 3D1.2(d), and 3D1.3(b) are supposed operationalize this decision.

1. Grouping

Turn once again to the Sentencing Table in Chapter Five. It contemplates that there will be one singular "offense level" applicable at sentencing. But what about the many cases in which the indictment contains multiple counts, often involving different statutory offenses? How can one arrive at one "offense level" for a multi-count, multi-offense indictment?

One begins by conducting the above-described Chapter Two and Chapter Three analysis for each count in the indictment. Let us assume, for example, that our hypothetical, the prosecutor chooses to charge ten counts of wire fraud. One would figure out the offense level for all ten counts by applying the applicable Chapter Two Guideline and Chapter Three adjustments to each count.

Now we have ten offense levels, and we need to get to one for purposes of the Sentencing Table in Chapter Five. How does one do it? **One *does* not simply add up the offense levels for the ten counts.**

Instead, one turns to Chapter Three, Part D's "grouping rules." In the grouping rules, the Commission sought a way to distinguish between two types of situations.

(1) Cases in which the multiple counts concern discrete harms that warrant additional punishment.

Take, for example, an indictment charging multiple counts of murder. Each murder is a discrete harm to the victim and society. It would make no sense to say that a defendant should receive the same sentence whether the government chooses to charge the defendant with murdering one victim or five. Such "non-aggregable" offenses, then, generally involve discrete harms attributable to "single episodes of criminal behavior,"[30] such as violent offenses, robberies, burglaries, and extortions. *These offenses are not "grouped."*

Instead, a punishment scale is assigned that yields an offense level that is higher than, but not a multiple of, the offense levels applicable to the non-aggregable offenses taken singly.[31] For example, the Guidelines dictate that a defendant convicted of six bank robberies receive more punishment than a defendant convicted of one robbery, but not six times more punishment. We will not further explore the sentencing rules applicable to such non-aggregable offenses because they are rare in white-collar practice.

(2) Cases in which multi-count indictments contain charges so closely intertwined—in terms of harm caused, victims affected, and temporal proximity—that the Guidelines range should not be higher for the multiple counts than it would be for a single count.

In this situation, the Commission sought in the grouping rules to minimize the effect that prosecutors could have on the eventual sentencing range by multiplying the charges brought. Thus, for example, it sought to avoid a situation in which a prosecutor could ensure greater Guidelines sentencing exposure by breaking up what was essentially a single fraud into multiple counts by charging each and every wiring in furtherance of that single scheme to defraud. *It decreed that in such situations, the count or counts should be "grouped" into one "group."*

30. *Id.* ch. 3, pt. D., former intro. cmt. (2004).
31. *See id.* §§ 3D1.2–3D1.4.

If one reads § 3D1.2(a)-(d), there are multiple theories under which one can "group" counts based on related harms, victims, or the like. For our purposes, we focus on one subsection, § 3D1.2(d), which provides that multiple counts should be "grouped" into one "group":

> When the offense level is determined largely on the basis of the total amount of harm or loss, the quantity of a substance involved, or some other measure of aggregate harm, or if the offense behavior is ongoing or continuous in nature and the offense guideline is written to cover such behavior.

In our fraud case, all ten counts comprise one "group" under § 3D1.2(d) because the offense level under § 2B1.1 largely turns on the "aggregated" amount of loss involved in the case. So-called "aggregable offenses" that fall within § 3D1.2(d) include most financial (fraud) crimes, drug offenses, and property crimes (except armed robberies, burglary, and extortion).[32] Note that when one brings multiple counts under different statutes, but the applicable Guidelines turn largely on aggregated harm, those counts also will be grouped together. So, for example, if an indictment contains one count of wire fraud and one count of money laundering that is related to the fraud, they will constitute one group.

We now have one "group" that contains ten counts. What does one do now? **No, one does not add up the offense levels for the ten counts.**

Instead, we turn the page and consult § 3D1.3(b), which states:

> In the case of counts grouped together pursuant to § 3D1.2(d), the offense level applicable to a Group is the offense level corresponding to the aggregated quantity, determined in accordance with Chapter Two and Parts A, B and C of Chapter Three. When the counts involve offenses of the same general type to which different guidelines apply, apply the offense guideline that produces the highest offense level.

What does *this* mean? In our wire fraud case, it means we total up the "aggregated quantity" of loss—here $10 million—and apply the relevant Chapter Two guideline, § 2B1.1, to that quantity, add whatever Chapter Three adjustments apply, and the resultant offense level is the offense level for the entire group and, in our hypothetical, for the entire indictment.

If we have grouped together different offenses of conviction—say wire fraud and money laundering—and they constitute one "group" under § 3D1.2(d), we will take the aggregated loss and apply it to § 2B1.1 and to the applicable Chapter Two money laundering Guideline, § 2S1.1, add the relevant Chapter Three adjustments, and simply pick whichever offense level is higher.

---

32. *See id.* § 3D1.2(d) & App. N. 6; *id.* § 3D1.3(b).

Once one has internalized these rules, one can skip a lot of the above steps. Where multiple counts of conviction charge such aggregable crimes, § 3D1.2(d) dictates that those crimes be considered one "group." And § 3D1.3(b) tells us that, to come up with a single offense level for that group, one simply totals the fungible items (e.g., dollar amount or quantity of drugs) and (1), where one Chapter Two Guideline applies, as in our hypothetical, simply apply that Guideline to the total aggregated amount and add the relevant Chapter Three adjustments; or (2) where more than one Guideline applies, apply the total aggregated quantity to each of the Chapter Two Guidelines applicable to the counts in the group, pick the highest offense level that results from this analysis, and add the relevant Chapter Three adjustments to that offense level. And voila! One can now turn to the Chapter Five chart with a single offense level.

2. The Interaction of Grouping and Relevant Conduct

But what if a prosecutor instead chooses to charge just one count of wire fraud based on the $1 million loss one victim suffered? When dealing with a one-count indictment, do we simply factor the $1 million loss into § 2B1.1's loss chart, apply Chapter Three's adjustments, and call it a day? **No.**

Recall that the Commission wished, when dealing with "aggregable" crimes, to avoid situations in which the prosecutor could affect a defendant's guidelines sentencing range by charging ten counts as opposed to one or by charging one count as opposed to ten. This is where the third dimension of relevant conduct—embodied in § 1B1.3(a)(2)—comes into play.

Subsection 1B1.3(a)(2) requires that a judge calculating a defendant's offense level, specific offense characteristics, and Chapter Three adjustments include:

> [S]olely with respect to offenses of a character for which § 3D1.2(d) would require grouping of multiple counts, all acts and omissions [before during and after the offense of conviction and within the scope of the reasonably foreseeable jointly undertaken criminal activity by the defendants and his accomplices or coconspirators] that were part of the same course of conduct or common scheme or plan as the offense of conviction.

We know that "offenses of a character for which § 3D1.2(d) would require grouping of multiple counts" are aggregable offenses—that is, crimes in which the "offense level is determined largely on the basis of the total amount of harm or loss, the quantity of a substance involved, or some other measure of aggregate harm." In other words, most white-collar offenses.

Section 1B1.3(a)(2) instructs that where a defendant commits such "aggregable" crimes as part of the "*same course of conduct or common scheme or plan* as the offense of conviction," the entire amount of loss resulting from that common scheme or course of conduct should be used when figuring out the appropriate Chapter Two offense level and specific offense characteristics and Chapter Three adjustments for the one count indictment.[33]

In our hypothetical, if the government chose to bring only one count of wire fraud, § 1B1.3(a)(2) requires that one use the total loss from the entire common scheme or course of conduct—$10 million—rather than just the $1 million loss reflected in the count of conviction when applying the applicable wire fraud Chapter Two Guidelines section, § 2B1.1. To be clear, one uses the aggregated loss from the entire course of conduct even if the prosecutor only chose to charge, and the jury only convicted the defendant of, one count involving one wiring to one victim.

In sum, the relevant conduct rule in § 1B1.3(a)(2) and the grouping rules in § 3D1.2(d) and § 3D1.3(b) are designed to complement each other, with the goal of together reducing the effect of prosecutorial charging choices. Where grouping rules § 3D1.2(d) and § 3D1.3(b) ensure that a prosecutor cannot secure a more severe sentence by bringing a variety of "aggregable" counts, relevant conduct rule § 1B1.3(a)(2) prevents a prosecutor from obtaining a more lenient sentence by failing to charge or dismissing related "aggregable" counts. The linkage of the relevant conduct rules to the grouping rules in aggregable crime cases means (at least in theory) that whether ten wirings are charged or simply one, the Guidelines range will be the same.

Defense counsel, in particular, must understand this reality. When the Guidelines first came into force, many in the defense bar did not understand the implications of the concededly puzzling text of relevant conduct § 1B1.3(a)(2). Thus, they regularly accepted plea deals in which, for example, the government agreed to allow the defendant to plead to one count of wire fraud and dismiss the remaining nine counts that related to the same course of conduct or scheme or plan. Counsel were appalled to realize at sentencing that, by virtue of § 1B1.3(a)(2), this "deal" was no deal at all because courts were required to aggregate the harm caused by all ten counts and use that amount in computing the defendant's offense level for the single count. Do not make that mistake.

F. Chapter Four: Criminal History

The defendant's criminal history category is determined by scoring the frequency, recency, and seriousness of the defendant's prior convictions. Thus, for example, under § 4A1.1(a), a defendant receives three points for each

33. *See id.* § 1B1.3, App. N. 5.

prior sentence of imprisonment exceeding one year and one month and under 4A1.1(b) he receives an additional two points for each prior sentence of imprisonment of at least sixty days not counted in (a). Additional points will be assessed if the crime of conviction was committed while the defendant was under any criminal justice sentence (e.g., probation or parole), or was a crime of violence.[34] The Guidelines significantly enhance a defendant's offense level and criminal history category for career offenders under § 4B1.1, armed career criminals under § 4B1.4, and repeat and dangerous sex offenders against minors under § 4B1.5.

Effective November 2023, defendants can claim a "zero-point offender" adjustment to their offense level under § 4C1.1. Section 4C1.1 provides a decrease of two levels from the offense level determined under Chapters Two and Three for offenders who did not receive any criminal history points under Chapter Four, Part A and whose offense(s) of conviction did not involve specified aggravating factors.

Because most white-collar offenders are not career criminals or recidivists, they will find themselves in Category I and will be able to claim a two-level credit against their offense level under § 4C1.1.

G. Acceptance of Responsibility

Under § 3E1.1(a), "[i]f the defendant clearly demonstrates acceptance of responsibility for his offense," he receives a credit of two points against his offense level. Basically, this means the defendant gets a two-point credit for pleading guilty. Under § 3E1.1(b), the defendant may qualify for an additional one point credit if his offense level is sixteen or greater and the government makes a motion stating that "the defendant has assisted authorities in the investigation or prosecution of his own misconduct by timely notifying authorities of his intention to enter a plea of guilty, thereby permitting the government to avoid preparing for trial and permitting the government and the court to allocate their resources efficiently." This basically means that the defendant gets a three-point credit by pleading guilty early.

In crafting the "acceptance of responsibility" credit, the Commission accepted that prosecutors can and often do offer defendants deals to incentivize them to plead guilty. But the Commission recognized that prosecutors could choose to give some defendants a sweet deal through whatever sentencing or charge discounts they wish based on their own druthers or case management needs, thus potentially subverting the uniformity and proportionality goals of the Guidelines. The Commission, then, created this provision to avoid such results where possible by providing a *uniform* plea discount.

---

34. *See id.* § 4A1.1(d), (e).

This is not called the "pleading guilty" credit because it if were, it would likely be unconstitutional: it would effectively penalize defendants who exercise their constitutional trial rights vis á vis those who don't. It is entitled "acceptance of responsibility" because it is supposed to recognize that those who admit their responsibility and express remorse are more likely to stay on the straight and narrow. The Commission notes that this adjustment "is not intended to apply to a defendant who puts the government to its burden of proof at trial by denying the essential factual elements of guilt, is convicted, and only then admits guilt and expresses remorse."[35] But it is possible that the defendant can be considered for such a reduction even if he goes to trial:

> In rare situations a defendant may clearly demonstrate an acceptance of responsibility for his criminal conduct even though he exercises his constitutional right to a trial. This may occur, for example, where a defendant goes to trial to assert and preserve issues that do not relate to factual guilt (*e.g.*, to make a constitutional challenge to a statute or a challenge to the applicability of a statute to his conduct).[36]

H. Chapter Five: Departures

The Guidelines sections covered to this point concentrate on *offense* characteristics such as loss, drug amount, and the like. But the only factor relevant to the history, circumstances, or character of the *offender* included in the sentencing calculus thus far is the defendant's prior criminal history. Offender circumstances are often viewed as important to decisions about both culpability and dangerousness, but they are difficult to quantify the way that loss figures can be. Judges may, of course, consider the defendant's background and personal qualities in picking the sentence within the applicable Guidelines range. But it was originally contemplated that judge could also consider the offender's circumstances in deciding whether to make a *departure* from the otherwise applicable range.

When the Guidelines were mandatory, departures were a crucial part of defense practice because they were the only means by which a judge could deviate from the applicable sentencing range. Now that the Guidelines are no longer mandatory, some circuits deem "departure" analysis "obsolete."[37] The Ninth Circuit, for example, holds that "the scheme of downward and upward departures [is treated] as essentially replaced by the requirement that judges impose a 'reasonable' sentence."[38] But most other circuits have

35. *Id.* § 3E1.1, App. N.2.
36. *Id.*
37. United States v. Arnaout, 431 F.3d 994, 1003 (7th Cir. 2005).
38. United States v. Volp, 479 F.3d 715, 722 (9th Cir. 2007) (internal quotation marks omitted).

held that departures are still an important part of the post-*Booker* sentencing system and that district courts must continue to assess their authority to depart under the advisory Guidelines.[39]

Accordingly, Chapter 5, Parts H and K, which control departures, are still worth consulting in most of the country. In Part H, the Commission takes the view that defendant's education and vocational skills (§ 5H1.2), employment record (§ 5H1.5), and family ties and responsibilities (§ 5H1.6) are not "ordinarily" relevant to determining whether a departure is warranted, and drug or alcohol dependence or abuse is "ordinarily" not a reason to depart downward (§ 5H1.4). The Commission counsels that mental and emotional conditions and military service may be relevant (§ 5H1.3) but race, sex, national origin, creed, religion, and socio-economic status (§ 5H1.10), as well as lack of guidance as a youth and circumstances indicating a disadvantaged upbringing (§ 5H1.12), are not relevant.

Part K provides various specific grounds for departures. The most important is § 5K1.1, which provides that "[u]pon motion of the government stating that the defendant has provided substantial assistance in the investigation or prosecution of another person who has committed an offense, the court may depart from the guidelines." Although this means of escaping the applicable sentencing range is less critical in the post-*Booker* advisory Guidelines era, substantial assistance departures are still very common. In 2023, for example, 17.7 percent of the sentences imposed that fell outside of the Guidelines range involved substantial assistance motions.[40]

Example

1. Pontus Kjellsson was a trust and estates lawyer with the law firm of Able & Able. During his two-year tenure there, he diverted $1 million from client trust accounts to his offshore account in the Cayman Islands. Kjellsson was recruited to move to the law firm of Better & Better, where he engaged in the same practice. He immediately began diverting clients' trust funds to his Cayman's account and, over the course of the next two years, stole $1 million from those accounts. The government charged him with two counts of wire fraud based on one wiring of $10,000 from an Able & Able client account to his offshore account (Count One) and another wiring of $100,000 from a Better & Better client to the Caymans account (Count Two). Kjellsson has no criminal record.

39. *See, e.g.*, United States v. Robertson, 568 F.3d 1203, 1210 n.5 (10th Cir. 2009) (collecting cases); United States v. McBride, 434 F.3d 470, 477 (6th Cir. 2006) (Guidelines relating to departures, non-binding as they are, remain "a relevant consideration for determining the appropriate Guideline sentence").
40. *See* 2023 Sourcebook, *supra* note 13, Table 33.

Kjellsson is considering taking a government plea deal pursuant to which he would plead guilty to Count One of the indictment. Assume that § 2B1.1 is the applicable Chapter Two Guideline and that the only relevant specific offense characteristic is the loss from the offense. As his lawyer, explain to Kjellsson the sentencing consequences of going to trial versus pleading to Count One of the indictment.[41] What concessions—or Guidelines stipulations—might defense counsel wish to ask the government to make to sweeten the plea deal?

Explanation

1. This problem is designed to illustrate that application of the Guidelines is not always straightforward and may require the exercise of judicial discretion. It also demonstrates the types of matters over which the defense and prosecutors may bargain.

We would begin by figuring out the Guidelines range the defendant would face if he went to trial and was convicted of both counts of wire fraud.

Chapter Two Guideline: Consulting Appendix A, two Guidelines can be used for § 1343: USSG § 2B1.1 and § 2C1.1. Because this is a "money or property" fraud, not an "honest services" fraud (see Chapter 6, Fraud), § 2B1.1 is the applicable Chapter Two Guideline.

We apply § 2B1.1 to each count.

Count One

Base Offense Level: +7

The defendant was convicted of an offense referenced to this guideline in Appendix A and the offense of conviction, § 1343, has a statutory maximum of "not more than 20 years" and thus has, under § 2B1.1(a)(1), a "statutory maximum term of imprisonment of 20 years or more."

Specific Offense Characteristics:

§ 2B1.1(b)(1) Loss Chart: **+16**

Count One charges Kjellsson with a specific $10,000 wire transfer of funds but the total amount he stole from all the Able & Able clients totals $1 million. And he stole another $1 million from the clients of Better & Better. What loss figure do we use in determining the loss amount for purposes of the § 2B1.1(b)(1) loss chart?

Because § 1343 is the kind of aggregable offense for which § 3D1.2(d) requires grouping, relevant conduct rule § 1B1.3(a)(2) instructs that where a defendant commits such "aggregable" crimes as part of the "*same course of conduct or common scheme or*

41. When conducting this analysis, it may help readers to use the Sentencing Commission's worksheet for individual sentencing, available at https://www.ussc.gov/education/training-resources/worksheets-sentenced-individuals.

plan as the offense of conviction," the entire amount of loss resulting from that common scheme should be used when figuring out the appropriate Chapter Two offense level and specific offense characteristics, and Chapter Three adjustments. Are the crimes committed against *all* the Able & Able clients part of the same "*common scheme or plan*" as the crime charged in this count? Application Note 5(B)(i) following § 1B1.3 provides definitional assistance in applying this test:

> For two or more offenses to constitute part of a common scheme or plan, they must be substantially connected to each other by at least one common factor, such as common victims, common accomplices, common purpose, or similar modus operandi.

Because the crimes against Able & Able's other clients involved a common purpose and similar *modus operandi*, they are part of the same "*common scheme or plan*" as Count I so we could use the $1 million figure. If that is the relevant loss figure, the offense level would be augmented by **14** (§ 2B1.1(b)(1)(H)).

But would we also use the $1 million that the defendant garnered from the clients of Better & Better as relevant conduct for Count One? The two counts relate to fraud perpetrated on the clients of two different firms. But they may qualify under the above definition of a "common scheme or plan." Even if that were not the case, do the two frauds appear to be part of the same "*course of conduct*"? Application Note 5(B)(ii) explains that:

> Offenses that do not qualify as part of a common scheme or plan may nonetheless qualify as part of the same course of conduct if they are sufficiently connected or related to each other as to warrant the conclusion that they are part of a single episode, spree, or ongoing series of offenses. Factors that are appropriate to the determination of whether offenses are sufficiently connected or related to each other to be considered as part of the same course of conduct include the degree of similarity of the offenses, the regularity (repetitions) of the offenses, and the time interval between the offenses.

Recall that a preponderance of the evidence standard applies. Although this is a judgment call, many judges would conclude that because the two offenses are identical in terms of the modus operandi, and Kjellsson engaged in repeated violations over a virtually uninterrupted period of four years, the loss from both firms reflects the same "course of conduct or scheme or plan." If the judge so concludes, the entire loss amount from both firms' victims—$2,000,000—would be used as relevant conduct, and **16** (§ 2B1.1(b)(1)(I)) would be added to the base offense level. In the author's judgment, if the government pushes this theory a judge is likely to accept it. Thus, we will use **16** in the loss chart.

Total Chapter Two Offense Level for Count One: 23

Chapter Three Adjustments: +2

Part A: *Victim Related Adjustments*

§ 3A1.1: If the trust accounts were held for vulnerable individuals, it may be appropriate to assess points if the defendant knew or should have known of their vulnerability, but we do not have sufficient evidence to make this determination.

Part B: *Role in the Offense Adjustments*

Aggravating or Mitigating Rule

§§ 3B1.1, 3B1.2: The defendant apparently acted alone so no aggravating or mitigating role adjustment is called for.

Abuse of a Position of Trust/Special Skill

§ 3B1.3: **+2** The defendant abused a position of private trust—his position as a lawyer (fiduciary) in charge of client trust accounts—in a manner that significantly facilitated the commission the offense.

Part C: *Obstruction Adjustment*

§ 3C1.1,etc.: There is no evidence of obstruction.

Adjusted Offense Level for Count One: 25

Count Two

Base Offense Level: +7

Same as above.

Specific Offense Characteristics:

§ 2B1.1(b)(1) Loss Chart: **+16**

Count Two charges Kjellsson with a specific $100,000 wire transfer of funds from one Better & Better client account but the total amount he stole from all of the Better & Better clients totals $1 million. And if one considers his conduct at Able & Able, the total loss is $2 million. What loss figure do we use in determining the loss amount for purposes of the § 2B1.1(b)(1) loss chart?

The above analysis would apply here as well. Given that a court is likely to conclude that all the losses due to his work at Better & Better were part of a "common scheme or plan" and that the losses he caused the clients of Able & Able were part of the same "course of conduct," § 1B1.3(a)(2) requires that the total amount of loss flowing from these aggregable offenses be used in determining Kjellsson's offense level—that is, $2 million.

Total Chapter Two Offense Level for Count Two: 23

Chapter Three Adjustments: **+2**

The same analysis would apply to Count Two.

Adjusted Offense Level for Count Two: 25

Grouping, Chapter Three, Part D

How Many Groups? One

§ 3D1.2(d): Because the offense level for both counts is determined largely on the basis of the total amount of loss, the two counts constitute one "group."

What Is the Offense Level for the One "Group"? 25

§ 3D1.3(b): Because these counts were grouped together pursuant to § 3D1.2(d), "the offense level applicable to a Group is the offense level corresponding to the aggregated quantity, determined in accordance with Chapter Two and Parts A, B and C of Chapter Three." The aggregated quantity of loss is $2 million. We apply that number to the applicable Chapter Two Guideline, § 2B1.1, and the relevant Chapter Three adjustments, and the final offense level for both counts is **25**.

Preliminary Offense Level for the Indictment (Counts One and Two): 25

Other Adjustments to Offense Level

§ 3C1.1 Acceptance of Responsibility: 0

If the defendant was convicted of both counts after trial, he would receive no credit.

§ 4C1.1 Adjustment for Certain Zero-Point Offenders: −2

Under the "zero-point offender" adjustment, the defendant would earn a two-point credit because he has no criminal history points under Chapter Four, Part A and his offenses conviction did not involve specified aggravating factors.

Final Offense Level for the Indictment (Counts One and Two): 23

Criminal History Category Under Chapter Four

Criminal History Category: I

Kjellsson has no criminal history points

Final Offense Level for the Indictment: 23
Criminal History Category: I
Chapter 5 Sentencing Chart: **46-57 months**

Next we would determine Guidelines range the defendant would face if he pled guilty just to Count One.

Count One Pursuant to Plea Bargain

Base Offense Level: +7

Specific Offense Characteristics:
§ 2B1.1(b)(1) Loss Chart: **+16**

Total Chapter Two Offense Level for Count One: 23

Chapter Three Adjustments: +2

Adjusted Offense Level for Count One: 25

Other Adjustments to Offense Level

§ 3C1.1 Acceptance of Responsibility: −2

Because of the guilty plea, the defendant will receive a 2 point credit.

§ 4C1.1 Adjustment for Certain Zero-Point Offenders: −2

Final Offense Level for Count One assuming a Guilty Plea: 21

Criminal History Category: I

Offense Level 21
Criminal History Category I
Chapter 5 Sentencing Chart: **37-46 months**

Assuming the judge accepts that the thefts from the clients at the two firms are part of the "same course of conduct or scheme or plan" for relevant conduct purposes, the only difference between the sentencing range for both counts and the sentencing range for only Count One would be the credit the defendant would secure for pleading guilty, −2 (or −3 points if he pleads out early).

Additional concessions—and Guidelines stipulations—to ask the government to make:

If the government agrees to stipulate that a sentence on the low end of the Guidelines range is appropriate and the judge agrees, pleading guilty would mean that instead of facing a potential maximum of imprisonment of 57 months, Kjellsson could receive a sentence of 37 months—a significant discount.

The defense also could try to persuade the prosecution to stipulate that Count One was not part of the same course of conduct as Count Two and thus that the loss from Count Two should not be included as relevant conduct for purposes of the § 2B1.1 loss chart. If the judge agrees, the defendant's offense level will be:

Count One Pursuant to Plea Bargain with Stipulation

Base Offense Level: +7

Specific Offense Characteristics:

§ 2B1.1(b)(1) Loss Chart: **+14**

Because of the stipulation, Count Two's loss will not be considered part of the same course of conduct or scheme or plan as Count One. We will consider only the $1 million lost by virtue of the losses Able & Able clients suffered from Kjellsson's common scheme or plan. Accordingly, the loss is only $1 million, which translates into a specific offense characteristics on the loss chart of **+14** (§ 2B1.1(b)(1)(H)) instead of 16.

Total Chapter Two Offense Level for Count One: 21

Chapter Three Adjustments: +2

Adjusted Offense Level for Count One: 23

Other Adjustments to Offense Level

§ 3C1.1 Acceptance of Responsibility: −2

Because of the guilty plea, the defendant will receive a 2 point credit.

§ 4C1.1 Adjustment for Certain Zero-Point Offenders: −2

Final Offense Level for Count One assuming a Guilty Plea: 19

Criminal History Category: I

Offense Level 19
Criminal History Category I
Chapter 5 Sentencing Chart: **30-37 months**

III. OUTLINE OF ORGANIZATIONAL GUIDELINES ANALYSIS

The Organizational Guidelines—found in Chapter Eight of the Guidelines Manual—became effective on November 1, 1991. In crafting the Organizational Guidelines, the Commission adopted a "carrot and stick approach" that flowed from the Commission's belief in three propositions.

The Commission first recognized that the respondeat superior standard of corporate liability does not necessarily accurately reflect the relative blameworthiness of the corporation itself. The Commission also concluded that prevention and detection of corporate crime would most efficiently be achieved through reforming the corporations—particularly instantiating a law-abiding corporate culture and instituting an effective compliance program. Finally, and critically, the Commission concluded that it could create the appropriate incentives for these changes by adopting "carrots" to reward responsible corporate behavior and "sticks" that ensured certain and harsh sanctions for truly culpable corporations.

After *Booker*, the Organizational Guidelines are advisory only; § 3553(a) controls but it requires courts to consider the Guidelines in formulating a sentence for organizational defendants. The number of organizations sentenced under the Guidelines are few, and their numbers are inching downward. They have gone from a high of 181 entities in 2015 to 99 in 2022 and 113 in 2023.[42] Many of these cases involved negotiated pleas and Guideline stipulations; other cases are resolved by various types of diversion agreements. The Organizational Guidelines provides a useful yardstick by which the parties negotiate the terms—and particularly the sanctions—in such agreements. The following is a summary of how that calculus proceeds, and readers are encouraged to read the Organizational Guidelines for more detailed coverage.

As is true in all Guidelines calculations, the statutory maximum (or where applicable, minimum) sentence always trumps the Guidelines calculation. This means that if the Organizational Guidelines suggest a fine range that exceeds the maximum set by statute, the court may not exceed the statutory maximum.[43] Prosecutors seeking to secure large Guidelines fines after conviction of an organization, then, would be well advised to consider, when making their charging choices, the applicable statutory maximums provided by statute, 18 U.S.C. § 3571. In general, the statutory maximum for a given felony count if an organization is the defendant is the *greatest* of (1) the amount (if any) specified in the law setting forth the offense; (2) for an organization convicted of a felony, $500,000; or (3) "[i]f any person derives pecuniary gain from the offense, or if the offense results in pecuniary loss to a person other than the defendant, the defendant may be fined not more than the greater of twice the gross gain or twice the gross loss, unless the imposition of a fine under this subsection would unduly complicate or prolong the sentencing process."[44]

42. *See* 2023 Sourcebook, *supra* note 13, Fig. O-2.
43. *See* USSG, *supra* note 4, § 8C3.1(b), (c).
44. 18 U.S.C. § 3571(d).

Turning to Chapter Eight, the appropriate sentence to be imposed requires reference to two principal parts: (1) Part B—"Remedying the Harm from Criminal Conduct" and (2) Part C—"Fines." Part B, dealing with remedying the harm from the offense, applies to the sentencing of all organizations[45] for felony and Class A misdemeanor offenses.[46] But the fine provisions of Part C do not apply to all organizational sentencings. Counsel must consult § 8C2.1 to determine whether the offense is one that is covered by the Part C fine Guidelines. Important categories of cases, such as environmental offenses, are not presently covered by the fine Guidelines. The fines for such excluded offenses must be determined by reference to traditional criteria contained in the general sentencing provisions discussed above.

Part D, which controls organizational probation, is worth brief mention. This Part, like the restitution provisions of Part B, applies to all organizations convicted of federal felonies or Class A misdemeanors. It gives judges the power to impose terms and conditions of probation that most companies would view as intrusive, disruptive in terms of business functioning, and expensive. "The court may order the organization, at its expense and in the format and media specified by the court, to publicize the nature of the offense committed, the fact of conviction, and the nature of the punishment imposed, and the steps that will be taken to prevent the recurrence of similar offenses."[47] Courts can require the organization to make "periodic submissions to the court or probation officer, at intervals specified by the court, (A) reporting on the organization's financial conditions and results of business operations, and accounting for the disposition of all funds received and (B) reporting on the organization's progress in implementing" an effective compliance and ethics program.[48] And probation can include an order requiring the organization to submit to regular or unannounced examinations of its books and records by the probation officers or experts hired by the court (but paid by the organization) and "interrogation of knowledgeable individuals within the organization."[49]

A. Part B—Remedying the Harm from Criminal Conduct—Restitution

Part B is intended to be remedial, not punitive. The Commission determined that all convicted organizations—regardless of their perceived culpability—should be required to remedy any harm caused by the offense

45. *See* USSG, *supra* note 4, § 8A1.1, App. N.1 (definition of "organization").
46. *Id.* § 8A1.1, App. N. 2.
47. *Id.* § 8D1.4(a).
48. *Id.* § 8D1.4(b)(3).
49. *Id.* § 8D1.4(b)(5).

whenever practicable.[50] This will generally take the form of an order of restitution "for the full amount of the victim's loss."[51] It may also take the form of remedial orders requiring the organization "to remedy the harm caused by the offense and to eliminate or reduce the risk" that the offense will cause future harm.[52] There will be circumstances, however, in which an order of restitution may not be appropriate.[53]

B. Part C—Fines

If the Organizational Guidelines' fine provisions apply and there is no statutory maximum issue, the organizational fine provisions proceed through three basic steps. In general terms, the fine range is said to be a *product* of the *seriousness* of the offense and the *culpability* of the organization.

1. Seriousness of the Offense: The Base Fine

The *seriousness of the offense* is reflected in a dollar amount called the "Base Fine."[54] This number is generally the greatest of (1) the amount from a table corresponding to a calculation under the individual Guidelines; (2) the pecuniary gain to the organization from the offense; or (3) the pecuniary loss from the offense caused by the organization, "to the extent that the loss was intentionally, knowingly, or recklessly caused."[55] In many cases, this simply boils down to the loss caused by the crime.

2. The Culpability of the Organization: The Culpability Score

The *culpability of the organization* is reflected in the organization's "Culpability Score."[56] One begins the computation with a score of five. Points are then added or subtracted depending upon the existence or absence of certain factors that the Commission concluded aggravate or mitigate the organization's culpability in the crime. Among the factors that add to an organization's score are:

- the size of the organization and the hierarchical level and degree of discretionary authority of the individuals who participated in or tolerated the illegal behavior

50. *Id.*, Chap. 8, intro. cmt.
51. *Id.* § 8B1.1(a)(1).
52. *Id.* § 8B1.2(a).
53. *See id.* § 8B1.1(b).
54. *Id.* § 8C2.4.
55. *Id.* § 8C2.4(a).
56. *Id.* § 8C2.5.

- any recent prior history of similar misconduct
- the commission of the offense violated a judicial order or injunction or a condition of probation, and
- the organization willfully obstructed or attempted to obstruct justice during the investigation, prosecution, or sentencing of the offense.

There are two provisions under which organizational defendants may have points deducted from their culpability score.

a. Effective Compliance Programs

First, a credit of 3 points is permitted, subject to certain caveats,[57] if "the offense occurred even though the organization had in place at the time of the offense an effective compliance and ethics program."[58] Under § 8B2.1(a), an "effective" compliance and ethics program requires that an organization "(1) exercise due diligence to prevent and detect criminal conduct; and (2) otherwise promote an organizational culture that encourages ethical conduct and a commitment to compliance with the law."

These two primary determinants of an effective program can be proved by the satisfaction of seven criteria embodied in § 8B2.1(b). The criteria mandate certain governance commitments, including ensuring that the company's governing authority exercises reasonable oversight over the compliance function, assigning responsibility for compliance to specific persons in the high-level personnel of the company, and specifying that persons charged with compliance functions have the ability to report problems to high-level personnel or, if necessary, the governing authority of the company. With respect to the specifics of its program, the company must establish standards and procedures to prevent and detect criminal conduct and disseminate its standards and procedures by conducting training programs. The company must ensure that the organization's compliance and ethics program is followed by monitoring and auditing to detect criminal conduct and periodically testing the effectiveness of the program. The organization must have a system, which may include mechanisms that allow for anonymity or confidentiality, through which the organization's agents may report or seek guidance regarding potential or actual criminal conduct without fear of retaliation. The organization must create incentives to comply with its dictates and take disciplinary measures against employees who do not. Finally, when criminal conduct has been detected, the organization must take reasonable steps to respond appropriately to the criminal conduct and to prevent further similar criminal conduct, including making any necessary modifications to the organization's program.

---

57. *See id.* § 8C2.5(f)(3).
58. *Id.* § 8C2.5(f)(1).

b. Self-Reporting, Cooperation, and Acceptance of Responsibility

Second, an organization can reduce its culpability score by self-reporting, cooperating, and/or accepting responsibility.[59] An organization earns just one point for acceptance of responsibility—that is, for pleading guilty. If the organization is willing to "fully cooperate[] in the investigation" and plead guilty, it may secure two credit points.[60] And if the organization, "prior to an imminent threat of disclosure or government investigation," and "within a reasonably prompt time after becoming aware of the offense," self-reports the offense to government authorities, fully cooperates, and then pleads guilty, the organization will gain five credit points.[61]

3. Identification and Application of the Minimum and Maximum Multipliers

After the culpability score has been computed, one references a chart that allots to each culpability score a "minimum multiplier" and a "maximum multiplier."[62] These multipliers are then applied to the Base Fine amount, and the result is a fine range. Note that the multipliers range from a minimum of .05 to a maximum of four depending upon the seriousness of the crime and culpability of the organization.

Example

1A. Assume that the offense of conviction is covered by the fine provisions of Chapter Eight. The loss from the criminal episode is $10 million and that is the Base Fine amount. The culpability score for the case is ten: the five points with which one begins with five points added for the organization's large size and high level of management participation. What is the fine range?

1B. Now assume that the organization earned a three-point effective compliance program credit. What is the fine range?

1C. Finally, assume that the organization earned a further five-point credit for self-reporting, cooperating, and accepting responsibility.

59. Id. § 8C2.5(g).
60. Id. § 8C2.5(g)(2).
61. Id. § 8C2.5(g)(1).
62. Id. § 8C2.6.

Explanation

1A. Reference to the multiplier chart in § 8C2.6 tells one that a culpability score of ten means that one multiplies the base fine (here, $10 million) by the culpability multipliers of a minimum of 2.0 and maximum of 4.0, to arrive at a fine range of $20 million to $40 million.

1B. The culpability score would now be seven, the multipliers would be 1.4 (minimum) and 2.8 (maximum), and the final fine range would be $14 million to $28 million.

1C. The culpability score would now be two, the multipliers would be .40 (minimum) and .80 (maximum), and the final fine range would be $4 million to $8 million.

CHAPTER 16

Plea Bargaining and Cooperation

I. Justifications for, and Arguments Attacking, Plea Bargaining
II. Constitutional Limitations on Prosecutorial Discretion
- **A. Equal Protection**
- **B. Vindictive Prosecution**

III. Guilty Plea Procedures
IV. Rule 11 and Guidelines Bargaining
- **A. Charge Bargains Under Fed. R. Crim. P. 11(c)(1)(A)**
- **B. Guidelines Fact and Factor Bargaining Under Fed. R. Crim. P. 11(c)(1)(B) and (C)**
- **C. Sentence Bargains Under Fed. R. Crim. P. 11(c)(1)(B) and (C)**

V. Plea Agreements Generally
VI. Cooperation Agreements

A defendant who has been criminally charged in the federal system has a number of plea options, the most obvious of which are "guilty" and "not guilty." In pleading guilty, a defendant may concede guilt or, if permitted by the judge, enter what is known as an *Alford* plea pursuant to which he continues to maintain his innocence.[1] Under Fed. R. Crim. P. 11(a)(1), (3), a defendant may enter a plea of nolo contendere, which constitutes a judgment of conviction but which, under Fed. R. Evid. 410(a)(2), is not admissible against

1. *See* North Carolina v. Alford, 400 U.S. 25 (1970); *see also* U.S. Dept of Justice, Justice Manual § 9-27.440 ("[d]espite the constitutional validity of *Alford* pleas, such pleas should be avoided except in the most unusual circumstances") [hereinafter Justice Manual].

the defendant in subsequent federal criminal or civil cases. Nolo contendere pleas may be entered only with the consent of the court after the court has considered the views of the parties and the public interest.

Finally, Fed. R. Crim. P. 11 provides for a conditional plea of guilty or nolo contendere. The conditional plea was created because a defendant normally waives all non-jurisdictional[2] objections to the prosecution when he pleads guilty. This means that defendants who lose potentially dispositive pre-trial objections—e.g., challenges to the admissibility of evidence or the legal theory of the prosecution's case—will sometimes go to trial solely to secure appellate review of these objections. To avoid this drain on prosecutorial and judicial resources, Rule 11(a)(2) permits a defendant, with the consent of the government and the court, to enter a conditional plea, reserving the right to appeal the adverse pre-trial ruling and, if successful on appeal, to withdraw the guilty or nolo contendere plea.

For at least the last twenty years, the federal guilty plea rate has hovered around ninety-seven percent. In some cases, defendants enter a "straight" plea to the indictment without any bargaining or concessions from the government. Many cases, however, involve some sort of bargained-for disposition. Plea bargaining is defined as an exchange of a defendant's consent to the entry of a criminal judgment against him in exchange for official concessions. Fed. R. Crim. P. 11 allows parties to bargain in charges, sentences or sentencing ranges, or the application of U.S. Sentencing Guidelines policies, factors, or provisions. But "[a]lmost anything lawfully within the power of a prosecutor acting in good faith can be offered in exchange for guilty plea," including, for example, an agreement not to indict the defendant's mother or to waive the usual immigration consequences of a criminal conviction.[3] One kind of plea deal is very common: the defendant agrees both to plead guilty and to cooperate with the government in the investigation and prosecution of other wrongdoers in exchange for consideration that includes a motion for a downward departure under the U.S. Sentencing Guidelines § 5K1.1.

This chapter discusses the pros and cons of plea bargaining, the constitutional constraints on prosecutorial charging and bargaining decisions, and the rules governing plea bargaining in federal cases under Rule 11 and

2. In United States v. Cotton, 535 U.S. 625 (2002), the Supreme Court clarified that "jurisdiction" in this context refers to the "'courts' statutory or constitutional power to adjudicate the case.'" *Id.* at 630. The Court held that "defects in an indictment do not deprive a court of its power to adjudicate a case," and that the question whether the indictment "'does not charge a crime against the United States goes only to the merits of the case.'" *Id.* at 630-31. A guilty plea bars appellate consideration of some alleged constitutional violations, such as Fourth Amendment claims. *See, e.g.*, Class v. United States, 583 U.S. 174, 182 (2018). But a guilty plea does not extinguish due process vindictive prosecution claims, *see id.* at 179, double jeopardy claims, *see id.* at 180-81, or challenges to the constitutionality of the statute of conviction on direct appeal, *see id.* at 176.

3. United States v. Pollard, 959 F.2d 1011, 1021 (D.C. Cir. 1992).

the U.S. Sentencing Guidelines. It concludes by discussing plea agreements that contemplate defendants' cooperation in the investigation and prosecution of others.

These materials are critical to effective practice because, as the Supreme Court recognized in *Missouri v. Frye*, 566 U.S. 134 (2012):

> The reality is that plea bargains have become so central to the administration of the criminal justice system that defense counsel have responsibilities in the plea bargain process, responsibilities that must be met to render the adequate assistance of counsel that the Sixth Amendment requires in the criminal process at critical stages. Because ours "is for the most part a system of pleas, not a system of trials," it is insufficient simply to point to the guarantee of a fair trial as a backstop that inoculates any errors in the pretrial process. "To a large extent . . . horse trading [between prosecutor and defense counsel] determines who goes to jail and for how long. That is what plea bargaining is. It is not some adjunct to the criminal justice system; it is the criminal justice system." In today's criminal justice system, therefore, the negotiation of a plea bargain, rather than the unfolding of a trial, is almost always the critical point for a defendant.[4]

I. JUSTIFICATIONS FOR, AND ARGUMENTS ATTACKING, PLEA BARGAINING

The primary justification advanced for plea bargaining is that absent such dealing, the federal justice system would grind to a halt, overwhelmed by a surfeit of trials. Even if the practice were banned, it would through necessity be resurrected in clandestine dealing. Plea bargaining is also justified as serving both parties' interests by providing them with flexibility in structuring a resolution that furthers interests not possible in a binary trial result.

From the government's point of view, trial on the merits is time- and resource-consuming. Through plea bargaining, prosecutors can hold more offenders criminally accountable. "[W]ith the avoidance of trial, scarce judicial and prosecutorial resources are conserved for those cases in which there is a substantial issue of the defendant's guilt or in which there is substantial doubt that the State can sustain its burden of proof."[5] A defendant's prompt acknowledgment of his guilt is said to prevent further criminality and enhance the defendant's potential for

4. *Frye*, 566 U.S. at 143-44. In *Frye* and *Lafler v. Cooper*, 566 U.S. 156 (2012), the Court recognized that defendants' Sixth Amendment right to effective assistance of counsel extends to the plea bargaining process.

5. Brady v. United States, 397 U.S. 742, 752 (1970).

rehabilitation.[6] Perhaps more important from the prosecutor's point of view, plea agreements are a form of insurance. Trial outcomes are uncertain for a variety of reasons—the case may not go in as well as anticipated, witnesses may disappear or develop amnesia, and the jury may nullify. By agreeing to a plea deal, the government secures a conviction that presumably, in the prosecutor's mind, serves the interests of justice and justifies the commitment of investigative resources to the matter while avoiding the risk of loss. Finally, guilty pleas mean that victims and other witnesses need not be put through the wringer of a trial.

From the defendant's perspective, a trial on the merits can be expensive, extremely stressful, and embarrassing for oneself and one's family. "For a defendant who sees slight possibility of acquittal, the advantages of pleading guilty and limiting the probable penalty are obvious—his exposure is reduced, the correctional processes can begin immediately, and the practical burdens of a trial are eliminated."[7] Once again, trial outcomes are uncertain; a plea provides certainty regarding the level of culpability that is assigned. And the sentence after trial may exceed what the defendant expected and certainly what he could have bargained for.

Plea bargaining is not without its critics. The literature surrounding this practice is extensive, but three challenges to the legitimacy of plea bargaining are worth brief mention.

First, one could argue that when a defendant pleads guilty out of fear of receiving a harsher sentence if he goes to trial, he has effectively been coerced into waiving his constitutional trial rights in violation of due process. Conversely, when a defendant refuses a plea deal and receives a greater sentence after trial than he would have if he pleaded out, one could argue that the defendant has been penalized for exercising his constitutional trial rights, again in violation of due process guarantees. The Supreme Court, however, has rejected both arguments.

In *Brady v. United States*, 397 U.S. 742 (1970), the defendant, by operation of a federal statute, faced a choice between going to trial and potentially receiving a death sentence, and pleading guilty and receiving a lesser penalty. The Supreme Court rejected Brady's claim that, under due process, "a guilty plea is coerced or invalid if influenced by the fear of a possibly higher penalty for the crime charged" after trial.[8] It noted that the government "to some degree encourages pleas of guilty at every important step in the criminal process"—such as by accumulating sufficient evidence to persuade the defendant that a trial is not worth the effort—and ruled that this plea was as

---

6. *See id.*
7. *Id.*
8. *Id.* at 750-51.

valid as others in which the state bears some responsibility for the impetus to plead.[9]

In *Bordenkircher v. Hayes*, 434 U.S. 357 (1978), the Court ruled that a prosecutor did not violate due process by following through on a threat presented in plea bargaining to indict on harsher charges if the defendant elected to go to trial. It recognized that "confronting a defendant with the risk of more severe punishment clearly may have a 'discouraging effect on the defendant's assertion of his trial rights,'" but concluded that the imposition of these choices is inevitable and permissible in plea bargaining.[10] "[B]y tolerating and encouraging the negotiation of pleas, this Court has necessarily accepted as constitutionally legitimate the simple reality that the prosecutor's interest at the bargaining table is to persuade the defendant to forgo his right to plead not guilty."[11]

A second objection turns on issues of accuracy and public confidence in the integrity of the criminal process. Defendants, prosecutors, and society generally have an interest in ensuring that a defendant suffer the penalties of the criminal sanction only if he is in fact guilty. Not only does it offend justice to have innocents languishing in jail, but wrongful convictions also mean that those who actually committed the crime are free to re-offend. The Constitution provides defendants with many protections at trial—the right against compelled self-incrimination, the right to counsel, the right to a presumption of innocence and to have the government bear the burden proof beyond a reasonable doubt, the right to confront witnesses, and the right to call witnesses for the defense. The framers believed that these constitutional trial rights were necessary provide the degree of accuracy in criminal adjudication that society requires to justify the imposition of the criminal stigma and the sanction of imprisonment. These guarantees are also supposed to ensure to some extent that the assessed level of culpability is actually commensurate with the facts. Some argue, then, that the procedures the Constitution mandates for criminal trials should not be short circuited by a practice that undermines the accuracy of the process and, consequentially, public confidence in the fairness of the criminal justice system.

The counter-argument, of course, is that if a defendant says he is guilty, these protections are unnecessary, assuming the defendant knowingly, intelligently, and voluntarily enters the plea with a full understanding of its consequences. This rests on the intuitive judgment that innocent persons would never plead guilty to crimes they did not commit. According to data gathered by, among others, the Innocence Project, this intuition is demonstrably not true.[12] The reasons for false self-inculpation are many. But the concern most relevant to this chapter is that prosecutors, in plea bargaining,

---

9. *Id.* at 750.
10. *Bordenkircher*, 434 U.S. 364.
11. *Id.*
12. *See* Innocence Project, DNA Exonerations in the United States (1989-2020), available at: https://innocenceproject.org/dna-exonerations-in-the-united-states/ (44 of 375 people

can offer defendants such a stark choice between a lenient plea offer and a threat of more serious charges if the plea is rejected that innocent but risk-averse defendants will be coerced into a guilty plea. And prosecutors offer defendants the most irresistible plea offers precisely in instances in which the government's case is the weakest.

In white-collar cases, the "innocence" issue is often more subtle. It is less about what happened or who "did it"—the drug deal, bank robbery, or the like—and more about what the defendant's state of mind was at the time or whether the conduct at issue should be sanctioned under an expansive theory of the law. Where a defendant's culpability is arguable, prosecutors can avoid the adjudication of difficult questions of intent or novel legal theories by pressuring a plea. Some of these cases may be ones in which the defendant's mental state is truly difficult to ascertain. Other cases may not involve a complete "innocent," but they may be ones where formal adjudication would reveal that what the defendant did (or what he thought while doing it) should not be sanctioned or should be sanctioned much less stringently than charged.

Finally, one of the principal concerns presented by plea bargaining is the opportunity it presents for prosecutors to subject offenders to unequal treatment under the law. Prosecutors may offer some defendants a sweet deal, while dealing severely with others, based on their idiosyncratic views about relative culpability: they may conclude that "the kid comes from a good family," or that they don't want to ruin a promising sports star's career, or that the defendant reminds them of their beloved grandfather. Such preferences have no real relationship to the defendant's culpability and thus introduce arbitrary differences in the treatment of like offenders, but they cannot be attacked on constitutional grounds. It is only when prosecutorial charging choices are founded on racial, gender, or other constitutionally suspect types of bias that they are subject to judicial scrutiny. Unfortunately, there is a great deal of evidence that racial bias, in particular, pervades the criminal justice system, and prosecutors are not immune from it. But, as we shall see, equal protection claims founded on such selective prosecutions are very difficult for defendants to prove.

The above discusses differential treatment by prosecutors as an equal protection issue, but inequality also undermines the degree to which the purposes of punishment will be effectively served at sentencing. As we saw in the Chapter 15 (Sentencing), a major impetus for the current Guidelines sentencing system was a concern about disparities in sentences among those similarly situated in light of just deserts and crime control goals. The Guidelines were designed to promote uniformity and proportionality in sentencing by cabining judicial discretion. Congress and the Sentencing

---

exonerated by DNA pled guilty to crimes they did not commit; 24 percent involved false confessions).

Commission did not—and probably constitutionally could not—directly restrict the charging and plea-bargaining practices of the Department of Justice. Instead, the Commission consciously designed the Guidelines' mechanics to blunt the effect of prosecutorial charging choices on defendants' sentencing ranges. And, cognizant of plea rates, the Commission created a uniform discount for pleading guilty and formulated standards governing judicial acceptance or rejection of plea agreements that turn on whether those agreements undermine the uniformity and proportionality goals of the Guidelines. But the Commission could not completely eliminate the disparities between like offenders that prosecutors' charging and plea decisions introduce into the criminal justice system.

II. CONSTITUTIONAL LIMITATIONS ON PROSECUTORIAL DISCRETION

The Supreme Court has decreed that a "'presumption of regularity supports' . . . prosecutorial decisions and, 'in the absence of clear evidence to the contrary, courts presume that [prosecutors] have properly discharged their official duties.'"[13] Thus, "[i]n the ordinary case, 'so long as the prosecutor has probable cause to believe that the accused committed an offense defined by statute, the decision whether or not to prosecute, and what charge to file or bring before a grand jury, generally rests entirely in his discretion.'"[14]

The Court has recognized two constitutional constraints on this discretion: the Equal Protection Clause[15] bars the consideration of "race, religion or other arbitrary classification" in charging decisions[16] and the Due Process Clauses[17] prohibit prosecutors from engaging in vindictive prosecutions.

A. Equal Protection

Defendants may claim that a prosecutor violated the Equal Protection Clause by selecting them for prosecution on the basis of race or other forbidden considerations. In *United States v. Armstrong*, 517 U.S. 456 (1996), the Court held that such claims are subject to "'ordinary equal protection standards'": "The claimant must demonstrate that the federal prosecutorial policy 'had a discriminatory effect and that it was motivated by a discriminatory purpose.'"[18]

13. United States v. Armstrong, 517 U.S. 456, 464 (1996).
14. *Id.*
15. U.S. Const., amend. XIV, § 1.
16. *Armstrong*, 517 U.S. at 464.
17. U.S. Const., amend. XIV, § 1; *id.* amend. V.
18. *Armstrong*, 517 U.S. at 465.

To establish discriminatory effect in a race case, the claimant must show that similarly situated individuals of a different race were *not* prosecuted. But prosecutors rarely share or make public information regarding persons federal prosecutors have declined to charge, making it extremely difficult for defendants to provide concrete proof of discriminatory effect without a means of forcing the government to turn over the relevant information. And the Supreme Court has demonstrated a strong disinclination to allow the defendant such discovery.

In *Armstrong*, the defendants, who were indicted for selling crack and using guns in relation to a drug trafficking offense, moved for discovery on a claim that they had been selected for federal, as opposed to state, prosecution because they are African American. (Federal sentences for this offense are generally much harsher than those authorized under state law.) The Court held that to establish an entitlement to discovery on a claim of selective prosecution based on race, the defendants had to produce credible evidence regarding discriminatory effect—that is, that the government could have prosecuted similarly situated defendants of a different race for the offense but did not. The Supreme Court rejected the Ninth Circuit's presumption that "'people of *all* races commit *all* types of crimes'" and that no crime is the exclusive province of any particular racial or ethnic group.[19]

In so doing, the Court cited federal *sentencing* statistics that showed that more than ninety percent of the persons sentenced in 1994 for crack cocaine trafficking were Black.[20] Such statistics, of course, merely show that the defendants federal prosecutors chose to charge were overwhelmingly Black, not that the ninety percent of the people who deal crack are Black. Given that the *Armstrong* defendants alleged that they were selected for federal prosecution for crack offenses precisely because of their race, this sentencing statistic would seem to support the defendant's claim rather than the Court's apparent belief—contradicted by other data sources—that African Americans were the predominant consumers and sellers of crack cocaine. The Court went on to find the study the defendants tendered to show discriminatory effect insufficient, leaving defendants with the obvious Catch-22 of not being able to find sufficient evidence (most of which is in the government's possession) of a discriminatory effect absent discovery but not being able to obtain discovery absent a clear showing of such an effect.

The Supreme Court underscored its intent to enforce this stringent discovery standard when it summarily overturned a Sixth Circuit decision affirming a district court discovery order in *United States v. Bass*, 536 U.S. 862 (2002). Bass, who is Black, alleged that the government had determined to seek the death penalty against him because of his race. The district court ordered that the government provide discovery and, when it refused,

19. *Id.* at 469.
20. *See id.*

dismissed the death penalty notice. The Sixth Circuit upheld the discovery order, finding that the defendant had met the test articulated in *Armstrong*. The defendant had introduced a report released by the Department of Justice in September 2000 entitled *The Federal Death Penalty System: A Statistical Survey* (1988-2000). He also put into evidence public comments regarding the survey on the day of its release by then-Attorney General Janet Reno and then-Deputy Attorney General Eric Holder to the effect that the study's results demonstrated a clear racial disparity in the DOJ's charging decisions in capital cases and raised questions warranting further study to determine whether that disparity was caused by intentional racial discrimination. Finally, the court noted the evidence introduced from other official sources indicating that Black people are no more likely to commit violent federal offenses than are whites.

The Supreme Court granted review in *Bass* and, without briefing or oral argument, summarily reversed in a *per curiam* decision. The Court's two-paragraph analysis explained that "[e]ven assuming that the *Armstrong* requirement can be satisfied by [the DOJ report's] nationwide showing (as opposed to a showing regarding the record of the decisionmakers in respondent's case), raw statistics regarding overall charges say nothing about charges brought against *similarly situated defendants*."[21]

B. Vindictive Prosecution

In *North Carolina v. Pearce*, 395 U.S. 711 (1969), the Supreme Court held that due process "requires that vindictiveness against a defendant for having successfully attacked his first conviction must play no part in the sentence he receives after a new trial."[22] To "assure the absence of such a motivation," the Court held that "whenever a judge imposes a more severe sentence upon a defendant after a new trial, the reasons for his doing so must affirmatively appear" and those reasons "must be based upon objective information concerning identifiable conduct on the part of the defendant occurring after the time of the original sentencing proceeding."[23] In *Blackledge v. Perry*, 417 U.S. 21 (1974), state procedures allowed a defendant convicted of a misdemeanor in an inferior court to demand a trial de novo in a higher court. The Supreme Court held that prosecutor was barred from reindicting a convicted misdemeanant on a felony charge after the defendant had asked for a new trial because, in the Court's view, this situation also created a "realistic likelihood of 'vindictiveness.'"[24]

---

21. *Bass*, 536 U.S. at 863-64 (emphasis original).
22. *Pearce*, 395 U.S. at 725.
23. *Id.* at 726.
24. *Blackledge*, 417 U.S. at 27.

Since *Blackledge*, however, the Court has not recognized another type of judicial or prosecutorial practice to which it is willing to attach a presumption of vindictiveness. In *United States v. Goodwin*, 457 U.S. 368 (1982), the Court held that a presumption of prosecutorial vindictiveness was not warranted in a case in which a prosecutor responded to a defendant's request for a jury trial on a misdemeanor charge by reindicting him on a felony count. In so doing, the Court strongly indicated a disinclination to apply a presumption of vindictiveness to prosecutors' *pre-trial* charging decisions.[25] A defendant remains free to argue that although a presumption of vindictiveness may not be appropriate, the prosecutor actually acted vindictively in his case.[26] Such claims are very difficult to make out given the presumption of regularity accorded prosecutorial decisions.

For purposes of this chapter, it is important to recognize that prosecutors do not act vindictively by presenting the defendant with very difficult choices in plea bargaining, even if the prosecutor's intention in so doing is to pressure the defendant to waive his trial rights and plead out. In *Bordenkircher v. Hayes*, 434 U.S. 357 (1978), the Court reasoned that "[t]o punish a person because he has done what the law plainly allows him to do is a due process violation of the most basic sort," and rationalized *Pearce* and *Blackledge* as cases in which the state acted improperly by *unilaterally* imposing a penalty upon a defendant who chose to exercise a legal right.[27] It concluded, however, that such vindictiveness is "'very different from the give-and-take negotiation common in plea bargaining between the prosecution and defense, which arguably possess relatively equal bargaining power.'"[28] In such "give-and-take" bargaining, "there is no such element of punishment or retaliation so long as the accused is free to accept or reject the prosecution's offer."[29] Thus where a prosecutor "openly presented the defendant with the unpleasant alternatives of forgoing trial or facing charges on which he was plainly subject to prosecution," the imposition of these difficult choices is "an inevitable—and permissible—attribute of any legitimate system which tolerates and encourages the negotiation of pleas."[30]

---

25. *See Goodwin*, 457 U.S. at 382 ("A prosecutor should remain free before trial to exercise the broad discretion entrusted to him to determine the extent of the societal interest in prosecution. An initial decision should not freeze future conduct.").
26. *See, e.g.*, Jordan v. Epps, 756 F.3d 395, 406 (5th Cir. 2014).
27. *Bordenkircher*, 434 U.S. at 363.
28. *Id.* at 362.
29. *Id.* at 363.
30. *Id.* at 364, 365 (internal quotation marks omitted).

III. GUILTY PLEA PROCEDURES

Only the parties—the defense and the prosecution—may engage in plea negotiations. Under Fed. R. Crim. P. 11(c)(1) the "court must not participate in these discussions." As absolute as this prohibition is supposed to be, judges are able to indirectly shape plea deals through their authority, under Rule 11, to accept or reject deals. A judge can reject a proposed plea agreement, stating why it is, in her view, unsatisfactory, and leave the parties to decide whether they can live with a deal that is responsive to the judge's concerns.

The *Brady* Court noted that "[w]e would have serious doubts about this case if the encouragement of guilty pleas by offers of leniency substantially increased the likelihood that defendants, advised by competent counsel, would falsely condemn themselves."[31] But, the Court ruled, "our view is to the contrary and is based on our expectations that [1] the courts will satisfy themselves that [2] pleas of guilty are voluntary and intelligently made by [3] competent defendants [4] with adequate advice of counsel and [5] there is nothing to question the accuracy and reliability of the defendants' admissions that they committed the crimes with which they are charged."[32] These safeguards are reflected in Fed. R. Crim. P. 11, which describes the requirements for a valid guilty plea.

If a defendant decides to plead guilty, the district court must hold a plea hearing, also known as a Rule 11 proceeding. Given that, in entering a plea of guilty, the defendant waives his right against compelled self-incrimination and all his trial rights, the waiver of these rights must be knowing, intelligently, and voluntarily made. The judge will normally inquire of the defendant whether circumstances exist that may undermine the "knowing" and "intelligent" character of the plea (such as whether the defendant is intoxicated). The court must inform the defendant of, and determine that the defendant understands, the constitutional rights he is giving up by pleading. It must ensure that the defendant understands the charges to which he is pleading, including any maximum and minimum sentences and other potentially applicable penalties or obligations. The court can rely on counsel's representation that she advised the defendant of the nature of the charges and the elements of the crimes to which he is pleading guilty.[33] Among the matters about which the judge must advise the defendant under Rule 11, and ensure he understands, are the terms of any appeal waiver in the plea agreement.[34] The court's most important function

31. *Brady*, 397 U.S. at 758.
32. *Id.*
33. *See, e.g.*, Bradshaw v. Stumpf, 545 U.S. 175, 183 (2005).
34. Fed. R. Crim. P. 11(b)(1)(N).

in a Rule 11 guilty plea proceeding is to ensure that the defendant's plea is "done voluntarily, knowingly, and intelligently, 'with sufficient awareness of the relevant circumstances and likely consequences.'"[35]

Some types of plea deals are perceived to be sufficiently coercive that courts will review them with particular care in Rule 11 hearings. For example, defendants often attack the voluntariness of plea deals in which the defendant agrees to plead guilty in return for the government's undertaking to ensure that his family will not be charged or serve jail time. The circuit courts do not find such inducements per se objectionable. But, recognizing that these bargains can "pose a danger of coercion" and "increase the leverage possessed by prosecutors," the government must abide by a "high standard of good faith" in using such tactics.[36] "The government acts in good faith when it offers leniency for an indicted third party or threatens to prosecute an unindicted third party in exchange for a defendant's plea when the government has probable cause to prosecute the third party."[37]

During the course of a plea allocution under Rule 11(b)(3), the court "must determine that there is a factual basis for the plea." How this criterion is satisfied may depend upon the court's practice. Sometimes, courts will put the defendant under oath, warn the defendant of the government's right to use against the defendant any statement he makes in a prosecution for perjury or false statements,[38] and ask the defendant to attest to his guilt. In other courts, no such personal admission is required.[39]

If the defendant does not object and seeks a reversal of his conviction on the ground that the district court committed plain error under Rule 11 in connection with advice or warnings omitted, the defendant must show a reasonable probability that he would not have pleaded guilty but for the error.[40]

IV. RULE 11 AND GUIDELINES BARGAINING

If the plea is entered pursuant to an agreement between the government and defense in which the government agrees to give the defendant some

35. *Bradshaw*, 545 U.S. at 183 (quoting *Brady*, 397 U.S. at 748); *see also* Fed. R. Crim. P. 11(b)(2).
36. Miles v. Dorsey, 61 F.3d 1459, 1468 (10th Cir. 1995) (internal quotation marks omitted).
37. *Id.*
38. Fed. R. Crim. P. 11(b)(1)(A).
39. In *Mitchell v. United States*, 526 U.S. 314 (1999), the Supreme Court held that a guilty plea does not waive the defendant's Fifth Amendment privilege in the sentencing phase of the case, either as a result of the plea colloquy or by operation of law when the plea is entered. Moreover, the Court ruled that a trial court, in determining facts about the crime which bear upon the severity of the sentence under the Sentencing Guidelines, may not draw an adverse inference from the defendant's silence at sentencing.
40. *See* United States v. Dominguez Benitez, 542 U.S. 74, 83 (2004).

consideration in return for a plea, this should be reflected in a written plea agreement. Rule 11 provides the basic rules for such plea bargaining. It contemplates three types of plea agreements:

(1) a "charge" bargain under Fed. R. Crim. P. 11(c)(1)(A): under this subsection, the government agrees to "not bring, or . . . move to dismiss, other charges" in return for a plea
(2) a "recommended sentence" bargain under Fed. R. Crim. P. 11(c)(1)(B): under this subsection, the government agrees to recommend, or agrees not to oppose the defendant's request, "that a particular sentence or sentencing range is appropriate or that a particular provision of the [U.S.] Sentencing Guidelines, or policy statement, or sentencing factor does or does not apply (such a recommendation or request does not bind the court)."
(3) a "specific sentence" bargain under Fed. R. Crim. P. 11(c)(1)(C): this subsection contemplates agreements "that a specific sentence or sentencing range is the appropriate disposition of the case, or that a particular provision of the Sentencing Guidelines, or policy statement, or sentencing factor does or does not apply (such a recommendation or request binds the court once the court accepts the plea agreement)."

Note that agreements in fact need not fit neatly into one category or another. For example, a plea agreement that reflects a charge bargain may also involve a government promise to not oppose a recommended sentence.

Judges have broad discretion in deciding whether to accept or reject a proffered plea agreement, but the U.S. Sentencing Guidelines (Guidelines or USSG) contain non-binding criteria for judges to consider in making these calls. These policy statements, found in Guidelines Chapter Six, contemplate that the judge will compare the Guidelines sentence that the defendant would receive under the plea bargain with that which would be applicable to the defendant and other offenders similarly situated in absence of a plea. The Guidelines advise that where a plea agreement contemplates a charge bargain under Rule 11(c)(1)(A)—that is, the dismissal of charges or an undertaking not to pursue potential charges—a judge should accept the agreement only if "the remaining charges adequately reflect the seriousness of the actual offense behavior and . . . accepting the agreement will not undermine the statutory purposes of sentencing or the sentencing guidelines."[41] In cases where the plea agreement contains a non-binding sentence recommendation under Rule 11(c)(1)(B) or an agreement on a specific

41. U.S. Sentencing Guideline § 6B1.2(a) (2023 ed.) [hereinafter USSG].

sentence under Rule 11(c)(1)(C), the judge should accept the deal only if the recommended or agreed "sentence is within the applicable guideline range"[42] or the recommended or agreed sentence "is outside the applicable guideline range for justifiable reasons."[43]

Sometimes the judge will want more information before deciding on whether to accept the parties' plea agreement. The Probation Department is charged with independently investigating the facts of the offense and preparing a pre-sentence report (PSR) for the judge and the parties. The judge may be worried, for example, that the bargain constrains her sentencing discretion in ways she suspects she will not like once the Probation Department has done an investigation and come up with its PSR. In such circumstances, the judge may accept the guilty plea but defer acceptance of the plea bargain itself until after receipt of the PSR.[44]

With respect to the first type of plea bargain (charge bargains) and the third (specific sentence bargains), if the judge decides to reject the plea agreement, the defendant can elect to withdraw his plea under Fed. R. Crim. P. 11(c)(5)(B). But a defendant may not withdraw a plea entered pursuant to a recommended sentence bargain under Rule 11(c)(1)(B) even if the court ultimately rejects the sentencing recommendation or request in the plea agreement; accordingly, under Fed. R. Crim. P. 11(c)(3)(B), the court must so advise the defendant during the Rule 11 proceeding.

A. Charge Bargains Under Fed. R. Crim. P. 11(c)(1)(A)

As was explained in Chapter 15 (Sentencing), the U.S. Sentencing Commission attempted to blunt the effect of prosecutorial charging choices on a defendant's sentencing range in certain types of cases—those involving aggregable offenses, including most financial crime violations. Thus, in theory at least, it is more difficult for the parties to affect sentencing ranges through charge bargaining in white-collar cases. That said, charge bargains continue to be useful in such matters in at least two circumstances.

First, the maximum and minimum sentences embedded in the statutes under which the defendant has been convicted always trump the Guidelines. In some white-collar cases—particularly those in which the victims have

42. *Id.* § 6B1.2(b)(1), (c)(1).
43. *Id.* § 6B1.2(b)(2), (c)(2).
44. For the standards that control whether a defendant can, as of right, withdraw his plea during the period between the time the judge accepts his plea and the time at which the judge issues a decision on the plea agreement, see Fed. R. Crim. P. 11(d); United States v. Hyde, 520 U.S. 670 (1997).

suffered substantial losses—the parties can manipulate the advisory sentencing range by agreeing on a charge or charges for which the maximum statutory penalty is less than the range that would result from application of the Guidelines to the facts of the criminal conduct at issue. For example, assume that a defendant committed a series of wire frauds. Assume further that the defendant's Guidelines exposure is well over five years because of the large amount of loss involved. In such circumstances, the parties can bargain to "cap" the defendant's exposure to five years by agreeing to a plea to only one conspiracy count under 18 U.S.C. § 371, which carries a five-year maximum sentence, rather than conspiracy to commit wire fraud under 18 U.S.C. § 1349, which carries a twenty-year maximum and would not therefore operate to "cap" the defendant's Guidelines' exposure.[45]

Second, the Commission attempted to dampen the effect of prosecutorial charging choices in part by making one Guideline apply to all like offenses. Whether a prosecutor chooses to charge securities, health care, wire, or mail fraud, the sentencing range will generally be computed according to the same rules. There remain a few instances, however, where a prosecutor's theory of the case can change the applicable Chapter Two Guideline and thus the eventual sentencing range. For example, § 371 has two clauses: it allows prosecutors to charge a conspiracy to commit a crime against the United States (offense clause) or a conspiracy to defraud the United States (defraud clause). The prosecutor's choice of legal theory will affect what Chapter Two Guideline applies and may thereby change the applicable Guidelines sentencing range.[46] Similarly, a "money or property" mail or wire fraud count will be sentenced under a different Chapter Two Guideline than an "honest services" fraud count.[47]

---

45. As explained in Chapter 15, white-collar offenses are almost entirely deemed "aggregable"—meaning that the seriousness of the offense "is determined largely on the basis of the total amount of harm or loss, the quantity of a substance involved, or some other measure of aggregate harm"—and thus groupable (under USSG, *supra* note 41, § 3D1.2(d)); the relevant conduct rules (*see id.* § 1B1.3(a)(2)) apply in such cases. When such aggregable counts are at issue, the Commission attempted through the grouping and relevant conduct rules to blunt the extent to which prosecutors could change the sentencing range through manipulation of the number of counts. These rules do not apply to non-aggregable offenses. Thus, a prosecutor can induce pleas by agreeing to forgo or drop certain non-aggregable counts. Because these are rare in white-collar cases, they are not further discussed.

46. *See, e.g.*, *id.* §§ 2X1.1 (applicable to offense clause conspiracies), 2C1.1 (applicable to defraud clause conspiracies); *see also* Chapter 5 (Conspiracy) (discussing the difference between offense and defraud clause cases).

47. *See, e.g.*, USSG, *supra* note 41, §§ 2B1.1 (applicable to money or property frauds), 2C1.1 (applicable to honest services frauds); *see also* Chapter 6 (Fraud) (explaining the difference between "money or property" and "honest services" fraud cases).

B. Guidelines Fact and Factor Bargaining Under Fed. R. Crim. P. 11(c)(1)(B) and (C)

Prosecutors may bargain away "facts" that the Guidelines make relevant or Guidelines "factors" to induce a plea. This is commonly known as Guidelines "fact" or "factor" bargaining and is reflected in Fed. R. Crim. P. 11(c)(1)(B) and (C). For example, in financial crime cases the loss from the offense is a huge driver of sentence; in such prosecutions, the prosecutor and defense might stipulate to the "fact" of a lesser loss amount than a full investigation would reveal (fact bargaining). Or the parties might stipulate that an arguable adjustment—such as one for abusing a position of trust—should not be assessed ("factor" bargaining). Such bargains should be made in good faith and disclosed to the court. A prosecutor who misrepresents the true scope of the defendant's relevant conduct or the factual or legal applicability of other aggravating factors to affect the applicable Guidelines range or departure analysis could, at least in theory, risk professional and ethical censure.

C. Sentence Bargains Under Fed. R. Crim. P. 11(c)(1)(B) and (C)

Prosecutors have a number of options regarding sentence negotiation: "taking no position regarding the sentence; not opposing the defendant's request; requesting a specific type of sentence (e.g., a fine or probation), a specific fine or term of imprisonment, or not more than a specific fine or term of imprisonment; and requesting concurrent rather than consecutive sentences."[48]

Fed. R. Crim. P. 11(c)(1)(B) and (C) authorize the parties to agree to a recommended or specific sentence. The DOJ notes that specific or recommended sentence bargains come in two basic types: those in which prosecutors bargain for a sentence that is within the Guidelines range, and those in which they bargain in departures from the applicable Guidelines range.[49] The latter type of bargain involves a prosecutor agreeing to stipulate to, or at least not to oppose, a given departure. As was discussed in Chapter 15, the degree to which the parties and judges feel the need to even discuss departures after *United States v. Booker*, 543 U.S. 220 (2005), rendered the Guidelines advisory, rather than mandatory, is subject to some question. This may not, then, be the most fruitful area for negotiation going forward, at least in some districts.

48. Justice Manual, *supra* note 1, § 9-27.400.
49. *See id.*

V. PLEA AGREEMENTS GENERALLY

The factors a prosecutor ought to consider in deciding on whether to enter into a plea agreement with the defense are many: the defendant's willingness to cooperate in the investigation or prosecution of others; the defendant's criminal history; the nature and seriousness of the offense or offenses charged; the defendant's remorse or contrition and her willingness to assume responsibility for her conduct; the desirability of prompt and certain disposition of the case; the likelihood of obtaining a conviction at trial; the probable effect on witnesses; the probable sentence or other consequences if the defendant is convicted; the public interest in having the case tried rather than disposed of by a guilty plea; the expense of trial and appeal; the need to avoid delay in the disposition of other pending cases; and the interests of the victim, including any effect upon the victim's right to restitution.[50] If the prosecutor concludes that a plea agreement is appropriate, DOJ policy instructs that:

> [T]he defendant should be required to plead to a charge or charges: (1) That ordinarily include the most serious readily provable offense consistent with the nature and extent of his/her criminal conduct; (2) That have an adequate factual basis; (3) That make likely the imposition of an appropriate sentence and order of restitution, if appropriate, under all the circumstances of the case; and (4) That do not adversely affect the investigation or prosecution of others.[51]

The DOJ and sentencing courts require that plea agreements be reduced to writing. Courts use normal contract principles to resolve disputes about the terms of such agreements. If the government is deemed to have violated the parties' bargain, the defendant can enforce the agreement in court. In *Santobello v. New York*, 404 U.S. 257 (1971), the prosecutor agreed in a plea deal not to make a recommendation as to sentence, but a new prosecutor recommended the maximum sentence, which the judge imposed. The Supreme Court ruled that even if the prosecutor's lapse was inadvertent and even though the judge was uninfluenced by the prosecutor's recommendation, the "interests of justice and appropriate recognition of the duties of the prosecution in relation to promises made in the negotiation of pleas of guilty will be best served by remanding the case."[52] In terms of remedy, the Court left it up to the court on remand to determine whether specific performance of the agreement, which would involve resentencing by

50. *Id.* § 9-27.420.
51. *Id.* § 9-27.430.
52. *Santobello*, 404 U.S. at 262.

a different judge, or allowing the defendant to withdraw his plea was the appropriate remedy.

A defendant has no similar obligation to comply with the terms of his plea bargain. In case of a defense breach, the parties are left to whatever remedies or consequences were specified in the plea agreement.

In federal cases, prosecutors regularly ask that the defendant agree to a variety of waivers in plea agreements. Many U.S. Attorney's Offices have incorporated so-called *Brady* waivers in their agreements. In these waivers, defendants agree to waive any rights to impeachment evidence under *Brady* and *Giglio*; in some cases, they are also asked to waive *Brady* rights to substantive evidence of innocence.[53] In *United States v. Ruiz*, 536 U.S. 622 (2002), the Supreme Court ruled that a defendant has no right to pre-plea impeachment material under *Giglio* and that a plea agreement requiring defendant to waive her right to receive such pre-plea *Brady* material did not offend the Constitution or render the defendant's plea involuntary.

Prosecutors also regularly require the defendant to waive his right to appeal or collaterally attack whatever sentence is eventually imposed as well as any other issues as part of the plea agreement. All the circuits have held that appeal waivers are generally permissible and enforceable.[54] Some circuits, however, will make exceptions, for example where the defendant establishes that the appeal waiver in the plea agreement was not made knowingly, intelligently, and voluntarily.[55] Many circuits will not enforce the appeal waiver where the defendant claims ineffective assistance of counsel "directly related to the knowing, voluntary nature of the waiver."[56] Some circuits have also indicated that certain challenges to sentencing decisions other than ineffective assistance claims will be entertained despite an otherwise valid waiver, for example, where the sentence was imposed in excess of the maximum penalty provided by law,[57] where the sentence was based on a constitutionally impermissible factor such as race,[58] or where the sentence violated a material term of the plea agreement.[59]

VI. COOPERATION AGREEMENTS

Chapter 14 (Fifth Amendment) discussed agreements in which the defendant trades his cooperation in return for a government grant of immunity.

53. *See also* Chapter 13 (Discovery).
54. *See, e.g.*, United States v. Khattak, 273 F.3d 557, 560-61 (3d Cir. 2001) (collecting cases).
55. *See, e.g.*, United States v. Rollings, 751 F.3d 1183, 1189 (10th Cir. 2014).
56. United States v. White, 307 F.3d 336, 341 (5th Cir. 2002) (collecting cases).
57. *See, e.g.*, United States v. Brown, 232 F.3d 399, 403 (4th Cir. 2000).
58. *See id.*
59. *See* DeRoo v. United States, 223 F.3d 919, 923 (8th Cir. 2000).

In this Chapter, what is meant by a "cooperation agreement," is the far more common agreement in which the defendant agrees to enter a guilty plea and cooperate with the government in return for consideration in the form of a charge and/or sentence bargain and the potential of a departure motion under USSG § 5K1.1 ("Substantial Assistance to Authorities").

The process by which cooperation deals are hammered out—including the necessity of a defendant's proffer—is described in Chapter 14. Once such an agreement is concluded, the government, again, has an obligation to comply with the terms of the cooperation agreement and the consequences of a defendant's breach of his obligations are spelled out in the agreement. Cooperation agreements generally provide that, in the event of the defendant's breach, the government will be free from its obligations under the agreement and the cooperator will be fully subject to criminal prosecution for any crimes about which the government has information, including perjury and obstruction of justice, regardless of the charge or sentence bargain contained in the original agreement. In such circumstances, the defendant's conviction under the plea agreement may be vacated and the original charges—and more—can then be brought. The Supreme Court held in *Ricketts v. Adamson*, 483 U.S. 1 (1987), that a similar agreement contained an implicit waiver of double jeopardy protections. Such agreements also typically state that the government is free to use any statements the cooperator made or any information or materials he provided in the course of his cooperation against him in any subsequent prosecution.

The usual inducement offered cooperating defendants in federal court is the potential for a motion made pursuant to U.S. Sentencing Guidelines § 5K1.1. Section 5K1.1 provides that "[u]pon motion of the government stating that the defendant has provided substantial assistance in the investigation or prosecution of another person who has committed an offense, the court may depart from the guidelines."

Before the Supreme Court's decision in *Booker*, a judge was required to sentence a defendant within the Guidelines' sentencing range absent some ground for departure. For many defendants against whom the government had a strong case, a § 5K1.1 departure constituted their only chance to substantially reduce or eliminate the possibility of jail time. Section 5K1.1, then, is credited with significantly increasing defendants' incentives to lend the government "substantial assistance." Pre-*Booker*, § 5K1.1 was by far the most common ground for departure from the otherwise applicable sentencing ranges. At the time *Booker* was decided, the government made substantial assistance motions in nearly 20 percent of all federal prosecutions.

The § 5K1.1 departure is, by the terms of that section, contingent on a government motion. Prior to *Booker*, courts generally held that they could not, in the absence of a government motion, base a downward departure for a defendant's substantial assistance to federal prosecutors on other provisions of the Guidelines, including the general departure provision, § 5K2.0.[60] And judicial review of the government's refusal to file a § 5K1.1 motion was extremely limited.

These circumstances made § 5K1.1 controversial. First, many cooperators complained that prosecutors refused to make the promised § 5K1.1 motion without just cause and with impunity. A second, related concern was that the incentives the Guidelines created to cooperate—and in particular for cooperators to do whatever was necessary to secure a government motion—dramatically increased the risk of perjury. Such a risk is always present when the government rewards witnesses for their testimony. As the Supreme Court has recognized, "[c]ommon sense would suggest that [an accused accomplice] often has a greater interest in lying in favor of the prosecution rather than against it, especially if he is still awaiting his own trial or sentencing. To think that criminals will lie to save their fellows but not to obtain favors from the prosecution for themselves is indeed to clothe the criminal class with more nobility than one might expect to find in the public at large."[61] Many argued, however, that § 5K1.1's motion requirement created too great an incentive for cooperators to say whatever the government wanted them to say to escape the otherwise applicable Guideline sentence.

The government countered that there are a variety of means by which cooperators' deceit will be deterred or exposed. These include the requirement that government disclose exculpatory information, including impeachment information, to a defendant. The terms of any cooperation agreement must be turned over to the defense, and testifying accomplices can be extensively cross-examined about the likely effect of such agreements on their testimony. The jury is often instructed that it may regard cooperators' testimony with caution. And a prosecutor who knowingly procures false testimony could be prosecuted for subornation of perjury, 18 U.S.C. § 1622, or at the very least be subjected to professional sanctions. Whether these are sufficient to counter cooperators' incentives to falsely inculpate a defendant in hopes of a § 5K1.1 motion is an unanswerable empirical question. It is worth noting, however, that the Innocence Project analyzed 375 cases of DNA exoneration, and 17 percent of the cases involved government informants.[62]

In response to these criticisms, a variety of proposals were made to eliminate or qualify the government motion requirement. It appears that *Booker* has done what Congress did not. Because the Guidelines are now only advisory, the government motion requirement no longer binds courts seeking to

---

60. *See* In re Sealed Case No. 97-3112, 181 F.3d 128, 136 (D.C. Cir. 1999) (*en banc*).
61. Washington v. Texas, 388 U.S. 14, 22-23 (1967).
62. *See* Innocence Project, *supra* note 12.

reward defendants—over government opposition—for cooperation with government investigators. It does not appear, however, that district courts are embracing this freedom in many cases; government-sponsored § 5K1.1 departures still appear to be the norm.

Examples

1. Teodoro Ribeiro was one of a group of co-conspirators who laundered money for the mob. Two of Ribeiro's ten co-conspirators hatched the scheme, controlled the offshore accounts through which the money was funneled, and were the primary beneficiaries of the scheme. Ribeiro was a relatively minor player who joined the conspiracy a month before it was uncovered. The government offered all eleven participants in the scheme a plea bargain that provided that if all the co-conspirators pleaded guilty to one count of wire fraud, the government would stipulate that no sentencing enhancements were appropriate. This is a very good deal for the two leaders of the scheme, less of a bargain for the more minor players. The government takes the position, however, that if any one of the co-conspirators elects to go to trial, the government will withdraw the deal for everyone. Is this offer permissible?

2. Durga Sharma entered a plea of guilty to one count of wire fraud pursuant to a plea agreement under Fed. R. Crim. P. 11(c)(1)(B). The parties stipulated that the Sharma's Guidelines range was 21 to 27 months imprisonment and the government agreed not to oppose Sharma's argument that a sentence at the lowest point of the applicable Guidelines range—21 months—was appropriate. After a Rule 11 hearing, the district court accepted both the guilty plea and the plea agreement. The judge, after receiving the Probation Department's PSR, sentenced Sharma to 27 months in jail. Can he withdraw his plea?

3. Lockie Eldridge faced misdemeanor domestic abuse-related charges. Events transpired during trial that warranted a mistrial motion. Assistant District Attorney Julie Williams was the prosecutor who was trying the case, but she had taken it over from another ADA who had made the decision to bring only misdemeanor charges. Williams told defense counsel, Sieful Saad, that, if a mistrial motion were made and granted, the state would file more serious charges. Nonetheless Saad filed the mistrial motion and it was granted. About a year later Williams brought a second round of charges, including nine felonies and two misdemeanors. These eleven counts incorporated the conduct underpinning the original misdemeanor charges and also included new allegations of misconduct dating back to 2019. (Assume that this charging decision was consistent with double jeopardy rules.)

Eldridge moved to dismiss the new case as a vindictive prosecution. He contended that the prosecutors leveled the expanded charges against him in retaliation for his seeking and receiving a mistrial in the misdemeanor case. He supported his motion with an affidavit from Sieful Saad, his counsel at the first trial. Saad's affidavit recounted statements ADA Williams made about why she brought additional charges in the second case. According to Saad, "ADA Williams stated that although her assignment within the Office of the District Attorney [was] changing, she was not going to allow the case against Mr. Eldridge to be assigned to another ADA. ADA Williams stated that even if she were to leave the District Attorney's Office and go into private practice, she would return under the District Attorney's pro bono program to personally see to the prosecution" of Eldridge.

The court held a hearing on the vindictiveness claim at which ADA Williams testified: "I can tell the Court, in all candor, when I heard about what he had done to her to inflict these injuries in the past during the course of their relationship, considering my oath as a prosecutor, I was convinced that I had no choice but to file these charges." Can Eldridge succeed on a vindictive prosecution claim?

4. The prosecutors' office in a small college town has an unwritten policy to go easy on students who are arrested for non-violent offenses. The office shows particular solicitude when deciding whether to indict star student athletes, regardless of the offense. Shabani Zawadi, a senior citizen and town resident, was charged with public drunkenness and disturbing the peace and moved to dismiss the indictment based on a selective prosecution argument, pointing to this unwritten policy. Is he likely to succeed on an equal protection claim?

5. Graeme Roy has entered into a plea agreement with the government in which he agreed to plead guilty to one count of conspiring to commit wire fraud under 18 U.S.C. § 371 and to cooperate with the government in the investigation and prosecution of his co-conspirators. In return, the government agreed to dismiss a wire fraud count that, under the Guidelines, would yield an advisory Guidelines range of 78-97 months' imprisonment. (Section 371 carries a statutory maximum of five years and wire fraud's maximum penalty is ordinarily twenty years; recall from Chapter 15 that the statutory maximum always trumps the advisory Guidelines range.) The government also agreed to make a motion for a departure under § 5K1.1 if Roy did in fact provide substantial assistance in the prosecution of others. Should the judge accept the plea agreement under the standards laid out in the Guidelines?

Explanations

1. The consideration the government may offer in exchange for a guilty plea is limited only by constitutional due process and equal protection constraints and, as we saw, those are few. This is what is called a "wired" or "package deal" plea. Under such agreements, several confederates plead together, and the government gives them a "volume discount—a better deal than each could have gotten separately."[63] The nature of the deal is that all must plead guilty, or no one gets the deal. Although not per se impermissible, courts will be concerned that "one defendant will be happier with the package deal than his codefendant(s); looking out for his own best interests, the lucky one may try to force his codefendant(s) into going along with the deal."[64] Accordingly, a number of circuits recognize that package deals present "special risks" and they therefore require that such package deals be disclosed to the court and that district courts conduct colloquies with the pleading defendants "with special care."[65]

2. No. This is a recommended sentence bargain under Fed. R. Crim. P. 11(c)(1)(B). A disappointed defendant may not withdraw his guilty plea as of right if the judge does not follow the recommended sentence. (By contrast, if the judge ultimately rejects a charge bargain under Fed. R. Crim. P. 11(c)(1)(A) and/or a specific sentence bargain under 11(c)(1)(C), a defendant may withdraw their plea.) Under Rule 11(c)(3)(B), the judge should have warned Sharma that this is the case before Sharma entered his guilty plea during the Rule 11 hearing. If the judge failed to do so, and Sharma did not timely object, he would have to show plain error—that is, to secure relief, he would need to demonstrate a reasonable probability that he would not have pleaded guilty but for the lack of warning.

3. In this case, Eldridge would first argue that a presumption of vindictiveness is appropriate on these facts. Under *Goodwin*, a presumption of vindictive prosecution does not apply when a prosecutor adds charges in a criminal case, in advance of trial, after discovering new information that supports additional charges. But in *Blackledge*, the Supreme Court applied a presumption of vindictiveness where a prosecutor reindicted a convicted misdemeanant on a felony charge after the defendant had asked for a new trial. Courts may be persuaded that *Blackledge* argues for a presumption of vindictiveness when a prosecutor adds new felony charges to

63. United States v. Caro, 997 F.2d 657, 658 (9th Cir. 1993).
64. *Id.* at 659.
65. United States v. Hodge, 412 F.3d 479, 490-91 (3d Cir. 2005) (collecting cases).

retaliate against a defendant for a successful mistrial motion. The argument against such a presumption is that this was not a case in which the prosecutor unilaterally imposed this penalty; rather, she warned defense counsel that this would be the result.

Eldridge would further argue that even if a presumption is not applied, the prosecutor actually acted vindictively in this case. If a court accepts the prosecutor's explanation, it is likely that it would find that the prosecutor did not act vindictively and that whatever presumption applied was rebutted on the facts.

In the case from which this was drawn, the court "credited the prosecutor's account that, at around the time of the misdemeanor trial, the prosecutor learned additional information that reflected a deeper and broader history of domestic violence between [the defendant and his victim] than the prosecution had not been aware of before."[66] It found that the prosecutor could not have charged the defendant with the felony counts the first time around because she did not yet have knowledge of the full scope of his criminal conduct. And the court accepted

> as true trial counsel's account that the prosecutor had told trial counsel that, if a mistrial motion were made and granted, the State would file more serious charges. The court did not view this as a threat, but instead only as the prosecutor's frank explanation of where the case was headed in the event of a mistrial.[67]

4. No. It will be difficult for Zawadi to prove the necessary discriminatory effect of this unwritten policy—that is, that students and star athletes receive preferential treatment in public drunkenness and disturbing the peace cases—without discovery, and we know that discovery is not ordinarily allowed unless the defendant can prove this effect. Even assuming the defendant has the data, ordinary equal protection law applies in selective prosecution cases. Being a "non-student" or a "non-athlete" is not a protected class entitled to strict scrutiny. The presumption that the prosecutor is acting reasonably is likely to remain unrebutted because "[i]n the ordinary case, 'so long as the prosecutor has probable cause to believe that the accused committed an offense defined by statute, the decision whether or not to prosecute, and what charge to file or bring before a grand jury, generally rests entirely in his discretion.'"[68]

5. If the prosecutor had not dismissed the wire fraud count, Roy would be facing a Guidelines range of well over five years, and this sentence could be imposed given that wire fraud carries a statutory maximum of twenty years. By agreeing to this charge bargain, the parties have capped the

66. State v. Lass, 393 Wis. 2d 594, at *5 (Ct. App. 2020) (unpublished)
67. *Id.*; *see also* Lass v. Wells, 105 F.4th 932 (7th Cir. 2024).
68. *Armstrong*, 517 U.S. at 464.

judge's sentencing discretion at five years—§ 371's statutory maximum penalty—which controls regardless of the Guidelines range.

This is a charge bargain under Rule 11(c)(1)(A). The Guidelines advise that the judge accept the agreement only if the remaining charges adequately reflect the seriousness of Roy's offense and accepting the agreement would not undermine the uniformity and proportionality goals of the Guidelines. In theory, then, the judge would be justified in rejecting the deal. But the Guidelines are advisory only and these plea standards are simply statements of policy. The judge has the discretion to accept the plea deal; she is constrained only by "reasonableness" appellate review of the ultimate sentence imposed.[69]

69. *See* Chapter 15 (Sentencing) (discussing "reasonableness" standard of appellate review for Guidelines sentences).

CHAPTER 17

Parallel Proceedings

In white-collar matters—particularly those involving potential organizational misconduct—it is very common for those under criminal investigation to be subjected to concurrent civil investigations and lawsuits as well as the scrutiny of prosecutors.[1] Potential plaintiffs in such matters may include private litigants, qui tam relators,[2] shareholders launching derivative suits, and a variety of federal, state, and local governmental agencies. Corporate clients, in particular, will be very concerned about their potential liability in such matters because civil judgments can exceed any fine imposed in the criminal cases. Criminal defense counsel faced with collateral litigation will be called upon to coordinate their client's responses to the demands of those seeking criminal sanctions and civil remedies so as to minimize the extent to actions in one matter prejudice the client in another.

In 2018, the Department of Justice issued a policy that increases the likelihood that those subject to criminal investigation will also experience parallel federal agency enforcement actions. The DOJ's Justice Manual § 1-12.000 stresses that every U.S. Attorney's Office and litigating component at Main Justice ought to prioritize "early, effective, and regular communication between criminal, civil, and agency attorneys to the fullest extent appropriate to the case and permissible by law." From the beginning of a case, government attorneys are instructed to "consider potential civil, administrative, regulatory, and criminal remedies, and discuss those remedies with the investigative agents and other government personnel." And at every point in the case, government attorneys should consider what effect their proposed resolution of a matter will have on other criminal, civil, regulatory, and administrative proceedings. "While parallel proceedings must be handled carefully in order to avoid allegations of improper release of grand jury material or abuse of civil process, when conducted properly, they can complement one another and serve the best interests of law enforcement and the public."[3] In short, the Department of Justice is promoting the coordination of civil and criminal investigations to remedy and punish misconduct "to the fullest extent appropriate and permissible by law."[4] At the same time, as is discussed within, the DOJ encourages the various components of the federal government to work together to prevent duplicative penalties in its "anti-piling on" policy.[5]

1. With respect to parallel state, federal, or tribal or foreign criminal proceedings, see Chapter 2's discussion of the dual sovereignty doctrine. In brief, this doctrine means that the Double Jeopardy Clause does not preclude different "sovereigns" (including federal, state, tribal, and foreign governments) from bringing criminal cases concerning the same offense.
2. *See* Chapter 4 (discussing False Claims Act qui tam cases).
3. U.S. Dept of Justice, Justice Manual § 1-12.000 [hereinafter Justice Manual].
4. *Id.*
5. *See id.* § 1-12.100.

I. CONSTITUTIONAL CONSTRAINTS ON PARALLEL FEDERAL CRIMINAL AND CIVIL ENFORCEMENT ACTIONS

A. Due Process

United States v. Kordel, 397 U.S. 1 (1970), involved a criminal prosecution for violations of the federal Food, Drug and Cosmetic Act and a concurrent civil enforcement action by the Food and Drug Administration (FDA) based upon the same events. The issue was whether the vice-president who answered interrogatories addressed to the corporation in the civil enforcement proceeding was "compelled" to do so within the meaning of the Fifth Amendment. The Court held that he was not given that he was free to assert his individual Fifth Amendment right. In the course of so holding, the Supreme Court rejected the individual defendant's argument that the government's conduct in pursuing both the criminal and civil cases "reflected such unfairness and want of consideration for justice as independently to require the reversal of their convictions."[6] The Court concluded that, "[o]n the record before us, we cannot agree that the respondents have made out either a violation of due process or a departure from proper standards in the administration of justice requiring the exercise of our supervisory power."[7]

The *Kordel* Court did, however, hypothesize that in "special circumstances" such proceedings may be impermissible, either as a matter of due process or under federal courts' supervisory power.[8] It cautioned that "[w]e do not here deal here with a case in which the Government has brought a civil action solely to obtain evidence for its criminal prosecution or has failed to advise the defendant in its civil proceeding that it contemplates his criminal prosecution."[9] The Court further noted that *Kordel* did not involve a situation in which "the defendant is without counsel or reasonably fears prejudice from adverse pretrial publicity or other unfair injury."[10]

Defendants subject to double-barreled criminal and civil enforcement actions are rarely successful in claiming one of the *Kordel* exceptions. Occasionally, however, courts have found that the government "has departed from the proper administration of criminal justice where it 'manipulate[s] the simultaneous [criminal and civil] investigations for its own purposes.'"[11] In the cases in which district courts have granted relief,

6. *Kordel*, 397 U.S. at 11.
7. *Id.*
8. *Id.* at 12.
9. *Id.* at 11-12.
10. *Id.* at 12.
11. United States v. Mahaffy, 446 F. Supp. 2d 115, 124 (E.D.N.Y. 2006); *see, e.g.*, United States v. Scrushy, 366 F. Supp. 2d 1134 (N.D. Ala. 2005).

judges have expressed outrage when they find that government actors misled or lied to defense counsel about the existence of parallel proceedings and where the civil case was brought "solely" to serve the interests of the prosecutors.[12] But "the 'mere failure' of a government official to warn that an investigation may result in criminal charges does not constitute fraud, deceit, or trickery."[13] In the usual case where there is no proof that prosecutors "hid behind or manipulated" the civil investigators with the "intention of misrepresenting its true intentions," or improperly used the civil process to further the criminal case, such claims will be denied.[14]

B. Double Jeopardy

As a general rule, one cannot argue that the Double Jeopardy Clause precludes successive criminal and civil actions because that clause has traditionally been read to preclude only successive *criminal* prosecutions for the same offense by the same sovereign.[15] Moreover, until the Supreme Court's decision in *United States v. Halper*, 490 U.S. 435 (1989), defendants could not prevail by arguing that a nominally civil sanction actually constituted "criminal punishment" for double jeopardy purposes.

In 1989, the *Halper* Court began a litigation landslide by holding that in certain circumstances courts should look through the nominally "civil" nature of certain types of penalties and treat them as criminal punishment for purposes of double jeopardy analysis. The government indicted Halper on sixty-five counts of making false claims on the government in violation of 18 U.S.C. § 287. He was convicted on all counts and was sentenced to imprisonment for two years and fined $5,000. The government then brought a civil action against Halper under the False Claims Act. Having violated the act sixty-five separate times, Halper's statutory civil penalty was assessed at more than $130,000. Harper argued that this penalty was clearly punitive in light of the government's actual loss of $585.

The Supreme Court agreed, ruling that "a civil as well as a criminal sanction constitutes punishment when the sanction as applied in the individual case serves the goals of punishment."[16] It held that "[w]here a defendant previously has sustained a criminal penalty and the civil penalty sought in the subsequent proceeding bears no rational relation to the goal of compensating the Government for its loss, but rather appears to qualify as

---

12. *See, e.g.*, United States v. Stringer, 408 F. Supp. 2d 1083 (D. Or. 2006), *rev'd*, 535 F.3d 929 (9th Cir. 2008); United States v. Tweel, 550 F.2d 297 (5th Cir. 1977).

13. United States v. Posada Carriles, 541 F.3d 344, 355 (5th Cir. 2008).

14. *Mahaffy*, 446 F. Supp. 2d at 126.

15. *See, e.g.*, One Lot Emerald Cut Stones v. United States, 409 U.S. 232, 235-36 (1972).

16. *Halper*, 490 U.S. at 448.

'punishment' in the plain meaning of the word, then the defendant is entitled to an accounting of the Government's damages and costs to determine if the penalty sought in fact constitutes a second punishment."[17]

In a series of subsequent cases, the Court struggled with the application of this standard, particularly in cases in which a civil forfeiture was sought parallel to a criminal proceeding.[18] In 1997, the Court's obvious discomfort with the unforeseen consequences of its *Halper* analysis was made explicit in *Hudson v. United States*, 522 U.S. 93 (1997). The *Hudson* Court "disavow[ed]the method of analysis used in *United States v. Halper*," identifying two deficits in its reasoning.[19] First, the *Hudson* Court criticized the *Halper* decision for bypassing the threshold question: whether the successive punishment at issue is a "criminal" punishment. Instead, *Halper* improperly "focused on whether the sanction, regardless of whether it was civil or criminal, was so grossly disproportionate to the harm caused as to constitute 'punishment.'"[20] *Hudson* clarified that the punitive nature of the sanction should be only one of a variety of factors to be considered. The second significant departure from precedent in *Halper* was "the Court's decision to 'asses[s] the character of the actual sanctions imposed,' rather than, as [precedent] demanded, evaluating the 'statute on its face' to determine whether it provided for what amounted to a criminal sanction."[21]

The *Hudson* Court then reaffirmed the two-part test to distinguish between civil and criminal penalties that it had previously employed in *United States v. Ward*, 448 U.S. 242 (1980). Under *Ward*, a court first must determine whether the legislature intended to establish a civil or criminal penalty.[22] Second, the court must consult a variety of factors to decide whether the nominally civil statutory penalties are "'so punitive in form and effect'" as to render them criminal despite Congress' intent to the contrary.[23] Importantly, courts are to evaluate the statute on its face, and only the "clearest proof" will suffice to override legislative intent and transform what has been denominated a civil remedy into a criminal penalty.[24]

---

17. *Id.* at 449.
18. *See, e.g.*, United States v. Ursery, 518 U.S. 267 (1996).
19. *Hudson*, 522 U.S. at 95.
20. *Id.* at 101.
21. *Id.*
22. *Id.* at 99.
23. *Id.* at 104. The seven factors relied on in *Hudson* are: "(1) '[w]hether the sanction involves an affirmative disability or restraint'; (2) 'whether it has historically been regarded as punishment'; (3) 'whether it comes into play only on a finding of scienter'; (4) 'whether its operation will promote the traditional aims of punishment—retribution and deterrence'; (5) 'whether the behavior to which it applies is already a crime'; (6) 'whether an alternative purpose to which it may rationally be connected is assignable for it'; (7) 'whether it appears excessive in relation to the alternative purpose assigned.'" *Id.* at 99-100.
24. *See id.* at 104, 105.

Obviously, *Hudson* renders arguments that civil sanctions are jeopardy-barred, or in fact jeopardy-bar subsequent criminal proceedings, much more difficult—indeed generally impossible—to win. In effect, the Court has once more made virtually dispositive the label Congress affixed to a given sanction and has further insulated nominally civil sanctions from double jeopardy scrutiny by permitting only facial challenges.

II. FIFTH AMENDMENT RIGHT AGAINST COMPELLED SELF-INCRIMINATION AND PARALLEL PROCEEDINGS

A. The Dangers of Not Taking the Fifth in Collateral Litigation: Gifts to Prosecutors and Potential Waiver Issues

The Fifth Amendment "not only protects the individual against being involuntarily called as a witness against himself in a criminal prosecution but also privileges him not to answer official questions put to him in any other proceeding, civil or criminal, formal or informal, where the answers might incriminate him in future criminal proceedings."[25] This means that those involved in civil litigation, when called to answer a complaint, respond to interrogatories, or sit for a deposition, can assert their right against compelled self-incrimination if what they say could eventually be used against them in a criminal prosecution.

Many experienced defense counsel will advise clients who are targets of a grand jury investigation to exercise their Fifth Amendment right in the course of related civil litigation.[26] First, the statements themselves can be used in the criminal case: they likely will be admissible as a party admission or a co-conspirator's statement and can be used for impeachment should the defendant take the stand. If the government believes that the defendant lied in the course of the civil deposition, at least where the deposing party was a federal agency or department, it can potentially bring a perjury, false statement, or obstruction case against the defendant.[27] The potential peril goes beyond evidentiary use of the statements. The defendant will often reveal the defense theory, thus locking the defense in prematurely—that is, before the defense team learns what the government has to rebut their theory. The government can also use what the defendant says in the civil case

25. Lefkowitz v. Turley, 414 U.S. 70, 77 (1973).
26. *See, e.g.*, Watts v. Indiana, 338 U.S. 49, 59 (1949) (Jackson, J., concurring in part) ("[A]ny lawyer worth his salt will tell the suspect in no uncertain terms to make no statement to the police under any circumstances.").
27. *See* Chapters 4 (Perjury and False Statements) and 7 (Obstruction).

to develop its criminal case, find new witnesses or sources of evidence, and develop rebuttal arguments.

Another consideration in counseling a client whether to take the Fifth in the course of a parallel investigation is the possibility that speaking in one forum may threaten a broader waiver in that forum or may constitute a waiver in other proceedings. The test for waiver of one's right against compelled self-incrimination is generally whether the statement was voluntary.[28] With certain exceptions, a witness who answers a question, even if the witness is not aware of the danger of incrimination or possibility of waiver, will not be deemed to have been "compelled" to be a witness against himself.[29] And by waiving his Fifth Amendment right in answering the question, the defendant faces the possibility that a wider waiver will be implied.

The Supreme Court articulated the relevant standard in *Rogers v. United States*, 340 U.S. 367 (1951). In *Rogers*, a witness testified before a federal grand jury that as Treasurer of the Communist Party of Denver she had turned membership records over to another person. The witness then refused to name the person to whom she had given the records, grounding her refusal upon her Fifth Amendment privilege against compelled self-incrimination. The Supreme Court held that she no longer could claim the privilege with respect to further questions on the same subject. The Court ruled that "[d]isclosure of a fact waives the privilege as to details," and found that, on these facts, the witness's privilege was not implicated because answering the question would not incriminate her further.[30]

Although *Rogers* concerned the scope of a waiver in the context of sequential questions in a single grand jury appearance, courts often use the *Rogers* "further incrimination" analysis in determining whether a witness's statement in one proceeding constitutes a waiver for purposes of subsequent proceedings. They ask whether the answer to the same or related questions in a subsequent proceeding would "subject the witness to a 'real danger' of further crimination."[31] In making this determination, however, a clear majority of courts apply an irrebuttable presumption of further

---

28. As noted in Chapter 14 (Fifth Amendment), the safeguards the Court constructed in *Miranda v. Arizona* generally do not apply in business crime cases because defendants are only infrequently subjected to custodial interrogations. Accordingly, the knowing, intelligent, and voluntary waiver standard required by *Miranda* does not apply.

29. *See* Minnesota v. Murphy, 465 U.S. 420, 427 (1984); United States v. Monia, 317 U.S. 424, 427 (1943).

30. *Rogers*, 340 U.S. at 373. Where the question is the scope of a privilege waiver in the same proceeding, courts sometimes apply a test articulated by the Second Circuit in Klein v. Harris, 667 F.2d 274, 287-89 (2d Cir. 1981) as well as *Rogers*.

31. *Rogers*, 340 U.S. at 374.

incrimination where the witness is asked to reiterate his earlier statement in a "separate proceeding."[32]

B. The Danger of Taking the Fifth in Collateral Litigation: Adverse Inferences

A defendant who takes the Fifth in the course of civil proceedings against him avoids the above perils but runs into another potential difficulty. The Supreme Court has held that while no adverse inference may be drawn against a defendant's failure to testify in a criminal case, "the Fifth Amendment does not forbid adverse inferences against parties to civil actions when they refuse to testify in response to probative evidence offered against them, at least where refusal to waive the privilege does not lead automatically and without more to [the] imposition of sanctions."[33]

The Court's caveat is important: "although inferences based on the assertion of the privilege are permissible, the entry of judgment based only on the invocation of the privilege and 'without regard to the other evidence' exceeds constitutional bounds."[34] The Seventh Circuit explained how this rule applies in civil litigation in *LaSalle Bank Lake View v. Seguban*, 54 F.3d 387 (7th Cir. 1995).

The court in *LaSalle Bank* cautioned that the failure to answer the allegations in a civil complaint based on the Fifth Amendment cannot alone justify a default judgment. "[D]eeming an allegation of the complaint to be admitted based on the invocation of the Fifth Amendment privilege without requiring the complainant to produce evidence in support of its allegations would impose too great a cost."[35] Circumstances may be different when the plaintiff moves for summary judgment contending that, based on the evidence uncovered in discovery, there is no genuine issue of material fact, and that the movant is entitled to judgment as a matter of law.

At issue in *LaSalle Bank* was a local rule that required the party opposing a summary judgment motion to file a response setting forth the reasons, based on the evidence, that the movant was not entitled to relief. The Seventh Circuit held that if the responding party asserts the Fifth rather

---

32. *See* United States v. Cain, 544 F.2d 1113, 1117 (1st Cir. 1976) ("[i]t is hornbook law that the waiver is limited to the particular proceeding in which the witness appears"). Although not relying upon the above rule, the Supreme Court also has made clear that the privilege against self-incrimination survives a guilty plea. *See* Mitchell v. United States, 526 U.S. 314 (1999). Thus a defendant who had pleads guilty can assert her Fifth Amendment right not to testify at sentencing and a sentencing judge may not draw an adverse inference from her assertion of her right.

33. *Mitchell*, 526 U.S. at 326 (internal quotation marks omitted).

34. LaSalle Bank Lake View v. Seguban, 54 F.3d 387, 391 (7th Cir. 1995).

35. *Id.*

than file the required response, the judge is entitled to draw an adverse inference—that is, that the facts set forth by the movant are true. In such a case, the responding party's assertion of the Fifth "*does not* lead directly and without more to the entry of summary judgment, but merely establishes the factual basis" upon which the judge will decide whether to grant the motion.[36]

Corporations have no Fifth Amendment right, but their individual employees and agents do, except when they are producing corporate records in response to a government subpoena in their representative capacity.[37] Companies cannot control whether their agents take the Fifth in collateral litigation, but they will suffer the consequences of agents' decisions. Thus, if the employees choose to respond to civil discovery, Fed. R. Evid. 801(d)(2)(D) provides that a statement "made by the party's agent or employee on a matter within the scope of that relationship while it existed" is not hearsay and is therefore admissible against a corporate party. If, by contrast, the corporate agent takes the Fifth, the decision-maker may draw a negative inference against the corporation based on this assertion, even if the agent is no longer employed by the company.[38]

III. OBTAINING A STAY OF CIVIL OR ADMINISTRATIVE PROCEEDINGS

To avoid the Fifth Amendment dilemma discussed above, as well as to avoid the distractions and expense of conducting parallel litigation, a defendant embroiled in concurrent criminal and civil cases may ask the court in the civil case to stay the action pending resolution of the criminal prosecution. Although defendants' requests for stays of pending civil or administrative proceedings until the conclusion of a prospective or pending criminal case are fairly common, they are very infrequently granted.

Just as there are pros and cons to the assertion of the Fifth Amendment privilege in civil litigation, there are pros and cons to seeking a stay. Indeed, there is a potentially significant upside for the defense in allowing discovery to continue in the parallel civil matters. As we have seen in Chapter 13 (Discovery), the discovery a defendant receives in a criminal case is minimal in comparison to civil cases. In particular, the defense generally has no opportunity to depose or serve interrogatories on potential

36. *Id.* at 392.

37. *See* Chapter 14 (Fifth Amendment).

38. *See, e.g.*, Rad Services Inc. v. Aetna Cas. & Sur. Co., 808 F.2d 271, 274-75 (3d Cir. 1986).

government witnesses or to secure impeachment materials from third parties. The defense, then, may wish to engage in at least some discovery in the civil case to secure critical information and impeachment materials it otherwise would not have access to under the Federal Rules of Criminal Procedure.

To preclude the defense from using civil discovery to help it prepare for the criminal trial, the government may intervene where necessary and move for a stay. Once an indictment has been returned, the government "often moves for and frequently obtains relief preventing a criminal defendant from using parallel civil proceedings to gain premature access to evidence and information pertinent to the criminal case."[39]

Courts generally consider five factors in deciding whether to grant a stay:

1. *The effect on the plaintiff's interests.* Among the relevant considerations are whether a delay will prejudice the plaintiffs' ability to put on a case because his witnesses may die or disappear, and his evidence may degrade, over time. Another concern is whether the defendant will dissipate the assets necessary to satisfy a judgment.
2. *The effect on the defendant's interests.* The Fifth Amendment dilemma discussed above is the primary consideration here, but courts rarely find it sufficient to grant a stay. Another issue is whether adverse publicity from the civil trial may taint the jury pool in the criminal case.
3. *The convenience of the court in the management of its cases, and the efficient use of judicial resources.* Many judges do not wish to leave matters to languish on their dockets. But they may also decide that a stay is the efficient option because a conviction in the criminal case may make trial in the civil case unnecessary given the application of collateral estoppel.
4. *The interests of third parties.*
5. *The public interest.* Courts will look at whether the civil matter involves important public policy or health and safety considerations relating, for example, to environmental harms or consumer safety. If such considerations are present and can be remedied through a civil injunction or damages, the court may decline to stay the civil matter.[40]

39. SEC. v. Doody, 186 F. Supp. 2d 379, 381 (S.D.N.Y. 2002).
40. *See, e.g.*, Keating v. Office of Thrift Supervision, 45 F.3d 322, 324-25 (9th Cir. 1995).

IV. OBTAINING A PROTECTIVE ORDER IN CIVIL OR ADMINISTRATIVE PROCEEDINGS BARRING DISCLOSURE TO PROSECUTORS OR THE GRAND JURY

If the defendant does not wish to seek, or the court does not agree to grant, a stay of the parallel civil action, the subject of a criminal investigation may seek to secure a more easily obtainable civil protective order that precludes the parties from turning over evidence revealed in the course of civil discovery to prosecutors or the grand jury. Thus, if the client insists on participating in civil discovery, counsel may seek a protective order, hoping to guard the client against the consequences of failing to take the Fifth discussed above. But the circuits are split on whether a protective order under Fed. R. Civ. P. 26(c) can shield evidence given during the course of civil discovery from a federal grand jury subpoena.

The Second Circuit holds that to enforce a grand jury subpoena and gain access to civil discovery protected by a protective order, the government must show either "improvidence in the grant of the Rule 26(c) protective order or some extraordinary circumstance or compelling need."[41] The First Circuit applies the opposite presumption and burden of proof. It holds that a grand jury subpoena trumps a Rule 26(c) protective order "unless the person seeking to avoid the subpoena can demonstrate the existence of exceptional circumstances that clearly favor subordinating the subpoena to the protective order."[42] The Fourth, Ninth, and Eleventh Circuits are not willing to consider the individual circumstances of the case; they have articulated a per se rule that protective orders cannot shield civil discovery from grand jury subpoenas.[43]

V. OBTAINING GRAND JURY MATERIALS FOR USE IN CIVIL CASES

A. Private Litigants' Ability to Secure Grand Jury Transcripts

We have thus far concerned ourselves with circumstances in which civil litigation may impact the criminal case. There are circumstances, however, in

41. Martindell v. ITT, 594 F.2d 291, 296 (1979).

42. In re Grand Jury Subpoena (Served Upon Stephen A. Roach), 138 F.3d 442, 445 (1st Cir. 1998).

43. *See* In re Grand Jury Subpoena (Served on Meserve, Mumper & Hughes), 62 F.3d 1222, 1224-27 (9th Cir. 1995) (collecting cases).

which the parties to a civil proceeding will seek to secure evidence gathered in the course of a criminal case. Consider, for example, a case in which a corporation cooperates with the government in its investigation in an effort to secure a declination of charges or a deferred prosecution agreement. In so doing, the company may share materials with, and encourage its agents to testify before, the grand jury. The company will vigorously resist providing similar assistance to plaintiffs seeking to extract civil damages for the same alleged misconduct. The company's opponents in civil litigation, then, may seek to gain access to the grand jury transcript and exhibits.

Fed. R. Crim. P. 6(e) prohibits any disclosure of matters occurring before the grand jury except in limited circumstances specifically enumerated in the rule. Once grand jury information is disclosed at trial or through other authorized means and becomes part of the record in a criminal case, the materials lose their protected status and can be used in a civil proceeding. And under certain circumstances, civil litigants may secure orders modifying Rule 6(e)'s protections even where the grand jury information is not publicly disclosed. But disclosure may be made to a litigant involved in a parallel proceeding only when ordered by a court preliminary to, or in connection with, a judicial proceeding and upon a showing of particularized need for the materials.

In *Douglas Oil Co. v. Petrol Stops Northwest*, 441 U.S. 211 (1979), the Supreme Court decreed that "[p]arties seeking grand jury transcripts under Rule 6(e) must show that the material they seek is needed to avoid a possible injustice in another judicial proceeding, that the need for disclosure is greater than the need for continued secrecy, and that their request is structured to cover only material so needed."[44] This rigorous standard applies even when the grand jury whose transcripts are sought has concluded its operations. The *Douglas Oil* Court explained that "[i]t is clear . . . that disclosure is appropriate only in those cases where the need for it outweighs the public interest in secrecy, and that the burden of demonstrating this balance rests upon the private party seeking disclosure. It is equally clear that as the considerations justifying secrecy become less relevant, a party asserting a need for grand jury transcripts will have a lesser burden in showing justification."[45] The application of this balancing test is obviously fact intensive, and thus "a court called upon to determine whether grand jury transcripts should be released necessarily is infused with substantial discretion."[46]

The government's investigative file may well contain materials that civil litigants would like to see and that are not subject to the grand jury secrecy requirements of Rule 6(e). Prosecutors—and those agencies conducting parallel governmental enforcement investigations—consider even

44. *Douglas Oil*, 441 U.S. at 222.
45. *Id.* at 223.
46. *Id.*

non-grand jury investigative materials to be highly confidential. Certainly, much of it will be protected by the work product doctrine. Civil litigants may seek the production of materials held by prosecutors, investigators or administrative agencies through civil discovery processes or requests submitted under the Freedom of Information Act (FOIA), 5 U.S.C. § 552. But FOIA contains a variety of disclosure exemptions, the most important of which is an investigatory files exemption.[47]

B. Sharing Grand Jury Materials with Federal Government Lawyers in Civil Matters

Given the degree of cooperation the Department of Justice would like to see between its criminal and civil divisions, the question of whether criminal assistants can share grand jury materials with their civil colleagues is an important one. Fed. R. Crim. P. 6(e)(3)(A)(i) provides that disclosure of materials occurring before the grand jury may be made (without court order) to "an attorney for the government for use in performing that attorney's duty." But government attorneys concerned only with civil matters do not fall within the definition of an "attorney for the government" in Fed. R. Crim. P. 1(b)(1). Disclosure of grand jury protected materials to government attorneys and their assistants for use in a civil suit, then, is permissible only with a court order under Rule 6(e)(3)(E)(i).

In *United States v. Sells Engineering, Inc.*, 463 U.S. 418 (1983), the Supreme Court held that government civil attorneys seeking grand jury materials are held to the same "particularized need" standard as private parties. In *United States v. John Doe, Inc. I*, 481 U.S. 102 (1987), however, the Supreme Court ruled that a government attorney involved in a grand jury investigation may make *continued* use of grand jury materials if the attorney is subsequently involved in the civil phase of the same or a related matter without having to obtain court approval under Fed. R. Crim. P. 6(e)(3)(E)(i). The Court relied on the plain language of the rule, finding that the government attorney's continued use of the grand jury information did not constitute a "disclosure" under Rule 6(e).

Justice Manual § 1-12.000 encourages cooperation between civil and criminal attorneys "to the fullest extent appropriate to the case and permissible by law." Likely in recognition of the *Sells* limit on the sharing of grand jury materials, the policy counsels that attorneys ought to consider investigative strategies that "maximize the government's ability to share information among criminal, civil, and agency administrative teams, including the

---

47. *See* 5 U.S.C. § 552(b)(7).

use of investigative means other than grand jury subpoenas for documents or witness testimony."

VI. COLLATERAL ESTOPPEL

In general, collateral estoppel principles provide that "a party who has had issues of fact determined against him after a full and fair opportunity to litigate . . . is collaterally estopped from obtaining a subsequent . . . trial of these same issues of fact."[48] In *Parklane Hosiery v. Shore*, 439 U.S. 322 (1979), the Supreme Court ruled that where an issue of fact—the falsity of defendants' proxy statements—was resolved against a defendant in the course of an enforcement proceeding brought by the SEC, the defendant was collaterally estopped from relitigating the issue in a derivative suit brought by shareholders. The Court, in deciding that "a litigant who was not a party to a prior judgment may nevertheless use that judgment 'offensively' to prevent a defendant from relitigating issues resolved in the earlier proceeding,"[49] ruled that trial courts have broad discretion to determine when offensive collateral estoppel should be applied.

"The general rule should be that in cases where a plaintiff could easily have joined in the earlier action or where . . . the application of offensive estoppel would be unfair to a defendant, a trial judge should not allow the use of offensive collateral estoppel."[50] Some of the factors courts consider in applying this rule argue for allowing plaintiffs to use a criminal conviction to collaterally estop the defendant from contesting civil liability. The criminal conviction is founded upon the beyond a reasonable doubt standard, which is higher than the preponderance standard that prevails in civil litigation.[51] And the "application of offensive collateral estoppel will not . . . reward a private plaintiff who could have joined in the previous action" because private parties cannot intervene in criminal prosecutions.[52] Finally, criminal defendants have a very strong incentive to contest their guilt "fully and vigorously."[53]

Under *Parklane Hosiery*, then, issues of fact tried and conclusively determined against a defendant in a criminal case are generally binding on a defendant in a subsequent civil proceeding brought by the government or outside parties based upon the same acts or transactions. A defendant who

48. Parklane Hosiery Co. v. Shore, 439 U.S. 322, 325 (1979).
49. *Id.* at 326.
50. *Id.* at 331.
51. *See One Lot Emerald Cut Stones*, 409 U.S. at 235.
52. *Parklane Hosiery*, 439 U.S. at 331-32.
53. *Id.* at 332.

is negotiating a plea with the government must obviously take into account the possibility that whatever plea is entered may preclude the defendant from resisting liability in collateral civil suits.

Collateral estoppel does not present similar problems for the government. Although *Parklane Hosiery* holds that mutuality of parties need not exist under federal collateral estoppel principles as applied to private litigants, the Supreme Court has held that there must be mutuality of parties for collateral estoppel to be asserted successfully against the federal government.[54]

VII. GLOBAL SETTLEMENTS

Those attempting to defend against parallel civil, regulatory, and criminal actions will wish to secure a so-called "global settlement" of all the various proceedings against them. The advantages of such settlements are substantial. Defending multi-front litigation can be enormously distracting and expensive, can generate continuing adverse publicity as each case is resolved, and can pose continuing business headaches in a variety of ways, including extended disclosure obligations, depressed stock prices, the maintenance of reserves on the company's books to meet future judgments, and the possibility that large civil and administrative judgments against the company will result from the application of collateral estoppel principles.

Global settlements offer peace and the elimination of risk, but they can be difficult to achieve. Those parties sought to be brought together in one deal—e.g., prosecutors, plaintiffs, state attorneys general, and federal and state regulatory agencies—operate independently of each other and often have different priorities and goals. Some may view themselves as competing with the others to secure the greatest glory and the largest settlement amount. As a practical matter, not all of the matters will proceed in tandem and thus parties may feel that they need further investigation or discovery before committing themselves to an overall resolution. And global settlements become even more complex where, as is increasingly the case, foreign regulators and prosecutors are conducting their own investigations and proceedings and must somehow be brought into the fold for settlement purposes.

Normally, the prosecutorial agency involved—usually the Department of Justice—must take the lead in crafting the agreement. But prosecutors are normally reluctant to enter into agreements that will bind other federal

54. *See* United States v. Mendoza, 464 U.S. 154, 158 (1984); *cf.* United States v. Stauffer Chem. Co., 464 U.S. 165 (1984) (the doctrine of mutual defensive collateral estoppel is applicable against the government to preclude re-litigation of the same issue already litigated against the same party in another case involving virtually identical facts).

agencies or interfere with their enforcement actions for fear of stepping on the toes of regulators with whom they must work in future or provoking intra-government criticism of any settlement reached. Certainly, prosecutors have no control over private plaintiffs. Finally, many prosecutors do not want to be accused of unethically using the power of the criminal sanction to "unfairly to extract, or to attempt to extract, additional civil or administrative monetary payments."[55]

Although the global resolutions were relatively rare in the past, the DOJ has promulgated policies that give defendants hope that the DOJ will be more active in encouraging such resolutions at least among prosecutors and federal agencies. In the so-called "anti-piling on" policy embodied in Justice Manual § 1-12.100, the Department cautions that "in resolving a case with a company that multiple Department components are investigating for the same misconduct, Department attorneys should coordinate with one another to avoid the unnecessary imposition of duplicative fines, penalties, and/or forfeiture against the company." In particular, prosecutors "from each component should consider the amount and apportionment of fines, penalties, and/or forfeiture paid to the other components that are or will be resolving with the company for the same misconduct, with the goal of achieving an equitable result."

Finally, prosecutors should endeavor, "as appropriate, to coordinate with and consider the amount of fines, penalties, and/or forfeiture paid to other federal, state, local, or foreign enforcement authorities that are seeking to resolve a case with a company for the same misconduct." In transnational cases, U.S. authorities are increasingly coordinating with foreign regulators and prosecutors with whom they have relationships, enhancing the possibility that multiple national investigations can be resolved in a coordinated fashion.

Examples

1A. Acme Pharma, Inc., and its CEO, Chantrea Keo, are under federal criminal investigation for engaging in a price-fixing conspiracy with competitors in violation of U.S. antitrust laws. The Federal Trade Commission (FTC) is conducting a parallel investigation. Acme's shareholders have filed a shareholder's derivative suit against Keo and Acme's board of directors alleging that the corporation was injured through their illegal conduct. Keo has been noticed for a deposition by both the FTC investigators and counsel in the shareholder's derivative suit. As Keo's lawyer, please explain to him how appearing or not appearing for these depositions will affect his criminal defense.

55. Justice Manual, *supra* note 3, § 1-12.100.

1B. Federal prosecutors believed that Keo was more likely to agree to be interviewed or deposed by the FTC if prosecutors kept a low profile and delayed serving grand jury subpoenas on Keo and Acme until the FTC was able to depose Keo. Assume Keo's counsel counsel was unaware of the parallel criminal investigation. Keo appeared for his FTC deposition and the FTC shared the transcript with federal prosecutors. As Keo's counsel, what constitutional argument would you make to preclude the government from using Keo's sworn statements in its criminal case?

1C. Acme's former Chief Financial Officer, Rozenn Alana, is cooperating with the government and has appeared before the grand jury. Alana has refused to be interviewed by the plaintiffs in the shareholder derivative suit and has asserted her Fifth Amendment right when they sought to depose her. In what circumstances can the plaintiffs get a transcript of Alana's grand jury testimony?

1D. The FTC attorneys have asked the prosecutors for access to the grand jury testimony of potential witnesses. In what circumstances may the prosecutors share such materials with their FTC colleagues?

1E. If Keo and Acme are acquitted after trial on the criminal antitrust indictment, can they use that judgment to collaterally estop the FTC or the plaintiffs in the shareholder derivative action from pursuing their claims?

Explanations

1A. If Keo appears for the deposition, the government can use what he says against him in the investigation and prosecution of the criminal case. It will lock in the defense prematurely. What he says can be used by the government to develop a rebuttal case and to impeach him if he takes the stand at a criminal trial. If Keo lies, he may open himself up to a prosecution for perjury and other charges. Waiver, however, turns out to be not that big an issue.

If Keo instead takes the Fifth, that assertion of the privilege can lead to a (non-determinative) adverse inference being drawn against him and the company.

Keo may ask the judge in the shareholders' suit to stay the action to avoid this dilemma, but judges are very reluctant to stay a parallel proceeding on behalf of the defense especially where, as here, a criminal case has not yet been filed so the duration of any stay is uncertain. Keo may also wish to avoid staying the civil matter because he may be able to secure valuable discovery that he can use in defending a later criminal case.

Keo could ask for a Fed. R. Civ. P. 26(c) protective order to guard against disclosure of his deposition to the government. But in much of the country (that is, outside the Second Circuit) an investigative target who is also subject to discovery in parallel civil litigation and who wishes to avoid exposing his statements to prosecutors is well advised to take the Fifth rather than rely on the dubious protection of a Rule 26(c) protective order.

1B. Under *Kordel*, parallel federal criminal investigations and civil enforcement actions generally do not raise due process concerns. There are exceptions, but they are limited to situations "where the government made affirmative misrepresentations or conducted a civil investigation solely for purposes of advancing a criminal case."[56] It is clear that the FTC is conducting its own independent investigation and that it is not being used as a proxy for prosecutors. The fact that the prosecutors and civil attorneys coordinated the timing of Keo's deposition, and that the U.S. Attorney's Office wanted to keep its investigation confidential in hopes of getting Keo to appear for his civil deposition, are probably insufficient to create a due process problem absent active misrepresentations to the defense.

1C. The shareholders would seek a court order under Fed. R. Crim. P. 6(e)(3)(E)(i) for the transcript of Alana's testimony from the court supervising the grand jury. The rule requires that the disclosure be preliminary to, or in connection with, a judicial proceeding—here, the shareholders' suit—and that the plaintiffs show of particularized need for the materials. To meet that burden, plaintiffs would have to show "that the material they seek is needed to avoid a possible injustice in another judicial proceeding, that the need for disclosure is greater than the need for continued secrecy, and that their request is structured to cover only material so needed."[57] The plaintiffs, then, must show not just that they are interested in Alana's testimony, but also that it is needed for a fair result in their case. This is a heavy burden and cannot be met by mere speculation about the value a witness may hold. A court is *very* unlikely to order the disclosure of transcripts from a grand jury investigation that has not yet concluded for fear of interfering with the executive branch's responsibility for investigating and prosecuting crimes.

1D. In *Sells Engineering*, the Supreme Court held that government civil attorneys seeking grand jury materials are held to the same "particularized need" standard as private parties. One could argue that sharing of grand jury materials with federal civil enforcement agents does not present the same concerns raised by release of "secret" grand jury minutes to

56. United States v. Stringer, 535 F.3d 929, 937 (9th Cir. 2008).
57. *Douglas Oil*, 441 U.S. at 222.

private litigants. Government attorneys are unlikely to harass the grand jury witnesses or suborn perjury from them and, because such attorneys have an incentive to keep matters that they do not use in court confidential, they will not undermine future witnesses' belief that their testimony will remain secret. Courts will also be less concerned that disclosing materials from a pending grand jury will interfere with criminal investigation if it is the DOJ attorneys who petition the court for permission to share such materials with their colleagues at the FTC. That said, the court may wish to know why FTC attorneys, who have a variety of means of securing information, cannot get the materials directly from the witnesses rather than invading the secrecy of the grand jury. It is unlikely that the government attorneys can take advantage of the Court's decision in *John Doe, Inc. I*, because the FTC attorneys were not part of the grand jury investigation and thus giving them access to the grand jury transcripts would assuredly be a "disclosure" of materials protected by Rule 6.

1E. An acquittal in a criminal case does not have a collateral estoppel effect on civil proceedings because it simply represents a judgment that the government did not prove its case beyond a reasonable doubt. It does not reflect a determination that the defendant did not commit the acts complained of by a preponderance of the evidence—the applicable civil standard.

Index

www.ingramcontent.com/pod-product-compliance
Lightning Source LLC
LaVergne TN
LVHW082006200926
848481LV00010B/2812
* 9 7 9 8 8 9 2 0 7 0 6 9 0 *